Manufacturing Planning and Control for Supply Chain Management

The McGraw-Hill/Irwin Series in Operations and Decision Sciences

Manufacturing Planning and Control for Supply Chain Management

Fifth Edition

Thomas E. Vollmann
International Institute for Management Development

William L. Berry
The Ohio State University

D. Clay Whybark
University of North Carolina

F. Robert Jacobs
Indiana University

McGraw-Hill Irwin

Boston   Burr Ridge, IL   Dubuque, IA   Madison, WI   New York   San Francisco   St. Louis
Bangkok   Bogotá   Caracas   Kuala Lumpur   Lisbon   London   Madrid   Mexico City
Milan   Montreal   New Delhi   Santiago   Seoul   Singapore   Sydney   Taipei   Toronto

The *McGraw·Hill* Companies

MANUFACTURING PLANNING AND CONTROL FOR SUPPLY CHAIN MANAGEMENT

Published by McGraw-Hill/Irwin, a business unit of The McGraw-Hill Companies, Inc., 1221 Avenue of the Americas, New York, NY, 10020. Copyright © 2005, 1997, 1992, 1988, 1984 by The McGraw-Hill Companies, Inc. All rights reserved. No part of this publication may be reproduced or distributed in any form or by any means, or stored in a database or retrieval system, without the prior written consent of The McGraw-Hill Companies, Inc., including, but not limited to, in any network or other electronic storage or transmission, or broadcast for distance learning.

Some ancillaries, including electronic and print components, may not be available to customers outside the United States.

This book is printed on acid-free paper.

domestic 1 2 3 4 5 6 7 8 9 0 DOC/DOC 0 9 8 7 6 5 4
international 1 2 3 4 5 6 7 8 9 0 DOC/DOC 0 9 8 7 6 5 4

ISBN 0–07–229990–8

Vice president and editor-in-chief: *Robin J. Zwettler*
Editorial director: *Brent Gordon*
Executive editor: *Richard T. Hercher, Jr.*
Editorial assistant: *Lee Stone*
Marketing manager: *Greta Kleinert*
Senior media producer: *Anthony Sherman*
Senior project manager: *Pat Frederickson*
Freelance project manager: *Margaret Haywood*
Production supervisor: *Gina Hangos*
Designer: *Adam Rooke*
Supplement producer: *Betty Hadala*
Senior digital content specialist: *Brian Nacik*
Typeface: *10/12 Times New Roman*
Compositor: *Interactive Composition Corporation*
Printer: *R. R. Donnelley*

Library of Congress Control Number: 2004100115

INTERNATIONAL EDITION ISBN 0–07–112133–1
Copyright © 2005. Exclusive rights by The McGraw-Hill Companies, Inc. for manufacture and export. This book cannot be re-exported from the country to which it is sold by McGraw-Hill.
The International Edition is not available in North America.

www.mhhe.com

We dedicate this book to our great mentors, who continue to have so much influence on our lives:

Elwood S. Buffa

Frank Gilmore

William K. Holstein

John F. Muth

Larry P. Ritzman

Harvey M. Wagner

Brief Contents

Table of Contents

Preface

Over the editions of this book, we have modified the material, dropped sections, and added new concepts in response to changing needs. In one area, however, we held fast—until now. We stayed with the original organization and flow of the book despite many appeals to change it one way or another. This time it is different! True, we have done the usual editing, adding, and deleting, but we've also changed the basic organization of the book. This is in response to changes in the environment in which manufacturing planning and control (MPC) systems operate. We have known about some of these forces for some time, but others were not as well predicted. In this section, we'll describe some of these changes in the MPC environment and the responses we've made in this edition of the book.

Changes in the Manufacturing World

One of the more pervasive and least well forecast changes in the manufacturing environment is the implementation of enterprise resource planning (ERP) systems. At the end of the last century, there was an enormous amount of investment in computing hardware, software, and ancillary systems. Much of this was in response to the anticipated year 2000 problem. Some companies were investing in order to prevent major catastrophes should there be problems with software that couldn't accept 00 for the year 2000. Others were worried that the internal clocks might create havoc with programs when the year turned over. The spur of the Y2K issue led to a considerable amount of other activity as well.

Many firms argued that, since major investments in information technology had to be made anyway, they should go ahead and invest in the replacement and/or upgrading of legacy systems. For lots of companies, these systems were a hodge-podge of commercial, proprietary, and hybrid programs that performed functions independently of one another for different departments in the company. The argument was extended to say the replacement programs should be integrated. They should be able to "talk" to one another. They should be able to provide common information to all areas of the firm and between firms. Companies like J. D. Edwards, PeopleSoft, SAP, Oracle, and others responded. They created integrated programs that they called "enterprise solutions." These programs were very large, reportedly integrated all functions of the organization, and were called enterprise resource planning (ERP) systems.

Many of the ERP systems were based on the material requirements planning (MRP) logic and factory integration that MRP systems already had in place. Nevertheless, they often displaced the existing manufacturing planning and control systems or were implemented alongside of them. The result is that MPC systems are now imbedded in ERP systems in a great number of organizations. This both increases the opportunities for effective management and the complexity of integration required. No MPC activity can now ignore the pervasiveness of ERP systems.

Another major force that has created the need to respond in material planning and control systems is the continuing decentralization of decision making to the factory floor. Floor level teams that are now organized to solve problems, run manufacturing cells, and improve processes need information at this operating level of the organization. Status information, performance metrics, and planning data are all required in order to make the kinds of decisions and perform the kinds of activities that are now delegated to the factory floor. This is a continuing trend, however, and one that was not as much under forecast as that of the installation of ERP systems.

The customer still remains king in the competitive manufacturing environment. The capabilities of manufacturing plus the expectations of customers has led to increased pressure for both speed and variety. Customers are demanding more tailoring in the products that they order and want them faster than ever. Part of this is derived from the expectation of shortened product life cycles, while part is derived from customers wanting more individualized treatment.

Another major change that has continued over all the editions of this book is that of globalization. Even small and medium-size enterprises now have manufacturing facilities in countries other than their home country. In some instances this is a complex network of facilities. In others it's a single manufacturing or manufacturing/marketing subsidiary. The implications of this are that the geographic reach and diversity of environments within which the material planning and control system must operate has increased and will continue to do so.

Partly as a consequence of the internationalization of business and partly as a response to outsourcing as companies focus on their core competencies, the interconnectedness of manufacturing firms has increased substantially. The implication of this is that companies are now often integrated as customers of their suppliers and integrated with the customers whom they supply in complicated ways. This has created the need to manage some very complex supply chains or networks. In some instances, firms in these supply networks will find themselves competing with customers and suppliers while simultaneously trying to develop mutually beneficial relationships for some portion of their product line. Increasingly, firms have a mixture of industrial and consumer markets that require different channels, which also increases the complexity of the manufacturing relationships. These relationships must be incorporated in the MPC system of the firm.

Responses to the Changing Manufacturing Environment

The response in this book to all of these changes has been twofold. The organization of the book has been changed and the contents have been adjusted to more closely reflect contemporary needs. In terms of reordering the book for this edition, we have brought the front-end activities of the MPC system up front. We've moved demand management and independent demand issues much closer to the beginning of the book. This reflects the importance of the customer in setting the agenda for manufacturing. Since the firm is also a customer for its suppliers, this change also brings the issue of supply chain (network) integration into the early chapters.

Indeed the material on managing the supply chain has been extended and deepened throughout. This is an important response to the increasing interconnectedness of manufacturing firms and the necessity to pay specific management attention to those interconnections. It also substantially increases the scope of manufacturing planning and control from just the connections inside the factory to more broadly looking at the totality of the supply chain.

It's no longer sufficient, however, to look just at the connections inside the factory and between the factory and suppliers and customers. The presence of ERP systems means that the connections to other functional areas inside the firm need to be addressed as well. As a consequence, we've added material on ERP and its relationship to the material planning and control system that directly addresses some of these other internal interconnections.

To make space for this newer material, we have substantially reduced the scope of some of the technical material in the book. Specifically, we have removed techniques that have had limited practical application. We have added some new technical material in the new chapters, however. We still maintain the division between the more managerial chapters in the first part of the book and the more technical support chapters in the latter part of the book.

It may sound from our response to these forces and the reorganization of this edition of the book that we've abandoned our position that materials requirement planning (MRP) records need to be "tattooed on the back of an MPC professional's eyelids." This is certainly not the case! We do argue in this edition, however, that the increased integration between customers and suppliers has strengthened the need for understanding independent-demand issues and the management of the interface between customers and suppliers. We reflect this need in bringing the independent–demand management material forward in the book. We also spend much more time looking specifically at the issues that govern the conversion of independent- into dependent-demand information. It is here that a clear understanding of time-phased planning and control records is important and, indeed, it is essential to the integration with modern enterprise resource planning systems.

Comments on the Fifth Edition

Much of what we have said over the years in the preface to the various editions of this text remains true today. We pointed out a number of the areas of change that will continue to be important for the future. For instance, there is no question that globalization and multinational collaboration will continue to grow and influence MPC system needs.

The information revolution will continue, but it is difficult to predict the directions that it will take. Certainly, more communications capabilities, decreased communications costs, and increased information storage are in the future. However, the systems that will be devised to integrate the information and the algorithms that will be developed to make use of it are yet to be disclosed.

Finally, the roles of people in the organization will continue to change. The devolution of decision making to the people most proximate to the problem will continue. This will require information linkages for decision making and coordination. All of these forces that will continue and those we have not yet identified will shape the MPC system configurations of the future.

The pervasiveness of ERP systems heightens another tension that will shape the development of MPC systems in the future. This is the tension between organization and information centralization versus decentralization, a debate that has permeated the management literature for decades. The ERP systems that we have seen being implemented tilt the organizational model toward centralization and certainly move the information closer to a centralized position. This has not, however, removed the debate nor decreased the tension between the ideologies.

Complementary to, but different from, the centralization/decentralization issue is the issue of complexity versus simplicity. At the moment, the ERP forces are moving organizations toward using complex, highly integrated systems that require an enormous amount of discipline and tactical conformity to be used effectively. Indeed, in the early editions of this book, the MPC systems that we were describing were complex integrated systems and we argued strongly for maintaining the disciplines necessary for them to operate effectively. ERP systems take this to a whole new level.

As we revised the book over time, simpler, less integrated (often decentralized) systems for managing aspects of the MPC systems were introduced. Much of this philosophy came from the concepts applied in the Japanese automobile industry in the latter part of the last century: concepts like JIT, lean manufacturing, and cellular organization. Our position in this debate is that simple, effective mechanisms for managing manufacturing resources must be developed and integrated into the material planning and control systems—ultimately into the enterprise resource planning systems. It may be that the combination of the information revolution, the next resolution of the centralization versus decentralization issue, and the invention of effective techniques to use information will be the strongest forces changing the specifics of MPC systems in the future.

The one constant that remains throughout all these changes, however, is that the manufacturing planning and control systems now and into the future must do all of the things that we've advocated all along. They must provide the platform for enhancing the company strategy, for effective manufacturing resource planning, for providing execution information, and for supporting the control function. Moreover, to be successful these all must be performed well. That's why we think this material has endured and will continue to do so.

APICS Certification Examination Program

APICS, the Educational Society of Resource Management, has a series of programs of certification. The broadest of these programs is Certification in Integrated Resource Management (CIRM). Becoming certified in integrated resource management involves taking five examinations covering material from several functional areas of business and concepts of enterprise integration. Many of the chapters in this book contain background material relevant to the CIRM exams. In particular, the first four chapters provide information on intra- and interorganizational integration. Chapters 8, 11, 17, and 19 contain material on interorganizational integration and on emerging concepts. Additional references are available at the APICS website: http://www.apics.org/.

The other certification programs revolve around Certification in Production and Inventory Management (CPIM). Becoming certified in this field requires passing examinations covering five areas of production and inventory management. There is also a fellow's level certification (CFPIM) that requires additional demonstrations of professional competence in the field. Another important aspect of the CPIM and CFPIM certification programs is that they have sunset clauses. The dynamic nature of the field means that material is continually being updated and continual maintenance of the certification is required.

The specific content of the examinations is constantly being updated, so it is very important to secure copies of the study guides and sample examination questions from APICS as part of any plan of study. Each study guide has a list of references, as do the chapters in this book. APICS also provides training aids and books of reprinted articles that show the concepts in practice. One important general reference for all five areas of the certification examinations is the *APICS Dictionary,* 10th ed., by James F. Cox III and John H. Blackstone Jr., American Production & Inventory Control Society, 2002.

Using the combination of this textbook and the materials provided by APICS is an excellent way to prepare for the certification examinations. The APICS publications tend to focus on case examples rather than on basic methods. The latter type of material is better provided in a text. A similar difference applies to the problems furnished from both sources. The sample tests provided by APICS use a short answer format. In this book, we provide more open ended kinds of problems that require calculation and discussion. In the discussion questions, occasionally there are no single right answers; discussion of the alternatives leads to a deeper understanding of manufacturing planning and control systems.

Before describing the relationship between the certification exams and this book, we feel the need to add a few words of caution. Manufacturing planning and control cannot be easily partitioned into five parts. This is a dynamic, ever-changing field that needs to be understood in its entirety. Moreover, the changes will continue, and professionals in this area need a framework for understanding change and seeing the opportunities for their companies. We feel that the framework will come from reading all of this book, or at least the first 11 chapters. This set of chapters is recommended reading before going into the more detailed study of each area in the remaining chapters.

In the rest of this section, we detail the primary and linkage chapters that address the subject matter of each examination. We also provide information on what is not in our book, sources where the gaps can be filled, and at least one more reference that complements the materials presented here. Again the APICS website is an important source of current information on the exams. The presentation is organized around the five areas covered by the certification exam.

Basics of Supply Chain Management

This part of the certification covers the basic concepts of managing the flow of materials in a supply chain. It encompasses a complete overview of material flow, from internal and external suppliers, to and from the company. The topics included are:

- Elements of the supply chain.
- Just-in-time (JIT).
- Total quality management (TQM).
- Manufacturing resources planning (MRP II).
- Demand planning.
- Capacity management.

With the exception of total quality management, there is a chapter for each of these topics in this book. Chapters 17 (Supply Chain Management), 9 (Just-in-Time), 7 (Material Requirements Planning), 2 (Demand Management), and 10 (Capacity Planning and Utilization) are those that line up directly with the topics above. In addition, supplementary basic material on inventory management is found in Chapter 5. More advanced material on MRP is found in Chapter 14 (Advanced MRP) and for JIT in Chapter 15 (Advanced JIT). One of the recommended books for this section is *Introduction to Materials Management,* 4th ed., by J. R. Tony Arnold and Stephen N. Chapman, Prentice Hall, 2000.

Master Planning of Resources

This section explores the processes used to develop sales and operations plans and the internal and external demand forecasting requirements. The objective is to produce achievable master schedules that are consistent with business policies, objectives, and resource constraints. The topics covered are:

- Demand management.
- Sales and operations planning.
- Master scheduling.
- Measuring the business plan.

There is a chapter for each of these topics, though the coverage of measuring the business plan is not as comprehensive as the exam requires. Chapters 2 (Demand Management), 3 (Sales and Operations Planning), and 6 (Master Production Scheduling) are directly associated with the first three topics. In Chapter 13 (Strategy and MPC System Design) we relate the MPC system to the company strategy that is reflected in the business plan. Supplementary material is found in Chapter 18 (Implementation) and Chapter 4 [Enterprise Resources Planning (ERP)—Integration]. Advanced material is found in Chapters 12 and 16 on sales and operations planning and scheduling. Another reference for this section is *Master Scheduling,* 2nd ed., by John F. Proud, John Wiley & Sons, 1999.

Detailed Scheduling and Planning

This section focuses on the various techniques for material and capacity scheduling. The exam covers the details of material requirements planning (MRP), capacity requirements planning (CRP), inventory management practices, and procurement and supplier planning. There are four topics:

- Recognizing techniques and practices of inventory management.
- Mechanics of the detailed material planning process.
- Planning operations to support the priority plan.
- Planning procurement and external sources of supply.

For this section, the directly relevant Chapters are 5 (Supply Chain Inventory Management—Independent-Demand Items), 6 (Master Production Scheduling), 7 (MRP), and 11 (Production Activity Control). Supplementary Chapters include 4 (ERP), 9 (JIT), and 10 (Capacity Planning and Utilization). Advanced material for this area is found in Chapters 14 (MRP), 15 (JIT), and 16 (Scheduling). Two additional references for this section are *Integral Logistics Management,* by Paul Schönsleben, CRC Press, 2000, and *World Class Supply Chain Management,* 7th ed., by Donald W. Dobler, David N. Burt, and Stephen S. Starling, McGraw-Hill/Irwin, 2002.

Execution and Control of Operations

This part of the exam is concerned with prioritizing and sequencing work, executing work plans and implementing controls, reporting activity results, and providing feedback on performance. It includes techniques for scheduling and controlling production processes, the execution of quality initiatives and continuous improvement plans, and the control and handling of inventories. The topics covered are:

- Prioritizing and sequencing work.
- Executing plans and implementing controls.
- Authorizing and reporting activities for push and pull systems.
- Evaluating performance and providing feedback.

The chapters in this book that are directly relevant to this section are 11 (Production Activity Control), 18 (Implementation), and 9 (Just-in-Time). Supplemental material is available in Chapter 5 (Supply Chain Inventory Management) and advanced material is covered in Chapter 16 (Advanced Concepts in Scheduling). One additional reference for this part of the exam is *Production and Inventory Management,* 2nd ed., by Donald W. Fogarty, John H. Blackstone Jr., and Thomas R. Hoffmann, South-Western, 1999. A reference for the quality aspects of this section is *Quality Planning and Analysis,* 4th ed., by J. M. Juran and Frank M. Gryna, McGraw-Hill Science, 2000.

Strategic Management of Resources

The final section explores the relationship of existing and emerging processes and technologies to manufacturing strategy and supply-chain-related functions. The objective of the material is to align resources with the strategic plan, configure and integrate operating processes to support the strategic plan, and to implement change. The topics included here are:

- Competitive market issues.
- Choices affecting facilities, supply chain, information technology, and organizational design.
- Configuring and integrating internal processes.
- Evaluating and managing projects.

The chapters that are directly relevant to this part of the exam include Chapter 1 (Manufacturing Planning and Control), Chapter 18 (Implementation), Chapter 13 (Strategy and MPC System Design), and Chapter 19 (MPC: The Next Frontier). Supplemental material is available in Chapter 5 (Supply Chain Inventory Management), Chapter 3 (Sales and Operations Planning) and Chapter 4 [Enterprise Resources Planning (ERP)—Integrated Systems]. Advanced material is in Chapter 16 (Advanced Concepts in Scheduling). Two references for some of the other topics in this section are *Project Management,* 5th ed., by Jack R. Meredith and Samuel J. Mantel Jr., John Wiley & Sons, 2002, and *Operations Strategy,* by Peter W. Stonebraker and G. Keong Leong, Prentice Hall, 1994.

Acknowledgments

All editions of *Manufacturing Planning and Control Systems* have benefited from the comments of reviewers. In the first edition, we had:

Gene Groff
Georgia State University

Robert Millen
Northeastern University

Richard Penlesky
Carroll College

Reviewers for the second edition were:

Jeff Miller
Boston University

William Sherrard
San Diego State University

Urban Wemmerlov
University of Wisconsin

In the third edition, we were helped by the reviews of:

Stanley Brooking
University of Southern Mississippi

Henry Crouch
Pittsburgh State University

Marilyn Helms
University of Tennessee

Robert Johnson
Pennsylvania State University

Ted Lloyd
Eastern Kentucky University

Dan Reid
University of New Hampshire

Dwight Smith-Daniels
Arizona State University

Herman Stein
Bellarmine College

Glen Wilson
Middle Tennessee State University

In the fourth edition, we enjoyed, were challenged by, and are very grateful for the thoughtful reviews by:

Paul M. Bobrowski
Syracuse University

Philip S. Chong
California State University–Long Beach

Ted Lloyd
Eastern Kentucky University

Daniel S. Marrone
SUNY Farmingdale

R. Dan Reid
University of New Hampshire

William Sherrard
San Diego State University

Herman Stein
Bellarmine College

Urban Wemmerlov
University of Wisconsin—Madison

In this edition of the book, the following reviewers provided comments that shaped our thinking for the current revisions in content and organization:

William Sherrard
San Diego State University

Victor Sower
Sam Houston State University

Robert Vokurka
Texas A&M University

Ted Lloyd
Eastern Kentucky University

Stephen Chapman
NC State University

Donna Summers
University of Dayton

Jeffrey Herrmann
University of Maryland

Harish Bahl
California State University–Chico

Kim LaScola Needy
University of Pittsburgh

Daniel Steele
University of South Carolina

As before, our ideas have been greatly shaped by the manufacturing practitioners and college students whom we teach and by the colleagues at our schools. The education executives who have supported us in this edition are Dean Robert Sullivan, University of North Carolina; Dean Joseph Alutto, The Ohio State University; Dean Dan Dalton, Indiana University; and President Peter Lorange, IMD. We thank all of these friends and associates for their support and help.

Bob Fetter, our consulting editor for the first and second editions, was a champion as well as a critical reviewer. Dick Hercher has exhausted his patience with us but is still there to help when we need him.

The three original authors welcome Bob Jacobs to the team. The task of revising was made much more tolerable by the support of our very understanding families. Thanks folks!

Thomas E. Vollmann

William L. Berry

D. Clay Whybark

F. Robert Jacobs

1

Manufacturing Planning and Control

In this chapter we set the stage for the remainder of the book. We put the manufacturing planning and control (MPC) system into perspective and provide a framework for its exploration. The MPC system is concerned with planning and controlling all aspects of manufacturing, including managing materials, scheduling machines and people, and coordinating suppliers and key customers. Since these activities change over time and respond differently to different markets and company strategies, this chapter provides a model for evaluating responses to changes in the competitive environment. We believe that the development of an effective manufacturing planning and control system is key to the success of any company. Moreover, truly effective MPC systems coordinate supply chains—joint efforts across company boundaries. Finally, MPC systems design is not a one-time effort; MPC systems need to continuously adapt and respond to changes in the company environment, strategy, customer requirements, particular problems, and new supply chain opportunities. The critical question is not what one has accomplished; it is "What should the firm, together with its supply chain partners, do next?" To put these ideas in perspective, this chapter is organized around the following five managerial concerns:

- *The context for MPC:* What are the market, economic, technological, and organizational elements that influence MPC system design?
- *The MPC system defined:* What are the typical tasks performed by the MPC system and how do these tasks affect company operations?
- *An MPC system framework:* What are the key MPC system components and how do they respond to a company's needs?
- *Matching the MPC system with the needs of the firm:* How do supply-chain, product, and process issues affect MPC system design?
- *Evolution of the MPC system:* What forces drive changes in the MPC system and how do companies respond to the forces?

An additional role of this chapter is to provide a model for the remaining chapters in the book. Each chapter will start with an introduction describing the chapter's content and will highlight the managerial concerns addressed. It will also direct you to other parts of the book that are related to the chapter. We have not included, within the chapters, footnotes or references to other pages or chapters of the book, since these tend to interrupt the flow of ideas. Finally, each chapter concludes with a set of principles, references, and problems.

The Context for MPC

Perhaps the most important aspect of the context for development and maintenance of a manufacturing planning and control system is the continual change in its competitive environment. Changes range from technological to political and strategic. Three key areas of influence on MPC system design are the degree of internationalization, the role of the customer in the system, and the increasing use of information technology.

Internationalization

The increase in breadth and depth of internationalization of manufacturing continues apace. Growth in international markets, both demand and supply, has had a major impact on MPC system design and execution. Even small firms have customers around the world, and many have foreign sources of supply as well. The reach of national markets through trade blocs like NAFTA, the European Common Market, the Andean Market, and others will continue to expand. These markets expand the sources of demand and locations of suppliers for firms of all sizes. It is a competitive imperative to adapt MPC systems to this wide environment.

Internationalization has given rise to a whole new form of company. An expression from the 1980s, "hollow corporation," has taken on a new meaning. The original concept had to do with a firm that had very little manufacturing and focused primarily on product design and marketing. But companies like Nike have taken this concept to a new level. Whole networks of manufacturing firms around the world have grown up to support the likes of such companies as Nike. The MPC systems necessary to support these supply chain networks are much more complex than those of the traditional manufacturing company.

At the same time, there are firms that have capitalized on distinctive competence in manufacturing. Firms like Solectron and Flextronics perform subcontract manufacturing of products for many different companies around the world. Their distinctive competence is manufacturing first and foremost and, secondarily, the capability to coordinate their activities with their suppliers and their customers in global networks. They do this with high levels of flexibility—to ramp up production and deliver new products to the marketplace and respond to changing market needs.

These new arrangements have given rise to what can be called "plug compatibility." This is a concept not unlike the original Macintosh computer concept of "plug and play." The idea here is to have the ability to plug into a manufacturer in Malaysia for a particular product component for assembly and be able to move that capacity to Indonesia or Chile when demands shift or requirements change. Thus, for example, the Microsoft Xbox was launched in the U.S. market by manufacturing in Mexico and Hungary. The manufacturing was done by Flextronics, which was able to rapidly ramp up production to meet a target launch date. Thereafter, Flextronics concentrated Xbox manufacturing in China. All of this requires new levels of excellence in MPC system design.

These shifting requirements in international collaborations have given new meaning to the expression *supply chains* (sometimes called demand or value chains) or *supply networks*. As opportunities arise and conditions change, the members of a particular supply network will change with unpredictable timings. There are occasions when a firm will be both a supplier and a customer to the same firm, while supplying their competitors and their customers. These shifting networks have given rise to a very special need to have material planning and control systems that are transportable, international, transparent, and effective.

The Role of the Customer

The competitive demands of the marketplace have not diminished over the last decade; the push for lower inventories, faster response, and lower transaction costs is relentless. The requirements for customer responsiveness and improved service must also match the global expansion of business itself. The demands on MPC systems are those of customer integration and responsiveness.

One way of viewing this requirement is to think of both product and process flexibility. Mass customization implies flexibility to produce a variety of products to meet increasing customer demands and flexibility of processes to meet whatever volume responsiveness is required. As our technological capabilities to produce a greater variety of products from our processes increases, the need to manage the material flows necessary to support this flexibility increases as well. As customers demand more individualization, our processes need to be made more flexible. In turn, this flexibility needs a degree of responsiveness in the MPC system that can manage an ever-increasing variety of material, capacity, and capability requirements.

Manufacturing planning and control systems continually encompass larger supply and demand networks. Clearly, as responsiveness and flexibility increase, the implications for coordination among our partners on the supply and demand sides increase proportionally. Here we're not talking just about plug compatibility, but operational compatibility. The capability to recognize changes in consumer preferences and move them through the supply network in response to customer demands is an important dimension of the MPC system. Moreover, these changes must be accommodated without excessive inventory or shortages. In order to respond effectively in global markets, responsiveness must move throughout the supply network in a timely and effective manner. Geographical dispersion creates additional complexity and is an important component of the environment within which the MPC system must be designed and operated.

In order to be an effective competitor in today's marketplace, firms must have MPC systems with the ability to determine, transmit, revise, and coordinate requirements throughout a global supply chain system. Changing customer requirements and shifting consumer preferences make this an extraordinarily dynamic task.

Increasing Use of Information Technology

One response to the global need for coordination and communication has been the rapid deployment of information technology, particularly enterprise resource planning (ERP) systems. Recognizing the need for common definitions of data, compatible procedures for handling information, effective communications within and between firms, and a common means for accomplishing tasks, ERP systems have come to the forefront. These gigantic information systems built over a common database have provided the means for linking functionally disparate, geographically dispersed, and culturally different organizational units into a uniform system. The hope and promise of ERP systems is to provide common data, common procedures, and real-time data availability for coordinated decision making in globally dispersed organizations.

ERP systems need to be seen in the context of greater internationalization and more global optimization. Originally, MPC systems were designed to support individual factory operations. ERP allowed firms to move beyond the concept of "lean manufacturing" with its factory focus to "lean organization" with a business unit focus. Here, integration encompasses several factories as well as functions such as accounting, human resources, and sales. The new frontier is to move toward "lean enterprise" where integration is achieved across business units. This is particularly valuable when cumulative purchasing volumes are large or when responding to global customers such as Wal-Mart and Carrefour. But lean enterprise is not the end of the road. "Lean supply chains" focus on optimizing activities across company boundaries.

The MPC System Defined

In this section we define what the MPC system does and some of the costs and benefits associated with effective MPC systems. The essential task of the MPC system is to manage efficiently the flow of material, the utilization of people and equipment, and to respond to customer requirements by utilizing the capacity of our suppliers, that of our internal facilities, and (in some cases) that of our customers to meet customer demand. Important ancillary activities involve the acquisition of information from customers on product needs and providing customers with information on delivery dates and product status. An important distinction here is that the MPC system provides the information upon which managers make effective decisions. The MPC system does not make decisions nor manage the operations—managers perform those activities. The MPC system provides the support for them to do so wisely.

Typical MPC Support Activities

The support activities of the MPC system can be broken roughly into three time horizons: long term, medium term, and short term. In the long term, the system is responsible for providing information to make decisions on the appropriate amount of capacity (including equipment, buildings, suppliers, and so forth) to meet the market demands of the future. This is particularly important in that these decisions set the parameters within which the firm responds to current demands and copes with short-term shifts in customer preferences. Moreover, long-term planning is necessary for the firm to provide the appropriate mix of human resource capabilities, technology, and geographical locations to meet the firm's future needs. In the case of supply chain planning, the long term has to include the same kind of capacity planning for the key suppliers. For companies that outsource their manufacturing to outside companies, like Solectron, the planning of supplier capacity can be more critical than internal capacity planning. Moreover, the choice of outsourcing partners has to consider their capabilities to ramp up and adjust capacities to the actual dictates of the marketplace.

In the intermediate term, the fundamental issue addressed by the MPC system is matching supply and demand in terms of both volume and product mix. Although this is also true in the longer term, in the intermediate term, the focus is more on providing the exact material and production capacity needed to meet customer needs. This means planning for the right quantities of material to arrive at the right time and place to support product production and distribution. It also means maintaining appropriate levels of raw material, work in process, and finished goods inventories in the correct locations to meet market needs. Another aspect of the intermediate term tasks is providing customers with information on expected delivery times and communicating to suppliers the correct quantities and delivery times for the material they supply. Planning of capacity may require determining employment levels, overtime possibilities, subcontracting needs, and support requirements. It is often in the intermediate time frame that specific coordinated plans, including corporate budgets, sales plans and quotas, and output objectives, are set. The MPC system has an important role in meeting these objectives.

In the short term, detailed scheduling of resources is required to meet production requirements. This involves time, people, material, equipment, and facilities. Key to this activity is people working on the right things. As the day-to-day activities continue, the MPC system must track the use of resources and execution results to report on material consumption, labor utilization, equipment utilization, completion of customer orders, and other important measures of manufacturing performance. Moreover, as customers change their minds, things go wrong, and other changes occur, the MPC system must provide the information to managers, customers, and suppliers on what happened, provide problem-solving support, and report on the resolution of the problems. Throughout this process, communication with customers on production status and changes in expectations must be maintained.

In order to effectively manage the manufacturing processes, a number of manufacturing performance indicators need to be compiled. Among these are output results, equipment utilization, and costs associated with different departments, products, labor utilization, and project completions. Also, measures of customer satisfaction such as late deliveries, product returns, quantity errors, and other mistakes are needed. The implications physically and financially of the activities on the manufacturing floor are collected, summarized, and reported through the MPC system.

Costs and Benefits of MPC Systems

The initial costs for a material planning and control system can be substantial. Moreover, the ongoing operational costs are also significant. An effective MPC system requires a large number of professionals and all their supporting resources, including computers, training, maintenance, and space. It's not uncommon to find the largest number of indirect employees at a manufacturing firm to be involved in the MPC area. Frustratingly, many companies have invested large amounts of money in MPC systems and have not achieved the requisite benefits. These companies are characterized by poor customer service; excessive inventories; inappropriate assignment of materials, workers, and equipment; and large numbers of expediters dedicated to putting out fires.

These symptoms of an inappropriate or ineffective MPC are the bane of many managers. In fact, poor MPC performance has often been a major cause of firm bankruptcy. In one instance, a large U.S. producer of farm equipment allowed its inventory of finished goods to get so large and unmatched to the required market mix, that the firm was acquired by another company—for a fraction of what the farm equipment company might have been worth. Many instances of failed mergers in China have been attributed to substantial mismatches in the MPC capabilities of the firms in China and their partners. Other examples abound of companies that have missed major opportunities because of their inability to respond quickly.

A notable example is the widely reported difficulty that Hershey had in meeting the demand for candy on Halloween because of a failure in the implementation of its ERP system.

On the other hand, many companies have realized substantial payoffs from their investments in MPC systems. Consider, for example, the following results:

- A division of the Timken Company operates a plant in North Carolina that produces special-purpose engineered bearings. Unlike most of its sister plants, this plant produces bearings to order under very stringent conditions of quality, delivery speed, and advanced engineering. It competes for business around the world, with one sister plant in Eastern Europe producing similar products. Its MPC system has enabled them to achieve a number of advantages including:

  A carefully controlled level of work-in-process inventory and smooth production flows.

  Very short and consistent delivery times for most products, with extraordinarily rapid response for a few emergency orders.

  Efficient production of lot sizes as small as one unit.

  Labor productivity that provides a cost advantage over competitors.

- Even during a difficult time in the industry, Nortel Networks has succeeded in streamlining its supply chain. After divesting and outsourcing much of its manufacturing, it was able to focus more intently on its core competencies of engineering design, system configuration, and system integration. These moves resulted in substantial physical, geographical, organizational, and system changes in the supply chain and necessitated major modifications in the MPC system that supports supply chain management. The resulting system has enabled Nortel to achieve such objectives as the following:

  A several-fold reduction in manufacturing and distribution overhead that enables it to continue to operate during a very turbulent period.

  Substantially reduced throughput times enabling them to be more responsive to customer requests.

  A focus on core competencies that enables the company to achieve substantial improvements in revenue per employee.

- A large Korean company with many suppliers, Korean Heavy Industries Co., Ltd. implemented a just-in-time-based MPC system that provided:

  A reduction of manufacturing lead time of 40 percent.

  An overall reduction of inventories of nearly 50 percent.

  Direct labor productivity increases of 40 percent.

- A major chemical manufacturer, through careful analysis of demand patterns, product lines, and customer preferences, was able to substantially enhance its material planning and control system. Among the benefits achieved by incorporating its research into the system were:

  Much improved prepositioning of inventory prior to seasonal sales, with a corresponding improvement in customer service.

  A substantial reduction in transshipment costs and risks of aging inventory by better matching demand with supply.

Improved relationships with customers (suppliers to homeowners) that helped build customer loyalty for the future.

- The worldwide boom in wireless communication has provided opportunities for products and services for many companies. One of the best-known purveyors of cell phones is Nokia. The company's MPC system is designed to enable it to match product capability with market demand on both price and feature dimensions. Its global system has enabled Nokia to achieve several advantages, among which are:

A wide variety of products that meet customer needs all around the world from high sophistication to minimal functionality.

An efficiency of production that enables it to provide cell phones to the wireless carriers at very low cost, thereby expanding global volumes.

The ability to incorporate innovative concepts into its product with great speed and frequency.

An MPC System Framework

It is most typical now to find the MPC system imbedded in an enterprise resource planning (ERP) system. Many essential activities that need to be performed in the MPC system have not changed. However, the details have evolved as changes in our knowledge, technology, and markets have occurred. The MPC activities are now carried out in more areas of the firm and differ to meet the strategic requirements of the company. In this section, we'll provide our framework for understanding the MPC system.

MPC System Activities

Figure 1.1 is a schematic of the general MPC system that would be used within a firm for planning and controlling its manufacturing operations. But linking customer and supplier firms in a supply chain requires coordinating the MPC activities between the firms. The model shown in Figure 1.1 is essentially what one will find as a key part of any packaged ERP system. The figure is divided into three parts or phases. The top third, or front end, is the set of activities and systems for overall direction setting. This phase establishes the overall company direction for manufacturing planning and control. Demand management encompasses forecasting customer/end product demand, order entry, order promising, accommodating interplant and intercompany demand, and spare parts requirements. In essence, demand management coordinates all activities of the business that place demands on manufacturing capacity.

Sales and operations planning balances the sales/marketing plans with available production resources. The result is an agreed-on company game plan that determines the manufacturing role in meeting company strategy. Increasingly, this activity is receiving more management attention as the need for coordination is recognized in progressive firms. The master production schedule (MPS) is the disaggregated version of the sales and operations plan. That is, it states which end items or product options manufacturing will build in the future. The MPS must support the sales and operations plan. Resource planning determines the capacity necessary to produce the required products now and in the future. In the long run this means bricks and mortar, while in the short run it means labor and machine hours. Resource planning provides the basis for matching manufacturing plans and capacity.

FIGURE 1.1
Manufacturing Planning and Control System (simplified)

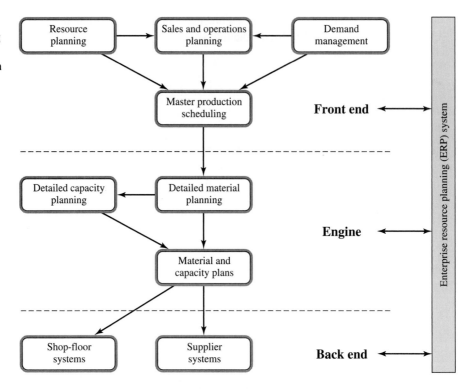

The middle third, or engine, in Figure 1.1 encompasses the set of MPC systems for detailed material and capacity planning. The master production schedule feeds directly into the detailed material planning module. Firms with a limited product range can specify rates of production for developing these plans. However, for firms producing a wide variety of products with many parts per product, detailed material planning can involve calculating requirements for thousands of parts and components, using a formal logic called material requirements planning (MRP). MRP determines (explodes) the period-by-period (time-phased) plans for all component parts and raw materials required to produce all the products in the MPS. This material plan can thereafter be utilized in the detailed capacity planning systems to compute labor or machine center capacity required to manufacture all the component parts.

The bottom third, or back end, of Figure 1.1 depicts MPC execution systems. Here, again, the system configuration depends on the products manufactured and production processes employed. For example, firms producing a large variety of products using thousands of parts often group all equipment of a similar type into a single work center. Their shop floor system establishes priorities for all shop orders at each work center so the orders can be properly scheduled. Other firms will group mixtures of equipment that produce a similar set of parts into work centers called production cells. For them, production rates and just-in-time (JIT) systems for execution are appropriate.

The supplier systems provide detailed information to the company suppliers. In the case of arm's length relationships with these suppliers, the supplier systems will produce purchase orders that will be transmitted to the suppliers. Thereafter, the company MPC systems should provide suppliers with updated priority information, based on current conditions in the company—as well as in their customers' companies. In the case of closer (partnership) relations with suppliers, information can also include future plans—to help the suppliers understand expected needs. In a general sense the receiving end of this information is the demand management module of the front end in the suppliers' MPC systems.

In firms using MRP systems, execution of the detailed material and capacity plans involves detailed scheduling of machines and other work centers. This scheduling must reflect such routine events as starting and completing orders for parts and any problem conditions, such as breakdowns or absenteeism. These schedules are often available on a real-time basis from the ERP system database. Real-time data is particularly important in factories with complex manufacturing processes and/or customers demanding responsiveness to volume, design, or delivery schedule changes.

Components and materials sourced from outside the organization require an analogous detailed schedule. In essence, purchasing is the procurement of outside work center capacity. It must be planned and scheduled well to maximize final customer satisfaction. Best-practice purchasing systems typically separate the procurement or contractual activity from routine order release and follow up. Procurement, a highly professional job, involves contracting for vendor capacity and establishing ground rules for order release and order follow-up. These tasks take on extra dimensions as procurement involves global sourcing and multinational coordination of schedules.

An important activity that is not depicted in Figure 1.1 is the measurement, follow-up, and control of actual results. As products are manufactured, the rate of production and timing of specific completion can be compared to plans. As shipments are made to customers, measures of actual customer service can be obtained. As capacity is used, it too can be compared to plans. If actual results differ from plan, appropriate actions to bring the results back to plan or modifications of the plan must be made. These measurements and control actions are part of all three of the phases of the MPC system.

The three-phase framework for manufacturing planning and control is supported by widely available MPC systems and software, from master production scheduling to the back-end systems. This software is not only integrated to follow the framework, it is also linked to other business activities in the ERP systems of many firms. That means that the MPC systems provide inputs to the financial, distribution, marketing, and human resources systems that require the information.

Matching the MPC System with the Needs of the Firm

The specific requirements for the MPC system design depend on the nature of the production process, the degree of supply chain integration, customers' expectations, and the needs of management. As the MPC system is required to integrate with other company systems in the supply chain and/or with the ERP system of the firm, additional design parameters are introduced. Moreover, these MPC system requirements are not static. As competitive conditions, customer expectations, supplier capabilities, and internal needs change, the MPC system needs to change. In addition, the changes that are being addressed as we make one set of modifications may well be different when we move to another change that needs addressing. The result is a different emphasis on various MPC system modules over time.

MPC technology continues to change over time as well. The present trend is to more on-line data access and systems. MPC status is also a product of the increasing speeds, decreasing costs, and increasing storage capabilities of modern computers. On-line systems provide multiple advantages, particularly between firms. Internet-based systems are becoming an important way to support intrafirm coordinated efforts. For these firms the amount of paper moving between departments of a company or between companies has been greatly reduced. Planning cycles have been speeded up. Inventories between partners in the supply chain are being replaced by speedier information. All of these changes dramatically affect the way users interact with the MPC system. As information processing capabilities increase, MPC systems have evolved to utilize the latest technologies.

MPC systems must also reflect the physical changes taking place on the factory floor. Outsourcing, contract manufacturing, and the hollowing out of the corporation dramatically affect MPC systems design. Moves from job shops to flow processes to cellular manufacturing approaches affect the MPC systems design as well. Providing information at the level where decisions are made in appropriate time frames has greatly augmented the use of computers on the factory floor and the speed of interaction between planning and execution.

It's not, however, just on the factory floor that changes dictate the MPC system needs. As the firm shapes its manufacturing strategy, different modules of the MPC system may need to be modified to respond. As an example, firms that are increasing product variety may need to strengthen the master production scheduling and detailed material planning modules in order to more quickly phase in and phase out new products. Firms that are competing on delivery speed may need to improve shop floor execution and feedback systems to more closely monitor the progress of products through the manufacturing facility. This matching of strategic direction with MPC system design is as dynamic as any of the other elements that shape the MPC system requirements.

An MPC Classification Schema

Figure 1.2 shows the relationship between MPC system approaches, the complexity of the manufactured product as expressed in the number of subparts, and the repetitive nature of production, expressed as the time between successive units. Figure 1.2 also shows some example products that fit these time and complexity scales.

Several MPC approaches presented in Figure 1.2 are appropriate for products that fit in various points in the schema. The figure demonstrates that the MPC emphasis changes as the nature of the product, process, or both change. For example, as a product's sales volume grows over time, the MPC emphasis might shift from right to left. Regardless of where the company

FIGURE 1.2
MPC
Classification
Schema

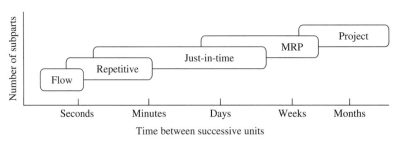

is on Figure 1.2, it's necessary to perform all the activities depicted in Figure 1.1. However, how they are performed can be quite different for firms at different points on Figure 1.2.

The lower left-hand corner of Figure 1.2 shows a flow-oriented manufacturing process typical of many chemical, food, petroleum, and bulk product firms. Since products are produced in streams instead of discrete batches, virtually no time elapses between successive units. With these processes, the front-end concern of the MPC system is primarily the flow rates that become the master production schedule. Typically, these products have relatively few component parts, so engine management is straightforward. Depending on how components are purchased, the back end may involve some complexity. Typically, these firms' major cost is for raw materials, although transportation costs can also be significant.

Repetitive manufacturing activities are found in many plants that assemble similar products (e.g., automobiles, watches, personal computers, pharmaceuticals, and televisions). For such products, component-part management is necessary, but everything is coordinated with the flow or assembly rate for the end items.

In the middle of the figure we show a large application area for just-in-time systems. Using lean manufacturing approaches, many firms today try to move their processes from right to left in the figure. That is, they try to make processes more repetitive as opposed to unique in order to achieve the operational advantages of repetitive manufacturing (shorter production cycles, reduced lead times, lower inventories, and the like). JIT is shown as spanning a wide variety of products and processes. This MPC approach is increasingly being integrated with more traditional MRP-based systems. The goal is to achieve better MPC system performance and to reduce costs of maintaining the MPC system.

Figure 1.2 also shows material requirements planning as spanning a wide area. MRP is often the platform for ERP applications and is key to any MPC system involving management of a complicated parts situation. The majority of manufacturing firms have this sort of complexity, and MRP-based systems continue to be widely applied. For many firms, successful use of MRP is an important step in evolving their approaches to MPC. Once routine MRP operation is achieved, portions of the product and processes that can be executed with JIT methodologies can be selected.

The last form of MPC depicted in Figure 1.2, the project type, is applied to unique long-lead-time products, such as ships and highly customized products. Here the primary concern is usually management of the time dimension. Related to time is cost. Project management attempts to continually assess partially completed projects' status in terms of expected completion dates and costs. Some firms have successfully integrated MRP approaches with the problems of project management. This is particularly effective in planning and controlling the combined activities of engineering and manufacturing.

Evolution of the MPC System

In several parts of this chapter, we have discussed the dynamism of the MPC system. This notion is so important that we devote an entire section to the topic. Although the activities shown in Figure 1.1 are performed in every manufacturing company, whether large or small, MPC system configuration depends strongly on the company's attributes at a particular point in time. The key to keeping the MPC system matched to evolving company needs

FIGURE 1.3
Evolutionary
Responses to
Forces for
Change

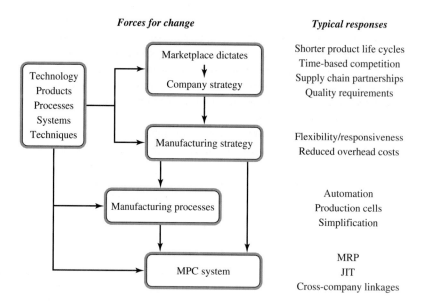

Forces for change

Typical responses

Shorter product life cycles
Time-based competition
Supply chain partnerships
Quality requirements

Flexibility/responsiveness
Reduced overhead costs

Automation
Production cells
Simplification

MRP
JIT
Cross-company linkages

is to ensure system activities are synchronized and focused on the firm's strategy. This ensures that detailed MPC decision making is in harmony with the company's game plan. But the process is not static—the need for matching is ongoing.

The Changing Competitive World

Figure 1.3 depicts some manufacturing firms' typical responses to changing marketplace dictates. New technology, products, processes, systems, and techniques permit new competitive initiatives; global competition intensifies many of these forces. Marketplace dictates drive revisions in company strategy, which in turn often call for changes in manufacturing strategy, manufacturing processes, and MPC systems.

Shorter product life cycles come about partly because consumers have access to products from all over the world. This has spawned the move to "time-based competition." Who can get to the market quickest? Similarly, today's market insists on ever-higher quality, which in turn has led to many changes in manufacturing practices. Cost pressures have translated into reductions of all manufacturing cost components from material and labor to overhead and energy.

But increasingly, cost and quality are the ante to play the game—winning requires flexibility and responsiveness in dealing with even more fickle customer demands. Clearly, these pressures and responses require changes in both the MPC system and the underlying manufacturing process. As Figure 1.3 shows, typical MPC responses are MRP and JIT. Process responses include automation, simplification, and production cells for cellular manufacturing.

Reacting to the Changes

If the MPC system has remained unchanged for a significant length of time, it may no longer be appropriate to the company's needs. The system, like the strategy and processes themselves, must change to meet the dictates of the market. In many instances, this may simply imply a different set of evaluative criteria for the MPC system. In other cases, new modules or information may be required. In yet other cases, entire MPC activities may need to be eliminated. For example, JIT systems frequently move materials so quickly through the factory that MRP and shop-floor scheduling systems to track them are not needed. In supply chain management approaches, the emphasis shifts to the total costs (and values created) in the joint activities of more than one firm. The typical focus is on the dyad: two firms where time and inventories are substantially reduced.

The need for evolution in MPC systems implies the need for periodic auditing that compares system responses to the marketplace's requirements. The audit must address not only the system's focus but also the concomitant training of people and match with current objectives. Although the MPC framework in Figure 1.1 is general, its application is specific and evolving. Keeping it on track is an essential feature of MPC itself.

Concluding Principles

This chapter lays the groundwork for the rest of the book. Defining and adjusting the MPC system to support the manufacturing activity are an ongoing challenge. We hope that, as you read the rest of the book, you constantly ask how the general framework applies in specific instances, and what is happening to ensure a better match between MPC system design and marketplace dictates. From the chapter we draw the following principles:

- The framework for MPC is general, and all three phases must be performed, but specific applications necessarily reflect particular company conditions and objectives.
- In supply chain environments, the MPC system must coordinate the planning and control efforts across all companies involved.
- Manufacturing planning and control systems should support the strategy and tactics pursued by the firm in which they are implemented.
- Different manufacturing processes often dictate the need for different designs of the MPC system.
- The MPC system should evolve to meet changing requirements in the market, technology, products, and manufacturing processes.
- The manufacturing planning and control system should be comprehensive in supporting the management of all manufacturing resources.
- An effective MPC system can contribute to competitive performance by lowering costs and providing greater responsiveness to the market.
- In firms that have an integrated ERP system and database, the MPC system should integrate with and support cross-functional planning through the ERP system.

References

Anderegg, Travis. *ERP: A–Z Implementer's Guide for Success*. Cibres Inc, 2000.

Artiba, A., and S. E. Elmaghraby, eds. *The Planning and Scheduling of Production Systems: Methodologies and Applications*. Chapman & Hall, 1997.

Biemans, F. P. M. *Manufacturing Planning and Control: A Reference Model*. New York: Elsevier, 1990.

Blackburn, Joseph D. *Time-Based Competition: The Next Battle Ground in American Manufacturing.* Homewood, Ill.: Business One Irwin, 1991.

Bodington, C. Edward. *Planning, Scheduling, and Control Integration in the Process Industries.* New York: McGraw Hill, 1995.

Dennis, D. R., and Jack R. Meredith. "An Analysis of Process Industry Production and Inventory Management Systems," *Journal of Operations Management* 18, no. 6 (November 2000), pp. 683–699.

Duplaga, Edward A., and Peter A. Pinto. "Adapting Production Processes to Respond to Evolutionary Changes in Market Conditions: A Case Study," *Production and Inventory Management Journal,* 1st–2nd quarter, 2002.

Ehie, Ike C. "Determinants of Success in Manufacturing Outsourcing Decision: A Survey Study," *Production and Inventory Management Journal,* first quarter, 2001.

Eversheim, Walter; F. Klocke; T. Pfeifer; and M. Weck. *Manufacturing Excellence in Global Markets.* Chapman & Hall, 1997.

Fine, C. H. *Clockspeed—Winning Industry Control in the Age of Temporary Advantage.* Perseus Publishing, 1999.

Flynn, B. B.; Roger G. Schroeder; and E. James Flynn. "World Class Manufacturing: An Investigation of Hayes and Wheelwright's Foundation," *Journal of Operations Management* 17, no. 3 (March 1999), pp. 249–269.

Fogarty, D. W.; J. H. Blackstone, Jr.; and T. R. Hoffmann. *Production and Inventory Management Journal,* 2nd ed. Cincinnati: Southwestern, 1991.

Geoffrion, A. M. "Progress in Operations Management, *Production and Operations Management* 11, no. 1 (2002), pp. 92–100.

Goodwin, B.; M. Seegert; J. Cardillo; and E. Bergmann. "Implementing ERP in a Big Way," *The Performance Advantage,* June 1996.

Greene, James H., ed. *American Production and Inventory Control Society Production and Inventory Control Handbook,* 3rd ed. New York: McGraw-Hill, 1997.

Hax, Arnoldo C. *Production and Inventory Management.* Englewood, N.J.: Prentice Hall, 1983.

Howard, Alexander. "A Rule-Base for the Specification of Manufacturing Planning and Control System Activities," *International Journal of Operations & Production Management* 22, no. 1 (2002), p. 7.

Jacobs, F. R., and V. A. Mabert. *Production Planning, Scheduling, and Inventory Control: Concepts, Techniques, and Systems,* 3rd ed. Atlanta: Institute of Industrial Engineering, Monograph Series, 1986.

Kehoe, Dennis. "Internet Based Supply Chain Management: A Classification of Approaches to Manufacturing Planning and Control," *International Journal of Operations & Production Management* 21, no. 4 (2001), p. 516.

Landvater, Darryl V. *World Class Production and Inventory Management,* 2nd ed. New York: John Wiley & Sons, 1997.

Li, Lode; Evan L. Porteus; and Hongtao Zhang. "Optimal Operating Policies for Multiplant Stochastic Manufacturing Systems in a Changing Environment," *Management Science* 47, no. 11 (November 2001), p. 1539.

Mabert, Vincent A., and F. Robert Jacobs, eds. *Integrated Production Systems Design, Planning, Control, and Scheduling,* 4th ed. Institute of Industrial Engineers, November 1992.

Mabert, Vincent A.; Ashok Soni; and M. A. Venkataramanan. "Enterprise Resource Planning Survey of U.S. Manufacturing Firms," *Production and Inventory Management Journal,* 2nd quarter, 2000.

McGrath, M. E., and Hoole, R. W. "Manufacturing's New Economies of Scale," *Harvard Business Review* 70, no. 3 (May/June 1992), p. 94.

Miller, Jeffrey; Arnoud De Meyer; and Jinichiro Nakane. *Benchmarking Global Manufacturing: Understanding International Suppliers, Customers, and Competitors.* New York: McGraw-Hill, 1992.

Narasimhan, S. L.; Dennis W. McLeavey; and Peter J. Billington. *Production Planning and Inventory Control,* 2nd ed. Englewood Cliffs, N.J.: Prentice Hall, 1994.

Papke-Shields, K. E.; Manoj K. Malhotra; and Varun Grover. "Strategic Manufacturing Planning Systems and Their Linkage to Planning System Success," *Decision Sciences Journal* 33, no. 1 (Winter 2002), pp. 1–30.

Parker, G. "Progress in Operations Management," *Production and Operations Management* 11, no. 1 (2002), pp. 92–100.

Plossl, George W., and Oliver W. Wight. *Production and Inventory Control: Principles and Techniques,* 2nd ed. Englewood Cliffs, N.J.: Prentice Hall, 1985.

Plossl, George. *Managing in the New World of Manufacturing: How Companies Can Improve Operations to Compete Globally.* Englewood Cliffs, N.J.: Prentice Hall, 1991.

Pontrandolfo, P., and O. G. Okogbaa. "Global Manufacturing: A Review and a Framework for Planning in a Global Corporation," *International Journal of Production Research* 37, no. 1 (1999), p. 1.

Prasad, S., and Sunil Babbar. "International Operations Management Research," *Journal of Operations Management* 18, no. 2 (February 2000), pp. 209–247.

Ptak, Carol A., and Eli Schragenheim, eds. *ERP: Tools, Techniques, and Applications for Integrating the Supply Chain.* Boca Raton, Fla.: CRC Press, 1999.

Rondeau, Patrick J., and Lewis A. Litteral. "Evolution of Manufacturing Planning and Control Systems: From Reorder Point to Enterprise Resources Planning," *Production and Inventory Management Journal* 42, no. 2 (2nd quarter 2001), p. 1.

Schmenner, R. W., and Morgan L. Swink. "On Theory in Operations Management," *Journal of Operations Management* 17, no. 1 (December 1998), pp. 97–113.

Schroeder, Roger G., and Barbara B. Flynn. *High Performance Manufacturing: Global Perspectives.* New York: John Wiley & Sons, 2001.

Silver, Edward; David F. Pyke; and Rein Peterson. *Inventory Management and Production Planning and Scheduling,* 3rd ed. New York: John Wiley & Sons, 1998.

St. John, C. H.; Alan R. Cannon; and Richard W. Pouder. "Change Drivers in the New Millennium: Implications for Manufacturing Strategy Research," *Journal of Operations Management* 19, no. 2 (February 2001), pp. 143–160.

Tersine, Richard J. *Principles of Inventory and Materials Management,* 4th ed. Englewood Cliffs, N.J.: Prentice Hall, 1993.

Tully, Shawn. "Following the Money," *Fortune,* Dec. 3, 2002.

Vollmann, Thomas E.; William Lee Berry; and David C. Whybark. *Integrated Production and Inventory Management: Revitalizing the Manufacturing Enterprise.* New York: Irwin/McGraw-Hill, 1992.

Wallace, Thomas F., and Michael H. Kremzar. *ERP: Making It Happen: The Implementers' Guide to Success with Enterprise Resource Planning,* 3rd ed. New York: John Wiley & Sons, 2001.

West, Martin. *Flexibility and Productivity: Two Fundamental Properties of Production Processes in International Manufacturing Networks,* The Department of Production Economics, Linköping Institute of Technology, Linköping, Sweden, 2002.

Whybark, D. C., and Gyula Vastag, eds. *Global Manufacturing Practices: A Worldwide Survey of Practices in Production Planning and Control.* Elsevier Science, 1993.

Wortmann, J. C.; J. Wijngaard; and J. W. M. Bertrand. *Production Control.* North-Holland, 1990.

Discussion Questions

1. In this chapter we have identified three forces that influence the changes in which MPC systems must function and adapt: internationalization, the role of the customer, and the use of information (such as ERP) systems. At times these all work together. Identify some of the ways in which international customers use information systems to interact with the MPC system of a company.

2. The discussion of the framework for manufacturing planning and control seems to imply that overall direction setting must be done before detailed material and capacity planning activities can be accomplished. The latter must be done before executing and controlling the plans is possible. Do you agree? Give an example supporting your position.

3. Apply the MPC framework to a college setting. In particular, identify the front end, engine, and back end.

4. We have suggested that as changes take place in the world, the MPC system would require modifications to adapt. What changes can you see that will require changes in the MPC system?

5. One of the local company's production managers asked you to advise her on installing an MPC system. She starts by asking you which particular software brand you prefer and if you believe in ERP systems. What questions would you ask her?

Chapter

2

Demand Management

This chapter covers issues concerned with how a firm integrates information from and about its customers, internal and external to the firm, into the manufacturing planning and control system. It is in this module that all potential demands on manufacturing capacity are collected and coordinated. Demand management includes activities that range from determining or estimating the demand from customers, through converting specific customer orders into promised delivery dates, to helping balance demand with supply. A well-developed demand management system within the manufacturing, planning, and control (MPC) system brings significant benefits to the firm. Proper planning of all externally and internally generated demands means capacity (ultimately, supply) can be better managed and controlled. Information that helps to integrate the needs of the customers with the capabilities of the firm can be developed. Timely and *honest* customer order promises are possible. Physical distribution activities can be improved significantly. This chapter shows how to achieve these benefits. The focus is a combination of techniques and management concepts necessary to perform this integrative activity. This chapter is organized around the following topics:

- *Demand management in MPC systems:* What role does demand management play in the manufacturing planning and control system?
- *Demand management and the MPC environment:* How do the different manufacturing environments shape the demand management activities?
- *Communicating with other MPC modules and customers:* What are the communication linkages between demand management, other MPC modules and customers?
- *Providing appropriate forecast information:* What are the needs for forecast information within the firm?
- *Information use in demand management:* How is information converted to knowledge and manufacturing plans?
- *Producing and evaluating detailed forecasts:* What techniques for providing detailed forecasts have proved useful in practice, and what are the metrics of forecast quality?
- *Using the forecasts:* What techniques are useful in keeping the detailed forecasts and aggregate management plans synchronized?
- *Managing demand:* What day-to-day management activities are required to manage demand?
- *Company examples:* Effective demand management in practice.

Several chapters in this book closely relate to demand management. Sales and operations (Chapter 3) is the area where much of the demand management information is used to develop formal company plans. Externally, as we are satisfying customers, we in turn are a customer, so this chapter is closely related to supply chain management (Chapter 17). Demand management provides information to the company that is used in master production scheduling (Chapter 6), capacity planning (Chapter 10), and production activity control (Chapter 11). Additional technical detail on the management of inventories is found in basic inventory concepts (Chapter 5).

Demand Management in MPC Systems

Demand management is a gateway module in manufacturing planning and control (MPC), providing the link to the marketplace, sister plants, warehouses, and other important "customers." As such, it is in demand management that we gather information from and about the market doing things like forecasting customer demand, entering orders, and determining specific product requirements. Moreover, it is through this module that we communicate with our customers by promising delivery dates, confirming order status, and communicating changes. Demand management is also concerned with identifying all sources of demand for manufacturing capacity, including service-part demands, intracompany requirements, and promotional inventory buildup or other needs for pipeline inventory stocking.

The position of demand management in the MPC system is shown in Figure 2.1. It is the key connection to the market in the front end of the MPC system. The external aspects of the demand management module are depicted as the double-ended arrow connected to the marketplace outside the MPC system. This simply underscores the need to communicate with the customers as well as to gather information from and about them. The other linkages are with the sales and operations planning (SOP) module and the master production scheduling (MPS) module. The information provided to SOP is used to develop sales and operations (including manufacturing) plans covering a year or more in duration at a fairly high level of aggregation. Both forecast and actual demand information is provided to the MPS module. It is in the MPS module that short-term, product-specific manufacturing plans are developed and controlled as actual demand becomes available and information is provided to provide delivery promises and order status to customers.

FIGURE 2.1 **Demand Management in the MPC System**

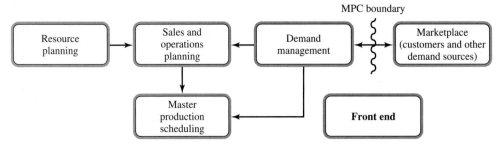

It is through these linkages that quantities and timing for all demands must be collected and coordinated with the **planning** and **control** activities of the company. The planning part of manufacturing planning and control (MPC) involves determining the capacity that will be made available to meet actual future demands for products. Much of this planning activity occurs in the sales and operations module. The control part determines how the capacity will be converted into products as the orders come in. The company **executes** the plan as actual demand information becomes available. The control function determines how the company will modify the plans in light of forecast errors and other changes in assumptions that inevitably occur. A substantial portion of the control activity is conducted in the master production scheduling module. Both the SOP and MPS modules require the information provided through the demand management module.

For many firms, planning the execution and controlling demand quantities and timings are a day-to-day interactive dialogue with customers. For other firms, particularly in the process industries, the critical coordination is in scheduling large inter- and intracompany requirements. For still others, physical distribution is critical, since the factory must support a warehouse replenishment program, which can differ significantly from the pattern of final customer demand.

The difference between the pattern of demand and the response by the company points out the important distinction between **forecasts** and **plans.** In demand management, forecasts of the quantities and timing of customer demand are developed. These are estimates of what might occur in the marketplace. Manufacturing plans that specify how the firm will respond are based on these forecasts. The plan for response can look quite different from the forecasts. Take a highly seasonal product like snowboards as an example. The actual pattern of customer demand will be high in the fall and winter months and very low at other times. The manufacturing plan, however, might be constant throughout the year.

This distinction between forecasts and plans is important for two reasons. First, a manager cannot be held responsible for not getting a forecast right. We can and should hold managers responsible for making their plans, however. Much of what the MPC system is about is providing the means for making as good a set of executable plans as possible and then providing the information to execute them. When conditions change, the control function should change the plans and the new plans should be executed faithfully. As much as we like to hold the weatherman responsible for not forecasting the rain, the forecast is only a guess, albeit an intelligent one. If the forecast is for rain, an intelligent plan would be to carry an umbrella. If you don't, it is hard to feel sorry for you when you get wet. You have control over the plan and execution, and not the demand.

This brings us to the second reason for making a distinction between the plan and the forecast. The demands of customers are **independent demands.** When (and if) a customer decides to buy our product, that decision is independent of the actions of the company. Obviously, we can influence the timing (and quantities) through advertising, pricing, promotions, and so forth, but the ultimate decision rests with the customer. On the other hand, if we have plans for building snowboards at a constant rate throughout the year, the demand for the decals that are needed can be calculated. The demand for the decals depends on our plans for producing the snowboards. It is **dependent demand.** Similarly, the "demand" from our warehouses for snowboards depends on our plans for replenishing the warehouses. When conditions change, the plans may need to change and this, in turn, could change the dependent demands that need to be coordinated in the demand management module.

It also may be necessary to reconcile different sources of demand information, provide forecasts for new products, and modify forecasts to meet the requirements of the users or otherwise adjust the information for use in the company. All these considerations are taken into account in the demand management process. Techniques for forecasting, aggregating (pooling) demand, and disaggregating demand can facilitate this process.

The linkage between demand management, sales and operations planning, and master production scheduling in the front end makes clear the importance of providing complete forecasts and providing them at the appropriate level of detail. The importance of identifying all sources of demand is obvious, but sometimes overlooked. If material and capacity resources are to be planned effectively, we must identify *all* sources of demand: spare parts, distribution, inventory changes, demonstration stock, new items, promotions, and so on. Only when we have accounted for all demand sources can we develop realistic MPC plans.

Demand Management and the MPC Environment

Demand management activities must conform to the strategy of the firm, the capabilities of manufacturing, and the needs of customers. Different strategies, capabilities, and customer needs define different MPC environments within which demand management activities are carried out. In order to understand how the activities might differ from environment to environment, we first develop a broad classification of manufacturing environments. Key to this classification is the concept of the **customer order decoupling point** or, as it is sometimes called, the **order penetration point.**

The customer order decoupling point can be looked at as the point at which demand changes from independent to dependent. It is the point at which the firm—as opposed to the customer—becomes responsible for determining the timing and quantity of material to be purchased, made, or finished. Consider for a moment a small tailor shop. If customers go into the shop and buy suits from the available stock (off the rack), the customer order decoupling point is the finished suit (the finished goods inventory). In this case, the customer decides which suit to buy and when to buy it (independent demand for the suits). The tailor decides what suits to make and when to make them (dependent demand for the fabric).

If, on the other hand, customers look over the available inventory of fabrics, make their choice, and request a specific suit design, the customer order decoupling point is the raw material inventory of fabric. Similarly, if the customer looks at catalogs of fabrics, chooses one, and requests the tailor to make a specific design, the customer order decoupling point is the supplier. In this latter case, both the customer and the supplier are included in the tailor's manufacturing decisions. In the examples of buying or making suits, the customer order decoupling point has moved deeper into the tailor's organization.

Figure 2.2 provides a means for visualizing the customer order decoupling point as it might move from finished goods inventory through the company all the way back to the supplier. The different locations of the customer order decoupling point give rise to different categories of manufacturing environments. Firms that serve their customers from finished goods inventory are known as **make-to-stock** firms. Those that combine a number of options together to meet a customer's specifications are called **assemble-to-order** firms. Those that make the customer's product from raw materials, parts, and components are **make-to-order firms.** An **engineer-to-order** firm will work with the customer to design the product,

FIGURE 2.2
Customer Order Decoupling Point in Different Environments

Inventory location	Suppliers	Raw materials	Work-in-process (WIP) parts and components	Finished goods
Customer order decoupling point				
Environment	Engineer-to-order (ETO)	Make-to-order (MTO)	Assemble-to-order (ATO)	Make-to-stock (MTS)

then make it from purchased materials, parts, and components. Of course, many firms will serve a combination of these environments and a few will have all simultaneously.

For our purposes in describing the role of demand management in different situations, we will characterize the MPC environments as make-to-stock, assemble-to-order, or make-to-order (we will consider the engineer-to-order and make-to-order environment together).

The Make-to-Stock (MTS) Environment

In the make-to-stock (MTS) environment, the key focus of the demand management activities is on the maintenance of finished goods inventories. In this environment, since the customers buy directly from the available inventory, customer service is determined by whether their item is in stock or not. As we saw with the tailor that sold suits, the customer order decoupling point is the finished goods inventory. It is at this point that the independent demand of the customer for suits becomes the dependent demand for fabric to support the tailor's plans for making suits. Unlike the tailor, however, inventory of manufactured goods may be located very far from the manufacturing plant. Moreover, there may be several locations from which the customers buy their goods. This means that there is both a geographical and temporal dimension to the maintenance of finished goods inventory. Thus tracking of demand by location throughout the supply chain is an important activity in the MTS environment.

A key aspect of the management of the finished goods inventory is the determination of when, how much, and how to replenish the stock at a specific location. This is the **physical distribution** concern in demand management. This can be an extremely broad concern, encompassing numerous locations in many countries, and involving several levels of distribution and storage. Some MTS firms employ plant warehouses, distribution centers, local warehouses, and even **vendor-managed inventory** inside their customers' locations. Management of this supply chain requires information on the status of inventory in the various locations, relationships with transportation providers, and estimates of the customers' demands by location and item. Formal methods of forecasting customer demand can help in this process.

The essential issue in satisfying customers in the make-to-stock environment is to balance the level of inventory against the level of service to the customer. If unlimited inventory were possible and costless, the task would be trivial. Unfortunately, that is not the case. Providing more inventory increases costs, so a trade-off between the costs of the inventory and the level of customer service must be made. The trade-off can be improved by better estimates (or knowledge) of customer demand, by more rapid transportation alternatives, by speedier production, and by more flexible manufacturing. Many MTS firms are investing in such **lean manufacturing** programs in order to shift the trade-off, i.e., to achieve higher service levels for a given inventory investment. Regardless of how the trade-off comes out, the focus of demand management in the make-to-stock environment is on providing finished goods where and when the customers want them.

The Assemble-to-Order (ATO) Environment

Returning to our tailor for a moment, imagine that you were interested in buying an ensemble consisting of a jacket, a matching pair of slacks, a contrasting pair of slacks, and a vest. You would make your choices from the finished items of each and the tailor would then cut and sew them to your size. This is a form of assemble-to-order (ATO) business. Many manufacturing examples exist. You may have experienced this yourself when you ordered a personal computer. You decided what components you wanted and the company assembled the components to complete your order. Many people buy their cars this way, and some industrial products are assembled to meet the users' specifications.

In the assemble-to-order environment, the primary task of demand management is to define the customer's order in terms of alternative components and options, e.g., a two-door versus four-door car, with or without antilock brakes. It is also important to assure that they can be combined into a viable product in a process known as **configuration management.** This is a critical step, since it might not be possible to assemble certain combinations. In a sports car, for example, mounting the center "boom box" of a deluxe sound system might fill the cavity in which the convertible top fits. Not only is that not desirable, it may not be physically possible to assemble that combination. In addition to combinations that can't go together there may be combinations that must go together. For example, a heavy-duty radiator might be required for certain air conditioning units in a car. One of the capabilities required for success in the assemble-to-order environment is engineering design that enables as much flexibility in combining **components, options,** and **modules** into finished products as possible.

The assemble-to-order environment clearly illustrates the two-way nature of the communication between customers and demand management. Customers need to be informed of the allowable combinations, and the combinations should support marketplace desires, such as sports trim for cars. Moreover, customers' orders must be configured and the customers must be informed of the delivery date of the finished product. In this environment, the independent demand for the assembled items is transformed into dependent demand for the parts required to produce the components needed. The inventory that defines customer service is the inventory of components, not the inventory of finished product.

Some ATO firms have applied lean manufacturing principles to dramatically decrease the time required to assemble finished goods. By so doing they are delivering customers' orders so quickly that they appear to be MTS firms from the perspective of the customer.

There are some significant advantages from moving the customer order decoupling point from finished goods to components. The number of finished products is usually substantially greater than the number of components that are combined to produce the finished product. Consider, for example, a computer for which there are four processor alternatives, three hard disk drive choices, four CD-DVD alternatives, two possible speaker systems, and four monitors available. If all combinations of these 17 components are valid, they can be combined into a total of 384 different final computer configurations. It is much easier to manage and forecast the demand for 17 components than for 384 computers. If N_i is the number of alternatives for component i, the total number of combinations for n components (given all are viable) is:

$$\text{Total number of combinations} = N_1 * N_2 * \cdots * N_n \qquad \textbf{(2.1)}$$

The Make (Engineer)-to-Order (MTO) Environment

The focus of demand management in the MTS and ATO environments was largely on satisfying customers from the appropriate inventory—finished goods or components. In the make-to-order and engineer-to-order environments, there is another resource that needs to be taken into account—engineering. Moving the customer order decoupling point to raw materials or even suppliers puts independent demand information further into the firm and reduces the scope of dependent demand information. Moreover, the nature of the information needed from customers changes. We knew what the customers could buy in the MTS and ATO environments, but not if, when, or how many; in the make (engineer)-to-order environment, on the other hand, we are not sure what they are going buy. We need, therefore, to get the product specifications from the customers and translate these into manufacturing terms in the company. This means that a task of demand management in this environment is to coordinate information on customers' product needs with engineering.

The need for engineering resources in the engineer-to-order case is somewhat different than in the make-to-order case. In the make-to-order environment, engineering determines what materials will be required, what steps will be required in manufacturing, and the costs involved. The materials can come from the company's inventory or be purchased from suppliers. In the engineer-to-order environment, more of this same information is needed from customers, although more of the detail design may be left to the engineers than the customer. Because of the need for engineering resources in this environment, demand management's forecasting task now includes determining how much engineering capacity will be required to meet future customer needs. This may be complicated because some orders can be in progress, even though they aren't completely specified and engineered, so material coordination is still important. Although there is certainly some overlap among them, a summary of the major tasks in demand management for each of the environments is provided in Figure 2.3.

The customer order decoupling point could actually be with the supplier in the engineer-to-order case. In all the environments, suppliers' capabilities may limit what we are able to do, so coordination with them is essential. This span of involvement from

FIGURE 2.3 **Key Demand Management Tasks for Each Environment**

Tasks	MTS	ATO	MTO
Information	Provide forecast	Configuration management	Product specifications
Planning	Project inventory levels	Determine delivery dates	Provide engineering capacity
Control	Assure customer service levels	Meet delivery dates	Adjust capacity to customer needs

customer to supplier gives rise to the term **supply chain** (sometimes called the **demand chain**) and the coordination of activities along the supply chain is referred to as **supply chain management.** This is a concept that we will see again in our discussion of demand management.

Communicating with Other MPC Modules and Customers

Regardless of the environment, demand management has important internal and external communication tasks. Forecast information must be provided to sales and operations planning (SOP). Detailed demand information must be communicated to master production scheduling (MPS) and information on product availability must be made available to customers both for planning purposes and to manage the day-to-day customer order activities. Some of the major communication needs are shown in Figure 2.4.

Sales and Operations Planning

A key requirement for demand management communication with sales and operations planning is to provide demand forecast information. In turn, sales and operations planning will provide coordinated sales and operations plans. In order for these plans to be comprehensive, all sources of demand must be accounted for, both in quantity and timing. It is not sufficient to simply determine the market needs for product. To get a complete picture of the requirements for manufacturing capacity, engineering resources, and material needs, we must gather demand information for spare parts, inter- and intracompany transfers, promotion requirements, pipeline buildups, quality assurance needs, exhibition or pilot project requirements, and even charitable donations. Sometimes this is more difficult than it appears. The difficulty seems to be greatest for companies with a significant number of inter-plant transfers. We've often heard plant managers complain that their worst customer is a sister plant or division.

Choosing the appropriate measure for determining capacity needs is important to effective communication between demand management and SOP. The measure can vary with the environment. For instance, material capacity may be most important in the make-to-stock environment, while it may be machine and/or labor hours in the make-to-order case. Engineering capacity is often most critical in the engineer-to-order environment. It is essential that the demand management communication with sales and operations planning be in the proper units for the development of their plans. Moreover, both internal and external

FIGURE 2.4 **Demand Management Communication Activities for Each Environment**

Connection	MTS	ATO	MTO
SOP	Demand forecasts	Demand forecasts, product family mix	Demand forecasts, engineering detail
MPS	Actual demands	Mix forecasts, actual demands	Final configuration
Customer(s)	Next inventory replenishment	Configuration issues, delivery date	Design status, delivery date

timing issues need to be communicated. For instance, if changes in the timing of deliveries to a significant customer could affect the plans, this information must be communicated to sales and operations planning. Similarly, a major change in distribution inventory policy might influence the plan.

Sales and operations planning may develop plans by product families, geographical regions, organizational units, or even combinations of these and other categories. This means the plans may not line up completely with the market. For instance, some customers may want only some units from each of several families, while others may want several complete families. Moreover, the sales and operations plans may be stated in dollars or some other aggregate measure, while the market buys specific products. This creates the need for demand management to translate and synchronize the communication of data between market activities and SOP.

Master Production Scheduling

Interactions between demand management and master production scheduling (MPS) are frequent and detailed. As customer orders are received and entered into the MPS, the detailed order information must be provided to the master production scheduler as the orders occur. Similarly, demand management needs information on the status of orders, capacity consumed, and capacity available so customers can be kept informed. Details vary significantly between make-to-stock, assemble-to-order, and make-to-order environments. In all instances, however, the underlying concept is that forecasts are consumed over time by actual customer orders, as Figure 2.5 shows. In each case, forecast future orders lie to the right and above the line, while actual customer orders are to the left and below the line.

Observe in Figure 2.5 that the lines for the three environments are quite different. For the make-to-stock environment, there are very few actual customer orders, since demand is generally satisfied from inventory. This reflects the need to manage the finished goods inventory. In the assemble-to-order environment there are customer orders already booked for several periods into the future, reflecting the need to provide accurate delivery promise dates to the customers. Still different demand management problems confront the firm with a make (engineer)-to-order environment, even though there's a larger backlog of customer orders. Communication between the firm and the customer first involves engineering, as orders become completely specified, and then project management status and delivery date promising.

FIGURE 2.5
Forecasts Consumed by Orders

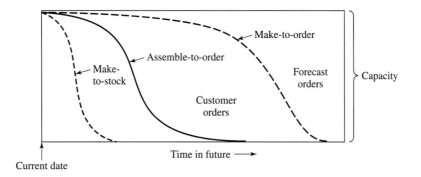

The types of uncertainty also differ between these environments. In the make-to-stock case, uncertainty is largely in the demand variations around the forecast at each of the inventory locations. In this case, additional levels of inventory **(safety stock)** are held in order to provide the service levels required. In the assemble-to-order case, the uncertainty involves not only the quantity and timing of customer orders but product mix as well. For the make-to-order environment, the uncertainty is often not the timing or quantity of the customer order but, rather, what level of company resources will be required to complete the engineering and produce the product once the exact requirements are determined. One aspect of the communications between master production scheduling and demand management is to facilitate buffering against the uncertainties that exist.

Dealing with Customers on a Day-to-Day Basis

A primary function of the demand management module is converting specific day-to-day customer orders into detailed MPC actions. Through the demand management function, actual demands consume the planned materials and capacities. Actual customer demands must be converted into production actions regardless of whether the firm manufactures make-to-stock, assemble-to-order, or make-to-order products. Details may vary, depending on the nature of the company's manufacturing environment.

In make-to-order environments, the primary activity is controlling the progress of customer orders in order to meet the promised delivery dates. Any engineering or manufacturing changes must be related to the master production scheduler to determine their impact on the final delivery to the customer. While firms often perform this function the same way for assemble-to-order products, only limited communication with engineering would be needed to determine promise dates. In both these environments, there's communication from the customer (a request for a product) and to the customer (a delivery date) through the demand management module. Later there may be additional communication with the customer to respond to order status requests. These aspects of demand management have such names as **order entry, order booking,** and **customer order service.**

In a make-to-stock environment, demand management doesn't ordinarily provide customer promise dates. Since finished goods are stocked, the customer is most often served from inventory. If there's insufficient inventory for a specific request, the customer must be told when more will be available or, if there's allocation, told what portion of the request can be satisfied. Conversion of customer orders to MPC actions in the make-to-stock environment triggers resupply of the inventory from which sales are made. This conversion is largely through forecasting, since the resupply decision is in anticipation of customer orders.

In all these environments, extraordinary demands often must be accommodated. Examples include replacement of items after a disaster, advance orders in the make-to-stock environment, unexpected interplant needs, large spare-part orders, provision of demonstration units, and increased channel inventories. These all represent "real" demands on the material system.

Some clear principles emerge from this consideration of the relationship between demand management and the other modules in the front end of the MPC system. It is essential that all sources of demand be identified and incorporated in the planning and control activities of the firm. Demand management is responsible, as well, for communicating with the customers. Keeping the customer honestly informed of the status of an order is important to customer satisfaction, even if it is bad news that must be communicated.

Information Use in Demand Management

The information gathered in demand management can be used to enhance current and future performance of the firm. Some ways in which this is done are discussed below.

Make-to-Knowledge

As shown in Figure 2.5, a basic concept of demand management is that there is a "pipe" of capacity, which is filled in the short run with customer orders and the long run with forecasts; order entry is a process of consuming the forecast with actual orders. Performance has improved for many state-of-the-art situations, where supply chain partnerships are created. Between these suppliers and customers the goal is to improve the competitiveness of the entire chain, not just that of each of the companies independently. In some cases this allows the two firms to operate with **knowledge** of the other firm's needs. Figure 2.6 depicts this situation where a supplier has a forecast of demand, a set of actual orders, and also knowledge of the situation in some key customers. Examples of such knowledge would include the customer's inventory position (when using vender managed inventories, for example) and/or production schedule. This information allows one to know as closely as the customer when an order will be needed. This reduces the dependency on forecasts.

The knowledge comes from a natural evolution in the use of **electronic data interchange (EDI)** and **Internet**-based systems. The first interfirm applications of these communication means tends to consist of electronically processing transactions, such as orders, invoices, and payments. But a logical next step is to use the information channels to enhance knowledge. This requires determining the key data in the customers' and suppliers' companies that could be accessed by the partnership for better overall effectiveness. There are important potential implications from using knowledge. One example is the decreasing number of order transactions. If the goal is to maximize effectiveness of the overall supply chain, many of these types of transactions can be eliminated.

Philips Consumer Electronics (USA) is operating in this mode with Wal-Mart. Philips, using EDI, knows what the stock positions are in the Wal-Mart stores' warehouses. This allows Philips to know (not forecast) when Wal-Mart will need more of Philips' products. A similar communication exists between many large supermarkets and their suppliers. **Point-of-sale (POS)** data are electronically passed to the suppliers, so they know when a delivery is needed. In fact, some partnerships are trying to implement payment to the supplier on the basis of actual sales measured through POS data, with no order or delivery transactions.

FIGURE 2.6
Replacing Forecasts with Knowledge

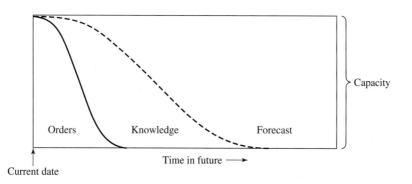

Data Capture and Monitoring

Data capture and monitoring activities of demand management fall into two broad categories: the overall market and the detailed product mix. The data most appropriate for sales and operations planning is overall market trends and patterns for the product familes. The intent is to determine on an ongoing basis any changes in the general levels of actual business for input to the sales and operations planning process. The second activity concerns monitoring the product mix for master production scheduling and customer order promising. The intent is to quickly determine changes in customer preferences for adjusting manufacturing and providing delivery information.

For both the overall market and the detailed product mix, it's important to capture actual demand data where possible. Many companies use sales instead of demand for purposes of making demand projections. Unless all demands have been satisfied, sales can understate actual demand. In other instances we know of firms that use shipments as the basis for projecting demands. In one such instance, the company concluded its demand was increasing since its shipments were increasing. Not until they had committed to increased raw-material purchases did they realize the increased shipments were replacement orders for two successive overseas shipments lost at sea.

It's in demand management that we explicitly define service levels and resultant safety stocks. The requisite degree of production flexibility for responding to mix or engineering design changes is set here as well. Then, through conversion of day-to-day customer orders into product shipments, we realize the company's actual service levels. Careful capture and management of actual demands can provide the stability needed for efficient production, and that stability provides the basis for realistic customer promises and service. Booking actual orders also serves to monitor demand against forecasts. As changes occur in the marketplace, demand management can and should routinely pick them up, indicating when managerial attention is required.

Customer Relationship Management

An important tool for gathering information on customers is **customer relationship management (CRM).** This is a very broad topic in its own right, so we discuss only a few of the demand management uses of the tool. In many consumer product companies, particularly those establishing supply chain relationships over the Internet, individual customer data is being captured and monitored by using CRM software. Since the data comes from requests by individual customers, it reflects more closely actual customer demand. In addition, it can provide closer insights on the real current needs of customers than historical data or projected trends. For MTS firms, capturing information at this level of detail can help to discern early demand and mix trends, provide the basis for new products and services, and lead to the development of knowledge-gaining activities that improve efficiency along the supply chain.

In the make- or assemble-to-order environments, CRM can be a useful means for developing similar insights into the customers. Data from CRM can be used to develop make-to-knowledge plans on an individual customer basis. Gathering current information on the customers' preferences can provide early warnings of shifts in design and mix preferences. This can be a big advantage to engineering and also provide information that could be useful in the development of raw material purchasing and manufacturing scheduling. Although not as explicit as the knowledge available with vendor-managed inventories, it can be useful in managing mix and service levels.

Outbound Product Flow

Physical distribution (outbound product flow) activities are planned on the basis of the information developed in the demand management function. Customer delivery promise dates, inventory resupply shipments, interplant shipments, and other such information from demand management are used to develop short-term transportation schedules. Information on the specific timing for resupply shipments can be integrated with distribution planning as well. For example, the information can be used to schedule resources at the warehouse and provide for the delivery capacity needed.

The distribution equivalent of the SOP and MPS function is the determination of the overall plans for moving the product to the customer and scheduling the shipments through the distribution system. This means determining the transportation and warehouse capacity, scheduling the movement of product and accounting for product availability so customers can be kept informed. The management of product distribution requires the same comprehensiveness of demand determination that the other functions need, since it is within this capacity derived from that demand that the day-to-day distribution function operates. Adequate planning of the capacity needs greatly facilitates day-to-day distribution operations.

Providing Appropriate Forecast Information

In this chapter, we deal primarily with preparing forecast information for the MPC linkages within the MPC front end (e.g., those between SOP and MPS and demand management). Forecasting information can come from a variety of sources, have different levels of aggregation, incorporate different assumptions about the market, and manifest other differences that need reconciliation before it can be used for planning and control. Here we look at some of the bases upon which forecasting methods are determined, some of the reasoning behind aggregating forecasts, and some of the means by which forecasts are reconciled for planning purposes.

A Forecasting Framework

Managers need forecasts for a variety of decisions. Among these are strategic decisions involving such things as constructing a new plant, developing more supplier capacity, expanding internationally, and other long-run company-wide considerations. Forecasts for this type of decision are highly aggregated estimates of general business trends over the long term. These broadly based forecasts are much too general for sales and operations planning, even though some aggregation is necessary for SOP. The forecast needs for both these applications (strategic considerations and sales and operations planning) are different, as well, from the forecasts that are needed for short-term scheduling and execution decision making in master production scheduling. Not only is the basis of the forecast different for each of these applications, but the investment in forecasting, the nature of the techniques used, and the frequency varies as well. A framework for some of the differences is provided in Figure 2.7.

FIGURE 2.7 **A Framework for Forecasting**

Nature of the Decision	Strategic Business Planning	Sales and Operations Planning	Master Production Scheduling and Control
Level of aggregation	Total sales or output volume	Product family units	Individual finished goods or components
Top management involvement	Intensive	When reconciling functional plans	Very little
Forecast frequency	Annual or less	Monthly or quarterly	Constantly
Length of forecast	Years by years or quarters	Several months to a year by months	A few days to weeks
Management investment in the forecast(s)	Very large	Moderate	Very little
Cost of data processing and acquisition	High	Moderate	Minimal
Useful techniques	Management judgment, economic growth models	Aggregation of detailed forecasts, customer plans	Projection techniques (moving averages, exponential smoothing)

The general principle indicated here is that the nature of the forecast must be matched with the nature of the decision. The level of aggregation, the amount of management review, the cost, and the time frame of the forecast needed really depends on the nature of the decision being made. Moreover, the source of the forecast can vary by need as well, as indicated by the useful techniques line in Figure 2.7. The frequency and number of forecasts needed for most short-term operating decisions don't warrant extensive management involvement, so computer-generated forecasts are utilized. Strategic decisions, on the other hand, are less frequent and involve more risk, thus justifying use of more expensive procedures and management involvement.

Forecasting for Strategic Business Planning

Among the decisions that require long-term, broadly based forecasts are those involving capital expansion projects, proposals to develop a new product line, and merger or acquisition opportunities. The forecasts are usually stated in very general terms such as total sales dollars or some output measure such as total tons, board feet, or engineering hours. This level of aggregation can be related to economic and business indicators such as the gross national product, net disposable income or market share of a particular industry. In turn, it is related to measures of capacity that may be required to meet the future demands. Substantial managerial judgment is required in preparing and reviewing these forecasts since the risk from making (or not making) an investment can be very large.

Causal models and the statistical tools of regression and correlation analysis can be used to augment the managerial insight and judgment needed for making these forecasts. Such models relate the firm's business to indicators that are more easily forecast or are available as general information. For example, household fixtures and furniture sales are closely related to housing starts. Housing starts and building permits in an area are usually public information, readily available to the firm. The relationship between housing starts and furniture sales may be statistically modeled to provide another forecast of demand. In addition, there are accuracy measures available with the statistical techniques to help determine the usefulness of the forecast. Moreover, using these models can lead to improved forecasting results and can help neutralize any emotion involved in the decision.

Forecasting for Sales and Operations Planning

The forecasts needed for sales and operations planning ultimately provide the basis for plans that are usually stated in terms of planned sales and output of product families in dollars or some other aggregate measure. The plans extend for a few months up to a year into the future for each of the product lines they cover. The forecasts, then, must also be aggregated to the product family level and cover the same (or a greater) number of periods.

One important input into the forecasts for SOP is information on customer plans and current demand information. Insights into the customers' future plans are gained through discussions with marketing and communication with customers through demand management. This information can be augmented with current data on inventory balances, demand levels, and product mix preferences through programs like CRM and vendor-managed inventory (VMI). These are important sources of information for the development of the sales and operations plans.

A common means for producing an aggregated forecast for SOP is to sum the forecasts for the individual products in each product line. These totals can then be adjusted by incorporating knowledge of customers' plans, current trends, and any marketing plans that would influence demand. However the forecasts are developed, managerial insight and judgment are important in using them to develop the plans. Developing the forecast is not the same as developing the plan.

Forecasting for Master Production Scheduling and Control

Demand management supports the decisions made in the master production scheduling module by providing detailed forecasts on a nearly continuous basis. The result of the MPS decisions is a statement of how many of a finished product or component to make and when to do so. These decisions occur constantly as conditions change in the market and in manufacturing. Consequently, the flow of forecast information to the MPS is frequent and detailed.

Also occurring constantly are control decisions that change priorities for production, allocation of inventory, and destinations of shipments. As products move from purchasing of raw material to distribution of finished goods, changes that require adjustments occur in all areas of the process. To compensate for these changes, control decisions must be made quickly and efficiently to keep the product moving to the customer. If the demand for the product is dependent, then the timing and quantities can be calculated from the plans for their **parents** (the products that they are used on); if the demand is independent, then it must be forecast. Forecasting to support these day-to-day control decisions must be frequent, detailed, and timely.

To produce these detailed forecasts, it is most common to use mechanical procedures, procedures that can be incorporated into the demand management software. Most often, these are models for "casting forward" historical information to make the "fore cast." Implicit in this process is a belief that the past conditions that produced the historical demand won't change. However, we shouldn't draw from this the impression that managers can always rely on past information to estimate future activity. In the first place, in certain instances, we simply have no past data. This occurs, for example, when a new product is introduced, a future sales promotion is planned, a new competitor appears, or new legislation affects our business. These circumstances all illustrate the need for managerial review and modification of the forecast where special knowledge should be taken into account.

These different approaches simply underscore the variety of sources, aggregation, and purposes of forecasts. In the next section we illustrate two very common techniques for producing the forecasts used to support MPS and control decisions. We'll also provide common measures of forecast quality.

Producing and Evaluating Detailed Forecasts

In this section, we'll introduce two very common short-term forecasting techniques: **moving averages** and **exponential smoothing.** We choose these procedures since they are commonly available in commercial software and meet the criteria of low cost and little management involvement. The techniques are simple mathematical means for converting past information into forecasts. The procedures, often called *statistical forecasting models,* can easily be automated and incorporated into demand management activities.

There are a number of more complicated forecasting procedures that have been developed and we contemplated including some of them in this book, but research has shown the simple procedures to be at least as effective, especially for detailed, frequent forecasts. For example, Bernard Smith developed a novel approach to short-term forecasting called *focus forecasting.* It involves evaluating several simple forecasting models and choosing the one that performed best in the past to make the current forecast. Flores and Whybark compared focus forecasting and an average of all the forecasts produced with simple exponential smoothing. Simple exponential smoothing performed the best.

In another study, Spyros Makridakis and his colleagues challenged experts to a forecasting competition. A total of 21 forecasting models were tested on 1,001 actual data sets. Forecasting accuracy was determined with five different measures. There was no one model that consistently outperformed all the others for all series, but one conclusion was very clear. Simple methods do better than the more sophisticated models for detailed forecasts, especially over short periods. Another conclusion was that any special knowledge about demand patterns should be used to develop the forecast. If you ignore the seasonal sales pattern of swimsuits, you do so at your peril.

Moving-Average Forecasting

Moving-average and exponential smoothing forecasting are both concerned with averaging past demand to project a forecast for future demand. This implies that the underlying demand pattern, at least for the next few days or weeks, is constant with random fluctuations about the average. Thus the objective is to smooth out the random fluctuations while being sensitive to any possible changes that may be taking place with the underlying average.

Figure 2.8 shows the number of cases of a household cleaning liquid shipped to retail stores from an East Coast distribution center in each of the last nine weeks. If there were requests for shipments that couldn't be fulfilled, it would be desirable to capture that

FIGURE 2.8 **Demand for Household Cleaning Liquid (Past Nine Weeks)**

	Week Number								
	24	25	26	27	28	29	30	31	32
Cases shipped	1,600	1,500	1,700	900	1,100	1,500	1,400	1,700	1,200

information to get better estimates of the actual demand. For our examples, though, we will consider the shipments to represent the demand. The past demand is plotted in Figure 2.9.

A tempting procedure would be to simply draw a line through the data points and use that line as our estimate for week 33 and subsequent weeks. This would require constant management involvement in making the forecasts, however. Rather than draw a line through the points in Figure 2.9 to find the average, we could simply calculate the arithmetic average of the nine historical observations. Since we're interested in averaged past data to project into the future, we could even use an average of all past demand data available for forecasting purposes. There are several reasons, however, why this may not be a desirable way of smoothing. In the first place, there may be so many periods of past data that storing them all is an issue. Second, often the most recent history is most relevant in forecasting short-term demand in the near future. Recent data may reveal current conditions better than data several months or years old. For these reasons, the moving average procedure uses only a few of the most recent demand observations.

The moving-average model for smoothing historical demand proceeds, as the name implies, by averaging a selected number of past periods of data. The average moves because a new average can be calculated whenever a new period's demand is determined. Whenever a forecast is needed, the most recent past history of demand is used to do the averaging.

Equation (2.2) shows the model for finding the moving average. The equation shows the moving average forecast always uses the most recent n periods of historical information

FIGURE 2.9
Plot of the Past Demand for Household Cleaning Liquid

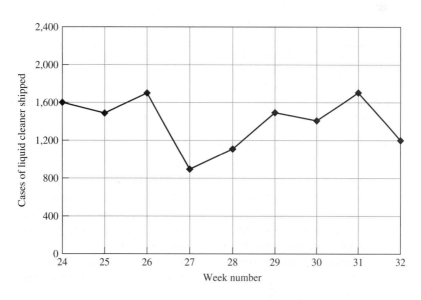

FIGURE 2.10   **Example Moving-Average Calculations**

	Period					
	27	**28**	**29**	**30**	**31**	**32**
Actual demand	900	1,100	1,500	1,400	1,700	1,200

$$\text{6-period MAF made at the end of period } 32 = \sum_{27}^{32} \text{actual demand}/6$$

$$= (900 + 1{,}100 + 1{,}500 + 1{,}400$$
$$+ 1{,}700 + 1{,}200)/6 = 1{,}300 \qquad (2.2)$$

$$\text{3-period MAF made at the end of period } 32 = \sum_{30}^{32} \text{actual demand}/3$$

$$= (1{,}400 + 1{,}700 + 1{,}200)/3 = 1{,}433 \qquad (2.2)$$

available for developing the forecast. Notice the moving average is the forecast of demand for the next and subsequent periods. This timing convention needs to be clearly understood. We are at the end of period t; we know the demand in period t and forecasts are made for periods $t + 1$, or $t + X$ periods into the future. Forecasts are not made for period t since that period's demand is known. Figure 2.10 shows sample calculations for the number of cases shipped.

$$\text{Moving average forecast (MAF)} \atop \text{at the end of period } t\text{: MAF}_t = \sum_{i=t-n+1}^{t} \text{actual demand}_i/n \quad \textbf{(2.2)}$$

where:

  $i = $ period number

  $t = $ current period (the period for which the most recent actual demand is known)

  $n = $ number of periods in the moving average

You'll note the moving-average model does smooth the historical data, but it does so with an equal weight on each piece of historical information. We could adjust this, of course, by incorporating different weights on past periods. In fact the *weighted-moving-average* model does exactly that, but at the cost of complexity and more data storage. In addition, some data play no part in making a moving average forecast. For example, the demand of 900 in week 27 has no weight in the 3-period moving average forecast for period 33. Exponential smoothing addresses both of these considerations in making forecasts.

Exponential Smoothing Forecasting

The exponential smoothing model for forecasting doesn't eliminate *any* past information, but so adjusts the weights given to past data that older data get increasingly less weight (hence the name exponential smoothing). The basic idea is a fairly simple one and has a great deal of intuitive appeal. Each new forecast is based on an average that's adjusted each time there's a new forecast error. For example, if we forecast 90 units of demand for an item in a particular period and that item's actual demand turns out to be 100 units, an appealing

FIGURE 2.11 **Example Exponential Smoothing Calculations**

	Period	
	27	28
Actual demand	900	1,100

Assume:

ESF_{26} = exponential smoothing forecast made at the end of period 26 = 1,000, α = .1

ESF_{27} (made at the end of period 27 when actual demand for period 27 is known but actual demand in period 28 is not known) =

$$1,000 + .1(900 - 1,000) = 990 \tag{2.3}$$

$$.1(900) + (1 - .1)1,000 = 990 \tag{2.4}$$

$$ESF_{28} = .1(1,100) + (1 - .1)990 = 1001 \tag{2.4}$$

idea would be to increase our forecast by some portion of the 10-unit error in making the next period's forecast. In this way, if the error indicated demand was changing, we would begin to change the forecast. We may not want to incorporate the entire error (i.e., add 10 units), since the error may have just been due to random variations around the mean.

The proportion of the error that will be incorporated into the forecast is called the **exponential smoothing constant** and is identified as α. The model for computing the new average appears in Equation (2.3) as we've just described it. Equation (2.4) gives the most common computational form of the exponentially smoothed average. The new exponentially smoothed average is again the forecast for the next and subsequent periods. The same timing convention is used; that is, the forecast is made at the end of period t for period $t + X$ in the future. Figure 2.11 shows example calculations for the number of cases shipped.

Exponential smoothing forecast (ESF) at the end of period t:

$$ESF_t = ESF_{t-1} + \alpha(\text{actual demand}_t - ESF_{t-1}) \tag{2.3}$$

$$= \alpha(\text{actual demand}_t) + (1 - \alpha)ESF_{t-1} \tag{2.4}$$

where:

α = the smoothing constant $(0 \leq \alpha \leq 1)$

t = current period (the period for which the most recent actual demand is known)

ESF_{t-1} = exponential smoothing forecast made one period previously (at the end of period $t - 1$)

Let's compare exponential smoothing and moving average forecasting procedures. Figure 2.12 compares a 5-period MAF with an ESF using α = .3. In preparing the forecast for period 28, the 5-period MAF would apply a 20 percent weight to each of the five most recent actual demands. The ESF model (with α = .3) would apply a 30 percent weight to the actual demand in period 27 as seen here:

$$ESF_{27} = \text{period 28 forecast} = .3 \,(\text{period 27 actual demand}) + .7 \,(ESF_{26})$$

FIGURE 2.12 **Relative Weights Given to Past Demand by a Moving Average and Exponential Smoothing Model**

	Period								
	20	**21**	**22**	**23**	**24**	**25**	**26**	**27***	**28**
5-period MAF weights	0%	0%	0%	20%	20%	20%	20%	20%	—
ESF weights ($\alpha = .3$)	2%	4%	5%	7%	10%	15%	21%	30%	—

*Forecast made at the end of period 27.

By looking at the ESF for period 27, made at the end of period 26 (i.e., ESF_{26}), we see it was determined as

$$\text{ESF}_{26} = .3 \text{ (period 26 actual demand)} + .7 \text{ } (\text{ESF}_{25})$$

By substitution, ESF_{27} can be shown to be

$$\text{ESF}_{27} = .3 \text{ (period 27 actual demand)}$$
$$+ .7 \text{ } [.3 \text{ (period 26 actual demand)} + .7 \text{ } (\text{ESF}_{25})]$$

The result of this calculation is a weight of 0.21 ($.7 \times .3$) being applied to the actual demand in period 26 when the forecast for periods 28 and beyond is made at the end of period 27. By similar substitution, we can derive the entire line for the ESF weights in Figure 2.12.

Figure 2.12 shows, for the forecast made at the end of period 27, 30 percent of the weight is attached to the actual demand in period 27, 21 percent for period 26, and 15 percent for period 25. The sum of these weights, 66 percent, is the weight placed on the last three periods of demand. The sum of all the weights given for the ESF model in Figure 2.12 is 94 percent. If we continue to find the weights for periods 19, 18, and so on, the sum for all weights is 1.0, as intuition would tell us. If the smoothing constant were .1 instead of .3, a table like Figure 2.12 would have values of .1, .09, and .081 for the weights of periods 27, 26, and 25, respectively. The sum of these three (27 percent) is the weight placed on the last three periods. Moreover, ($1 - 27\% = 73\%$) is the weight given to all actual data *more than* three periods old.

This result shows larger values of α give more weight to recent demands and utilize older demand data less than is the case for smaller values of α; that is, larger values of α provide more responsive forecasts, and smaller values produce more stable forecasts. The same argument can be made for the number of periods in an MAF model. This is the basic trade-off in determining what smoothing constant (or length of moving average) to use in a forecasting procedure. The higher the smoothing constant or the shorter the moving average, the more responsive forecasts are to changes in underlying demand, but the more "nervous" they are in the presence of randomness. Similarly, smaller smoothing constants or longer moving averages provide stability in the face of randomness but slower reactions to changes in the underlying demand. Ultimately, however, the trade-off between stability and responsiveness is reflected in the quality of the forecasts, a subject to which we now turn.

Evaluating Forecasts

Ultimately, of course, the quality of any forecast is reflected in the quality of the decisions based on the forecast. This leads to suggesting the ideal comparison of forecasting procedures would be based on the costs of producing the forecast and the value of the forecast for the

FIGURE 2.13
Example Bias
Calculation

	Period (i)			
	1	**2**	**3**	**4**
(1) Actual demand	1,500	1,400	1,700	1,200
(2) Forecast demand	1,600	1,600	1,400	1,300
Error (1) − (2)	−100	−200	300	−100

$$\text{Bias} = \sum_{i=1}^{4} \text{error}_i / 4 = (-100 - 200 + 300 - 100)/4$$

$$= -100/4 = -25. \tag{2.5}$$

decision. From these data, the appropriate trade-off between the cost of developing and the cost of making decisions with forecasts of varying quality could be made. Unfortunately, neither cost is easily measured. In addition, such a scheme suggests that a different forecasting procedure might be required for each decision, an undesirably complex possibility. As a result of these complications, we rely on some direct measures of forecast quality.

For any forecasting procedure we develop, an important criterion is honesty, or lack of bias; that is, the procedure should produce forecasts that are neither consistently high nor consistently low. Forecasts shouldn't be overly optimistic or pessimistic, but rather should "tell it like it is." Since we're dealing with projecting past data, lack of **bias** means smoothing out past data's randomness so that forecasts that are too high are offset by forecasts that are too low. To measure bias, we'll use the **mean error** as defined by Equation (2.5). In this equation, the **forecast error** in each period is actual demand in each period minus forecast demand for that period. Figure 2.13 shows an example calculation of bias.

$$\text{Mean error (bias)} = \frac{\sum_{i=1}^{n} (\text{actual demand}_i - \text{forecast demand}_i)}{n} \tag{2.5}$$

where:

i = period number

n = number of periods of data

As Figure 2.13 shows, when forecast errors tend to cancel one another out, the measure of bias tends to be low. Positive errors in some periods are offset by negative errors in others, which tends to produce an average error, or bias near zero. In Figure 2.13, there's a bias and the demand was over forecast by an average of 25 units per period for the four periods.

Having an unbiased forecast is important in manufacturing planning and control, since the unbiased estimates, on average, are about right. But that's not enough. We still need to be concerned with the errors' magnitude. Note, for the example in Figure 2.13, we obtain the identical measure of bias if actual demand for the four periods had been 100, 100, 5,500, and 100, respectively. (This is shown as part of the calculations in Figure 2.14.) However, the individual errors are much larger, and this difference would have to be reflected in extra inventory if we were to maintain a consistent level of customer service. Let's now turn to a widely used measure of forecast error magnitude, the **mean absolute**

FIGURE 2.14
Sample MAD Calculations

	Period (i)			
	1	**2**	**3**	**4**
(1) Actual demand	1,500	1,400	1,700	1,200
(2) Forecast demand	1,600	1,600	1,400	1,300
Error (1) − (2)	−100	−200	300	−100

$$\text{MAD} = \sum_{i=1} |error_i|/4$$
$$= (|-100| + |-200| + |300| + |-100|)/4 = 175 \tag{2.6}$$

	Period (i)			
	1	**2**	**3**	**4**
(1) Actual demand	100	100	5,500	100
(2) Forecast demand	1,600	1,600	1,400	1,300
Error (1) − (2)	−1,500	−1,500	4,100	−1,200

$$\text{Bias} = \sum_{i=1}^{4} error_i/4 = (-1,500 - 1,500 + 4,100 - 1,200)/4$$
$$= -100/4 = -25 \tag{2.5}$$
$$\text{MAD} = \sum_{i=1}^{4} |error_i|/4$$
$$= (|-1,500| + |-1,500| + |4,100| + |-1,200|)/4$$
$$= 8,300/4 = 2,075 \tag{2.6}$$

deviation (MAD). The equation for calculating MAD is provided in Equation (2.6), while Figure 2.14 shows example calculations.

$$\text{Mean absolute deviation (MAD)} = \frac{\sum_{i=1}^{n} |\text{actual demand}_i - \text{forecast demand}_i|}{n} \tag{2.6}$$

The mean absolute deviation expresses the size of the average error irrespective of whether it's positive or negative. It's the combination of bias and MAD that allows us to evaluate forecasting results. Bias is perhaps the most critical, since we can compensate for forecast errors through inventory, expediting, faster delivery means, and other kinds of responses. MAD indicates the expected compensation's size (e.g., required speed). However, if a forecast is consistently lower than demand, the entire material-flow pipeline will run dry; it will be necessary to start over again with raw materials. Inventory buildups can arise with a consistently high forecast.

Before turning to some managerial issues concerning forecasting, we would like to provide one other relationship that is quite useful. The most widely used measure of deviation or dispersion in statistics is the **standard deviation.** MAD also measures deviation (error) from an expected result (the forecast). When the forecast errors are distributed normally, there is a direct relationship between the two measures that can be used to develop statistical insights and conclusions. The standard deviation of the errors is arithmetically related to MAD by Equation (2.7):

$$\text{Standard deviation of forecast errors} = 1.25 \text{ MAD} \qquad \textbf{(2.7)}$$

In the demand management module we are interested in providing the appropriate level of detail and frequency of the forecast to the other modules in the front end of the MPC system. This may require modification of the forecasts or reconciliation with other forecast sources before they can be used for decision making.

Using the Forecasts

Using the forecasts requires a heavy dose of common sense, as well as application of techniques. In this section, we'll look at some technical reasons for aggregating forecasts and some of the methods for readying the forecasts for use in sales and operations planning. We'll also review some means for incorporating management information into the forecasts.

Considerations for Aggregating Forecasts

In Figure 2.7 we pointed out different means of developing forecasts for different uses in the company. For sales and operations planning, one source of forecast might be the aggregation by product family of the detailed forecasts for individual products. Other inputs might come from marketing and our knowledge of customers. The result of reconciling all these sources is an aggregate demand forecast that is used for developing the sales and operations plans.

There are several reasons for aggregating product items in both time and level of detail for forecasting purposes. We must do it with caution, however. Aggregating individual products into product lines, geographical areas, or customer types, for example, must be done in ways that are compatible with the planning systems. Product groupings must also be developed, so that the forecast unit is sensible to forecasters. Provided we follow these guidelines, we can use product groupings to facilitate the forecasting task.

It's a well-known phenomenon that long-term or product-line forecasts *are more accurate than short-term and/or detailed forecasts*. This merely verbalizes a statistical verity. Consider the example in Figure 2.15. Monthly sales average 20 units but vary randomly with a standard deviation of 2 units. This means 95 percent of the monthly demands lie between 16 and 24 units when demand is normally distributed. This corresponds to a forecast error of plus or minus 20 percent around the forecast of 20 units per month.

FIGURE 2.15
Effect of Aggregating on Forecast Accuracy

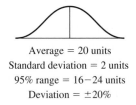

Monthly sales distribution

Average = 20 units
Standard deviation = 2 units
95% range = 16−24 units
Deviation = ±20%

Yearly sales distribution

Average = 240 units
Standard deviation = 6.9 units
95% range = 226−254 units
Deviation = ±5.8%

Now suppose, instead of forecasting demand on a monthly basis, we prepare an annual forecast of demand—in this case, 240 (12 months × 20 units/month) units for the year. If monthly sales are independent, the resulting standard deviation is 6.9 units. This is found by noting that the variance of the monthly distribution is 4 units (2^2). The variance of the yearly distribution is 48 (12 months × 4), so the standard deviation is 6.9 ($\sqrt{48}$). This corresponds to a 95 percent range of 226 to 254 units or a ±5.8 percent deviation. The reduction from ±20 percent to ±5.8 percent is due to using a much longer time period. The same effect can be seen in forecasting demand for product lines instead of for individual items.

In the assemble-to-order environment, Equation (2.1) shows the number of items that need to be forecast when finished products are used instead of the components. This is often a substantial increase in the number and, because of the detail, often results in very poor forecasting performance. For example, what is the forecast for red, two-door, small engine, antilock-brake cars with sport stripes. It is much easier to forecast demand for the components than the detailed component combinations. Many of the same advantages of error reduction that accrue to aggregating are possible here as well.

An issue arises whenever aggregations of products, regions, or time periods are used to develop strategic or sales and operations plans. The total forecast must be consistent with the individual product forecasts. The whole must be equal to the sum of the parts. Very often an individual product's share of the aggregate product line totals remains fairly constant. That is, there is more uncertainty in the day-to-day demand for the item than for its share in the demand for the total line. We can use this knowledge to disaggregate the aggregate forecasts and thereby maintain the consistency between the detail and the totals. We may even be able to show improvements in the accuracy of the detail forecasts by doing it this way. One formal method for achieving consistency is described next.

Pyramid Forecasting

When the basis of the aggregated forecast for sales and operations planning is the sum of product level forecasts produced by, say, exponential smoothing, it is unlikely that this sum would match the aggregate forecasts developed by other sources. Yet, for example, knowledge of customers' and marketing plans need to be taken into account at the individual item level. In addition, there may be budget restrictions, income goals, or other company considerations that shape the aggregate forecasts that need to be taken into account in developing the final forecasts at the item level. One procedure for doing this is **pyramid forecasting.** It provides a means of coordinating, integrating, and assuring consistency between the various sources of forecasts and any company constraints or goals.

Figure 2.16, from a paper written by Newberry and Bhame, provides the basic framework for pyramid forecasting. The procedure used in implementing the approach often begins with individual product item forecasts at level 3, which are rolled up into forecasts for product lines shown as level 2. We then aggregate forecasts for product lines into a total business forecast (in dollars) at level 1 in Figure 2.16. Once the individual item and product line forecasts have been rolled up and considered in finalizing the top management forecast (plan), the next step is to force down (constrain) the product line and individual item forecasts, so they're consistent with the plan.

In the example shown in Figure 2.17, the 11 individual product items are divided into two product lines. Two of these items, X_1 and X_2, form product line X (which we'll study in detail), while the remaining products, Z_1 through Z_9, are included in product line Z. These two product lines, X and Z, represent the firm's entire range of products. Figure 2.17 shows unit prices and initial forecasts for each level.

FIGURE 2.16
Pyramid
Forecasting
Example

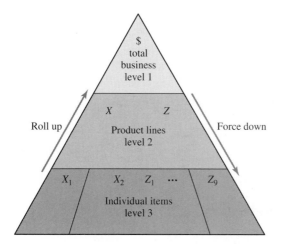

FIGURE 2.17
Initial and
Roll-Up
Forecasts

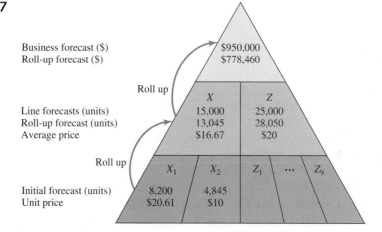

The roll-up process starts by summing the individual item forecasts (level 3) to provide a total for each line (level 2). For the X line, the roll-up forecast is 13,045 units (8,200 + 4,845). The sum of the individual Z line items gives a forecast of 28,050 units. Note that the X line roll-up doesn't correspond to the forecast of 15,000 units for the line. If there's substantial disagreement at this stage, reconciliation could occur or an error might be discovered. If there's to be no reconciliation at this level, we needn't prepare independent forecasts for the lines. If dollar forecasts are required at level 2, prices at level 3 can be used to calculate an average price.

To roll up to the level 1 dollar forecasts, the average prices at the line level are combined with the line roll-up forecasts. The total of $778,460 [(13,045 × 16.67) + (28,050 × 20.00)] is less than the independent business forecast of $950,000. For illustrative purposes, we'll assume management has evaluated the business forecast and the roll-up forecast and has decided to use $900,000 as the forecast at level 1. The next task is to make the line and individual item forecasts consistent with this amount. To bring about the

FIGURE 2.18
Forcing down the Management Forecast of Total Sales

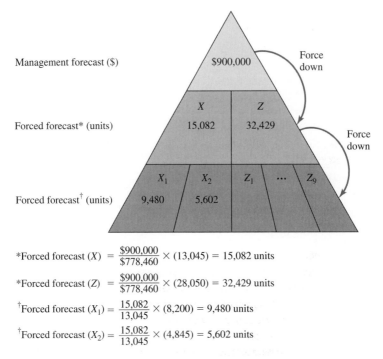

Management forecast ($) $900,000 Force down

Forced forecast* (units)

X	Z
15,082	32,429

Force down

Forced forecast† (units)

X_1	X_2	Z_1	...	Z_9
9,480	5,602			

$$*\text{Forced forecast } (X) = \frac{\$900,000}{\$778,460} \times (13,045) = 15,082 \text{ units}$$

$$*\text{Forced forecast } (Z) = \frac{\$900,000}{\$778,460} \times (28,050) = 32,429 \text{ units}$$

$$^{\dagger}\text{Forced forecast } (X_1) = \frac{15,082}{13,045} \times (8,200) = 9,480 \text{ units}$$

$$^{\dagger}\text{Forced forecast } (X_2) = \frac{15,082}{13,045} \times (4,845) = 5,602 \text{ units}$$

consistencies, we use the forcing-down process. The ratio between the roll-up forecast at level 1 ($778,460) and the management total ($900,000) is used to make the adjustment.

The forecasts at all levels appear in Figure 2.18. The results are consistent forecasts throughout the organization, and the sum of the parts is forced to equal the whole. Note, however, the process of forcing the consistency needs to be approached with caution. In the example, forecasts at the lower level are now higher than they were originally and incorporate the plans at the higher levels. Even though the sum of the parts equals the whole, it's possible the people responsible for the forecast won't "own" the number. They mustn't be made to feel they're simply being given an allocation of someone else's wish list.

Incorporating External Information

Many kinds of information can and should be used to make good forecasts. For example, in a college town on the day of a football game, traffic around the stadium is a mess. An intelligent forecaster adjusts travel plans on game days to avoid the stadium traffic, if possible. He or she modifies the forecast, knowing the game's impact on traffic. A mechanical procedure based on observations during the week would probably forecast very little traffic around the stadium. We certainly wouldn't use such a forecast without adjusting it for game day. That simple principle is applicable to business forecasting as well, but it's surprising how often people fail to make these adjustments.

Examples of activities that will influence demand and perhaps invalidate the use of a routine exponential forecasting model are special promotions, product changes, competitors' actions, and economic changes. One of the primary ways to incorporate information about such future activities into the forecast is to change the forecast directly. We might do this if we knew, for example, there was to be a promotion of a product in the future, or we were going to open more retail outlets, or we were going to introduce a new product that would cannibalize the sales of an existing product. In these instances, we could adjust the forecast directly to account for the activities, just as we do for the game day. By recognizing explicitly that future conditions won't reflect past conditions, we can modify the forecast directly to reflect our assessment of the future.

We may need to change the forecasting method as well. If technology has prolonged the life of our products, we may need to change the parameters in the model that relates replacement sales to the average life of our products in the field. If, for example, we know one of our competitors is going to introduce a new product, we suspect the market will change, but we may not be sure of the change's direction or magnitude. In this case, we may want to do frequent forecasting and model testing to assess the effect of the new product. We could also make the smoothing constant larger in an exponential smoothing model and be more responsive to any changes. There may be circumstances where our knowledge would lead us to change both the forecast and the forecasting parameters.

Key in all of these adjustments is that intelligence must be included in the forecasts, and the forecasts must be readied for use in preparing and controlling the plans of the firm. Determining the appropriate level of aggregation and reconciling various forecasting approaches (perhaps with pyramid forecasting) are important steps in making the modifications.

Managing Demand

As we said at the start of this chapter, demand management is the gateway module between the company and marketplace. As such, it is where market intelligence is gathered, forecasts of demand are developed, and status information on customer orders is maintained. Much of what is required in managing demand is the discipline to be honest with both the internal and external customers. This is partly political, partly organizational, and partly a systems issue. In this section we look at some of the internal demand management activities that are required to effectively manage demand, including organization and systems monitoring. We'll also look at demand management's role in balancing supply and demand.

Organizing for Demand Management

Most companies already perform many, if not all, the activities associated with demand management. In many instances, organizational responsibility for these activities is widely scattered throughout the firm. The finance or credit department performs credit checks and order screening associated with customer orders. Sales, customer service, or supply chain management departments handle order entry or booking. Outbound product activities are associated with the distribution, traffic, or logistics departments of firms.

Organizational responsibility for demand management tends to be a function of the organization's history and nature. In marketing-oriented firms (where success requires close contact with demand trends and good customer relations), demand management might well be performed by the marketing or sales organization. In firms where product development requires close interaction between engineering and customers, a technical services department might manage demand. Some companies establish a materials or supply chain management function to coordinate demand management activities. These tend to be firms that feel it important to manage the flow of materials from purchasing raw materials through the production process to the customer. In all instances, we must clearly assign responsibilities to make sure nothing is left to chance.

If flexibility is a key objective, then management must carefully design and enforce rules for interacting with the system and customers so the system can provide this flexibility. By this we mean customer order processing must be established and enforced through the communication to the master production scheduling module. It involves carefully establishing rules for serving particular special customers. For example, if an extraordinarily large order is received at a field warehouse, procedures need to be established for determining whether that order will be allowed to consume a large portion of the local inventory or be passed back to the factory. We must define and enforce limits within which changes can be made. If a manager violates any of these procedures—for example, by saying, "I don't care how you do it, but customer X must get the order by time Y"—demand management is seriously undercut.

A useful technique for defining and managing these areas of responsibility is to require higher and higher levels of approval the nearer to the current date that a change is requested. This procedure doesn't preclude a change but does force a higher level of review for schedule changes to be made near term. The underlying concept is to take the informal bargaining out of the system. By establishing and enforcing such procedures for order entry, customer delivery date promising, changes to the material system, and responses to mix changes in the product line, everyone plays by the same rules. Clearly this is more a matter of management discipline than technique. The ability to respond "What don't you want?" to the statement "I have to have it right away" for a particular customer request helps establish this discipline.

Monitoring the Demand Management Systems

If demand management is to perform its role in the MPC system well, the data that are produced must be accurate, timely, and appropriate. This goes not only for the information that is consumed internally, but also for information that is provided to customers. Obviously this means that the data (both input and output) must be monitored and it also means that the systems themselves must be monitored. If forecasts for a particular product line suddenly increase fourfold, there had better be a way that someone can find this out and start tracking down why. To do this requires data monitoring capability, not only of the input data but the calculated data as well. The last thing you want is to be communicating patently wrong information to your customers. Think of the implications of either a too short or a too long delivery date promise, for example.

Monitoring the input and output of the configuration management system can disclose product opportunities and provide insights for managing the priorities for producing product modules and options. If customers are increasingly requesting product combinations that can't be built, it might be a signal to engineering to work on making the products feasible. These combinations could represent new product offerings. If the combinations that are being correctly configured are changing, it might mean that the demand for specific components is changing and manufacturing priorities should be adjusted. When manufacturing and/or engineering starts complaining that too many "bad" combinations are getting through configuration, it could mean that something has gone awry in the configuration management system.

Similar opportunities and concerns can arise in the order entry system. At order entry time there is an opportunity to pick up market intelligence through CRM, cross-sell complementary products, and further customer relationships. The essence of the complaints from customers, incorrect orders, missing information, and other such tips may signal the need for more training. Complaints from manufacturing about insufficient information from the customer may also mean more training is needed or could disclose a problem in the system itself. Consistent late or early delivery could signal a problem in the MPS–demand management communication link or some other aspect of delivery date promising.

The common theme in all of these examples is that data must be captured and evaluated to keep the system honest. As a key communication link to the market, it is particularly important to monitor the systems in demand management. An effective demand management module will gather marketing information, generate forecast information, screen and monitor performance information, and provide detailed action instructions to the material planning and control system. Only by careful monitoring of the system can we be assured that this is done effectively.

Balancing Supply and Demand

A key element of the demand management module is providing the information to help balance the supply of products with the demand. Gathering intelligence on actual conditions in the marketplace provides the basis for deciding whether to change the company's plans. We saw, in the forecasting section, the use of pyramid forecasting to harmonize various forecasts, other sources of information on the market, and company goals. At times this process will leave some potential demand unfulfilled. There are a myriad of legitimate reasons for this. Investments in capacity may not be warranted, some product lines may not be sufficiently profitable, key materials may be in short supply, and so forth.

At this time real management discipline is required. Purposely leaving some demand on the table is extremely difficult. A pleading customer is hard to turn away. Perhaps the most important activity in demand management is to be honest with customers. In our experience, customers prefer honest answers (even if they're unpleasant) to inaccurate information. A demand management module with discipline in the management and effective systems provides the basis for honest communication with customers. They can be told when to expect delivery or when inventory will be replenished—and they can count on it. Providing the basis for honest communication with customers can pay handsome dividends in terms of customer loyalty.

Company Examples

In this section, we illustrate actual demand management practice as well as records that demonstrate key concepts discussed in this chapter. These illustrations use material gathered from Dell Computer, Ross Products Division of Abbott Laboratories, and Kirk Motors, Ltd.

Configuration Management at Dell Computer Corporation

Dell Computer Corporation is a worldwide supplier of computer hardware and peripherals. In the manufacturing world, Dell is best known for its ability to **mass-customize** consumer products. It employs an assemble-to-order approach to build computers to customer specifications, often within a few hours of receiving the order. The orders can be for a single desktop or laptop for an individual or an order for a number of workstations and desktops for a company.

Using the Internet, Dell has turned configuration management over to the customer. The customer enters the Dell on-line store through the Internet and selects the product line of interest. For our example here, we'll use the Dell Dimension 8200 series desktop PC. Once the line is selected the customer can see the Dell recommended configuration and decide if

FIGURE 2.19

Dell Computer Corporation's Configuration System

CD or DVD Drive   *Learn More*

○ 48x Max CD-ROM Drive [subtract $50]

○ 16x Max DVD-ROM Drive [subtract $20]

○ 16x Max DVD-ROM Drive for Altec Lansing ADA 995 Speakers [subtract $50]

○ 40x/10x/40x Max CD-RW Drive with Roxio's Easy CD Creator® [add $30]

◉ 24x/10x/40x Max CD-RW Drive with Roxio's Easy CD Creator®

○ New 32x/10x/40x Max CD-RW/DVD Combo Drive w/ Roxio's Easy CD Creator® [add $99]

○ 32x/10x/40x Max CD-RW/DVD Combo Drive for Altec Lansing 995 Speakers [add $99]

○ DVD+RW/CD-RW Combo Drive with 1 DVD+RW disc [add $329]

○ DVD+ RW/CD-RW Combo Drive for ADA 995 Speakers (includes 1 DVD+RW disc) [add $329]

CD or DVD Burner for 2nd bay   *Learn More*

○ None [subtract $219]

○ 24x/10x/40x Max CD-RW Drive with Roxio's Easy CD Creator® [subtract $140]

○ 40x/10x/40x Max CD-RW Drive with Roxio's Easy CD Creator® [subtract $120]

◉ New 32x/10x/40x Max CD-RW/DVD Combo Drive w/ Roxio's Easy CD Creator®

○ 32x/10x/40x Max CD-RW/DVD Combo Drive for Altec Lansing 995 Speakers

○ DVD+RW/CD-RW Combo Drive with 1 DVD+RW disc [add $180]

○ DVD+ RW/CD-RW Combo Drive for ADA 995 Speakers (includes 1 DVD+RW disc) [add $180]

! Requires that you select the 48x Max CD-ROM Drive as your CD or DVD Drive selection

! Not compatible with your current CD or DVD Drive selection

that will be satisfactory. A customer who wants a different configuration can go into the configuration software to make the choices. The choices range from the system components such as the processor, memory, keyboard, and monitor to services such as on-line training and system support.

Customers make their choices by clicking on a circle next to the appropriate item. Figure 2.19 shows the choices for the CD, DVD, and DVD burner drives. Note that there is an opportunity to learn more about the choices available. At the bottom of the example, the configuration management system has pointed out to the customer that the choices are not compatible and what must be done to rectify the problem. In Figure 2.20 the choices for the video driver and a second monitor are shown. Here the customer is told that a second monitor won't work without one of the more expensive video cards.

The computer can be completely configured by the customer and the order placed without having to speak with anyone at Dell at all (though it remains an option, of course).

FIGURE 2.20
Additional Dell Choices

Video Card   *Learn More*

⦿ New 64MB DDR NVIDIA GeForce4™ MX Graphics Card with TV-Out

○ New 64MB DDR NVIDIA GeForce4™ TI 4200 Graphics Card with TV-Out and DVI [add $80]

○ New 128MB DDR NVIDIA GeForce4™ TI 4600 Graphics Card w/DVI and TV-Out [add $310]

A second monitor is only available for sale with video cards that support dual monitor (128mb Nvidia Geforce4 Ti 4600 or 64mb Nvidia Geforce4 Ti 4200 Graphics Cards). If you purchase two VGA (analog) monitors for these cards, you will also need to purchase the DVI-VGA Adapter.

Optional Second Monitor   *Learn More*

⦿ None

○ New 17 in (16.0 in v.i.s., .27dp) E772 Monitor [add $110]

○ 17 in (16.0 in viewable, .25dp) M782 Flat Screen CRT Monitor [add $160]

○ New 19 in (18.0 in v.i.s., .26dp) M992 Flat Screen CRT Monitor [add $300]

○ 19 in (17.9 in viewable, .24.25AG) P992 FD Trinitron® Monitor [add $429]

○ 21 in (19.8 in viewable, .24AG) P1130 FD Trinitron® Monitor [add $699]

○ New 15 in 1504FP Dell Ultrasharp™ Digital Flat Panel Display [add $450]

○ 17 in (17.0 in viewable) 1702FP Digital Flat Panel Display [add $800]

○ New 18 in 1800FP Dell Ultrasharp™ Digital Flat Panel Display [add $950]

○ 19 in (19.0 in viewable) 1900FP Digital Flat Panel Display [add $1100]

Moreover, once the order has been placed, the Dell order tracking system is available to the customer via the Internet. The customer can follow his or her system through to completion and delivery. This not only provides the best available information to the customer, it also avoids the necessity of having to answer status requests from a majority of the customers.

Forecasting at Ross Products

Ross Products Division of Abbott Laboratories is headquartered in Columbus, Ohio. The company produces a variety of nutritional products, including adult medical nutrition supplements and pediatric infant formulas, as well as ancillary equipment. An example of this equipment is a pump that supplies nutritional liquids to the stomach and that can also monitor the rate of flow. There are four manufacturing facilities in the United States, and Ross markets its products in the United States and overseas. Managers use a program entitled Log*Plus to perform demand management activities.

The firm uses a comprehensive approach to assure that all demands on capacity are included in the forecast. Figure 2.21 illustrates the system's key features. The demand management aspects of Log*Plus produces forecasts from national inputs and monitors actual demand against these forecasts. The process of producing the forecast used for planning starts with forecasts from marketing and sales in dollars by product groups. These are broken out by region in Log*Plus to provide plant-level forecasts of national demand. These data are

FIGURE 2.21
Forecasting Procedure for Ross Products Division, Abbott Laboratories

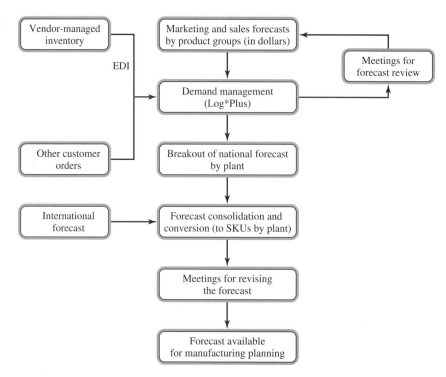

consolidated with the forecast for international sales and the total is converted to an item level forecast by plant. The process is not finished, however, until marketing, the product manager, and the production and inventory manager review the forecasts. Three times a year, meetings are held to review forecasts for all products in conjunction with budget meetings. These meetings can be held monthly for products that are experiencing changes, promotions, or other factors that could change demand.

To provide a service to customers and directly capture information on the market, Ross manages product inventory in some of its customers' facilities using VMI. Information on the use of these products is transmitted to Ross by electronic data interchange (EDI). These data are combined with the forecasts to produce reports such as the one shown in Figure 2.22 for SKU XYZ, a medical nutrition product in 8-ounce cans. The top of the figure shows several years' actual sales with two years and three months of forecast sales. (The current month is shown with an asterisk in year 0.) To facilitate any review of the forecasts, the data are plotted in the bottom half of the report. Here the seasonality is quite evident as is a sales peak about a year and a half ago (because of a promotion). These forecasts are a basic input to the master production scheduling module of the firm.

Customer Order Promising at Kirk Motors, Ltd.

Kirk Motors, Ltd., is a licensed motor vehicle dealer for Mitsubishi cars and trucks. Headquartered just outside of Wellington, New Zealand, Kirk has outlets in several cities in New Zealand. The company is a full-service distributor offering a complete range of Mitsubishi cars and trucks, with full maintenance and used-vehicle facilities. The company sells products that are assembled in New Zealand, Australia, and Japan. The wide variety of

FIGURE 2.22 Example Forecast for Ross Products Division, Abbott Laboratories

FCST: 8/31
PLAN: 9/20
STOCK: 9/20

MPS OPERATIONS DATA BASE

INDEX = 150

LEVEL	104	REPLN DB FRC	
TREND	0.0000	DATE TO MPS	
MSE	0.00	PLANNER	
MODEL TERMS		SRC NAME	
MODLFT EXPT	1	LEADTIME	0.00
MODLFT DATE	6/19	PWD LBS CONV	0.0000
TRND DISCNT	0.00	UNITS/CASE	0

HIST LENGTH		FORCE PLT	61396
HIST USED		67 KNO/BE	
OUTLRS FND		DEFAULT	
OUTLIER THR		DEFAULT	1.6552
SMOOTH CONST			24
PER FAST SMT			
MAX SS/LT	409681		

LEAD TIME	0.00
STK ON HAND	19313
INTRANSIT	430
SCHEDULED IN	8100
CURR PR FCST	58,971
EST. MONTH	53,491
MTD USAGE	48,142

DEMAND

	year −3	year −2	year −1	year 0	year +1	year +2
JAN	43344	63774	69839	64317	58507	54903
FEB	43492	61651	70819	60291	55323	57160
MAR	57933	56175	75732	57044	55528	54626
APR	54347	57004	61323	56381	55863	52434
MAY	50963	69295	72861	58564	57226	56359
JUN	59525	75039	81655	51098	60778	61925
JUL	58633	65850	70063	66546	61189	62623
AUG	61982	89558	81310	60501	60610	60790
SEP	63433	69850	69198	*58971	61638	60834
OCT	57188	62077	73592	66375	62563	59988
NOV	62559	58514	62432	59910	58150	55395
DEC	71563	67954	55607	63417	55834	
TOT	684962	796741	844431	723415	703209	637037

DEMAND DETAIL

PERIOD ENDING	STAT MODEL	MKT INTEL	PROMO	SCHED BACKLOG	DEP DEMAND	DIST DEMAND	TOTAL
9/30		58971					58971
10/31		66375					66375
11/30		59910					59910
12/31		63417					63417
1/31		58507					58507
2/27		55323					55323
3/31		55528					55528
4/30		55863					55863
5/31		57226					57226
6/30		60778					60778
7/31		61189					61189
8/31		60610					60610
TOTAL		713697					713697

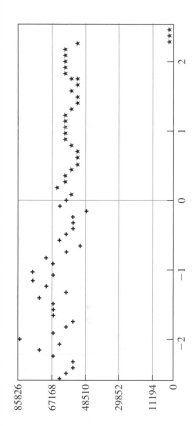

FIGURE 2.23   Kirk Motors Available to Promise from Stock

Vehicle Search								
Dealer		**Kirkwe**						
Model Package Options PT		KS6P41						
Dealer	**Order**		**PT**	**TM**	**BS**	**RS**	**AM**	**Locn**	**Due**
KIRKWE	631194		DF	A5	BABS	RSTD	AIM	KIRKWE	STOCK
			JX	A5	BABS	RSTD	AIM	TODDPK	STOCK
			JX	A5	BABS	RSTD	AIM	TODDPK	STOCK
			WP	A5	BABS	RSTD	AIM	TODDPK	STOCK
			WP	A5	BABS	RSTD	AIM	TODDPK	STOCK
			AE	A5	BABS	RSTD	AIM	TODDPK	STOCK
KIRKLH	631426		AE	A5	BABS	RSTD	AIM	KIRKLH	STOCK
MCVEMA	631294		DF	A5	BABS	RSTD	AIM	MCVEMA	STOCK
TOUR	626477		LR	A5	BABS	RSTD		TOUR	STOCK

production/option combinations means that keeping a complete inventory is impossible. Moreover, because of the multiple geographical sources of product, customer order promising is complicated. In order to facilitate customer order promising and to provide customers with information on the specific models they are interested in, the company uses an availability record. This record provides inventory and final-assembly schedule information. Consequently, the firm can provide very reliable product and delivery information to its customers.

The information to produce a response to a customer request is stored centrally, and individual requests for a specific model and options are run when a customer wants the information. Figure 2.23 is an example of part of the record for the Wellington, New Zealand, location. The header information gives the name of the dealer (Kirk, Wellington), and the salesperson specifies the vehicle model number (KS6P41, containing information on engine, doors, etc.), special packages, other options, and any paint (PT) specifications. Specifying the options does limit the search but doesn't provide any information for the customer to use for trading off, say, color for availability. For each vehicle listed, the paint (PT), trim (TM), brakes (BS), air bags (RS), alarm system (AM), location (Locn), and availability (Due) codes are provided. The vehicles in stock are listed first, starting with those at the Wellington dealership (KIRKWE) and continuing with those in stock at the New Zealand assembly plant (Todd Park, located near Wellington) and then those at other dealers at ever-increasing distances from Wellington. If the customer finds the desired vehicle in stock, then arrangements are made for delivery at the Wellington location.

The salesperson can use the system to look at the automobile assembly schedule to determine availability if the vehicle is not in stock (or is too far away for delivery). An example is shown in Figure 2.24, again for the Wellington dealership. The information is the same except that now the assembly dates are provided in the Due column. Vehicles that are not already promised to a dealer are available to promise to customers. In addition, for vehicles to be assembled in the future there is some flexibility for the customer to change

FIGURE 2.24   **Kirk Motors Available to Promise from Assembly**

Vehicle Search									
Dealer	**Kirkwe**								
Model	KS6P41								
Package									
Options									
PT									
Dealer	**Order**		**PT**	**TM**	**BS**	**RS**	**AM**	**Locn**	**Due**
DONNDN	630606		LQ	A5	BSTD	RSTD	AIM	TODDPK	01MAR
KIRKNM	630675		DF	A5	BSTD	RSTD	AIM	TODDPK	01MAR
DALLHA	630678		DA	A5	BSTD	RSTD	AIM	TODDPK	01MAR
KIRKMA	630761		WP	A5	BSTD	RSTD	AIM	TODDPK	01MAR
			DA	A5	BABS	RSTD	AIM	TODDPK	01MAR
			DF	A5	BABS	RBDR	AIM	TODDPK	01MAR
KIRKLH	631426		DA	A5	BSTD	RSTD	AIM	TODDPK	28MAR
DALLHA	631461		LQ	A5	BSTD	RSTD	AIM	TODDPK	28MAR
WRPH	631463		LQ	A5	BABS	RSTD	AIM	TODDPK	28MAR
			DF	A5	BSTD	RSTD	AIM	TODDPK	28MAR
			DF	A5	BSTD	RSTD	AIM	TODDPK	28MAR
			WP	A5	BSTD	RSTD	AIM	TODDPK	29MAR
			WP	A5	BSTD	RSTD	AIM	TODDPK	29MAR
			DF	A5	BABS	RSTD	AIM	TODDPK	29MAR

the options that are specified for the schedule. Since the system has been installed, the salespeople have been very satisfied with their ability to provide reliable information to their customers and to close sales that might not have been possible before. The system has been such an effective device that the company is now using it in its advertising, inviting customers to come in and configure their own vehicle.

Concluding Principles

In this chapter we have reviewed the pivotal role of demand management in communicating with the market. Through the demand management module, information on the market is gathered, orders are entered, products are configured, manufacturing specifications are developed, and customers are informed of product availability and delivery times. The following principles will help managers to effectively carry out these tasks.

- Demand management systems and procedures must be aligned with the market environment of the firm.
- All demands on product resources must be identified and accounted for in providing forecast information to sales and operations planning and master production scheduling.
- Data capture must not be limited to sales (demand) but should include knowledge, trends, systems performance, and demand management performance.
- The forecasting models should not be any more complicated than necessary. Simple models often work better than more complicated ones.
- Input data and output forecasts should be routinely monitored for quality and appropriateness.

- Information on the sources of variation in sales, such as seasonality, market trends, and company policies, should be incorporated into the forecasting system.
- Forecasts from different sources must be reconciled and made consistent with company plans and constraints.
- Customers must be provided honest information, even if it is bad news.

References

Ahmad, S., and R. Schroeder. "The Impact of Electronics Data Interchange on Delivery Performance," *Production and Operations Management* 10, no. 1 (2001), pp. 16–30.

Boyer, K. K.; Cecil Bozarth; and Christopher McDermott. "Configurations in Operations: An Emerging Area of Study," *Journal of Operations Management* 18, no. 6 (November 2000), pp. 601–604.

Browne, Jim. "Analyzing the Dynamics of Supply and Demand for Goods and Services," *Industrial Engineering* 26, no. 6 (June 1994), p. 18.

Bylinsky, Gene. "America's Elite Factories," *Fortune,* Aug. 16, 1999.

Calantone, R.; Cornelia Dröge; and Shawnee Vickery. "Investigating the Manufacturing-Marketing Interface in New Product Development: Does Context Affect the Strength of Relationships?" *Journal of Operations Management* 20, no. 3 (June 2002), pp. 273–287.

Carr, A. S., and John N. Pearson. "Strategically Managed Buyer-Supplier Relationships and Performance Outcomes," *Journal of Operations Management* 17, no. 5 (August 1999), pp. 497–519.

Carroll, Brian J. *Lean Performance ERP Project Management—Implementing the Virtual Supply Chain,* 1st ed. Boca Raton, Fla.: CRC Press, February 27, 2002.

Chorafas, Dimitris N. *Integrating ERP, CRM, Supply Chain Management, and Smart Materials,* Auerbach Publications, 2001.

Cooper, R. *When Lean Enterprises Collide: Competing Through Confrontation,* Harvard Business School Press, 1995.

Dobson, G., and C. Yano. "Product Offering, Pricing, and Make-to-Stock/Make-to-Order Decisions with Shared Capacity," *Production and Operations Management* 11, no. 3 (2002), pp. 293–312.

Dowling, Grahame. "Customer Relationship Management: In B2C Markets, Often Less is More," *California Management Review* 44, no. 3 (Spring 2002), p. 87.

Fliedner, E. B., and B. Lawrence. "Forecasting System Parent Group Formulation: An Empirical Application of Cluster Analysis," *Journal of Operations Management* 12, no. 2 (1995).

Flores, B. E., and D. C. Whybark. "A Comparison of Focus Forecasting with Averaging and Exponential Smoothing Strategies," *Production and Inventory Management,* 3rd quarter 1986.

Fransoo, Jan C. "Demand Management and Production Control in Process Industries," *International Journal of Operations & Production Management* 12, no. 7/8, (1992), p. 187.

Freeland, John G., ed. *The Ultimate CRM Handbook: Strategies and Concepts for Building Enduring Customer Loyalty and Profitability.* New York: McGraw-Hill, 2002.

Fullerton, R. R., and Cheryl S. McWatters. "The Production Performance Benefits from JIT Implementation," *Journal of Operations Management* 19, no. 1 (January 2001), pp. 81–96.

Gardner, E. S.; E. A. Anderson-Fletcher; and A. M. Wicks. "Further Results on Focus Forecasting and Exponential Smoothing," *International Journal of Forecasting* 17, no. 2 (2001).

Gefen, David. "Implementation Team Responsiveness and User Evaluation of Customer Relationship Management: A Quasi-Experimental Design Study of Social Exchange Theory," *Journal of Management Information Systems* 19, no. 1 (Summer 2002), p. 47.

Gilbert, S. M., and Ronald H. Ballou. "Supply Chain Benefits from Advanced Customer Commitments," *Journal of Operations Management* 18, no. 1 (December 1999), pp. 61–73.

Graves, S. C.; A. H. G. Rinnooy Kan; and P. H. Zipkin, eds. *Logistics of Production and Inventory,* 2nd ed. North-Holland, 2002.

Gray, G. N. "Basic Q2 Forecasting," *APICS—The Performance Advantage,* October 1995.

Guerrero, Hector H. "Demand Management Strategies for Assemble-to-Order Production Environments," *International Journal of Production Research* 29, no. 1 (January 1991), p. 39.

Gupta, S., and P. C. Wilton. "Combination of Forecasts: An Extension," *Management Science* 33, no. 3 (March 1987).

Heikkilä, J. "From Supply to Demand Chain Management: Efficiency and Customer Satisfaction," *Journal of Operations Management* 20, no. 6 (November 2002), pp. 747–767.

Helms, Marilyn M.; Lawrence P. Ettkin; and Sharon Chapman. "Supply Chain Forecasting—Collaborative Forecasting Supports Supply Chain Management," *Business Process Management Journal* 6, no. 5 (2000), p. 392.

Hill, C. A., and Gary D. Scudder. "The Use of Electronic Data Interchange for Supply Chain Coordination in the Food Industry," *Journal of Operations Management* 20, no. 4 (August 2002), pp. 375–387.

Johnson, Lauren Keller. "New Views on Digital CRM," *Sloan Management Review* 44, no. 1 (Fall 2002), p. 10.

Lawrence, M. J.; R. H. Edmundson; and M. J. O'Connor. "The Accuracy of Combining Judgmental and Statistical Forecasts," *Management Science* 32, no. 12 (December 1986).

Lee, T. S., and E. E. Adam, Jr. "Forecasting Error Evaluation in Material Requirements Planning Production-Inventory Systems," *Management Science* 32, no. 9 (September 1986).

Makridakis, S., and M. Hibon. "The M3 Competition: Results, Conclusions, and Implications," *International Journal of Forecasting* 16, no. 4 (2000), pp. 451–476.

Makridakis, S., ed. "Special Issue on the Forecasting Competition," *International Journal of Forecasting* 17, no. 4 (2001).

Moodie, D. "Demand Management: The Evaluation of Price and Due Date Negotiation Strategies Using Simulation," *Productions and Operations Management* 8, no. 2 (1999), pp. 151–162.

Moodie, D. R., and Bobrowski, P. M. "Due Date Demand Management: Negotiating the Trade-off Between Price and Delivery," *International Journal of Production Research* 37, no. 5 (1999), p. 997.

Newberry, T. L., and Carl D. Bhame. "How Management Should Use and Interact with Sales Forecasts." *Inventories and Production Magazine,* July–August 1981.

Rigby, Darrell K.; Frederick F. Reichheld; and Phil Schefter. "Avoid the Four Perils of CRM," *Harvard Business Review* 80, no. 2 (February 2002), p. 101.

Ritzman, L. P., and B. E. King, "The Relative Significance of Forecast Errors in Multi-Stage Manufacturing," *Journal of Operations Management* 11, no. 1 (1993).

Smith B. T., and V. Brice. *Focus Forecasting Computer Techniques for Inventory Control Revised for the Twenty-First Century,* B. T. Smith and Associates, 1997.

Stock, G. N.; Noel P. Greis; and John D. Kasarda. "Enterprise Logistics and Supply Chain Structure: The role of fit," *Journal of Operations Management* 18, no. 5 (August 2000), pp. 531–547.

Tanwari, Anwar Uddin, and James Betts. "Impact of Forecasting on Demand Planning," *Production and Inventory Management Journal* (3rd quarter 1999).

Tyagi, Rahul. "How to Evaluate a Demand Planning and Forecasting Package," *Supply Chain Management Review,* Sept. 1, 2002, p. 48.

Van Landeghem, Hendrik, and Hendrik Vanmaele. "Robust Planning: A New Paradigm for Demand Chain Planning," *Journal of Operations Management* 20, no. 6 (November 2002), p. 769.

Winer, Russell S. "A Framework for Customer Relationship Management," *California Management Review* 43, no. 4 (Summer 2001), p. 89.

Wortmann, J. C.; D. R. Munstlag; and P. J. M. Timmermans. *Customer-driven Manufacturing,* London: Chapman & Hall, 1997.

Zhang, O.; Mark A. Vonderembse; and Jeen-Su Lim. "Manufacturing Flexibility: Defining and Analyzing Relationships Among Competence, Capability, and Customer Satisfaction," *Journal of Operations Management* 21, no. 2 (March 2003), pp. 173–191.

Zotteri, Giulio, and Roberto Verganti, "Multi-level Approaches to Demand Management in Complex Environments: An Analytical Model," *International Journal of Production Economics* 71, no. 1–3 (Mar. 6, 2001), p. 221.

Discussion Questions

1. The customer order decoupling point was described as the point at which the demand changed from independent to dependent. Describe what this means and why it is important to managers.

2. Provide examples of make-to-stock, assemble-to-order, and make-to-order products available in your area. What advantages do you see in moving from make-to-stock to assemble or make-to-order?

3. In the lower levels of the pyramid forecasting system, how would you prevent abdication of the responsibility for forecasting?

4. Can a grocery store capture true demand data? How might a warehouse capture demand data?

5. Some experts have argued it's more important to have low bias (mean error) than to have a low MAD. Why would they argue this way?

Problems

1. The Flaglet Company is considering investing in a complete redesign of its products and manufacturing process in order to produce on an assemble-to-order basis. It will still sell to the same wholesalers as in the past, so demand and prices won't change, but it will need to use premium transportation to deliver the products. The company anticipates that the premium transportation will increase its transportation costs by $100,000 per year. It estimates that it can reduce its inventory of finished goods inventory by $1 million while increasing the component inventory by only $200,000. It costs 25 percent of the investment in finished goods and 20 percent of the component investment to store the inventory. If Flaglet wanted a 20 percent return on its investment, how much could the company invest in the project?

2. The Hunter and Levin Company has capacity to produce 200 Transtar 3000s per week. The firm currently has booked orders as follows:

Week	Orders
1	196
2	220
3	210
4	192
5	150
6	165
7	135
8	80
9	45
10	50
11+	0

a. Plot booked orders against capacity by week.

b. Assume the following transactions. In week 1, 198 Transtar 3000s were shipped. Orders for eight Transtar 3000s were canceled in week 2, and two more were canceled in week 5. Additional orders were booked for 5 in week 2, 20 in week 3, 10 in week 4, 5 in week 6, 4 in week 7, 2 in week 9, and 1 in week 11. What does the plot look like as of week 2?

c. What problems do you foresee?

3. In an effort to improve customer service and reduce the cost of inventory, the Thanskavel Company invested in a number of lean manufacturing initiatives. One result of these investments was a reduction of the manufacturing lead time for the company's specialty product, Eggsbar, from six weeks to four weeks. A study of Eggsbar disclosed that the demand averages 200 units per week, with a standard deviation of 22 units. The demand from one week to the next week was found to be independent.

   a. What was the mean and standard deviation of the demand during manufacturing lead time for this product before and after the initiatives?

   b. Thanskavel has a policy of holding safety stock of finished goods inventory in the amount of 2.5 times the standard deviation of demand during manufacturing lead time. In the past, this amounted to $10,000 of safety stock inventory for this product. What reduction in safety stock for this product resulted from the reduction of the manufacturing lead time?

4. When a firm is able to move to an assemble-to-order capability from a make-to-stock approach, there can be a substantial reduction in the number of things that must be stored and kept track of. For example, the Northland Computer Shop had decided to stop stocking assembled computers and moved to an assemble-to-order approach. Northland even invited customers to the work area to see their computer being assembled, a great customer relations ploy. The company estimated that there were seven hard disk choices, six mother boards (including the processor), five CD/DVD alternatives, three operating systems, and four other options.

   a. What was the total number of potential finished products?

   b. If it cost $10 per item to make a forecast each week, what is the weekly savings from forecasting just the components and options as compared to the potential number of finished products?

5. Five individual products in a product family of the Cumberland Company have identical sales patterns. Each averages 100 units per month, with a standard deviation of 10 units. Assuming normal distributions and independent demands:

   a. What is the yearly sales distribution of each product?

   b. What is the monthly sales distribution for all products together?

   c. What is the yearly sales distribution for all products together?

6. Using ±3 standard deviations for the values obtained in parts a, b, and c of problem 5, compare your results to the results of a Polysar International survey of its managers concerning the accuracy of the company's forecasts.

		Forecast for a Period of:	
Level of Detail	1 Month	1 Quarter	1 Year
Total Volume			
Family	12*	8	8
Type in Family	15	10	8
Grade in Type	15	NF[†]	12
SKU[‡]	30	NF	NF

*±12%.

[†]NF = no forecast.

[‡]Stockkeeping unit.

7. The demand manager of Maverick Jeans is responsible for ensuring sufficient warehouse space for the finished jeans that come from the production plants. It has occasionally been necessary to rent public warehouse space, something that Maverick would like to avoid. In order to estimate

the space requirements the demand manager is evaluating moving-average forecasts. The demand (in 1,000 case units) for the last fiscal year is shown below.

Month	1	2	3	4	5	6	7	8	9	10	11	12
Demand	20	18	21	25	24	27	22	30	23	20	29	22

a. Use a three-month moving average to estimate the month-in-advance forecast of demand for months 4–12 and generate a forecast for the first month of next year. Calculate the average forecast error and mean absolute error.

b. Use a three-month weighted moving average with weights of 0.6, 0.3, 0.1 (most recent to last recent, respectively) to calculate month-in-advance forecasts for months 4–12 and forecast for the first month of next year. Calculate the average forecast error and mean absolute error.

c. Compare the average forecast error and MAD for the forecasting methods in parts a and b. Based on these error calculations, which of the two forecast methods would you recommend? Why?

8. Maverick Jeans' demand manager decided to evaluate exponential smoothing. To maintain comparability, she used the data from problem 7.

a. Use a starting forecast of 20 for month 4 to develop forecasts for months 5–12 and the first month of next year. Use smoothing constants (α) of .2, .5, and .8. Calculate the average forecast error and mean absolute error.

b. What observations do you have? How does exponential smoothing compare to the results for moving averages from problem 6?

9. Talbot Publishing Company's production planning manager has provided the following historical sales data for its leading textbook on forecasting:

Year	4	5	6	7
Sales (in 1,000 units)	21	18	20	17

The firm is considering using a basic exponential smoothing model with $\alpha = .2$ to forecast this item's sales.

a. Use the sales average of 20,000 units through year 3 as the forecast for period 4. Prepare forecasts for years 5 through 7 as of the end of year 4.

b. Calculate the average error and MAD value for the three forecasts using the actual sales data provided. Estimate the standard deviation of the forecast errors using the calculated MAD.

c. Redo the forecasts and MAD calculations, updating the forecasts for years 6 and 7 at the end of years 5 and 6, respectively. What do you observe?

10. Use a spreadsheet program to compare a three-period moving average forecasting model with a basic (ESF) exponential smoothing model. Five periods of past data exist (27, 26, 32, 41, and 28); the five future periods to be forecast have demands of 35, 43, 47, 28, and 38. Develop MAD values for each technique (forecasting one period ahead) for the five periods.

a. Using the average of the five periods of history to start the exponential smoothing model, what smoothing constant produces the MAD value closest to that of the moving average approach? Which model gives the lower MAD?

b. What changes when you use the average of the past three periods to start the exponential smoothing model?

11. The following two demand sets are to be used to test two different basic exponential smoothing models. The first model uses $\alpha = .1$, and the second uses $\alpha = .5$. In both cases, the model should be initialized with a beginning forecast value of 50; that is, the ESF forecast for period 1 made at the end of period 0 is 50 units. In each of the four cases (two models on two demand sets), compute the average forecast error and MAD. What do the results mean?

Demand Set I		Demand Set II	
Period	Demand	Period	Demand
1	51	1	77
2	46	2	83
3	49	3	90
4	55	4	22
5	52	5	10
6	47	6	80
7	51	7	16
8	48	8	19
9	56	9	27
10	51	10	79
11	45	11	73
12	52	12	88
13	49	13	15
14	48	14	21
15	43	15	85
16	46	16	22
17	55	17	88
18	53	18	75
19	54	19	14
20	49	20	16

12. MacRonald's Restaurant uses a monthly exponential smoothing forecast for demand of each of its products. MacRonald's has four product families: burgers, chicken, hoagies, and pizza. MacRonald's also asks the shift managers to come up with a forecast for each product family. The exponential forecast for each product and the family forecast are given below.

Family	Product	Forecast	$/Unit
Burgers	Regular	1,200	1.00
	Super	2,700	1.50
	Super-Duper	2,100	1.80
Chicken	Regular	1,800	2.50
	Cajun	2,700	2.75
Hoagies	Italian	2,250	3.50
	French	1,650	3.00
	American	1,350	3.25
Pizza	Cheese	750	1.75
	Pepperoni	1,200	2.25

Family	$ Sales
Burgers	10,000.00
Chicken	15,000.00
Hoagies	20,000.00
Pizza	5,000.00

a. Calculate a roll-up of the individual forecasts and compare it to the product family forecast.

b. Roll up the individual product forecast to the top level and compare it to an overall corporate forecast of $65,000. Roll the forecast back down to families and individual forecast (dollars and units).

13. The general sales manager at Knox Products Corporation has just received next year's sales forecast (in units) for two of the firm's major products (Less Knox and More Knox) from sales managers of the Eastern and Western sales regions:

Eastern Region Forecast		Western Region Forecast	
Less Knox	**More Knox**	**Less Knox**	**More Knox**
150	300	300	450

Less Knox sells for $4.50 per unit and More Knox sells for $8.50 per unit.

a. The corporate economist has forecast a total corporation-wide sales volume for these two products of $11,000 for next year. What's the disparity between the two forecasts at the item level?

b. If top management agrees to a total corporation-wide sales forecast volume of $9,000, what's the sales forecast at the item level?

14. The Gonzales Electric Company's 12 products are further grouped into four product families. Products A, B, and C compose family 1; D, E, and F compose family 2; G, H, and I compose family 3; and products J, K, and L make up family 4. Dick Gonzales has the following exponential smoothing forecasts of monthly demand for each product.

Family	Product	Forecast	$/Unit	Family	Product	Forecast	$/Unit
1	A	10	1,000	3	G	100	250
	B	15	1,200		H	180	100
	C	20	900		I	220	100
2	D	5	5,000	4	J	2	10,000
	E	3	7,000		K	4	9,000
	F	2	9,000		L	3	8,000

Gonzales's sales force has also come up with the monthly forecasts of sales for each product family.

Family	$ Sales
1	50,000
2	50,000
3	75,000
4	75,000

a. Top management has independently set a $300,000 overall monthly sales goal for the company. Roll up the individual product forecasts and compare them with the family data. Use a spreadsheet and the family forecasts to revise the individual item forecasts (in both dollars and units).

b. Roll up the family forecasts to the top level, compare these to the overall forecasts, and roll the forecasts back down to families and to individual unit forecasts (dollars and units).

15. The analysts at Gonzales were kept busy performing "what-if" analyses of the data in problem 14.

a. Suppose a top-management meeting produces a decision that the family forecast for product family 3 (products G, H, and I) in problem 12 can't be increased. At the same meeting, the company's overall forecast ($300,000) is maintained. Roll the forecasts up and down to determine the dollar and unit forecasts.

b. Suppose the family forecast data in problem 14 are assumed to be correct, except in any case where the sum of the exponential smoothing forecast data for items exceeds the family forecast. In these cases, the sum of the item forecasts will be used instead of the family forecast. Roll up the resultant overall forecast and roll down the resultant item forecasts.

c. Suppose a major customer order has just been received for 10 units of product J. This order wasn't expected and is in addition to any other forecasts for product J. The company still wants to plan a total monthly sales volume of $300,000. Use the family forecasts (revised) to roll the forecasts up and down to get revised individual product forecasts.

3

Sales and Operations Planning

Sales and operations planning (SOP) is probably the least understood aspect of manufacturing planning and control. However, the payoffs from a well-designed and -executed sales and operations plan are large. Here we discuss the process for determining aggregate levels of production. The managerial objective is to develop an overall business plan, which integrates the various functional planning efforts in a company whose manufacturing portion is embodied in the operations plan. The sales and operations plan links strategic goals to production and coordinates the various planning efforts in a business, including marketing planning, financial planning, operations planning, human resource planning, etc. If the sales and operations plan does not represent an integrated, cross-functional plan, the business can fail to succeed in its markets.

Our discussion of sales and operations planning is organized around four topics:

- *Sales and operations planning in the firm:* What is sales and operations planning? How does it link with strategic planning and other MPC functions?

- *The sales and operations planning process:* What are the fundamental activities in sales and operations planning and what techniques can be used?

- *The new management obligations:* What are the critical issues in developing an effective sales and operations planning function?

- *Operating with sales and operations planning:* What is the state of the art in practice?

This chapter focuses on managerial concepts for sales and operations planning. Advanced concepts in sales and operations planning are emphasized in Chapter 12. Useful background for the concepts in this chapter appears in Chapter 2, on demand management; Chapter 6, which deals with master production scheduling (MPS); Chapter 17, which deals with supply chain management; and Chapter 10, which concerns capacity planning.

Sales and Operations Planning in the Firm

Sales and operations planning provides the key communication links for top management to coordinate the various planning activities in a business. These linkages are shown in Figure 3.1. For example, marketing initiatives dealing with the entry of a new product in the

FIGURE 3.1
Key Linkages in Sales and Operations Planning

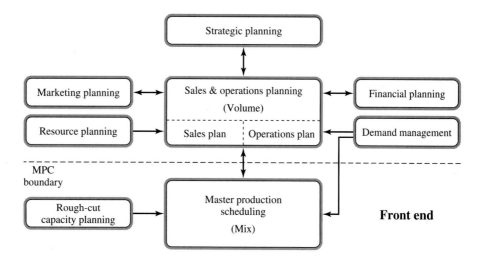

market can be coordinated with an increase in manufacturing capacity to support the marketing promotional plans at the same time financial resources are coordinated to support the working capital for the buildup of pipeline inventories.

From a manufacturing perspective, sales and operations planning provides the basis to focus the detailed production resources to achieve the firm's strategic objectives. The sales and operations plans provide the framework within which the master production schedule is developed, subsequent MPS decisions can be planned and controlled, and material resources and plant capacities can be coordinated in ways that are consistent with strategic business objectives. We now describe the sales and operations planning function in terms of its role in top management, necessary conditions for effective planning, linkages to other MPC system functions, and the payoffs from effective sales and operations planning.

Sales and Operations Planning Fundamentals

There are four fundamentals in sales and operations planning: demand, supply, volume, and mix. First, let's consider the **balance between demand and supply.** When demand exceeds supply, customer service suffers because manufacturing cannot provide the volume of products required by the customer. Costs increase because of overtime and premium freight rates, and quality suffers because of the rush to ship products, all of which are unfavorable to the business. Likewise, when supply exceeds demand, the effect on the business is unfavorable. Inventories increase because of the imbalance between demand and manufacturing capacity; layoffs result from production rate cuts, causing plant efficiency and morale to decline; and profit margins are squeezed because of price cuts and discounting. Therefore, the key to good business performance is to maintain a proper balance between demand and supply. It is important to have business processes in place to maintain a proper balance between demand and supply, and to provide early warning signals when they are becoming unbalanced. This is the role of sales and operations planning, and it can be accomplished through the effective coordination of the plans of the different functional areas in a business with the active involvement of top management.

Two other fundamentals are **volume and mix.** These need to be treated separately in managing the manufacturing planning and control function. Volume concerns big-picture decisions about how much to make and the production rates for product families, while mix concerns detailed decisions about which individual products to make, in what sequence, and for which customer orders. What happens in many companies is that the focus is on mix decisions because these are urgent as a result of customer pressures. Volumes are only considered once a year when the business plan is developed and production rates must be fixed to establish overhead absorption. These companies don't spend enough time forecasting and planning their volumes. Instead of focusing on the big picture, they focus on the details in trying to predict mix. Smart companies carefully plan their volumes first and then focus on mix decisions. This is done because if volumes are planned effectively, mix decisions become much easier to cope with. These companies find that imbalances in demand and supply occur frequently over the course of a year, and as a result volume decisions need to be reviewed and adjusted on a monthly basis.

Sales and operations planning is concerned with getting the big picture right and then attending to the details of manufacturing planning and control. The role of sales and operations planning is to balance demand and supply at the volume level. Volume concerns rates: overall sales rates, production rates, aggregate inventories, and order backlogs. Once volume (rates and levels) is effectively planned, the problems of mix (individual products and orders) become easier to cope with. Understanding the fundamentals of sales and operations planning makes this function easier to understand as a part of a company's manufacturing planning and control system.

Sales and Operations Planning and Management

Sales and operations planning provides a direct and consistent dialogue between manufacturing and top management as well as between manufacturing and the other business functions. As Figure 3.1 shows, many key linkages of sales and operations planning are *outside* the manufacturing planning and control (MPC) system. Therefore the plan necessarily must be in terms that are meaningful to the firm's nonmanufacturing executives. Only in this way can the sales and operations planning function noted in Figure 3.1 become consistent for each basic functional area in the business. Likewise, the operations portion of the overall plan must be stated in terms that the MPC functions can use, so detailed manufacturing decisions are kept in concert with the overall strategic objectives reflected in the sales and operations plan.

The basis for consistency of the functional plans in a business is the resolution of broad trade-offs at the top management level. Suppose, for example, there's an opportunity to expand into a new market, and marketing requests additional production to do so. When a given operations plan has been authorized, this could be accomplished only by decreasing the currently authorized production for some other product group. If this is seen as undesirable—i.e., the new market is to be a direct add-on—by definition a new sales and operations plan is required, with an updated and consistent set of plans in marketing, finance, and production. The feasibility of the added volume must be determined and agreed on before detailed execution steps are taken. This debate is of the type typically discussed in regular sales and operations planning meetings, and illustrates why top management involvement in sales and operations planning is critical.

The operations portion of the sales and operations plan states the mission manufacturing must accomplish if the firm's strategic objectives are to be met. How to accomplish the operations plan in terms of detailed manufacturing and procurement decisions is a problem for manufacturing management. Within an agreed-on operations plan, the job in manufacturing is to "hit the operations plan." Similar job definitions hold for sales, marketing, and finance.

Figure 3.1 also indicates that the planning in other MPC system functions is necessarily detailed, and the language is quite different from that required for the operations plan. The operations plan is normally stated in terms of aggregate units of output per month, while the master production schedule (MPS) is stated in terms of end product units per week. The MPS might be stated in units that use special bills of materials to manage complicated options and do not correspond to the units used to communicate with top management.

To perform the necessary communication role, the operations plan must be stated in commonly understood, aggregated terms. In many companies the operations plan is stated in total units for each product line (or major product family groupings). In other companies the operations plan is stated as the dollar value of total monthly output. Still other firms need to break the total output down by individual factories. Some firms also use measures that relate to capacity, such as direct labor hours and tons of product. The key requirement is that the operations plan be stated in some commonly understood homogenous unit that thereafter can be kept in concert with other functional plans.

The operations plan needs to be expressed in meaningful units, but it also needs to be expressed in a manageable number of units. Experience indicates that 6 to 12 family groups seem to be about right for a top management group to handle. Each family grouping has to be considered in terms of expectations on sales, manufacturing, and the resultant inventories and backlogs. The cumulative result, expressed in monetary units, also has to be examined and weighed against overarching business plans.

The operations plan is *not* a forecast of demand! It's the planned production, stated on an aggregate basis, for which manufacturing management is to be held responsible. The operations plan is not necessarily equal to a forecast of aggregate demand. For example, it may not be profitable to satisfy all of the demand in a peak monthly period, but the production would be leveled over the course of a seasonal cycle. Likewise, a strategic objective of improved customer service could result in aggregate production in excess of aggregate demand. These are important management trade-offs to be debated in the context of the sales and operations plan.

The operations plan is a result of the sales and operations planning process. Inputs to the process include sales forecasts, but these need to be stated on the basis of shipments (not bookings) so that the inventory projections match physical inventories and so that manufacturing goals are expressed correctly with respect to time.

Operations Planning and MPC Systems

So far we have emphasized sales and operations planning linkages to activities outside MPC system boundaries. Because of these linkages, the sales and operations plan is often called "top management's handle on the business." To provide execution support for the operations plan, we need linkages to the MPC systems. The most fundamental linkage is that to the master production schedule, which is a disaggregation of the operations plan. The result drives the detailed scheduling through detailed material planning and other MPC functions.

The MPS must be kept in concert with the operations plan. As the individual daily scheduling decisions to produce specific mixes of actual end items and/or options are made, we must maintain parity between the sum of the MPS quantities and the operations plan. If the relationship is maintained, then "hitting the schedule" (MPS) means the agreed-on operations plan will be met as well.

Another critical linkage shown in Figure 3.1 is the link with demand management. Demand management encompasses order entry, order promising, and physical distribution coordination as well as forecasting. This function must capture every source of demand against manufacturing capacity, such as interplant transfers, international requirements, and service parts. In some form, one or more of these demand sources may be of more consequence than others. For the firm with distribution warehouses, for example, replenishing those warehouses may create quite a different set of demands on manufacturing than is true for other firms. The contribution of demand management, insofar as operations planning is concerned, is to ensure that the influence of all aspects of demand is included and properly coordinated.

As a tangential activity, the match between actual and forecast demand is monitored in the demand management function. As actual demand conditions depart from forecast, the necessity for revising the operations plan increases. Thus, the assessment of changes' impact on the operations plan and the desirability of making a change depend on this linkage. It's critical for top management to change the plans, rather than to let the forecast errors in themselves change the aggregate production output level.

The other direct MPC linkage to sales and operations planning shown in Figure 3.1 is that with resource planning. This activity encompasses long-range planning of facilities. Involved is the translation of extended operations plans into capacity requirements, usually on a gross or aggregate basis. In some firms the unit of measure might be constant dollar output rates; in others, it might be labor-hours, head counts, machine-hours, key-facility–hours, tons of output, or some other output measure. The need is to plan capacity, at least in aggregate terms, for a horizon at least as long as it takes to make major changes.

Resource planning is directly related to operations planning, since, in the short term, the resources available provide a set of constraints to operations planning. In the longer run, to the extent that operations plans call for more resources than available, financial appropriations are indicated. A key goal of the linkage between operations planning and resource planning is to answer what-if questions. Maintaining current resource planning factors related to the product groupings used for planning is the basis for performing this analysis.

Much of the very near term operations plan is constrained by available material supplies. Current levels of raw material, parts, and subassemblies limit what can be produced in the short run, even if other resources are available. This is often hard to assess unless information links from the detailed material planning and shop status databases are effective.

Links through the MPS to material planning and other MPC functions provide the basic data to perform what-if simulations of alternative plans. Being able to quickly evaluate alternatives can facilitate the sales and operations planning process. This is not an argument to always change the operations plan. On the contrary, having the ability to demonstrate the impact of proposed changes may reduce the number of instances in which production "loses" in these negotiations.

The value of the sales and operations planning function is certainly questionable if there's no monitoring of performance. This requires linkages to the data on shipment/sales, aggregated into the sales and operations planning groupings. Measuring performance is an important input to the planning process itself. Insofar as deviations in output are occurring, they must be taken into account. If the plan can't be realized, the entire value of the sales and operations planning process is called into question.

One final performance aspect where effort must be expended is in the reconciliation of the MPS with the operations plan. As day-to-day MPS decisions are made, it's possible to move away from the operations plan unless constant vigilance is applied. Like other performance monitoring, it requires a frequent evaluation of status and comparison to plan.

Payoffs

Sales and operations planning is top management's handle on the business. It provides important visibility of the critical interactions between sales, marketing, production, and finance. If sales and marketing wants higher inventories, but top management decides there's not sufficient capital to support the inventories, the operations plan will be so designed. Once such critical trade-off decisions are made, the operations plan provides the basis for monitoring and controlling manufacturing performance in a way that provides a much more clear division of responsibilities than is true under conventional budgetary controls.

Under sales and operations planning, manufacturing's job is to hit the schedule. This can eliminate the battle over "ownership" of finished-goods inventory. If actual inventory levels don't agree with planned inventory levels, it's basically not a manufacturing problem, if they hit the schedule. It's either a sales and marketing problem (the products didn't sell according to plan) or a problem of product mix management in the demand management activity (the wrong individual items were made).

The operations plan provides the basis for day-to-day, tough-minded trade-off decisions as well. If sales and marketing want more of some items, it must be asked, "Of what do you want less?" There's no other response, because additional production without a corresponding reduction would violate the agreed-on operations plan. In the absence of a new, expanded operations plan, manufacturing, sales, and marketing must work to allocate the scarce capacity of the completing needs (via the master production schedule).

The reverse situation is also true. If the operations plan calls for more than sales and marketing currently needs, detailed decisions should be reached about which items will go into inventory. Manufacturing commits people, capacities, and materials to reach company objectives. The issue is only how best to convert these resources into particular end products.

Better integration between functional areas in a business is one of the major payoffs from sales and operations planning. Once a consistent sales and operations plan between top levels of the functional areas is developed, it can be translated into detailed plans that are in concert with top-level agreements. This results in a set of common goals, improved communication, and transparent systems.

Without a sales and operations plan, the expectation is that somehow the job will get done—and in fact, it does get done, but at a price. The price is organizational slack: extra inventories, poor customer service, excess capacity, long lead times, panic operations, and poor response to new opportunities. Informal systems will, of necessity, come into being. Detailed decisions will be made by clerical-level personnel with no guiding policy except "get it out the door as best we can." The annual budget cycle won't be tied in with the detailed plans and will probably be inconsistent and out of date before it's one month old. Sales and marketing requests for products won't be made so as to keep the sum of the detailed end products in line with the budget. In many cases detailed requests for the first month are double the average monthly volume. Only at the end of the year does the reconciliation between requests and budget take place, but in the meantime it has been up to manufacturing to decide what's really needed.

We've seen many companies with these symptoms. Where are these costs reflected? There's no special place in the chart of accounts for them, but they affect the bottom-line profit results. More and more firms are finding that a well-structured monthly sales and operations planning meeting allows the various functional areas to operate in a more coordinated fashion and to better respond to the marketplace. The result is a dynamic overall plan for the company, one that changes as needed and fosters the necessary adaptation in each function.

The Sales and Operations Planning Process

This section views aids to managing the sales and operations planning process. Specifically, we'll be concerned with the monthly sales and operations planning process, the tabular spreadsheet display, and the basic operations planning trade-offs. We will examine these techniques with an example.

The Monthly Sales and Operations Planning Process

Sales and operations planning involves making decisions on each product family concerning changes to the sales plan, the operations plan, and the inventory/backlog. These decisions are made on the basis of recent history, forecasts, and the recommendations of middle management and top management's knowledge of business conditions. A formal process for accomplishing sales and operations planning developed by Tom Wallace is shown in Figure 3.2. This process

FIGURE 3.2
The Monthly Sales and Operations Planning Process

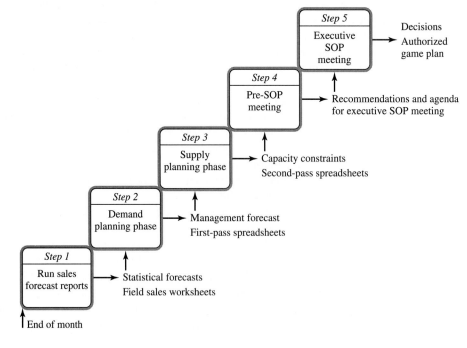

begins shortly after a month's end and continues for some days. These steps involve middle management and others throughout the company as well as top management, and include:

- Updating the sales forecast.
- Reviewing the impact of changes to the operations plan and determining whether adequate capacity and material will be available to support them.
- Identifying alternatives where problems exist.
- Formulating agreed-on recommendations for top management regarding overall changes to the plans and identifying areas of disagreement where consensus is not possible.
- Communicating this information to top management with sufficient time for them to review it prior to the executive SOP meeting.

Having accomplished this work with the appropriate staff personnel during the month means that a productive two-hour Executive SOP meeting can be held each month to make the appropriate decisions regarding changes to the sales and operations plan.

Five steps form the basis for the monthly planning cycle:

1. *Run the sales forecasting reports.* This step occurs shortly after the month end and involves the information systems department updating the files with data from the month just ended—actual sales, production, inventories, etc. This information is disseminated to the appropriate people, and forms the basis for sales and marketing people to use in developing sales analysis reports, and changes to sales forecasts.

2. *The demand planning phase.* The information received in step 1 for new and existing products is reviewed by sales and marketing and discussed with the view of generating a new management forecast covering the next 12 or more months. For example, in the case of consumer make-to-stock products, price changes, competitive activity, economic conditions, and field sales input regarding large customers are considered in revising the sales forecast. The task here is to override the statistical forecasts when appropriate, and to bring senior marketing and sales management into the loop. It is also necessary to consider the new forecast along with the actual sales, production, and inventory data from the past month. Once the new forecast has been authorized by sales and marketing, it is applied to last month's operations plan. Once this is done it is easy for the operations people to see where the operations plan needs to be changed, and where it is acceptable. The necessary changes are then made that produce the new operations plan.

3. *The supply (capacity) planning phase.* Here is where the capacity planning activity (resource planning) takes place. The new operations plan for each product family grouping is compared with any changes made in the sales forecast or changes that have occurred in inventory or customer order backlog levels. It may be necessary to modify the operations plan if, for example, demand exceeds supply by a margin that is too large to reach with the current plant, or vendor, capacity. In cases where a change in the operations plan is necessary, spending authorization by top management may be required. These are the types of issues that are carried into the pre-SOP meeting.

4. *The pre-SOP meeting.* The purpose of this meeting involving representatives from the various business functions is to (1) make decisions regarding the balance of demand and supply, (2) resolve problems where differences in recommendations exist,

(3) identify areas that cannot be resolved to be discussed in the executive SOP meeting, (4) develop alternative courses of action, and (5) set the agenda for the executive SOP Meeting. This meeting includes a review of the plans for each product family grouping, the development of an updated financial view of the business, recommendations for each product family grouping, recommendations for changes in resource requirements, and recommendations regarding alternatives to be discussed in the Executive SOP Meeting.

5. *The Executive SOP Meeting.* The culminating meeting each month is one that includes the senior executives in the business. Its purpose is to (1) make decisions on the sales and operations plans for each product family, (2) authorize spending for changes in production/procurement rate changes, (3) relate the collective impact of the dollarized version of the product grouping sales and operations plans to the overall business plan, (4) break ties in areas where the pre-SOP team was unable to reach consensus, and (5) to review customer service and business performance.

The discipline required in routinizing the sales and operations planning process is to replan when conditions indicate it's necessary. If information from the demand management function indicates differences between the forecast and actual have exceeded reasonable error limits, replanning may be necessary. Similarly, if conditions change in manufacturing, a new market opportunity arises, or the capital market shifts, replanning may be needed.

Since the purpose of the planning process is to arrive at a coordinated set of plans for each function, mechanisms for getting support for the plans are important. Clearly, a minimum step here is to involve the senior executive team in the business in the process. This does more than legitimize the plan; it involves the people who can resolve issues in the trade-off stage. A second step used by some firms is to virtually write contracts between functions on what the agreements are. The contracts serve to underscore the importance of each function performing to plan, rather than return to informal practices.

To illustrate the nature of the sales and operations planning decisions, we now turn to an example based on a firm with a seasonal sales pattern on its make-to-stock products. We raise the issues in the context of a single product family produced in a dedicated production facility. In this context, there are two issues for discussion:

1. The sales and operations plan must be adjusted frequently to bring sales and production into a proper balance.
2. It is important to find a low cost operations plan when the cost of inventories, overtime, changes in the work force levels, and other capacity variations that meet the company's sales and operations requirements are considered.

This example presents both a cumulative charting and a tabular representation of alternative strategies to resolve these issues.

Sales and Operations Planning Displays

Figure 3.3 shows the aggregate sales forecasts for our example, the AA product family at XYZ Company, for the year. Monthly totals vary from a high of $15.8 million to a low of $7 million. Figure 3.4 shows these monthly sales data in the form of a **cumulative chart display** (solid line). In addition, the dashed straight line represents the cumulative

FIGURE 3.3
XYZ Company
AA Product
Family
Monthly Sales
Forecast

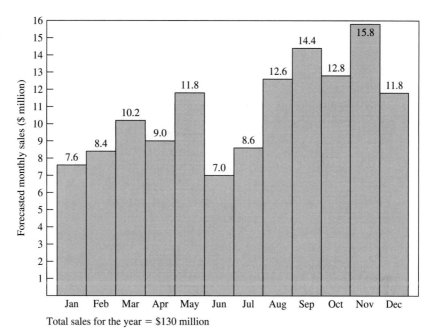

Total sales for the year = $130 million

FIGURE 3.4
XYZ Company
Cumulative
Chart

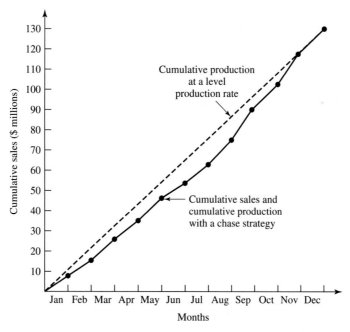

production plan at a constant rate of production. One issue in sales and operations planning is to choose a low-cost cumulative operations plan, which is depicted by a line on the cumulative chart that's always on or above the cumulative forecast line.

The cumulative chart shows clearly the implications of alternative plans. For example, the vertical distance between the dashed line and the solid line represents the expected inventory at each point of time. If no inventory were to be held, the cumulative production line would equal the cumulative sales line. This policy is a **chase strategy** where production output is changed to chase sales. The opposite extreme is a level policy, where production is at a constant uniform rate of output, with inventory buildups and depletions. Changing production output incurs the costs of changing the workforce level, hours worked, and subcontracting. Keeping production at a constant rate incurs inventory holding and backorder costs.

The more typical way of displaying the sales and operations planning information is to use **time-phased planning** and a **tabular display.** The advantage of this approach is that it is easily captured and communicated using an electronic spreadsheet. This information can be used for two important management purposes: evaluating current performance against the sales and operations plan, and modifying the current sales and operations plan. An example of this display is shown in Figure 3.5. This display requires several important information inputs each month: the sales forecast; the operations and inventory plans; and the actual operating results for the past three months covering the sales, production, and inventory levels. The information used for assessing current performance is shown to the left of the vertical line in Figure 3.5, while the information to the right of the vertical line represents the current sales and operations plan.

In the XYZ Company example shown in Figure 3.5, a planning factor is used to convert sales dollar output into production capacity terms for planning purposes. In our example, the XYZ Company keeps a planning statistic to convert the sales dollars for this product family, the AA product family, into total product units. This statistic, obtained from accounting records, indicates each product unit is valued at $30 in sales on the average. This factor is used to convert the sales forecast data in Figure 3.3 into product unit forecast shown in Figure 3.5.

Figure 3.5 is the statement of the sales and operations for the AA product family over the coming year. Here the sales plan is shown in both million dollars and 1,000 product units. Likewise, the operations plan is shown in both 1,000 product units and the number of people employed. Here each employee is assumed to produce 8 product units per day. Figure 3.5 also presents the number of working days in each month for the year. This is an important addition, since the number varies sharply from month to month. The lowest number occurs in July, which only has 10 working days as a result of the XYZ Company's annual two-week summer shutdown. In addition, Figure 3.5 shows a projection of the finished goods inventory in both 1,000 product units and in sales dollars. Since Figure 3.5 shows the chase sales strategy, the level of the finished goods inventory is constant over the one-year plan.

Modifying the Sales and Operations Plan

Figure 3.5 also shows the recent history covering the last three months of sales, production, and inventory levels for this product line. This information is useful in updating the sales and operations plan on a monthly basis. The data provided in Figure 3.5 illustrate the types of conclusions that are typically drawn during the sales and operations planning cycle in companies. Note that in this case the actual sales have fallen short of the forecast sales each month during the past quarter. This is indicated as a negative difference in the fourth row of Figure 3.5, and amounts to a cumulative difference of $-100,000$ product units (or about 40% of the January sales forecast) as of the end of the last quarter as shown in the table. This trend in sales indicates the need to focus on re-forecasting to better estimate sales during the demand planning phase of the sales and operations planning cycle.

FIGURE 3.5 Chase Sales Operations Plan

XYZ Company Sales and Operations Planning Spreadsheet
AA Product Family (Make-to-Stock)
Target Finished Inventory: 5 days

		History			Plan											
		October	November	December	January	February	March	April	May	June	July	August	September	October	November	December
Sales																
Forecast	(in million $)	10	13.1	6.9	7.6	8.4	10.2	9	11.8	7	8.6	12.6	14.4	12.8	15.8	11.8
	(in 1,000 units)	333	437	230	253	280	340	300	393	233	287	420	480	427	527	393
Actual	(in 1,000 units)	300	400	200												
Diff. month		−33	−37	−30												
Diff. cumulative			−70	−100												
Operations																
Plan	(in 1,000 units)	333	437	230	253	280	340	300	393	233	287	420	480	427	527	393
	(in 1,000 employees)	1,892	2,731	1,437	1,583	1,667	1,848	1,875	2,235	1,326	3,583	2,283	3,000	2,424	3,292	2,458
Number working days/mo.		22	20	20	20	21	23	20	22	22	10	23	20	22	20	20
Actual	(in 1,000 units)	360	455	300												
Diff. month		27	18	70												
Diff. cumulative			45	115												
Inventory																
Plan	(in 1,000 units)	100	100	100	215	215	215	215	215	215	215	215	215	215	215	215
	(in 1,000 $)	3,000	3,000	3,000	6,450	6,450	6,450	6,450	6,450	6,450	6,450	6,450	6,450	6,450	6,450	6,450
Actual	(in 1,000 units)	60	115	215												
Days of supply		4	6	21	17	15	13	14	11	18	15	10	9	10	8	11
Customer service (%)		98	100	100												

Furthermore, the actual production has exceeded the operations plan every month during the past quarter, and the cumulative difference equals +115,000 product units. The fact that actual sales are less than that the sales plan, and that production has exceeded the operations plan in each month, has produced a major increase in the finished goods inventory. As shown in Figure 3.5, the number of days of inventory has increased from 4 to 21 over this period, exceeding the target of 5 days. In this example the number of days of inventory was calculated by dividing the actual inventory by the average sales per day. Here, the average of sales per day was determined by dividing the actual monthly sales by 20 days.

These results signal a need to adjust the operations plan to bring sales and production into balance. There are many ways in which this could be accomplished. One way would be to reduce the January production plan in Figure 3.5 by 100,000 units in order to bring the inventory level back to 115,000 (or 6 days of sales). Alternatively, the reduction in production and inventory levels could be made over several months in order to reduce the impact of layoffs on the workforce. Such feedback on sales and production performance each month is a critical input to the sales and operations planning discussion and revision of the business plans.

In the next section we consider the basic cost trade-offs involved in developing the sales and operations plan. To provide a common basis for comparing different sales and operations plans, we will reduce the January sales figure of 253,000 units to 153,000 units in order to bring production and sales into balance, and to bring the finished goods inventory back to a level of 6 days. There are, of course, many other ways of achieving this, including spreading the inventory adjustment over several future months in order to reduce the impact of the workforce adjustment.

The Basic Trade-Offs

The second issue in sales and operations planning is *to find a low cost operations plan*. Figure 3.5 represents one approach to a pure chase strategy. For this example, the working week is held at 40 hours, and the labor force size is varied as needed to produce only the forecast sales. For example, January forecast sales are $7.6 million. When that number is divided by $30, the result is 253,333 product units. In order to compare the total cost of alternative operation plans on a consistent basis, the January sales of 253,333 units is reduced to 153,333 units in order to take into account the process inventory adjustment of 100,000 units. Dividing this result by 20 working days, we obtain a need for 7,667 units each day. If each worker produces 8 units per day, the implied workforce for January is 958 workers.

Month-to-month differences between implied workforce levels represent hire-fire decision. For example, the decision for February would be to hire 709 more workers over the January total (1,667 − 958). The hire-fire decision's impact is even more severe during the summer. It would be necessary to fire 909 workers in June, but to hire 2,257 in July.

In most circumstances, only a firm like a summer resort or a farm that harvests an agricultural commodity could consider such a high level of hiring and firing. In many Western countries, it's difficult to hire and fire workers. In Western Europe and parts of South America, it's virtually impossible to fire workers—the cost is very high.

The operations plan shown in Figure 3.6 represents an alternative to the chase strategy. In this case, the labor force is kept at a constant level of 2,178, using a "pure" level strategy.

FIGURE 3.6 Level Operations Plan

XYZ Company Sales and Operations Planning Spreadsheet
AA Product Family (Make-to-Stock)
Target Finished Inventory: 5 days

	History			Plan											
	October	November	December	January	February	March	April	May	June	July	August	September	October	November	December
Sales															
Forecast (in million $)	10	13.1	6.9	7.6	8.4	10.2	9	11.8	7	8.6	12.6	14.4	12.8	15.8	11.8
(in 1,000 units)	333	437	230	253	280	340	300	393	233	287	420	480	427	527	393
Actual (in 1,000 units)	300	400	200												
Diff. month	−33	−37	−30												
Diff. cumulative		−70	−100												
Operations															
Plan (in 1,000 units)	333	437	230	348	366	401	348	383	383	174	401	348	383	348	348
(in employees)	1,892	2,731	1,437	2,178	2,178	2,178	2,178	2,178	2,178	2,178	2,178	2,178	2,178	2,178	2,178
Number working days/mo.	22	20	20	20	21	23	20	22	22	10	23	20	22	20	20
Actual (in 1,000 units)	360	455	300												
Diff. month	27	18	70												
Diff. cumulative		45	115												
Inventory															
Plan (in 1,000 units)	100	100	100	310	396	457	506	496	646	534	514	383	339	161	116
(in 1,000 $)	3,000	3,000	3,000	9,314	11,892	13,714	15,168	14,878	19,388	16,005	15,428	11,482	10,172	4,817	3,481
Actual (in 1,000 units)	60	115	215												
Days of supply	4	6	21	41	28	27	34	25	55	37	24	16	16	6	6
Customer service (%)	98	100	100												

If the total product units for the year's sales (4,333,333 units less the 100,000 units inventory adjustment in January) is divided by the number of working days (243), the result (17,421) is the number of units necessary each day if level production is to be employed. Dividing the result by 8 units per day gives an implied constant labor force of 2,178 workers required to produce the year's forecast. This is essentially the dashed line in Figure 3.3, with allowances for the exact numbers of working days in each month. In this example, 2,178 workers would need to be employed on each of the 243 working days in the year to meet the forecast sales levels.

In January, the 2,178 workers, working 20 days each, create $10,454,400 of goods, using the planning factor of $30 of output per unit. Since the sales forecast for January is $7.6 million (minus the $3 million inventory adjustment), the expected inventory at the end of January is $9,314,000. Figure 3.6's value for February, $11,892,000, includes the January ending inventory plus the net addition to inventory created during February. (Figure 3.6 shows all values rounded to the nearest $1,000.)

This example clearly shows the basic trade-offs in operations planning. They may involve inventory accumulations, hiring and firing, undertime and overtime, and alternative capacity forms, such as outside contracting. Evaluating these trade-offs is very firm-specific.

Evaluating Alternatives

The cumulative chart in Figure 3.4 and the tabular presentation in Figures 3.5 and 3.6 show the implications of the pure chase and level production strategies. So far in the example, we've said nothing about evaluating the trade-offs involved. The management issue is how to choose between them or how to construct an alternative that's superior to either pure strategy. To do this rigorously, we must establish cost data that relate to the alternative operations planning methods. But in many firms, relevant cost data aren't readily available. In such cases, analysis could be done by using executive opinion.

Suppose, for example, no explicit cost data exist for operations planning at the XYZ Company. In that case, XYZ executives could evaluate such data as those in Figures 3.5 and 3.6 to point out situations they don't like. Implications of revised plans could be quickly calculated, using spreadsheet analysis, for subsequent evaluation by the executives. For example, the workforce could be allowed to build up as indicated from January through May for the chase strategy and be held at 2,235 for June, instead of dropping to 1,326. The resulting inventory would be included in the analysis performed for July and beyond. If this process of revising and evaluating were continued until the managerial group was satisfied, it could be possible to imply, from the choices made, the relative importance of costs assigned to various conditions.

To illustrate the analysis when cost data are available, we assume Figure 3.7's cost data were provided for the XYZ Company. The cost to hire an employee is estimated to be $200, whereas the cost to fire is $500. The final cost element, inventory carrying cost, is estimated to be 2 percent per month, on the basis of monthly ending inventory value.

We must establish the starting conditions before beginning the operations planning analysis. One way of proceeding is to identify those costs associated with making changes in the operations plan given the current actual employment status and a January inventory adjustment of −100,000 units. Therefore, in Figures 3.7 and 3.8 we have assumed a beginning and ending inventory of 115,000 units and a current workforce of 1,437.

FIGURE 3.7
XYZ Company
Operations
Planning Data

Hiring cost	$200 per employee
Firing cost	$500 per employee
Inventory carrying cost	2% per month (applied to the monthly ending inventory)
Beginning and ending inventory	115,000 product units
Beginning labor force	1,437 persons

FIGURE 3.8
Costs of
Alternative
Operations
Plans

Cost of:	Chase Sales Plan*	Level Production Plan	Mixed Plan
Hiring	$1,023,781	$ 148,200	$ 369,750
Layoff	2,048,787	0	413,875
Carrying inventory	828,000	2,914,805	1,039,474
Total	$3,900,568	$3,063,005	$1,823,099

*Note: The chase sales plan costs have been adjusted to reflect the −100,000 unit adjustment made in January.

In Figure 3.8 we have considered the monthly adjustments made in the workforce level shown previously in Figure 3.5 for the Chase Sales Plan. The cost of making these changes is simply the hire and fire cost for these actions. No regular labor costs are shown in Figure 3.8, since they'll be the same for each alternative plan considered; that is, the same number of working hours will be used for every plan. This results in an incremental cost of a pure hire-fire policy, with the given cost values of $3,900,568.

The second alternative in Figure 3.8 is the level strategy. In this case, enough people are added to the workforce in January to raise it from 1,437 to 2,178 workers. Each worker puts in a constant 40-hour week, and inventories are varied, as Figure 3.6's inventory plan shows. When each of these planned inventory values is multiplied by 2 percent, the total cost of carrying inventory shown in Figure 3.7 is obtained.

The last alternative, evaluated in Figure 3.8 and shown in Figure 3.9, is a mixed strategy calling for adding employees as necessary from January through May, but thereafter keeping the resultant workforce constant (2,235) until September. This means some inventories are held during June, July, and August. In September, the workforce is again expanded, this time by 570 workers, to provide the necessary output levels for the months of September, October, and November to meet the sales plan and to bring the finished goods inventory to the desired level (116,000 units). The lower demand forecast in December results in a layoff of 347 workers.

This plan may not be the best plan possible. For example, it's less costly to carry the extra inventory produced by 347 workers in December ($33,312) than to lay off all 347 workers ($173,500). The analysis thus far hasn't considered the desirable ending conditions in terms of workforce levels. The valuation of any particular ending workforce level must be made in light of the following year's sales forecast. The determination of mixed strategies that improve cost over those obtained by employing pure strategies can be guided by mathematical models.

FIGURE 3.9 Mixed Operations Plan

XYZ Company Sales and Operations Planning Spreadsheet
AA Product Family (Make-to-Stock)
Target Finished Inventory: 5 days

		History			Plan											
		October	November	December	January	February	March	April	May	June	July	August	September	October	November	December
Sales																
Forecast	(in million $)	10	13.1	6.9	7.6	8.4	10.2	9	11.8	7	8.6	12.6	14.4	12.8	15.8	11.8
	(in 1,000 units)	333	437	230	253	280	340	300	393	233	287	420	480	427	527	393
Actual	(in 1,000 units)	300	400	200												
Diff. month		−33	−37	−30												
Diff. cumulative			−70	−100												
Operations																
Plan	(in 1,000 units)	333	437	230	153	280	340	300	393	393	179	411	449	494	449	393
	(in employees)	1,892	2,731	1,437	956	1,667	1,848	1,875	2,235	2,235	2,235	2,235	2,805	2,805	2,805	2,458
Number working days/mo.		22	20	20	20	21	23	20	22	22	10	23	20	22	20	20
Actual	(in 1,000 units)	360	455	300												
Diff. month		27	18	70												
Diff. cumulative			45	115												
Inventory																
Plan	(in 1,000 units)	100	100	100	115	115	115	115	115	276	168	159	128	194	116	116
	(in 1,000 $)	3,000	3,000	3,000	3,450	3,452	3,453	3,453	3,463	8,274	5,028	4,765	3,829	5,830	3,484	3,492
Actual	(in 1,000 units)	60	115	215												
Days of supply		4	6	21	15	8	7	8	6	24	12	8	5	9	4	6
Customer service (%)		98	100	100												

The New Management Obligations

Implementing sales and operations planning requires major changes in management, particularly in top management coordination of functional activities in the business. If the sales and operations plan is to be the game plan for running a manufacturing company, it follows that top management needs to provide the necessary direction.

Top Management Role

Top management's first obligation is to commit to the sales and operations planning process. This means a major change in many firms. The change involves establishing the framework for sales and operations planning: getting the right team together, setting meetings, participating in the process, and so on. The change may also imply modifications of performance measurement and reward structures to align them with the plan. We should expect at the outset that many existing goals and performance measures will be in conflict with the integration provided by the sales and operations planning activity. These should be rooted out and explicitly changed. Enforcing changes implies a need to abide by and provide an example of the discipline required to manage with the planning system. This implies even top management must act within the planned flexibility range for individual actions and must evaluate possible changes that lie outside the limits.

As part of the commitment to the planning process, top management *must force* the resolution of trade-offs between functions prior to approving plans. The sales and operations plan provides a transparent basis for resolving these conflicts. It should provide basic implications of alternative choices even if it doesn't make decisions any easier. If trade-offs aren't made at this level they'll be forced into the mix of day-to-day activities of operating people who'll have to resolve them—perhaps unfavorably. If, for example, manufacturing continues long runs of products in the face of declining demand, the mismatch between production and the market will lead to increased inventories.

One of the benefits of sales and operations planning is to be able to run the business with one set of numbers. Top management should lead the cultural change to make that happen. Sales and operations activities must encompass all formal plans in an integrated fashion. If budgeting is a separate activity, it won't relate to the sales and operations plan and operating managers will need to make a choice. Similarly, if the profit forecast is based solely on the sales forecast (revenue) and accounting data (standard costs) and doesn't take into account implications for production, its value is doubtful. The sales and operations planning process intention is to produce complete and integrated plans, budgets, objectives, and goals that are used by managers to make decisions and provide the basis for evaluating performance. If other planning activities or evaluation documents are in place, the end result will be poor execution. An unfortunate but frequent approach is to invest management time in the sales and operations planning activity, but thereafter allow the company to be run by a separate performance measurement system or budget.

Functional Roles

The primary obligation under sales and operations planning is to "hit the plan" for all functions involved: manufacturing, sales, engineering, finance, and so on. A secondary obligation is the need to communicate when something will prevent hitting the plan. The sooner a problem can be evaluated in terms of other functional plans, the better. The obligation for communication provides the basis for keeping all groups' plans consistent when changes are necessary.

The purpose of the monthly planning cycle shown in Figure 3.2 is to facilitate cross-functional communication. This cycle ensures that critical demand and supply issues and important business trade-offs are considered on a routine basis. Further, the pre-SOP and executive SOP meetings are structured to ensure that decisions are made to resolve important demand and supply issues. In managing this process, it is important to have a cross-functional team with the appropriate skills to implement and execute sales and operations planning. There are six areas to be addressed in terms of roles and responsibilities.

1. *Executive champion/sponsor.* This role needs to be filled by a senior executive in the business who can keep top management focused on the process, clear major obstacles, and acquire the necessary resources. Either the president or a senior executive who has a solid working relationship with the president is a good candidate.

2. *SOP process owner.* This needs to be a person who can lead the implementation effort and can provide the leadership for the sales and operations planning process, normally as a part of other responsibilities. A well-organized person who has good people skills and can run meetings is a good choice. This person might come from any of the following jobs: director of sales administration, demand manager, materials manager, production control manager, controller, or sales manager.

3. *Demand planning team.* This team typically includes people with the following job titles: demand manager, product manager, forecast analyst, sales manager, salesperson, customer service manager, sales administration manager, new products coordinator, and SOP process owner.

4. *Supply planning team.* This team is made up of the following group: plant manager, materials manager, purchasing manager, master scheduler, distribution manager, production control manager, new products coordinator, and SOP process owner.

5. *Pre-SOP team.* This team needs to provide effective cross-functional skills within the business and could include the demand manager, materials manager, customer service manager, forecast analyst, product manager, master scheduler, plant manager, purchasing manager, controller, new products coordinator, and SOP process owner.

6. *Executive SOP team.* This group should include the president (general manager, chief operating officer), vice presidents of sales, marketing, operations, product development, finance, logistics, and human resources, and the SOP process owner.

In addition, information technology support is needed to support the sales and operations planning team because the planning process is most often carried out with electronic spreadsheets. This role might be filled by a spreadsheet developer or by having an appropriate level of spreadsheet skills in the team.

Other cross-functional issues involve defining product families and determining how many of them to consider in developing the sales and operations plan. Experience suggests that if more that a dozen are used, that is too many. Six to twelve appears to be the best number. A larger number involves getting into too much detail and losing top management's attention during the monthly planning meetings. Figure 3.10, from Tom Wallace's book *Sales and Operations Planning,* shows a range of possibilities to consider in defining the product

FIGURE 3.10
Product Family Grouping

Total company

Business unit

Product family

Product subfamily

Model/brand

Package size

Stockkeeping unit (SKU)

SKU by customer

SKU by customer by location

family groupings. It is difficult to do sales and operations planning at the top of the pyramid because there is not enough granularity at that level on which to base the demand/supply decisions. Likewise, at the bottom of the pyramid there is too much detail, and it will be difficult to see an overall picture of volume in aggregate planning.

The other problem in defining the product families is how to structure these families in a way that is convenient for the different functions in the business. Some of the possibilities include structuring the product family groupings by product type, product characteristics, product size, brand, market segment, or customer. The fundamental question is simply "How do you go to market?" Since products are what a company provides to customers, the product family groupings should be set up on that basis. Setting up the product family groupings in a way that is consistent with how the sales and marketing people think about the market is best. However, when the product groupings line up with the market segments or customer groups, they often do not line up with the resources—plants, departments, and processes. This can, however, be handled by identifying the production resources and reviewing their status separately.

A final problem in structuring the product families is to choose the appropriate unit of measure for each family. Choices include: units, pounds, gallons, cases, etc. Here the best approach is to select a measure that is based on how the company goes to market. If the plants need to use a different measure, this can be handled in capacity planning through conversion routines.

Still another cross-functional issue is that the process of budgeting usually needs to change and to be integrated with sales and operations planning and subsequent departmental plans. In many firms, budgeting is done on an annual basis, using data that aren't part of the manufacturing planning and control system. Manufacturing budgets are often based on historical cost relationships and a separation of fixed and variable expenses. These data aren't as precise as data obtained by utilizing the MPC system database. By using the database, we can evaluate tentative master production schedules in terms of component part needs, capacities, and expected costs. We can then analyze the resultant budgets for the effect of product mix changes as well as for performance against standards.

Another important aspect of relating budgeting to the sales and operations planning activity and underlying MPC systems and database is that the cycle can be done more frequently. We won't need to collect data—they always exist in up-to-date form. Moreover, inconsistencies are substantially cut. The budget should always agree with the sales and operations plan, which, in turn, is in concert with the disaggregated end-item and component plans that support the operations plan. As a result, an operating manager should have to choose between a budget and satisfying the operations plan far less often.

With budgeting and sales and operations planning done on the same basis with the same underlying dynamic database, it's natural to incorporate cost accounting. This enables us to perform detailed variance accounting as well as cross-check transaction accuracy.

The most obvious need for integrated planning and control is between sales, marketing, and production. Yet it's often the most difficult to accomplish. Firms must ensure product availability for special promotions, match customer orders with specific production lots, coordinate distribution activities with production, and deal with a host of other cross-functional problems.

The sales and marketing job under integrated sales and operations planning is to sell what's in the sales plan. We must instill the feeling that overselling is just as bad a underselling. In either case, there will be a mismatch with manufacturing output, financial requirements, and inventory/backlog levels. If an opportunity arises to sell more than the plan, it needs to be formally evaluated via a change in the sales and operations plan. By going through this process, we can time this increase so it can be properly supported by both manufacturing and finance. And once the formal plan has been changed, it's again each function's job to achieve its specified objectives—no more and no less.

Similarly, it's manufacturing's job to achieve the plan—exactly. Overproduction may well mean that too much capacity and resources is being utilized. Underproduction possibly means the reverse (not enough resources) or means poor performance. In either case, performance against the plan is poor. This can be the fault of either the standard-setting process or inadequate performance. Both problems require corrective action.

When manufacturing is hitting the schedule, it's a straightforward job for sales and marketing to provide good customer order promises and other forms of customer service. It's also a straightforward job for finance to plan cash flows and anticipate financial performance.

If the sales and operations planning results can't be achieved, whatever component can't meet its plan must be clearly responsible for reporting this condition promptly. If, for example, a major supplier can't meet its commitments, the impact on the detailed sales, marketing, and operations plans must be quickly ascertained.

Integrating Strategic Planning

An important direction-setting activity, strategic planning can be done in different ways. Some companies approach it primarily as an extension of budgeting. Typically, these firms use a bottom-up process, which is largely an extrapolation of the departmental budgets based on growth assumptions and cost-volume analysis. One key aspect of these firms' strategic plans is to integrate these bottom-up extrapolations into a coherent whole. Another is to critically evaluate the overall outcome from a corporate point of view.

A more recent approach to strategic planning is to base the plan more on products and markets, and less on organizational units. The company's products/markets are typically grouped into strategic business units (SBUs), with each SBU evaluated in terms of its strength and weakness vis-à-vis competitors' similar business units. The budgetary process in this case is done on an SBU basis rather than an organizational unit basis. Business units are evaluated in terms of their competitive strengths, relative advantages, life cycles, and cash flow patterns (e.g., when does an SBU need cash and when is it a cash provider?). From a strategic point of view, the objective is to carefully manage a portfolio of SBUs to the firm's overall advantage.

Sales and operations planning and departmental plans to support these strategic planning efforts can be important. In the case of the operations plan, the overall database and systems must ensure that the sales and operations plans will be in concert with disaggregated decision making. In other words, the MPS and related functions ensure that strategic planning decisions are executed!

All the advantages of integrating sales and operations planning with budgeting also apply when the SBU focus is taken. It makes sense to state the sales and operations plan in the same SBU units; that is, rather than use dollar outputs per time unit, the sales and operations plan should be stated in SBU terminology.

Controlling the Operations Plan

A special responsibility in sales and operations planning involves control of performance against the plan. As a prerequisite to control, the sales and operations planning process should be widely understood in the firm. The seriousness with which it's regarded should be communicated as well as the exact planned results that pertain to each of the organization's functional units. In other words, the planning process must be transparent, with clear communication of expectations, to control actual results. For the operations plan, this means wide dissemination of the plan and its implications for managers.

Another dimension of control is periodic reporting. Performance against the sales and operations plans should also be widely disseminated. When actual results differ from plans, we must analyze and communicate the source of these deviations.

The Tennant Company provides an example of this communication. Some of its more important measures of operations performance and reporting frequency are:

Measure	Reporting
Conformity of the master production schedule to the operations plan	Weekly
Capacity utilization	Weekly
Delivery performance	Daily
Actual production to master production schedule performance	Weekly
Inventory/backlog performance	Weekly

Tennant hadn't missed a quarterly operations plan for the previous 2.5 years. Moreover, it had met the monthly operations plan in 10 out of 12 months for each of the previous years. These results are well known inside the company and widely disseminated outside too. All levels of the firm understand the operations plan's importance.

Key issues in sales and operations planning are when and how to change the plan, and how stable to keep the operations portion of the plan from period to period. No doubt a stable operations plan results in far fewer execution problems by the detailed master production scheduling, material planning, and other execution functions. Stability also fosters achievement of some steady-state operations where capacity can be more effectively utilized.

At Tennant, operations plan changes are batched until the next review, unless they're required to prevent major problems. In other companies, stability in the plan is maintained by providing time fences for changes and permissible ranges of deviation from the plan. Tennant provides flexibility within the plan by planning adequate inventories or other forms of capacity to absorb deviations within an agreed-on range.

Increasingly, companies are using lean manufacturing concepts, with many aspects of the system based on manual controls. One key to making lean manufacturing work is a stable operations plan. The output rate is held constant for long time periods and is modified only after extensive analysis. This means the production rate at each step of the manufacturing process can be held to very constant levels, providing stability and predictability.

We can see the other side of this coin by reviewing one U.S. auto manufacturer's approach. In the face of diminishing sales, the company continued to produce in excess of sales. This led to a buildup of finished-goods inventory exceeding 100 days of sales. The results on the financial statements were significant: adjustments in manufacturing were even more severe. Finished-goods inventories and order backlogs can buffer manufacturing from day-to-day shocks, but long-run changes have to be reflected in the basic operations plan itself.

Operating with Sales and Operations Planning

In this section, we show examples of sales and operations planning practice. In particular, we present organizational aspects of sales and operations planning at the Compugraphic Corporation, the entire process at the Delta Manufacturing Company, and the Hill-Rom Company's use of SBU-related bills of material for tying the operations plan to its strategic business units.

Sales and Operations Planning at Compugraphic

Compugraphic Corporation makes typesetters and related equipment for the printing industry in five separate factory locations in Boston's northern suburbs. Figure 3.11 shows how sales and operations planning fits in the corporation. Figure 3.12 details its relationship with master production scheduling.

The sales and operations planning committee is made up of the company's top management group representing all functional areas. It develops and monitors the sales and operations plan that determines the manufacturing resources to support the business plan and corporate objectives. The committee's mission is further delineated as:

- To assure that sales and operations plans are consistent with the annual business plan.
- To establish performance measurements for evaluating the sales and operations planning process.

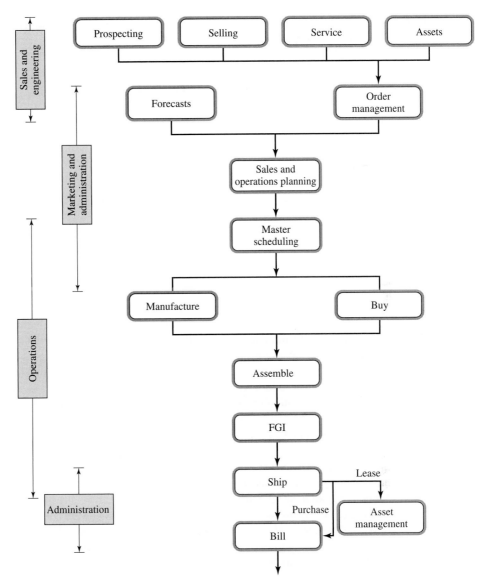

FIGURE 3.11
Compugraphic Sales and Operations Planning

- To communicate sales forecasts for product families on a monthly basis.
- To assure that manufacturing capabilities are consistent with the operations plan.
- To monitor actual results against plans and make adjustments as required.
- To manage the finished-goods inventory with the targets established in the sales and operations plans.
- To provide direction to the development and execution of the master production schedule.

FIGURE 3.12
Compugraphic's Sales and Operations Planning and the MPS

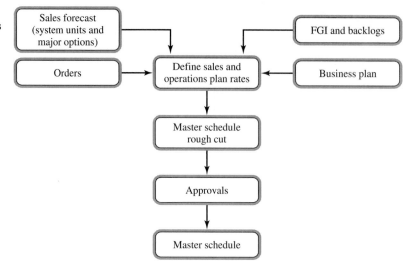

At each monthly meeting, each of the 11 product family groups are reviewed. For each family, forecast and order performance for the current month are reviewed and the outlook for the coming 12 months is reviewed as well. Next, manufacturing performance is reviewed. Was the operations plan for the past month met? Are there any expected sales or manufacturing deviations in the future? If so, are they to be compensated for in other months? The other major review point is the finished goods inventories in relation to plans, including consideration of established safety stock levels. Projected inventory levels are based on netting the sales and manufacturing data, but they're reviewed independently to see if revisions in either sales or manufacturing are needed.

Also reviewed at the meeting are several other items that could affect a particular family group's performance. This includes customer backlogs, customer service levels achieved, new marketing plans (such as price changes or sales incentives), and product requirements for demonstration or other nonsales purposes.

Figure 3.13 shows records for one product family. Data were collected during the month of May. The sales and operations planning process is essentially made up of three parts, each corresponding to one of the records. The top third of Figure 3.13 is devoted to this product family's marketing outlook. At the end of April, actual shipments and backlog to be shipped were exactly equal to the baseline sales plan (43 units). The original forecast for May was 128 units, but as of the date the data were collected, it appeared the actual shipments would exceed this plan by 7 units. June was expected to fall short by 54 units (47 cumulative), but marketing expected to catch up during July.

The bottom third of Figure 3.13 indicates production performance. In April manufacturing overbuilt the schedule by 14 units. However, the plan shows manufacturing underbuilding in May to get back on the baseline schedule for the year.

The middle third of Figure 3.13 nets sales (shipment) plans against the operations plan to project inventories. This allows top management to examine the overall impact of both forecast errors and manufacturing performance deviations.

FIGURE 3.13
Compugraphic's
Sales and
Operations
Planning:
Sample Family

Product family *Sunline 25*   Month *May*

Shipment Performance

	–	–	Apr	May	June	July	Aug	Sept	Oct	Nov	Dec	Jan	Feb	Mar
Baseline (plan)			43	128	228	222	311	356	288	288	383	232	232	308
Actual & backlog			43	–	–	–	–	–	–	–	–	–	–	–
Shipment outlook			–	135	174	269	311	356	288	288	383	232	232	308
Variance			0	7	<54>	47	0	0	0	0	0	0	0	0
Cum. variance			0	7	<47>	0	0	0	0	0	0	0	0	0

Inventory Performance

	–	–	Apr	May	June	July	Aug	Sept	Oct	Nov	Dec	Jan	Feb	Mar
Baseline (plan)			89	193	32	8	27	1	33	65	2	10	18	10
Actual*		15	103	–			–		–		–	–	–		
Outlook			–	86	79	8	27	1	33	65	2	10	18	10
Variance			<14>	7	<47>	0	0	0	0	0	0	0	0	0

Production Performance

	–	–	Apr	May	June	July	Aug	Sept	Oct	Nov	Dec	Jan	Feb	Mar
Baseline (plan)			117	132	167	198	330	330	320	320	320	240	240	300
Actual			131	–	–	–	–	–	–	–	–	–	–	–
Outlook			–	118	167	198	330	330	320	320	320	240	240	300
Variance			14	<14>	0	0	0	0	0	0	0	0	0	0

Compugraphic's sales and operations planning process has had an important impact, particularly on its MPC systems. When the firm implemented a new on-line MRP-based system, it became clear that the sales and operations plan was critical to provide the necessary direction to master production scheduling and resulting MPC functions. Before sales and operations planning was developed, there was a tendency to not react rapidly to market shifts (particularly downturns). The result was larger than necessary inventories, which, in turn, required more radical adjustments in production. The monthly sales and operations planning process's goal was to make more frequent, smaller adjustments on a regular basis, according to top management's ongoing assessment of where the business was headed.

Delta Manufacturing Company's Integrated Sales and Operations Planning Process

The sales and operations planning process is a top-down process that begins with a senior management commitment to orchestrating the process. It is focused on positioning the business enterprise to support expected future sales requirements. The end results of this activity are (1) a financial projection of the future sales and operations plans and (2) a road map for the company activities so the individual areas in the business arrive at the same destination at the same time.

Delta's management believes that the following criteria are necessary for the successful implementation of sales and operations planning:

1. The development of a company unit of measure that all of the business functions agree can be used for the process of sales and operations planning.
2. An understanding of the capacity of the producing entity that is stated in the company's standard unit of measure.
3. Agreement on the product level that will be used in the process, e.g., end items or some agreed-on grouping of end items.
4. Establishment of the business requirement for each product item. This involves determining whether the product will be built to stock or built to order, and determining the appropriate level of inventory or back orders to be maintained.

Delta Manufacturing Company's Operations

Delta manufactures plastic components for products that are sold to major retailers and to the health care industry. The company has two major business units, and annual sales are approximately $200 million. Delta produces 750 end products that are grouped into 150 product groupings for planning purposes. The 150 product groupings can be further aggregated into 12 market segments that relate to the two business units. The 150 product groupings were developed so that each category is defined in terms of similar manufacturing capabilities. The company's products are produced in two plants that include a total of 14 manufacturing work centers. Approximately 70 percent of the production volume is shipped directly from inventory. For sales and operations planning purposes, the company uses pounds of extruded plastic as the sales and operations planning measure. The total annual production output exceeds 100 million pounds of product.

Delta's Sales and Operations Monthly Planning Cycle

Each month the sales and operations planning process develops a full sales and operations plan covering the next 12 months. Figure 3.14 provides an example of an SOP calendar that shows the timing for each step during the monthly SOP cycle. This calendar is prepared and sent one quarter in advance to all of the SOP participants. During one of the SOP monthly cycles each year, a five-year SOP is completed as a part of the annual budgeting process.

The sales forecast is a key input to the monthly SOP process. The sales forecast is the result of an interactive process involving the manufacturing planning group and the sales representatives for each of the 750 end items forecast. This forecasting activity begins with a statistical forecast that utilizes several moving-average and exponential smoothing techniques and that identifies the forecasting technique that provides the "best fit" to the actual sales history data. Figure 3.15 provides an example of the one-year sales forecast for one of the product groupings, "Market 005 Patient Care." This product grouping includes five individual products.

A statistical sales forecast is sent electronically to each of the sales representatives that covers their individual products and accounts. The sales representatives update the statistical forecast with additional information received from customers. The statistical forecast for each of the 750 items is then updated and aggregated into product categories. These product categories represent the product level used in the SOP process. The final updated

FIGURE 3.14 Sales and Operations Planning Calendar, August Year 1

Monday	Tuesday	Wednesday	Thursday	Friday
			1 **12:00 PM** Sales closing complete **12:00 PM** Scheduled trials due to master scheduler **12:00 PM** Inventory reports due to demand manager from plants	2 **12:00 PM** Send on-time shipments reports (e-mail)
5 **12:00 PM** Production plan to operations	6 **2:00 PM** On-time shipments	7 **2:00 PM** Supply planning meeting	8 **9:00 AM** Final forecast due to operations analysis	9 **12:00 PM** Send on-time shipments reports (e-mail)
12	13 **2:00 PM** On-time shipments	14 **2:00 PM** Capacity call	15 **12:00 PM** Send SOP agenda/spreadsheets (e-mail)	16 **12:00 PM** Send on-time shipments reports (e-mail)
19	20 **1:00 PM** Operations & engineering meeting **2:00 PM** On-time shipments **5:00 PM** Forecast feedback to sales	21 **8:00 AM** Operations & engineering meeting **1:00 PM** SOP meeting	22	23 **12:00 PM** Send on-time shipments reports (e-mail) **4:00 PM** Send SOP meeting notes (e-mail)
26 **9:00 AM** Sales forecast due to demand manager **5:00 PM** Sales forecast due to business unit directors (BUDs)	27 **2:00 PM** On-time shipments	28 **1:00 PM** Final forecast due to demand manager from BUDs **2:00 PM** Capacity call	29 **8:30 AM** Production planning **1:00 PM** Forecast due to master scheduler	30 **12:00 PM** Send on-time shipments reports (e-mail)

FIGURE 3.15 Final Sales Forecast, August Year 1

Market 005 Patient Care	Historical Demand			Forecast												Total
	May Y1	Jun Y1	Jul Y1	Aug Y1	Sept Y1	Oct Y1	Nov Y1	Dec Y1	Jan Y2	Feb Y2	Mar Y2	Apr Y2	May Y2	Jun Y2	Jul Y2	
Product Code:																
05A PP Patient Care Embossed Pad	48,158	70,051	60,887	65,000	78,000	65,000	65,000	50,000	65,000	65,000	65,000	65,000	65,000	65,000	65,000	**778,000**
05B PP Patient Care Nonembossed	0	0	0	0	0	0	0	0	0	0	0	0	0	0	0	**0**
05C RP Patient Care Embossed Pad	0	0	0	120,000	200,000	200,000	200,000	200,000	200,000	200,000	200,000	200,000	200,000	200,000	200,000	**2,320,000**
05D BP Patient Care Nonembossed Pad	39,632	68,535	54,584	55,002	55,000	55,000	55,002	45,001	55,000	55,000	55,000	55,000	55,002	54,998	55,001	**650,006**
05E SP Patient Care Embossed Pad	28,475	29,148	27,689	30,000	35,999	29,999	30,001	25,000	30,000	30,000	30,000	30,000	30,000	30,000	35,999	**366,998**
Total for Patient Care	116,356	167,734	143,160	270,002	358,999	349,999	350,003	320,001	350,000	350,000	350,000	350,000	350,002	349,998	356,000	**4,115,004**

forecast with all the customer modifications included is sent to the business unit directors for their review and approval.

At midnight on the last day of the month, the finished goods inventory status (organized by product category and net of any past due orders) is updated for use in the SOP process. At this point all of the information needed in the SOP monthly cycle is available. This information includes the currently available capacity, the sales forecasts, and the inventory status.

Figure 3.16 shows the sales and operations plan spreadsheet for the Market 005 Patient Care product grouping. These plans can be displayed for various levels of aggregation in Delta's planning process, including the company level, the business unit level, and at a product grouping level. In the case of Figure 3.16 the inventory goal is a 20-day supply. At the end of July the actual inventory was at a 16-day supply. This means that the production plan for some of the items in Market 005 Patient Care product grouping will have to be increased beyond the forecast in order to increase the inventory to the required level. For example, the planned production in September is 403,000 pounds and the forecast sales are 369,000 pounds.

Once the production plan for each product grouping has been determined, the detailed planning for individual production facilities is developed. For example, the product category 05C RP embossed pad (which is a part of the Market 005 Patient Care product grouping) is planned for production on extrusion line 2. This is shown in Figure 3.17. This particular product category did not require any inventory adjustments to increase the number of days' supply, and the planned production will equal the forecast sales amount. Since the product category 05A PP embossed pad requires more production than is available on extrusion line 2, this will result in a portion of the requirements being planned on an alternative line.

The resulting plan for extrusion line 2 shows that the required production days will equal the scheduled production days (available capacity) for the next 12 months. (Rounding the numbers shows a slight difference.) After the planning is complete for each extrusion line, the plans are reviewed with the plants for their agreement. This step is indicated on the SOP calendar in Figure 3.14. These plans may be further modified as necessary during this plant review. This review is completed approximately one week before the monthly SOP meeting in order to allow time for the needed changes to be incorporated into the plan.

SOP Monthly Meeting

The formal agenda shown in Figure 3.18 is sent to the SOP meeting attendees prior to each meeting. The senior operating officer of the company chairs this meeting, and attendance is mandatory.

The first item on the agenda is a review of customer satisfaction performance as shown by the example in Figure 3.19. The percentage of time that shipments met both the company's promise of shipment and the customer's request for shipment is charted and reviewed. For each area where the company failed to meet either of these criteria, a discussion is held and corrective action plans are assigned.

The second agenda item is a review of plant capacity. The graphs in Figure 3.20 show the planned downtime and capacity by line, the actual sales, and the production over the past three months. Actual performance is compared to plan. In addition, the sales and production planned for the next 12 months is compared to the planned capacity. This review begins with the overall company performance and continues through each production line.

FIGURE 3.16 Sales and Operations Plan

Business: Unit A
Unit of measure: 1,000 pounds

Market: Patient Care

Segment: Pads

August Y1

Budget Dollars X $1,588

Target On-Time to Promise 95%

	May	Jun	Jul	FYTD	Aug	Sep	Oct	Nov	Dec	Jan	3rd 3 mos.	4th 3 mos.	Next 12 months	Latest Call	Budget Plan
						Inventory Goal—20 Days' Supply									
Sales															
Old forecast	150	150	155	1562	150	169	150	150	120	150	450	450	1,789	1,817	1,800
New forecast					270	369	350	350	320	350	1,050	1,056	4,115	2,117	
New vs. old fcst.					120	200	200	200	200	200	600	606	2,326	320	
Open orders					20	0	0	0	0	0	0	0	20		
Excess deficit					250	369	350	350	320	350	1,050	1,056	4,095		
Actual sales	116	168	143	1,498											
Diff. month	-34	18	-12	-64											
Cum.	-34	-16	-28												
Operations															
Old plan	113	115	102	1,096	170	149	154	122	148	150	448	450	1,791		
New plan					270	403	380	370	330	348	1,043	1,054	4,198		
New vs. old plan					100	254	226	248	182	198	595	604	2,407		
Actual	154	193	103	1,561											
Diff. month	41	78	1	465											
Cum.	41	119	120												
Inventory															
Plan FGI					8	22	32	32	32	32	32	32			
Plan cons.					134	154	174	194	204	202	195	193			
Finished	41	37	35												
Consignment	115	144	106												
Master rolls	0	-7	0												
Doctor	0	0	0												
Actual	156	174	142												
Days' supply	24	53	16		12	16	18	22	21	20	20	20			
On time—request date	100	99	100												
On time—promise date	100	99	100												

FIGURE 3.17 Production Plan, August Y1

	Daily Capacity	Aug Y1	Sep Y1	Oct Y1	Nov Y1	Dec Y1	Jan Y2	Feb Y2	Mar Y2	Apr Y2	May Y2	Jun Y2	Jul Y2
Extrusion line 2													
05A PP embossed pad	12,031	65,000	0	0	22,800	34,872	42,273	7,182	42,273	31,000	42,816	30,336	36,075
05D BP nonembossed pad	11,812	55,002	69,000	65,000	55,002	45,001	55,000	55,000	55,000	55,000	55,002	54,998	55,001
05C RP embossed pad	11,812	120,000	200,000	200,000	200,000	200,000	200,000	200,000	200,000	200,000	200,000	200,000	200,000
17R PP label	14,074	80,000	32,000	29,000	0	0	0	0	0	0	0	0	0
22Y SP cover	12,426	21,260	21,260	21,260	21,260	25,000	25,000	25,000	25,000	25,000	25,000	25,000	25,000
05E SP embossed pad	10,567	30,000	22,172	39,999	40,001	25,000	30,000	30,000	30,000	30,000	30,000	30,000	35,999
Forecast pounds		371,262	344,432	355,259	339,063	329,873	352,273	317,182	352,273	341,000	352,818	340,334	352,075
Estimated capacity		365,745	346,147	355,359	339,298	329,661	352,828	316,758	352,828	340,814	352,840	340,799	352,011
Excess/(deficit)		−5,517	1,716	100	235	−212	555	−424	555	−186	22	465	−64
Required production days		30.5	28.9	30.0	29.0	28.0	30.0	27.0	30.0	29.0	30.0	29.0	30.0
Scheduled production days		30.0	29.0	30.0	29.0	28.0	30.0	27.0	30.0	29.0	30.0	29.0	30.0
Excess/(deficit)		−0.5	0.1	0.0	0.0	0.0	0.0	0.0	0.0	0.0	0.0	0.0	0.0
Cumulative excess/(deficit)		−0.5	−0.3	−0.3	−0.3	−0.3	−0.3	−0.3	−0.2	−0.3	−0.3	−0.2	−0.2

FIGURE 3.18

Agenda,
Executive Sales
and Operations
Planning
Meeting

August 23, Y1
2:00 PM

1. On-time shipments review
   a. Review of July and August-to-date performance

2. Capacity issues
   a. Planned downturns
   b. Production line graphs and summary

3. Inventory review
   a. Inventory turns
   b. Total inventory value graphs
   c. Finished goods DOH (days on hand) graphs
   d. Raw materials DOH graphs

15-minute break

4. SOP follow-ups and spreadsheet review
   a. Process of review
   b. Follow-ups from prior meeting
   c. Spreadsheet review and decisions

5. Critique of meeting

For example, the data shown in Figure 3.20 indicate that actual sales exceeded the forecast in June, and was less than forecasted in May and July. This has resulted in adjustments in planned production in order to achieve targeted inventory levels.

The third area of discussion is a review of inventory performance. Here the past 12-month actual statistics are charted and trends developed. The example shown in Figure 3.21 is the raw materials inventory. This review also begins with overall company totals, and continues with each plant's performance. The on-hand dollar amount and the number of days' supply are compared with the goals. If the goals are not being met, specific problem areas are discussed and corrective action is assigned.

The fourth part of the meeting is a review of the sales and operations plans that were developed during the SOP process. Figure 3.16 provides an example of these plans. The majority of the meeting is spent in this area. During this discussion, the business unit directors discuss these plans for each market, the performance during the past three months, and the plans during the next 12 months for sales, production, and inventory. The final part of the meeting is a critique of the process and suggested improvements.

Results

From the beginning of the implementation of the SOP process two years ago, Delta has improved its delivery reliability by raising the on-time shipment to promise performance from 65 percent to the current level of more than 95 percent. During this same period of time the company also reduced the investment in finished goods inventories by over $2,000,000, and the raw materials inventory by $2,500,000.

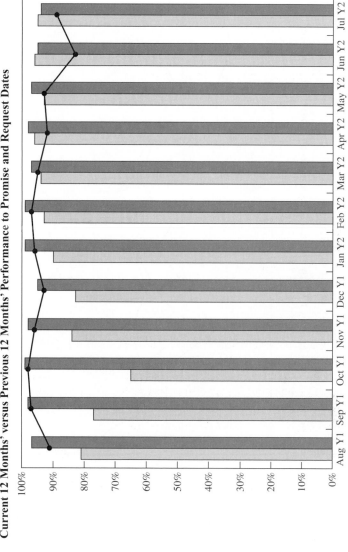

FIGURE 3.19 Current 12 Months' versus Previous 12 Months' Performance to Promise and Request Dates

	Aug Y1	Sep Y1	Oct Y1	Nov Y1	Dec Y1	Jan Y2	Feb Y2	Mar Y2	Apr Y2	May Y2	Jun Y2	Jul Y2
Prev. 12 mo. on time (prom.)	81%	77%	65%	84%	83%	90%	93%	94%	96%	93%	96%	95%
Cur. 12 mo. on time (prom.)	97%	98%	99%	98%	95%	99%	99%	97%	98%	97%	95%	94%
Cur. 12 mo. on time (req.)	91%	97%	98%	96%	93%	96%	97%	95%	92%	93%	87%	89%

94

FIGURE 3.20 Company Total Pounds versus Estimated Capacity, Including Actual Sales and Production (Unit of Measure: Million Pounds)

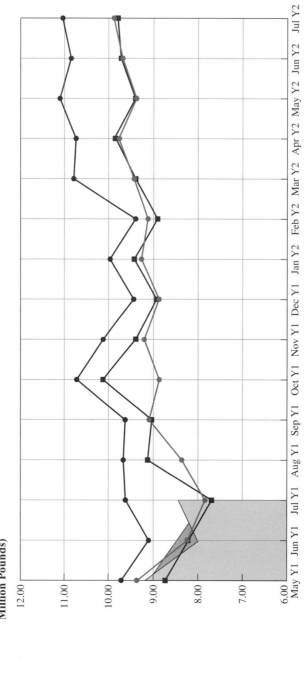

	May Y1	Jun Y1	Jul Y1	Aug Y1	Sep Y1	Oct Y1	Nov Y1	Dec Y1	Jan Y2	Feb Y2	Mar Y2	Apr Y2	May Y2	Jun Y2	Jul Y2
Actual sales	9.10	8.56	7.82												
Actual production	9.14	8.04	8.51												
Production plan	8.74	8.31	7.64	9.15	9.09	10.14	9.50	8.93	9.53	8.85	9.41	9.84	9.41	9.67	9.82
Sales forecast	9.37	8.32	7.84	8.43	9.17	8.87	9.27	8.86	9.36	9.15	9.45	9.77	9.40	9.63	9.88
Staffed capacity	9.83	9.12	9.60	9.68	9.62	10.73	10.20	9.41	9.93	9.41	10.78	10.74	11.06	10.84	11.05

FIGURE 3.21 **Plant 2 Total Raw Materials Inventory**

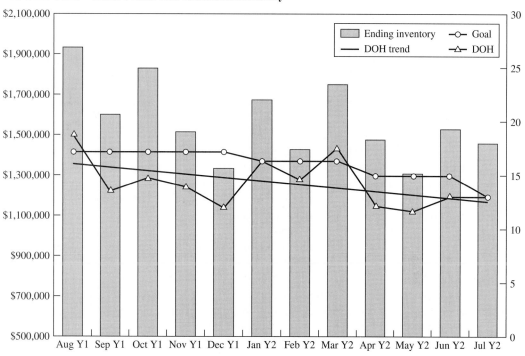

While these improvements are impressive in and of themselves, the most important improvement was expressed by the vice president of operations during a recent SOP meeting when he commented, "The company is no longer running us, we are running the company."

Lessons Learned

Several lessons were learned during the successful implementation of sales and operations planning at Delta. They include the importance of:

- Senior management owning the SOP process.
- The SOP plans being visible to all parts of the company.
- Having one set of books, which include the sales, operations, and financial plans of the company.
- Preparing the SOP plans on a global basis for the company.
- The impact of the SOP process on the return-on-assets performance achieved by the company.
- Having no surprises in the SOP process homework.
- The SOP process in reducing uncertainty in demand and supply, which enables important inventory reductions.
- Viewing the SOP process as a planning process instead of a scheduling process.
- Not second-guessing the sales forecasts.

Overall, the company considers continuous improvement to be an important ingredient in further improving the SOP process. It views SOP as a journey, not a destination!

Hill-Rom's Use of Planning Bills of Materials

The use of planning bill of materials concepts can be very helpful in the sales and operations planning process. An example is the application developed at Hill-Rom, a manufacturer of hospital beds, related equipment, and accessories for hospitals and nursing homes.

Hill-Rom has expanded the planning bill concept to what it calls the "super-duper" bill. Figure 3.22 shows an abbreviated example. In this approach, only one item is forecast: total bed sales. All other forecasts are treated as bill of materials relationships. For example, the forecast for over-bed tables is a percentage of overall bed sales.

One marketing person at Hill-Rom found the super-duper bill concept ideal for implementing an idea he'd been thinking about for some time. He believed the company makes trigger products and trailer products. Beds are trigger products, whereas over-bed tables, chairs, and add-ons (such as trapezes or intravenous fluid rods) are trailer products. Purchase of trailer products is dependent on purchase of trigger products in somewhat the same relationship as component sales depend on end-item sales. This relationship means that, rather than forecast demand for over-bed tables, Hill-Rom tracks and maintains the percentage relationship between sales of beds and over-bed tables.

This bill of materials relationship will probably be a better estimate than a direct forecast of over-bed tables. If we expect bed sales to go up or down, by treating over-bed tables as a trailer product with a bill of materials linkage, we have an automatic adjustment in over-bed table forecasts, as in all trailer products.

FIGURE 3.22 **Hill-Rom's "Super-Duper" Bill**

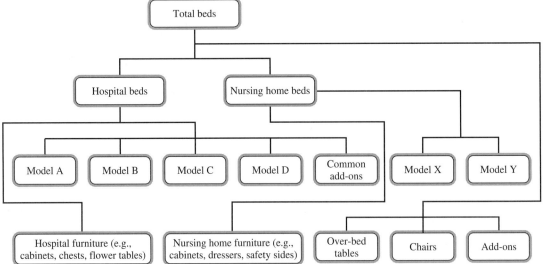

Using bill of materials approaches to forecasting also forces a logical consistency. At one time the forecast for 84-inch mattresses at Hill-Rom exceeded combined forecasts for beds using 84-inch mattresses. Treating these relationships with bill of materials approaches reduces these inconsistencies, which always result from independent estimating.

The sales and operations planning unit for these products at Hill-Rom is total beds. Furthermore, the percentage split into hospital beds and nursing home beds is not only estimated, it's managed. Sales personnel are held to specified tolerance limits on this split because the capacity and net profit implications of the percentage split are important.

Below each of these two super-duper bills are "super" bills for the various model series. Finally, there's another trigger-trailer relationship between total hospital bed sales and sales of hospital furniture such as cabinets and flower tables. The same kind of bill of materials relationship is used to forecast nursing home furniture sales. These various bill of materials relationships pass the planning information down through the MPC system in a logically consistent way.

Finally, this entire approach is consistent with the way the firm does its strategic planning, which is in terms of strategic business units (SBUs). SBUs are established as super bills. The result is a very close integration of MPC and strategic planning.

Concluding Principles	Sales and operations planning provide key inputs to MPC systems. It represents management's handle on the business. This chapter emphasizes the key relationships of top management and functional management in developing and maintaining an effective sales and operations plan. The following important principles summarize our discussion.

- The operations plan is not a forecast; it must be a managerial statement of desired production output.

- The operations plan should be a part of the sales and operations planning process so it will be in complete agreement with the other functional plans (sales plan, budget, and so on) that make up the business plan.

- The trade-offs required to frame the operations plan must be made *prior* to final approval of the plan.

- There must be top-management involvement in the sales and operations planning process, which should be directly related to strategic planning.

- The MPC system should be used to perform routine activities and provide routine data, so management time can be devoted to important tasks.

- The MPC system should be used to facilitate what-if analyses at the sales and operations planning level.

- Reviews of performance against sales and operations plans are needed to prompt replanning when necessary.

- The operations plan should provide the MPS parameters, and flexibility should be specifically defined. The sum of the detailed MPS must always equal the operations plan.

- The operations plan should tie the company's strategic activities directly through the MPS to the MPC's execution functions.

References

Brander, Arne. "Drive the Business with Sales & Operations Planning," *APICS—The Performance Advantage,* August 1998, pp. 48–51.

Hausman, W. H.; David B. Montgomery; and Aleda V. Roth. "Why should Marketing and Manufacturing Work Together?: Some exploratory empirical results," *Journal of Operations Management* 20, no. 3 (June 2002), pp. 241–257.

Konijnendijk, P. A. *Coordination of Production and Sales.* Eindhoven, The Netherlands: Technical Eindhoven University, 1992.

Ling, R. C., and W. E. Goddard. *Orchestrating Success: Improved Control of the Business with Sales and Operations Planning.* New York: John Wiley & Sons, 1995.

Malhotra, M. K., and Subhash Sharma. "Spanning the Continuum Between Marketing and Operations," *Journal of Operations Management* 20, no. 3 (June 2002), pp. 209–219.

O'Leary-Kelly, S. W., and Benito E. Flores. "The Integration of Manufacturing and Marketing/Sales Decisions: Impact on Organizational Performance," *Journal of Operations Management* 20, no. 3 (June 2002), pp. 221–240.

Palmatier, George E., and Joseph S. Shull. *The Marketing Edge: The New Leadership Role of Sales & Marketing in Manufacturing.* New York: John Wiley & Sons, 1989.

Rucinski, David. "Game Planning," *Production and Inventory Management Journal* (1st quarter) 1982, pp. 63–68.

Sari, John F. "Why Don't We Call It Sales and Operations Planning, Not Production Planning?" *APICS 29th Annual Conference Proceedings* (1986), pp. 22–24.

Sheldon, Donald J. "The S&OP Process—An Old Idea Gaining New Interest and Praise," *Mid-Range ERP,* January–February, 1998.

Wallace, T. F. *Sales and Operations Planning: The How To Handbook.* Cincinnati: Tom Wallace Publications, 1999.

Wallace, Tom F. "Sales & Operations Planning—Report from the Field," *APICS—The Performance Advantage,* February 1997, pp. 34–38.

Wallace, T. F. "Sales and Operations Planning: Top Management's Handle on the Business," in *World-Class Manufacturing: Instant Access Guide,* T. F. Wallace, ed. Essex Junction, Vt.: Oliver Wight Publications, 1994.

Discussion Questions

1. The sales and operations plan is sometimes called "management's handle on manufacturing." Discuss.
2. What would you guess would be the aggregate terms used in managing a university as a whole? The computer center? Buildings and grounds? An individual major?
3. The operations plan is stated in aggregate terms; therefore, there will be some error in resource planning. Wouldn't it be better to use the MPS where the specific product mix is either anticipated or incorporated directly?
4. What are the differences between sales and operations planning and budgeting?
5. Some experts argue the sales and operations planning process ought to be done only on exception, that is, only when conditions have changed enough to warrant replanning. Others argue it should be done on a periodic basis and when required by exception. What's your view?
6. Discuss the relative merits of cumulative charts (e.g., Figure 3.4) and tabular plans (e.g., Figure 3.5) for sales and operations planning.
7. What are some implications of not making the trade-offs explicit in the sales and operations planning process?
8. In incorporating the firm's strategic objectives into the sales and operations planning process, what differences exist between such firms as coal mines or cardboard manufacturers versus fashion or manufacturers of machine tools?
9. In the university setting, what is an analogue to the Hill-Rom super-duper bill and its trigger-and-trailer notions?

Problems

1. Complete the history portion of the Elm Co. sales and operations planning spreadsheet given below. Inventory is valued at $700 per unit. The actual inventory at the end of September was 150 units.

Elm Co. Sales and Operations Planning Spreadsheet

		History		
		October	November	December
Sales				
Forecast	(in million $)	0.80	0.85	0.90
	(in units)	800	850	900
Actual	(in units)	826	851	949
Diff. month				
Diff. cumulative				
Operations				
Plan	(in units)	800	800	800
	(in employees)	6	8	8
Number working days/mo.		23	19	19
Actual	(in units)	798	802	800
Diff. month				
Diff. cumulative				
Inventory				
Plan	(in units)			
	(in 1,000 $)			
Actual	(in units)	122	73	−76
Days of supply				

2. The Trapper Lawn Equipment Company manufactures a line of riding mowers. The company currently uses a chase strategy in its sales and operations planning. Management attempts to maintain a line fill rate of at least 99 percent and hold inventory of five days. Employees can produce three units a day on average. The historical records for the last three months and the plan for the next six months are given as follows:

Trapper Lawn Equipment Company Sales and Operations Planning Spreadsheet: Riding Mowers Product Group (Make-to-Stock)

		History			Plan					
		Oct	Nov	Dec	Jan	Feb	Mar	Apr	May	Jun
Sales										
Forecast	(in million $)	12.50	10.00	16.25	5.00	5.00	7.50	10.00	12.50	17.50
	(in units)	5,000	4,000	6,500	2,000	2,000	3,000	4,000	5,000	7,000
Actual	(in units)	4,384	3,626	6,065						
Diff. month		−616	−374	−435						
Diff. cumulative			−990	−1,425						

			History			Plan					
		Oct	Nov	Dec	Jan	Feb	Mar	Apr	May	Jun
Operations											
Plan	(in units)	5,000	4,000	6,500	2,000	2,000	3,000	4,000	5,000	7,000
	(in employees)	72	70	114	33	32	43	67	76	106
Number working days/mo.		23	19	19	20	21	23	20	22	22
Actual	(in units)	5,649	4,091	7,279						
Diff. month		649	91	779						
Diff. cumulative			740	1,519						
Inventory											
Plan	(in units)	1,270	1,270	1,270	3,944	3,944	3,944	3,944	3,944	3,944
	(in 1,000 $)	2,223	2,223	2,223	6,902	6,902	6,902	6,902	6,902	6,902
Actual	(in units)	2,265	2,730	3,944						
Days of supply		10	15	13	39	39	26	20	16	11

a. Given this information, suggest a revised production plan for the next three months (January, February, March) that will hit the five days of inventory supply target if you accept the sales forecast. Assume all days of supply calculations are based on a 20-day month.

b. What are the implications of this plan, considering the qualitative factors?

3. As production manager for the Trapper Lawn Equipment Company, you are concerned about the impact of marketing's forecast accuracy on inventory performance. If the future actual sales for January through June are off by the same average historical error percentage as the last three months (see table in problem 2):

a. What is the historical forecast error?

b. What would your estimate of actual sales be for January through June?

c. What would the days of supply and inventory level be assuming the production plan is executed according to the current plan and your estimate in part b is correct?

d. What options would you consider to address this problem?

4. On December 20 (the end of the fourth quarter), Ivar Jorgenson, head operations planner for Ski & Sea, Inc., is in charge of developing a sales and operations plan for the coming year. Ski & Sea assembles jet skis and snowmobiles from subassemblies and component parts provided by reliable vendors. Both products (end items) utilize the same small engines and many of the same parts. They require the same assembly time and employee labor skills. The available planning information is as follows:

Demand Forecasts

Quarter	Jet Skis	Snowmobiles
1	10,000	9,000
2	15,000	7,000
3	16,000	19,000
4	3,000	10,000

Anticipated Quarter 1
Beginning inventory   600 skis   400 Snowmobiles

Production and costs
   Regular time $15.00 per unit

   Overtime $22.50 per unit

   Subcontract $30.00 per unit

   Part-time $36.00 per unit

   Inventory $3.00 per unit per quarter, based on average
                              inventory during each quarter

   Back order $24.00 per unit per quarter (based on back
                              orders at end of quarter)

   Hiring $300.00 per full-time employee (no cost if part-time)

   Layoff $1,500.00 per full-time employee (no cost if part-time)

Production rates
   Regular   500 units per full-time employee per
                              quarter (of either unit)

   Overtime (max.)   200 units per full-time employee per
                              quarter (of either unit)

   Part-time   400 units per part-time employee per
                              quarter (of either unit)

   Initial workforce size   44 full-time employees (beginning of quarter 1)

Additional assumptions

1. Part-time employees may not work overtime.

2. Assume 100% utilization of employees on regular time (i.e., all employees on the payroll during a period produce at least 500 units). If overtime is used, up to another 200 units can be produced per employee.

---

  a. Develop an operations plan that utilizes a level, or constant, rate of output each quarter using full-time regular employees only. Ending inventory and back orders for quarter 4 must be equal to zero. Summarize the plan, its costs, and its consequences.

  b. Prepare a cumulative chart for your plan in part a of this problem.

  c. If each shipping container for completed jet skis and snowmobiles requires 20 cu. ft. of space, what is the maximum finished-goods warehouse space you will need next year if the plan in part b of this problem is adopted.

  d. If the cost of each completed end item is $600, what is the maximum amount of capital that will be tied up in finished-goods inventory during the year?

5. Suppose that Ivar Jorgenson finds out on December 21 that the long-range weather forecast was revised by the weather service and now more snow than normal is predicted. As a result, the marketing department at Sea & Ski raises its forecast for quarter 1 sales of snowmobiles from 9,000 to 11,000 units. He will now have to develop and analyze several alternative level plans for next year. Keep in mind that each of these plans must consider:

- Beginning inventory of 600 skis and 400 snowmobiles.

- Ending inventory and back orders for quarter 4 must be zero.

- Each plan must have the same level total-output rate each quarter.

    a. Develop a level plan that uses overtime by regular, full-time employees to meet the new demand conditions (with no additional hiring). Calculate the total annual cost of this plan.

   b. Develop a second plan that will use regular employees (no overtime) plus subcontracting to meet the new demand conditions (with no additional hiring). Calculate the total annual costs.

   c. Another possibility would be to hire an additional full-time employee on January 2 and employ him/her for the full year. Calculate the total annual cost.

6. Susie Svensen, the VP of marketing at Ski & Sea, is not happy with having back orders in any sales and operations plan for the future. She asks Ivar to develop a plan that requires no back orders at any time during the year. The VP of manufacturing, Josef Jaeger, says he will insist that any such plan specify the same output each quarter and use full-time employees on a regular time only. The VP of finance, Thor Ledger, states that quarter 4 ending inventory need not be zero, but it should be as low as possible.

   a. Use the original forecasts, beginning inventory, and other data from problem 4. Develop a plan that will meet the requirement of all three VPs. (*Hint:* Examine the graphs you prepared for problem 4b. What slope is required for the output line to eliminate backlogs?)

   b. What will the ending inventory for quarter 4 be?

7. On December 22, Thor Ledger informs Ivar that the cost of capital will be extremely high next year. As a consequence he asks him to develop a radically different type of sales and operations plan based on a chase strategy and the data from problem 4. Ending inventory is to be *zero* at the end of each quarter. The VP of manufacturing says he realizes this type of strategy will require him to adandon his beloved "level" strategy and asks Ivar to vary the total output rate from one quarter to the next. When necessary to do so, the following options and priorities should be used in developing the required output each period.

Priority	Option	Limit (maximum)
1	Full-time employees (FTE)	500 units/quarter/worker
2	Overtime (FTE)	Up to 200 units/worker
3	Subcontract	Up to 5,000 units/quarter
4	Part-time employees	Up to 25 workers/quarter

Finally, the personnel manager reports that because of end-of-year retirements, only 36 (not 44) full-time employees will be on the payroll as of January 2.

   a. Develop a chase plan that varies the number of full-time workers per quarter to meet demand without using overtime, subcontracting, or part-time employees.

   b. Develop a chase plan following the guidelines noted above. Summarize your plan on the worksheet (you may not hire any additional regular-time workers, but you can lay them off).

   c. What hiring/layoff actions will the personnel department need to take each quarter in parts a and b, above?

8. An operations planner, Lovell Bradley, is developing a sales and operations plan that involves back orders. The company's demand and production rates for the next four periods are as follows:

Period	Demand	Production
1	8,200	8,000
2	10,000	8,000
3	7,000	8,000
4	6,600	7,600

Beginning inventory at the start of period 1 is 400 units. Calculate beginning inventory, ending inventory, average inventory, and the back order amount, if any, for each of the next four periods.

9. The VP of manufacturing for the N. L. Hyer Company is ready to decide on her sales and operations plan for next year. The firm's single product (known throughout the adult puzzle trade as "Hyer's Hexagon") is "red hot," according to the VP of marketing, so she insists that backorders are not acceptable next year. Since the United Puzzlemakers Union is trying to organize the plant, the manufacturing VP decided the number of employees must remain constant (i.e., level) throughout all four quarters. Pertinent information is as follows:

Quarter	Production Days	Demand Forecast
1	60	12,000
2	58	13,000
3	61	13,590
4	70	9,000

Beginning inventory = 1,000 units
Regular time output rate = 10 units/day employee

a. What daily production rate and number of employees will be required?

b. How many units will be in inventory at the end of quarter 4?

10. Below is the plotted cumulative demand for Joan's Joyous Nature Food (in pounds) for the next four months. Beginning inventory is 10 pounds.

Month	Demand
1	120
2	160
3	20
4	70

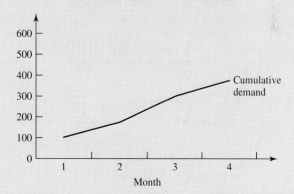

a. How much should Joan produce each month if she wishes to have a level operations plan with no back orders or stockouts? Plot your cumulative production on the preceding graph.

b. What is ending inventory for month 4 under this plan?

c. Joan decides to have a level-production, level-employment sales and operations plan with no ending inventory at the end of the planning horizon. How much should she make each month? What are the monthly back orders?

d. Given inventory carrying costs of $5/pound/month (based on the average inventory) and back orders of $8/pound/month (based on month-end back orders), calculate the cost of back orders and inventory for the plan in part c.

11. The Oro del Mar Company's forecast (in 1,000 pounds) for the first three months of next year is: January—100. February—0, March—300. Beginning inventory is 100,000 pounds.

   a. Plot cumulative demand and a level operations plan that meets demand with no back orders and no ending inventory in March.

   b. What production each month is needed to meet part a's conditions?

12. Crazy Tubb Thumpers uses a level plan to produce its snowshoe covers. Beginning inventory for January is zero. Demand for covers in January, February, and March is as follows:

Month	Demand
January	5,000
February	0
March	20,000

   a. Graph cumulative production for a level operations plan of 10,000 units per month. Show cumulative demand for the months January through March and indicate the ending inventory for March.

   b. Consider the following additional data for Crazy Tubb Thumpers:

   Employment = 9 people.

   Production = 1,000 units/month/employee (regular time).

   Standard hours/months = 166 hours (regular time).

   Regular-time labor rate = $1,200/month.

   Overtime rate = 1.5 times regular-time rate.

   Assuming a production rate of 10,000 units per month, what's the labor cost of one month's production at Crazy Tubb Thumpers?

13. The Bi-Product Company produces two products (A and B) that are similar in terms of labor content and skills required. Company management wishes to "level" the number of employees needed each day so no hiring or layoffs will be required during the year. A complication to this problem is that the number of working days in each quarter varies.

	Demand		
Quarter	Product A	Product B	Working Days
1	9,800	14,500	68
2	12,000	30,000	56
3	14,000	19,500	62
4	31,000	25,000	58

Beginning inventory: 2,400 units of Product A
                     900 units of Product B
Inventory holding cost: $10 per unit per quarter (either product)
No back orders allowed
No variations in size of workforce allowed
Output rate = 25 units of either product per day per employee

    a. What daily production rate will be required to meet the demand forecast and yield zero inventory at the end of quarter 4?

    b. How many employees will be required each day? What are the inventory levels each quarter?

14. Cubby Compressors has had relatively steady sales volume for years. The introduction of a new high-end "biscuit" model for the professional contractor market has added the potential for additional sales. The operations manager is also concerned about losing sales if product is not readily available. The current sales and operations plan is given below. Assume all days-of-supply calculations are based on a 20-day month and that back orders are to be filled from current production.

    a. Propose a revised production plan that brings the days of supply to the target of five days for the next six months.

    b. What would the plan look like if you had a hiring freeze at 45 employees maximum and still want to achieve the target five days of supply?

    c. What other options are available to not exceed the 45-employee limit and still not experience inventory shortages and related customer service problems?

Cubby Compressors Sales and Operations Planning Spreadsheet

		History			Plan					
		Oct	Nov	Dec	Jan	Feb	Mar	Apr	May	Jun
Sales										
Forecast	(in million $)	0.56	0.60	0.63	0.63	0.63	0.63	0.63	0.63	0.63
	(in units)	800	850	900	900	900	900	900	900	900
Actual	(in units)	826	851	949						
Diff. month		26	1	49						
Diff. cumulative			27	76						
Operations										
Plan	(in units)	800	800	800	900	900	900	900	900	900
	(in employees)	34	42	42	45	43	39	45	41	41
Number working days/mo.		23	19	19	20	21	23	20	22	22
Actual	(in units)	758	842	824						
Diff. month		−42	42	24						
Diff. cumulative			0	24						
Inventory										
Plan	(in units)	150	100	0	−52	−52	−52	−52	−52	−52
	(in 1,000 $)	74	49	0	0	0	0	0	0	0
Actual	(in units)	82	73	−52						
Days of supply		2.0	1.7	−1.1						

15. The ABC Consumer Electronics Company has a hard time forecasting demand on its current mix of products. In order to be sure to not run out during periods of unforecast high demand, the management team has decided to raise the inventory target from 5 to 10 days of supply. They currently use a chase production strategy. Their 5-day target plan follows. Propose a level build plan that gradually brings the days of supply to the 10-day level over the next 3 months. Use 30 days per month for all days of supply calculations. Employees can build an average of 1,000 units per workday. Note that July is a short work month due to a two-week vacation shutdown.

ABC Sales and Operations Planning Spreadsheet

		History			Plan		
		Apr	May	Jun	Jul	Aug	Sep
Sales							
Forecast	(in million $)	$22.50	$25.50	$28.50	$31.50	$34.50	$37.50
	(in million units)	1.50	1.70	1.90	2.10	2.30	2.50
Actual	(in million units)	0.78	1.95	1.63			
Diff. month		−0.72	0.25	−0.27			
Diff. cumulative			−0.47	−0.74			
Operations							
Plan	(in million units)	1.50	1.70	1.90	2.10	2.30	2.50
	(in employees)	75	77	86	210	110	109
Number working days/mo.		20	22	22	10	21	23
Actual	(in million units)	1.51	1.70	1.88			
Diff. month		0.01	0.00	−0.02			
Diff. cumulative			0.01	−0.01			
Inventory							
Plan	(in units)	250,000	250,000	250,000	250,001	250,001	250,001
	(in 1,000 $)	$2,625	$2,625	$2,625	$2,625	$2,625	$2,625
Actual	(in units)	250,001	250,000	250,001			
Days of supply		9.6	3.9	4.6	3.6	3.3	3.0

16. Mike Blanford, master scheduler at General Avionics, has the following demand forecast for one line in his factory:

Quarter	Unit Sales
1	5,000
2	10,000
3	8,000
4	2,000

At the beginning of quarter 1, there are 1,000 units in inventory. The firm has prepared the following data:

Hiring cost per employee = $200

Firing cost per employee = $400

Beginning workforce = 60 employees

Inventory carrying cost = $2 per unit per quarter of ending inventory

Stock cost = $5 per unit

Regular payroll = $1,200 per employee per quarter

Overtime cost = $2 per unit

Each employee can produce 100 units per quarter. Demand not satisfied in any quarter is lost and incurs a stockout penalty. If Mike produces exactly enough to meet demand each quarter, with no inventories at the end of quarters and no overtime, how much will he produce each quarter, and what is the overall cost? (Use a spreadsheet model for the calculations.)

17. Use the data in problem 16 to calculate production amounts and costs for a level rate of output with no ending inventory. Stockouts (or back orders) are allowed.

18. For the data in problem 16, at the end of the first quarter, inventory is 2,000 units. Marketing has revised the forecasts for quarters 2, 3, and 4 with a 20 percent reduction (i.e., remaining sales = 16,000). Develop a level and chase plan for the revised forecast that provides for an inventory of at least 1,000 units at the end of each quarter. (Assume 50 people were in the workforce in the first quarter.)

Chapter 4

Enterprise Resource Planning (ERP)—Integrated Systems

This chapter concerns the integrated enterprise resource planning (ERP) systems that are now commonly used by large companies to support MPC decisions. Major software vendors such as SAP, Oracle, PeopleSoft, and i2 Technologies offer state-of-the art systems designed to provide real-time data to support better routine decision making, improve the efficiency of transaction processing, foster cross-functional integration, and to provide improved insights into how the business should be run. This chapter is organized around five major questions:

- *What ERP is:* What is the scope of ERP implementations and how are the various modules of the software organized?
- *How ERP connects the functional units:* That is, how does ERP help integrate overall company operations?
- *How manufacturing planning and control (MPC) decisions are supported by ERP:* What are the detailed MPC issues addressed by ERP, and how does an ERP package help address these issues?
- *Performance metrics to evaluate integrated system effectiveness:* Why do we need overall metrics to break out of "functional silo" thinking?
- *What the experience with ERP is:* How have some example firms gone about implementation and what have been the results?

In most companies, ERP provides the information backbone needed to manage day-to-day execution. Many of the standard production planning and control functions are supported by ERP. In particular, standard applications include demand management covered in Chapter 2, sales and operations planning in Chapters 3 and 12, master production scheduling found in Chapter 6, materials requirements planning in Chapters 7 and 14, production activity control in Chapter 11, inventory control in Chapter 5, forecasting covered in Chapter 2, and project management. The software is often extended through either commercial software designed to work with the ERP system, or through custom programmed modules built with spreadsheets and other general purpose software.

What Is ERP?

The term *enterprise resource planning* (ERP) can mean different things, depending on one's viewpoint. From the view of managers in a company, the emphasis is on the word *planning;* ERP represents a comprehensive software approach to support decisions concurrent with planning and controlling the business. On the other hand, for the information technology community, ERP is a term to describe a software system that integrates application programs in finance, manufacturing, logistics, sales and marketing, human resources, and the other functions in a firm. This integration is accomplished through a database shared by all the functions and data processing applications in the firm. ERP systems typically are very efficient at handling the many transactions that document the activities of a company. For our purposes, we begin by describing our view of what ERP should accomplish for management, with an emphasis on planning. Following this, we describe how the ERP software programs are designed and provide points to consider in choosing an ERP system. Our special interest is in how the software supports MPC systems.

ERP systems allow for integrated planning across the functional areas in a firm. Perhaps more importantly, ERP also supports integrated *execution* across functional areas. Today the focus is moving to coordinated planning and execution across companies. In many cases this work is supported by ERP systems.

Consistent Numbers

ERP requires a company to have consistent definitions across functional areas. Consider the problem of measuring demand. How is demand measured? Is it when manufacturing completes an order? When items are picked from finished goods? When they physically leave the premises? When they are invoiced? When they arrive at the customer site? What is needed is a set of agreed-on definitions that are used by all functional units when they are processing their transactions. Consistent definitions of such measures as demand, stockouts, raw materials inventory, and finished goods inventory, for example, can then be made. This is a basic building block for ERP systems.

ERP, with the emphasis on planning, is designed to allow much tighter integration, thus eliminating the problem of local optimization. Tom Wallace and Mike Kremzar, noted manufacturing industry experts, describe ERP as:

- An enterprise-wide set of management tools that helps balance demand and supply,
- Containing the ability to link customers and suppliers into a complete supply chain,
- Employing proven business processes for decision making, and
- Providing high degrees of cross-functional integration among sales, marketing, manufacturing, operations, logistics, purchasing, finance, new product development, and human resources, thereby
- Enabling people to run their business with high levels of customer service and productivity, and simultaneously lower costs and inventories, and providing the foundation for effective e-commerce.

Companies implementing ERP strive to derive benefits through much greater efficiency gained by an integrated MPC planning and control process. In addition, better responsiveness to the needs of customers is obtained through the real-time information provided by the system. To better understand how this works, we next describe features of ERP software.

Software Imperatives

There are four aspects of ERP software that determine the quality of an ERP system:

1. The software should be **multifunctional in scope** with the ability to track financial results in monetary terms, procurement activity in units of material, sales in terms of product units and services, and manufacturing or conversion processes in units of resources or people. That is, excellent ERP software produces results closely related to the needs of people for their day-to-day work.

2. The software should be **integrated.** When a transaction or piece of data representing an activity of the business is entered by one of the functions, data regarding the other related functions is changed as well. This eliminates the need for reposting data to the system. Integration also ensures a common vision—we all sing from the same sheet of music.

3. The software needs to be **modular** in structure so it can be combined into a single expansive system, narrowly focused on a single function, or connected with software from another source/application.

4. The software must **facilitate classic manufacturing planning and control activities** including forecasting, production planning, and inventory management.

An ERP system is most appropriate for a company seeking the benefits of data and process integration supported by its information system. Benefit is gained from the elimination of redundant processes, increased accuracy in information, superior processes, and improved speed in responding to customer requirements.

An ERP software system can be built with software modules from different vendors, or it can be purchased from a single vendor. A multivendor approach can provide the opportunity to purchase "best in class" of each module. But this is usually at the expense of increased cost and greater resources needed to implement and integrate the functional modules. On the other hand, a single-vendor approach may be easier to implement, but the features and functionality may not be the best available.

Routine Decision Making

It is important to make a distinction between the transaction processing capability and the decision support capability of an ERP system. **Transaction processing** relates to the posting and tracking of the activities that document the business. When an item is purchased from a vendor, for example, a specific sequence of activities occurs. The solicitation of the offer, acceptance of the offer, delivery of goods, storage in inventory, and payment for the purchase are all activities that occur as a result of the purchase. The efficient handing of the transactions as goods move through each step of the production process is the primary goal of an ERP system.

A second objective of an ERP system is decision support. **Decision support** relates to how well the system helps the user make intelligent judgments about how to run the business. A key point here is that *people,* not software, make the decisions. The system *supports* better decision making. In the case of manufacturing planning and control, for example, decisions concerning the amount to purchase, the selection of the vendor, and how it should be delivered will need to be determined. These decisions are made by MPC professionals while ERP systems are oriented toward transaction processing. But over time, they evolve using decision logic based on parameters set in the system. For example, for items stored in inventory, the specific reorder points, order quantities, vendors, transportation vendors, and storage locations can be established when the items are initially entered in the system. At a later point, the decision logic can be revisited to improve the results. A major industry has been built around the development of **bolt-on** software packages designed to provide more intelligent decision support to ERP systems.

Choosing ERP Software

Key considerations when evaluating ERP software are:

1. The complexity of the business, degree of vertical integration, and level of international operations.
2. The size of the business.
3. The scope of functionality needed—is decision making reasonably routine, or is complex optimization required?
4. The differences in the conversion processes. Is discrete manufacturing used or process manufacturing, or both? The needs of these entities are different and perhaps difficult to accommodate with a single system.
5. The degree of sophistication and unique requirements of the firm's processes. Are there unique customer information requirements? How much of a custom solution is needed?
6. The alignment of the manufacturing planning and control modules with the needs of the firm. For example, are the mechanisms for aggregating demand for forecasting purposes adequate? Can the inventory control module accommodate the requirement to uniquely identify production batches?
7. The money available for implementing the system. Are radical process changes needed?
8. The computer hardware and telecommunications availability. Is the existing infrastructure compatible? Where does the company see the future? Where is the industry going? Do we need to be state of the art?

How ERP Connects the Functional Units

A typical ERP system is made up of functionally oriented and tightly integrated modules. All the modules of the system use a common database that is updated in real time. Each module has the same user interface, similar to that of the familiar Microsoft Office products, thus making the use of the different modules much easier for users trained on the system. ERP systems from various vendors are organized in different ways, but typically modules are focused on at least the following four major areas: finance, manufacturing and logistics, sales and marketing, and human resources.

One can see the evolution of ERP systems in much the same way as car models evolve at automobile manufacturers. Automobile manufacturers introduce new models every year or two and make many minor refinements. Major (platform) changes are made much less frequently, perhaps every 5 to 8 years. The same is true of ERP software. ERP vendors are constantly looking for ways to improve the functionality of their software, so new features are often added. Many of these minor changes are designed to improve the usability of the software through a better screen interface or added features that correspond to the "hot" idea of the time. Major software revisions that involve changes to the structure of the database, changes to the network, and computer hardware technologies, though, are made only

FIGURE 4.1
The Scope of ERP Applications

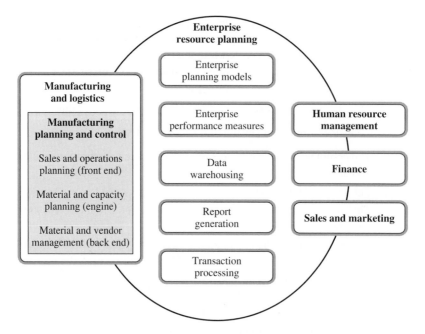

every 3 to 5 years. The basic ERP platform cannot be easily changed because of the large installed base of users and support providers. But these changes do occur. As an example, SAP has moved from version R/2 to R/3, a major change in the software.

Figure 4.1 depicts the scope of ERP applications. The diagram is meant to show how a comprehensive information system uses ERP as the core or backbone of the information system. Many other software-based functions may be integrated with the ERP system, but are not necessarily included in the ERP system. The use of more specialized software such as decision support systems can often bring significant competitive advantage to a firm. The following brief descriptions of typical module functionality give an indication of how comprehensive the applications can be.

Finance

As a company grows through acquisition, and as business units make more of their own decisions, many companies find themselves with incompatible and sometimes conflicting financial data. An ERP system provides a common platform for financial data capture, a common set of numbers, and processes, facilitating rapid reconciliation of the general ledger. The real value of an ERP system is in the automatic capture of basic accounting transactions from the source of the transactions. The actual order from a customer, for example, is used not only by manufacturing to trigger production requirements, but also becomes the information for the update of accounts payable when the order is actually shipped.

Manufacturing and Logistics

This set of applications is the largest and most complex of the module categories. The MPC system components discussed in this book (front end, engine, back end) are concentrated in this area. Typical components include:

- *Sales and operations planning* coordinates the various planning efforts including marketing planning, financial planning, operations planning, and human resource planning.

- *Materials management* covers tasks within the supply chain, including purchasing, vendor evaluation, and invoice management. It also includes inventory and warehouse management functions to support the efficient control of materials.
- *Plant maintenance* supports the activities associated with planning and performing repairs and preventive maintenance.
- *Quality management* software implements procedures for quality control and assurance.
- *Production planning and control* supports both discrete and process manufacturing. Repetitive and configure-to-order approaches are typically provided. Most ERP systems address all phases of manufacturing, including capacity leveling, material requirements planning, JIT, product costing, bill of materials processing, and database maintenance. Orders can be generated from sales orders or from links to a World Wide Web site.
- *Project management* systems facilitate the setup, management, and evaluation of large, complex projects.

Sales and Marketing

This group of systems supports customer management; sales order management; forecasting, order management, credit checking configuration management; distribution, export controls, shipping, transportation management; and billing, invoicing, and rebate processing. These modules, like the others, are increasingly implemented globally, allowing firms to manage the sales process worldwide. For example, if an order is received in Hong Kong, but the products are not available locally, they may be internally procured from warehouses in other parts of the world and shipped to arrive together at the Hong Kong customer's site.

Human Resources

This set of applications supports the capabilities needed to manage, schedule, pay, hire, and train the people who make an organization run. Typical functions include payroll, benefits administration, applicant data administration, personnel development planning, workforce planning, schedule and shift planning, time management, and travel expense accounting.

Customized Software

In addition to the standard application modules, many companies utilize special add-on modules that link to the standard modules, thus tailoring applications to specific needs. These modules may be tailored to specific industries such as chemical/petrochemical, oil and gas, hospital, and banking. They may also provide special decision support functions such as optimal scheduling of critical resources.

Even though the scope of applications included in standard ERP packages is very large, it is usually the case that additional software will be required because of the unique characteristics of each company. A company generates its own unique mix of products and services that are designed to provide a significant competitive advantage to the firm. This unique mix of products and services will need to be supported by unique software capability, some of which may be purchased from vendors and others that will need to be custom designed. Customized software applications are also widely used to coordinate the activities of a firm with its supply chain customers and suppliers.

Data Integration

The software modules, as described above, form the core of an ERP system. This core is designed to process the business transactions to support the essential activities of an enterprise in an efficient manner. Working from a single database, transactions document each of the activities that compose the processes used by the enterprise to conduct business. A major value of the integrated database is that information is not reentered at each step of a process, thus reducing errors and reducing work.

Transactions are processed in **real time,** meaning that as soon as the transaction is entered into the system, the effect on items such as inventory status, order status, and accounts receivable is known to all users of the system. There is no delay in the processing of a transaction in a real-time system. A customer could, for example, call into an order desk to learn the exact status of an order—or determine the status independently through an Internet connection. From a decision analysis viewpoint, the amount of detail available in the system is extremely rich. If, for example, one wishes to analyze the typical lead time for a product produced to order, the analyst could process an information request that selects all of the orders for the product over the past 3 months, then a calculation of the time between the order date and delivery date for each order would be done, and finally the average of this time for the whole set of orders can be calculated. Analyses, such as this lead time, can be valuable for evaluating improvements designed to make the process more responsive, for example.

To facilitate queries not built into the standard ERP system software, a separate **data warehouse** is commonly employed. A data warehouse is a special program (often running on a totally separate computer) that is designed to automatically capture and process data for uses that are outside the basic ERP system applications. For example, the data warehouse could, on an ongoing basis, capture and perform the calculations needed for the average lead time question. The data warehouse software and database is set up so that users may access and analyze data without placing a burden on the operational ERP system. This is a powerful mechanism to support higher-level decision support applications.

A good example of a company making use of a data warehouse is Wal-Mart. Wal-Mart is now able to put two full years of retail store sales data on line. The data are used by both internal Wal-Mart buyers and outside suppliers—sales and current inventory data on products sold at Wal-Mart and Sam's Club stores. Vendors, who are restricted to viewing products they supply, use a Web-based extranet site to collaborate with Wal-Mart's buyers in managing inventory and making replenishment decisions. A vendor's store-by-store sales results for a given day are available to vendors by 4 A.M. the following day. The database is over 130 terabytes in size. Each terabyte is the equivalent of 250 million pages of text. At an average of 500 pages per book, a terabyte is a half million books. For Wal-Mart as a whole, that is about 20 major university libraries.

How Manufacturing Planning and Control (MPC) Fits within ERP

MPC is concerned with planning and controlling all aspects of manufacturing, including managing materials, scheduling machines and people, and coordinating suppliers and key customers. The coordination required for success runs across all functional units in the firm. Consider the following simple example to illustrate the degree of coordination required.

Simplified Example

The Ajax Food Services Company has one plant that makes sandwiches. These are sold in vending machines, cafeterias, and small stores. One of the sandwiches is peanut butter and jelly (PBJ). It is made from bread, butter, peanut butter, and grape jelly. When complete, it is wrapped in a standard plastic package used for all Ajax sandwiches. One loaf of bread makes 10 sandwiches, a package of butter makes 50 sandwiches, and containers of peanut butter and jelly each make 20 sandwiches.

Consider the information needed by Ajax for manufacturing planning and control. First Ajax needs to know what demand to expect for its PBJ sandwich in the future. This might be forecast by analyzing detailed sales data from each location where the sandwiches are sold. Since sales are all handled by sales representatives who travel between the various sites, data based on the actual orders and sales reports provided by the reps can be used to make this forecast. The same data are used by human resources to calculate commissions owed to the reps for payroll purposes. Marketing uses the same data to analyze each current location and evaluate the attractiveness of new locations.

Freshness is very important to Ajax, so daily demand forecasts are developed to plan manufacturing. Consider, for example, that Ajax sees that it needs to make 300 PBJ sandwiches to be delivered to the sales sites this Friday. Ajax will actually assemble the sandwiches on Thursday. According to the usage data given above, this requires 30 loaves of bread, 6 packages of butter, and 15 containers of peanut butter and jelly. Freshness is largely dictated by the age of the bread, so it is important that Ajax works closely with the local baker since the baker delivers bread each morning on the basis of the day's assembly schedule. Similarly, the delivery schedules for the butter, peanut butter, and jelly need to be coordinated with the vendors of these items.

Ajax uses college students who work on a part-time basis to assemble the sandwiches. Manufacturing knows that a student can make 60 sandwiches per hour and that sandwiches must be ready for loading into the delivery trucks by 4:00 P.M. on the day prior to delivery. Our 300 sandwiches require 5 hours of work, so any one student doing this work needs to start at or before 11:00 A.M. on Thursday to make the sandwiches on time.

An ERP system is designed to provide the information and decision support needed to coordinate this type of activity. Of course, with our simplified example, the coordination is trivial, but consider if our company were making hundreds of different types of sandwiches in 1,000 cities around the world, and these sandwiches were sold at hundreds of sites in each of these cities. This is exactly the scale of operations that can be handled by a modern ERP system.

Precisely how all of these calculations are made is, of course, the main focus of this book. All of the details for how material requirements are calculated, how capacity is planned, and how demand forecasts are made, for example, are explained in great detail. To illustrate the MPC features within ERP systems, the following section describes mySAP Supply Chain Management, a software package offered by SAP, a major ERP vendor.

Supply Chain Planning with mySAP SCM

In this section we see how SAP has approached the details of manufacturing planning and control. Detailed discussions of these applications are the topic of other sections of this book. Here, we are using SAP to show how one vendor organizes the functions. Other major vendors like PeopleSoft, Oracle, and BAAN each have a unique approach to packaging supply chain software.

SAP, in its Spring 2003 marketing, labeled all MPC applications as part of its supply chain software, divided into four main functions: supply chain planning, supply chain execution, supply chain collaboration, and supply chain coordination. Note that vendors make frequent changes in their products. Current information about products is on vendors' websites and readers are encouraged to download the white papers that describe a vendor's current thinking. These publications are informative and indicate where a vendor will move in the future. Moreover, comparing/contrasting this information can be very educational—and help in making key choices as to which business processes can be supported by standard (plain vanilla) software.

The *supply chain design module* provides a centralized overview of the entire supply chain and key performance indicators, which helps identify weak links and potential improvements. It supports strategic planning by enabling the testing of various scenarios to determine how changes in the market or customer demand can be addressed by the supply chain. Here, for our simplified example of Ajax food services, we could evaluate the relative profitability of particular market channels and locations such as vending machines versus shops in train stations.

Collaborative demand and supply planning helps match demand to supply. Demand-planning tools take into account historical demand data, causal factors, marketing events, market intelligence, and sales objectives and enable the supply chain network to work on a single forecast. Supply planning tools create an overall supply plan that covers materials management, production, distribution and transportation requirements, and constraints. Here Ajax would be able to anticipate the demands for each kind of sandwich in each location and plan replenishments accordingly.

Supply Chain Execution with mySAP SCM

Materials management shares inventory and procurement order information to ensure that the materials required for manufacturing are available in the right place and at the right time. This set of applications supports plan-driven procurement, inventory management, and invoicing, with a feedback loop between demand and supply to increase responsiveness. In this set of applications, Ajax would plan for all the sandwich components to be delivered to the right places at the right times. Inventories might be maintained on some items such as peanut butter, while others such as bread might be planned on a just-in-time basis.

Collaborative manufacturing shares information with partners to coordinate production and enable everyone to work together to increase both visibility and responsiveness. These applications support all types of production processes: engineer-to-order, configure-to-order, make-to-order, and make-to-stock. They create a continuous information flow across engineering, planning, and execution and can optimize production schedules across the supply chain, taking into account material and capacity constraints. Here Ajax might do joint planning with key suppliers, and perhaps organize the planning of special promotions.

Collaborative fulfillment supports partnerships that can intelligently commit to delivery dates in real time and fulfill orders from all channels on time. This set of applications includes a global available-to-promise (ATP) feature that locates finished products, components, and machine capacities in a matter of seconds. It also manages the flow of products through sales channels, matching supply to market demand, reassigning supply and demand to meet shifts in customer demand, and managing transportation and warehousing. Clearly all these logistics activities are critical to Ajax in order to deliver fresh sandwiches in the right amounts.

Supply Chain Collaboration with mySAP SCM

The *inventory collaboration hub* uses the Internet to gain visibility to suppliers and manage the replenishment process. Suppliers can see the status of their parts at all plants, receive automatic alerts when inventory levels get low, and respond quickly via the Web. The hub can also be integrated with back-end transaction and planning systems to update them in real time. Here Ajax could provide real-time inventory views to its suppliers—not only of material suppliers, but also of down stream inventories (i.e., sandwiches).

Collaborative replenishment planning is particularly useful in the consumer products and retail industries. These applications allow manufacturers to collaborate with their strategic retail customers to increase revenue, improve service, and lower inventory levels and costs. They enable an exception-based collaborative planning, forecasting, and replenishment (CPFR) process that allows the firm to add retail partners without a proportional increase in staff. This set of applications would be particularly useful to Ajax, as it grows its global business and adds new channels of distribution.

Vendor-managed inventory (VMI) is a set of processes to enable vendor-driven replenishment and can be implemented over the Web. Now Ajax vendors would no longer receive "orders." They would replenish Ajax inventories as they like—but be paid for their materials only when consumed by Ajax.

Enterprise portal gives users personalized access to a range of information, applications, and services supported by the system. It uses role-based technology to deliver information to users according to their individual responsibilities within the supply chain network. It can also use Web-based tools to integrate third-party systems in the firm's supply chain network. Here, for example, marketing people at Ajax might like to examine the detailed sales data (and perhaps customer questionnaires) in relation to a new product introduction.

Mobile supply chain management is a set of applications so that people can plan, execute, and monitor activity using mobile and remote devices. Mobile data entry using personal data assistant devices and automated data capture using wireless "smart tags," for example, are supported. Here Ajax can have marketing and even delivery personnel report on actual store conditions—not just sales but also category management. For example, how well does the actual assortment of sandwiches match the standard?

Supply Chain Coordination with mySAP SCM

Supply chain event management monitors the execution of supply chain events, such as the issue of a pallet or the departure of a truck, and flags any problems that come up. This set of applications is particularly useful for product tracking/traceability. For Ajax, if there is a customer complaint about a sandwich, it is critical to quickly determine if this is an isolated instance or whether there might be a large group of bad quality sandwiches—and how to find them.

Supply chain performance management allows the firm to define, select, and monitor key performance indicators, such as costs and assets, and use them to gain an integrated, comprehensive view of performance across the supply chain. It provides constant surveillance of key performance measures and generates an alert if there is a deviation from plan. It can be used with mySAP Business Intelligence and SAP's data warehousing and data analysis software. Here Ajax needs to not only assess profit contribution by sandwich type and location, it also needs to determine which are the best supplier and customer partners.

Performance Metrics to Evaluate Integrated System Effectiveness

As indicated, one significant advantage that a firm gains from using an integrated ERP system is the ability to obtain current data on how the firm is performing. An ERP system can provide the data needed for a comprehensive set of performance measures to evaluate strategic alignment of the various functions with the firm's strategy. An example of the comprehensiveness of the measures is tracking the time from spending cash on purchases until the cash is received in sales.

The balance sheet and the income and expense statements contain financial measures, such as net profit, that traditionally have been used to evaluate the success of the firm. A limitation of traditional financial metrics is that they primarily tell the story of past events. They are less helpful to guide decision makers in creating future value through investments in customer infrastructure, suppliers, employees, manufacturing processes, and other innovations.

Our goal is a more holistic approach to management of the firm. Figure 4.2 depicts three major functional areas that make up the internal supply chain of a manufacturing enterprise: purchasing, manufacturing, and sales and distribution. Tight cooperation is required between these three functions for effective manufacturing planning and control. Considered independently, purchasing is mainly concerned with minimizing materials cost, manufacturing with minimum production costs, sales that result in selling the greatest amount, and distribution with minimum distribution and warehousing costs. Let us consider how each independently operating function might seek to optimize its operation.

The "Functional Silo" Approach

The purchasing function is responsible for buying all of the material required to support manufacturing operations. When operating independently, this function wishes to know what materials and quantities are going to be needed over the long term. The purchasing group then solicits bids for the best price for each material. The main criterion is simply the cost of the material, and the purchasing function is *evaluated* on this criterion: what is latest actual cost versus standard cost? Of course, quality is always going to be important to the group, so typically some type of quality specification will need to be guaranteed by the supplier. But quality is more of a constraint than a goal; suppliers must achieve some minimal level of specification. Consideration of delivery schedules, quantities, and responsiveness are also important, but again these considerations are often secondary at best in how the purchasing function is evaluated in a traditional firm.

For manufacturing, making the product at the lowest possible cost is the classic metric. To do this requires minimum equipment downtime, with high equipment and labor utiliza-

FIGURE 4.2
Manufacturing Operating Cycle

- Purchase cost of material
- Accounts payable

- Raw materials inventory
- Work in process
- Finished goods inventory

- Distribution inventory
- Accounts receivable

tion. Stopping to set up equipment is not the desire of this group. This group is focused on high-volume output, with minimum changeovers. Quality is again "important"—but as in purchasing it is more of a minimum hurdle. Large batches foster better quality performance, since defects often occur during changeovers. Once production reaches some steady state, it is easier to maintain a quality standard.

Long production runs lead to lower unit costs, but they also generate larger cycle stock inventories. For sales, larger inventories appear at first to be desirable, since these should support customer service. Alas, it is not so; a one-year supply of product A is of no help when we are out of product B.

Distribution can be equally narrow-minded and suboptimal. In the classic case its job is moving the product from the manufacturing site to the customer at the lowest possible cost. Depending on the product, it may need to be stored in one or more distribution centers and be moved via one or more different modes of transportation (truck, rail, etc.). Evaluation of distribution activities tends to focus on the specific distribution activity involved. For example, many firms focus on the lowest price quotation for moving a product from one stage of the distribution chain to another, rather than on the *total* costs of moving materials *into* and *out of* the overall firm. And even here this cost focus needs to be integrated with other objectives such as lower inventories, faster response times, and customer service.

Consider the implications if all three areas are allowed to work independently. In order to take advantage of discounts, purchasing will buy the largest quantities possible. This results in large amounts of raw material inventory. The manufacturing group desires to maximize production volumes in order to spread the significant fixed costs of production over as many units as possible. These large lot sizes result in high amounts of work-in-process inventory, with large quantities of goods pushed into finished goods whether they are needed or not. Large lot sizes also mean that the time between batches increases; therefore, response times to unexpected demand increase. Finally, distribution will try to fully load every truck that is used to move material to minimize transportation cost. Of course, this may result in large amounts of inventory in distribution centers (perhaps the wrong ones) and might not match well with what customers really need. Given the opportunity, the sales group might even sell product that cannot possibly be delivered on time. After all, they are evaluated on sales, not deliveries. A more coordinated approach is facilitated by the use of an ERP system. The following is an example of a consistent set of metrics useful for managing supply chain functions effectively.

Integrated Supply Chain Metrics

The Supply Chain Council has developed many metrics to measure the performance of the overall supply chain. It has used these standardized measures to develop benchmarks for comparisons between companies. Figure 4.3 contains a list of some of these measures with average and best-in-class benchmarks. The average and best-in-class measures are for typical large industrial products. The Supply Chain Council has developed sets of measures similar to these for many different categories of companies.

A particularly useful approach to measuring performance captures not only the integrated impact that the three classic functions have on the entire business supply chain; the best metrics also integrate the finance function. A metric that does so in measuring the relative efficiency of a supply chain is **cash-to-cash cycle time.** Cash-to-cash cycle time integrates the purchasing, manufacturing, and sales/distribution cycles depicted in

FIGURE 4.3
Supply Chain Metrics

Source: Supply Chain Council.

Measure	Description	Best in Class	Average or Medium
Delivery performance	What percentage of orders is shipped according to schedule?	93%	69%
Fill rate by line item	Orders often contain multiple line items. This is the percentage of the actual line items filled.	97%	88%
Perfect order fulfillment	This measures how many complete orders were filled and shipped on time.	92.4%	65.7%
Order fulfillment lead time	The time from when an order is placed to when it is received by the customer.	135 days	225 days
Warranty cost of % of revenue	This is the actual warranty expense divided by revenue.	1.2%	2.4%
Inventory days of supply	This is how long the firm could continue to operate if all sources of supply were cut off.	55 days	84 days
Cash-to-cash cycle time	Considering accounts payable, accounts receivable, and inventory, this is the amount of time it takes to turn cash used to purchase materials into cash from a customer.	35.6 days	99.4 days
Asset turns	This is a measure of how many times the same assets can be used to generate revenue and profit.	4.7 turns	1.7 turns

Figure 4.2. But it also relates well to the financial maxim: cash is king! Calculating the measure requires the use of data related to purchasing, accounting, manufacturing, and sales.

Actually, cash-to-cash cycle time is a measure of cash flow. Cash flow indicates where cash comes from (its source), where cash is spent (its use), and the net change in cash for the year. Understanding how cash flows through a business is critical to managing the business effectively. Accountants use the term *operating cycle* to describe the length of time that it takes a business to convert cash outflows for raw materials, labor, etc. into cash inflows. This cycle time determines, to a large extent, the amount of capital needed to start and operate a business. Conceptually, cash-to-cash cycle time is calculated as follows:

$$\text{Cash-to-cash cycle time} = \text{inventory days of supply} + \text{days of sales outstanding}$$
$$- \text{average payment period for material} \qquad \textbf{(4.1)}$$

The overall result is the number of days between paying for raw materials and getting paid for the product. Going through the details of calculating cash-to-cash cycle time

FIGURE 4.4
Integrated
ERP Data for
Cash-to-Cash
Cycle Time
Calculation

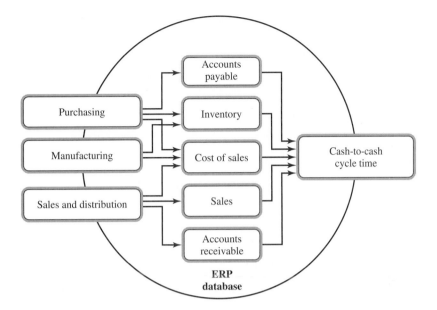

demonstrates the power of integrated information. These calculations are straightforward in an ERP system. The calculation can be divided into three parts: the accounts receivable cycle, the inventory cycle, and the accounts payable cycle.

Figure 4.4 shows the data that are used for calculating cash-to-cash cycle time. The data are controlled by different functions within the company. The current accounts payable amount, an account that is dependent on the credit terms that purchasing negotiates with suppliers, gives the current money that that firm owes its suppliers. As will be seen in the calculation, this is a form of credit to the company.

The inventory account gives the value of the entire inventory within the company. This includes raw materials, work in process, finished goods, and distribution inventory. The value of inventory depends on the quantities stored and also the cost of the inventory to the firm. All three major functional areas affect the inventory account. Purchasing has the major influence on raw materials. Manufacturing largely determines work in process and finished goods. Sales/distribution influences location of finished goods—as well as amounts through their forecasts and orders.

Just as inventory is affected by all three functions, the cost of sales is dependent on costs that are incurred throughout the firm. For the purposes of the cash-to-cash cycle time calculation, this is expressed as a percentage of total sales. This percentage depends on such items as material cost, labor cost, and all other direct costs associated with the procurement of materials, manufacturing process, and distribution of the product.

Sales are simply the total sales revenue over a given period of time. Finally, accounts receivable is the amount owed the firm by its customers. The accounts receivable amount will depend on the firm's credit policy and its ability to deliver product in a timely manner. Figure 4.4 shows how the three major functional areas influence the cash-to-cash cycle calculation.

Calculating the Cash-to-Cash Time

As noted, the first task in determining the cash-to-cash cycle time is to calculate accounts receivable cycle time. This measures the length of time it takes a business to convert a sale into cash. In other words, how long does it take a business to collect the money owed for goods already sold? One way is to calculate the number of days of sales invested in accounts receivable:

$$S_d = \frac{S}{d} \tag{4.2}$$

where

S_d = average daily sales

S = sales over d days

$$AR_d = \frac{AR}{S_d} \tag{4.3}$$

where

AR_d = average days of accounts receivable

AR = accounts receivable

The next part of the calculation is the inventory cycle time. This is the number of days of inventory measured relative to the cost of sales:

$$C_d = S_d CS \tag{4.4}$$

where

C_d = average daily cost of sales

CS = cost of sales (percent)

$$I_d = \frac{I}{C_d} \tag{4.5}$$

where

I_d = average days of inventory

I = current value of inventory (total)

Next, the accounts payable cycle time measures the level of accounts payable relative to the cost of sales:

$$AP_d = \frac{AP}{C_d} \tag{4.6}$$

where

AP_d = average days of accounts payable

AP = accounts payable

Finally, the cash-to-cash cycle time is calculated from the three cycle times.

$$\text{Cash-to-cash cycle time} = AR_d + I_d - AP_d \tag{4.7}$$

Figure 4.5 shows an example of the cash-to-cash cycle time calculation.

The cash-to-cash cycle time is an interesting measure for evaluating the relative supply chain effectiveness of a firm. Some firms are actually able to run a negative value for the

FIGURE 4.5
Example of
Cash-to-Cash
Cycle Time
Calculation

Data: Sales over last 30 days = $1,020,000
Accounts receivable at the end of the month = $200,000
Inventory value at the end of the month = $400,000
Cost of sales = 60% of total sales
Accounts payable at the end of the month = $160,000

$$S_d = \frac{S}{d} = \frac{1{,}020{,}000}{30} = 34{,}000$$

$$AR_d = \frac{AR}{S_d} = \frac{200{,}000}{34{,}000} = 5.88 \text{ days}$$

$$C_d = S_d CS = 34{,}000(0.6) = 20{,}400$$

$$I_d = \frac{I}{C_d} = \frac{400{,}000}{20{,}400} = 19.6 \text{ days}$$

$$AP_d = \frac{AP}{C_d} = \frac{160{,}000}{20{,}400} = 7.84 \text{ days}$$

Cash-to-cash cycle time = $AR_d + I_d - AP_d = 5.88 + 19.6 - 7.84 = 17.64$ days

measure. Dell Computer, for example, typically runs cash-to-cash cycle times of -10 to -20 days. This implies the ability to invest in the business as needed—with no requirement for additional funds! Metrics, such as cash-to-cash cycle time, can be efficiently reported using ERP data. These metrics can even be reported in real time if needed.

What Is the Experience with ERP?

In this section we examine the implementation trials and tribulations of several firms. ERP implementation is not easy, but the results can be dramatic, and there are some key lessons to be learned.

Eli Lilly and Company—Operational Standards for Manufacturing Excellence

Eli Lilly is a multinational company with 35,000 people, manufacturing plants in 16 countries, and medicine sales in over 150 different countries. Eli Lilly uses ERP to manage the coordination of its manufacturing, sales, and research facilities around the globe as new products are developed and introduced. Developing and deploying a new product is a complex process that requires extensive research, a complex government approval process, marketing plans, and manufacturing coordination. The promise of ERP information integration was compelling for this global company managed from its corporate headquarters in Indianapolis.

Managing such a large company can be done in one of two ways. One approach is to essentially decentralize the company around autonomous units located in the United States, Europe, Japan, and other major world centers. Each entity might operate independently from a sales and manufacturing standpoint, sharing products developed by the research centers operated by the company. This is largely the way the company operated prior to standardizing processes beginning in the 1990s.

The company felt that a single-vendor ERP system would generate the following benefits:

- *Process improvements.* Significant reduction in the number of transactions processed and reconciliations needed.
- *Training.* Simplified employee training and more efficient job rotation because of the similarity of operations across different functions.
- *Information technology.* Significantly reduced support and infrastructure costs, since hundreds of legacy systems could be replaced.
- *Strategic direction.* Resources more efficiently allocated because of visibility from all operating entities.
- *Organization flexibility.* Changing more quickly with new products more quickly deployed, quicker response to changing market conditions.

The decision to move to ERP certainly seemed sound to Eli Lilly, but the details have proved to be difficult. Implementing an ERP system is only part of true enterprise integration. Reengineering processes to fully utilize the integrated information support is essential. In practice, process reengineering is more difficult to achieve than the implementation of ERP computer hardware and software. Moreover, if processes are not changed, the ERP system will usually create additional work for people rather than less.

At Eli Lilly, a set of global policies was adopted. These policies are documented (and updated) in a book entitled *Operational Standards for Manufacturing Excellence: Materials Management Policies.* The book has been extremely important to integration of manufacturing processes in the company, defining a common set of measures to guide the manufacturing management. The book contains a comprehensive set of policies, activities, measures, and goals that defines how manufacturing activities are evaluated across Eli Lilly global operations. Figure 4.6 is an example of how customer service level is defined.

Figure 4.6 defines precisely the manufacturing policy related to customer service satisfaction, integrated with a set of essential activities to support the policy, and a specific set of measures and goals. In a similar manner, Eli Lilly defines policies for the following:

- Independent demand management
- Dependent demand management
- Sales and operations planning/requirements and operations planning
- Master scheduling
- Material requirements planning
- Shop floor control
- Inventory control
- Capacity management
- Lead time reduction
- Data quality
- Training
- Evaluation

Deployment of this common set of policies to all manufacturing units set the stage for a unified vision of manufacturing excellence around the world. Further, processes as well as measurements and goals are also commonly based on the activities defined in the policies.

FIGURE 4.6
Eli Lilly
Definition of
Customer
Service Level

Rationale: *Service level* is a critical element of customer satisfaction and is defined as consistently meeting customer needs related to delivery of product.

Policy: Our *service level goal* to all customers (external and internal) is to fully satisfy valid orders 100% of the time and to position Lilly as one of the best suppliers in the industry.

Fundamental activities:
1. Develop a site program directing efforts toward attainment of the service level goal.
2. Establish a monthly measurement system to report the number of "fully satisfied" *orders* delivered "on time" versus the total number of orders delivered.
3. Report the number of *lines* delivered "on time" versus the total number of lines delivered.
4. Publish order lead times (at least annually) for make-to-order and make-to-stock products that meet the customers' needs and make economic sense.
5. Document the number of incompatible orders, determine causes, and take corrective action as necessary.

Measurements and goals:
1. For both internal and external customers, monthly measure and report the number and percentage of valid customer orders not fully satisfied. Pareto root causes for *not* fully satisfying a customer's valid order so that appropriate corrective action can be taken.
2. Compare results of the "customer service surveys" with your service level measurement to assure that your perceptions of service match those of your customers.
3. Customer inquiries should receive a response before the end of the next work day.
4. When delivery dates change, customers should be notified within 2 work days after the problem causing the change occurs. This must be measured and documented.
5. Incompatible orders must be routinely measured and should not exceed 10% of the total orders per month.

At Eli Lilly, terms were precisely defined so that the meaning of the measures and goals is understood. This was facilitated through diagrams such as Figure 4.7, the order management process. Horizontally across the middle of the diagram is a sequential list of all the major processes associated with make-to-order and make-to-stock orders. Vertically, various lead times are defined on the basis of beginning and ending points of the required processes.

A final feature of Lilly's book is the precise definition of how measurement calculations should be done. These calculations are illustrated by examples. Consider the following calculation of days of stock (DOS). Assume 30 days/month and these data:

March ending inventory (at standard cost)	$1,000,000
Forecast demand (at standard cost)	
April	$400,000
May	$300,000
June	$500,000

To calculate DOS, consider how many full months can be covered with inventory on hand. In this case March inventory will fully cover April and May demand ($1,000,000 − $400,000 − $300,000 = $300,000), projecting that $300,000 worth of inventory will be

FIGURE 4.7   **Lilly Order Management Processes and Lead Time Definitions**

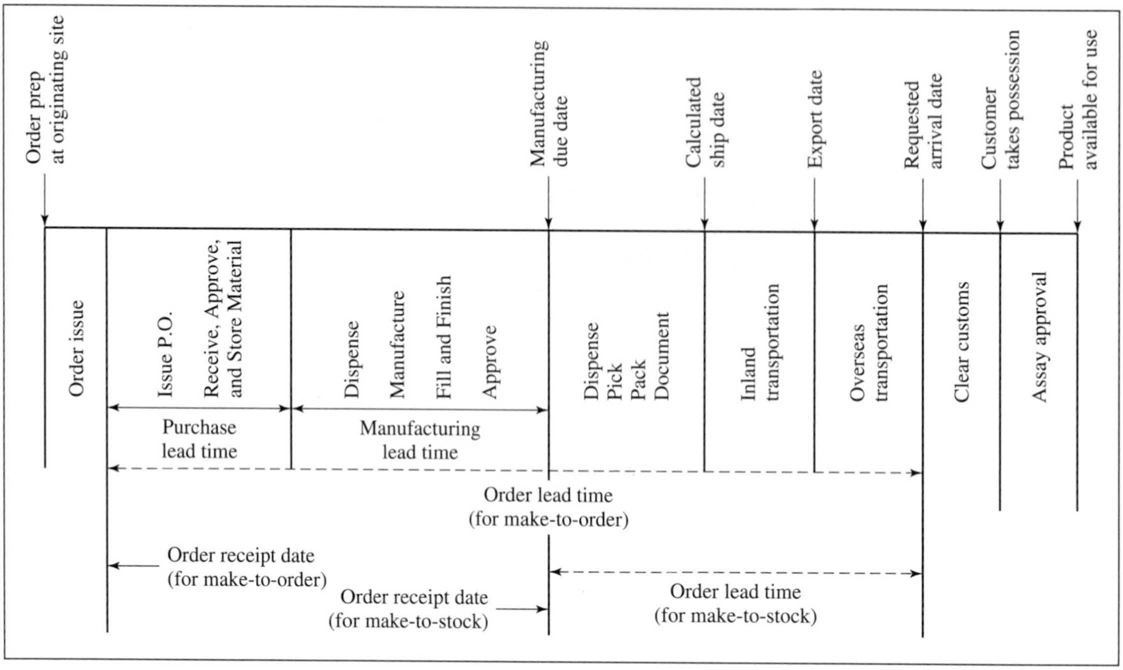

left for June. Sixty percent of June demand can be met ($300,000/$500,000 = 0.6). Sixty percent of June demand is equivalent to 18 days ($0.6 \times 30 = 18$). The total DOS is 78 days (30 for April + 30 for May + 18 for June = 78 days).

In the mid-1990s Lilly began implementing an SAP ERP product, R/3. The ideas from the company's policy book have been embedded in the ERP system. Processes have been defined to correspond to those outlined, as have performance measures and reports. In essence, the ERP system has now replaced the policy book, since the concepts are part of the logic of the processes used by the company and supported by the ERP system. In the case of Lilly, developing these common standards began years before the actual implementation of the ERP system.

The Journey at "United Computer"

A recent survey of APICS members by Mabert, Soni, and Venkataramanan indicates that close to 75 percent of the firms represented are pursuing the ERP approach and 44 percent have already implemented the software. The survey also indicates that 40 percent of the firms expect a single system to provide complete functionality for all expected business needs. For about half the firms, a single package will be employed as the backbone of support, with some supplemental systems handling special requirements. The survey indicated that on average 5.6 percent of annual revenue was being spent on ERP, but there is wide variation of this statistic.

An important question is whether implementing this technology actually results in an improvement in operational performance. Of course, actual results vary greatly, since much depends on how poorly the company performed prior to the ERP implementation and on the extent of the changes to actual processes implemented as part of the project.

Andrew McAfee has studied a manufacturer of high-end computer equipment at a single facility in the United States. The pseudonym adopted to protect the confidentiality of the company is "United Computer." The company employs 800 people, with approximately 400 in direct labor. Annual revenues for the company at the time of the study were approximately US$2 billion.

The facility is completely make-to-order, and no production work takes place before a customer order is received. United's products are a combination of logic devices, memory, mass storage, operating and applications software, networking and input/output equipment and other peripherals, and metal and plastic cabinets, all purchased from external suppliers. United offers four product lines, differentiated largely by processing power. Production consists of assembling these components to customer specifications. United ships between 8,000 and 10,000 customer orders each month. Approximately 80 percent of these orders do not include any products assembled by United. Instead, these orders are for upgrades, additions, or replacements to input/output devices; networking equipment; memory; peripherals; and other stocked items.

At United the term *availability* refers to both response time (the time elapsed between receipt and completion of a customer order) and on-time completion rates. To remain competitive, response time was considered a top priority, even higher than product cost or quality. The four processes that most directly affected United's ability to complete customer orders quickly and on time were production plan development, material supply, order confirmation, and manufacturing. Coordination is required between the planning, purchasing, order management, and production functions to successfully complete an orders. Prior to implementing ERP, United Computer was using approximately 40 separate technical and business legacy applications. These systems sent periodic batch updates to each other, which made getting accurate, timely reports on basic business information, such as inventory levels, difficult. These delays made it difficult to deliver properly configured orders on schedule and at the lowest possible cost.

United management decided that the existing information system environment could not support an efficient operation and decided to implement SAP's R/3 product. The plan was for replacement to take place during a single large-scale changeover. During the changeover, the facility was to be shut down for 10 days while final tests were performed, all required data were uploaded to R/3, and a total factory inventory taken. The actual changeover period was delayed twice, largely for technical reasons. At the end of the changeover period all legacy systems became inactive. By United's estimate, R/3 replaced 75 percent of the company's legacy information systems. The total elapsed time from the decision to move to ERP until actual changeover was approximately $3\frac{1}{2}$ years.

The adoption of ERP at United Computer involved major changes to the company's technology infrastructure. However, the adoption did not involve large changes to United's business processes, especially during the study time period. The time period of the study included the 90 days prior to the 10-day changeover period and 280 days following the changeover. Although there were some changes made to the existing business processes, they were made before the 370-day window.

The data used for the study were the actual orders processed during the 370-day window. Three performance measures were collected from the orders: the daily fraction of orders shipped late, the average lead time for the orders shipped during a day, and the standard deviation of order lead time. For each of these performance measures, observed and fitted values were plotted for all orders, as shown in Figure 4.8.

FIGURE 4.8
Pre- and Post-ERP Data

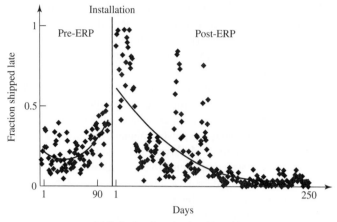

(a) Daily fraction of order shipped late

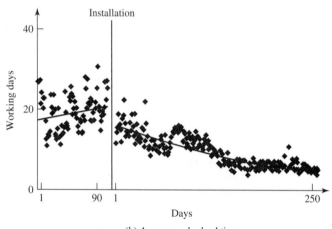

(b) Average order lead time

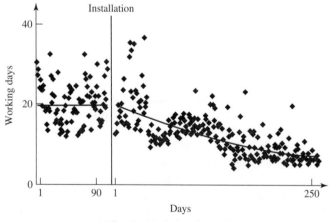

(c) Standard deviation of order lead time

FIGURE 4.9
Comparison of Performance at United Computer

Measure	Pre-ERP	Immediate Post-ERP	Post-ERP
Fraction of orders shipped late	0.228	0.672 (+195%)	0.03 (−87%)
Average lead time of orders shipped	19.46 (days)	14.97 (−23%)	6.32 (−68%)
Standard deviation of lead time	20.32	19.8 (−2.6%)	8.7 (−57%)

Figure 4.8a shows the fraction of orders shipped late before and after ERP. Clear differences are shown between the periods. Before ERP, approximately 20 percent of the orders were shipping late. Notice how this statistic increased during the period just prior to the changeover. Immediately after ERP was in place, late shipments increased and these rates approached 100 percent on several days. However, these rates began to decrease after approximately 30 days. United personnel indicated there were severe shortages in mass-storage components during this period, so not all was attributable to ERP. The post-ERP values follow a learning curve with progressively decreasing late shipment rates. Figure 4.8b plots the average order lead times by day and shows a before and after ERP pattern similar to that of the late order data. Figure 4.8c gives observed and fitted values for the standard deviation of order lead time before and after ERP. Once again, we see a similar performance pattern, with significant improvement after approximately 30 days of using the ERP system.

Figure 4.9 has statistics on the pre-, immediate post-, and post-ERP implementation periods. The results are impressive, with the fraction of orders shipped late decreasing by 86 percent, lead time decreasing 68 percent, and standard deviation of lead time reduced 57 percent. The study expended considerable effort to verify that the performance improvement could actually be related to the new information system and not caused by other factors such as included volume of customer orders shipped, material shortages, inventory levels, quality, employee head counts, and new product introductions. None of these factors was found to be significant in explaining the results.

Lessons Learned at Scotts

The Scotts Company is a leading global producer and marketer of products for do-it-yourself lawn care, gardening, and professional horticulture, with major product offerings in the the United States, the United Kingdom, and Europe. The company has implemented a state-of-the-art ERP system that has been globally deployed at sales, distribution, and production sites. Joe Petite, senior vice president for business development, identified the following lessons learned that may be of value to others in the quest for ERP success:

- Ensure top management visibly supports the project—at kickoff, status meetings, etc.
- Hold the line on project scope and management expectations.
- Assign ownership of deliverables to business leaders.
- Effective change management and user training is imperative.
- Have a solid, integrated project plan down to the people/task level so everyone understands accountabilities.
- Manage to critical path delivery dates and make timely decisions.

- Get management performance objectives tied to savings and deliverables from the start.
- A full-time project team is required.
- Locate the project team together in open space.
- Avoid interfaces wherever possible and do not change software source code from the vendor.
- Always challenge consultants to do better than the timelines. Set high expectations for the entire project team.
- Ensure knowledge transfer from consultants to internal employees.
- Write procedures and ensure they are part of end-user training.
- Whenever possible, change processes before technology.
- Do not underestimate the "people change" side of the equation. Implementing new technology is fairly straightforward compared to getting people to adapt to new roles, responsibilities, and measurement systems.

| **Concluding Principles** | The value of ERP to a company depends to a great extent on the potential savings that can be derived from the ability to centralize information and decision making. For example, a company like Eli Lilly that makes and distributes drugs around the world can derive great benefit from an ERP system because of the similarity of manufacturing and distribution at its sites around the world. It is important to recognize that the value of the system is derived from the synergies obtained from quick access to information from multiple functions in the company. ERP is especially valuable when these functions are located at many different sites within a country or around the world. |

In addition to the suggestions from Scotts, we provide the following principles regarding implementation of an ERP system:

- To achieve efficiencies, redundant transactions must be reduced.
- Data accuracy and efficiencies can be realized if information is captured at the initial entry and the transactions that document a process are preserved.
- Installing the computer hardware and implementing the software is only a part of the process of implementing ERP. Processes need to be changed in a manner that efficiently supports the data needs of the ERP system.
- The company must define a comprehensive set of performance measures together with policies and goals that correspond to these measures.
- Information technology–related economies of scale can be obtained from the need to support fewer software and hardware platforms with an ERP implementation.

References

Bartholomew, D. "SAP: America's Trojan Horse," *Information Week,* April 24, 1995.

Boyle, Robert D. "Unlocking ROI," *The Performance Advantage,* June 2003, pp. 37–39.

Eli Lilly and Company. *Operational Standards for Manufacturing Excellence: Materials Management Policies,* 1993.

Goodwin, B.; M. Seegert; J. Cardillo; and E. Bergmann. "Implementing ERP in a Big Way," *The Performance Advantage,* June 1996.

Inmon, W. H.; Claudia Imhoff; and Ryan Sousa. *Corporate Information Factory,* 2nd ed., New York: John Wiley & Sons, New York, 2001.

Jacobs, F. Robert, and D. Clay Whybark. *Why ERP? A Primer on SAP Implementation.* New York: McGraw-Hill, 2000.

Mabert, Vincent A. "Enterprise Resource Planning: Measuring Value," *Production and Inventory Management Journal* 42, nos. 3–4 (3rd quarter 2001) p. 46.

Mabert, Vincent A.; Ashok Soni; and M. A. Venkataramanan. "Enterprise Resource Planning Survey of U.S. Manufacturing Firms," *Production and Inventory Management Journal* (2nd quarter 2000).

McAfee, Andrew. "The Impact of Enterprise Information Technology Adoption on Operational Performance: An Empirical Investigation," *Production and Operations Management* 11, no. 1 (spring 2002) pp. 33–53.

Martin, Ian, and Yen Cheung. "SAP and business process re-engineering," *Business Process Management Journal* 6, no. 2 (2000) p. 113.

Nenakis, J. "Taming SAP," *CFO,* March 1996.

Ptak, Carol A., and Eli Schragenheim. *ERP Tools, Techniques, and Applications for Integrating the Supply Chain.* St. Lucie Press/APICS Series on Resource Management, 2000.

Softselect Systems. "2003 ERP Software Scorecard," *The Performance Advantage,* June 2003, pp. 60–69.

Supply-Chain Council. "Supply-Chain Operations Reference-Model: SCOR Version 5.0." Supply-Chain Council Inc. (www.supply-chain.org), 2001.

Wallace, Thomas F., and Michael H. Kremzar. *ERP: Making It Happen: The Implementers' Guide to Success with Enterprise Resource Planning.* New York: John Wiley & Sons, 2001.

Discussion Questions

1. What are the essential attributes of ERP systems?

2. Consultants often argue strongly that processes need to be reengineered at the same time that a new ERP system is installed. Do you agree with the consultants? Why or why not?

3. What is the value of real-time data?

4. Access the websites for the following companies: SAP (www.sap.com), Oracle (www. oracle.com), and PeopleSoft (www.peoplesoft.com). Compare the product offerings of these leading ERP software vendors.

5. i2 Technologies is a leading vendor of bolt-on software. Access the i2 website (www.i2. com) and develop a list of the features of this company's offerings.

Problems

1. The following data were obtained from a recent quarterly report for Dell Computer (in millions):

Net revenue	$8,028
Cost of revenue	$6,580
Inventories:	
Production materials	$126
Work-in-process and finished goods	$224
Accounts receivable	$2,689
Accounts payable	$4,326

Calculate the cash-to-cash cycle time for Dell.

2. Obtain from the Internet the current data needed to calculate cash-to-cash cycle time for Dell Computer, Gateway, and Cisco Systems. Calculate the measure for each company and critically evaluate the differences in how the companies operate their supply chains.

3. Evaluate the effect of the following changes that a company makes on cash-to-cash cycle time. Indicate simply the direction of movement of the measurement (i.e., up, down or no change).

   Reduction in cost-of-goods sold

   More frequent deliveries from suppliers

   Reductions in time customers are allowed to pay for goods

   Change from paying suppliers on receipt of goods to waiting 60 days to pay suppliers

Write-off of obsolete inventory

Reduction in labor content in a production process

Outsourcing the production of a major product

4. Return to the Ajax sandwich example on page 115. Suppose that in addition to the 300 peanut butter and jelly sandwiches to be delivered on Friday, Ajax also needs to make 2,000 sandwiches of other varieties. Assume that the same amount of time is needed to assemble sandwiches and that each part-time student can work for five hours. How many students are needed on Thursday?

5. If the average selling price per sandwich is $2.00 and the cost of materials and labor is $1.25, what is the daily profit if Ajax sells 2,100 sandwiches (unsold sandwiches are discarded at the end of the day)? What if it is a really bad day and it only sells 1,500?

6. Supposing a new bread supplier provides bread that increases the shelf life for sandwiches from one day to two. What does this imply for the calculations in problem 5? What kind of MPC system linkages would be required from Ajax to its customers?

7. Suppose that in one college location Ajax typically sells 500 tuna and 500 roast beef sandwiches per day. Every week, the sales of roast beef are going down by 10% because some students are concerned about eating beef. About one-half of these students now buy tuna instead. How many of each sandwich should be made per day for the third week?

8. Continuing with the data in problems 5 and 7, how much are the profits to Ajax reduced in problem 6 by the new student behavior in the third week?

9. Suppose that the peanut butter for the 300 daily peanut butter and jelly sandwiches is delivered once per week and one delivery costs $20. A week's supply of peanut butter is valued at $100 and the cost of capital is 15%. Further suppose that the invoice for peanut butter is paid immediately. What would be the costs and benefits of delivering monthly, using VMI, where payment is made immediately upon use by Ajax?

10. Continuing problem 9, what information linkages might be established from the Ajax ERP systems to the peanut butter supplier to make the VMI work? What would the information links be if the payment to the supplier was paid based on sale of the sandwiches? What else would need to be included?

11. Ajax has established a new sandwich shop format for airports and train stations. Here, the sandwiches are only made from a specially made, long, individual loaf of bread. But the innovation is that the sandwiches are not made ahead in large batches. Instead, a few of each variety of sandwich are made at a time, in the shop, with the result being a better ability to exactly match supply to demand. If prior to this change the shop had roughly 5% leftovers of one-half of the sandwich varieties each day, but could have sold 10% more of the two best sellers that day, what are the potential benefits of the new format if the store sells 12 different sandwiches each with an average demand of 20 per day?

12. Continuing with problem 11, how might an ERP system help plan the replenishment orders for sandwich ingredients?

13. A leading company in the electronics industry estimates that a reduction of 10 days of supply held in inventory is the equivalent of an increase of 1% of sales. What would be the difference between average performance and best in class according to Figure 4.3?

14. Returning to the ideas of problem 13 and Figure 4.3, what might be said about the difference between two firms in the same industry with average and best in class results for asset turns?

15. In the Eli Lilly example, how much would be saved by reducing inventory by 10 days?

Chapter 5

Supply Chain Inventory Management— Independent-Demand Items

This chapter concerns managing inventory items that are found at many points in a supply chain, including finished goods in factories, field warehouses, and distribution centers; spare-parts inventories; office and factory supplies; and maintenance materials. Such items are subject to independent random demand, and not the dependent demand on inventories of raw materials and component parts used in the production of end products. However, many of the underlying principles of the inventory management techniques described in this chapter apply to the management of dependent-demand items as well as independent-demand items, and we will indicate these similarities in our discussion.

The inventory management techniques described in this chapter are commonly referred to as *order point methods.* They are used to determine appropriate order quantities and timing for individual independent-demand product items that are characterized by random customer demand. If we perform these inventory management functions well, we can provide appropriate levels of customer service without excess levels of inventory or management costs.

This chapter is organized around six topics:

- *Basic concepts:* What is independent demand and what are the functions of independent demand inventory?
- *Management issues:* How can routine inventory decisions be implemented and how is performance measured?
- *Inventory-related costs:* How are costs of the inventory system measured and used?
- *Economic order quantity model:* What techniques are used to determine the quantity to order?
- *Order timing decisions:* How can we determine timing of orders and set the level of safety stock?

- *Multi-item management:* What techniques are available for focusing management attention on the important items?

Chapter 5 is related to distribution requirements planning and material requirements planning in Chapters 7, 8, and 14. These chapters discuss lot sizing (order quantity) and order timing decisions for independent-demand items under time-phased planning. Principles of independent-demand inventory management apply, even though MRP decisions are based on dependent demand. Chapters 9 and 15 present JIT concepts that consider inventory management when the order cost is very low and speed is the key criterion. The forecasting material in Chapter 2 provides a key input into the inventory management system. Systems for supply chain networks and associated inventories appear in Chapter 17.

Basic Concepts

The investment in inventory typically represents one of the largest single uses of capital in a business, often over 25 percent of total assets. In this section, we discuss different types of inventory, distinguishing between **independent- and dependent-demand items.** We also describe functions of different types of inventories (transit, cycle, safety, and anticipation stock).

Independent- versus Dependent-Demand Items

This chapter concerns managing **independent demand inventories.** The demand for items contained in independent demand inventories (such as those stocked in the distribution center and field warehouses in Figure 5.1) is primarily influenced by factors outside of company decisions. These external factors induce random variation in demand for such items. As a result, demand forecasts for these items are typically projections of historical demand patterns. These forecasts estimate the average usage rate and pattern of random variation.

Demand for inventory items at the manufacturing stage in Figure 5.1 (e.g., raw material and component items) is directly dependent on internal factors well within the firm's control, such as the final assembly schedule (FAS) or master production schedule (MPS); that is, demand for raw materials and component items is a derived demand, which we can calculate exactly once we have the FAS or MPS. Therefore, demand for end-product items is called *independent demand,* while demand for items contained in manufacturing inventories is called *dependent demand.*

There are other examples of independent-demand inventories in a supply chain context. Items subject to random use such as spare parts for production equipment, office supplies, and production supplies used to support the process all have independent demands. The techniques described in this chapter are suitable for all such items. Demand for these items can't be calculated from a production schedule or other direct management program.

Functions of Inventory

An investment in inventory enables us to decouple successive operations or anticipate changes in demand. Inventory also enables us to produce goods at some distance from the actual consumer. This section describes four types of inventories that perform these functions.

FIGURE 5.1 **Dependent and Independent Demand Inventories**

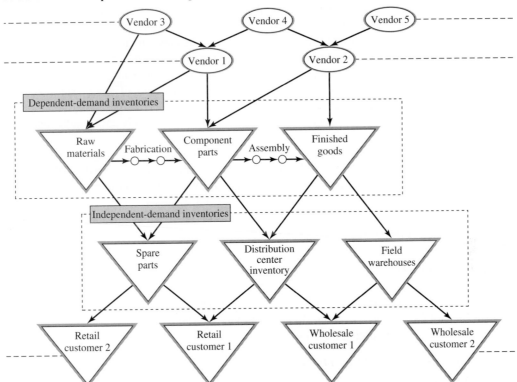

Transit stock depends on the time to transport goods from one location to another. These inventories (along with those in distribution centers, field warehouses, and customers' locations) are also called *pipeline inventories*. Management can influence the magnitude of the transit stock by changing the distribution system's design. For example, in-transit inventory between the raw material vendor and factory can be cut by (1) changing the transportation method (e.g., switching from rail to air freight) or (2) switching to a supplier closer to the factory to reduce transit time. These choices, however, involve cost and service trade-offs, which need to be considered carefully. For example, shipping raw material by air freight instead of by rail may cut transit time in half and therefore reduce average pipeline inventory by 50 percent, but it might increase unit cost because of higher transportation costs. Therefore, the consequences of changing suppliers or transport modes should be weighed against investing in more (or less) inventory.

Cycle stock exists whenever orders are made in larger quantities than needed to satisfy immediate requirements. For example, a distribution center may sell two units of a given end item weekly. However, because of scale economies with larger shipping quantities, it might choose to order a batch of eight units once each month. By investing in cycle stock, it can satisfy many periods of demand, rather than immediate need, and keep shipping costs down.

Safety stock provides protection against irregularities or uncertainties in an item's demand or supply—that is, when demand exceeds what's forecast or when resupply time is longer than anticipated. Safety stock ensures that customer demand can be satisfied immediately, and that customers won't have to wait while their orders are backlogged. For example, a portion of the inventory held at distribution centers may be safety stock. Suppose average demand for a given product in a distribution center is 100 units a week, with an average restocking lead time of one week. Weekly demand might be as large as 150 units with replenishment lead time as long as two weeks. To ensure meeting the maximum demand requirements in this situation, a safety stock of 200 units might be created.

An important management question concerns the amount of safety stock actually required; that is, how much protection is desirable? This question represents an inventory-investment trade-off between protection against demand and supply uncertainties and costs of investing in safety stock.

Anticipation stock is needed for products with seasonal patterns of demand and uniform supply. Manufacturers of children's toys, air conditioners, and calendars all face peak demand conditions where the production facility is frequently unable to meet peak seasonal demand. Therefore, anticipation stocks are built up in advance and depleted during the peak demand periods. Again, trade-offs must be considered. An investment in additional factory capacity could reduce the need for anticipation stocks.

Management Issues

Several issues surround the management of independent-demand inventories. In this section we look at three: making routine inventory decisions, determining inventory system performance, and timing implementation.

Routine Inventory Decisions

Basically only two decisions need to be made in managing independent-demand inventories: *how much to order (size)* and *when to order (timing)*. These two decisions can be made routinely by using any one of the four inventory control *decision rules* in Figure 5.2. The decision rules involve placing orders for either a fixed or a variable order quantity, with either a fixed or a variable time between successive orders. For example, under the commonly used order point (Q, R) rule, an order for a fixed quantity (Q) is placed whenever the stock level reaches a reorder point (R). Likewise, under the S, T rule, an order is placed once every T periods for an amount equaling the difference between current on-hand balance and a desired inventory level (S) on receipt of the replenishment order.

Effective use of any of these decision rules involves properly determining decision rule parameter values (e.g., Q, R, S, and T). This chapter details procedures for determining order quantity (Q) and reorder point (R) parameters for the order point rule, and it gives references covering determination of parameter values for the other decision rules in Figure 5.2.

FIGURE 5.2
Inventory
Decision Rules

	Order Quantity	
	Fixed Q^*	Variable $S^\dagger$
Order frequency Variable $R^\ddagger$	Q, R	S, R
Fixed $T^\S$	Q, T	S, T

$^*Q$ = order a fixed quantity Q.
$^\dagger S$ = order up to a fixed expected opening inventory quantity S.
$^\ddagger R$ = place an order when the inventory balance drops to R.
$^\S T$ = place an order every T periods.

Determining Inventory System Performance

A key management issue is determining the inventory control system's performance. We've already mentioned how large the investment in inventory can be. That investment's size makes it a visible performance measure. Because of this, some managers simply specify inventory reduction targets as the performance measure. Unfortunately this is usually too simplistic. It doesn't reflect trade-offs between the inventory investment and other benefits or activities in the company, nor does it account for the magnitude of the demand on the inventory.

To overcome the latter concern, a common measure of inventory performance, **inventory turnover,** relates inventory levels to the product's sales volume. Inventory turnover is computed as annual sales volume divided by average inventory investment. Thus, a product with annual sales volume of $200,000 and average inventory investment of $50,000 has inventory turnover of 4. That is, the inventory was replaced (turned) four times during the year.

Turnover is often used to compare an individual firm's performance with others in the same industry or to monitor the effects of a change in inventory decision rules. High inventory turnover suggests a high rate of return on inventory investment. Nevertheless, though it does relate inventory level to sales activity, it doesn't reflect benefits of having the inventory.

To capture a major benefit of inventory, some firms use customer service to assess their inventory system performance. One common measure of customer service is the **fill rate** (the percentage of units immediately available when requested by customers). Thus, a 98 percent fill rate means only 2 percent of the units requested weren't on the shelf when a customer asked for them. A 98 percent fill rate sounds good. On the other hand, a 2 percent rate of unsatisfied customers doesn't. Some firms now use a dissatisfaction measure to focus attention on continuous improvement of customer service.

Other measures of inventory-related customer service can be used, but all attempt to formalize trade-offs in costs and benefits. Common among the alternatives are the percentage of the different items ordered that were available, number of times any shortage occurred in a time period, length of time before the item was made available, and percentage of customers who suffered a lack of availability. The correct measure or measures depend on the reason for having the inventory, the item's importance, the nature of the business, and the firm's objectives.

Implementing Changes in Managing Inventory

After analysis of the appropriate decision rules and performance measures, the critical management task is making the changes to improve inventory performance. Appropriate timing of these changes is important. Informal procedures may be quite effective for managing inventories in a small-scale warehouse; as the number of products and sales volumes increases, more formal inventory control methods are needed to assure continued growth. Further improvements might be warranted as the business grows and as inventory management technology improves.

Some of this chapter's concepts require new mindsets, such as the distinction between dependent and independent demand. Other concepts require new organizational objectives and role changes throughout the company. Both these issues must be explicitly considered in timing implementation. One final caveat in implementation, especially for highly automated computer systems: the basic systems must be in place first. If inventory accuracy is poor, computerizing only means that mistakes can be made at the speed of light! If the warehouse currently runs on informal knowledge of what's where and how much is available, or if some inventory is held back by salespersons for "their" customers, a formal system won't help. Basic disciplines and understandings must be in place before formal decision rules are developed.

Inventory-Related Costs

Investment in inventory isn't the only cost associated with managing inventories, even though it may be the most visible. This section treats three other cost elements: cost of preparing an order for more inventory, cost of keeping that inventory on hand until a customer requests it, and cost implied when there is a shortage of inventory. We'll also discuss incremental costs in the context of inventory management.

Order Preparation Costs

Order preparation costs are incurred each time an inventory replenishment order is placed. Included are the variable clerical costs associated with issuing the paperwork, plus any one-time costs involved in, for example, transporting goods between plants and distribution centers. Work measurement techniques, such as time study, can be used to measure the labor content of order preparation. Determining other order preparation costs is sometimes more subtle. For instance, the inventory balance might need to be verified before ordering. Sometimes there may be a fixed cost for filling out a form and a variable cost for each item ordered. Companies frequently bear large costs of maintaining files, controlling quality, and verifying accurate receipts, as well as other hidden costs.

Inventory Carrying Costs

Inventory commits management to certain costs that are related to inventory quantity, items' value, and length of time the inventory is carried. By committing capital to inventory, a firm forgoes use of these funds for other purposes (e.g., to acquire new equipment, to develop new products, or to invest in short-term securities). Therefore, a cost of capital, which is expressed as an annual interest rate, is incurred on the inventory investment.

The cost of capital may be based on the cost of obtaining bank loans to finance the inventory investment (e.g., 5 to 20 percent), the interest rate on short-term securities the firm could earn if funds weren't invested in inventory (e.g., 5 to 15 percent), or the rate of return on capital investment projects that can't be undertaken because funds must be committed to inventory. For example, the cost of capital for inventory investment might be 25 percent in the case where a new machine would yield a 25 percent return on investment. In any case, capital cost for inventory might be determined by alternative uses for funds. Cost of capital typically varies from 5 to 35 percent, but climbs substantially higher in some cases.

The cost of capital is only one part of inventory holding cost. Others are the variable costs of taxes and insurance on inventories, costs of inventory obsolescence or product shelf life limitations, and operating costs involved in storing inventory—for example, rental of public warehousing space, or costs of owning and operating warehouse facilities (such as costs of heat, light, and labor). One example of product obsolescence is that of freshly cut flowers, which must be replaced each week. This implies at least a 5,200 percent annual cost to carry fresh flowers.

As an example, if capital cost is 10 percent, and combined costs of renting warehouse space, product obsolescence, taxes, and insurance come to an additional 10 percent of the average value of the inventory investment, total annual cost of carrying inventory is 20 percent of the cost of an inventory item. In this example, an inventory item costing $1 per unit would have an inventory carrying cost of $0.20/unit/year.

Shortage and Customer Service Costs

A final set of inventory-related costs consists of those incurred when demand exceeds the available inventory for an item. This cost is more difficult to measure than the order preparation or inventory carrying costs.

In some cases, shortage costs may equal the product's contribution margin when the customer can purchase the item from competing firms. In other cases, it may involve only the paperwork required to keep track of a back order until a product becomes available. However, this cost may be very substantial in cases where significant customer goodwill is lost. The major emphasis placed on meeting delivery requirements in many firms suggests that, while shortage and customer service costs are difficult to measure, they're critical in assessing inventory performance.

Customer service measures are frequently used as surrogate measures for inventory shortage cost—for example, the fill rate achieved in meeting product demand (i.e., the percentage of demand supplied directly from inventory on demand). If the annual demand for an item is 1,000 units and 950 units are supplied directly from inventory, a 95 percent fill rate is achieved.

The level of customer service can be measured in several ways; examples include the fill rate, average length of time required to satisfy back orders, or percentage of replenishment order cycles in which one or more units are back-ordered. Level of customer service can also be translated into level of inventory investment required to achieve a given level of customer service. As an example, a safety stock of 1,000 units may be required to achieve an 85 percent customer service level, while 2,000 units of safety stock may be required to achieve a 98 percent customer service level. Translating customer service level objectives into the inventory investment required often is useful in determining customer service level/inventory trade-offs.

Incremental Inventory Costs

Two criteria are useful in determining which costs are relevant to a particular inventory management decision: (1) Does the cost represent an actual out-of-pocket expenditure or a forgone profit? (2) Does the cost actually vary with the decision being made? Determining the item cost used in calculating inventory carrying cost is a good illustration of applying these criteria. The item's cost should represent the actual out-of-pocket cost of purchasing or producing the item and placing it in inventory (i.e., an item's variable material, labor, and overhead costs). An element of the overhead cost, such as a cost allocation for general administrative expenses, isn't an actual out-of-pocket expenditure.

Another example involves measuring clerical costs incurred in preparing replenishment orders. If clerical staff size remains constant throughout the year, regardless of the number of replenishment orders placed, this cost is not relevant to the decision being made (i.e., the replenishment order quantity). These examples are not meant to be exhaustive, but rather

illustrative of the careful analysis required in determining costs to be considered in evaluating inventory management performance.

An Example Cost Trade-Off

Order quantity decisions primarily affect the amount of inventory held in cycle stocks at
various stocking points in the different stages of the supply chain in Figure 5.1. Large order
quantities mean orders are placed infrequently and lead to low annual costs of preparing replenishment orders, but they also increase cycle stock inventories and annual costs of carrying inventory. Determining replenishment order quantities focuses on the question of
what quantity provides the most economic trade-off between order preparation and inventory carrying costs. A deluxe television set stocked in a distribution center is used to illustrate this trade-off.

The 14-inch stereo television is sold to several hundred retail stores from a distribution
center. To avoid excessive inventories, stores place orders frequently and in small quantities. The demand for the 14-inch stereo television at a typical retail store was obtained from
past sales records. It averages 5 units per weekday (or 1,250 units per year). The 14-inch
stereo television can be obtained within a one-day lead time from the distribution center
(DC) serving the retail stores. This requires preparing an order and faxing it to the DC. The
variable cost of preparing a replenishment order is estimated to be $6.25. The firm's cost of
carrying inventory is estimated at 25 percent of the item cost per year, including variable
costs of capital, insurance, taxes, and obsolescence. Since the 14-inch stereo television unit
cost is $100, inventory carrying cost is $25/unit/year.

Currently, the retail stores order the 14-inch stereo television on a daily basis in lots of
5 units. The solid line in Figure 5.3 plots the inventory level versus time for this decision
rule. This plot assumes demand is constant at 5 units per day, and the resulting average
inventory level is 2.5 units. Since orders are placed daily, 250 orders are placed per year,

FIGURE 5.3
**Inventory
Level versus
Time for
14-Inch Stereo
Television**

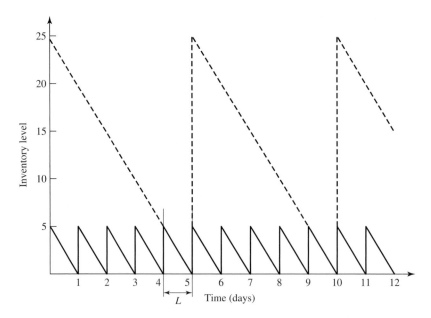

costing a total of $1,562.50/year ($6.25 × 250). The average inventory of 2.5 units represents an annual inventory carrying cost of $62.50 a year (2.5 × $25), yielding an overall combined cost of $1,625/year for placing orders and carrying inventory.

The dashed line in Figure 5.3 shows the inventory level plot for an alternative order quantity of 25 units, or placing orders weekly. In this case, average inventory is 12.5 units and 50 orders are placed annually. The larger order quantity in this case provides important savings in ordering cost ($312.50 versus the previous $1,562.50) with an increase in annual inventory cost ($312.50 versus the previous $62.50). Overall, a shift to a larger order quantity produces a favorable trade-off between ordering and inventory carrying costs, which cuts total cost to $625 per year.

A number of order quantities could be evaluated to determine the best trade-off between ordering and inventory carrying costs. The economic order quantity model, however, enables us to determine the lowest-cost order quantity directly.

Economic Order Quantity Model

The order quantity decision is formally stated in the **economic order quantity (EOQ) model.** This equation describes the relationship between costs of placing orders, costs of carrying inventory, and the order quantity. This model makes several simplifying assumptions: the demand rate is constant, the costs don't change, and production and inventory capacity are unlimited. Despite these seemingly restrictive assumptions, the EOQ model provides useful guidelines for ordering decisions—even in operating situations that depart substantially from these assumptions.

The total annual cost equation for the economic order quantity is

$$\text{TAC} = (A/Q)C_P + (Q/2)C_H. \tag{5.1}$$

This equation contains two terms. The first term, $(A/Q)C_P$, represents annual ordering cost, where A is annual demand for the item, Q is order quantity, and C_P is cost of order preparation. Therefore, the total ordering cost per year is proportional to the number of orders placed annually (A/Q).

The second term, $(Q/2)C_H$, represents annual inventory carrying cost, where average inventory is assumed to be half the order quantity (Q), and C_H is the inventory carrying cost per unit per year; that is, item cost (v) times the annual inventory carrying cost rate (C_r).

Combined costs of ordering and carrying inventory are expressed as a function of the order quantity (Q) in Equation (5.1), enabling us to evaluate the total cost of any given order quantity.

Determining the EOQ

One method of determining the lowest-cost ordering quantity is to graph the total cost equation for various order quantities. Figure 5.4 plots the total cost equation for the 14-inch stereo television for several different order quantities for the following data:

$$A = 1,250$$
$$C_P = 6.25$$
$$C_H = 25$$
$$\text{TAC} = (1,250/Q)6.25 + (Q/2)25$$

FIGURE 5.4

Cost versus Order Quantity for 14-Inch Stereo Television

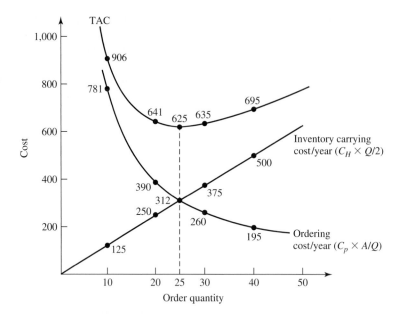

Minimum total cost can be found graphically to equal 25 (i.e., placing orders weekly). Both terms of the total-cost equation are also plotted. We should note several facts in these graphs. First, inventory carrying costs increase in a straight line as order quantity is increased, while ordering cost diminishes rapidly at first and then at a slower rate as the ordering cost is allocated over an increasing number of units. Second, for this cost structure, the minimum cost solution exists where the ordering cost per year equals annual inventory carrying cost. (This observation is used in developing lot-sizing decision rules for dependent-demand items.) Finally, total cost is relatively flat around the minimum cost solution ($Q = 25$ in this case), indicating inventory management performance is relatively insensitive to small changes in order quantity around the minimum-cost solution.

A second and more direct method of solving for the minimum-cost order quantity is by using the EOQ formula in Equation (5.2):

$$EOQ = \sqrt{\frac{2C_p A}{C_H}} \qquad (5.2)$$

This formula is derived from the total cost equation (5.1) by using calculus. That is, Equation (5.1) is differentiated with respect to the decision variable Q and solved by setting the resulting equation equal to zero, as Equations (5.3) through (5.6) show:

$$dTAC/dQ = -C_p(A/Q^2) + C_H/2 \qquad (5.3)$$

$$C_p A/Q^2 = C_H/2 \qquad (5.4)$$

$$Q^2 = 2C_p A/C_H \qquad (5.5)$$

$$EOQ = \sqrt{\frac{2C_p A}{C_H}} \qquad (5.6)$$

where EOQ = the optimal value of Q.

Using the EOQ formula for the 14-inch stereo television produces a lot size of 25; that is, $\sqrt{[(2)(6.25)(1250)]/25}$. In using this expression, we must make sure both demand and inventory carrying costs are measured in the same units (1,250 units/year and $25/unit/year, in this case).

In addition to its use in determining order quantities, the EOQ formula can also be used to develop another important measure in the control of inventories, the **economic time between orders (TBO).** The formula to calculate TBO in weeks is

$$\text{TBO} = \text{EOQ}/\bar{D} \qquad\qquad\qquad (5.7)$$

where $\bar{D}$ = average weekly usage rate.

For the 14-inch stereo television, the TBO equals one week (25 units/order)/(25 units/week). This measure can be used to determine an economic ordering frequency or time between inventory reviews. In the case of the 14-inch stereo television, we might consider using a Q, T decision rule; that is, order an economic lot size weekly.

Order Timing Decisions

In this section we describe timing of replenishment orders under the order point rule Q, R from Figure 5.2. This means calculating the reorder point (R). The inventory level is assumed to be under continuous monitoring (review), and, when the stock level reaches the reorder point, a replenishment order for a fixed quantity Q is issued. Setting the reorder point is influenced by four factors: demand rate, lead time required to replenish inventory, amount of uncertainty in the demand rate and in the replenishment lead time, and management policy regarding the acceptable level of customer service.

When there's no uncertainty in an item's demand rate or lead time, safety stock isn't required, and determination of the reorder point is straightforward. For example, if the 14-inch stereo television's demand rate is assumed to be exactly 5 units per day, and replenishment lead time is exactly one day, a reorder point of 5 units provides sufficient inventory to cover demand until the replenishment order is received.

Using Safety Stock for Uncertainty

The assumptions of fixed demand rate and constant replenishment lead time are rarely justified in actual operations. Random fluctuations in demand for individual products occur because of variations in the timing of consumers' purchases of the product. Likewise, the replenishment lead time often varies because of machine breakdowns, employee absenteeism, material shortages, or transportation delays in the factory and distribution operations.

The 14-inch stereo television illustrates the amount of uncertainty usually experienced in demand for end-product items. Analysis of this item's retail sales and inventory records indicates replenishment lead time is quite stable, requiring a one-day transit time from the distribution center to the retail stores. However, daily demand D varies considerably from day to day. While daily demand averages five units, demands of from one to nine units have been experienced, as the demand distribution in Figure 5.5 shows.

If the reorder point is set at 5 units to cover average demand during the one-day replenishment lead time, inventory shortages of 1 to 4 units can result when daily demand

FIGURE 5.5

14-Inch Stereo
Television
Daily Demand
Distribution

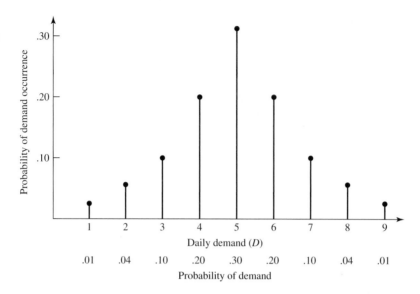

Daily demand (D)	1	2	3	4	5	6	7	8	9
Probability of demand	.01	.04	.10	.20	.30	.20	.10	.04	.01

exceeds the average of 5 units, that is, when demand equals 6, 7, 8, or 9 units. Therefore, if we're to protect against inventory shortages when there's uncertainty in demand, the re-order point must be greater than average demand during the replenishment lead time. The difference between the average demand during lead time and the reorder point is called **safety stock** (S). Increasing the reorder point to 9 units would provide a safety stock of 4 units, for example, as long as the 14-inch stereo television's historical pattern of demand does not change.

The Introduction of Safety Stock

Figure 5.6 illustrates introducing safety stock into the reorder point setting. The reorder point R in this diagram has two components: safety stock level S, and level of inventory ($R - S$) required to satisfy average demand $\bar{d}$ during the average replenishment lead time L. The reorder point is the sum of these two: $R = \bar{d} + S$. To simplify this explanation, lead time in Figure 5.6 is assumed to be constant while demand rate varies.

When a replenishment order is issued (at point a), demand variations during the replenishment lead time mean the inventory level can drop to a point between b and e. In the 14-inch stereo television's case, the inventory level may drop by 1 to 9 units (points b and e, respectively) before a replenishment order is received. When demand equals the average rate of five units or less, the inventory level reaches a point between b and c, and the safety stock isn't needed. However, when the demand rate exceeds the 5-unit average and inventory level drops to a point between c and e, a stockout will occur unless safety stock is available. (We can construct a similar diagram when both demand rate and lead time vary.)

Determining the Safety Stock

Before deciding the safety stock level, we must establish a criterion for determining how much protection against inventory shortages is warranted. One of two different criteria is often used: the probability of stocking out in any given replenishment order cycle, or the desired level of customer service in satisfying product demand immediately out of

FIGURE 5.6
Introducing
Safety Stock
as a Buffer
against
Demand
Variability

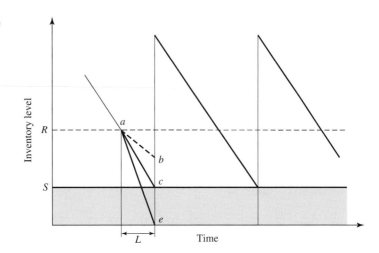

inventory (the fill rate). We illustrate both criteria using the demand distribution for the 14-inch stereo television in Figure 5.5.

Stockout Probability

One method for determining the required level of safety stock is to specify an acceptable risk of stocking out during any given replenishment order cycle. Figure 5.5 provides demand distribution data for this analysis for the 14-inch stereo television. There is a .05 probability of demand exceeding 7 units (i.e., a demand of either 8 or 9 units occurring). A safety stock level of 2 units (meaning a reorder point of 7 units) would provide a risk of stocking out in 5 percent (1 out of 20) of the replenishment order cycles. This safety stock level provides a .95 probability of meeting demand during any given replenishment order cycle. Note this means there is a .05 probability of stocking out by *either* 1 or 2 units when demand exceeds 7 units.

We can reduce the risk of stocking out by investing more in safety stock; that is, with safety stock of 3 units, the probability of stocking out can be cut to .01, and with 4 units of safety stock the risk of stocking out is 0, assuming the demand distribution doesn't change. Thus, one method of determining the required level of safety stock is to specify an acceptable trade-off between the probability of stocking out during a replenishment order cycle and investment of funds in inventory.

Customer Service Level

A second method for determining the required level of safety stock is to specify an acceptable fill rate. For doing this, we define the customer service level as the percentage of demand, measured in units, that can be supplied directly out of inventory. Figure 5.7 provides data for calculations for the 14-inch stereo television. It shows a safety stock of 1 unit, which enables 95.8 percent of the annual demand of 1,250 units for this item to be supplied directly out of inventory to the customer. We compute the service level as follows:

$$SL = 100 - (100/Q) \sum_{d=R+1}^{d_{MAX}} P(d)(d - R) \qquad \textbf{(5.8)}$$

FIGURE 5.7

Safety Stock Determination for Specified Service Levels

Reorder Point R	Safety Stock S	Demand Probability, $P(d) = R$	Probability of Stocking Out, $P(d) > R$	Average Number of Shortages per Replenishment Order Cycle*	Service Level[†] SL, %
5	0	.30	.35	.56	88.8
6	1	.20	.15	.21	95.8
7	2	.10	.05	.06	98.8
8	3	.04	.01	.01	99.8
9	4	.01	.00		100.0

*Calculated by $\sum_{d=R+1}^{d_{MAX}} P(d)(d - R)$.
[†]Assuming the replenishment order quantity is 5 units.

where

$$Q = \text{order quantity}$$

$$R = \text{reorder point}$$

$$P(d) = \text{probability of a demand of } d \text{ units during the replenishment lead time}$$

$$d_{MAX} = \text{maximum demand during the replenishment lead time}$$

For example, when the safety stock is set at one unit in Figure 5.7, we compute the service level as

$$SL = 95.8 = 100 - (100/5)[(.01)(3) + (.04)(2) + (0.1)(1)] \quad \textbf{(5.9)}$$

A service level of 95.8 percent means 4.2 percent of the annual demand, or $(.042)(1,250) = 52.5$ units, can't be supplied directly out of inventory. Returning to when the store was ordering 5 units, and the item was ordered 250 times per year, the average number of stockouts per reorder cycle would be 0.21 (i.e., 52.5/250), as shown in Figure 5.7.

Figure 5.7 shows the effect of increasing the safety stock level on both the service level and the average number of shortages per replenishment order cycle. The service level can be raised to 100 percent by increasing safety stock to 4 units. Again, as in the case of the stockout probability method described previously, choice of the required safety stock level depends on determining an acceptable trade-off between customer service level and inventory investment.

So far, the safety stock and order quantity parameters for an order point system have been determined separately. These two parameters are, however, interdependent in their effect on customer service level performance. We can see this interactive effect in Equation (5.8), since both safety stock level and order quantity size affect the level of customer service. We will demonstrate the interdependent effects of these two parameters later in this chapter.

Continuous Distributions

Two different criteria for determining the required safety stock level and the reorder point have been described (i.e., use of a stockout probability and a desired level of customer service). In discussing both criteria, we used a discrete distribution to describe the uncertainty in demand during the replenishment lead time. It's frequently convenient to approximate a

FIGURE 5.8 Normal Approximation to the Empirical Demand Distribution*

Midpoint X	Discrete Distribution Probability	Interval	Normal Distribution Probability	Probability of Demand Exceeding $(X + 0.5)$	Expected Number of Stockouts When Reorder Point $= X$[†]
1	.01	.5–1.5	.0085	.9902	4.0068
2	.04	1.5–2.5	.0380	.9522	3.0128
3	.11	2.5–3.5	.1109	.8413	2.0591
4	.20	3.5–4.5	.2108	.6305	1.2303
5	.30	4.5–5.5	.2610	.3695	0.5983
6	.20	5.5–6.5	.2108	.1587	0.2255
7	.10	6.5–7.5	.1109	.0478	0.0641
8	.04	7.5–8.5	.0380	.0098	0.0127
9	.01	8.5–9.5	.0085	.0013	0.0018

*A χ^2 test indicates that these two distributions are not significantly different. ($\chi^2 = 8.75$ versus 20.09 at the 0.01 level of significance.)
[†]This is $\sigma_d E(Z)$ based on the $E(Z)$ values from R. G. Brown, *Decision Rules for Inventory Management*. New York: Holt, Rinehart & Winston, 1967, pp. 95–103.

discrete distribution with a continuous distribution to simplify the safety stock and reorder point calculations. One distribution that often provides a close approximation to empirical data is the normal distribution. In this section, we indicate the changes required in the calculations when the normal distribution is used to describe uncertainty in demand during the replenishment lead time.

Figure 5.8's data enable us to compare the empirically derived probability values for the 14-inch stereo television demand in Figure 5.5, with similar values derived from the normal distribution. The comparison shows the normal distribution closely approximates the empirical observations and can be used to determine safety stock and reorder point levels.

Probability of Stocking Out Criterion

When the probability of stocking out is used as the safety stock criterion, the required level of safety stock and the reorder point values are easily computed by using the normal distribution. First, we determine the mean and standard deviation for the distribution of demand during the replenishment lead time. These values have been calculated for the empirical distribution data for the 14-inch stereo television in Figure 5.5 and are shown in Figure 5.9 along with examples of the area (probability) under the normal distribution. (Refer to the appendix at the end of the book for a table of normal distribution probabilities.)

Next, we can calculate the safety stock (or reorder point) value using a table of normal probability values. For example, suppose sufficient safety stock is desired for the 14-inch stereo television that the probability of stocking out in any given replenishment order cycle is .05. We determine the safety stock level and the reorder point as follows:

$$\text{Safety stock} = Z\sigma_d \tag{5.10}$$

$$\text{Reorder point} = \text{mean demand during the replenishment lead time} + Z\sigma_d \tag{5.11}$$

where

$Z =$ appropriate value from a table of standard normal distribution probabilities

$\sigma_d =$ demand during the replenishment lead time standard deviation.

FIGURE 5.9

Daily Demand Distribution

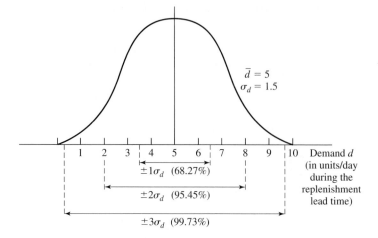

The Z value for a .05 probability of stocking out is 1.645 (from a table of standard normal distribution probabilities). The required level of safety stock, therefore, is 2.5 units—that is, $(1.645)(1.5)$—and the reorder point is 7.5 (or 8) units. The reorder point can also be determined directly from the data in Figure 5.8, where the probability of demand exceeding 7.5 is .0478.

Customer Service Criterion

When the customer service level is used as the safety stock criterion, we can also determine the desired level of safety stock using the normal distribution approximation. For this case, we need the average number of stockouts per replenishment order cycle. To get this, the quantity

$$\sum_{d=R+1}^{d_{\text{MAX}}} P(d)(d - R)$$

shown in Equations (5.8) and (5.9) is replaced by $\sigma_d E(Z)$. The σ_d still equals the standard deviation of the normal distribution being used to approximate demand during replenishment lead time. The $E(Z)$ value is the partial expectation of the normal distribution called the service function. It's the expected *number* of stockouts when Z units of safety stock are held in the standard normal curve. A graph of the service function $E(Z)$ is plotted in Figure 5.10. Note when Z is less than -1, the service function $E(Z)$ is approximately linear.

The safety stock and reorder point calculations are similar to those shown earlier in Equations (5.8) and (5.9). As an illustration, suppose we want a 95 percent service level for the 14-inch stereo television, and we go back to using an order quantity of 5 units. The required value for $E(Z)$ is computed by using Equation (5.13), which we derive from Equation (5.12):

$$\text{SL} = 100 - (100/Q)(\sigma_d E(Z)) \tag{5.12}$$

or

$$E(Z) = [(100 - \text{SL})Q]/100\sigma_d \tag{5.13}$$

In this case, the service function value, $E(Z)$, equals .167; that is,

$$E(Z) = \frac{(100 - 95)(5)}{(100)(1.5)} = .167 \tag{5.14}$$

FIGURE 5.10

Service Function

Source: R. G. Brown, *Decision Rules for Inventory Management.* New York: Holt, Rinehart & Winston, 1967, pp. 95–103.

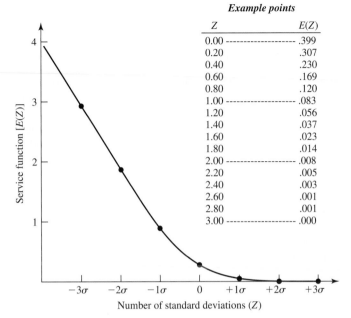

Example points

Z	E(Z)
0.00 -----------------	.399
0.20	.307
0.40	.230
0.60	.169
0.80	.120
1.00 -----------------	.083
1.20	.056
1.40	.037
1.60	.023
1.80	.014
2.00 -----------------	.008
2.20	.005
2.40	.003
2.60	.001
2.80	.001
3.00 -----------------	.000

and

$$\sigma_d E(Z) = 0.25 \qquad (5.15)$$

From the service function table in Figure 5.10, we find an $E(Z)$ of .167 represents a Z value of approximately $+0.6\sigma_d$. The safety stock level therefore is $0.9 = (0.6)(1.5)$. The reorder point would be 5.9. Alternatively, from Figure 5.8, we find $R = 6$ when $\sigma_d E(Z) = 0.2255$. Note this is the same result we got by using the empirical discrete distribution earlier.

Time Period Correction Factor

In the preceding examples, the demand data were expressed as units per day and the lead time was one day. Sometimes the demand data are provided in a different number of time units than the lead time. For example, we might have weekly demand and a two-week lead time. In such cases, adjustments must be made in calculating safety stock as shown in Equation (5.16).

$$\text{Average demand during replenishment lead time} = \bar{D}m \qquad (5.16)$$

The standard deviation of demand during replenishment lead time is

$$\sigma_d = \sigma_D \sqrt{m} \qquad (5.17)$$

and

$$\text{Safety stock} = Z\sigma_D \sqrt{m} \qquad (5.18)$$

where:

$\bar{D}$ = average demand per period

m = lead time expressed as a multiple of the time period used for the demand distribution

σ_d = standard deviation of the demand during replenishment lead time

σ_D = standard deviation of the demand per period

Z = appropriate value from a table of standard normal distribution probabilities

If lead time for the 14-inch stereo television were three days instead of one day, required safety stock would be 4.3 units [that is, $(1.645)(1.5)\sqrt{3}$] and the reorder point would be 19.3 units [(3 days)(5 units/day) + 4.3 units]. Since lead time in this example is 3 times the demand interval of one day, the factor has been included in calculating required safety stock. The resulting safety stock level increases for the three-day lead time to allow for the possible increase in variation in demand over the additional two days.

Up to this point we have considered variability in the demand only, and have considered the lead time to be known and constant. Clearly, transportation difficulties, lack of inventory at the supplier, miscommunications, and other problems can introduce uncertainty into the lead time as well. With globalization increasing distances between companies in the supply chain, uncertain lead times are a growing reality and an increasingly important issue to address. The correction for uncertain lead time is substantially more complicated than for multiple but certain periods.

The parameters of the demand during the replenishment lead time distribution when both lead time and demand are uncertain are found by using Equations (5.19) and (5.20), as reported by Nahmias.

$$\text{Average demand during replenishment lead time} = \bar{D}\bar{L} \qquad \textbf{(5.19)}$$

The standard deviation of demand during replenishment lead time is

$$\sigma_d = \sqrt{\bar{D}\sigma_D^2 + \bar{L}\sigma_L^2} \qquad \textbf{(5.20)}$$

where

$\bar{D}$ = average demand per period

$\bar{L}$ = average lead time in periods

σ_D = standard deviation of the demand per period

σ_L = replenishment lead time standard deviation

The authors have had many comments on the fact that the standard deviation equation (15.20) doesn't look dimensionally correct. We have derived the equations ourselves, and one approach to the mathematical proof is found in Hadley and Whiten (see references).

To verify that the equations presented here can be used in practice, we performed a simulation experiment using Excel. Three demand distributions were generated, using 5,000 periods of simulated demands. The first distribution, demand during a single period, used possible demands for the period of 1, 2, 3, 4, and 5 with probabilities of 0.1, 0.2, 0.4, 0.2, and 0.1, respectively. The second distribution was the sum of the demand during two periods. The same demand distribution as for the single period case was used for each period, and the demands in each period were determined independently. The final distribution was for the demand during a variable lead time. The lead time was either one or two periods long (with equal probability) and the same one period demand distribution was used for each period. The results are shown in Figure 5.11.

FIGURE 5.11　**Comparison of Theoretical and Observed Parameters for Different Lead Times**

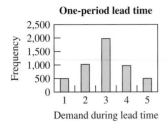

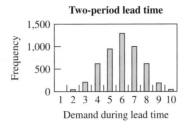

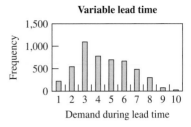

	Lead time					
	One period		Fixed two period		Variable two period	
Factor	Theory	Observed	Theory	Observed	Theory	Observed
Mean	3.00	2.99	6.00	5.99	4.50	4.50
Standard deviation	1.10	1.11	1.55	1.57	2.01	2.02
Variance	1.20	1.22	2.40	2.45	4.05	4.09

Note: Sample size is 5,000 for the observed distributions and theoretical parameter calculations.

The observed distributions are very close to the theoretical distributions, too close to show any differences on the graphs. The theoretical calculations of mean, standard deviation, and variance are obtained from direct calculations for the one-period case, from equations 5.16, 5.17, 5.19, and 5.20, and from the fact that the variance of a distribution is the square of the distribution's standard deviation. The observed values are calculated from the 5,000 individual periods of data for each of the three cases. The theoretical values are very close to the observed values, confirming empirically the correction factors reported here.

Forecast Error Distribution

In many inventory management software packages, demand values for the economic order quantity and reorder point calculations are forecast by using statistical techniques such as exponential smoothing. When these forecasting techniques are used, the required safety stock level depends on the forecasting model's accuracy—how much variation there is around the forecast. Very little safety stock is required when forecast errors are small, and vice versa, for a fixed level of customer service. One commonly used measure of forecasting model accuracy is the mean absolute deviation (MAD) of the forecast errors.

The methods for determining the safety stock and reorder point levels described earlier in this chapter are relevant when product demand is forecast and a MAD value is maintained for the forecasting model. We make use of the fact that the value of σ_E can be approximated by 1.25MAD when the forecast errors are normally distributed. We calculate the safety stock values as follows:

$$\sigma_E = 1.25\text{MAD} \qquad\qquad \textbf{(5.21)}$$

$$\text{Safety stock} = Z\sigma_E = Z(1.25\text{MAD}) \qquad\qquad \textbf{(5.22)}$$

where

σ_E = forecast error distribution standard deviation

Z = appropriate value from a table of standard normal distribution probabilities

FIGURE 5.12

14-Inch Stereo Television Forecast Error Distribution

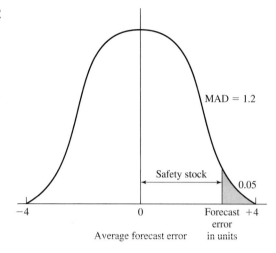

As an illustration, suppose an exponential smoothing model is used to forecast demand for the 14-inch stereo television, a .05 probability of stocking out during a reorder cycle is specified, and the forecast errors are normally distributed, as Figure 5.12 shows. Since the Z value is 1.645 for a .05 probability of stocking out and the MAD value equals 1.2 from Figure 5.12, the required level of safety stock is 2.5 units; that is, (1.645) (1.25) (1.2). The reorder point would be 7.5 units, as we found before. The use of MAD values to approximate the standard deviation can be used in any of the formulas in this chapter for calculating safety stock, reorder points, and service levels.

Order Quantity and Reorder Point Interactions

We saw earlier that there is an interaction between the reorder point and the order quantity in terms of their effect on the customer service level. In this section we use an example problem to explore this interaction. The problem allows us to determine the demand during lead time distribution using discrete probability distributions for lead time and demand. We also introduce the shortage cost concept, which we use to expand the total cost equation. We then present an iterative procedure as a way of jointly determining the reorder point and order quantity using a total cost criterion.

Service Levels and Order Quantities

Figure 5.13 provides data for a single inventory item that will serve as our example throughout this section. Note both lead time and weekly demand are uncertain. This means the process of determining distribution of demand during lead time must account for both uncertainties. We use a tree diagram to illustrate all possible combinations of demand and lead time that can occur. These are then summarized to give the distribution of demand during lead time.

The lead time and weekly demand distribution data in Figure 5.13 have been used to develop the tree diagram in Figure 5.14. As an example of the calculations, we'll use the branch at the bottom of Figure 5.14. The 4-unit demand occurs during the replenishment lead time only when the lead time is 2 weeks and 2 units are demanded each week. The probability of these events occurring is: (.2)(.2)(.2) = .008. Figure 5.14 enumerates the remaining combinations of daily demand and lead time values; the results are summarized in the demand during lead time distribution in Figure 5.15.

FIGURE 5.13
Data for Interaction Example

Quantity	Notation	Value
Item cost	v	$500 per unit
Annual demand	A	35 units per year
Fixed ordering cost	C_p	$45 per order
Shortage cost	C_s	$60 per unit short
Inventory carrying cost rate	C_r	25% of item cost per year
Economic order quantity	EOQ	5 units
Replenishment lead time	L	1 week, probability = .8
		2 weeks, probability = .2
Average lead time	$\bar{L}$	1.2 weeks
Weekly demand	D	0 units, probability = .5
		1 unit, probability = .3
		2 units, probability = .2
Average weekly demand	$\bar{D}$	0.7 unit

FIGURE 5.14
Tree Diagram of Possible Occurrences of Lead Time and Demand for Example Problem

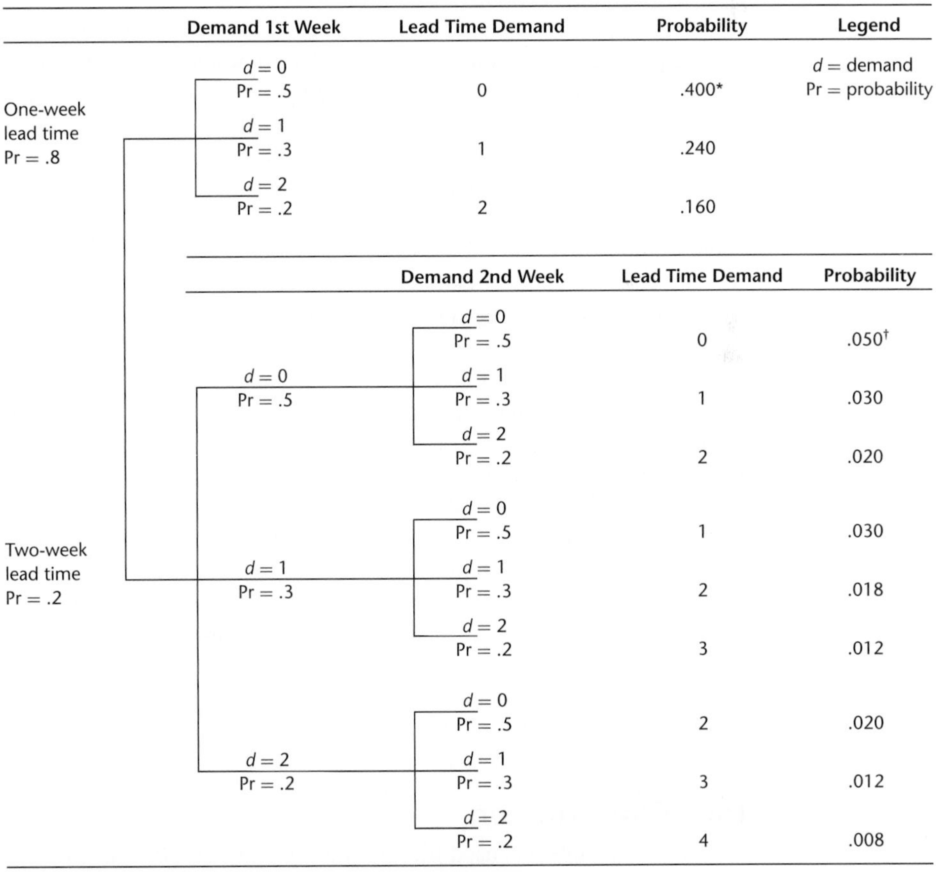

	Demand 1st Week	Lead Time Demand	Probability	Legend
One-week lead time Pr = .8	$d = 0$ Pr = .5	0	.400*	d = demand Pr = probability
	$d = 1$ Pr = .3	1	.240	
	$d = 2$ Pr = .2	2	.160	

		Demand 2nd Week	Lead Time Demand	Probability
	$d = 0$ Pr = .5	$d = 0$ Pr = .5	0	.050†
		$d = 1$ Pr = .3	1	.030
		$d = 2$ Pr = .2	2	.020
Two-week lead time Pr = .2	$d = 1$ Pr = .3	$d = 0$ Pr = .5	1	.030
		$d = 1$ Pr = .3	2	.018
		$d = 2$ Pr = .2	3	.012
	$d = 2$ Pr = .2	$d = 0$ Pr = .5	2	.020
		$d = 1$ Pr = .3	3	.012
		$d = 2$ Pr = .2	4	.008

*$L = 1$ week (Pr = .8) and $d = 0$ for that week (Pr = .5). Probability of both occurring is .4 = (.8 × .5).
†$L = 2$ weeks (Pr = .2) and $d = 0$ (Pr = .5) for each week. Probability of all three occurring is .05 = (.2 × .5 × .5).

FIGURE 5.15
Demand During Lead Time Distribution

Demand d	Probability that Demand $= d$	Probability that Demand $> d$	Reorder Point R	Expected Number of Units Short ($E\{s\}$) When Reorder Point $= R$
0	.450	.550	0	0.840 unit
1	.300	.250	1	0.290 unit
2	.218	.032	2	0.040 unit
3	.024	.008	3	0.008 unit
4	.008	0	4	0 units
Expected demand during lead time $= 0.840$				

Figure 5.15 also shows the expected number of units short, $E\{s\}$, for specified reorder points. A shortage can only occur when demand exceeds the reorder point. So, for example, when the reorder point is 4, no shortages can occur. If the reorder point is 2, there's a 1-unit shortage if the demand is 3, and a 2-unit shortage if demand is 4. The probabilities of these demands occurring are .024 and .008, respectively. This means the expected number of stockouts is $(.024 \times 1) + (.008 \times 2) = .040$ when the reorder point is 2.

To show the interaction between reorder point and order quantity, we use the data in Figure 5.15. Suppose the item was currently ordered about five times per year in quantities of 7. If the reorder point was set to 1 unit, the expected number of units short *per reorder cycle* would be 0.29. This would mean, for the 5 cycles per year, about 1.5 units would be out of stock in a year. This corresponds to a service level of about 95 percent $[(35 - 1.5)/35]$.

If the order quantity is changed to 35, only one reorder cycle per year would occur. There would be an expected 0.29 unit short in the cycle if the reorder point was 1, but that's now the expected number short for the year, as well. This corresponds to a service level of 99 percent $[(35 - 0.29)/35]$. Even a reorder point of 0 would provide a level of service of about 97 percent $[(35 - 0.84)/35]$ when 35 units are ordered at a time.

The order quantity of 35 requires more cycle stock than the order quantity of 7. For the larger order, the exposure to stockout is only once a year, as opposed to 5 times per year when the order quantity is 7. The increased cycle stock when the order quantity is 35 protects against demand fluctuations, acting much like safety stock.

So far we have seen that the order quantity and reorder point both affect service levels and inventory costs. One way of providing useful data for management's consideration is to develop tables that make explicit the trade-off between inventory costs (carrying, ordering, and safety stock costs) and customer service levels for various order quantities and reorder points. Figure 5.16 shows such a table using the example data.

To illustrate the calculations for Figure 5.16, consider a reorder point of 2 and an order quantity of 4. Annual ordering costs would be $(35/4)(45) = \$393.75$. Cycle stock carrying cost would be $(4/2)(.25)(500) = \$250$, while cost of safety stock would be $(2 - 0.84)(.25)(500) = \$145$. This totals $\$788.75$.

Total Cost Criterion

So far, our example has used fill rate (percentage of units ordered met from stock) as the measure of customer service. In some cases, the cost of not having the units in stock (e.g., lost profits, penalty costs, and loss of customer goodwill) can be quantified. Use of this

FIGURE 5.16   Inventory Costs* and Service Levels

	Order Quantity					
	4		5		6	
Reorder Point	Inventory Cost, $	Service Level, %	Inventory Cost, $	Service Level, %	Inventory Cost, $	Service Level, %
0	643.75	79	627.50	83	637.50	86
1	663.75	93	647.50	94	657.50	95
2	788.75	99	772.50	99	782.50	99

*Ordering costs plus cycle and safety stock carrying costs.

cost, the *shortage cost* (C_s), permits a more comprehensive examination of inventory decisions since the ordering, carrying, and shortage costs can all be considered in determining inventory parameters.

The equation for total annual cost (TAC) [Equation (5.23)] contains terms for the costs of placing orders, carrying inventory, and incurring inventory shortages. This equation requires estimates for all the costs, the most difficult of which is probably the shortage cost. Once cost estimates are made, the expression can be used to find the lowest total cost set of order quantity (Q) and reorder point (R) parameter values. The equation is

$$\text{TAC} = A/Q \left[C_P + C_S \left(\sum_{d=R+1}^{d_{max}} (d - R)P(d) \right) \right] + C_H[Q/2 + (R - \bar{d})] \quad \textbf{(5.23)}$$

where

A = annual demand

Q = order quantity

C_P = fixed ordering costs

C_H = annual inventory carrying cost per unit = vC_r

v = item unit cost

C_r = annual inventory carrying cost rate

d = demand during the replenishment lead time

$\bar{d}$ = average demand during the replenishment lead time

$P(d)$ = probability that demand during lead time will equal d

R = reorder point

$(R - \bar{d})$ = safety stock level

C_s = shortage cost per unit

The first part of Equation (5.23) includes the ordering costs and the stockout cost. The number of reorder cycles per year is A/Q, which can be used to convert costs per cycle to annual costs. The expression $(A/Q)C_P$ is the cost per year of placing orders. The expected number of units short, $E\{s\}$, for a reorder point of R is

$$E\{s\} = \sum_{d=R+1}^{d_{max}} (d - R)P(d)$$

Multiplying this by $(A/Q)C_s$ gives cost per year of inventory shortages. Cost per year of carrying cycle stock is $(Q/2)C_H$, and cost per year of carrying safety stock inventory is $C_H(R - \bar{d})$.

Any particular solution to Equation (5.23) provides total cost per year for a given setting of the order quantity Q and the reorder point R. If the unit cost of acquiring an item depends on quantity ordered, this model requires additional terms. This can occur when volume or transportation discounts are available.

The next section describes a method for using Equation (5.23) to determine the least cost order point/order quantity value. We'll use the example problem to illustrate this approach.

The Iterative Q, R Procedure

Figure 5.17 summarizes the iterative procedure developed by Felter and Dalleck. It starts with the EOQ, as we did with the grid search. The value of $P(d > R)$ at step 2 is found by equating the extra annual inventory carrying cost C_H incurred by increasing the reorder point by 1 unit to savings in shortage costs that can be attributed to the additional unit of inventory; that is,

$$C_H = (A/Q)C_s(E\{s\}_R - E\{s\}_{R+1})$$

Since $(E\{s\}_R - E\{s\}_{R-1}) = P(d > R)$,

$$C_H = (A/Q)C_s P(d > R)$$

The calculation of Q at step 4 is obtained by differentiating Equation (5.23) with respect to Q, setting the resulting expression equal to 0, and solving for Q:

$$Q = \sqrt{\frac{2A[C_P + C_s E\{s\}_R]}{C_H}}$$

To illustrate the procedure, we'll use the example problem. Since the procedure iterates from calculating Q to calculating R, it's sometimes called the Q, R procedure.

Step 1. $Q = \sqrt{(2)(35)(45)/(.25)(500)} = 5$.

Step 2. $P(d > R) = (5)(.25)(500)/(35)(60) = .30$. The closest value in
Figure 5.15 is .250 at $R = 1$.

FIGURE 5.17
The Iterative Procedure for Finding Q and R

1. Compute $Q = \sqrt{2AC_P/C_H}$.
2. Compute $P(d > R) = QC_H/AC_s$ and determine the value of R by comparing the value of $P(d > R)$ with the cumulative demand during lead time distribution values.
3. Determine $E\{s\}$, the expected inventory shortage, using the value of R from step 2.
4. Compute $Q = \sqrt{2A[C_P + C_s E\{s\}_R]/C_H}$.
5. Repeat steps 2 through 4 until convergence occurs, i.e., until sequential values for Q at step 4 and R at step 2 are equal.

Step 3. $E\{s\} = 0.290$ (from Figure 5.15 when $R = 1$).

Step 4. $Q = \sqrt{(2)(35)[45 + (0.29)(60)]/(.25)(500)} = 5.91 \approx 6$.

Step 5. $P(d > R) = (6)(.25)(500)/(35)(60) = .36$. $R = 1$.

The five-step procedure converges quickly on the solution values for Q and R. Since the procedure considers the expected shortage cost in determining Q in step 4, and since the computation effort is minimal, it's often a useful approach for determining the order quantity and reorder point values. In cases where the magnitude of the shortage cost C_s is large, this procedure takes that fact into account and adjusts the order quantity and reorder point accordingly. This may mean that an increase in the order quantity over the EOQ and a reduction in the reorder point are required to reduce total cost. The five-step procedure explicitly accounts for the interaction between inventory shortages and ordering costs in solving for the minimum-cost reorder point/order quantity values.

Multi-Item Management

In this section we consider the management of multiple items in inventory. In particular we look at a method for categorizing items so the most important will receive management attention. The technique is called **ABC analysis.** It's first discussed with a single criterion for classification and later with multiple criteria.

Single-Criterion ABC Analysis

A single-criterion ABC analysis consists of separating the inventory items into three groupings according to their annual cost volume usage (unit cost × annual usage). These groups are: A, items having a high dollar usage; B, items having an intermediate dollar usage; and C, items having a low dollar usage.

Figure 5.18 shows the results of a typical ABC analysis. For this inventory, 20 percent of the items are A items, which account for 65 percent of the annual dollar usage. The B category constitutes 30 percent of the items and 25 percent of the dollar usage, while the remaining 50 percent of the items are C items accounting for only 10 percent of the annual dollar usage. While percentages may vary from firm to firm, it's common to find a small percentage of the items accounting for a large percentage of the annual cost volume usage.

ABC analysis provides a tool for identifying those items that will make the largest impact on the firm's overall inventory cost performance when improved inventory control procedures are implemented. A perpetual inventory system, improvements in forecasting procedures, or a careful analysis of the order quantity and timing decisions for A items will provide a larger improvement in inventory cost performance than will similar efforts on the C items. Therefore, ABC analysis is often a useful first step in improving inventory performance.

ABC analysis helps focus management attention on what is really important. Managers concentrate on the "vital few" (the A items) and spend less time on the "trivial many" (the C items). Unfortunately, classifying items into A, B, and C categories on the basis of just one criterion may overlook other important criteria.

Multiple-Criteria ABC Analysis

Several noncost criteria are important in inventory management. Among them are lead time, obsolescence, availability, substitutability, and criticality. Flores and Whybark looked

FIGURE 5.18

ABC Analysis

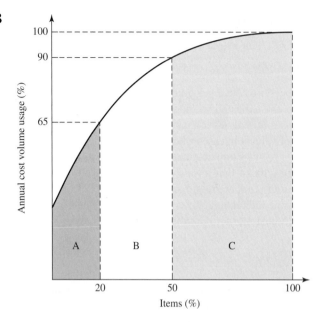

into the use of noncost criteria in managing maintenance inventories. Criticality seemed to sum up managers' feelings about most noncost aspects of the maintenance items. It takes into account such factors as severity of the impact of running out, how quickly the item could be purchased, whether a substitute was available, and even political consequences of being out. Some of these criticality notions may even weigh more heavily than dollar usage in managing the item—much like the proverbial cobbler's nail.

That isn't to say managers shouldn't still be concerned about dollar usage implications of maintenance inventory. To have separate ABC categories for dollar usage and criticality, however, could lead to a large number of combinations, each of which could require a different management policy. The potentially large number of different policies violates the principle of simplicity (a recurring theme in this book). To keep the number of inventory management policies to a workable few, the number of combinations of criteria needs to be kept small. This means combining criteria somehow (e.g., combining high-cost noncritical items with low-cost critical items).

The procedure for doing this consists of several steps. First we produce the dollar usage distribution and associated ABC categories. The second step involves establishing the ABC categories of criticality. To keep confusion down, we use I, II, and III to designate the criticality categories. The criteria to establish these categories are more implicit and intuitive. Category I, for example, might include items that would bring the plant to a stop and for which there's no easy substitute, alternative supply, or quick fix. The III items, on the other hand, are the ones for which there would be little if any effect if there were a shortage. The II items are the ones left over. Figure 5.19 shows the distributions of dollar usage and criticality for a sample of maintenance inventory items at a consumer durable manufacturing plant.

There's substantially less dollar usage in category I than in category A. This should not be surprising, given that the criteria for I included things like impact of outage and ease of replacement. Figure 5.20 presents a matrix of the dollar usage and criticality classifications. There's an entry for every combination. That means both low dollar usage and high dollar

FIGURE 5.19 **Distributions of Dollar Usage and Criticality for a Sample of Maintenance Inventory Items**

	Dollar Usage				Criticality		
Category	Number of Items	Percentage of Items	Percentage of Dollar Usage	Category	Number of Items	Percentage of Items	Percentage of Dollar Usage
A	15	11%	84%	I	5	4%	40%
B	25	15	15	II	48	39	56
C	88	74	1	III	75	57	4
Total	128	100	100		128	100	100

Source: B. E. Flores and D. C. Whybark, "Implementing Multiple Criteria ABC Analysis," *Journal of Operations Management* 7, no. 1 (Fall 1987).

FIGURE 5.20
Number of Items Classified by Dollar Usage and Criticality

	Criticality			
Dollar Usage	I	II	III	Total
A	2	12	1	15
B	1	19	5	25
C	2	17	69	88
Total	5	48	75	128

Source: B. E. Flores and D. C. Whybark, "Implementing Multiple Criteria ABC Analysis," *Journal of Operations Management* 7, no. 1 (Fall 1987).

usage items can have high criticality (or low criticality). It also means the problem of combining still remains.

Multiple-Criteria ABC Management Policies

There are nine possible combinations in Figure 5.20 that could each require a different management policy. The next step is to reduce the number, although R. G. Brown argues this isn't necessary when the computer can keep track of any number of policies. We, however, are concerned about having a number with which people can cope. A simple mechanical procedure is used to combine classifications to provide three initial categories of items. These categories, AA, BB, and CC, provide a starting point for management to reassess the item's classifications. The procedure simply assigns every item in A-I (see Figure 5.20), A-II, and B-1 to AA; every item in A-III, C-I, and B-II to BB; and every item in B-III, C-II, and C-III to CC. This results in 15 AA items, 22 BB items, and 91 CC items.

The next step is to ask management to review each item's classification. The final step is to define specific policies for managing each category. In fact, it's helpful to develop tentative policies first. These can be a guideline in reviewing each item's classification. With the policies in mind, the question to ask when reviewing each item is: Should it be managed with the procedures that apply to its classification? Figure 5.21 shows the manager's reclassification of the items. There were changes from the mechanical assignments in each category. Managers even created a fourth category, although we haven't shown it. In evaluating the items, they found nearly half shouldn't be carried in inventory at all. This demonstrated our observation that it's hard to enhance a system that doesn't have sound basics.

FIGURE 5.21
Multiple-
Criteria
Distributions

Combined Category	Number of Items	Percentage of Items	Percentage of Dollar Usage
AA	14	11%	78%
BB	16	13	12
CC	98	76	10
Total	128	100	100

Source: B. E. Flores and D. C. Whybark, "Implementing Multiple Criteria ABC Analysis," *Journal of Operations Management* 7, no. 1 (Fall 1987).

FIGURE 5.22
Inventory
Management
Policy
Parameters for
Multiple-
Criteria ABC
Items

	Category		
	AA	BB	CC
Counting frequency	Monthly	Every six months	Yearly
Order quantity	Small for costly items	Medium: EOQ-based	Large quantities
Safety stock	Large for critical items	Large for critical items	Low or none
Reclassify review	Every six months	Every six months	Yearly

Source: B. E. Flores and D. C. Whybark, "Implementing Multiple Criteria ABC Analysis," *Journal of Operations Management* 7, no. 1 (Fall 1987).

Specific inventory management policies are needed for each category to bring meaning to phrases like "closer management" or "more management attention." Policies are developed to cover four areas: inventory record verification, order quantity, safety stock, and classification of the item itself. The first area, verification, is to prevent the unpleasant surprises that often occur when the computer record doesn't agree with the physical count. To improve accuracy, more frequent counts should be made. This implies a higher frequency for the AA items than for the BB or CC items. Order quantity and safety stock levels are established for each item depending on both the economics and criticality. Finally, since it's a changing world, a specific period for reconsidering the item's classification is established.

Figure 5.22 shows the specific values chosen for each area. The frequency of counting was established for an average counting rate of 40 items per labor-hour and taking into account past difficulties with the inventory records and transaction reporting system. The order quantities were roughly based on the EOQ values, while safety stock was based on the item's criticality. For both order quantity and safety stock, each part was considered individually. Finally, in order not to leave the impression the item's category was "frozen," a specific frequency of review of each item's classification was established.

The multiple-criteria ABC categories take into account many factors not normally considered in classifying inventory items for management purposes. When combined with clear, specific policies for each category, they can substantially improve the use of scarce talent in managing the inventories.

Software Example

Figure 5.23 illustrates software to support multiple-criteria ABC analysis. The block labeled "Value class rules" contains the different criteria reported here: lead time, unit cost, and annual value (annual usage value). In this example, the various criteria haven't been combined into a single category, but are kept separate by their individual A, B, C, and D

FIGURE 5.23 Multicriterion ABC Analysis Software

XYZ COMPANY
REPORT NO. IC-480A
REQUESTED BY—YOUR NAME

ABC Inventory Classification Value Class Rules

Value Class	Lead Time	Unit Cost	Annual Value	Perct. Value	Usage Weight Factors	Post Value Class
A	20	100.00	100.000	25	YTD 50	N
B	15	50.00	50.000	50	Gross 50	
C	10	5.00	5.000	80		
D	0	.00	0	100		

①(Value Class A B C D) ②(Usage Weight Factors)

Part No./Desc.	TY	AC	Part Count	Perct. Total Count	Annual Usage	Lead Time Days	Unit Cost	Current Unit Cost	Annual Value	Annual Usage Value		Cum. Usage Value	Perct. Total Value		CURR	PREV
AA-05 center member	1	3	1	14.3	11,000	15	B	10.00	C	111,000	A	110,000	24.5	A	A	A
AA-09 raw material	3	4	2	28.6	12,500	30	A	7.50	C	93,750	B	203,750	45.4	B	A	A
AA-11 knob & lock	1	3	3	42.8	20,000	15	B	4.50	D	90,000	B	293,750	65.5	C	B	B
AA-10 glue	3	4	4	57.1	15,000	10	C	5.00	C	75,000	B	368,750	82.2	D	B	C
AA-13 hinge	1	3	5	71.4	240,000	10	C	.25	D	60,000	B	428,750	95.6	D	B	B
AA-12 lock catch	1	3	6	85.7	30,000	10	C	.50	D	15,000	C	443,750	98.9	D	C	C
AA-14 screw	1	3	7	100.0	480,000	5	D	.01	D	4,800	D	448,550	100.0	D	D	D

③(Value Class)

① User-specified ABC parameters for lead time, unit cost, annual dollar value, and percent total value determine value class rules.
② Annual usage can be weighted by year-to-date and/or planned usage percentages for more effective ranking.
③ Value class ranking based on highest value in accordance with specified parameters.

classifications. Thus, for example, the first part, AA-O5, is classified as B in terms of lead time, C in unit cost, and A in annual usage value. Note that it represents almost 25 percent of the annual usage value ("Perct total value").

| Concluding Principles | This chapter presents considerable theory on independent demand inventory management. Despite the material's technical nature, several management principles emerge: |

Concluding Principles

This chapter presents considerable theory on independent demand inventory management. Despite the material's technical nature, several management principles emerge:

- The difference between dependent and independent demand must serve as the first basis for determining appropriate inventory management procedures.
- Organizational criteria must be clearly established before we set safety stock levels and measure performance.
- A sound basic independent demand system must be in place before we attempt to implement the advanced techniques presented here.
- Savings in inventory-related costs can be achieved by a joint determination of the order point and order quantity parameters.
- All criteria should be taken into account in classifying inventory items for management priorities.
- The policies developed for each ABC classification should be used to guide the classification of each item as well as to manage its inventories.
- Management must be sure the organization is prepared to take on advanced systems before attempting implementation.

References

Arnold, J. R. Tony, and Chapman, Stephen N. *Introduction to Materials Management,* 4th ed. Englewood Cliffs, N.J.: Prentice Hall, 2001.

Axsater, S. *Inventory Control,* Kluwer Academic Publishers, 2000.

Barancsi, E., and Attila Chikan, eds. *Inventory Models* (Theory and Decision Library. Series B, Mathematical and Statistical Methods, Vol. 16). Kluwer Academic Publishers, February 1991.

Bernard, P. *Integrated Inventory Management.* New York: John Wiley & Sons, 1999.

Brown, R. G. *Decision Rules for Inventory Management.* New York: Holt, Rinehart & Winston, 1967, pp. 95–103.

Evers, Philip T. "The Effect of Lead Times on Safety Stocks," *Production and Inventory Management Journal,* 2nd quarter 1999.

Felter, R. B., and W. C. Dalleck. *Decision Models for Inventory Management.* Homewood, IL: Irwin, 1961.

Flores, B. E., and D. C. Whybark. "Multiple Criteria ABC Analysis," *International Journal of Operations and Production Management* 6, no. 3 (fall 1986).

Flores, B. E., and D. C. Whybark. "Implementing Multiple Criteria ABC Analysis," *Journal of Operations Management* 7, no. 2 (September 1987).

Greene, J. H. *Production and Inventory Control Handbook,* 3rd ed. New York: McGraw-Hill, 1997.

Harris, T. "You Make the Choice," *APICS—The Performance Advantage,* June 1996.

Hadley, G. J., and T. M. Whiten. *Analysis of Inventory Systems,* Englewoods Cliffs, N.J.: Prentice Hall, 1963, p. 153.

Inderfurth, K. "Nervousness in Inventory Control: Analytical Results," *OR Spektrum* 16 (1994), pp. 113–123.

Inventory Management Reprints. Falls Church, Va.: American Production and Inventory Control Society, 1993.

Karmarkar, U. S. "A Robust Forecasting Technique for Inventory and Lead Time Management," *Journal of Operations Management* 12, no. 1 (1994).

Krupp, J. A. G. "Safety Stock Management," *Production and Inventory Management Journal* 38, (3rd quarter 1997), pp. 11–18.

LaLonde, B. J., and D. M. Lambert. "A Methodology for Calculating Inventory Carrying Costs," *International Journal of Physical Distribution* 7, no. 4 (1977), pp.193–231.

Lambert D. M., and J. T. Mentzer. "Inventory Carrying Costs: Current Availability and Uses," *International Journal of Physical Distribution and Materials Management* 9, no. 6 (1979), pp. 256–271.

Minner, Stefan. *Strategic Safety Stocks in Supply Chains.* New York: Springer Verlag, October 2000.

Nahmias, S. *Production and Operations Analysis,* 4th ed. Burr Ridge, Ill.: McGraw-Hill Irwin, 2001, p. 270.

Porteus, Evan L. *Foundations of Stochastic Inventory Theory,* Stanford University Press, 2002.

Robinson Jr., E. P., and Funda Sahin. "Economic Production Lot Sizing with Periodic Costs and Overtime," *Decision Sciences Journal* 32, no. 3 (summer 2001), pp. 423–452.

Silver, E. A., and R. Peterson. *Decision Systems for Inventory Management and Production Planning,* 2nd ed. New York: John Wiley & Sons, 1985.

Silver, Edward; Pyke, David F.; and Peterson, Rein. *Inventory Management and Production Planning and Scheduling,* 3rd ed. New York: John Wiley & Sons, January 9, 1998.

Tang, O. "Modeling Stochastic Lead Times in a Production-Inventory System Based on the Laplace Transform Method." *International Journal of Production Research* 38, no. 17 (2002), pp. 4217–4227.

Toomey, John W. *Inventory Management: Principles, Concepts and Techniques,* New York: Kluwer Academic Publishers, June 2000.

Woolsey, R. E. D. *Inventory Control,* Southwestern Publishing, January 1996.

Woolsey, Robert E. D., and Ruth Maurer. *Inventory Control (For People Who Really Have to Do It).* Marietta, Ga.: Lionheart Publishing, March 2001.

Zipkin, Paul Herbert. *Foundations of Inventory Management,* Burr Ridge, Ill.: McGraw-Hill Irwin, 2000.

Discussion Questions

1. The concepts of independent and dependent demand are important in inventory management, but sometimes they aren't clearly distinguishable. Can you find the elements of dependency and in-dependency in the following situations: selling snacks at a football game, producing bumpers for automobiles, and selling greeting cards at a shopping center.

2. What would you expect to find as the predominant type of inventory in the following businesses: a ski manufacturer, a make-to-order tugboat manufacturer, and a printer?

3. Which of the inventory costs (carrying, shortage, or preparation) are most difficult to measure? How would you determine if you needed more precision in the estimate of the cost?

4. Why might the EOQ model not be appropriate for a dependent-demand item?

5. A friend of yours wants to leapfrog the basic independent demand inventory ideas and go directly to implementing some of the more advanced concepts. What arguments would you raise against this strategy? What counterarguments might persuade you the leapfrog strategy would be OK?

6. How many pairs of socks do you own? How many dress suits? How does this relate to the ABC concept?

7. How would you classify the three following items using multiple criteria ABC analysis to decide between AA, BB, or CC: a car, a calculator, and writing paper?

8. Use the analogy of writing home for money to explain the concept of demand during lead time. Be sure to account for the fact that both lead time and demand are variables.

Problems

1. Michael Traci, the new inventory manager at Magyar Golf Supplies, is considering using the economic order quantity for controlling inventory. He wants you to apply the EOQ to a sample product, the Super-Z Wedge. The Super-Z Wedge has an average demand of 30 units/period with an ordering cost of $30/order. The cost of carrying a Super-Z Wedge in inventory is $2.00/unit/period. No safety stock is carried for this item.

   a. Calculate the economic order quantity.

   b. Calculate the average cycle stock for this item using the order quantity in question a.

   c. Assuming there are 12 periods per year, calculate total cost per year.

2. Demand during lead time for Louie's Lobster Pots is distributed as follows:

Probability:	.05	.15	.2	.3	.1	.15	.05
Demand:	20	21	22	23	24	25	26

   a. Use a spreadsheet program to evaluate the expected number of units short per reorder cycle for reorder points of 20 to 26. What's the expected shortage cost per reorder cycle when the reorder point is 20 and cost per unit short is $25?

   b. What happens to the expected shortage cost (when $R = 20$ and $C_s = \$25$) if the demand distribution shifts as follows?

Probability:	.2	.4	.2	.1	.1	0	0
Demand:	20	21	22	23	24	25	26

3. The ICU Optical Clinic has recently introduced a new line of eyeglasses that incorporates a highly fashionable frame and special lenses that darken in sunlight and lighten indoors, thus eliminating the need to purchase a separate pair of sunglasses. ICU purchases frames for the glasses from an outside vendor. The lenses are manufactured on site. The clinic has recently noted the following demand distribution for its new glasses:

Demand/month	Probability
12	.10
13	.15
14	.15
15	.20
16	.20
17	.10
18	.05
19	.05

   Purchase price to the ICU Optical Clinic is $30 per frame. The clinic has an ordering cost of $25. Cost of carrying inventory is 25 percent of the item value per unit per year. Order lead time is constant at one month. The work year consists of 12 months.

   a. Compute the economic order quantity for the frames ICU purchases.

   b. Compute the reorder point and buffer stock level for a 99 percent customer service level. Assume order quantity and reorder point can be computed independently.

   c. What's the total annual cost of carrying the buffer stock computed in question b?

4. Wally's World orders a 10-day supply of ice cream whenever on-hand inventory falls below the reorder point. Lead time for ice cream is one day. On Monday, September 30, the clerk found 18 gallons of ice cream in stock. The sales are normally distributed with a mean of 20 gallons per day and a standard deviation of 9 gallons per day. Desired customer service level is 99 percent.

   a. What reorder point for ice cream provides a 99 percent customer service level?

   b. How many gallons of ice cream should be ordered on September 30 if the store is open five days per week?

5. The Seldom Seen Ranch in Muckinfut, Texas, is in the process of developing an inventory control system for purchasing hay that will cope with Texas-size uncertainty. Seldom Seen foreman Horace Cints prepared the following information on Seldom Seen's hay use:

   Average demand during lead time = 1,000 bales

   Lead time = 1 month

   Economic order quantity = 2,500 bales

   Forecast interval = 1 month

   Mean absolute deviation of forecast error = 40 bales

   Desired probability of stocking out = 0.10

   a. How much safety stock will be required?

   b. What's the reorder point?

   c. What's the customer service level for this policy?

   d. What decision rule should Horace Cints use in ordering hay, assuming constant hay usage throughout the year?

6. Nathan Kurash, assistant manager at Breir Sporting Goods, is trying to determine the best ordering policy for Primo biking shorts. The biking shorts have an annual inventory carrying cost of $7 per unit per year, stockout cost is $3 per unit, ordering cost is $4 per order, and the annual requirement is 140 units. Demand during replenishment lead time has the following probability distribution:

Demand During Lead Time (in Units)	Probability
0	.12
1	.24
2	.26
3	.23
4	.07
5	.05
6	.03

Determine the minimum-cost lot size and reorder point for the Primo biking shorts.

7. Solihull Distributors stocks a product having an ordering cost of $216, inventory carrying cost of $5/unit/year, stockout cost of $100 per unit short, an annual requirement of 60 units, and

one-month production lead time. Demand during replenishment lead time has the following probability distribution

Demand During Lead Time (in Units)	Probability
0	.01
1	.04
2	.08
3	.12
4	.15
5	.20
6	.15
7	.12
8	.08
9	.04
10	.01

What's the minimum-cost lot size and reorder point for this item?

8. The Anderson Company produces a spare part with ordering cost of $101, inventory carrying cost of $20/unit/year, stockout cost of $100 per unit short, an annual requirement of 988 units, and one-week replenishment lead time. Demand during replenishment lead time has the following probability distribution:

Demand During Lead Time (in Units)	Probability
15	.02
16	.05
17	.09
18	.15
19	.38
20	.15
21	.09
22	.05
23	.02

Find the minimum-cost lot size and reorder point for this item.

9. Consider the following demand and lead time data for the Turtle Tent produced by Cleveland Tent and Awning:

Demand Per Day	Probability	Manufacturing Lead Time (in Days)	Probability
3	.4	2	.3
4	.6	3	.7

a. Calculate average demand during lead time and determine the distribution for demand during lead time.

b. For each reorder point from 6 to 12 units (assume the item is ordered 12 times per year and stockout cost is $14 per unit), what are the expected stockouts and shortage costs per year.

10. After a merger, Old Framkranz found himself the only inventory clerk left at Allied Breakwater Company (ABC). The merger had left ABC with only 10 parts in inventory, and he'd been told to manage them as effectively as possible. Each part was to be reviewed once a week. (ABC worked a very exhausting five-day week.) Framkranz knew inventory carrying cost was 20 percent per dollar of cost per year. He also knew, to really manage a part's inventory well, he would have to spend a full day on the review, but he could do a reasonably good job in half a day. Even the most cursory review would require one-quarter day per part, however. Files for the 10 parts contain the following information. How should Framkranz schedule the review of the parts?

Part No.	Vendor	Unit Cost ($)	Shipping Cost/Unit	Cost per Order ($)	Annual Usage	Reorder Point	Order Quantity
1	A	0.20	0	10	1,000	50	70
2	B	1.00	0.10	20	10	1	45
3	B	0.25	0.10	15	12	2	95
4	C	3.00	0.25	15	100	20	71
5	A	10.00	0	10	300	15	55
6	B	7.00	0.10	15	2	1	7
7	C	0.50	0.25	20	10	2	13
8	A	5.00	0	10	400	20	39
9	C	20.00	0.30	20	2	1	4
10	A	2.00	0	10	200	10	100

11. Here's a sample of items from the Soaring Eagle Hang Glider Company's maintenance inventory.

Item:	a	b	c	d	e	f	g	h	i	j
Cost ($)	83	68	23	45	10	2	94	51	87	24
Usage	14	47	105	24	75	43	56	5	48	81

a. Rank the items in descending dollar usage order using a spreadsheet. How many items does it take to represent 50 percent of the total? How many does it take to represent the last 10 percent?

b. Management made A, B, and C as well as I, II, and III assignments for dollar usage and criticality, respectively, as shown below. Using the mechanical procedure to develop AA, BB, and CC categories, what are the classifications for each item? What's the dollar usage distribution for AA to CC?

Item:	a	b	c	d	e	f	g	h	i	j
A-C	C	B	B	C	C	C	A	C	A	B
I-III	III	II	I	III	I	III	I	II	III	III

6

Master Production Scheduling

In this chapter, we discuss constructing and managing a master production schedule (MPS), a central module in the manufacturing planning and control system. An effective master production schedule provides the basis for making good use of manufacturing resources, making customer delivery promises, resolving trade-offs between sales and manufacturing, and attaining the firm's strategic objectives as reflected in the sales and operations plan. The prerequisites to master production scheduling are to define the MPS unit (and associated bill of materials) and to provide the master production scheduler with the supporting concepts and techniques described in this chapter.

This chapter is organized around the following eight topics:

- *The master production scheduling (MPS) activity:* What is the role of master production scheduling in manufacturing planning and control?
- *Master production scheduling techniques:* What are the basic MPS tasks and what techniques are available to aid this process?
- *Bill of materials structuring for the MPS:* How can nonengineering uses of the bill of materials assist the master production scheduling function?
- *The final assembly schedule:* How is the MPS converted into a final build schedule?
- *The master production scheduler:* What does a master production scheduler do and what are the key organizational relationships for this position?
- *Company examples:* How do actual MPS systems work in practice?
- *Master production schedule stability:* How can a stable MPS be developed and maintained?
- *Managing the MPS:* How can MPS performance be monitored and controlled?

This chapter is closely related to Chapter 2 on sales and operations planning and Chapter 3 on demand management. Both of these chapters describe modules that provide important inputs to the MPS function. Chapter 7 describes the material requirements planning activities and Chapter 10 describes the management of capacity. Both of these functions depend on the master production schedule to develop their plans. Chapter 13 describes the importance of aligning the production activities of the firm (largely operationalized through the MPS) with the firm's approach to the market and competition.

The Master Production Scheduling (MPS) Activity

We begin with a brief overview of the role of master production scheduling (MPS) in the manufacturing planning and control (MPC) system. We look at the fundamental role of the MPS in converting the disaggregated sales and operations plan into a specific manufacturing schedule. Next we consider how the environment in which the MPS activity takes place shapes the MPS task. Finally, we discuss the linkages between the MPS, other MPC modules, and other company activities.

At the conceptual level, the master production schedule translates the sales and operations plan of the company into a plan for producing specific products in the future. Where the sales and operations plan provides an aggregate statement of the manufacturing output required to reach company objectives, the MPS is a statement of the specific products that make up that output. The MPS is the translation of the sales and operations plan into producible products with their quantities and timing determined. Paraphrasing Tom Wallace, a noted MPC expert, the role of the sales and operations plan is to balance supply and demand volume, while the MPS specifies the mix and volume of the output.

On a day-to-day basis, the MPS provides the information by which sales and manufacturing are coordinated. The MPS shows when products will be available in the future, thereby providing the basis for sales to promise delivery to customers. These promises will be valid as long as manufacturing executes the MPS according to plan. When conditions arise that create customer promise dates that are unacceptable from a marketing or manufacturing perspective, the MPS provides the basis for making the required trade-offs.

At the operational level, the most basic concern is with the construction of the MPS record and updating it over time. The MPS record is developed to be compatible with the material requirements planning (MRP) system and to provide the information for coordinating with sales. Over time, as production is completed and products are used to meet customer requirements, the MPS record must be kept up to date. Doing this means implementing a periodic review and update cycle that we term "rolling through time." Updating the record involves processing MPS transactions, maintaining the MPS record, responding to exception conditions, and measuring MPS effectiveness on a routine basis. Performing these tasks effectively will keep manufacturing resources and output aligned with the sales and operations plan.

The MPS Is a Statement of Future Output

The master production schedule is a statement of planned future output. It specifies the products (or product options) that will be completed, the time of completion and the quantities to be completed. It is the anticipated build schedule for the company. As such, it is a statement of production, not a statement of demand. The MPS specifies how product will be supplied to meet future demand. We stress the fact that the MPS is *not* a forecast, since manufacturing is held responsible for meeting the MPS requirements.

The forecast is an important input into the planning process that determines the master production schedule, but the MPS differs from the forecast in significant ways. The MPS takes into account capacity limitations, the costs of production, other resource considerations, and the sales and operations plan. As a consequence, the MPS may specify large batches of product when the demand is for single units. Or production may take place in advance of market demand in order to better utilize production capacity. It is even possible that product for which there is forecast demand may not even be made.

As the statement of output, the master production schedule forms the basic communication link between the market and manufacturing. The MPS is stated in product specifications—in part numbers for which there are **bills of materials (BOM),** the language of product manufacturing. Since the MPS is a build schedule, it must be stated in terms used to determine component-part needs and other requirements. It can't, therefore, be stated in overall dollars or some other global unit of measure. It must be in terms that relate to a producible product.

The MPS can be stated in specific end-item product designations, but this is not always the case. The MPS units might be options or modules from which a variety of end products could be assembled. Alternatively, the MPS might be stated in a number of units of an "average" final product—for example, an average Dell Latitude D series laptop. Doing this requires a special **planning bill of materials** designed to produce the parts and components necessary to build a number of laptops whose "average" configuration would correspond to the average Latitude D laptop. Converting the options, parts, and components into specific end products would be controlled by a separate **final assembly schedule (FAS),** which isn't ascertained until the last possible moment. The choice of MPS unit is largely dictated by the environment in which the MPS is implemented, a topic to which we now turn our attention.

The Business Environment for the MPS

The business environment, as it relates to master production scheduling, encompasses the production approach used, the variety of products produced, and the markets served by the company. Three basic production environments have been identified: make-to-stock, make-to-order, and assemble-to-order. Each of these environments affects the design of the MPS system, primarily through the choice of the unit used for stating the MPS—that is whether the MPS is stated in end-item terms, some average end item, product modules or options, or specific customer orders.

The **make-to-stock** company produces in batches, carrying finished goods inventories for most, if not all, of its end items. The MPS is the production statement of how much of and when each end item is to be produced. Firms that make to stock are often producing consumer products as opposed to industrial goods, but many industrial goods, such as supply items, are also made to stock.

The choice of MPS unit for the make-to-stock company is fairly straightforward. All use end-item catalogue numbers, but many tend to group these end items into model groupings until the latest possible time in the final assembly schedule. Thus, the Ethan Allen Furniture Company uses a **consolidated item number** for items identical except for the finish color, running a separate system to allocate a lot size in the MPS to specific finishes at the last possible moment. Similarly, the Black & Decker tool manufacturing firm groups models in a series, such as sanders, which are similar, except for horsepower, attachments, and private-brand labels. All products so grouped are run together in batches to achieve economical runs for component parts and to exploit the learning curve in the final assembly areas.

The **make-to-order** (or **engineer-to-order**) company, in general, carries no finished-goods inventory and builds each customer order as needed. This form of production is often used when there's a very large number of possible production configurations, and, thus, a small probability of anticipating a customer's exact needs. In this business environment, customers expect to wait for a large portion of the entire design and manufacturing lead time. Examples include a tugboat manufacturer or refinery builder.

In the make-to-order company, the MPS unit is typically defined as the particular end item or set of items composing a customer order. The definition is difficult since part of the job is to define the product; that is, design takes place as construction takes place. Production often starts before a complete product definition and bill of materials have been determined.

The **assemble-to-order** firm is typified by an almost limitless number of possible end item configurations, all made from combinations of basic components and subassemblies. Customer delivery time requirements are often shorter than total manufacturing lead times, so production must be started in anticipation of customer orders. The large number of end-item possibilities makes forecasting exact end-item configurations extremely difficult, and stocking end items very risky. As a result, the assemble-to-order firm tries to maintain flexibility, starting basic components and subassemblies into production, but, in general, not starting final assembly until a customer order is received.

Examples of assemble-to-order firms include Dell and IBM with their endless variety of computer end-item combinations; the Hyster Company, which makes forklift trucks with such options as engine type, lift height, cab design, speed, type of lift mechanism, and safety equipment; and Mack Trucks, which produces trucks with many driver/owner-specified options. None of these firms know until the last minute the specific choices their customers will make.

The assemble-to-order firm typically doesn't develop a master production schedule for end items. The MPS unit is stated in planning bills of materials, such as an average Hyster forklift truck of some model series or an average Mack highway truck. The MPS unit has as its components a set of common part and options. The option usages are based on percentage estimates, and their planning in the MPS incorporates **buffering** or **hedging** techniques to maximize response flexibility to actual customer orders.

We've said here that the primary difference between make-to-stock, make-to-order, and assemble-to-order firms is in the definition of the MPS unit. However, most master production scheduling techniques are useful for any kind of MPS unit definition. Moreover, the choice of the MPS unit is somewhat open to definition by the firm. Thus some firms may produce end items that are held in inventory, yet still use assemble-to-order approaches. Also, some firms use more than one of these approaches at the same time, so common systems across all approaches are important.

Linkages to Other Company Activities

Figure 6.1 presents a partial schematic for the overall manufacturing planning and control system showing the linkages to master production scheduling. The detailed schedule produced by the MPS drives all the engine and, subsequently, the back-end systems, as well as the rough-cut capacity planning activities. All the feedback linkages aren't shown in the figure, however. For example, as execution problems are discovered, there are many mechanisms for their resolution, with feedback to the MPS and to the other MPC modules.

The linkages to the enterprise resource planning (ERP) system of the firm are shown as indirect, but they are important. All of the major ERP vendors have a master production

FIGURE 6.1

Master Production Scheduling in the MPC System

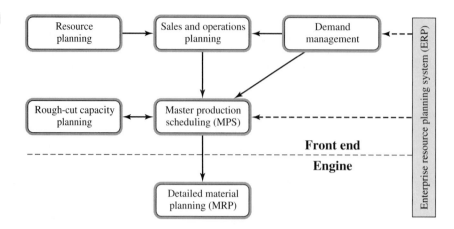

scheduling module. The role of the MPS in an ERP system is the same as we have described here: disaggregating the sales and operations plan, creating a statement of the output from the factory, and providing the information for coordinating sales and manufacturing. The records for a particular ERP system may look different from the version that we use here, but all of the functions will be included.

The demand management block in Figure 6.1 represents a company's forecasting, order entry, order promising, and physical distribution activities. Demand management collects data on all sources of demand for manufacturing capacity: customer orders, forecasts of future customer orders, warehouse replenishments, interplant transfers, spare parts requirements, and so forth. These forecasts are summarized and provided to sales and operations planning. Moreover, demand management books customer orders (enters the order, determines a delivery date with the customer and provides product details to manufacturing). These booked orders are also provided to master production scheduling to coordinate product availability with customer requirements.

In sales and operations planning, the forecasts from demand management will be consolidated and incorporated into the sales and operations plan. This is sometimes referred to as the *company game plan*. The operations plan is a statement of the aggregate output that will meet the objectives of the firm, both quantitatively and qualitatively. In some firms this plan is stated in terms of the sales dollars generated for the company as a whole or for individual plants or regions. In other firms it is stated as the number of units of output to be produced in the next year. The aggregate operations plan constrains the MPS, since the sum of the detailed MPS quantities must always equal the whole as defined by the operations plan.

Rough-cut capacity planning involves an analysis of the master production schedule to discover the existence of any manufacturing resources that represent potential bottlenecks in the production flow. This is the linkage that provides a rough evaluation of potential capacity problems with a particular MPS. If any problems are disclosed, they must be resolved before attempting to execute the MPS.

The disaggregation of the operations plan into production plans for specific products defines the product mix that will be produced. These plans also provide the basic demand "forecast" for each MPS production unit. It is on the basis of these forecast data that the master production schedule is developed. The MPS, in turn, provides the input (gross requirement) data to the material requirements planning system. The MPS, then, is the driver of all the detailed manufacturing activities needed to meet the output objectives of the firm.

The MPS also is the basis for key interfunctional trade-offs. The most profound of these is between production and sales. The specification of exact production output, in terms of products, dates, and quantities, provides the basis for promising delivery to customers. Moreover, when there is a request to increase the output for any one item, the MPS helps determine which item should be reduced in output in order to stay within the capacity constraints. If the production for no item can be reduced, by definition, the operations plan and resultant budget for manufacturing and the firm must be changed.

Since the MPS is an important input to the manufacturing budget, it follows that financial budgets should be integrated with master production scheduling activities. When the MPS is extended over a time horizon sufficient to make capital equipment purchases, a better basis is provided for capital budgets. On a day-to-day basis, both cash flow and profits can be better forecast by basing the estimates on the planned production output specified in the MPS.

Master Production Scheduling Techniques

This section presents some useful basic techniques for master production scheduling. We start out with the time-phased record to show relationships between production output, the "forecast" (derived from the sales and operations plan), and expected inventory balance. This record provides an integration of information that, up until the advent of ERP systems, was often scattered throughout the firm (and far too frequently still is). We then show how plans are revised as you roll through time during a review cycle. This is when actual conditions are taken into account and the record is updated. Finally, we present the process for promising delivery to customers. This process illustrates how the actual customer orders "consume" the forecast.

The Time-Phased Record

Using time-phased records as a basis for MPS preparation and maintenance means that they can be produced easily by computer, and they're consistent with MRP record formats. Figure 6.2 shows a highly simplified example of a master production schedule involving an item with a beginning inventory of 20 units, sales forecast of 10 units per week, and MPS of 10 units per week as well. The MPS row states the timing for *completion* of units available to meet demand. Data in this record show the expected conditions as of the current

FIGURE 6.2
MPS Example

	Week Number											
	1	2	3	4	5	6	7	8	9	10	11	12
Forecast	10	10	10	10	10	10	10	10	10	10	10	10
Available	20	20	20	20	20	20	20	20	20	20	20	20
MPS	10	10	10	10	10	10	10	10	10	10	10	10
On hand	20											

week (the first week in the master production schedule). The record covers a 12-week period (planning horizon) for which total sales forecast is 120 units. The total MPS is also 120 units.

The projected available inventory balance (available) is shown in the second row of the record in Figure 6.2. The "Available" row represents the expected inventory position at the end of each week in the 12-week schedule. It results from adding to the starting inventory of 20 units the MPS of 10 units per week, and subtracting the sales forecast of 10 units per week. Any negative values in the projected available inventory row represent expected back orders.

There are several reasons for maintaining a positive projected inventory balance. Forecasts involve some degree of error, and the MPS is a plan for production that may not be exactly achieved. The projected inventory balance provides a tolerance for errors that buffers production from sales variations. For example, in Figure 6.2, if actual sales in week 1 were 20 units and the MPS was achieved, there would be no back order. Furthermore, if the marketing department still expected total sales for the overall 12 weeks to be 120 units (implying some weeks' sales would be less than the forecast of 10), production can continue at the rate of 10 units per week and still end up with the same planned inventory at the end of week 12.

The MPS row indicates the quantity and time of completion of production. Details for starting production of the various components and assembly of the product are taken care of by the MRP system. In this sense, the MPS drives the MRP system, as shown in Figure 6.1. We'll discuss several of the many alternative MPS plans. All start from the basic logic used to project the expected available inventory balance.

Figure 6.3 presents a different sales forecast from that in Figure 6.2. In Figure 6.3, the marketing department expects sales of 5 units per week for the first 6 weeks and 15 units per week for the next 6 weeks. The overall result is the same: total sales of 120 units during the 12-week period, but sales are seasonal. Figures 6.3 and 6.4 show two different master production schedules to meet this sales forecast. The MPS in Figure 6.3 represents a level 10-unit-per-week production rate over the 12-week planning horizon. The MPS in

FIGURE 6.3
A Level Production MPS Approach to Seasonal Sales

					Week Number							
	1	2	3	4	5	6	7	8	9	10	11	12
Forecast	5	5	5	5	5	5	15	15	15	15	15	15
Available	25	30	35	40	45	50	45	40	35	30	25	20
MPS	10	10	10	10	10	10	10	10	10	10	10	10
On hand	20											

FIGURE 6.4
A Chase Sales MPS Approach to Seasonal Sales

					Week Number							
	1	2	3	4	5	6	7	8	9	10	11	12
Forecast	5	5	5	5	5	5	15	15	15	15	15	15
Available	20	20	20	20	20	20	20	20	20	20	20	20
MPS	5	5	5	5	5	5	15	15	15	15	15	15
On hand	20											

FIGURE 6.5
Lot Sizing in the MPS

	Week Number											
	1	2	3	4	5	6	7	8	9	10	11	12
Forecast	5	5	5	5	5	5	15	15	15	15	15	15
Available	15	10	5	30	25	20	5	20	5	20	5	20
MPS				30				30		30		30
On hand	20											

Figure 6.4, however, adjusts for the difference in sales forecasts, calling for 5 units of production per week for the first 6 weeks, and 15 units per week for the next 6 weeks.

Comparing the projected available rows in Figures 6.3 and 6.4 indicates the difference in inventory between the two MPS plans during the 12-week period. They start and end with the same inventory; but the MPS in Figure 6.3 builds up inventory during the first six weeks, which is gradually depleted during the last six weeks, while the MPS in Figure 6.4 maintains a constant inventory. These two master production schedules represent two extreme strategies. The MPS in Figure 6.3 is a **"leveling" strategy;** the MPS in Figure 6.4 is a **"chase" strategy.** The level MPS calls for no production, workforce, or other capacity adjustments. The chase MPS, on the other hand, requires production adjustments to chase the demands of the marketplace. There are, obviously, many alternative MPS plans between these two extremes. The goal is to find that plan that best balances the cost and benefits.

Figure 6.5 presents the same sales forecast as Figure 6.3, but it incorporates a lot size of 30 units. In Figure 6.5, a lot of 30 units is scheduled for completion in any week when projected available balance would fall below 5 units. This trigger quantity of 5 units reflects a managerial trade-off between carrying inventory and incurring possible back orders.

The projected available balance starts at the beginning inventory position of 20 units and would drop below the 5-unit trigger in the fourth week, so a 30-unit order is scheduled for the fourth week. This order lasts until the eighth week, when the 5-unit level again would be broken. Figure 6.5 shows a total of 4 batches of 30 units being produced over the 12-week planning horizon. The first batch lasts for 6 weeks, while subsequent batches last only for 2 weeks.

Manufacturing in batches of 30 units produces inventories that last between production runs. This inventory, called **cycle stock,** is part of the projected available inventory row in Figure 6.5. The cycle stock could be cut by reducing the lot size for the whole schedule or even just during the first 6 weeks. Similarly, if the company felt overall inventory investment was too high for this MPS, the 5-unit trigger could be reduced. This would provide less **safety stock** protection against forecast errors or manufacturing problems.

Rolling through Time

Now let's turn to Murphy's law: If anything can go wrong, it will. Rolling through time requires updating the record to define how the MPS reflects actual conditions. It's necessary not only to construct the MPS but also to process actual transactions and modify the MPS.

Figure 6.6 shows the situation at the start of the second week (now for weeks 2 through 13), using the original MPS for the 12-week period as given in Figure 6.5. No material was received during the first week, since none was planned by the MPS. But actual sales were 10 units instead of 5 units, and actual inventory at the end of the first week (also the start of week 2) is 10 units (instead of 15).

FIGURE 6.6
Using the Revised Forecast after One Week

	Week Number											
	2	3	4	5	6	7	8	9	10	11	12	13
Forecast	10	10	10	10	10	15	15	15	15	15	15	15
Available	0	−10	10	0	−10	−25	−10	−25	−10	−25	−10	−25
MPS			30				30		30		30	
On hand	10											

FIGURE 6.7
MPS Revisions to Accommodate Revised Forecast after One Week

	Week Number											
	2	3	4	5	6	7	8	9	10	11	12	13
Forecast	10	10	10	10	10	15	15	15	15	15	15	15
Available	30	20	10	30	20	5	20	5	20	5	20	5
MPS	30			30			30		30		30	
On hand	10											

In light of the higher-than-expected sales during the first week, it's reasonable to ask whether the sales forecast is still valid; that is, does the marketing department still believe that total sales for weeks 1 through 12 will be 120 units? What's the forecast for week 13? Let's say the marketing department has decided that the original forecast was incorrect. A new forecast at the end of the first week is for 10 units per week for the next 5 weeks (2 through 6) and 15 units per week for the following 7 weeks (7 through 13). This would total 155 units for the new 12-week planning horizon. Since the new 12-week forecast incorporates 35 more units than the original 12-week forecast, it's greater than the planned production indicated by the MPS of Figure 6.5. Figure 6.6 shows the implications of the new forecast without a revised MPS. Clearly, some adjustment to the MPS is required if anticipated customer needs are to be met. The first potential problem is seen in week 3 of the MPS, where projected available inventory goes negative. The original master production schedule called for the first batch of 30 units in week 4 and the next batch in week 8. That's not sufficient to meet the revised forecast made at the end of week 1.

The revised MPS in Figure 6.7 uses the same 5-unit trigger inventory logic used to establish the lot-sized master schedule in Figure 6.5. Figure 6.7 calls for five batches of 30 units to be produced during the MPS plan, instead of the four batches in Figures 6.5 and 6.6. This revision solves the problem of projected negative available inventory but puts in clear focus the question of feasibility. Does the company have the capacity to produce five batches during the next 12 weeks, or to immediately deliver a batch that was planned for 2 weeks hence? The capacity issue must be resolved before the new MPS is put into effect. Furthermore, high costs are typically associated with making production changes. The master production schedule should be buffered from overreaction, with changes made only when essential.

Order Promising

For many products, customers don't expect immediate delivery, but place orders for future delivery. The delivery date (promise date) is negotiated through a cycle of order promising,

FIGURE 6.8
Order
Promising
Example:
Week 1

	Week Number											
	1	2	3	4	5	6	7	8	9	10	11	12
Forecast	5	5	5	5	5	5	15	15	15	15	15	15
Orders	5	3	2									
Available	15	10	5	30	25	20	5	20	5	20	5	20
ATP	10			30				30		30		30
MPS				30				30		30		30
On hand =	20											

$$ATP = 20 - (5 + 3 + 2) = 10$$

FIGURE 6.9
Order
Promising
Example:
Week 2

	Week Number											
	2	3	4	5	6	7	8	9	10	11	12	13
Forecast	10	10	10	10	10	15	15	15	15	15	15	15
Orders	5	5	2									
Available	30	20	10	30	20	5	20	5	20	5	20	5
ATP	28			30			30		30		30	
MPS	30			30			30		30		30	
On hand =	10											

$$ATP = (30 + 10) - (5 + 5 + 2) = 28$$

where the customer either asks when the order can be shipped or specifies a desired shipment date. If the company has a backlog of orders for future shipments, the order promising task is to determine when the shipment can be made. These activities are illustrated in Figures 6.8 and 6.9.

Figure 6.8 builds on the lot-sized MPS depicted in Figure 6.5. The original sales forecast and MPS as of the beginning of week 1 are shown. In addition, we now consider the sales forecast row to be for shipments. That is, we're forecasting when items will be shipped; and we're closing out the forecast with shipments, not with sales. The distinction separates various forms of sales (e.g., receipt of order or billing) from the manufacturing concern with actual physical movement of the goods.

The row labeled "Orders" represents the company's backlog of orders at the start of the first week. Five units were promised for shipment in the first week, three more for week 2, and an additional two units were promised for delivery in week 3. Thus, the cumulative order backlog is 10 units over the three weeks. The **available-to-promise (ATP)** value of 10 units for week 1 is calculated in the bottom portion of Figure 6.8. The on-hand inventory (20 units) has to cover all existing customer orders until the next scheduled MPS (5 + 3 + 2).

As in our previous example, we assume actual shipments in week 1 were 10 units. This means five of the units shipped in week 1 weren't on the books as sold orders at the week's start; that is, 50 percent of the orders shipped during week 1 were received during the week. This percentage varies greatly among companies.

Figure 6.9 shows the status as of the start of week 2. Figure 6.8's sales forecast and MPS have been revised in the same way as the revision from Figure 6.5 to Figure 6.7. Furthermore, additional customer orders were received during the first week for shipping in weeks 2 through 4. At the start of week 1, we had three units due to be shipped during week 2. Two additional units have been booked during week 1 for week 2 shipment, so the total backlog at the beginning of week 2 for shipment during week 2 is five units. An additional three units have been booked for shipment during week 3 and an additional two units for week 4 shipment. We see then that the cumulative order backlog at the beginning of week 2 is 12 units over the 12-week planning horizon. The increase in the cumulative order backlog from 10 to 12 units over a three-week period may well have been one of the key inputs the marketing department used in revising its sales forecasts.

Orders booked for shipment in week 2 in Figure 6.9 are 5 units, while forecast total shipment in this week is 10 units. We expect to receive orders for 5 additional units during week 2 to be shipped during week 2. Carrying this analysis further, we see the cumulative backlog for weeks 2 and 3 to be 10 units, and the cumulative forecast for the same 2 weeks to be 20 units. This implies that, between the start of week 2 and the end of week 3, we expect to receive orders for 10 additional units to be shipped during that two-week period.

A more interesting relationship is seen between the order backlog and the MPS. The order backlog for week 2 in Figure 6.9 is 5 units, and the anticipated production plus beginning inventory is 40 units. This suggests we still have 35 units to use to meet additional customer requests; that is, it looks like we could make total shipments of up to 35 units in addition to what's already promised in week 2.

This isn't true; we can only accept 28 *additional* units for shipment during week 2; that is, we only have 28 units "available to promise." The reason is that the next scheduled production for this item isn't until week 5; therefore, as shown in the bottom portion of Figure 6.9, the beginning inventory of 10 units plus the 30 units in the master schedule for week 2 have to cover all existing orders for weeks 2 through 4. Since we already have orders for 12 units on the books for shipment during that period, we can only accept up to 28 additional units. That is why Figure 6.9 shows a value of 28 units in ATP for week 2. Those 28 units could be shipped any time during weeks 2, 3, or 4, or any other week in the future.

An important convention about the format of the time-phased MPS record in Figures 6.8 and 6.9 concerns the available row. The available row is the expected ending inventory. A frequently encountered convention is to use the greater of forecast or booked orders in any period for projecting the available inventory balance. In our example in Figures 6.8 and 6.9, actual customer orders never exceed forecasts for the periods. The general calculation for the available row is: previous available + MPS − (greater of forecast or orders).

The available-to-promise logic is a bit harder to state neatly. An ATP value is calculated for each period in which there is an MPS quantity. In the first period, it's the on-hand plus any first-period MPS minus the sum of all orders until the next MPS. For later periods, it's the MPS minus all orders in that and subsequent periods until the next MPS. Both of these rules, however, have to be modified to reflect subsequent-period ATP deficiencies. Figure 6.9 now shows 30 units as ATP in weeks 5, 8, 10, and 12. These quantities match the MPS quantities and reflect the lack of customer orders beyond week 4. Suppose an order for 35 units was booked for week 10 in Figure 6.9. The ATP for week 10 would be zero, and the ATP for week 8 would fall to 25. That is, the 35-unit order in week 10 is to be satisfied by 30 units produced in week 10 and 5 from the MPS produced in week 8.

Some companies choose to show the available-to-promise row as cumulative (58 in week 5). However, keeping the additional increments of ATP separate makes order promising easier and also has the advantage of not overstating the availability position; that is, there are not really 58 available to promise in week 5 as well as 28 in week 2. Some software packages provide ATP both as indicated in Figure 6.8 *and* in cumulative format.

In many firms, accurate order promising allows the company to operate with reduced inventory levels; that is, order promising allows the actual shipments to be closer to the MPS. Companies in effect buffer uncertainties in demand by their delivery date promises. Rather than carry safety stocks to absorb uneven customer order patterns, those firms "manage" the delivery dates.

Consuming the Forecast

One authority on master production scheduling, Richard Ling, originated the idea that actual customer orders "consume" the forecast; that is, we start out with an estimate (the forecast), and actual orders come in to consume (either partially, fully, or over) the estimate. We see this in Figure 6.9. Of the 10 units forecast for week 2, 5 have been consumed. For week 3, 5 of 10 have been consumed, as have 2 of the 10 for week 4.

Let's consider Figure 6.9 and see if, during week 2, we can accept the following hypothetical set of customer orders, assuming they were received in the sequence listed:

Order Number	Amount	Desired Week
1	5	2
2	15	3
3	35	6
4	10	5

The answer is yes to all but order number 4. Since the total amount requested is 65, and the cumulative amount available to promise is only 58 for weeks 2 through 6 (28 in week 2 plus 30 in week 5), only 3 units of order number 4 could be shipped in this period. Let's say the customer would not accept a partial delivery, so we negotiated for delivery in week 8. Figure 6.10 shows the time-phased record at the beginning of week 3 if no more orders were received in week 2 and the forecast for week 14 is incorporated.

FIGURE 6.10
Order Promising Example: Week 3

	Week Number											
	3	4	5	6	7	8	9	10	11	12	13	14
Forecast	10	10	10	10	15	15	15	15	15	15	15	15
Orders	20	2		35		10						
Available	10	0	20	−15	−30	−15	−30	−15	−30	−15	−30	−45
ATP	3		0			20		30		30		
MPS			30			30		30		30		
On hand	30											

Obviously, the set of orders received during week 2 represents a major deviation from the forecast. However, it does allow us to see clearly how we can use the record to make decisions as we roll through time. Let's first review the process's arithmetic. To calculate on-hand inventory at the beginning of week 3, we start with week 2's beginning inventory of 10. We add week 2's MPS of 30; then we subtract the orders for 5 units shipped in week 2 (shown in Figure 6.9) and we subtract the order for week 2 just promised (5 units). The result is $10 + 30 - 5 - 5 = 30$.

The available row provides the master production scheduler with a projection of the item availability throughout the planning horizon in a manner analogous to projecting an on-hand inventory balance in an MRP record. The convention of subtracting the "greater of forecast or orders" and adding the MPS quantities to calculate the available row has an effect here. For week 3 in Figure 6.10, for example, the available is the 30 units of inventory minus the 20 units on order, for a total of 10. In week 4, the available quantity is 0, the difference between the week 3 available of 10 and the forecast of 10. The use of the greater of forecasts or orders for calculating the available row is consistent with forecast consumption. If actual orders exceed forecast, there has been an "over" consumption that should be taken into account. As actual orders are less than forecasts, the result will appear in the on-hand balance (a gross-to-net process); this also impacts the available calculations.

The available position at the end of the planning horizon is important information for managing the master production schedule, as is the existence of negative available data during the planning horizon. During the planning horizon there is typically some length of time in which changes are to be made only if absolutely essential, to provide stability for planning and execution. At the end of this period, master production schedulers have maximum flexibility to create additional MPS quantities. If the projected available is positive in the time bucket at the end of this period, then scheduling more production of the item may not be necessary. Note, for example, at the start of week 2 in Figure 6.9 the week 13 available was 5 and no MPS quantity was entered for week 13. At the start of week 3 in Figure 6.10, the available for week 14 is −45, because of consumption of the forecast by orders booked in week 2. This indicates that in week 3 the master production scheduler should consider scheduling production for completion in week 14. The negative available numbers for weeks 6 through 14 indicate desire for more MPS during the planning horizon. Whether this can be achieved is a matter of response time, availability of materials, and competing needs (other items).

The convention of the greater of forecast or orders means large orders will be immediately reflected in the availability position. This signals the master production scheduler to consider responding to the order by increasing future item availability, which can be used for booking future orders. Separately the available-to-promise row controls the actual order promising. A related question for sales is whether a large order "consumes" forecast for only one period.

To calculate the available-to-promise position, we consider only actual orders and the scheduled production, as indicated by the MPS. We calculate only the incremental available to promise. Note that in Figure 6.10 the 30 units on hand must cover actual orders for weeks 3 and 4, since no additional production is scheduled. In week 5, 30 additional units are scheduled, but none of them is available to promise. The 3 units available to promise in week 3 come from the 30 on hand minus the 20 units ordered for week 3 and the 2 units ordered for week 4. Another 5 units of those on hand are needed for the order of 35 in week 6, since the MPS of

30 units in week 5 isn't sufficient. This leaves only 3 units available to promise for weeks 3 through 7. Of the 30 units to be produced in week 8, we see 10 will be used for the order in week 8. This leaves 20 units available to promise in week 8.

Note that the later customer orders are covered by the later MPS quantities. The 10-unit order for week 8 could have been covered by 3 units in week 3 plus 7 units in week 8 instead of all 10 in week 8. This would have left no units for promising from week 3 until week 8, greatly reducing promise flexibility. The convention is to preserve early promise flexibility by reducing the available to promise in as late a period as possible.

The use of both the "Available" row and the "ATP" row is the key to effective master production scheduling. Using the ATP to book orders means that no customer promise will be made that can't be kept. Note this may mean some orders must be booked at the end of a planning horizon concurrently with creating an additional MPS quantity. As actual orders are booked (the "Order" row), or anticipated (the "Forecast" row), or shipped (on-hand inventory), the "Available" row provides a signal for the creation of an MPS quantity. Once created, the MPS quantity provides the items available to promise for future orders.

The final item of interest in Figure 6.10 is to again focus on the negative available quantities from weeks 6 through 14. These negative quantities indicate potential problems—but only *potential* problems. However, costly MPS changes should not be made to solve "potential" problems. But a condition that created a negative ATP represents a "real" problem.

The time-phased records in Figures 6.9 and 6.10 are similar to MRP records. In fact, the same data can be integrated with standard MRP formats. The primary advantage of doing so is to obtain standard record processing. However, it's necessary to keep track of actual customer orders and the timings of MPS quantities to make ATP calculations. The result is the company database will need to be expanded.

Mitel Corporation: Order Promising with ATP

Mitel Corporation, headquartered in Kanata, Ontario, Canada, is an international supplier of telecommunications equipment and services. Its product lines include business telephone systems, semiconductors, public switching systems, network enhancement and gateway products, systems development, and software products. Mitel is active in major growth markets such as computer telephony integration and emerging technology systems. By combining its products, services, and knowledge, the company provides solutions to a variety of telecommunication problems for customers.

One of the company's products is a telephone, the Superset 430. The dark gray version of the phone is part number 9116-502-000-NA. The order promising record for this product is shown as Figure 6.11. At the top of the header information is the part number, and product description. Next, data on stock status and availability are given. The "Whs" is the warehouse where the stock is located. The "OH" is the on-hand balance, which might overstate availability because some product is already allocated ("Alc") for a customer, has been picked ("Opk") and is ready to ship to a customer, or is being inspected for damage ("Dmg"). The net result is the amount of product available ("Avl") for delivery to customers in the future. The record has a 13-month horizon, of which only 9 weeks are shown on the screen. The starting availability refers to the beginning of the first week of the record.

The detailed record itself is used to develop the available-to-promise quantities that are used to make order promises to customers. The record displays nine weeks of information

FIGURE 6.11 Order-Promising Record for Mitel

Product 9116-502-000-NA   Description SUPERSET 430 DARK GREY

Schedule/Stock-by-Week

```
----Whs------OH-----Alc-----OPk-----Dmg-----Avl-----BkO-----OnO-----Com-----InT-
     DIS   1,039                            1,039
APT Horizon: 13  Starting Avl: 1,039
```

Week Ending	3/8	3/15	3/22	3/29	4/5	4/12	4/19	4/26	5/3
Unal Ship	2	8	3	188	93				
Sch Rcpt / Mfg Rcpt							84		150
Prj OH	1,037	1,029	1,026	838	745	745	829	829	979
Cum B'log	294	292	284	281	93				
ATP	745	745	745	745	745	745	829	829	979

FIGURE 6.12 Update of ATP after Booking Order

```
-Product-------------Description----------------Extended Description----------
9116-502-000-NA   SUPERSET 430 DARK GREY
                                        Schedule/Stock-by-Week
----Whs------OH-----Alc-----OPk-----Dmg-----Avl-----BkO-----OnO-----Com-----InT-
     DIS   1,039                            1,039
ATP Horizon: 13  Starting Avl: 1,039
```

Week Ending	3/8	3/15	3/22	3/29	4/5	4/12	4/19	4/26	5/3
Unal Ship	2	8	3	188	93	100			
Sch Rcpt / Mfg Rcpt							84		150
Prj OH	1,037	1,029	1,026	838	745	645	729	729	879
Cum B'log	394	392	384	381	193	100			
ATP	645	645	645	645	645	645	729	729	879

using the week ending date as the indicator of the week. The row labeled "Unal Ship" (unallocated shipments) contains the booked customer orders that have not yet been allocated or picked. The second line shows scheduled receipts ("Sch Rcpt"), for items for which purchasing is an alternative, and manufacturing receipts ("Mfg Rcpt"), which come directly from the master production schedule and are managed using a different record. The projected on-hand balance ("Prj OH") is calculated from the booked orders directly, since there is no forecast information included in the Mitel order-promising record. For instance, the starting availability of 1,039 is reduced by the demand of 2 in the week of 3/8 to leave a balance of 1,037. Similarly, the demand of 8 in 3/15 further reduces the balance to 1,029.

The final row on the record totals the cumulative backlog for each week in the future for all subsequent weeks. For week 3/8 it is the sum of the booked orders for the first five weeks, 294. For week 3/15 it is the sum of the first five weeks minus the first week. Since the last booked order occurs in week 4/12, that is the last week for which there is a backlog. The ATP row shows that there are 745 units available to promise up to week 4/19 where an MPS quantity increases the availability. Another MPS quantity increases the ATP in week 5/3. The ATP amount (745) is just the difference between the starting availability and the cumulative backlog for the first six weeks. The record says that up to 745 units can be promised to customers anytime over the next six weeks and that another 84 will be available in seven weeks.

Figure 6.12 shows the results of booking an order for 100 telephones for the week of 4/12. The order increases the cumulative backlog by 100 units to 394 and reduces the ATP to 645 in the first six weeks. Salespeople use this record to inform customers when orders can be delivered. The actual booking of the orders is done formally, however, so there can be no game playing with the quantities. Once an order has been placed and is booked, the record is immediately updated for all subsequent order promises. The record is also updated when there is a change in the master production schedule.

Bill of Materials Structuring for the MPS

The assemble-to-order firm is typified by an almost limitless number of end-item possibilities made from combinations of basic components and subassemblies. For example, the number of unique General Motors automobiles runs into billions! Moreover, each new product option for consumers tends to double the number of end-item possibilities. This means the MPS unit in the assemble-to-order environment can't feasibly be based on end items. Defining other units for master production scheduling means creating special bills of material. In this section, we present a few key definitions to clarify what a bill of material is and is not. Thereafter, we discuss modular bills of materials and planning bills of materials that aid MPS management. With this background, it's possible to see how master production scheduling takes place in the assemble-to-order environment.

Key Definitions

The **bill of materials** is narrowly considered to be an engineering document that specifies the ingredients or subordinate components required physically to make each part number or assembly. A **single-level bill of materials** comprises only those subordinate components that are immediately required, not the components *of* the components. An **indented bill of**

materials is a list of components, from the end item all the way down to the raw materials; it does show the components of the components.

The **bill of materials files** are those computer records designed to provide desired output formats. The term **bill of materials structure** relates to the architecture or overall design for the arrangement of bill of materials files. The bill of materials structure must be such that all desired output formats or reports can be provided. A **bill of materials processor** is a computer software package that organizes and maintains linkages in the bill of materials files as dictated by the overall architecture (bill of materials structure). Most bill of materials processors use the single-level bill of materials and maintain links or chains between single-level files. It's the bill of materials processor that's used in MRP to pass the planned orders for a parent part to gross requirements for its components.

The single-level bill and the indented bill are two alternative output formats of the bill of materials. Alternative output formats are useful for different purposes. For example, the single-level bill supports order launching by providing the data for component availability checking, allocation, and picking. Industrial engineers often use the fully indented bill to determine how to physically put the product together; accountants use it for cost implosions. A fundamental rule is that a company should have one, and only one, set of bills of materials or **product structure** records. This set should be maintained as an entity and be so designed that all legitimate company uses can be satisfied.

An important element of the bill of materials is the designation of a **low-level code number** for each part, component, subassembly, or finished item in the BOM. These are numbers that indicate where in the product structure a particular part or subassembly is with respect to the end item. By convention the highest level (e.g., the end item) is designated level 0. The components of level 0 are designated as level 1 and so forth until the purchased parts and raw materials are designated. Designating level codes facilitates bill of material processing in that all requirements for items at level 0 can be determined and summarized before processing the requirements for level 2. In structuring bills of material for planning purposes, however, it is not always true that the end item is designated as level zero.

The rest of this section presents concepts providing another way of thinking about the bill of materials. The traditional approach is from an engineer's point of view, that is, the way the product is *built*. The key change required to achieve superior master production scheduling for assemble-to-order products is to include bill of materials structures based on the way the product is *sold*. In this way, the bill of materials can support some critical planning and management activities.

Constructing a bill of materials structure or architecture based on how the product is sold, rather than how it's built, offers important advantages. Achieving them, however, isn't without cost. The primary cost is that the resultant bills of materials may no longer relate to the way the product is built. Activities based on *that* structure (e.g., industrial engineering) will have to be based on some new source of data; that is, if the description of how the parts physically go together isn't found in the bill of materials, an alternative set of records must be maintained. Providing alternative means to satisfy these needs can be costly in terms of both file creation and maintenance.

The Modular Bill of Materials

A key use of bill of materials files is in translating the MPS into subordinate components requirements. One bill of materials structure or architecture calls for maintaining all end-

FIGURE 6.13
The MPS
Hourglass

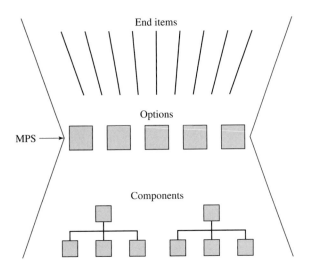

item buildable configurations. This bill of materials structure is appropriate for the make-to-stock firm, where the MPS is stated in end items. For each end item, a single-level bill is maintained, which contains those components that physically go into the item. For General Motors, with its billions of possible end items, this bill of materials structure isn't feasible.

Figure 6.13 shows the dilemma. A solution is to establish the MPS at the option or module level. The intent is to state the MPS in units associated with the "waist" of the hourglass. This necessitates that bill of materials files be structured accordingly; each option or module will be defined fully in the bill of materials files as a single-level bill of materials. Thus, the modular bill of materials structure's architecture links component parts to options, but it doesn't link either options or components to end item configurations. If the options are simply buildable subassemblies, then all that's required for the new architecture is to treat the subassemblies as end items; that is, designate them as level 0, instead of level 1. In most cases, however, the options aren't stated as buildable subassemblies but as options that provide features to the customer.

Consider, for example, the air-conditioning option for a car. The single-level bill of materials would show this option or module as consisting of a particular radiator, fan, hoses, compressor, and interior knobs and levers. These items are not, however, assembled together. They are assembled with still other parts as subassemblies, which eventually are assembled into the automobile.

Using the air-conditioning option as a bill of materials will pass demand from the customer who wants this option down to the necessary parts. It can also be used to forecast demand for air conditioners. However, this bill of materials isn't useful in the physical building process for air conditioners. For example, the air-conditioning knobs are planned by the bill for the air-conditioning option. They aren't planned by the bill of the dashboard assembly where they're installed. Thus, the industrial engineer needs other means to say how the dashboard is to be assembled and from what components. The modular bill of materials focuses on how the car is sold, not how it is made.

Using the modular bill of materials structure for a firm with a situation similar to that in Figure 6.13 permits the MPS to be stated in fewer different units. The MPS is stated in the terms in which the product is *sold,* not in terms in which it's built; that is, air conditioning, two doors, automatic transmission, fancy trim, and so on. The approach is compatible with marketing perceptions of models, options, and trends in options (e.g., more people buying cars with air conditioning), which tends to improve forecasting. Master scheduling may be made easier by using modular bills, but order entry tasks are more complex since each option must be evaluated.

Once the individual customer order (representing a unique collection of options) is entered, it serves the function of a one-time, unique single-level bill of materials; that is, it specifies which options or modules are to be included for the particular customer order. It's controlled by a separate final assembly schedule.

The Planning Bill of Materials

Restructuring the bill of materials to better perform MPS activities has led many people to see that alternative bill of materials approaches have additional applications. An example is the planning bill of materials, which is any use of bill of materials approaches for planning only, as opposed to use for building the products. The modular bill of materials approach just described involves one form of a planning bill, since it's used for developing material plans and modules not all of which are buildable.

The most widely used planning bill of materials is the **super bill.** The super bill describes the related options or modules that make up the *average* end item. For example, an average General Motors J-body car might have 0.6 Chevrolet unique parts, 2.6 doors, 4.3 cylinders, 0.4 air conditioners, and the like. This end item is impossible to build; but using bill of materials logic, it's very useful for planning and master production scheduling. Bill of materials processing dictates that the super bill be established in the product structure files as a legitimate single-level bill of materials. This means that the super bill will show all the possible options as components, with their average decimal usage. The logic of bill of materials processing permits decimal multiples for single-level component usages. The super bill combines the modules, or options, with the decimal usage rates to describe the average car. The bill of materials logic forces arithmetic consistency in the mutually exclusive options; for example, the sum of two possible engine options needs to equal the total number of cars.

The super bill is as much a marketing tool as a manufacturing tool. With it, instead of forecasting and controlling individual modules, the forecast is now stated in terms of total average units, with attention given to percentage breakdowns—to the single-level super bill of materials—and to *managing* module inventories by using available-to-promise logic on a day-to-day basis as actual customer orders are booked.

Let's consider an artificially small example. The Garden Till Company makes rototillers in the following options:

Horsepower: 3 HP, 4 HP, 5 HP.

Drive train: Chain, gear.

Brand name: Taylor, Garden Till, OEM.

The total number of end item buildable units is 18 ($3 \times 2 \times 3$). Management at the end-item level would mean each of these would have to be forecast. Figure 6.14 shows a super bill for 4-horsepower tillers. Using this artificial end item, an average 4-horsepower tiller, only one forecast is needed from marketing. More important, the MPS unit can be the super bill. The entry of 1,000 four-horsepower super bill units into the MPS would plan the

FIGURE 6.14
The
4-Horsepower
Super Bill

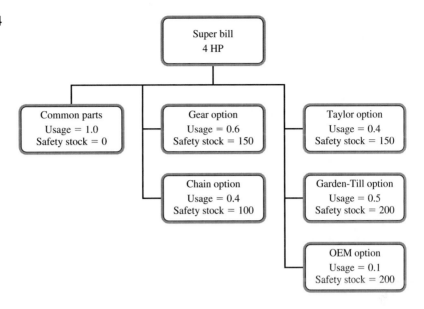

appropriate quantities of each of the options to build 1,000 four-horsepower units in the average option proportions. Actual orders may not reflect the average in the short run, however.

Figure 6.14 shows the use of safety stocks for the options to absorb variations in the mix.
No safety stock is shown for the common parts. This means protection is provided for product mix variances but not for variances in the overall MPS quantity of 4-horsepower tillers.
A commitment to an MPS quantity for the super bill means exactly that number of common
parts will be needed. In Figure 6.14's example, if 1,000 four-horsepower super bills were
entered, the bill of materials would call for 1,000 common-parts modules, 600 gear options, 400 chain options, 400 Taylor options, 500 Garden Till options, and 100 OEM options. The safety stocks allow shipments to customers to vary from the usages specified in
the bill of materials percentage usage.

Although 600 of the 1,000 four-horsepower tillers are expected to be finished in the gear
drive option, as many as 750 can be promised because of the safety stock. Similar flexibility exists for all other options. Safety stocks are maintained with MRP gross to net logic, so
appropriate quantities are maintained as actual conditions become reflected in replenishment orders. Moreover, the safety stock will exist in matched sets because of the modular
bill of materials structure. Matched sets occur because when one unit of the module is specified for safety stock, *all* parts required for that unit will be planned. Furthermore, costs
of all safety stocks are readily visible; marketing can and should have the responsibility to
optimize the mix.

Order entry using planning bill of materials concepts tends to be more complex than
when the structure is end-item based. To accept a customer order, the available-to-promise
logic must be applied to each option in the order, meaning it's necessary to check each of
the affected modules. Figure 6.15 shows the flow for a particular customer order, in this
case for 25 Taylor 4-horsepower units in the gear option (T4G). The safety stocks are available for promising and will be maintained by the gross to net logic as additional MPS quantities are planned.

FIGURE 6.15

Available-to-Promise Logic with Modular Bill Architecture (order for 25 T4Gs)

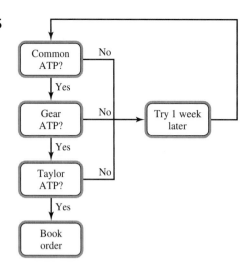

The Final Assembly Schedule

The final assembly schedule (FAS) states the exact set of end products to be built over some time period. It's the schedule that serves to plan and control final assembly and test operations; included are the launching of final assembly orders, picking of component parts, subassembly, painting or other finishing, scheduling the fabrication or purchase of any component items not under MPS control but needed for final assembly, and packing. In short, the FAS controls that portion of the business from fabricated components to completed products ready for shipment. It may be stated in terms of customer orders, end-product items, serial numbers, or special assembly order numbers.

Relation to the MPS

The master production schedule represents an anticipated build schedule. The FAS is the actual build schedule. The MPS disaggregates the production plan into end items, options, or groups of items, whereas the FAS is the last disaggregation—into exact end-item definitions. The distinction is that the MPS generally incorporates forecasts or estimates of actual customer orders in its preparation, with actual orders thereafter imperfectly consuming these forecasts; the FAS represents the last possible adjustment that can be made to the MPS; therefore, it's advisable to make that adjustment as late as possible. Any unsold items on the FAS will become part of the firm's finished-goods inventory.

The FAS is distinct and separate from the MPS. The distinction is most clearly seen in the assemble-to-order environment. There, the MPS is typically stated in super bills and options, whereas the FAS must be stated in terms of the exact end-item configurations. However, even in make-to-stock firms (such as Ethan Allen and Black & Decker), the MPS is stated in consolidated groups of items, such as all models of a table that differ only in finish, or all models of an electric drill that differ only in speed or gearing. In both cases, flexibility is so maintained that the final commitment to end items can be made as late as possible.

It's important to note that in make-to-stock firms a single-level bill of materials is typically maintained for each end item. This means that the conversion from MPS to FAS is simply the substitution of one end-item part number for another. Both are valid, and both explode to components in the same way. For some make-to-stock firms, the MPS is stated in terms of the most common or most complete end item. As actual sales information is received, other end items are substituted. This process continues until a time is reached when all final substitutions are made.

For assemble-to-order and make-to-order firms, end-item bills of materials are not maintained. If the FAS is stated in terms of customer orders, these orders must be translated into the equivalent of a single-level bill of materials; that is, these orders must lead to bill of materials explosion for order release, picking, and so on. This is easily accommodated if the customer order is stated in the same modules as the planning bill. For the tillers, this means that the customer order is stated in brand name, horsepower, and drive train terms.

Avoidance of firming up the FAS until the last possible moment means the time horizon for the FAS is only as long as dictated by the final assembly lead time (including document preparation and material release). Techniques that help to delay the FAS commitment include bill structuring, close coupling of order entry/promising systems, partial assembly, stocking subassemblies, and process/product designs with this objective.

The Hill-Rom FAS

The Hill-Rom Company, a division of Hillenbrand Industries, manufactures hospital furniture and other health-care equipment. One product, an over-bed table, comes in four different models, 10 alternative color high-pressure laminate tops, and four different options of chrome "boots" (to protect the base) and casters. The result is 160 (4 × 10 × 4) end-item possibilities. Let's examine a super bill approach to master production scheduling and final assembly scheduling in this environment.

Figure 6.16 shows a super bill of materials for this group of products. Manufacturing lead time for over-bed tables is 20 weeks, which means that the MPS must extend at least

FIGURE 6.16
Over-Bed Table
Super Bill

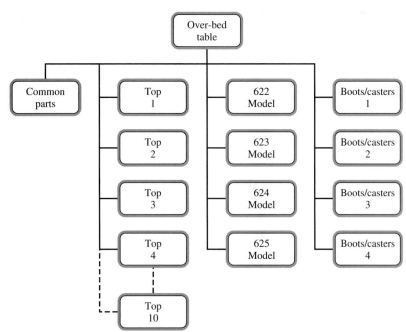

that far into the future. This means that an MPS time-phased record must be maintained over at least this time horizon for each of the 19 common part and option bills of materials shown in Figure 6.16.

The final assembly lead time for this product is four weeks. This involves part availability checking, order launching, component-part release, welding of subassemblies, snag grinding to smooth welded surfaces, degreasing, painting, subassembly, and final assembly.

Hill-Rom is basically an assemble-to-order company, but some finished-goods inventory is held. This means, for each of the 160 end-item over-bed tables, an on-hand balance record must be maintained. This is incorporated in a time-phased FAS record. The overall need is for 19 time-phased MPS records (1 for each option and the common parts) maintained for week 5 through at least week 20, plus 160 time-phased FAS records, maintained for each end item for weeks 1 through 4.

The FAS job is to convert MPS records into FAS records as we roll through time. This is done by the master production scheduler interacting with marketing, since the FAS represents the final culmination of the MPS process.

A related task is order promising, since customer orders may be promised out of the FAS system (on hand or in final assembly) or out of the MPS system (option by option, as done in Figure 6.15). Figures 6.17, 6.18, and 6.19 show this process. Figure 6.17 shows an FAS record for one of the 160 end items; it's maintained only for the length of the FAS lead time, four weeks. The record is for the 622 model, with "gunstock"-colored top, and 01B boots/caster combination; the finished-good item number, which identifies this configuration, is 17123-01B GUN.

FIGURE 6.17
FAS Record for 17123-01B GUN Table

Part No.	Item	FAS Lead Time	On Hand
7123-01B GUN	Over-bed Table	4	120

Week	1	2	3	4	
Orders	10			30	Before
Available	160	160	210	230	booking order
Available to promise	160		50	20	F 5264
FAS	50		50	50	

Week	1	2	3	4	
Orders	10		200	30	After
Available	160	160	10	30	booking order
Available to promise	10			20	F 5264
FAS	50		50	50	

MPS Pegging Detail				Actual Order Pegging Detail			
Week	Shop Order	Quantities	Action	Week	Quantity	Customer Order	Code
1	011	50		1	10	F 5117	F
3	027	50		3	200	F 5264	F
4	039	50		4	30	F 5193	F

FIGURE 6.18
MPS Record for Common Parts

Part No.	Item	MPS Lead Time						
1234	Common Parts	20						
Week		5	6	7	8	20	21	Before booking order
Forecast		75	75	75	75	75	75	
Orders		10						
Available		−15	210	235	160	125	50	
Available to promise		50	300	100				
MPS		50	300	100	0			
On hand = 10								

Week		5	6	7	8	20	21	After booking order
Forecast		75	75	75	75	75	75	
Orders		10	200					
Available		−15	85	110	35	0	−75	
Available to promise		50	100	100				
MPS		50	300	100				
On hand = 10								

FIGURE 6.19
Available-to-Promise Logic

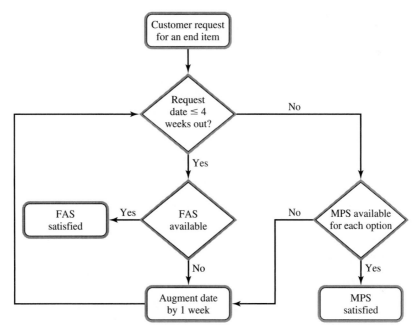

Note the record contains *only* orders (no forecasts), and they're used to compute the "Available" row. This convention recognizes that the FAS is finishing out products in a specific configuration. The 50 units that will be completed this week aren't subject to uncertainty. If no customer order is received for these, they'll go into stock; essentially, the company has written a "sales order."

Figure 6.17 also shows an order for 200 units being booked. The customer has requested shipment of the complete order as soon as possible. The available-to-promise (ATP) logic leads to putting the order into week 3, since only 160 units can be promised prior to week 3. This is shown in the "Before" and "After" sections of Figure 6.17. The bottom section gives supporting pegging data for the orders. Customer orders are pegged with an F code (satisfied from the FAS system).

Next we assume another customer order is received, requesting shipment in week 6. Since this is outside the FAS, it can be satisfied from MPS. Figure 6.18 shows the MPS record for the common-parts option. Note the MPS quantities are for common and option part numbers. Moreover, inventories for these options can exist, even though the physical inventory would be only a collection of parts. (The on-hand balance for common parts is 10.) The MPS option quantities can also be committed for final assembly of specific end items. When final assembly starts, it takes four weeks to finish out the end item. Figure 6.19 shows the ATP logic required to book any customer order in the Hill-Rom system.

The Master Production Scheduler

We turn now to the next topic in master production scheduling: Who's the master production scheduler, what does he or she do, and what's the appropriate job description? First, we briefly examine the use of some MRP concepts for the master scheduler.

The MPS as a Set of Firm Planned Orders

An interesting advantage of using standard MRP records to manage the master production schedule derives from the firm planned order concept. The firm planned order is similar to any planned order in that it explodes through product structures. However, it's *not* changed in either timing or amount as a result of MRP record processing. It's firm, and it can be changed only as the result of an action taken by a responsible person.

It's useful to think of the MPS as a set of firm planned orders. Thereafter, the master production scheduler's job is to convert planned orders to firm planned orders, and to *manage* the timing and amounts of the firm planned orders. The "available" row in the time-phased record provides the primary signal for performing this task. Standard MRP exception codes can provide indications of when and to what extent firm planned orders might not meet the needs.

Managing the timing and amounts of the firm planned orders means that any changes to the MPS have to be carefully evaluated in terms of their impact on material and capacity plans. The key need is to clearly understand trade-offs between customer needs and other MPC system objectives.

The Job

The master production scheduler has the primary responsibility for making any additions or changes to MPS records. He or she also has the primary responsibility for disaggregating the production plan to create the MPS and for ensuring that the sum of the detailed MPS production decisions matches the production plans. This involves analyzing trade-offs and telling top management about situations requiring decisions beyond the scheduler's authority level.

As part of the general feedback process, the master production scheduler should monitor actual performance against the MPS and production plan and distill operating results for higher management. The master production scheduler can also help in the analysis of what-if questions by analyzing the impact on the MPS of changes in plans.

The master production scheduler is often responsible for launching the final assembly schedule. This schedule represents the final commitment, taken as late as possible, to exact end items; that is, the final assembly schedule has to be based on specific finished-good items. Other master production scheduler activities include interface with order entry plus an ongoing relationship with production control to evaluate the feasibility of suggested changes.

Much of this activity involves resolving competing demands for limited capacity. Clearly, if several records for the master production schedule show a negative available at the end of the planning horizon, some trade-offs must be made. Not everything can be scheduled at once. Management of the firm planned orders must be done within capacity constraints. The available position indicates the priority for making those trade-offs. The lower the number of periods of supply or the larger the number of periods of backlog the available position shows, the more urgent the need. If too many are urgent, feedback to marketing may be necessary to change budgets.

Figure 6.20 shows the job description for the master production scheduler at Mitel Corporation. This formal job description makes it clear that the master production scheduler needs to constantly balance conflicting objectives and make trade-offs, especially between customer requirements and the need for stability in manufacturing. Moreover, there is a technical requirement to be able to use Fast-Man, the simulation software that Mitel uses to perform what-if analysis when extraordinary circumstances or opportunities are present. Such computer software can greatly aid the master production scheduler, but judgments will always be required.

Managing the MPS Database

For the master production scheduler to operate effectively, it's also critical that there be one single unified database for the MPS, that it links to the operations plan and to detailed material planning systems, and that clear responsibilities for all transactions be established. This involves not only the usual data integrity issues but also some organizational issues.

In the case of the MPS, many transactions occur in different functional areas. For example, receipts into finished goods may come from completed assemblies (production), shipments from order closing (marketing), or bills of lading (finance). It's critical that exact responsibilities be established for transaction processing, and that data linkages to MPS systems and files be rigorously defined and maintained.

Another critical database requirement for the MPS is proper control over both engineering and nonengineering changes to the bill of materials database. The MPS is often stated in planning bill units that may not be buildable (e.g., an average J-body car). This requires a more complex bill of materials or product structure database. The result is a greater need to procedurally control all changes to the bill of materials and to evaluate the impact of changes both from an engineering point of view and in terms of the effect on nonengineering bills of materials.

FIGURE 6.20 Mitel's Master Production Scheduler Job Description

A. Identifying Information

Job Title: *Master Scheduler*   Date: *February 17*
Department/Unit: *Planning & Administration*
Job Location: *Kanata, Ontario*

B. Job Purpose and Mandate

The incumbent of this position is responsible for the day to day management of the Master Production Schedule, as it relates to actioning unplanned forecast demand, forecast shortfalls, production and inventory changes, allowing accurate and up-to-date information which in turn drives material and capacity requirements and customer order dating. An advanced level of material planning and manufacturing process knowledge is required.

C. Organization Structure

The Master Production Scheduler reports to the Manager, Planning who reports to the Director, Planning and Administration.

D. Job Description

1. Specific Activities and Accountabilities:

- Responsible for the creation and continuous update of the master schedule that satisfies customer demand, maintains stability in terms of material and capacity requirements and minimizes RAW, WIP, and Finished Goods inventory levels by:
  • Managing day to day increases/decreases to the schedule through interface with Materials, Manufacturing, and Order Administration.
  • Working with Materials to ensure smooth E.C.O. transition into factory
  • Continuously monitor the impact of "Performance to Forecast" on inventory levels for the current month, and implement any necessary changes to the schedule; i.e. cut roll-over, increase availability through Fast-Man MRP tool.

- Act as a focal point between N.A. Order Administration, Manufacturing and Distribution to ensure configured system orders are:
  • Scheduled to meet customer cut-over requirements
  • Scheduled to meet manufacturing cell capacity.
  • Quoted and reviewed with manufacturing, initiating build and test.
  • Free of any discrepancies, with Order Administration notified to correct any problems.

- Continuously monitor problem inventory, taking advantage of any conversion opportunities, making recommendations for scrapping, or potential "Fire Sales."

- Assess the impact to capacity, inventory levels, purchase order activity and problem inventory levels that result from any proposed major change to the master schedule, utilizing the Fat-Man MRP tool.

2. Supervisory Responsibilities: Direct ( )   Indirect ( )

3. Key relationships (internal and external)
  • Internal and external auditors   • Traffic
  • Marketing   • Manufacturing
  • Order Administration   • Materials Planning
  • Distribution   • Product Management
  • All levels of management within Mitel

E. Job requirements
  • Superior product knowledge
  • 3-4 years progressive experience in materials or production control
  • Knowledge of internal Mitel processes and procedures
  • APICS Certification a definite asset
  • Knowledge gained through APICS Certification
  • Organizational and planning skills
  • Secondary education
  • High degree of initiative and personal motivation
  • Personal computer skills
  • Broad-based knowledge of supply/demand process

To support the master production scheduler, the time-phased MPS-record-oriented software system must produce the time-phased records to maintain the database, provide the linkages to other critical systems, provide MPS monitoring and exception messages, and provide for all MPS transactions. Included are entering of order quantities into the MPS, firm planned order treatment, removing MPS order quantities, changing the latter's timing or amount, converting MPS quantities to final assembly schedule (FAS) quantities, launching final assemblies, monitoring FAS scheduled receipts for timing or quantity changes, closing out FAS receipts into finished-goods inventory, and providing for all customer order entry pegging and promising activities.

Company Examples

We turn now to two actual MPS examples. First we'll show Ethan Allen's approach to master production scheduling. The approach uses a form of time-phased record. We'll see how standard MRP system approaches can be usefully applied and highlight aspects of the master production scheduler's job.

The second example illustrates how Jet Spray uses packaged software with an MPS module. The software incorporates available-to-promise logic and other features.

The Ethan Allen Master Production Schedule

The Ethan Allen Furniture Company produces case goods (wood furniture) in 14 geographically dispersed factories. Its total product line is 980 consolidated item numbers. (Different finishes for the same item make the number of end items about 50 percent larger.) Each consolidated item number is uniquely assigned to a particular assembly line or building station in one of the 14 factories. For each assembly line in each factory, a capacity is established in hours such that, if hours of capacity are fully utilized on all lines, overall company objectives as stated in its production plan will be met.

A forecast of demand is made for each consolidated item number, using statistical forecasting methods. A lot size for each item is also determined, based on economic order quantity concepts. For each assembly lot size, hours required on the assembly line are estimated. For each product, expected weekly priorities are established by dividing the expected beginning inventory by the weekly forecast. In weeks after the first, expected beginning inventory takes account of production and expected sales. The assembly line is loaded to capacity in priority sequence, smallest to largest. Figure 6.21 provides a simplified example for an assembly line with 35 hours of weekly capacity. The simplified example is based on only four products. Actual lines typically manufacture from 15 to 100 different items.

The top section of Figure 6.21 provides the basic data for each of the four products: the beginning inventory, weekly forecast of sales, lot size, and estimated hours to assemble one lot. Note that for product C, there's a beginning back order or oversold condition.

The middle portion of Figure 6.21 is the set of time-phased priority data. For product A in week 1, the beginning inventory of 20 is divided by the weekly forecast of 5, yielding a priority of 4; that is, at the beginning of week 1 there are four weeks of inventory for product A. Similar priority calculations are made for products B, C, and D in week 1.

The rule for assigning products to the assembly line is to first assign that product with the smallest priority—the most urgent need. Thus, product C is scheduled for production first. The assignment of product C to the assembly line in week 1 consumes all of the 35 hours of

FIGURE 6.21
Simplified
Ethan Allen
MPS Example

Basic Data:

Product	Beginning Inventory	Weekly Forecast	Lot Size	Hours Per Lot Size
A	20	5	50	20
B	50	40	250	80
C	−30	35	150	60
D	25	10	100	30

Priorities:

Product	P_1	P_2	P_3	P_4	P_5	P_6	P_7	P_8
A	4	3			0		−2	4.5
B	1.25	.25			3.5		1.5	.5
C	−.86	.64			−.57		.29	.71
D	2.5	1.5			−1.5		6.5	5.5

Schedule:

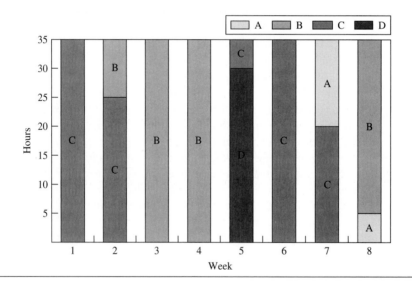

capacity in that week plus 25 hours in week 2. This is so since it takes 60 hours to assemble a batch of 150 of product C.

Moving to week 2, the expected beginning inventory for product A is 15, since forecast sales for week 1 is 5. Divide 15 by the weekly forecast (5) to get the expected priority for week 2 (15 ÷ 5 = 3). Alternatively, if four weeks of sales are in inventory at the beginning of week 1, we'd expect to have three weeks of sales at the beginning of week 2 if no production of product A takes place. This means, for each product not produced, its priority number in the succeeding week is reduced by 1. The expected priority for product C at the start of week 2 can be computed by finding 35/60 of 150, adding this to the beginning inventory of −30, subtracting 35 units of forecast demand for week 1, and dividing the result by the forecast of 35 to give a value of 0.64.

The lowest-priority product for week 2 is B (.25). Since a lot size of the product takes 80 hours, capacity is fully utilized until the end of week 4. This is why no priority data are given for weeks 3 and 4. A similar situation is true for week 6 when product C, started in week 5, uses the full week's capacity. By loading each line to its weekly capacity, no more and no less, the match between the production plan dictated for each assembly line and detailed MPS decision making is maintained. Calculations in subsequent weeks involve adding in any production and reducing inventories by expected sales. For example, product C's priority in week 5 can be calculated as follows:

$$
\begin{array}{ll}
\text{Beginning inventory} & = -30 \\
\text{Production} & = \underline{150} \\
& 120 \\
-4 \text{ weeks' sales at } 35 = & \underline{140} \\
& -20
\end{array}
$$

$$-20/35 = -.57$$

Figure 6.22 shows another way to create the Ethan Allen MPS. Here, the same four products are used. For each, a **time-phased order point (TPOP)** record is developed. The same schedule shown in the bottom portion of Figure 6.21 is achieved when the line is loaded to capacity in the sequence of when planned orders occur in the TPOP records; that is, product C has the first planned order, then B, then D, and so on. Of course, the planned order for D in week 3 isn't placed in week 3 because capacity isn't available until week 5. There's also a tie shown in week 8. Both products B and C have planned orders in that week. The tie-breaking decision could produce a schedule that differs slightly from that shown in Figure 6.21.

The great advantage to using TPOP approaches to developing the MPS is that specialized MPS software development is reduced. TPOP records are produced with standard MRP logic using the forecast quantities as gross requirements. The master production scheduler's job is to convert these planned orders to firm planned orders, so that capacity is properly utilized. At Ethan Allen, conversion of TPOP planned orders to firm planned orders is largely an automatic activity, so it has been computerized. Note, however, the objective is to load the assembly stations to their absolute capacity, in priority sequence. Other firms might use other criteria, such as favoring those jobs with high profitability, favoring certain customers, or allowing flexibility in the definition of capacity. If so, the master production scheduler's detailed decisions would be different.

Master Production Scheduling at Jet Spray

Jet Spray Corporation manufactures and sells dispensers for noncarbonated cold beverages and hot products (coffee and hot chocolate). Jet Spray uses an integrated on-line system encompassing MRP, capacity planning, shop-floor control, master production scheduling, inventory management, and other functions. The software package (Data 3) allows the user to designate part numbers as either being MRP or MPS; that is, MRP part numbers are driven by MPS numbers (but not the opposite). Bills of materials need to be designed accordingly (MPS part numbers are parents to MRP part numbers).

Any MPS part may also be designated as either a make-to-stock or make-to-order item. The distinction is that, when a shop order is created for a make-to-stock MPS item, the order is closed into finished-goods inventory. Subsequent shipment to a customer requires

FIGURE 6.22

Ethan Allen MPS Example Using Time-Phased Order Point

Week

		1	2	3	4	5	6	7	8	
Gross requirements		5	5	5	5	5	5	5	5	
Scheduled receipts										A
On hand	20	15	10	5	0	45	40	35	30	
Planned orders						50				

Week

		1	2	3	4	5	6	7	8	
Gross requirements		40	40	40	40	40	40	40	40	
Scheduled receipts			250							B
On hand	50	10	220	180	140	100	60	20	230	
Planned orders									250	

Week

		1	2	3	4	5	6	7	8	
Gross requirements		35	35	35	35	35	35	35	35	
Scheduled receipts										C
On hand	−30	85	50	15	130	95	60	25	140	
Planned orders		150			150				150	

Week

		1	2	3	4	5	6	7	8	
Gross requirements		10	10	10	10	10	10	10	10	
Scheduled receipts										D
On hand	25	15	5	95	85	75	65	55	45	
Planned orders				100						

another transaction to remove the items from finished goods into an area awaiting shipment. The inventory in turn is reduced by actual shipment. For a make-to-order item (which includes assemble-to-order), the shop order is driven by an actual customer order and is closed directly into the area awaiting shipment.

One of Jet Spray's best-known products is a two-product cold beverage dispenser, the Twin Jet 3 (TJ3), which is made to stock. Figure 6.23 is a portion of the basic MPS record for the TJ3. It shows the weeks of 11/17 through 1/12, but the system has data to support a one-year planning horizon. Notice that the available-to-promise rows are shown in the

FIGURE 6.23 Jet Spray Corporation Master Planning Schedule

PART NUMBER	DESCRIPTION	QUANTITY ON HAND	SAFETY STOCK	QUANTITY UNAVAIL	LEAD TIME	CUM L/T	FAM GRP	LOT HOR	PLN	TIME FENCE	MASTER SCHEDULE TYPE
S3568	TJ3 DOM. TWIN JET	279	0	21	0	92	TJ	5	001	50	MAKE TO STOCK

BEGIN DATE	11/17/	11/24/	12/01/	12/08/	12/15/	12/22/	12/29/	1/05/	1/12/
DAYS/PERIOD	7	7	7	7	7	7	7	7	7
FORECAST	28	63	147	147	147	146	146	181	181
ACTUAL DEMAND	9	26	8	5	4	4	963	4	1
PROJECTED BAL	240	402	680	830	1,116	1,112	374	493	312
TARGET INV BAL	0	0	0	0	0	0	0	0	0
AVAIL TO PROM	249	171						295	
CUMULATIVE ATP	249	420	420	420	420	420	420	715	715
MPS	0	225	286	155	290	0	225	300	0

format just described as well as in cumulative format. The cumulative date are always the sum of the prior period cumulative plus any ATP in the present period.

The available-to-promise for 11/17 is determined by taking the on-hand quantity (279), subtracting the unavailable (21), and thereafter subtracting the actual demand (9) in the week starting 11/17. The ATP for 11/24 requires looking all the way out to 12/29. In that week, an actual order for 963 completely consumes all MPS quantities for the month of December ($286 + 155 + 290 + 225 = 956$). Thus, 7 units from the MPS for 11/24 must be promised to the order in the week of 12/29. Additionally, the other actual demand quantities for December ($8 + 5 + 4 + 4 = 21$) and 11/24 (26) will have to be covered. Thus, the ATP for 11/24 is the MPS $(225) - 7 - 21 - 26 = 171$. The other ATP figures are relatively straightforward.

The projected balance row (available) for the record is based on a different convention than we've described. The forecast values shown are the *original* forecasts, whereas the software uses the *unconsumed* forecast plus the actual demand in decrementing the projected balance. The unconsumed forecast values are not shown in Figure 6.23. We'd argue for more transparency in the system, but in actual practice, absence of the unconsumed forecast data isn't a great problem. The system is on line, so this number can be obtained whenever it's needed.

The target inventory balance row in Figure 6.23 is worth explaining. The production plan for the TJ3 wasn't shown here. The actual production plan for the TJ3 is constantly monitored against the MPS. There are tolerances for inventory variations, and when projected inventory data exceed limits set by the production plan, this is where those differences are recorded.

This MPS software is an on-line system. Figure 6.23 is only one of several documents available to the master scheduler. Most of the master scheduler's work is supported with a video screen, not paper, and the MPS is reviewed on a daily basis.

Master Production Schedule Stability

A stable master production schedule translates into stable component schedules, which mean improved performance in plant operations. Too many changes in the MPS are costly in terms of reduced productivity. However, too few changes can lead to poor customer service levels and increased inventory. The objective is to strike a balance where stability is monitored and managed. The techniques most used to achieve MPS stability are firm planned order treatment for the MPS quantities, frozen time periods for the MPS, and time fencing to establish clear guidelines for the kinds of changes that can be made in various periods.

Ethan Allen Stability

Construction of the Ethan Allen MPS is based on TPOP records, with assembly lines loaded up to exact capacities, and the sequence of MPS items determined by the date sequence of planned orders. This process might seem to lead to a great deal of repositioning of MPS quantities; that is, as actual sales occur, forecast errors will tend to rearrange the MPS. In fact, this doesn't occur, because planned orders from TPOP records are "frozen," or firm planned, under certain conditions.

FIGURE 6.24
Ethan Allen
Firm Planned
Order
Approach

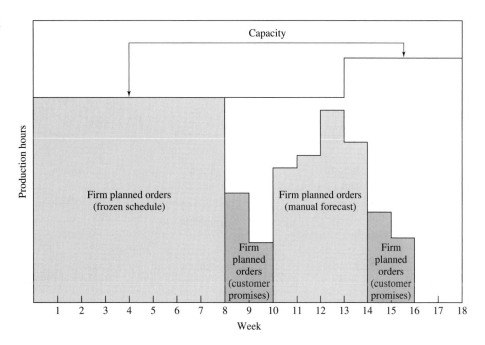

Ethan Allen uses three types of firm planned orders for the MPS, as Figure 6.24 shows. In essence, any firm planned order is frozen in that it won't be automatically repositioned by any computer logic. All MPS quantities for the next eight weeks are considered to be frozen or firm planned at Ethan Allen. In addition, any MPS quantity used to make a customer promise (i.e., a customer order is pegged to that MPS batch) is also a firm planned order. The third type of firm planned order used in Ethan Allen's MPS is for what the company calls the **manual forecast.** Included are contract sales (e.g., items to a motel chain), market specials (i.e., items to go on special promotion), and new items (MPS here being when the product is to be introduced). Finally, all blank space in Figure 6.24 is filled with the TPOP-based scheduling technique discussed earlier. Computerized MPS logic fills in the holes up to the capacity limit without disturbing any firm planned order.

Freezing and Time Fencing

Figure 6.24 shows the first eight weeks in the Ethan Allen MPS as **frozen.** This means *no* changes inside of eight weeks are possible. In reality, "no" may be a bit extreme. If the president dictates a change, it will probably happen, but such occurrences are rare at Ethan Allen.

Many firms don't like to use the term *frozen,* saying that anything is negotiable—but negotiations get tougher as we approach the present time. However, a frozen period provides a stable target for manufacturing to hit. It also removes most alibis for missing the schedule!

Time fencing is an extension of the freeze concept. Many firms set time fences that specify periods in which various types of change can be handled. A common practice, for example, is to have three time fences, say 8, 16, and 24 weeks. The marketing/logistics people could make any changes that they wanted beyond the 24-week fence as long as the sum of all MPS records is synchronized with the production plan. From weeks 16 to 24, substitutions of one end item for another would be permitted, provided required parts would be available and the production plan wasn't violated. From weeks 8 to 16, the MPS is quite rigid; but minor changes within the model series can be made if component parts are available. The period before 8 weeks is basically a freeze period similar to that of Ethan Allen, but occasional changes are made even within this period. In fact, assembly lines have been shut down to make changes—but it's so rare that everyone in the factory remembers when this happens! To achieve the productivity necessary to remain competitive, stability in short-range manufacturing plans is essential.

Two common fences are the **demand fence** and the **planning fence.** The demand fence is the shorter of the two. Inside the demand fence, the forecast is ignored in calculating the available. The theory is that customer orders—not the forecast—matter in the near term. The planning fence indicates the time at which the master production scheduler should be planning more MPS quantities. Within the demand fence it is very difficult to change the MPS. Between the demand fence and the planning fence, management trade-offs must be made to make changes; outside the planning fence, changes can be made by the master production scheduler. Some firms refer to these as the ice, slush, and water zones.

Managing the MPS

We turn now to managing the MPS: How do we measure, monitor, and control detailed day-to-day performance against the MPS? The first prerequisite for control is to have a realistic MPS. Most basic management textbooks say it's critical to hold people accountable only for performance levels that are attainable. This means the MPS can't be a wish list, and it shouldn't have any significant portion that's past due. In fact, we claim that the presence of a significant amount of past due is a major indication of a sick manufacturing planning and control system.

Stability and proper buffering are also important, because the objective is to remove all alibis and excuses for not attaining the performance for which the proper budget has been provided. Successful companies hit the production plan every month, and they do the best job possible to disaggregate the plan to reflect actual product mix in the MPS.

The Overstated MPS

Most authorities have warned that the MPS must not be overstated. To do so destroys the relative priorities developed by MRP and shop-floor control; more important, the overstated MPS erodes belief in the formal system, thereby reinstituting the informal system of hot lists and black books. Walter Goddard, a well-known MPS expert, no longer tells companies not to overstate the MPS, because at some point the temptation is overwhelming; he now tells them to learn from the experience so they won't do it again!

A key to not overstating the MPS is to always force the sum of the MPS to equal the production plan. Then, when someone wants to add something, the question is, "of what do you want less?" The company must give up what's referred to as *the standard manufacturing answer*. The standard manufacturing answer to whether more output of some product is possible is: "We don't know, but we'll try!"

The company *must* know. There should be an overall output budget for manufacturing. Capacity should be in place, and should match (not be more or less than) the budget. Manufacturing and marketing should work diligently to respond to product mix changes, but within the overall budgetary constraint. The correct response to whether more output of some product is possible is, "what else can be reduced?" If nothing, then the answer is either "No" or "The output budget and concomitant resources will have to be changed to increase capacities."

MPS Measures

There's an old Vermont story about the fellow who was asked: "How is your wife?" His answer: "Compared to what?" Likewise, measuring MPS has to be in concrete terms that reflect the firm's fundamental goals. This isn't as easy as it might seem. At one time, Ethan Allen evaluated each factory on the basis of dollar output per week. At one plant, an assembly line produced both plastic-topped tables and all-wood tables. Plastic-topped tables sold for more and could be assembled in roughly half the time, since the top was purchased as a completed subassembly. Obviously, the factory favored plastic-topped tables, even when inventories were high on those items and low on wood tables.

Ethan Allen had to change the measure for evaluating plant performance. Each line in each plant is now scheduled by the techniques we've described, and performance is based upon hitting the schedule.

Another important measure of MPS and other MPC system functions is customer service. In virtually every company, customer service is an area of concern. However, in many firms, a tight definition of precisely how the measure is to be made is lacking. Measurement is a critical step in control, and each firm will need to express how this important aspect of its operation is to be measured.

It's to be expected that whatever measure for customer service is chosen, the firm may have problems similar to those of Ethan Allen when evaluating plants using dollar output. However, the way to find the problems and thereafter eliminate them is, in fact, to start with *some* measure, no matter how crude, and evolve.

Appropriate measures vary a great deal from firm to firm, reflecting the type of market response typical in the industry and the particular company. Ethan Allen measures customer service in terms of hitting the order acknowledgment or promise dates. Jet Spray measures manufacturing performance against the MPS, as well as monthly performance in "equivalent units" of output versus the budget. The goal is a cumulative performance of at least 95 percent. Some assemble-to-order firms evaluate production against the production plan, which is to deliver a specific number of each model to marketing in the agreed upon time frame. They also evaluate customer service in terms of how long customers have to wait until they can get a specific end item. This indicates how well the sales and operations plan is being disaggregated.

Monitoring the MPS at Ethan Allen

Figure 6.24 shows Ethan Allen's planned order approach to its MPS. We also know that each plant is evaluated on hitting the MPS, so it should be useful to see how detailed monitoring takes place and how overall company operations have been affected.

FIGURE 6.25

Ethan Allen Summary MPS Performance

Source: W. L. Berry, T. E. Vollmann, and D. C. Whybark, *Master Production Scheduling: Principles and Practice* (Falls Church, Va.: American Production and Inventory Control Society, 1979), p. 54.

```
                                                    April 5,
To:  Bill Morrissey
From: Marty Stern

                     Production schedule review
                              4/1

Summary:
    Nine of the 14 factories operation hit their schedules 100 percent.
    Performance against schedule was poor this week at one of the factories:
    Boonville-75 percent
    Packed production was 196 million over total scheduled. 11 of the factories
    reporting met or exceeded their schedule.
    The outside suppliers produced 171 million under their schedule bringing total
    production to 25 million over scheduled goal.

cc:  Marshall Ames
     Barney Kvingedal
     Ray Dinkel
     Walter Blisky
     Andy Boscoe
     Steve Kammerer
     Tom Ericson
     Bob Schneble
     Hank Walker
```

Every Tuesday morning, Ethan Allen's vice president of manufacturing gets a report detailing each factory's performance in the prior week. Figure 6.25 shows this overall performance report. Figure 6.26 is the detail for one factory at Beecher Falls, Vermont.

Figure 6.25 shows one plant, Boonville, as having had poor performance. The last two comments about packed production and outside suppliers show total production achieved in these two categories.

The "STATION" column in Figure 6.26 shows the assembly lines; their capacities are stated in hours. The "PRIORITY" data reflect expected operating conditions 18 weeks in the future. If each priority number were 18, we'd expect the plant to exactly meet customer needs 18 weeks in the future. This particular factory will be seriously behind in terms of meeting anticipated customer demands. This is a question of capacity that's reflected in the comments about each station. For example, for the 06 station, the detail indicates 10 extra weeks of capacity are required to catch up. Note, however, lack of capacity doesn't mean the plant isn't meeting its schedule. All eight lines are reported as "no misses." This means, in the week covered by this report, the plant met its schedule exactly. Jobs in the schedule are being run. The schedule is loaded up to capacity—not in excess of capacity. Lack of adequate capacity means longer delivery times to customers, but not missed schedules.

By evaluating the reports in Figures 6.25 and 6.26, management can tell which plants are performing according to expectations. Life in the factories is much more calm with performance more clearly defined. No longer do salespeople, customers, marketing people, and executives call the factories. The interface between functions is reflected in the master production schedule, and each factory's job is to hit its MPS. In a sense, the entire master

FIGURE 6.26

Ethan Allen Detailed MPS Performance (for one factory)

SUMMARY OF SCHEDULE REVIEW

PLANT: <u>BEECHER FALLS</u>　　　　　　　　　　　　FROM:　　MARTY STERN

SCHEDULE DATE <u>3/27/78</u>
THRU WEEK OF　<u>8/28/78</u>

STATION	CAPACITY	PRIORITY	PROD. SCHED. DOLLARS	PRODUCTION GOAL
06-Cases	175.0	1	$240.1	232.0
07-C/Hutch	10.0	11	10.0	9.0
08-Hutch	15.0	14	17.9	19.0
20-Beds	60.0	1	85.7	84.0
21-Misc.	3.0	11	3.7	4.0
22-Bookstack	70.0	3	33.0	31.0
24-Desks	10.0	8	8.8	10.0
26-Mirrors	25.0	12	23.0	19.0
PLANT TOTAL			$422.2	408.0

Station 06 --- Cases: Other than misses caused by reporting date change (Canbury closed Good Friday) no misses. Items such as 10-4017, 4066, 4512P, 4522P, 11-5215, 5223 delayed 1 to 4 weeks. Nine items' service position improved. Some jobs outside frozen schedule should have been made "A" jobs and shifting would not have occurred. Priority down to 1 from 2. To schedule through priority 18 requires 10 weeks capacity, slightly higher than last months' 9 3/4 weeks.

Station 07 --- C/Hutch: No misses. Delayed 3 of 5 items on this line. Priority down to 11 from 14. 7 weeks capacity will schedule thru priority 18, up from 5 weeks.

Station 08 --- Hutch: No misses. Delayed 2 items, pulled 3 ahead. (Plant comments base the shift on purchase parts). Priority up to 14 from 3. To schedule thru priority 18 requires 3 weeks capacity, down from 6 weeks.

Station 20 --- No misses. Delayed the 11-5632-5. Pulled a number of beds ahead. Priority unchanged at 1. Eight weeks capacity, down from 10 3/4 weeks will schedule thru priority 18.

Station 21 --- Misc.: No misses. Some shifting but orders are O.K. Priority up from 10 to 11. Three weeks capacity, same as last month, will schedule thru priority 18.

Station 22 --- Bookstack: No misses. Built 1 assembly ahead. Priority up to 3 from 2. To schedule thru priority 18 requires 4 1/2 weeks capacity down from 6 weeks.

Station 24 --- Desks: No misses. Built 1 assembly ahead. Some shifting no delays. Priority up to 8 from 4. Three and one-half weeks capacity, down from 5 1/2 weeks, will schedule thru priority 18.

Station 26 --- No misses. Some shifting but ahead only. Priority up to 12 from 1. Two and three quarters weeks capacity, down from 8 weeks will schedule thru priority 18.

scheduling effort has enabled Ethan Allen to achieve centralized management of decentralized operations. Factory operations are geographically dispersed over wide areas, but those operations are carefully evaluated in the corporate offices. Execution responsibility and criteria are unambiguously defined for each plant.

One of the master production scheduling system's most important benefits for Ethan Allen is its upward compatibility; that is, the system is transparent and will work with 5 factories or 25 factories, with new ones easily added. Centralized coordination is maintained, and performance is very clear, with the result being an important tool to support orderly growth for the company. The company has roughly tripled in size since the start of the master production scheduling effort.

Concluding Principles

The master production schedule plays a key role in manufacturing planning and control systems. In this chapter, we've addressed what the MPS is, how it's done, and who does it. The following general principles emerge from this discussion:

- The MPS unit should reflect the company's approach to the business environment in which it operates.
- The MPS function should use the common ERP database if such a system is implemented in the firm.
- Common systems, time-phased processing, and MPS techniques facilitate effective scheduling regardless of the firm's environment.
- Customer order promising should be closely linked to the MPS.
- Available-to-promise information should be derived from the MPS and provided to the sales department.
- A final assembly schedule should be used to convert the anticipated build schedule into the final build schedule.
- The master production scheduler must keep the sum of the parts (the MPS) equal to the whole (the operations plan).
- The MPS activity and role of the master production scheduler must be clearly defined organizationally.
- The MPS can be usefully considered as a set of firm planned orders.
- The MPS should be evaluated with a formal performance measurement system.

References

Adenso-Diaz, B., and M. Laguna. "Modelling the Load Leveling Problem in Master Production Scheduling for MRP Systems," *International Journal of Production Research* 34 (1996), p. 483.

Campbell, G. M. "Establishing Safety Stocks for Master Production Schedules," *Production Planning and Control* 6 (1995), p. 404.

Chan, Joseph W. K., and N. D. Burns. "Benchmarking Manufacturing Planning and Control (MPC) Systems," *Benchmarking* 9, no. 3 (2002), pp. 256–277.

Chen, Chien-Yu; Zhenying Zhao; and Michael O Ball. "A Model for Batch Advanced Available-to-Promise," *Production and Operations Management* 11, no. 4 (winter 2002), p. 424.

Chu, S. C. K. "A Mathematical Programming Approach Towards Optimized Master Production Scheduling," *International Journal of Production Economics* 38 (1995), p. 269.

Davis, W. J.; A. Brook; and M. S. Lee. "A New Simulation Methodology for Master Production Scheduling," *1997 IEEE International Conference on Systems, Man, and Cybernetics* (1997), p. 1808.

Ebert, R. J., and T. S. Lee. "Production Loss Functions and Subjective Assessments of Forecast Errors: Untapped Sources for Effective Master Production Scheduling," *International Journal of Production Research* 33 (1995), p. 137.

Guerrero, Hector H., and Gary M. Kern. "How to More Effectively Accept and Refuse Orders," *Production & Inventory Management Journal* 29, no. 4 (1988), pp. 59–64.

Gundogar, E. "A Rule-Based Master Production Scheduling System for an Electro-Mechanical Manufacturing Company," *Production Planning and Control* 10 (1999), p. 486.

Hahn, Chan K.; Edward A Duplaga; and Kee Young Kim. "Production/Sales Interface: MPS at Hyundai Motor," *International Journal of Production Economics* 37, no. 1 (November 1994), p. 5.

Hill, J.; W. L. Berry; G. K. Leong; and D. Schilling. "Master Production Scheduling in Capacitated Sequence Dependent Process Industries," *International Journal of Production Research* 38, no. 18 (December 2000), p. 473.

Johnson, M. Eric, and Gary Scudder. "Supporting Quick Response Through Scheduling of Make-to-Stock Production/Inventory Systems," *Decision Sciences* 30, no. 2 (spring 1999), pp. 441–467.

Kadipasaoglu, Sukran N. "The Effect of Freezing the Master Production Schedule on Cost in Multilevel MRP Systems," *Production and Inventory Management Journal* 36, no. 3 (3rd quarter 1995), pp. 30–36.

Kern, Gary M., and Jerry C. Wei. "Master Production Rescheduling Policy in Capacity-Constrained Just-in-Time Make-to-Stock Environments," *Decision Sciences* 27, no. 2 (spring 1996), p. 365.

Kimms, A. "Stability Measures for Rolling Schedules with Applications to Capacity Expansion Planning, Master Production Scheduling, and Lot Sizing," *Omega* 26 (1998), p. 355.

Krajewski, L. J., and J. Wei. "Modeling MPS Policies for Supply-Chain Flexibility," *Proceedings of the First Asia-Pacific Decision Sciences Institute Conference,* 1996, p. 635.

Kulonda, Dennis J. "MRP in the Third World," *Production and Inventory Management Journal* (3rd quarter 2000).

Lin, N.-P., and L. J. Krajewski. "A Model for Master Production Scheduling in Uncertain Environments." *Decision Sciences* 23, no. 4 (fall 1992), pp. 839–861.

Ling, R. C., and W. E. Goddard. *Orchestrating Success.* New York: John Wiley & Sons, 1988.

Metters, R. D. "A Method for Achieving Better Customer Services, Lower Costs, and Less Instability in Master Production Schedules," *Production and Inventory Management* 34 (4th quarter 1993), pp. 61–65.

Metters, R., and V. Vargas. "A Comparison of Production Scheduling Policies on Costs, Service Level, and Schedule Changes," *Production and Operations Management* 8, no. 1 (spring 1999), pp. 76–91.

Proud, John F. *Master Scheduling: A Practical Guide to Competitive Manufacturing,* 2nd ed. New York: John Wiley & Sons, July 1999.

Spencer, M. S., and J. F. Cox, III. "Master Production Scheduling Development in a Theory of Constraints Environment," *Production and Inventory Management Journal* 36 (1995), p. 8.

Sridharan, V., and W. L. Berry. "Freezing the Master Production Schedule Under Demand Uncertainty," *Decision Sciences* 21, no. 1 (winter 1990), pp. 97–120.

Taylor, Sam G., and Gerhard J. Plenert. "Finite Capacity Promising," *Production and Inventory Management Journal* (3rd quarter 1999).

Vargas, V., and R. A., Metters. "A Master Production Scheduling Procedure for Stochastic Demand," *Proceedings,* Decision Sciences Institute 28th Annual Meeting, 1997, p. 1239.

Verganti, R. "Order Overplanning with Uncertain Lumpy Demand: A Simplified Theory," *International Journal of Production Research* 35 (1997), p. 3220.

Wacker, John G. "Configure-to-Order Planning Bills of Material: Simplifying a Complex Product Structure for Manufacturing Planning and Control," *Production and Inventory Management Journal* 41, no. 2 (2nd quarter 2000), p. 21.

Wallace, T. F., and R. A. Stahl. *Master Scheduling in the 21st Century.* Cincinnati: T. F. Wallace and Co., 2003.

Wright, Nevan. "Master Scheduling," *International Journal of Operations & Production Management* 15, no. 12 (1995), p. 99.

Xiande, Zhao, and Lam Kokin. "Lot-sizing Rules and Freezing the Master Production Schedule in Material Requirements Planning Systems," *International Journal of Production Economics* 53 (1997), p. 281.

Xie, Jinxing; Xiande Zhao; and T. S. Lee. "Freezing the Master Production Schedule Under Single Resource Constraint and Demand Uncertainty," *International Journal of Production Economics* 83, no. 1 (Jan. 25, 2003), pp. 65–84.

Yang, K. K., and F. Robert Jacobs. "Replanning the Master Production Schedule for a Capacity-Constrained Job Shop," *Decision Sciences Journal* 30, no. 3 (summer 1999), pp. 719–748.

Zhao, Xiande; Jinxing Xie; and Qiyuan Jiang. "Lot-sizing Rule and Freezing the Master Production Schedule under Capacity Constraint and Deterministic Demand," *Production and Operations Management* 10, no. 1 (spring 2001), pp. 45–67.

Discussion Questions

1. Why does the text stress that the master production schedule is *not* a forecast?

2. Some companies try to increase output simply by increasing the MPS. Discuss this approach.

3. What do you feel would be the key functions of the MPS in each of the following three environments: make-to-stock, make-to-order, and assemble-to-order?

4. What are the similarities and differences in "rolling through time" for MPS and MRP?

5. Much of the order-promising logic is directed at telling customers when they can honestly expect delivery. Several firms, on the other hand, simply promise their customers delivery within X weeks (often an unrealistic claim) and then deliver when they can. Contrast these two approaches.

6. One characterization of the available-to-promise record is that the "Available" row is for the master scheduler and the "Available-to-promise" row is for customers. What's meant by this contention?

7. Explain how determining the "Available" row with the "greater of forecast or orders" logic can overstate required production.

8. Many companies have come to view their master production schedulers as key people in profitably meeting the firm's strategic goals. Would you agree? What qualities would you look for in a master production scheduler?

9. Ethan Allen's approach to master production scheduling puts capacity into a primary position instead of a secondary consideration. What does this statement mean?

10. Discuss the relationship between stability and firm planned orders.

Problems

1. Excelsior Springs, Ltd., schedules production of one end product, Hi-Sulphur, in batches of 80 units whenever the projected ending inventory balance in a quarter falls below 10 units. It takes one quarter to make a batch of 80 units. Excelsior currently has 30 units on hand. The sales forecast for the next four quarters is:

	Quarter			
	1	2	3	4
Forecast	20	70	70	20

a. Prepare a time-phased MPS record showing the sales forecast and MPS for Hi-Sulphur.

b. What are the inventory balances at the end of each quarter?

c. During the first quarter, no units were sold. The revised forecast for the rest of the year is:

	Quarter		
	2	3	4
Forecast	30	50	70

How does the MPS change?

2. Neptune Manufacturing Company's production manager wants a master production schedule covering next year's business. The company produces a complete line of small fishing boats for both saltwater and freshwater use and manufactures most of the component parts used in assembling the products. The firm uses MRP to coordinate production schedules of the component part manufacturing and assembly operations. The production manager has just received the following sales forecast for next year from the marketing division:

Product Lines	Sales Forecast (Standard Boats for Each Series)			
	1st Quarter	2nd Quarter	3rd Quarter	4th Quarter
FunRay series	8,000	9,000	6,000	6,000
SunRay series	4,000	5,000	2,000	2,000
StingRay series	9,000	10,000	6,000	7,000
Total	21,000	24,000	14,000	15,000

The sales forecast is stated in terms of "standard boats," reflecting total sales volume for each of the firm's three major product lines.

Another item of information supplied by the marketing department is the target ending inventory position for each product line. The marketing department would like the production manager to plan on having the following number of standard boats on hand at the end of each quarter of next year:

Product Line	Quarterly Target Ending Inventory (in Standard Boats)
FunRay series	3,000 boats
SunRay series	1,000 boats
StingRay series	3,000 boats

The inventory position for each product is:

Product Line	Current Inventory Level (in Standard Boats)
FunRay series	15,000 boats
SunRay series	3,000 boats
StingRay series	5,000 boats

The master production schedule is to specify the number of boats (in standard units) to be produced for each product line in each quarter of next year on the firm's single assembly line. The assembly line can produce up to 15,000 standard boats per quarter (250 boats per day during the 60 days in a quarter).

Two additional factors are taken into account by the production manager in preparing the master production schedule: the assembly line changeover cost and the inventory carrying cost for the finished goods inventory. Each assembly line changeover costs $5,000, reflecting material handling costs of changing the stocking of component parts on the line, adjusting the layout, and so on. After some discussion with the company comptroller, the production manager concluded that the firm's inventory carrying cost is 10 percent of standard boat cost per year. The item value for each of the product line standard units is:

Product Line	Standard Boat Cost
FunRay series	$100
SunRay series	150
StingRay series	200

The master production scheduler has calculated the production lot sizes as 5,000, 3,000, and 4,000 units, respectively.

a. Develop a master production schedule for next year, by quarter, for each of Neptune's fishing boat lines. Identify any problems.

b. Verify the lot size calculations using the EOQ formula.

3. The Zoro Manufacturing Company has a plant in Murphysboro, Georgia. Product A is shipped from the firm's plant warehouse in Murphysboro to satisfy East Coast demand. Currently, the sales forecast for product A at the Murphysboro plant is 30 units per week.

The master production scheduler at Murphysboro considers product A to be a make-to-stock item for master scheduling purposes. Currently, 50 units of product A are on hand in the Murphysboro plant warehouse. Desired safety stock level is 10 units for this product. Product A is produced on a lot-for-lot basis. Currently, an order for 30 units is being produced and is due for delivery to the plant warehouse on Monday, one week from today.

The master production scheduler has heard that an MRP record that uses the forecast for gross requirements and has a lead time of zero can be used for master production scheduling. Complete the following MRP record. How can this be used for master production scheduling?

	Week					
Product A	1	2	3	4	5	6
Gross requirements						
Scheduled receipts						
Projected available balance						
Planned order release						

Q = lot for lot; LT = 0; SS = 10.

4. The MPS planner at Murphy Motors uses MPS time-phased records for planning end-item production. The planner is currently working on a schedule for the P24, one of Murphy's top-selling motors. The planner uses a production lot size of 70 and a safety stock of 5 for the P24 motor.

	Week							
Item: P24	1	2	3	4	5	6	7	8
Forecast	30	30	30	40	40	40	45	45
Orders	13	8	4					
Available								
Available to promise								
MPS								

On hand = 20.

a. Complete the MPS time-phased record for product P24.

b. Can Murphy accept the following orders? Update the MPS time-phased record for accepted orders.

Order	Amount	Desired Week
1	40	4
2	30	6
3	30	2
4	25	3

5. The Spencer Optics Company produces an inexpensive line of sunglasses. The manufacturing process consists of assembling two plastic lenses (produced by the firm's plastic molding department) into a finished frame (purchased from an outside supplier). The company is interested in using material requirements planning to schedule its operations and has asked you to prepare an example to illustrate the technique.

The firm's sales manager has prepared a 10-week sales forecast for one of the more popular sunglasses (the Classic model) for your example. The forecast is 100 orders per week. Spencer has customer orders of 110 units, 80 units, 50 units, and 20 units in weeks 1, 2, 3, and 4, respectively. The sunglasses are assembled in batches of 300. Presently, three such batches are scheduled: one in week 2, one in week 5, and one in week 8.

a. Complete the following time-phased record:

					Week					
Classic Model MPS Record	1	2	3	4	5	6	7	8	9	10
Forecast										
Orders										
Available										
Available to promise										
MPS										

On hand = 140.

b. Prepare the MRP record for the assembly of the sunglasses using the following record. The final assembly quantity is 300, lead time is 2 weeks, and there's a scheduled receipt in week 2. Note that no inventory is shown for the assembled sunglasses in this record, since it's accounted for in the MPS record.

						Week					
		1	2	3	4	5	6	7	8	9	10
Gross requirements											
Scheduled receipts			300								
Projected available balance	0										
Planned order release											

Q = 300; LT = 2; SS = 0.

6. Nino Spirelli has constructed the following (partial) time-phased MPS record:

	Week					
	1	2	3	4	5	6
Forecast	20	30	20	30	20	30
Orders	14	8	6			
Available						
Available to promise						
MPS	50		50		50	50

On hand = 5.

a. Complete the record.
b. Are there any problems?
c. What's the earliest Nino can promise an order for 44 units?
d. Assume that an order for 15 is booked for week 4. Assume the order for 44 units in part c is not booked; recompute the record.

7. The Cedar River Manufacturing Company produces a line of furnishings for motels and hotels. Among the items manufactured is an Executive water pitcher with the following product structure:

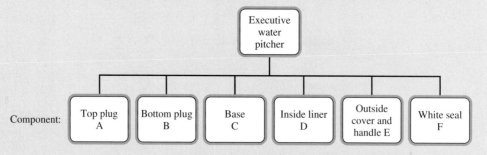

Component items A, B, C, and F are manufactured by the plastic molding shop; components D and E are purchased from a vendor. The Executive water pitcher is completed by the final assembly department.

Currently the following open shop orders for Executive water pitcher components are waiting to be processed at the #101 injection molding press in the plastic molding shop:

Plastic Molding Shop-Floor Control Report

Shop Order Number	Component Item	Order Quantity	Order Due Date	Molding Machine Time (Weeks)
10-XYZ	F	15	ASAP*	2
10-XXX	B	25	ASAP*	2
10-XZV	A	30	ASAP*	1
10-XXY	C	20	ASAP*	2

*As soon as possible.

All the orders shown have their last operation at the #101 injection molding press and are subsequently ready for the final assembly department. (Final assembly time is negligible.)

a. Given the preceding information, complete the MPS and MRP records for all of the Executive water pitcher items.

MPS Record: Executive Water Pitcher

	Week						
	1	2	3	4	5	6	7
Forecast	10	10	10	10	10	10	10
Orders	12	5	2				
Available							
Available to promise							
MPS							

On hand = 15.
MPS lot size = 20.

MRP Records

Component A		Week						
		1	2	3	4	5	6	7
Gross requirements								
Scheduled receipts		30						
Projected available balance	12							
Planned order releases								

Q = 30; LT = 5; SS = 0.

Component B		Week						
		1	2	3	4	5	6	7
Gross requirements								
Scheduled receipts		25						
Projected available balance	22							
Planned order releases								

Q = 25; LT = 5; SS = 0.

		Week						
Component C		1	2	3	4	5	6	7
Gross requirements								
Scheduled receipts		20						
Projected available balance	45							
Planned order releases								

Q = 20; LT = 5; SS = 0.

		Week						
Component F		1	2	3	4	5	6	7
Gross requirements								
Scheduled receipts		15						
Projected available balance	70							
Planned order releases								

Q = 15; LT = 5; SS = 0.

b. What conclusions can you make regarding the validity of the current order due dates for the open shop orders at the #101 injection molding press?

8. Georgia Clay and Gravel was updating the MPS record for one of its products, Smell Fresh Cat Litter.

a. Complete the following MPS time-phased record.

	Week							
Item: Smell Fresh	1	2	3	4	5	6	7	8
Forecast	20	20	20	30	30	30	30	30
Orders	5	3	2					
Available	50	30	10	30	50	20	40	10
Available to promise								
MPS	50			50	50		50	

On hand = 20; MPS Lot Size = 50.

The following events occurred during week 1:
- Actual demand during week 1 was 25 units.
- Marketing forecasted that 40 units would be needed for week 9.
- An order for 10 in week 2 was accepted.
- An order for 20 in week 4 was accepted.

- An order for 6 in week 3 was accepted.
- The MPS in week 1 was produced as planned.

b. Update the record below after rolling through time.

Item: Smell Fresh	Week							
	2	3	4	5	6	7	8	9
Forecast								
Orders								
Available								
Available to promise								
MPS								

On hand =   , MPS Lot Size = 50.

9. The following data have been prepared for master production scheduling purposes at the Pike's Peak Mountain Bike Company:

End Product	Beginning Inventory	Weekly Forecast	Lot Size	Hours Per Lot Size
A	60	10	30	30
B	20	5	20	20
C	30	15	50	50

(Current capacity = 40 hours per week).

a. Prepare the master production schedule for these items during the next four weeks using the Ethan Allen master production scheduling method.

b. Should the Pike's Peak Mountain Bike Company increase or decrease the capacity of the final assembly line? Justify your answer.

c. Suppose that the Pike's Peak master production schedule is frozen for the next three weeks. What specific impact would the policy have on the firm's performance?

10. Figure 6.21, the Ethan Allen example, is based on the following data:

Product	Beginning Inventory	Weekly Forecast	Lot Size	Hours Per Lot Size
A	20	5	50	20
B	50	40	250	80
C	−30	35	150	60
D	25	10	100	30

Priorities are calculated by dividing expected beginning inventory by forecast. In weeks after the first week, expected beginning inventory takes account of production and expected sales.

a. Calculate weekly priorities and determine the master production schedule for weeks 1 through 8 for these data. Check your answers against Figure 6.21.

b. Assume the actual sales in week 1 were as follows:

Product	Sales
A	10
B	30
C	25
D	25

Given these actual sales data, calculate the weekly priorities and determine the MPS for weeks 2 through 9, assuming the forecasts remain unchanged. What impact do these changes have?

c. Given the actual sales data in part b, calculate the priorities for weeks 7, 8, and 9. Determine the MPS for weeks 2 through 9, assuming the forecasts remain unchanged and weeks 2 through 6 are frozen; that is, the schedule in part a can be revised, but only from week 7 on. What impact would the frozen schedule have on the inventory and customer service levels for products A through D?

d. Assume that the time horizon date is extended to 18 weeks resulting in the following scheduling priorities for week 18:

Product	Priority
A	2
B	1.25
C	−1
D	1

Hours	Assembly Load (Week 18)
35	
30	
25	C
20	
15	
10	
5	B
0	

What capacity information can be inferred from this schedule?

11. The master production scheduler at the XYZ Company is concerned with determining the impact of using different MPS freezing intervals on component part shortages and inventory levels in the firm's fabrication shop. Currently, the firm's end products are produced on a make-to-stock basis. A four-period MPS planning horizon is used. Lot sizing is performed at the start of every period covering all four future periods. Assembly orders are issued at the start of each period. The assembly lead time equals zero periods; the beginning finished product inventory is zero.

TABLE A

Period	1	2	3	4
Forecast*	177	261	207	309
Available†	261	0	309	0
MPS	438	0	516	0

Period	2	3	4	5
Forecast	0	207	309	64
Available	0	373	64	0
MPS	0	580	0	0

Period	3	4	5	6
Forecast	207	309	64	182
Available	0	246	182	0
MPS	207	555	0	0

TABLE B

Period	1	2	3	4
Forecast*	177	261	207	309
Available†	261	0	309	0
MPS	438	0	516	0

Period	2	3	4	5
Forecast	0	207	309	64
Available	0	373	64	0
MPS	0	580	0	0

Period	3	4	5	6
Forecast	207	309	64	182
Available	373	64	0	0
MPS	580	0	0	182

*The forecast is net of beginning inventory.
†The available is the closing inventory balance.

Table A shows the forecast, projected inventory, and MPS for three consecutive periods for one of the firm's products, using the current freeze policy of one period and assuming perfect forecasts. Table B provides similar information using a two-period MPS freeze policy. Assuming the component part 1234 is used only on this end product, with a usage rate of one unit per unit of end product, prepare MRP records for this part as of the beginning of each of the three consecutive periods under both MPS freezing policies. Assume that component part 1234 has a planned lead time of two periods, that its lot size is the net requirement for the next two periods whenever a net requirement is observed, that it has zero safety stock and a beginning inventory of 450 units in period 1, and that there are no scheduled receipts.

a. What conclusions can you draw about the two different freezing policies' effectiveness?

b. What other freezing policies should be considered?

c. What are the appropriate time fences?

12. Falcon Sports Inc. makes a line of Jet Skis. There are eight different end items (catalog numbers) in the Jet Ski product line. The skis vary according to horsepower, seating capacity, and

starting mechanism. The company expects to sell one-half of the Jet Skis in the 12-horsepower model and one-half in the 10-horsepower model. The seating capacity breaks down to 60% for dual seating and 40% for single seating. The breakdown for starters is 25% manual and 75% automatic.

Catalog number	2100	2101	1100	1101	2120	2121	1120	1121
Horsepower	10	10	10	10	12	12	12	12
Seating style	Dual	Dual	Single	Single	Dual	Dual	Single	Single
Starter	Manual	Auto	Manual	Auto	Manual	Auto	Manual	Auto
Component parts	602	602	602	602	601	601	601	601
	350	350	360	360	350	350	360	360
	400	400	400	400	400	400	400	400
	235	230	235	230	235	230	235	230
	320	320	315	315	320	320	315	315
	600	600	600	600	600	600	600	600
	250	254	250	254	250	254	250	254
	410	410	410	410	610	610	610	610

   a. Group the component parts. Which are common? Which are associated with horsepower? Seating style? Starter?

   b. Create a super bill for Jet Skis matching the appropriate components with each option (include the usage percentages).

   c. What are the advantages and disadvantages of the super bill approach to planning?

13. The Ace Electronics Company produces printed circuit boards on a make-to-order basis.

   a. Prepare an MPS record for one of its items (catalogue #2400), including the available-to-promise information, using the following data:

      Final assembly production lead time = 2 weeks.
      Weekly forecast = 100 units.
      Current on-hand quantity = 0.
      Booked customer orders (already confirmed):
         95 units in week 1.
         105 units in week 2.
         70 units in week 3.
         10 units in week 5.

      Master production schedule:
         200 units to be completed at the start of week 1.
         200 units to be completed at the start of week 3.
         200 units to be completed at the start of week 5.
         200 units to be completed at the start of week 7.

   b. Suppose the cumulative lead time for the item (catalogue #2400) is eight weeks. What decision must the master scheduler make this week?

14. Brandy Boards produces circuit boards on a make-to-order basis. The company is currently planning production for one of its boards, the Sound Xapper. It has a weekly forecast of 50 boards, current inventory of 70 boards, and uses an MPS quantity of 150. MPS and order information for

the next seven weeks are given below:

Current Booked Orders		Master Production Schedule	
Week	Quantity	Week	Quantity
1	60	2	150
2	70	5	150
3	20		
4	70		
5	40		
6	30		

a. Prepare an MPS record for the Sound Xapper for the next seven weeks, including available-to-promise information.

b. Suppose the planning time fence is six weeks; what decision should the master scheduler make this week?

c. Sales received the following customer requests at the start of week 1. Using the information in the MPS record completed in part a, indicate to Sales which delivery commitments can be made to the customers.

Possible New Orders	
Week	Quantity
1	5
3	10
6	20

15. The Parker Corporation produces and sells a machine for tending golf course greens. The patented device trims the grass, aerates the turf, and injects a metered amount of nitrogen into the soil. Machines are marketed through the Taylor Golf Course Supply Company, under the Parker Company's own original equipment brand, and, recently, through a lawn and garden supply house (Brown Thumb), which serves both commercial and consumer accounts. Addition of the lawn and garden outlet and requests to add a 3-HP version have called into question the production planning and control process for the machines.

Forecasting the products to be produced is difficult. There are now two drive mechanisms (chain and gear), three different body styles (one for each outlet), and two sizes of engine (4- and 5-HP). This gives a total of 12 end items, all of which had some demand. (See Exhibit A.) The 3-HP motor would add six more end items. Forecasting demand for these new items would add to the difficulty of forecasting demand.

Lead times for some of the castings and for 5-HP motors have increased to the extent that it's not possible to wait until firm orders are received for the end items before the castings and motors have to be ordered. In addition, the firm's business is growing; it anticipates selling about 120 units next year. Consequently, the production manager has arranged to purchase enough material for 10 units per month. There's plenty of capacity for the small amount of parts fabrication required, but assembly capacity must be carefully planned. The current plan calls for assembly capacity of 10 units per month.

EXHIBIT A
Last Year's
Sales by
Catalog
Number

Catalog Number			Sales	Key
Body	Horsepower*	Drive	Total = 100	
T	4	C	1	
T	4	G	4	Body:
T	5	C	18	T = Taylor Supply
T	5	G	17	O = "OEM" Parker's
O	4	C	13	own
O	4	G	9	B = Brown Thumb
O	5	C	10	
O	5	G	8	
B	4	C	6	Drive
B	4	G	7	C = Chain
B	5	C	2	G = Gear
B	5	G	5	

*Note: The 3-HP machine would be offered in all three body styles and both drives.

With regard to the specific issue of forecasting, the marketing manager summarized the data on the sales of each end item over the past year. (See Exhibit A.) He felt that a 20 percent growth in total volume was about right, and that 3-HP machines will perhaps account for half that growth. Of course, once the forecasts were made, the production manager had to determine which motors and castings (gear or chain) to order. Each machine was made up of many common parts, but the motors, chain or gear drive subassemblies, and bodies were different (though interchangeable).

a. Suggest an improved method of forecasting demand for the firm's products.

b. As the production manager contemplated the difficulty of forecasting demand for the firm's products and determining exactly what to schedule into final assembly, two customers called. The first, from Taylor, wanted to know when the company could deliver a model T3G; the second wanted as early delivery as possible of one of Parker's own machines, an O4C. The Taylor representative said he felt that the three-horsepower models might "really take off."

Before making any commitment at all, it was necessary to check the material availability and get back to the two customers. It was the firm's practice not to promise immediate delivery, since units scheduled for final assembly were usually already promised. The planned assembly schedule called for assembly of three units next week, two units the following week, and alternating three and two thereafter. As a matter of practice, all parts for assembly and delivery in any week would need to be ready at the start of that week.

Exhibit B shows current inventory and on-order positions for the common part "kit," the motors, and the drives. (The production manager didn't concern himself with the body styles since all three styles can be obtained in a week.) Exhibit C lists all booked orders promised for delivery over the next few weeks. Organize this information to respond to the delivery promise requests. (Assume that no safety stocks are held.) What should the delivery promises be?

EXHIBIT B
Inventories and
On-Order

Item	Inventory	On Order in:	Due Date	Lot size
Common "kit"	0	5 each in:	weeks 1,3,5,7,9	5
5-HP motor	10	5 in:	week 5	5
4-HP motor	3	5 in:	weeks 3, 8	5
3-HP motor	0	5 in:	week 1	5
Chain drive	14	—	—	10
Gear drive	6	10 in:	week 3	10

EXHIBIT C
Booked Orders
and Delivery
Dates

		Delivery Week					
		1	2	3	4	5	6
Models		2T4G*	1B3G	1T5C	1O5G	1T5G	1O4G
		1O5C	1T4C	1B4C			
			1O4G				
	Total	3	3	2	1	1	1

*2 units of T4G.

7

Material Requirements Planning

This chapter deals with material requirements planning (MRP), a basic tool for performing the detailed material planning function in the manufacture of component parts and their assembly into finished items. MRP is used by many companies that have invested in batch production processes. MRP's managerial objective is to provide "the right part at the right time" to meet the schedules for completed products. To do this, MRP provides *formal* plans for each part number, whether raw material, component, or finished good. Accomplishing these plans without excess inventory, overtime, labor, or other resources is also important.

Chapter 7 is organized around the following five topics:

- *Material requirements planning in manufacturing planning and control:* Where does MRP fit in the overall MPC system framework and how is it related to other MPC modules?
- *Record processing:* What is the basic MRP record and how is it produced?
- *Technical issues:* What additional technical details and supporting systems should you recognize?
- *Using the MRP system:* Who uses the system, how is it used, and how is the exact match between MRP records and physical reality maintained?
- *System dynamics:* How does MRP reflect changing conditions, and why must transactions be processed properly?

MRP's relationship to other manufacturing planning and control (MPC) concepts is shown in Chapter 1. Many just-in-time (JIT) concepts have emerged as basic approaches for designing MPC systems in some companies. These concepts are discussed in Chapter 8. Advanced MRP techniques are presented in Chapter 14.

Material Requirements Planning in Manufacturing Planning and Control

For companies assembling end items from components produced in batch manufacturing processes, MRP is central to the development of detailed plans for part needs. It is often where companies start in developing their MPC systems. Facility with time-phased planning and the associated time-phased records is basic to understanding many other aspects of the MPC system. Finally, although introduction of JIT and investments in lean manufacturing processes have brought about fundamental changes in detailed material planning for some firms, companies continue to adapt the MRP approach or enhance their existing systems.

For firms using MRP, the general MPC framework depicted in Figure 7.1 shows that detailed requirements planning is characterized by the use of time-phased (period-by-period) requirement records. Several other supporting activities are shown in the front end, engine, and back end of the system as well. The front end of the MPC system produces the master production schedule (MPS). The back end, or execution system, deals with production scheduling and control of the factory and with managing materials coming from vendor plants.

FIGURE 7.1
Manufacturing Planning and Control System

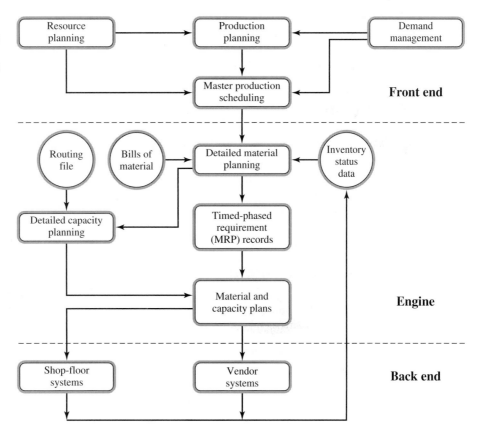

The detailed material planning function represents a central system in the engine portion of Figure 7.1. For firms preparing detailed material plans using MRP, this means taking a time-phased set of master production schedule requirements and producing a resultant time-phased set of component parts and raw material requirements.

In addition to master production schedule inputs, MRP requires two other basic inputs. A bill of material shows, for each part number, what other part numbers are required as direct components. For example, for a car, it could show five wheels required (four plus the spare). For each wheel, the bill of materials could be a hub, tire, valve stem, and so on. The second basic input to MRP is inventory status. To know how many wheels to make for a given number of cars, we must know how many are on hand, how many of those are already allocated to existing needs, and how many have already been ordered.

The MRP data make it possible to construct a time-phased requirement record for any part number. The data can also be used as input to the detailed capacity planning models. Developing material and capacity plans is an iterative process where the planning is carried out level by level. For example, planning for a car would determine requirements for wheels, which in turn determines requirements for tires, and so on. But planning for tires has to be done *after* the planning for wheels; if the company wants to build 10 cars (50 wheels) and has 15 complete wheels on hand, it only needs 35 more—and 35 tires. If 20 wheels have already been ordered, only 15 more must be made to complete the 10 cars.

An MRP system serves a central role in material planning and control. It translates the overall plans for production into the detailed individual steps necessary to accomplish those plans. It provides information for developing capacity plans, and it links to the systems that actually get the production accomplished.

Record Processing

In this section, we present the MRP procedures starting with the basic MRP record, its terminology, timing conventions, and construction. We then turn to an example illustrating coordination of planning component parts and end items. We examine several aspects of this coordination and the relationships that must be accounted for. We then look at linking MRP records to reflect all the required relationships. We intend to show clearly how each MRP record can be managed independently while the *system* keeps them coordinated.

The Basic MRP Record

At the heart of the MPC system is a universal representation of the status and plans for any single item (part number), whether raw material, component part, or finished good: the MRP time-phased record. Figure 7.2 displays the following information:

The anticipated future usage of or demand for the item *during* each period (i.e., **gross requirements**).

Existing replenishment orders for the item due in at the *beginning* of each period (i.e., **scheduled receipts**).

FIGURE 7.2
The Basic
MRP Record

		Period				
		1	2	3	4	5
Gross requirements			10		40	10
Scheduled receipts		50				
Projected available balance	4	54	44	44	4	44
Planned order releases					50	
Lead time = one period Lot size = 50						

The current and projected inventory status for the item at the *end* of each period (i.e., **projected available balance**).

Planned replenishment orders for the item at the *beginning* of each period (i.e., **planned order releases**).

The top row in Figure 7.2 indicates periods that can vary in length from a day to a quarter or even longer. The period is also called a **time bucket.** A widely used time bucket or period is one week. A timing convention is that the current time is the beginning of the first period. The initial available balance of four units is shown prior to period 1. The number of periods in the record is called the **planning horizon.** In this simplified example, the planning horizon is five periods. The planning horizon indicates the number of future periods for which plans are made.

The second row, "Gross requirements," is the anticipated future usage of (or demand for) the item. The gross requirements are **time phased,** which means they're stated on a unique period-by-period basis, rather than aggregated or averaged; that is, gross requirements are stated as 10 in period 2, 40 in period 4, and 10 in period 5, rather than as a total requirement of 60 or as an average requirement of 12 per period. This method of presentation allows for special orders, seasonality, and periods of no anticipated usage to be explicitly taken into account. A gross requirement in a particular period will be unsatisfied unless the item is **available** during that period. Availability is achieved by having the item in inventory or by receiving either a scheduled receipt or a planned replenishment order in time to satisfy the gross requirement.

Another timing convention comes from the question of availability. The item must be available at the *beginning* of the time bucket in which it's required. This means plans must be so made that any replenishment order will be in inventory at the beginning of the period in which the gross requirement for that order occurs.

The "Scheduled receipts" row describes the status of all open orders (work in process or existing replenishment orders) for the item. This row shows the quantities ordered and when we expect these orders to be completed. Scheduled receipts result from previously made ordering decisions and represent a source of the item to meet gross requirements. For example, the gross requirements of 10 in period 2 cannot be satisfied by the 4 units presently available. The scheduled receipts of 50, due in period 1, will satisfy the gross requirement in period 2 if things go according to plan. Scheduled receipts represent a commitment. For an order in the factory, necessary materials have been committed to the order, and capacity at work centers will be required to complete it. For a purchased item, similar commitments have been made to a vendor. The timing convention used for showing scheduled receipts is also at the *beginning* of the period; that is, the order is shown in the period during which the item will be available to satisfy a gross requirement.

The next row in Figure 7.2 is "Projected available balance." The timing convention in this row is the *end* of the period; that is, the row is the projected balance *after* replenishment orders have been received and gross requirements have been satisfied. For this reason, the "Projected available balance" row has an extra time bucket shown at the beginning. The bucket shows the balance *at the present time;* that is, in Figure 7.2, the beginning available balance is 4 units. The quantity shown in period 1 is the projected balance at the *end* of period 1. The projected available balance shown at the end of a period is available to meet gross requirements in the next (and succeeding) periods. For example, the 54 units shown as the projected available balance at the end of period 1 result from adding the 50 units scheduled to be received to the beginning balance of 4 units. The gross requirement of 10 units in period 2 reduces the projected balance to 44 units at the end of period 2. The term projected *available* balance is used, instead of projected *on-hand* balance, for a very specific reason. Units of the item might be on hand physically but not available to meet gross requirements because they are already promised or allocated for some other purpose.

The "Planned order releases" row is determined directly from the "Projected available balance" row. Whenever the projected available balance shows a quantity insufficient to satisfy gross requirements (a negative quantity), additional material must be planned for. This is done by creating a planned order release in time to keep the projected available balance from becoming negative. For example, in Figure 7.2, the projected available balance at the end of period 4 is 4 units. This is not sufficient to meet the gross requirement of 10 units in period 5. Since the lead time is one week, the MRP system creates a planned order at the beginning of week 4 providing a **lead time offset** of one week. As we have used a lot size of 50 units, the projected available balance at the end of week 5 is 44 units. Another way that this logic is explained is to note that the balance for the end of period 4 (4 units) is the beginning inventory for period 5, during which there's a gross requirement of 10 units. The difference between the available inventory of 4 and the gross requirement of 10 is a **net requirement** of 6 units in period 5. Thus, an order for at least 6 units must be planned for period 4 to avoid a shortage in period 5.

The MRP system produces the planned order release data in response to the gross requirement, scheduled receipt, and projected available data. When a planned order is created for the most immediate or current period, it is in the **action bucket.** A quantity in the action bucket means some action is needed now to avoid a future problem. The action is to release the order, which converts it to a scheduled receipt.

The planned order releases are *not* shown in the scheduled receipt row because they haven't yet been released for production or purchasing. No material has been committed to their manufacture. The planned order is analogous to an entry on a Christmas list, since the list comprises plans. A scheduled receipt is like an order mailed to a catalog firm for a particular Christmas gift, since a commitment has been made. Like Christmas lists versus mailed orders, planned orders are much easier to change than scheduled receipts. Not converting planned orders into scheduled receipts any earlier than necessary has many advantages.

The basic MRP record just described provides the correct information on each part in the system. Linking these single part records together is essential in managing all the parts needed for a complex product or customer order. Key elements for linking the records are the bill of materials, the explosion process (using inventory and scheduled receipt information), and lead time offsetting. We consider each of these before turning to how the records are linked into a system.

An Example Bill of Materials

Figure 7.3 shows a snow shovel, and item part number 1605. The complete snow shovel is assembled (using four rivets and two nails) from the top handle assembly, scoop assembly, scoop-shaft connector, and shaft. The top handle assembly, in turn, is created by combining the welded top handle bracket assembly with the wooden handle using two nails. The welded top handle bracket assembly is created by welding the top handle coupling to the top handle bracket. In a similar way, the scoop assembly combines the aluminum scoop with the steel blade using six rivets.

FIGURE 7.3
The 1605 Snow Shovel Shown with Component Parts and Assemblies

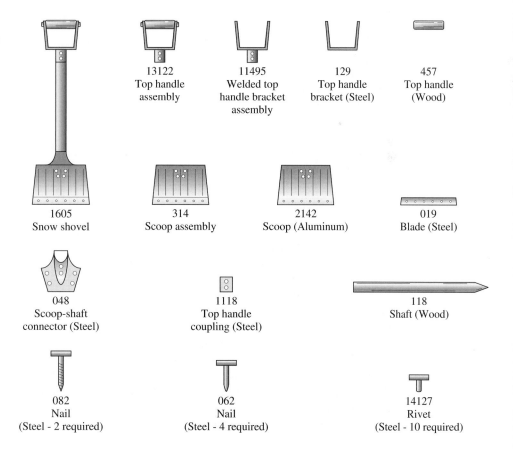

	13122 Top handle assembly	11495 Welded top handle bracket assembly	129 Top handle bracket (Steel)	457 Top handle (Wood)

1605 Snow shovel

314 Scoop assembly

2142 Scoop (Aluminum)

019 Blade (Steel)

048 Scoop-shaft connector (Steel)

1118 Top handle coupling (Steel)

118 Shaft (Wood)

082 Nail (Steel - 2 required)

062 Nail (Steel - 4 required)

14127 Rivet (Steel - 10 required)

Explaining even this simple assembly process is a cumbersome task. Moreover, such diagrams as Figure 7.3 get more complicated as the number of subassemblies, components, and parts used increases, or as they are used in increasingly more places (e.g., rivets and nails). Two techniques that get at this problem nicely are the **product structure diagram** and the **indented bill of materials (BOM)** shown in Figure 7.4. Both provide the detailed information of Figure 7.3, but the indented BOM has the added advantage of being easily printed by a computer.

FIGURE 7.4   Parts for Snow Shovel

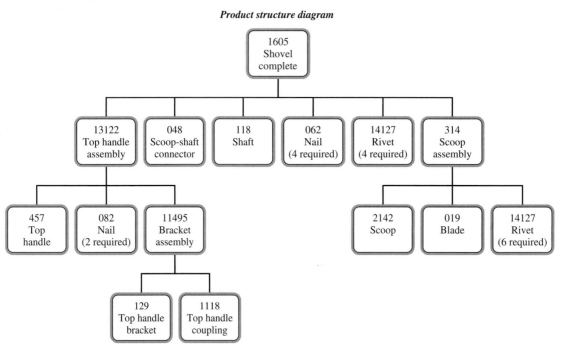

Product structure diagram

Indented bill of materials (BOM)

1605 Snow Shovel

    13122 Top Handle Assembly (1 required)
      457   Top Handle (1 required)
      082   Nail (2 required)
      11495 Bracket Assembly (1 required)
        129 Top Handle Bracket (1 required)
        1118 Top Handle Coupling (1 required)

    048   Scoop-Shaft Connector (1 required)
    118   Shaft (1 required)
    062   Nail (4 required)
    14127 Rivet (4 required)
    314   Scoop Assembly
      2142   Scoop (1 required)
      019   Blade (1 required)
      14127 Rivet (6 required)

Note that both the product structure diagram and the indented BOM show exactly what goes into what instead of being just a parts list. For example, to make one 13122 top handle assembly, we see by the product structure diagram that one 457 top handle, two 082 nails, and one 11495 bracket assembly are needed. The same information is shown in the indented BOM; the three required parts are indented and shown, one level beneath the 13122. Note also that we *don't* need a top handle bracket (129) or a top handle coupling (1118) to produce a top handle assembly (13122). These are only needed to produce a bracket assembly (11495). In essence, the top handle assembly does not care *how* a bracket assembly is made, only that it *is* made. Making the bracket assembly is a separate problem.

Before leaving our brief discussion of bills of material, it is important to stress that the bill of material used to support MRP may differ from other company perceptions of a bill of materials. The BOM to support MRP must be consistent with the way the product is manufactured. For example, if we're making red cars, the part numbers should be for red doors. If green cars are desired, the part numbers must be for green doors. Also, if we change to a different set of subassemblies, indentations on the BOM should change as well. Engineering and accounting may well not care what color the parts are or what the manufacturing sequence is.

Gross to Net Explosion

Explosion is the process of translating product requirements into component part requirements, taking existing inventories and scheduled receipts into account. Thus, explosion may be viewed as the process of determining, for *any* part number, the quantities of *all* components needed to satisfy its requirements, and continuing this process for *every* part number until all purchased and/or raw material requirements are exactly calculated.

As explosion takes place, only the component part requirements net of any inventory or scheduled receipts are considered. In this way, only the *necessary* requirements are linked through the system. Although this may seem like an obvious goal, the product structure can make determination of net requirements more difficult than it seems. To illustrate, let's return to the snow shovel example.

Suppose the company wanted to produce 100 snow shovels, and we were responsible for making the 13122 top handle assembly. We are given current inventory and scheduled receipt information from which the gross requirements and net requirements for each component of the top handle can be calculated, as shown in Figure 7.5.

FIGURE 7.5   **Gross and Net Requirement Calculations for the Snow Shovel**

Part Description	Part Number	Inventory	Scheduled Receipts	Gross Requirements	Net Requirements
Top handle assembly	13122	25	—	100	75
Top handle	457	22	25	75	28
Nail (2 required)	082	4	50	150	96
Bracket assembly	11495	27	—	75	48
Top handle bracket	129	15	—	48	33
Top handle coupling	1118	39	15	48	—

The gross and net requirements in Figure 7.5 may not correspond to what we feel they should be. It might at the outset seem that since one top handle coupling (1118) is used per shovel, the gross requirements should be 100 and the net requirement 46, instead of the 48 and zero shown. To produce 100 shovels means we need (have a demand for) 100 top handle assemblies (part 13122). Twenty-five of these 100 can come from inventory, resulting in a net requirement of 75. As we need to make only 75 top handle assemblies, we need 75 top handles and bracket assemblies. This 75 is the *gross* requirement for parts 457 and 11495 (as indicated by the circled numbers in Figure 7.5). Since 2 nails (part 082) are used per top handle assembly, the gross requirement for 082 is 150. The 25 units of top handle assembly inventory contain some implicit inventories of handles, brackets, and nails, which the gross to net process takes into account. Looking on down, we see that there are 27 units of the bracket assembly in inventory, so the net requirement is for 48. This becomes the gross requirement for the bracket and coupling. Since there are 39 top handle couplings in inventory and 15 scheduled for receipt, there is *no* net requirement for part 1118.

Gross to net explosion is a key element of MRP systems. It not only provides the basis for calculating the appropriate quantities but also serves as the communication link between part numbers. It's the basis for the concept of **dependent demand;** that is, the "demand" (gross requirements) for top handles depends on the net requirements for top handle assemblies. To correctly do the calculations, the bill of material, inventory, and scheduled receipt data are all necessary. With these data, the dependent demand can be exactly calculated. It need not be forecast. On the other hand, some **independent demand** items, such as the snow shovel, are subject to demand from outside the firm. The need for snow shovels will have to be forecast. The concept of dependent demand is often called the fundamental principle of MRP. It provides the way to remove uncertainty from the requirement calculations.

Lead Time Offsetting

Gross to net explosion tells us how many of each subassembly and component part are needed to support a desired finished product quantity. What it does not do, however, is tell us *when* each component and subassembly is needed. Referring back to Figures 7.3 and 7.4, clearly the top handle bracket and top handle coupling need to be welded together before the wooden top handle is attached. These relationships are known as **precedent relationships.** They indicate the order in which things must be done.

In addition to precedent relationships, determining when to schedule each component part also depends on how long it takes to produce the part (that is, the lead time). Perhaps the top handle bracket (129) can be fabricated in one day, while the top handle coupling (1118) takes two weeks. If so, it would be advantageous to start making the coupling before the bracket, since they are both needed at the same time to make a bracket assembly.

Despite the need to take lead time differences into account, many systems for component part manufacturing ignore them. For example, most furniture manufacturers base production on what is called a **cutting.** In the cutting approach, if a lot of 100 chairs were to be assembled, then 100 of each part (with appropriate multiples) are started at the same time. Figure 7.6 is a Gantt chart (time-oriented bar chart) showing how this cutting approach would be applied to the snow shovel example. (Note that processing times are shown on the chart.)

Figure 7.6 shows clearly that the cutting approach, which starts all parts as soon as possible, will lead to unnecessary work-in-process inventories. For example, the top handle bracket (129) doesn't need to be started until the end of day 9, since it must wait for the

FIGURE 7.6
Gantt Chart for Cutting Approach to Snow Shovel Problem (front or earliest start schedule)

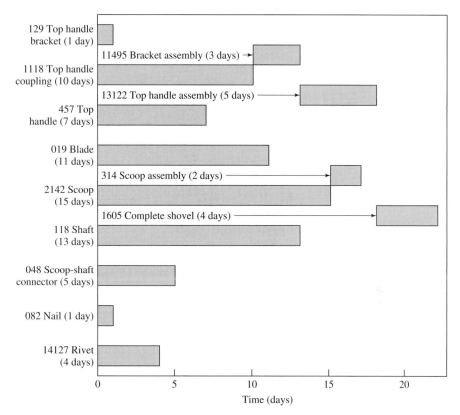

coupling (1118) before it can be put into its assembly (11495), and part 1118 takes 10 days. In the cutting approach, parts are scheduled earlier than need be. This results from using **front schedule** logic (that is, scheduling as early as possible).

What should be done is to **back schedule**—start each item as late as possible. Figure 7.7 provides a back schedule for the snow shovel example. The schedules for parts 1118, 11495, 13122, and 1605 don't change, since they form a critical path. All of the other parts, however, are scheduled later in this approach than in the front scheduling approach. A substantial savings in work-in-process inventory is obtained by this shift of dates.

Back scheduling has several obvious advantages. It will reduce work-in-process, postpone the commitment of raw materials to specific products, and minimize storage time of completed components. Implementing the back schedule approach, however, requires a system. The system must have accurate BOM data and lead time estimates, some way to ensure all component parts are started at the right times, and some means of tracking components and subassemblies to make sure they are all completed according to plans. The cutting approach is much simpler, since all component parts are started at the same time and left in the pipeline until needed.

MRP achieves the benefits of the back scheduling approach *and* performs the gross to net explosion. In fact, the combination of back schedules and gross to net explosion is the heart of MRP.

FIGURE 7.7
Gantt Chart
Based on Back
Schedule
(latest start)

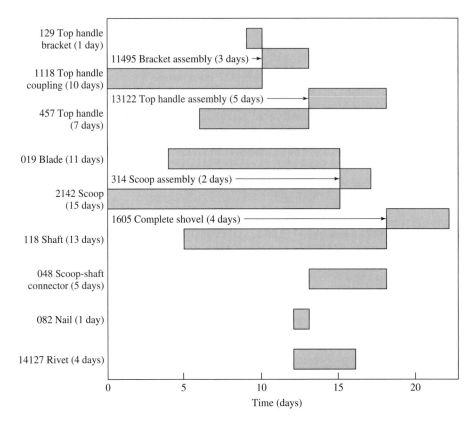

Linking the MRP Records

Figure 7.8 shows the linked set of individual time-phased MRP records for the top handle assembly of the snow shovel. We have already used the first five periods of the 082 nail record shown in Figure 7.8 as the record in Figure 7.2. To see how that record fits into the whole, we start with the snow shovels themselves. We said 100 snow shovels were going to be made, and now we see the timing. That is, the "Gross requirements" row in the MRP record for part number 13122 in Figure 7.8 shows the total need of 100 time phased as 20 in week 2, 10 in week 4, 20 in week 6, 5 in week 7, 35 in week 9, and 10 in week 10. Since each snow shovel takes a top handle assembly, the "Gross requirements" row for the top handle shows when shovel assembly is to begin. Note the total planned orders for the top handle assembly is the net requirement of 75 that we calculated before in the gross to net calculations of Figure 7.5.

The lead time for the top handle assembly is two weeks, calculated as the five days processing time shown in Figure 7.6 plus five days for paperwork. The lead time for each of the other records is similarly calculated; one week (five days) of paperwork time is added to the processing time and the total rounded to the nearest five-day week. The current inventories and scheduled receipts for each part are those shown in Figure 7.5. The scheduled receipts are shown in the appropriate periods. Using the two-week lead time and recognizing a net requirement of five units in week 4 for the top handle assembly, we see the need to plan an order for week 2 of five units.

FIGURE 7.8 **MRP Records for the Snow Shovel Top Handle Assembly**

			Week									
			1	2	3	4	5	6	7	8	9	10
13122 Top handle assembly Lead time = 2	Gross requirements			20		10		20	5		35	10
	Scheduled receipts											
	Projected available balance	25	25	5	5	0	0	0	0	0	0	0
	Planned order releases			(5)		20	5		35	10		
457 Top handle Lead time = 2	Gross requirements			(5)		20	5		35	10		
	Scheduled receipts				25							
	Projected available balance	22	22	17	42	22	17	17	0	0	0	0
	Planned order releases						18	10				
082 Nail (2 required) Lead time = 1 Lot size = 50	Gross requirements			10		40	10		70	20		
	Scheduled receipts		50									
	Projected available balance	4	54	44	44	4	44	44	24	4	4	4
	Planned order releases					50		50				
11495 Bracket assembly Lead time = 2	Gross requirements			5		20	5		35	10		
	Scheduled receipts											
	Projected available balance	27	27	22	22	2	0	0	0	0	0	0
	Planned order releases				3		35	10				
129 Top handle bracket Lead time = 1	Gross requirements				3		35	10				
	Scheduled receipts											
	Projected available balance	15	15	15	12	12	0	0	0	0	0	0
	Planned order releases					23	10					
1118 Top handle coupling Lead time = 3 Safety stock = 20	Gross requirements				3		35	10				
	Scheduled receipts			15								
	Projected available balance	39	39	54	51	51	20	20	20	20	20	20
	Planned order releases			4	10							

This planned order release of five units in week 2 becomes a gross requirement in week 2 for the top handles as shown by the circles in Figure 7.8. Note also the gross requirements for the nails and brackets in period 2 derive from this same planned order release (with two nails per top handle assembly). Thus, the communication between records is the dependent demand that we saw illustrated before in the gross to net calculations of Figure 7.5.

The remaining planned order releases for the top handle assembly exactly meet the net requirements in the remaining periods, offset for the lead time. The ordering policy used for these items is called **lot-for-lot** (i.e., as required) sizing. An exception to the lot-for-lot procedure is the ordering of nails, which is done in lots of 50. In the case of the nails, the total planned orders will not necessarily add up to the net requirements.

Another part for which there is a discrepancy between the planned orders and the net requirements calculated in Figure 7.5 is the top handle coupling. For this part, a safety stock of 20 units is desired. This means the planned order logic will schedule a planned order release to prevent the projected available balance from going below the safety stock level of 20 units. For the top handle couplings, this means a total of 4 units must be planned for period 2 and 10 for period 3 to maintain the 20-unit safety stock.

The one element we have yet to clearly show is the back scheduling effect. We saw in Figure 7.7 that it would be desirable to delay the start of the top handle bracket (part 129) so that this item is completed at the same time as the top handle coupling (part 1118). The MRP records show that the start of the first planned order for part 129 isn't until week 4, two weeks after the first planned order for part 1118. Both of these planned orders are to satisfy a gross requirement of 35 derived from the planned order for the bracket assembly in week 5. We see then that the orders are back scheduled. This relationship can be more complicated than our example, since the planned order release timing depends on the safety stock and inventory levels, as well as the lead times. The MRP system, however, coordinates all of that information and determines the appropriate planned order release dates, based on back scheduling.

At this point, we see fully the linking of the MRP time-phased records. The "Planned order releases" row for the top handle assembly (13122) becomes (with the appropriate multiplier) the "Gross requirements" row for each of its components (parts 457, 082, and 11495), and they are linked together. Once all the gross requirements data are available for a particular record, the individual record processing logic is applied and the planned order releases for the part are passed down as gross requirements to its components, following the product structure (BOM) on a level-by-level basis. In some cases, parts will receive their requirements from more than one source (common parts), as is true for the nails and rivets in the snow shovel. In these cases, gross requirements will reflect needs from more than one planned order release source. Again, the system accounts for this and incorporates it into the gross to net logic.

The MRP records take proper account of gross to netting. They also incorporate back scheduling and allow for explicit timings, desired lot sizing procedures, safety stocks, and part commonality. Even more important, however, is independence of the part number planning. With the MRP approach, the person planning snow shovels need not explicitly coordinate his planning with planning of the component parts. The MRP system accomplishes the coordination. Whatever is done to the MRP record for the snow shovels will result in a set of planned orders that the system will correctly pass down as gross requirements to its components. This means plans for each part number can be developed independently of the product structures, and the plans at each level will be communicated correctly to the other levels.

Technical Issues

In this section, we briefly introduce some technical issues to consider in designing MRP systems.

Processing Frequency

Thus far we've looked only at the static construction of the MRP records and how they're linked together. Since conditions change and new information is received, the MRP records must be brought up to date so plans can be adjusted. This means processing the MRP records anew, incorporating current information. Two issues are involved in the processing decision: how frequently the records should be processed and whether all the records should be processed at the same time.

Processing all of the records in one computer run is called **regeneration.** This signifies that *all* part number records are completely reconstructed each time the records are processed. When a regeneration run is conducted, all current planned orders are removed. Then, starting with the end items, each item is completely rescheduled. This can generate very large processing demands on the system. When initiated on line, the data-intensive run can negatively affect overall system performance and cause inconvenience to other users. To avoid this common problem, it is possible to conduct regeneration runs as background jobs. In addition to operating in the background, these jobs can be scheduled to take place automatically during periods of low system demand, such as late evenings or weekends.

The problem with processing less frequently is that the portrayal of component status and needs expressed in the records becomes increasingly out of date and inaccurate. This decrease in accuracy has both anticipated and unanticipated causes. As the anticipated scheduled receipts are received and requirements satisfied, the inventory balances change. As unanticipated scrap, requirement changes, stock corrections, or other such transactions occur, they cause inaccuracies if not reflected in all the time-phased records influenced by the transactions. Changes in one record are linked to other time-phased records as planned order releases become gross requirements for lower-level components. Thus, some change transactions may cascade throughout the product structure. If these transactions are not reflected in the time-phased records early enough, the result can be poor planning.

More frequent processing of the MRP records increases computer costs but results in fewer unpleasant surprises. When the records reflecting the changes are produced, appropriate actions will be indicated to compensate for the changes.

A logical response to the pressure for more frequent processing is to reduce the required amount of calculation by processing only the records affected by the changes. An alternative to regeneration is the **net change** approach. With net change, only those items that are affected by the new or changed information are reprocessed.

The argument for the net change approach is that it can reduce computer time enough to make daily or even real-time processing possible. Since only some of the records are reviewed at each processing, there's a need for very accurate computer records and transaction processing procedures. Some net change users do an occasional regeneration to clean up all records.

The most challenging aspect of net change is its hypersensitivity, or nervousness. The frequent replanning may result in continual revision of recommended user actions through the revision of planned order releases. Users may be frustrated with these frequent revisions to the plan.

Bucketless Systems

To some extent, the problems of timing are tied to the use of time buckets. When the buckets are small enough, the problems are reduced significantly. However, smaller buckets mean more buckets, which increases review, storage, and computation costs. A bucketless MRP system specifies the exact release and due dates for each requirement, scheduled receipt, and planned order. The managerial reports are printed out on whatever basis is required, including by exact dates.

Bucketless MRP systems are a better way to use the computer. Above and beyond that, the approach allows better maintenance of lead time offsets and provides more precise time-phased information. The approach is consistent with state-of-the-art software, and many firms now use bucketless systems. The major addition is that the planning cycle itself is bucketless. That is, plans are revised as necessary, not on a periodic schedule, and the entire execution cycle is also shortened.

Lot Sizing

In the snow shovel example of Figure 7.8, we use a fixed lot size (50 units for the nails) and the lot-for-lot procedure. The lot size of 50 for the nails could have been someone's estimate of a good lot size or the result of calculation. The time-phased information can be used in combination with other data to develop lot sizes conforming to organizational needs. We might reach the conclusion, for the top handle (1118) in Figure 7.8, that it's undesirable to set up the equipment for 4 parts in week 2, and again for 10 parts in week 3, so we'd combine the two orders. The time-phased record permits us to develop such **discrete lot sizes** that will exactly satisfy the net requirements for one or more periods.

Several formal procedures have been developed for lot sizing the time-phased requirements. The basic trade-off usually involves elimination of one or more setups at the expense of carrying inventory longer. In many cases, discrete lot sizes possible with MRP are more appealing than fixed lot sizes. Compare the residual inventory of nails in week 10, with that of the bracket assemblies in Figure 7.8, for example.

At first glance the lot-for-lot technique seems a bit too simple-minded since it does not consider any of the economic trade-offs or physical factors. However, batching planned orders at one level will increase gross requirements at the next level in the product structure. So larger lot sizing near the end-item level of the bill of materials cascades down through all levels. Thus, it turns out that lot-for-lot is better than we might expect in actual practice, particularly at the intermediate levels in the bill of materials. This is especially the case when a product structure has many levels, and the cascading effect becomes greatly magnified. This cascading effect can be mitigated to some extent for components and raw materials that are very common. When this is the case, again lot sizing may be appropriate. As a consequence, many firms employ lot sizing primarily at the end-item and basic component levels, while intermediate subassemblies are planned on a lot-for-lot basis.

Safety Stock and Safety Lead Time

Carrying out detailed component plans is sometimes facilitated by including **safety stocks** and/or **safety lead times** in the MRP records. Safety stock is a buffer of stock above and beyond that needed to satisfy the gross requirements. Figure 7.8 illustrates this by incorporating safety stock for the top handle coupling. Safety lead time is a procedure whereby shop orders or purchase orders are released and scheduled to arrive one or more periods before necessary to satisfy the gross requirements.

Safety stocks can be incorporated into MRP time-phased records. The result is that the projected available balance doesn't fall below the safety stock level instead of reaching zero. To incorporate safety lead time, orders are issued (planned) earlier and are scheduled (planned) to be received into inventory before the time that the MRP logic would indicate as necessary. Figure 7.9 shows the top handle bracket from Figure 7.8 being planned with a one-week safety lead time. Notice that both the planned release and planned receipt dates are changed. Safety lead time is not just inflated lead time.

Both safety stock and safety lead time are used in practice and can be used simultaneously. However, both are hedges indicating that orders should be released (launched) or that they need to be received when, in fact, this is not strictly true. To use safety stocks and safety lead times effectively, we must understand the techniques' influence on plans. If they are not well understood, wrong orders can be sent to the factory, meaning workers will try to get out part A because of safety lead time or safety stock when, in fact, part B will be required to meet a customer order.

Safety stock tends to be used in MRP systems where uncertainty about quantities is the problem (e.g., where some small amount of scrap, spare part demand, or other unplanned usage is a frequent occurrence). Safety lead time, on the other hand, tends to be used when the major uncertainty is the timing rather than the quantity. For example, if a firm buys from a vendor who often misses delivery dates, safety lead time may provide better results than safety stock.

FIGURE 7.9   **MRP Record with Safety Lead Time**

				1	2	3	4	5	6	7	8	9	10
Part 129	Gross requirements					3		35	10				
Top handle bracket lead time = 1	Scheduled receipts												
Lot-for-lot	Projected available balance	15	15	15	15	12	35	10	0	0	0	0	0
Safety lead time = 1	Planned order releases					23	10						

Low-Level Coding

If we refer once again to Figure 7.4, we see that the rivet (part 14127) is a common part. The "Planned order" row for completed shovels will be passed down as gross requirements to the rivet. But there are additional requirements for the rivets (14127) from the scoop assembly (314). If we process the time-phased record for this common part before all of its gross requirements have been accumulated, the computations must be redone.

The way this problem is handled is to assign **low-level code numbers** to each part in the product structure or the indented BOM. By convention, the top final assembly level is denoted as level 0. In our example, the snow shovel would have a low-level code of 0. All immediate component part numbers of this part (13122, 048, 118, 062, 14127, and 314 in Figure 7.4) are given the low-level code number 1. The next level down (part numbers 457, 082, 11495, 2142, 019, and 14127) are low-level coded 2. Note the common part (rivet) has just been recoded as level 2, indicating it is used lower in the product structure. The higher the level codes, the lower in the product structure the part is used. Consequently, the last level code assigned to a part indicates the lowest level of usage and is the level code retained for that part. We finish the example when part numbers 129 and 1118 are coded level 3. The level code assigned to any part number is based on the part's usage in all products manufactured by the organization.

Once low-level codes are established, MRP record processing proceeds from one level code to the next, starting at level code 0. This ensures all gross requirements have been passed down to a part before its MRP record is processed. The result is planning of component parts coordinated with the needs of all higher-level part numbers. Within a level, the MRP record processing is typically done in part number sequence.

Pegging

Pegging relates all the gross requirements for a part to all the planned order releases or other sources of demand that created the requirements. The pegging records contain the specific part number or numbers of the sources of all gross requirements. At level 0, for example, pegging records might contain the specific customer orders to be satisfied by the gross requirements in the end-item, time-phased records. For lower-level part numbers, the gross requirements are most often pegged to planned orders of higher-level items, but might also be pegged to customer orders if the part is sold as a service part.

Pegging information can be used to go up through the MRP records from a raw material gross requirement to some future customer order. In this sense, it's the reverse of the explosion process. Pegging is sometimes compared to **where-used data.** Where-used data, however, indicate for each part number, the part numbers of all items on which the part is used. Pegging, on the other hand, is a *selective* where-used file. Pegging shows only the specific part numbers that produce the specific gross requirements in each time period. Thus, pegging information can trace the impact of a material problem all the way up to the order it would affect.

Firm Planned Orders

The logic used to illustrate the construction of an MRP record for an individual part number is automatically applied for every processed part number. The result is a series of planned order releases for each part number. If changes have taken place since the last time the record was processed, planned order releases can be very different from one record-processing cycle to the next. Since planned orders are passed down as gross requirements to the next level, the differences can cascade throughout the product structure.

One device for preventing this cascading down through the product structure is to create a **firm planned order (FPO).** FPO, as the name implies, is a planned order that the MRP system *does not* automatically change when conditions change. To change either the quantity or timing of a firm planned order, managerial action is required. This means the trade-offs in making the change can be evaluated before authorization.

The FPO provides a means for temporarily overriding the system to provide stability or to solve problems. For example, if changes are coming about because of scrap losses on open orders, the possibility of absorbing those variations with safety stock can be evaluated. If more rapid delivery of raw material than usual is requested (say by using air freight) to meet a special need, lead time can be reduced for that one order. An FPO means the system will not use the normal lead time offset from the net requirement for that order.

Service Parts

Service part demand must be included in the MRP record if the material requirements are not to be understated. The service part demand is typically based on a forecast and is added directly into the gross requirements for the part. From the MRP system point of view, the service part demand is simply another source of gross requirements for a part, and the sources of all gross requirements are maintained through pegging records. The low-level code for a part used exclusively for service would be zero. If it's used as a component part as well, the low-level code would be determined the same way as for any other part.

As actual service part needs occur, it's to be expected that demand variations will arise. These can be partially buffered with safety stocks (inventories specifically allocated to service part usage) or by creative use of the MRP system. By careful examination of pegging records, expected shortage conditions for manufacturing part requirements can sometimes be satisfied from available service parts. Conversely, critical service part requirements can perhaps be met with orders destined for higher-level items. Only one safety stock inventory is needed to buffer uncertainties from both sources, however.

Planning Horizon

In Figure 7.8, the first planned order for top handle assemblies occurs in week 2 to meet period 4's gross requirement of 10 units. This planned order of 5 units in week 2 results in a corresponding gross requirement in that week for the bracket assembly (part 11495). This gross requirement is satisfied from the existing inventory of part 11495. But a different circumstance occurs if we trace the gross requirements for 35 top handle assemblies in week 9.

The net requirement for 35 units in week 9 becomes a planned order release in week 7. This, in turn, becomes a gross requirement for 35 bracket assemblies (part 11495) in week 7 and a planned order release in week 5. This passes down to the top handle coupling (part 1118), which creates a planned order release for 4 units in week 2. This means the **cumulative lead time** for the top handle assembly is 7 weeks (from release of the coupling order in week 2 to receipt of the top handle assemblies in week 9).

Scheduled Receipts versus Planned Order Releases

A true understanding of MRP requires knowledge of certain key differences between a scheduled receipt and a planned order. We noted one such difference before: the scheduled receipt represents a commitment, whereas the planned order is only a plan—the former is much more difficult to change than the latter. A scheduled receipt for a purchased item means a purchase order, which is a formal commitment, has been prepared. Similarly, a scheduled receipt for a manufactured item means there's an open shop order. Raw materials and component parts have *already* been specifically committed to that order and are no longer available for other needs. One major result of this distinction, which can be seen in Figure 7.8, is that planned order releases explode to gross requirements for components, but scheduled receipts (the open orders) do not.

A related issue is seen from the following question: Where would a scheduled receipt for the top handle assembly (13122) in Figure 7.8 of, say, 20 units in week 2 be reflected in the records for the component parts (457, 082, and 11495)? The answer is nowhere! Scheduled receipts are not reflected in the current records for component parts. For that scheduled receipt to exist, the component parts would have already been assigned to the shop order representing the scheduled receipt for part 13122 and removed from the available balances of the components. As far as MRP is concerned, the 20 part 457s, 40 part 082s, and 20 part 11495s don't exist! They're on their way to becoming 20 part 13122s. The 13122 record controls this process, not the component records.

Using the MRP System

In this section, we discuss critical aspects of using the MRP system to ensure that MRP system records are exactly synchronized with physical flows of material.

The MRP Planner

The persons most directly involved with the MRP system outputs are planners. They are typically in the production planning, inventory control, and purchasing departments. Planners have the responsibility for making detailed decisions that keep the material moving through the plant. Their range of discretion is carefully limited (e.g., without higher authorization, they cannot change plans for end items destined for customers). Their actions, however, are reflected in the MRP records. Well-trained MRP planners are essential to effective use of the MRP system.

Computerized MRP systems often encompass tens of thousands of part numbers. To handle this volume, planners are generally organized around logical groupings of parts (such as metal parts, wood parts, purchased electronic parts, or West Coast distribution center). Even so, reviewing each record every time the records are processed would not be an effective use of the planners' time. At any time, many records require no action, so the planner only wants to review and interpret those that do require action.

The primary actions taken by an MRP planner are:

1. Release orders (i.e., launch purchase or shop orders when indicated by the system).
2. Reschedule due dates of existing open orders when desirable.

3. Analyze and update system planning factors for the part numbers under her control. This would involve such things as changing lot sizes, lead times, scrap allowances, or safety stocks.
4. Reconcile errors or inconsistencies and try to eliminate root causes of these errors.
5. Find key problem areas requiring action now to prevent future crises.
6. Use the system to solve critical material shortage problems so actions can be captured in the records for the next processing. This means the planner works *within* formal MRP rules, *not* by informal methods.
7. Indicate where further system enhancements (outputs, diagnostics, etc.) would make the planner's job easier.

Order Launching

Order launching is the process of releasing orders to the shop or to vendors (purchase orders). This process is prompted by MRP when a planned order release is in the current time period, the **action bucket.** Order launching converts the planned order into a scheduled receipt reflecting the lead time offset. Order launching is the opening of shop and purchase orders; closing these orders occurs when scheduled receipts are received into stockrooms. At that time, a transaction must be processed—to increase the on-hand inventory and eliminate the scheduled receipt. Procedures for opening and closing shop orders have to be carefully defined so all transactions are properly processed.

The orders indicated by MRP as ready for launching are a function of lot sizing procedures and safety stock as well as timing. We saw this in Figure 7.8 where we worked with lot-for-lot approaches and fixed lot sizes. A key responsibility of the planner is managing with awareness of the implications of these effects. For example, not *all* of a fixed lot may be necessary to cover a requirement, or a planned order that's solely for replenishment of safety stock may be in the action bucket.

When an order is launched, it's sometimes necessary to include a shrinkage allowance for scrap and other process yield situations. The typical approach allows some percentage for yield losses that will increase the shop order quantity above the net amount required. To effect good control over open orders, the *total* amount, including the allowance, should be shown on the shop order, and the scheduled receipt should be reduced as actual yield losses occur during production.

Allocation and Availability Checking

A concept closely related to order launching is **allocation**—a step prior to order launching that involves an availability check for the necessary component or components. From the snow shovel example, if we want to assemble 20 of the top handle assembly (13122) in period 4, the availability check would be whether sufficient components (20 of part 457, 40 of part 082, and 20 of part 11495) are available. If not, the shop order for 20 top handle assemblies (13122) should not be launched, because it cannot be executed without component parts. The planner role is key here, as well. The best course of action might be to release a partial order. The planner should evaluate that possibility.

Most MRP systems first check component availability for any order that a planner desires to launch. If sufficient quantities of each component are available, the shop order can be created. If the order is created, then the system allocates the necessary quantities to the particular shop order. (Shop orders are assigned by the computer, in numerical sequence.) The allocation means this amount of a component part is mortgaged to the particular shop order and is, therefore, not available for any other shop order. Thus, the amounts shown in Figure 7.8 as projected available balances may not be the same as the physical inventory balances. The physical inventory balances could be larger, with the differences representing allocations to specific shop orders that have been released, but whose component parts have not been removed from inventory.

After availability checking and allocation, **picking tickets** are typically created and sent to the stockroom. The picking ticket calls for a specified amount of some part number to be removed from some inventory location, on some shop order, to be delivered to a particular department or location. When the picking ticket has been satisfied (inventory moved), the allocation is removed and the on-hand balance is reduced accordingly.

Availability checking, allocation, and physical stock picking are a type of double-entry bookkeeping. The result is that the quantity physically on hand should match what the records indicate is available plus what is allocated. If they don't match, corrective action must be taken. The resulting accuracy facilitates inventory counting and other procedures for maintaining date integrity.

Exception Codes

Exception codes in MRP systems are used "to separate the vital few from the trivial many." If the manufacturing process is under control and the MRP system is functioning correctly, exception coding typically means only 10 to 20 percent of the part numbers will require planner review at each processing cycle. Exception codes are in two general categories. The first, checking the input data accuracy, includes checks for dates beyond the planning horizon, quantities larger or smaller than check figures, nonvalid part numbers, or any other desired check for incongruity. The second category of exception codes directly supports the MRP planning activity. Included are the following kinds of exception (action) messages or diagnostics:

1. Part numbers for which a planned order is now in the most immediate time period (the action bucket). It's also possible to report any planned orders two to three periods out to check lead times, on-hand balances, and other factors while there's some time to respond, if necessary.

2. Open order diagnostics when the present timing and/or amount for a scheduled receipt is not satisfactory. Such a message might indicate that an open order exists that's not necessary to cover any of the requirements in the planning horizon. This message might suggest order cancellation caused by an engineering change that substituted some new part for the one in question. The most common type of open order diagnostic shows scheduled receipts that are timed to arrive either too late or too early and should, therefore, have their due dates revised to reflect proper factory priorities. An example of this is seen with each of the three scheduled receipts in Figure 7.8. The 457 top handle open order of 25 could be delayed one week. A one-week delay is also indicated for the 082 nail scheduled receipt. For part 1118 (the top handle coupling), scheduled receipt of 15 could be delayed from week 2 until week 5. Another open order exception code is to flag any past-due scheduled receipt (scheduled to have been received in previous periods, but

for which no receipt transaction has been processed). MRP systems assume a past-due scheduled receipt will be received in the immediate time bucket.

3. A third general type of exception message indicates problem areas for management; in essence, situations where level 0 quantities can't be satisfied unless the present planning factors used in MRP are changed. One such exception code indicates a requirement has been offset into the past period and subsequently added to any requirement in the first or most immediate time bucket. This condition means an order should have been placed in the past. Since it wasn't, lead times through the various production item levels must be compressed to meet the end-item schedule. A similar diagnostic indicates the allocations exceed the on-hand inventory—a condition directly analogous to overdrawing a checking account. Unless more inventory is received soon, the firm will not be able to honor all pick tickets issued, and there will be a material shortage in the factory.

Bottom-up Replanning

Bottom-up replanning—using pegging data to solve material shortage problems—is best seen through an example. Let's return again to Figure 7.8, concentrating on the top handle assembly and the nails (parts 13122 and 082). Let's suppose the scheduled receipt of 50 nails arrives on Wednesday of week 1. On Thursday, quality control checks them and finds the vendor sent the wrong size. This means only 4 of the 10 gross requirement in week 2 can be satisfied. By pegging this gross requirement up to its parent planned order (5 units of 13122 in week 2), we see that only 7 of the gross requirement for 10 units in week 4 can be satisfied (the 5 on hand plus 2 made from 4 nails). This, in turn, means only 7 snow shovels can be assembled in week 4.

The pegging analysis shows that 3 of the 10 top handle assemblies can't be available without taking some special actions. If none are taken, the planned assembly dates for the snow shovels should reflect only 7 units in week 4, with the additional 3 scheduled for week 5. This should be done if we cannot overcome the shortfall in nails. The change is necessary because the 10 snow shovels now scheduled for assembly in week 4 also explode to other parts—parts that won't be needed if only 7 snow shovels are to be assembled.

There may, however, be a critical customer requirement for 10 snow shovels to be assembled during week 4. Solving the problem with bottom-up replanning might involve one of the following alternatives (staying *within* the MRP system, as planners must do):

1. Issue an immediate order to the vendor for six nails (the minimum requirement), securing a promised lead time of two days instead of the usual one week. This will create a scheduled receipt for six in week 2.

2. Order more nails for the beginning of week 3, and negotiate a one-week reduction in lead time (from two weeks to one week) for fabricating this one batch of part 13122. The planned order release for five would be placed in week 3 and converted to a firm planned order, so it would not change when the record is processed again. The negotiation for a one-week lead time might involve letting the people concerned start work earlier than week 3 on the two part 13122s, for which material already exists, and a reduction in the one-week paperwork time included in the lead times.

3. Negotiate a one-week lead time reduction for assembling the snow shovels; place a firm planned order for 10 in week 5, which will result in a gross requirement for 10 top handle assemblies in period 5 instead of period 4.

FIGURE 7.10 Example MRP Record

```
DATE-01/21
********PART NUMBER********
NONJEK  OPTY  SSV  LAM  PP  UPHL
```

MATERIAL STATUS-PRODUCTION SCHEDULE

USTRO040	*****USAGE*****		DESCRIPTION	POLICY CODE	PLNR CODE	BYR COE	U/M		
YTD	LAST YR	YTD	3/16 × 7/8 MR P & C STL STRAP	3	01	9	LFT		
SCRAP									

****ORDER POLICY AND LOT SIZE DATA****

	REJECT QUANTITY	SAFETY STOCK 497	SHRINKG ALLOWNE 1	LEAD TIME 08	FAMILY DATA
PERIODS TO COMB. 04	MINIMUM QTY	MAXIMUM QTY	MULTIPLE QTY		MIN ORD POINT

Time-Phased Record

Weeks 563–573

	PAST DUE	563 01/22	564 01/29	565 02/05	566 02/12	567 02/19	568 02/26	569 03/05	570 03/12	571 03/19	572 03/28	573 04/02
REQUIREMENTS	495			483	25	25		516				
SCHEDULED RECEIPTS												
PLANNED RECEIPTS			508				491	516				337
AVAILABLE ON-HAND	1,500		508									
PLANNED ORDERS	491			337				334				

Weeks 574–585

	574 04/09	575 04/16	576 04/23	577 04/30	578 05/07	579 05/14	580 05/21	581 05/28	582 06/04	583 06/11	584 06/18	585 06/25
REQUIREMENTS	337		25		334	25						
SCHEDULED RECEIPTS			508									
PLANNED RECEIPTS			334	334								
AVAILABLE ON-HAND				334								
PLANNED ORDERS												

Weeks 586–612

	586 07/16	587 07/23	588 07/30	589-592 08/06	593-596 09/03	597-600 10/01	601-604 10/29	605-608 11/26	609-612 12/24
		VACATION							
REQUIREMENTS									
SCHEDULED RECEIPTS									
PLANNED RECEIPTS									
AVAILABLE									
PLANNED ORDERS									

```
********EXCEPTION MESSAGES********
PLANNED ORDER OF 491 FOR M-WK 568   OFFSET INTO A PAST PERIOD BY 03 PERIODS
********PEGGING DATA (ALLOC)********
790116  455  JN25220
********PEGGING DATA (REQMT)********
790205  483  F  17144
790305  516  F  19938
790409  337  F  17144
790507  334  F  19938
```

Thus, we see the solution to a material shortage problem might be made by compressing lead times throughout the product structure using the system and bottom-up replanning. Planners work within the system using firm planned orders and net requirements to develop workable (but not standard) production schedules. The creativity they use in solving problems will be reflected in the part records at the next MRP processing cycle. All implications of planner actions will be correctly coordinated throughout the product structure.

It's important to note that the resolution of problems cannot *always* involve reduced lead time and/or partial lots. Further, none of these actions are free. In some cases, customer needs will have to be delayed or partial shipments made. Pegging and bottom-up replanning will provide advance warning of these problems so customers can take appropriate actions.

An MRP System Output

Figure 7.10 is an MRP time-phased record for one part number out of a total of 13,000 at the Batesville, Indiana, facility of the Hill-Rom Company. The header information includes the date the report was run, part number and description, planner code number, buyer code number (for purchased parts), unit of measure for this part number (pieces, pounds, etc.), rejected parts that have yet to receive disposition by quality control, safety stocks, shrinkage allowance for anticipated scrap loss, lead time, family data (what other parts are similar to this one), year-to-date scrap, usage last year, year-to-date usage, and order policy/lot size data. The policy code of 3 for this part means the order policy is a **period order quantity (POQ).** In this case, "periods to comb. = 04" means each order should combine four periods of net requirements.

The first time bucket is "past due." After that, weekly time buckets are presented for the first 28 weeks of data; thereafter, 24 weeks of data are lumped into 4-week buckets. In the computer itself, a bucketless system is used with all data kept in exact days, with printouts prepared in summary format for one- and four-week buckets. The company maintains a manufacturing calendar; in this example, the first week is 563 (also shown as 1/22), and the last week is 612.

In this report, safety stock is subtracted from the on-hand balance (except in the past-due bucket). Thus, the exception message indicating that a planned order for 491 should have been issued three periods ago creates no major problem, since the planner noted that this amount is less than the safety stock. This report also shows the use of safety lead time. *Planned* receipts are given a specific row in the report and are scheduled one week ahead of the actual need date. For example, the 337-unit planned order of week 565 is a planned receipt in week 573, although it's not needed until week 574.

The final data in the report is the pegging data section tying specific requirements to the part numbers from which those requirements came. For example, in week 565 (shop order no. 790205), the requirement for 483 derives from part number F17144. MRP records are printed at this company only for those part numbers for which exception messages exist.

System Dynamics

Murphy's law states that if anything can go wrong, it will. Things are constantly going wrong, so it's essential that the MRP system mirror actual shop conditions; that is, both the physical system and the information system have to cope with scrap, incorrect counts,

FIGURE 7.11

MRP Record for Part 1234 as of Week 1

Lead time = 2
Lot size = 50

		1	2	3	4	5
Gross requirements		30	20	20	0	45
Scheduled receipts		50				
Projected available balance	10	30	10	40	40	45
Planned order releases		50		50		

changes in customer needs, incorrect bills of material, engineering design changes, poor vendor performance, and a myriad of other mishaps.

In this section, we look at the need for quick and accurate transaction processing and review the MRP planner's replanning activities in coping with change. We discuss sources of problems occurring as a result of database changes plus actions to ensure the system is telling the truth, even if the truth hurts.

Transactions During a Period

To illustrate transaction processing issues, we use a simple example for one part. Figure 7.11 shows an MRP record (for part 1234) produced over the weekend preceding week 1. The planner for part 1234 would receive this MRP record on Monday of week 1.

The planner's first action would be to try to launch the planned order for 50 units in period 1; that is, the MPC system would first check availability of the raw materials for this part and then issue an order to the shop to make 50, if sufficient raw material is available. Launching would require allocating the necessary raw materials to the shop order, removing the 50 from the "Planned order release" row for part 1234, and creating a scheduled receipt for 50 in week 3, when they're needed. Thereafter, a pick ticket would be sent to the raw material area and work could begin.

Let's assume during week 1 the following changes occurred, and the transactions were processed:

- Actual disbursements from stock for item 1234 during week 1 were only 20 instead of the planned 30.
- The scheduled receipt for 50 due in week 1 was received on Tuesday, but 10 units were rejected, so only 40 were actually received into inventory.
- The inventory was counted on Thursday and 20 additional pieces were found.
- The requirement date for the 45 pieces in week 5 was changed to week 4.
- Marketing requested an additional five pieces for samples in week 2.
- The requirement for week 6 has been set at 25.

The resultant MRP record produced over the weekend preceding week 2 is presented as Figure 7.12.

FIGURE 7.12
MRP Record
for Part 1234
as of Week 2

Lead time = 2
Lot size = 50

		2	3	4	5	6
Gross requirements		25	20	45	0	25
Scheduled receipts			50			
Projected available balance	50	25	55	10	10	35
Planned order release				50		

Rescheduling

The MRP record shown in Figure 7.12 illustrates two important activities for MRP planners: (1) indicating the sources of problems that will occur as a result of database changes and (2) suggesting actions to ensure the system is telling the truth. Note the scheduled receipt presently due in week 3 is not needed until week 4. The net result of all the changes to the database means it's now scheduled with the wrong due date, and the due date should be changed to week 4. If this change is not made, this job may be worked on ahead of some other job that is really needed earlier, thereby causing problems. The condition shown in Figure 7.12 would be highlighted by an MRP exception message, such as "reschedule the receipt currently due in week 3 to week 4."

Complex Transaction Processing

So far, we've illustrated system dynamics by using a single MRP record. However, an action required on the part of an MRP planner may have been caused by a very complex set of database transactions involving several levels in the bill of materials. As an example, consider the MRP records shown in Figure 7.13, which include three levels in the product structure. Part C is used as a component in both parts A and B as well as being sold as a service part. Part C, in turn, is made from parts X and Y. The arrows in Figure 7.13 depict the pegging data.

The part C MRP record is correctly stated at the beginning of week 1. That is, no exception messages would be produced at this time. In particular, the two scheduled receipts of 95 and 91, respectively, are scheduled correctly, since delaying either by one week would cause a shortage, and neither has to be expedited to cover any projected shortage.

While the two scheduled receipts for part C are currently scheduled correctly, transactions involving parts A and B can have an impact on the proper due dates for these open orders. For example, suppose an inventory count adjustment for part A resulted in a change in the 30-unit planned order release from week 1 to week 3. In this case, the 95 units of part C would not be needed until week 3, necessitating a reschedule. Similarly, any change in timing for the planned order release of 25 units of part A in week 4 would call for a reschedule of the due date for 91 units of part C. Finally, suppose a transaction requiring 75 additional units of part B in week 5 were processed. This would result in an immediate release of an order for 100 units of part C. This might necessitate rescheduling for parts X and Y. The point here is that actions required on the part of an MRP planner can occur because of

FIGURE 7.13
MRP Record Relationships for Several Parts

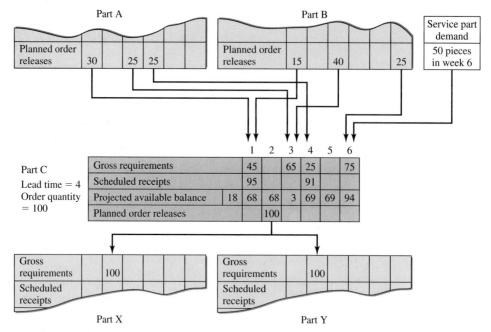

Note: This example is based on one originally developed by Joseph Orlicky. *Orlicky's Material Requirements Planning,* 2nd ed. New York: McGraw-Hill, 1994, chap. 4, pp. 69–99.

a complex set of database transactions involving many different parts. They may not necessarily directly involve the particular part being given attention by the MRP planner.

Procedural Inadequacies

MRP replanning and transaction processing activities are two essential aspects of ensuring the MPC database remains accurate. However, while these activities are necessary, they aren't sufficient to maintain accurate records. Some of the procedures used to process transactions simply may be inadequate to the task.

To illustrate inadequate transaction procedures, let's return to the example in Figure 7.13. Note that, if 4 or more pieces are scrapped on the shop order for 95, there will be a shortage in week 3, necessitating rescheduling of the order for 91 one week earlier.

It's even more interesting to see what would happen if 4 pieces were scrapped on the order for 95, and this scrap transaction weren't processed. If the scrap isn't reported, MRP records would appear as shown in Figure 7.13, indicating no required rescheduling—when, in fact, that's not true. *If* the shortage were discovered by the person in charge of the stockroom when he or she puts away this order, then only one week would be lost before the next MRP report shows the problem. If, however, the stockroom person doesn't count, or if the person who made the scrap puts the defective parts at the bottom of the box where they go undetected by quality control, then the problem will be discovered only when the assembly lines are trying to build As and Bs in week 3. Such a discovery comes under the category of unpleasant surprises. An interesting sidelight to this problem is that the cure will be to rush down to the shop to get at least 1 piece from the batch of 91. The very person who failed to report the earlier scrap may well now be screaming. "Why don't those idiots know what they need!"

Still another aspect of the scrap reporting issue can be seen by noting the 95 and 91 were originally issued as lot sizes of 100. This probably means 5 and 9 pieces of scrap have occurred already, and the appropriate adjustments have been made in the scheduled receipt data. Note that, if these adjustments had *not* been made, the two scheduled receipts would show as 100 each. The resultant 14 (or 5 + 9) pieces (that don't, in fact, exist) would be reflected in the MRP arithmetic. Thus, the projected available balance at the end of period 5 would be 83 (or 69 + 14); this is more than enough to cover the gross requirement of 75 in period 6, so the planned order release for 100 in period 2 would not exist and the error would cascade throughout the product structure. Further, even if shop orders are carefully counted as they are put into storage, the five-piece shortage in period 1 is not enough to cause the MRP arithmetic to plan an order. Only after period 4 (the beginning of period 5) will the additional nine pieces of scrap be incorporated in the MRP record showing a projected shortage in period 6. This will result in an immediate order, to be completed in one week instead of four! What may be obvious is that, if accurate counting isn't done, then the shortage is discovered in week 6, when the assembly line goes down. This means procedures for issuing scrap tickets when scrap occurs and procedures for ensuring good parts are accurately counted into inventory must be in place. If not, all the MPC systems will suffer.

The long and the short of all this is that we have to believe the numbers, and an error of as little as *one* piece can cause severe problems. We have to know the truth. We have to tightly control transactions. Moreover, we have to develop iron-clad procedures for processing MPC database transactions.

| **Concluding Principles** | Chapter 7 provides an understanding of the MRP approach to detailed material planning. It describes basic techniques, some technical issues, and how MRP systems are used in practice. MRP, with its time-phased approach to planning, is a basic building-block concept for materials planning and control systems. Moreover, there are many other applications of the time-phased record. We see the most important concepts or principles of this chapter as follows: |

- Effective use of an MRP system allows development of a forward-looking (planning) approach to managing material flows.
- The MRP system provides a coordinated set of linked product relationships, thereby permitting decentralized decision making on individual part numbers.
- All decisions made to solve problems must be done within the system, and transactions must be processed to reflect the resultant changes.
- Effective use of exception messages allows focusing attention on the "vital few," not on the "trivial many."
- System records must be accurate and reflect the factory's physical reality if they're to be useful.
- Procedural inadequacies in processing MRP transactions need to be identified and corrected to ensure material plans are accurate.

References

Conway, R. W. "Linking MRPII and FCS." *APICS—The Performance Advantage,* June 1996.

Fisher, D. "MRP at 'Lightspeed' without the MRP." *IE Solutions,* May 1996.

Hiquet, Bradley D. *SAP R/3 Implementation Guide: A Managers Guide to Understanding SAP.* Indianapolis: Macmillan Technical Publishing, 1998.

Miller, J. G., and L. G. Sprague. "Behind the Growth in Materials Requirements Planning." *Harvard Business Review,* September–October 1975.

Plossl, G. *Orlicky's Material Requirements Planning.* 2nd ed. New York: McGraw-Hill, 1994.

Ptak, Carol A. *ERP Tools, Techniques, and Applications for Integrating the Supply Chain.* Boca Raton, Fla.: St. Lucie Press, 2000.

Discussion Questions

1. Why is the MRP activity in the "engine" part of the MPC system shown in Figure 7.1?

2. What additional information would be helpful to you in using or following the basic MRP record?

3. Compare a bill of materials (BOM) and a cookbook recipe.

4. How does the *system* coordinate the individual item records and provide back schedule information?

5. Provide examples of potential differences between the information system and the physical reality for university activities. What are the consequences of some of these mismatches?

6. What are some of the reasons for wanting to process the records in an MRP system frequently? Provide examples and consequences of delaying the processing of the information.

7. The chapter uses a Christmas list and Christmas gift order analogy for planned order releases and scheduled receipts. What are other analogies of these two concepts? Why is it important to keep them separate in the MRP records?

8. What are the implications of *not* allocating material to a shop order after availability checking?

9. Give some examples of transaction processing for individual students at a university. What happens if they are not done well?

Problems

1. Joe's Burgers sells three kinds of hamburgers—Big, Giant, and The Football. The bills of materials are:

Big Burger		Giant Burger		Football Burger	
$\frac{1}{4}$ lb. patty	1.0	$\frac{1}{2}$ lb. patty	1.0	1 lb. patty	2.0
Regular bun	1.0	Sesame bun	1.0	Sesame bun	1.0
Pickle slice	1.0	Pickle slices	2.0	Pickle slices	4.0
Catsup	0.1 oz.	Catsup	0.2 oz.	Lettuce	0.3 oz.
		Onion	0.2 oz.	Catsup	0.2 oz.
				Cheese	0.5 oz.
				Onion	0.2 oz.

a. If the product mix is 20 percent Big, 45 percent Giant, and 35 percent Footballs, and Joe sells 200 burgers a day, how much hamburger meat is used per day?

b. How many pickle slices are needed per day?

c. Suppose buns are delivered every second day. Joe is ready to order. His on-hand balance of regular buns is 25, and his on-hand balance of sesame buns is 20. How many buns should be ordered?

d. Reconsider question c if Joe has 10 Big hamburgers, 5 Giant, and 15 Footballs all made.

2. The following illustration shows how to assemble your own computer.

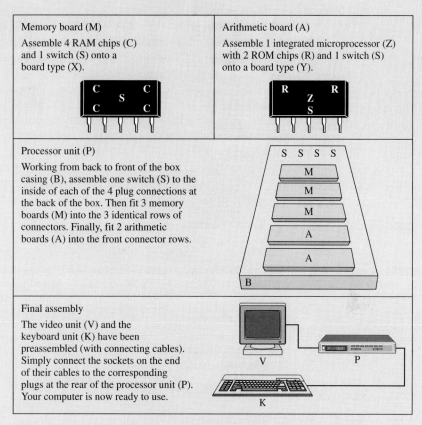

Memory board (M)	Arithmetic board (A)
Assemble 4 RAM chips (C) and 1 switch (S) onto a board type (X).	Assemble 1 integrated microprocessor (Z) with 2 ROM chips (R) and 1 switch (S) onto a board type (Y).

Processor unit (P)

Working from back to front of the box casing (B), assemble one switch (S) to the inside of each of the 4 plug connections at the back of the box. Then fit 3 memory boards (M) into the 3 identical rows of connectors. Finally, fit 2 arithmetic boards (A) into the front connector rows.

Final assembly

The video unit (V) and the keyboard unit (K) have been preassembled (with connecting cables). Simply connect the sockets on the end of their cables to the corresponding plugs at the rear of the processor unit (P). Your computer is now ready to use.

a. Draw the product structure tree corresponding to the assembly instructions.

b. Determine low-level codes for the following items: (1) A—Arithmetic board, (2) B—Box casing, (3) C—RAM chip, (4) K—Keyboard unit, (5) M—Memory board, (6) P—Processor unit, (7) R—ROM chip, (8) S—Switch, (9) V—Video unit, (10) X—Board type X, (11) Y—Board type Y, and (12) Z—Integrated microprocessor.

c. Assume no inventory of any item. How many of each part should be available to assemble one completed unit?

3. Power Tools (PT) has just received an order for 70 PT band saws, to be shipped at the beginning of week 9. Information concerning the saw assembly is given below:

	PT Band Saw	
Item	**Lead Time (weeks)**	**Components**
Saw	2	A(2*), B, C(3)
A	1	E(3), D
B	2	D(2), F(3)
C	2	E(2), D(2)
D	1	
E	1	
F	3	

*Number of parts required to make one parent.

   a. Draw the product structure tree.

   b. Construct a Gantt chart for the new order using front schedule logic.

   c. Construct a Gantt chart for the new order using back schedule logic.

4. The recipe for 6 servings of Martha's Triple Chocolate Smoothie calls for 4 dashes of cinnamon, $1\frac{1}{2}$ liters of vanilla ice cream, 2 liters of chocolate ice cream, $\frac{1}{2}$ liter of chocolate milk, and 1 bag of chocolate chips.

   a. Martha is planning an ice cream social for 12 people and wants to make Triple Chocolate Smoothies. How much chocolate ice cream does she need for 12 servings if her chocolate ice cream is totally gone?

   b. How many liters of vanilla ice cream must be bought if Martha already has one liter of vanilla on hand?

   c. Martha is planning her party for November 15. It's now November 11. The local dairy will deliver liters of ice cream and milk if given a one-day notice. Fill in the following MRP record for chocolate milk if Martha has $\frac{1}{2}$ liter on hand and wants the rest delivered. Assume she can make the Smoothies on the day of the social.

	November				
	11	12	13	14	15
Gross requirements					
Scheduled receipts					
Projected available balance					
Planned order release					

5. Develop an MRP spreadsheet record for six periods using the following parameters for the item:

Period	1	2	3	4	5	6
Gross requirements	20	20	40	30	30	30

Lead time	1 period
Lot size	50 units
Safety stock	0 units
Inventory	2 units
Scheduled receipt	50 units in period 1

   a. In what periods are there planned order releases?

   b. What happens to the timing, number of planned order releases, and average inventory (for periods 1 through 6) if 15 units of safety stock are required?

   c. What happens to the timing, number of planned order releases, and average inventory (for periods 1 through 6) if a one-week safety lead time is used instead of the safety stock?

6. Given the following product structure diagram, complete the MRP records for parts A, B, and C.

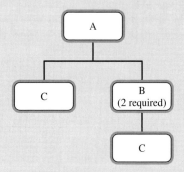

		Week					
Part A		1	2	3	4	5	6
Gross requirements		5	25	18	8	12	22
Scheduled receipts							
Projected available balance	21						
Planned order release							

Q = 20; LT = 1; SS = 0.

		Week					
Part B		1	2	3	4	5	6
Gross requirements							
Scheduled receipts		32					
Projected available balance	20						
Planned order release							

Q = 40; LT = 2; SS = 0.

		Week					
Part C		1	2	3	4	5	6
Gross requirements							
Scheduled receipts							
Projected available balance	70						
Planned order release							

Q = LFL; LT = 1; SS = 10.

7. Given the product structure diagrams at Traci's Tomahawk shown below, complete the MRP records for Parts A, F, and G using the data provided for each.

Product Structures

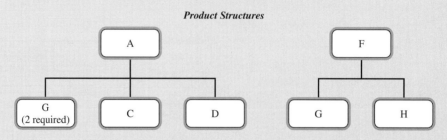

Part A		Week 1	2	3	4	5
Gross requirement		5	3	10	15	15
Scheduled receipt		5				
Projected available balance	10					
Planned order release						

Lead time = 1; Q = L4L; SS = 0.

Part F		Week 1	2	3	4	5
Gross requirement		10	20	25	15	5
Scheduled receipt			15			
Projected available balance	15					
Planned order release						

Lead time = 2; Q = L4L; SS = 0.

Part G		Week 1	2	3	4	5
Gross requirement						
Scheduled receipt		20				
Projected available balance	30					
Planned order releases						

Lead time = 1; Q = multiples of 20; SS = 10.

8. Ajax produces two basic products called A and B. Each week, Paul, the owner, plans to assemble 20 product As and 8 product Bs. Given this information and the following product structure dia-

grams for A and B, fill out the MRP records (inventory status files) for component parts G and Y for the next seven weeks.

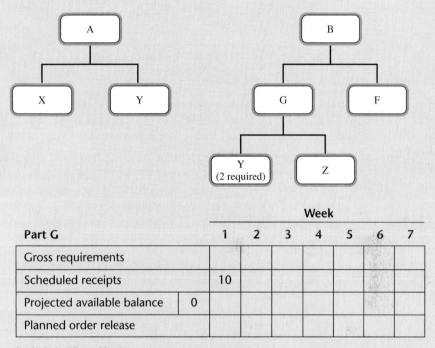

		Week					
Part G	1	2	3	4	5	6	7
Gross requirements							
Scheduled receipts	10						
Projected available balance 0							
Planned order release							

Q = lot for lot; LT = 1; SS = 0.

		Week					
Part Y	1	2	3	4	5	6	7
Gross requirements							
Scheduled receipts	10						
Projected available balance 48							
Planned order release							

Q = lot-for-lot; LT = 2; SS = 0.

Suppose 10 units of safety stock are required for part Y. What changes would result in the records? Would the MRP system produce any exception messages?

9. Consider the following product structure and inventory information:

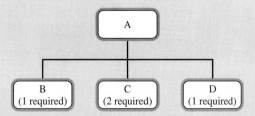

Item	Inventory
A	10
B	40
C	60
D	60

Lead time = 1 week for all items. There are no scheduled receipts for any item. How many units of product A can be delivered to customers at the start of next week (i.e., in one week) under each of the following circumstances? (Treat each independently; that is, only a, only b, or only c.)

a. The bill of materials for B is wrong. It actually takes 2 units of B to make an A.

b. The inventory for D is only 30 units.

c. There was need to scrap 5 units of the inventory for item C.

10. XYZ Manufacturing Company has collected 10 periods of data for two of its products, A and B. Using the two data sets as gross requirements data, construct MRP time-phased records. Using a spreadsheet program, create four time-phased records, two for each data set. For one case, use a lot size of 150 units, and for the other use an order quantity equal to the total net requirements for the next three periods. In all four records, start with a beginning inventory of 150 units, and compute the average inventory level held over the 10 periods. What do the results mean?

					Period					
Demand	1	2	3	4	5	6	7	8	9	10
A	71	46	49	55	52	47	51	48	56	51
B	77	83	90	22	10	10	16	19	27	79

11. Consider the information contained in the planned order row of the following MRP record. The planned order releases in weeks 2 and 4 are firm planned orders and cannot be changed without managerial approval.

		Period			
	1	2	3	4	5
Gross requirements	10	30	20	15	20
Scheduled receipts	40				
Projected available balance	10	40	10	30	15	35
Planned order release (firm)		40		40	

Q = 40; LT = 1; SS = 5.

Use an MRP spreadsheet to answer the following questions:

a. What transactions would cause an action message on the firm planned order in week 2?

b. What transactions would cause an action message on the firm planned order in week 4?

12. Consider the following MRP record:

		Week					
		1	2	3	4	5	6
Gross requirements		25	30	5	15	5	10
Scheduled receipts			50			15	
Projected available balance	35	10	30	25	10	20	10
Planned order releases							

Q = lot-for-lot; LT = 5; SS = 0.

Suppose 15 units of the scheduled receipt for 40 units due on Monday of week 2 are scrapped during week 1, and no scrap ticket is issued. Furthermore, assume this lot isn't counted before it's put away in the stockroom on Monday of week 2, but is recorded as a receipt of 50 units. What impact will these actions have on factory operations?

13. Complete the following MRP time-phased record:

			Week						
Item: Toaster		1	2	3	4	5	6	7	8
Gross requirements		20	20	35	25	35	35	35	35
Scheduled receipts		50							
Projected available balance	10								
Planned order release									

Q = 50; LT = 2; SS = 5.

The following events occurred during week 1:

1. Actual demand during week 1 was only 5 units.
2. A scheduled receipt of 45 was received during week 1.
3. A cycle count of on-hand units showed 17 units at the start of week 1.
4. Marketing forecasted that 40 easy chairs would be required in week 9.

Update the record below after rolling through time.

		Week						
Item: Easy Chair		2	3	4	5	6	7	8	9
Gross requirements		20	25	25	35	35	35	35	
Scheduled receipts									
Projected available balance									
Planned order release									

Q = 50; LT = 2; SS = 5.

14. The MPC system at ABC Manufacturing Company is run weekly to update the master production schedule (MPS) and MRP records. At the start of week 1, the MPS for end products X and Y is:

Master Production Schedule						
Week Number	1	2	3	4	5	6
Product X	10	—	25	5	10	—
Product Y	5	30	—	20	—	20

One unit of component C is required to manufacture one unit of either end product X or Y. Purchasing lead time for component C is two weeks, an order quantity of 40 units is used, and no (zero) safety stock is maintained for this item. Inventory balance for component C is 5 units at the start of week 1, and there's an open order (scheduled receipt) for 40 units due to be delivered at the beginning of week 1.

a. Complete the MRP record for component C as it would appear at the beginning of week 1:

	Week					
	1	2	3	4	5	6
Gross requirements						
Scheduled receipts						
Projected available balance						
Planned order releases						

b. During week 1, the following transactions occurred for component C:

1. The open order for 40 units due to be received at the start of week 1 was received on Monday of week 1 with a quantity of 30 (10 units of component C were scrapped on this order).

2. An inventory cycle count during week 1 revealed that five units of component C were missing. Thus, an inventory adjustment of −5 was processed.

3. Ten units of component C were actually disbursed (instead of the 15 units planned for disbursement to produce end products A and B). (The MPS quantity of 5 in week 1 for product B was canceled as a result of a customer order cancellation.)

4. The MPS quantities for week 7 include 15 units for product X and 0 units for product Y.

5. Because of a change in customer order requirements, marketing has requested that the MPS quantity of 25 units for product X scheduled in week 3 be moved to week 2.

6. An order for 40 units was released.

Given this information, complete the MRP record for component C as it would appear at the beginning of week 2:

	Week					
	2	3	4	5	6	7
Gross requirements						
Scheduled receipts						
Projected available balance						
Planned order releases						

What action(s) are required by the inventory planner at the start of week 2 as a result of transactions occurring during week 1?

15. Use a spreadsheet program to develop the MRP records for parts A and B from the following product structure. Use the data from the following table:

Part	A	B
Requirements	50/period	–
Initial inventory balance	63	8
Lead time	1	1
Lot size	lot-for-lot	250
Safety stock	10	–
Scheduled receipt	–	250 in period 1

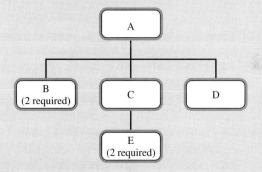

a. What are the planned orders for item B?

b. On an unlucky day (it must have been the 13th), the planner for part A found that the inventory was wrong by 13 units. Instead of 63, there were only 50 on hand. What happens to the planned orders for part B?

c. Use the spreadsheet model to generate a 10-period material plan for parts A and B. Assume that the 63 units of inventory for A were correct. Suppose that in period 1, actual demand for part A was 60 units instead of 50. Regenerate the spreadsheet for periods 2 through 11. What changes occur in the material plans for parts A and B?

8

Distribution Requirements Planning

Distribution requirements planning (DRP) provides the basis for integrating supply chain inventory information and physical distribution activities with the manufacturing planning and control (MPC) system. It is a bridge between the intrafirm MPC systems used to manage internal resources and the interfirm systems used to link members of the supply chain. The set of DRP techniques described in this chapter can help the firm link supply chain requirements with manufacturing activities. DRP relates current field inventory positions, forecasts, and knowledge of demand to manufacturing's master production scheduling and material planning modules. A well-developed DRP system helps management anticipate future requirements in the field, closely match material supply to demand, effectively deploy inventory to meet customer service requirements, and rapidly adjust to the vagaries of the marketplace. In addition, the system supports significant logistics savings through better planning of transportation capacity needs and dispatching of shipments. This chapter will show how DRP works, how it ties into the MPC system, and how it can be used to realize the potential savings.

This chapter is organized around four topics:

- *Distribution requirements planning in the supply chain:* How does DRP integrate the MPC system with the supply chain needs?
- *DRP techniques:* How does DRP work and how is it used to manage the demand and supply of field inventories?
- *Management issues with DRP:* What organizational questions must be addressed to fully realize the system's potential?
- *Company example:* How does DRP work in an actual firm?

This chapter closely relates to Chapter 2 on demand management, Chapter 6 on master production scheduling, and Chapter 17 on supply chain management. The DRP system links the demand management system to the supply chain. Record processing in DRP is consistent with that described for material requirements planning (MRP) in Chapter 7 and the theory on independent demand inventories as found in Chapter 5.

Distribution Requirements Planning in the Supply Chain

Managing the flow of materials in a contemporary supply chain is a difficult and complex task. The materials move between firms, warehouses, and distribution centers and can even return to their point of origin with value having been added or for remanufacturing. Moreover, the ownership might be different for any combination of the facilities among which the materials can flow.

Distribution requirements planning is a technique to help manage these material flows. DRP links firms in the supply chain by providing planning records that carry demand information from receiving points to supply points and returns supply information to the receiving points. Key linkages in the supply network can be integrated through DRP. The logistics activities of transportation, storage in warehouses and/or distribution centers, and ***breaking bulk*** (breaking large shipment quantities into customer-friendly units) can be incorporated, as can other value-adding activities like labeling, adding country-specific information, or providing special packaging.

Though several linkages in the supply network can be accommodated in a distribution requirements planning system, in our description of DRP we will take the perspective of a supplying firm distributing product to other manufacturers or to retail customers. Thus we will be concerned with the physical distribution (including transportation and warehousing) of the product(s). The key linkages that we will describe are those with our customer(s). They take us from intrafirm to interfirm MPC. These linkages can form the connection between our internal MPC system and our customers' internal MPC systems. They carry information to the market and provide us with information on the market.

Even though our description of DRP will be in terms of our supplying product to our customers, we are also a customer for our suppliers. Thus there can be a DRP connection from our internal system to the internal system of our suppliers. These DRP connections to or from us could extend deeply into the respective internal systems. This is especially true when we (or our suppliers) are using ***vendor-managed inventories.*** Under vendor-managed inventories, the replenishment of our products in inventory at customers' locations would be under our control.

When the quantities and timing of shipments to our customers is under our control rather than the customers, we need to know what the customers will need in the future. We can get this information, of course, from their MPC system. This degree of integration is what permits us to ***make to knowledge.*** Without this integration we would forecast what will be needed, provide safety stock for forecast errors, and still might be surprised. With the integration we can know as well as our customers what will be needed and can learn as soon as they do when their plans change.

DRP can be linked into our internal MPC system, both from our suppliers and to our customers. DRP, therefore, provides linkages that span the boundary from internal to external MPC systems. We take up those linkages in the rest of this section before moving on to the technical aspects of distribution requirements planning.

DRP and the MPC System Linkages

The distribution requirements planning (DRP) linkages that span the boundary from our internal systems to our customers' internal systems are shown in Figure 8.1. The link to the

FIGURE 8.1
DRP Links to
the Internal
MPC System

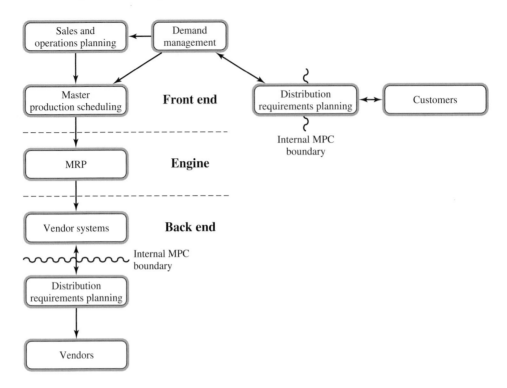

front end of the MPC system runs from demand management to the customers and back. Through this link with demand management, demand information is brought into master production scheduling and the sales and operations planning activity. For master production scheduling, the information is important for managing the balance of supply and demand within the current company plans and capacity. For sales and operations planning, the information is combined with other market data and company objectives to develop the company plans.

DRP has a central role in coordinating material flows through a complicated physical system consisting of field warehouses, intermediate distribution centers, central supplies, and customer locations. The role is similar to material requirements planning's role in coordinating materials in manufacturing. Moreover, the DRP information must be integrated into the internal MPC system. This is facilitated by using time-phased information on inventories, material in transit, and shipping plans. The key task is effectively managing the required flow of goods and inventories between the firm and the market. DRP's role is to provide the necessary data for matching customer demand with the supply of products at various stages in the physical distribution system and products being produced by manufacturing.

Key elements of these data are the planned timings and quantities for replenishing inventories throughout the physical distribution system. These data take into account currently available field inventories and forecasts. Planners use these data to evaluate the quality of the current match between supply and demand and to make adjustments as required.

Distribution requirements planning provides information to the master production scheduler in a format consistent with the MRP records. By using standard MRP software approaches for DRP, the full range of MRP techniques (such as firm planned orders, pegging, and exception messages) is available to manage distribution inventories. This also provides the basis for integrating the database throughout the MPC system—from supplier systems through distribution. Evaluation of alternative plans, with the integrated database, provides a complete view of the material planning implications. This is particularly valuable in master production scheduling.

DRP data provide the basis for adjusting the master production schedule (MPS) to reflect changes in demand or in the product mix. If manufacturing and distribution system priorities can't be adjusted to respond to these requirements, the implications can be evaluated and communicated to customers in a timely fashion. Common records and system integration mean there's complete visibility to see how best to use available inventories and to adjust future schedules. DRP provides a solid base of information to make these decisions, instead of relying on political negotiations between field and factory.

DRP and the Marketplace

DRP starts in the marketplace—or as close to it as possible. Increasingly, this could actually be at a customer location. Some firms gather information on inventory levels and on product usage directly from key customers, possibly directly from their MPC systems. This knowledge of their customers' requirements provides these firms the opportunity to make to knowledge. In the instance where they have vendor-managed inventories in a customer location, it enables them to even make the replenishment decision. This, in turn, offers them a major strategic advantage in providing products and service to these customers and gaining efficiencies in their own operations.

In most instances, however, DRP starts inside a company, linking its production unit to its field warehouse units. When the DRP records originate in a warehouse or distribution center, they start at the independent-demand interface; that is, they are derived from forecasts. Since customers of the distribution centers make their own ordering decisions, demand is *independent* of the firm's decisions. From the independent-demand interface point on, however, decisions are under the company's control. Timing and sizes of replenishment shipments, manufacturing batch sizes, and purchase order policies are all under management control.

The DRP approach allows us to pick up all the detailed local information for managing physical distribution and for coordinating with the factory. Since customer demand is independent, each warehouse needs detailed forecasts of end-item demand. However, careful attention to actual customer demand patterns may be useful in tailoring these forecasts to local conditions. We know of one instance, for example, where the local warehouse manager was able to identify several products purchased late in the month by some large customers. This produced a different demand pattern in the forecast than the constant weekly demand throughout the month that came from a standard forecasting software package. The modified forecasts produced important inventory savings by more closely matching demand with supply at this location.

Two types of demand data may be available locally that can help us manage field inventories. Information on special orders can help us provide service to regular orders while satisfying the special orders. Planned inventory adjustments by customers can also be reflected in the system, again providing data for more closely managing the distribution process. In each of these cases, the system allows the company to respond to advance notice of conditions, instead of treating them as surprises when they occur.

All management decisions for controlling inventories are reflected in the plans for re-supplying warehouses. Planned shipment information provides valuable data for managing the local facility. Personnel required for unloading incoming material and stocking shelves can be planned. If there are problems in satisfying local demands, realistic promises can be made to waiting customers. Also the amount of capital tied up in local inventory can be more realistically estimated for funds management.

In summary, DRP serves two purposes in the marketplace, be it in a warehouse, distribution center, or a customer location. First, DRP enables us to capture data, including local demand conditions, for modifying the forecast and to report current inventory positions. Second, DRP provides data for managing the distribution facility and the database for consistent communications with customers and the rest of the company.

DRP and Demand Management

The demand management module is the gateway between the manufacturing facility and the marketplace. In some systems with field inventories, it is where information on demand is taken in and where product for the field warehouses (and inventory status information) is sent out. This process requires detailed matching of supply to demand in every location—and requires providing supply to meet all sources of demand. DRP is a method for managing the resultant large volume of dynamic information and for generating the information to establish the plans for manufacturing and replenishing the inventories.

Plans derived from the DRP information and the resulting shipping requirements are the basis for managing the logistics system. Figure 8.2 shows the relationship between DRP and the logistics activities. Vehicle capacity planning is the process of planning the vehicle availability for the set of future shipments as generated by DRP. Shipping requirements also are used to determine vehicle loads, dispatch vehicles, and plan the resources necessary to receive the goods at the warehouse.

By planning future replenishment needs, DRP establishes the basis for more effective vehicle dispatching decisions. These decisions are continually adjusted to reflect current conditions. Long-term plans help to determine the necessary transportation capacity. Warehouses' near-term needs are used to efficiently load vehicles without compromising customer service levels. Data on planned resupply of the warehouses can be used for scheduling the labor force needed at the warehouses.

FIGURE 8.2
Distribution Requirements Planning and the Logistics System

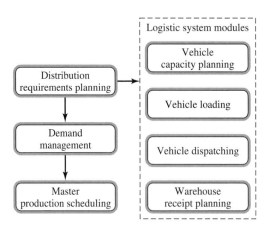

As actual field demands vary around the forecasts, adjustments to plans are required. DRP continually makes these adjustments, sending the inventories from the central warehouse to those distribution centers where they're most needed. In circumstances where insufficient total inventory exists, DRP provides the basis for deciding on allocations. The planning information facilitates applying whatever criteria are used for the allocation decision. These criteria are as varied as providing stock sufficient to last the same amount of time at each location or favoring the "best" customers. Moreover, DRP provides the data to be able to accurately say when availability will be improved and delivery can be expected.

DRP and Master Production Scheduling

Perhaps DRP's greatest payoff to master production scheduling is from integrating records and information. Since the formats of DRP and MRP records are compatible and all MPC modules are linked, DRP allows us to extend MPC visibility into the distribution system. This, however, has internal political implications. One company we know decided not to integrate the records. Instead it established a committee to resolve issues between logistics and manufacturing concerning inventories' size and composition. A sister company installed an integrated system using DRP. When it became evident that the integrated system was superior, the political cost of dismantling the committee was high since all committee members now had "permanent" jobs.

Moving the MPC boundaries into the supply chain, perhaps even into customers' MPC systems also has political costs. Crossing over into the area of interfirm MPC systems means negotiating with supply chain partners for sharing the costs and benefits. These negotiations sometimes require a major element of education for the partners—showing and convincing them of the value of integration. To overcome the natural reluctance to share internal MPC information requires that the customers have a very good understanding of the value you can provide by scheduling replenishments to knowledge instead of forecast. Providing the master scheduler with supply chain visibility makes this possible.

DRP collects detailed information in the field and summarizes it so MPC decisions can respond to overall company needs. DRP permits evaluation of current conditions to determine if manufacturing priorities should be revised. It provides insights into how they should be changed and into implications to the field if they aren't. Thus, more reasoned trade-offs can be made in the use of limited capacity or materials. The DRP shipping plans provide the master scheduler better information to match manufacturing output with shipping needs. Requirements based on shipments to the distribution centers can be quite different from demand in the field. Manufacturing should be closely coordinated with the former. For example, firms matching shipment timings and sizes with manufacturing batches can achieve substantial inventory savings. We turn next to DRP's technical details.

DRP Techniques

In this section, we develop the logic of DRP. We start by introducing the basic record and how DRP information is processed. Then we turn to the time-phased order point, how to link several warehouse records, ways to manage day-to-day variations from plans, and how to use safety stocks in a DRP-based system.

The Basic DRP Record

The DRP system's basic data elements are detailed records for individual products at locations as close to the final customer as possible. Records are maintained centrally as a part of the MPC system database, but continually updated information on inventory and demand are passed between the central location and the field sites either on some periodic basis or in real time, often on line. For illustrative purposes, we'll consider the record for a single **stockkeeping unit (SKU)** at a field warehouse.

To integrate DRP into the overall MPC system, we expand the bill of materials beyond its usual context. The zero level in the bill of material is defined as the SKU in a field warehouse. Thus, an item isn't seen as completed simply when the raw materials have been transformed into a finished product, but only after it has been delivered to the location where it satisfies a customer demand. This extension of the bill of materials into field locations allows us to use standard MRP explosion techniques to link the field with all other MPC systems. Note that the convention means that a product at location X is identified as different from the same product at location Y.

Regardless of the physical location (central inventory at the plant, a distribution center, a field warehouse, or even a customer's shelf), the item's ultimate demand comes from the customer. The warehouse is where the company's internal world of dependent demand must deal with the customer's independent demand. The customer, within wide ranges, decides how much and when to order; these decisions are usually independent of the company's decisions. Planners in the company, on the other hand, decide when and how much product to make. They also decide when and how much to send to field locations. To link company decisions with the customers' we must start with a forecast. This is recorded in the first row of the basic DRP record in Figure 8.3.

Even though the first row is labeled forecast, it may contain much more information than the typical "average weekly demand" forecast produced by a software package. For example, it may have information specific to the customers' buying patterns at a warehouse, as we alluded to before. It can be directly linked to the MPC system of a customer, in which case the information is not our forecast of the needs of that customer, but a reflection of their current plans. In all cases, however, the forecast requirements are subject to change as conditions change and the DRP system provides the means to adjust to those changes.

The record looks like an MRP record, but there are some subtle differences other than the use of forecast data in the requirements row. For example, since it's for a specific location, it not only provides time-phased data on how much and when, but also tells us where. It's not the differences, however, that are important. It's the consistency of format and

FIGURE 8.3
Field
Warehouse
DRP Record

		Period						
		1	2	3	4	5	6	7
Forecast requirements		20	20	20	20	30	30	30
In transit			60					
Projected available balance	45	25	65	45	25	55	25	55
Planned shipments				60		60		

Safety stock = 20; shipping quantity = 60; lead time = 2.

processing logic that provide many of DRP's benefits. To explain this, let's go through the record in some detail.

Figure 8.3 shows a change in the forecast in period 5. This could be due to a revision by someone at the warehouse who has information on local demand, or due to a sales promotion. The fact that these variations can be incorporated into the system at this level provides one of the advantages of using DRP for managing field inventories.

The second row shows shipments in transit to the warehouse. In Figure 8.3, one shipment is scheduled to arrive in time for use in period 2. Thus, time for unloading and shelving the products must be accounted for in setting lead time to show the order available for use in period 2. The equivalent row in a manufacturing MRP record is called "scheduled receipts" (open orders). However, more than the name of the in-transit row is different between manufacturing and distribution. In manufacturing, there is some flexibility in the timing of open orders. They can be speeded up or slowed down to a certain extent, by changing priorities in the shop-floor system. This is more difficult with goods in transit. Once a shipment is on a vehicle bound for a particular location, there's little opportunity to change the arrival time.

The projected inventory balance row contains the current inventory balance (45 for the example in Figure 8.3) and projections of available inventory for each period in the planning horizon (7 periods here). A safety stock value of 20 has been determined as sufficient to provide the customer service level desired for the item. The economics of transportation or packaging indicate a normal shipment of this product to this location is 60 units. Finally, it takes two periods to load, ship, unload, and store the product.

The projected available balance is generated by using the forecast requirements. The process is identical to that used for processing MRP records. In Figure 8.3, the available balance for the end of period 1 is determined by subtracting the forecast requirement of 20 from the initial inventory of 45. The 25 units at the end of period 1, plus the in-transit quantity of 60 to be received in period 2, minus the forecast of 20 for period 2, give the closing balance of 65 for period 2.

Planned shipments are indicated for those periods in which a shipment would have to be made to avoid a projected balance having less than the safety stock. The projected balance for period 4, for example, is 25 units. The forecast for period 5 is 30 units. Therefore, a shipment of product that will be available in period 5 is needed. Since lead time is two periods, a planned shipment of 60 units (the shipping quantity) is shown for period 3. Similarly, the planned shipment in period 5 is needed to cover the forecast of 30 in period 7, since there is only a 25-unit projected available balance at the end of period 6.

The result of these calculations for each product at each location is a plan for future shipments needed to provide the customer service levels the company desires. These plans depend on forecasts, but they incorporate management decisions for shipping quantities and safety stocks in planning resupply schedules. These plans provide the visibility planners need to match supply and demand.

Time-Phased Order Point (TPOP)

Many companies use economic order or shipping quantity/reorder point (Q, R) procedures based on demand forecasts for managing their field inventories. This means decisions for resupply are made independently at the field location, with no integrated forward planning;

FIGURE 8.4

Example Time-Phased Order Point (TPOP) Record

		Period						
		1	2	3	4	5	6	7
Forecast requirements		15	15	15	15	15	15	15
In transit								
Projected available balance	22	7	32	17	42	27	12	37
Planned shipments		40		40			40	

Safety stock = 5; shipping quantity = 40; lead time = 1.

that is, when the on-hand quantity at a location reaches the reorder point, the shipping quantity is ordered with no thought given to any other items ordered, to the situation at the factory, or to warehouses—or to when the next order might be needed. Also, Q, R assumes a constant usage. Whenever forecast information is used as the requirements and a time-phased MRP approach is used to develop planned shipments, it's called **time-phased order point (TPOP).** Time-phased order point can be used for constant usage situations and even when the usage forecast varies from period to period. We use Figure 8.4 to illustrate the approach.

If a Q, R system were used, the reorder point for the situation in Figure 8.4 would be 20 units, comprising the safety stock (5) plus the demand during lead time (15), assuming continuous review of inventory balances. Simulating the Q, R rules for Figure 8.4's data would lead to orders in periods 2, 4, and 7. If we use DRP logic, the planned shipments are in periods 1, 3, and 6. Thus, the timing of the orders in the TPOP record in Figure 8.4 doesn't exactly match the expected timing of orders using Q, R.

The results are, however, very close. The differences would largely disappear if the periods were made small (e.g., days instead of weeks) since they're primarily due to the fact that Q, R assumes continuous review. The TPOP approach is based on the MRP logic of planning a shipment that prevents the ending balance in the period from falling below the safety stock level.

One advantage of TPOP over Q, R is the TPOP record shows *planned* shipment data. These aren't part of the Q, R approach. In addition, TPOP isn't limited to use of constant requirement assumptions. When forecast usages vary, differences between TPOP and Q, R can be much larger than those in Figure 8.4.

Not only is it important to have planned shipment data, it's also critical to capture *all* demand information. Forecast sales requirements are only one source of demand input. DRP can use TPOP plus actual order data plus service part requirements plus interplant demands. *All* these demand sources can be integrated into the demand data driving DRP.

Linking Several Warehouse Records

Once DRP records are established for the field warehouses, information on planned shipments is passed through the distribution centers (if any) to the central facility. This process is sometimes referred to as **implosion.** The concept indicates we're gathering information from a number of field locations and aggregating it at the manufacturing facility. This is different from the explosion notion in manufacturing (where a finished product is broken

FIGURE 8.5
Field
Warehouse
to Central
Warehouse
Records for
DRP

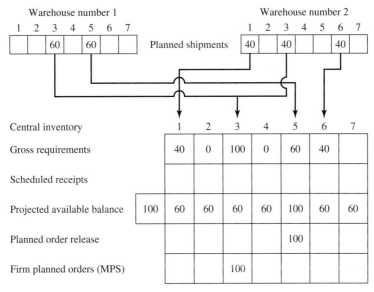

Safety stock = 50; order quantity = 100; lead time = 0

into its components), but the process is the same, and in both cases it's based on bills of material.

The record in Figure 8.5 is for the central warehouse inventory. The gross requirements correspond to planned shipments to the two warehouses in Figures 8.3 and 8.4. This relationship reflects the logic that, if there were a shipment of 40 units of product to warehouse number 2 in period 1, there would be a "demand" on the central warehouse for 40 units in period 1. The "demand," however, is dependent, having come from the company's shipping department. It is, therefore, a gross requirement and not a forecast requirement. We have crossed over from the independent demand world of the customers to the dependent demand world of the company.

The central warehouse's gross requirement is shown in the same period as the planned shipment, since lead time to ship, unload, and put away the product has already been accounted for in the field warehouse record. For example, the shipment of 60 units of product planned for period 3 in warehouse number 1 allows for the lead time before it's needed to meet forecast demand.

The logic for imploding planned shipment information holds also for much more complicated distribution systems. If there were intermediate distribution centers, they would have gross requirements derived from the warehouses they served. At distribution centers, gross requirements are established for any period in which replenishment shipments are planned to warehouses.

A primary task at the central facility is to create the master production schedule. The central inventory record in Figure 8.5 can be used for this purpose. The record shows projected available balances for the central inventory and the planned order releases, which provide the quantities needed to maintain the 50 units of safety stock. The master production schedule is created by using zero lead time and firm planned orders. Firm

FIGURE 8.6

FAS Record for
Packaging
Bulk Materials

Packaged Product		Period						
		1	2	3	4	5	6	7
Gross requirements		40	80	100	0	60	20	100
Scheduled receipts		40						
Projected available balance	10	10	10	10	10	10	10	10
Planned order release					60	20	100	
Firm planned orders		80	100					

Q = lot-for-lot; lead time = 1; SS = 10; planning fence: period 3.

planned orders are created by the planners and aren't under system control; that is, they aren't automatically replanned as conditions change but are maintained in the periods and quantities designated by the planners.

The MPS states when manufacturing is to have the product completed and available for shipment to the field warehouses. In the example in Figure 8.5, the MPS quantity (firm planned order) has replaced a planned order, although this need not be the case.

Our example implies creating an MPS for each end item. This may not be desirable in firms that assemble or package a large variety of end items from common modules, sub-assemblies, or bulk materials. If the MPS is stated in subassemblies or bulk materials, then a final assembly schedule (FAS) needs to be created for managing the conversion to as-semblies or packed products. The resultant records usually don't need to be frozen or firm planned over extensive planning horizons, since they only deal with conversion of, say, bulk material into some specific packaged products. Figure 8.6 shows how this conversion can be managed. This packaged product's gross requirements are exploded from the ship-ments planned to go to all the field locations. Packaging this specific product from the bulk material takes one period. Firm planned orders, up to the planning fence at period 3, are used to schedule the packaging operation. The record also shows 10 units of packaged product held at the central facility to provide flexibility in shipping to the field warehouses.

Figure 8.7 shows how the various sizes of packaged products can be combined into a bulk inventory record for creating the factory's MPS. In the example, two package sizes consume the bulk inventory. The packages are in grams, while the bulk item is in kilo-grams. The explosion process works from packaged item to bulk, but the grams have been converted to kilograms to get the gross requirements for the bulk material (e.g., for period 1: 100 units × 200 grams = 20,000 grams = 20 kilograms). The firm planned orders for the bulk material are the factory MPS, stating when the bulk inventory must be replenished to meet the packaging schedules.

Managing Day-to-Day Variations from Plan

On a daily basis, disbursals for actual customer demand, receipts of inventory, and other transactions are processed. These transactions are used to periodically update the DRP records. If forecasts and execution of plans were perfect, we wouldn't need to do anything but add the new period of information at the end of the planning horizon each time the

FIGURE 8.7
Bulk Material
Record and
MPS

200-Gram Product		Period						
		1	2	3	4	5	6	7
Planned orders						60	40	
Firm planned orders		100		100				

500-Gram Product		Period						
		1	2	3	4	5	6	7
Planned orders					10	10		20
Firm planned orders			20					

Bulk Material—Kilograms		Period						
		1	2	3	4	5	6	7
Gross requirements		20	10	20	5	17	8	10
Scheduled receipts								
Projected available balance	5	25	15	35	30	13	5	35
Planned orders								40
Firm planned orders (MPS)		40		40				

Q = 40; SS = 0; lead time = 0; planning fence: period 5.

records were processed. Unfortunately, we haven't found a company where such conditions hold. Figure 8.8 shows a more likely set of circumstances.

In this example, actual sales vary from 16 to 24 around the forecast of 20 units. The actual sales of 18 in period 1 have no impact on planned shipments, while actual sales of 24 units in period 2 change the plan. The additional sales in period 2 increase net requirements, which leads to planning a shipment in period 3 rather than period 4. Sales in period 3 were lower than expected, so net requirements are less and the planned shipment in period 5 is changed to period 6. Thus, the gross to net logic results in modifying shipping plans to keep them matched to the current market situation.

One negative aspect of the logic is clear from Figure 8.8's example. Actual sales' deviations around the forecast were reflected in changed shipping plans. These changes could have a destabilizing impact on the master schedule and shop. Two techniques for stabilizing the information flow are firm planned orders and error addback.

Figure 8.9 applies the firm planned order (shipment) concept to the warehouse example. By using firm planned shipments, the record shows the what-if results of maintaining the present order pattern. By using DRP records to display this pattern, we generate standard exception messages. For example, if a present plan violates a stated safety stock objective, exception messages highlight it.

In the Figure 8.9 record for period 3, the firm planned shipment of 40 in period 4 isn't rescheduled to period 3, even though the projected available inventory balance for period 4

FIGURE 8.8

Records for a Single SKU at One Warehouse over Four Periods

		Period				
		1	**2**	**3**	**4**	**5**
Forecast requirements		20	20	20	20	20
In transit		40				
Projected available balance	6	26	6	26	6	26
Planned shipments			40		40	

Actual demand for period 1 = 18.

		Period				
		2	**3**	**4**	**5**	**6**
Forecast requirements		20	20	20	20	20
In transit						
Projected available balance	28	8	28	8	28	8
Planned shipments		40		40		

Actual demand for period 2 = 24.

		Period				
		3	**4**	**5**	**6**	**7**
Forecast requirements		20	20	20	20	20
In transit		40				
Projected available balance	4	24	44	24	44	24
Planned shipments		40		40		

Actual demand for period 3 = 16.

		Period				
		4	**5**	**6**	**7**	**8**
Forecast requirements		20	20	20	20	20
In transit		40				
Projected available balance	28	48	28	8	28	8
Planned shipments				40		

Shipping Q = 40; SS = 6; lead time = 1.

is less than the safety stock. Thus, the master scheduler can review the implications of *not* changing before deciding whether changes should be made. In this case, the decision might be to opt for consistency in the information, knowing there still is some projected safety stock and the next order is due to arrive in period 5.

An alternative for stabilizing the information is the error addback method. This approach assumes forecasts are unbiased or accurate on the average. This means any

FIGURE 8.9

Record for a Single SKU at One Warehouse with Firm Planned Order (Shipments) Logic

		Period				
		1	**2**	**3**	**4**	**5**
Forecast requirements		20	20	20	20	20
In transit		40				
Projected available balance	6	26	6	26	6	26
Firm planned shipments			40		40	

Actual demand for period 1 = 18.

		Period				
		2	**3**	**4**	**5**	**6**
Forecast requirements		20	20	20	20	20
In transit						
Projected available balance	28	8	28	8	28	8
Firm planned shipments		40		40		40

Actual demand for period 2 = 24.

		Period				
		3	**4**	**5**	**6**	**7**
Forecast requirements		20	20	20	20	20
In transit		40				
Projected available balance	4	24	4	24	4	24
Firm planned shipments			40		40	

Actual demand for period 3 = 16.

		Period				
		4	**5**	**6**	**7**	**8**
Forecast requirements		20	20	20	20	20
In transit						
Projected available balance	28	8	28	8	28	8
Firm planned shipments		40		40		40

Shipping Q = 40; SS = 6; lead time = 1.

unsold forecast in one period will be made up for in a subsequent period, or any sales exceeding forecast now will reduce sales in a subsequent period. With this method, errors are added (or subtracted) from future requirements to reflect the expected impact of actual sales on projected sales. Figure 8.10 applies this concept to the warehouse example. Note the planned shipments are under system control; that is, firm planned orders aren't used.

FIGURE 8.10

Record for a Single SKU at One Warehouse with Error Addback

		Period				
		1	**2**	**3**	**4**	**5**
Forecast requirements		20	20	20	20	20
In transit		40				
Projected available balance	6	26	6	26	6	26
Planned shipments			40		40	

Period 1 demand = 18; cumulative error = +2.

		Period				
		2	**3**	**4**	**5**	**6**
Forecast requirements		22	20	20	20	20
In transit						
Projected available balance	28	6	26	6	26	6
Planned shipments		40		40		

Period 2 demand = 24; cumulative error = −2.

		Period				
		3	**4**	**5**	**6**	**7**
Forecast requirements		18	20	20	20	20
In transit		40				
Projected available balance	4	26	6	26	6	26
Planned shipments			40		40	

Period 3 demand = 16; cumulative error = +2.

		Period				
		4	**5**	**6**	**7**	**8**
Forecast requirements		22	20	20	20	20
In transit						
Projected available balance	28	6	26	6	26	6
Planned shipments		40		40		

Period 4 demand = 15; cumulative error = +7.
Shipping Q = 40; SS = 6; lead time = 1.

This example's records show the planned orders in exactly the same periods as in the firm planned shipment case. Adjustments to the forecast requirements ensure stability in the information. It's apparent this technique's effectiveness diminishes if the forecast isn't unbiased. For example, if the reduced demand in periods 3 and 4 is part of a continuing trend, the procedure will break down. DRP will continue to build inventory as though the reduced demand will be made up in the future. This means forecasts must be carefully monitored and changed when necessary so the procedure can be started again. One convenient measure for evaluating forecast accuracy is the cumulative forecast error. If this exceeds a specified quantity, the item forecast should be reviewed. For example, in period 4, cumulative error has reached a $+7$ (a value exceeding the safety stock); this might indicate the need to review the forecast for this item.

Safety Stock in DRP

Distribution requirements planning provides the means for carrying inventories and safety stocks at any location in the system. In the examples of Figures 8.3 through 8.5, we show safety stock in field locations and at the central facility. It is important to understand, however, that safety stock is less needed as errors in the forecast are washed out more frequently. With replenishments performed weekly or more often, safety stocks can be reduced.

With DRP, it's possible to use safety lead time as well. In those circumstances where the uncertainty is more likely to be in terms of timing (as in delivering product to the field), it may be better to use safety lead time. In the case of uncertainty in quantity (as with variable yields in manufacturing), safety stock is more typically used.

Where and how much safety stock (or safety lead time) to carry is still an open issue. Research and company experience are just now beginning to provide answers. In terms of quantity, the theory of relating safety stock to the uncertainty in our demand forecasts is clearly valid. The choice would be made on the basis of trade-offs between customer service levels and inventory required.

On the other hand, in distribution, we're not concerned just about how much uncertainty there is but where it is. Less is known about where to put safety stocks. One principle is to carry safety stocks where there's uncertainty. This implies the location closest to the customer and, perhaps, to intermediate points, where there's some element of independent demand. The argument would imply no safety stock where there's dependent demand.

If the uncertainty from several field locations could be aggregated, it should require less safety stock than having stock at each field location. This argument has led to the concept of a "national level" safety stock popularized by Robert G. Brown in his work on materials management. The idea is to have some central stock that can be sent to field locations as conditions warrant, or to permit transshipments between field warehouses. This added flexibility should provide higher levels of service than maintaining multiple field safety stocks. The issue is clouded, however, by the fact that stock in the central facility isn't where customers are.

In a comprehensive simulation study, Shitao Yang addressed the issue of where to hold inventory in a distribution system. He sent a portion of the inventory coming into the distribution system immediately out to the customers and held the rest back to send out later. He measured the ***fill rate*** (the amount of customer demand that was satisfied immediately from inventory) for different portions sent out immediately. He varied inventory levels, number of shipments, lead time, the number of customers, demand uncertainty, and inventory control system. Although it was not a key part of his study, Yang did find that no other inventory control system outperformed DRP.

A typical plot of service level versus the portion of inventory sent immediately to customers is shown in Figure 8.11. These results held across the entire study and lead to

FIGURE 8.11

Fill Rate as a Function of Percent of Distribution Inventory Sent Immediately to Customers

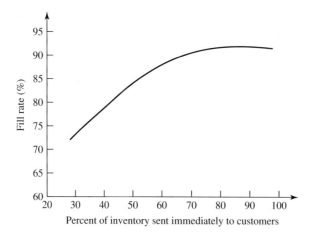

two strong conclusions. First, service levels improved as the percentage of inventory immediately sent to customers increased to about 90 percent. Second, the decrease in service level from sending 100 percent immediately was very small. The practical implication is clear. If you must have inventory available when and where your customers need it, you should hold very little, if any, back in the distribution system.

Other researchers have shown the same result in different situations. William Allen's work on service levels for repair parts showed that safety stock should be held at the repair facilities, not at the distribution center. Similar conclusions were reached for Phillips TV parts distribution in Europe. In a study at Eindhoven University in the Netherlands, van Donselar found the parts inventory should be sent to the field instead of being split between the field and a central facility.

Still another example of the benefits of positioning safety stocks in the field is seen in a large food company. In one division, the primary factory has little warehouse space and end items have considerable bulk. The result is a need to ship all production to distribution centers within hours of manufacture. This, in turn, forces the factory to keep in touch with actual demand and to continually adjust to actual circumstances. The company uses DRP to link distribution centers to all its factories. The products provided by this factory consistently have higher fill rates and fewer stockouts than other products sold through the same distribution centers. Also, inventory turnover on immediately shipped products is higher than for other products. Other plants have their own warehouses where stocks are held. These stocks reduce inventory turns and don't provide immediate service to customers.

Management Issues with DRP

With an operational DRP system integrated with other MPC systems, management has the ability to rationalize material flows from purchasing through distribution. Achieving this desired state, however, raises several critical management questions. We've already discussed some of the DRP issues, such as planning parameters, safety stock, stability, and the form of the master scheduling interface. More fundamental issues relate to assuring the system has appropriate data entry procedures, has an organizational setup facilitating an integrated MPC approach, and uses DRP to solve specific distribution problems. We now turn to each of these managerial topics.

Data Integrity and Completeness

Let's start by considering the record for an item at a location as close to the customer as possible. We've called this location the field warehouse, but it could be at a distribution center, at the customer location itself, or even at the central facility. The issue concerns *where* the forecast is to be input. Since this is the source of demand data for planning throughout the system, it must be correctly determined and maintained. For this record, there are two key data items on which all plans are based: forecast requirements and inventory balance (including any in transit). The axiom of garbage-in, garbage-out holds in DRP as elsewhere. To have confidence in the forecast data, we must assign responsibility for both forecast preparation and adjustments.

A key issue in forecast data integrity for DRP systems is use of aggregate forecasts, which are thereafter broken down into detailed forecasts. An example is a pharmaceutical firm that forecasts annual U.S. insulin sales in total ounces, based on the number of diabetics in the country. This total is multiplied by the company market share, which is in turn broken down into package sizes, weeks, and locations as the basis for field forecasts. As the total is broken down, relative errors increase, but the MPS is based on the totals as brought through the DRP system. This is the summation of the detailed forecasts, after field modifications, so the errors should tend to cancel out.

It's imperative, however, that adjustments of the detailed forecasts don't result in a systematic bias that doesn't balance out. DRP systems are designed to respond to forecast *errors,* but forecast bias is a problem we must avoid.

Once the basic forecast has been generated, people in the field can be given some authority to modify it according to local information and needs. This should be constrained by some rule, like "plus or minus 20 percent adjustment" or "only the timing can be changed but the monthly totals must remain the same." Some mechanism must be put in place for picking up this kind of local intelligence for adjusting forecasts, but it's important to define the limits for proper control.

Also, management programs should be established to monitor this process. Monitoring is more complex when records for items are at customer locations (e.g., a large hospital). In all cases, standard forecast monitoring techniques need to be applied, particularly to discover bias introduced through the adjustment process.

Inventory accuracy depends on transaction processing routines and discipline. Procedures for quick and accurate reporting of shipments to customers, allocations to customers, returns, adjustments, receipts, and the like must all be in place. Another source of errors is incorrect balances of material in transit; these will affect all calculations in the subsequent record processing. Computer auditing can help find outliers in the data for all these cases, but tight procedural controls are clearly needed.

FIGURE 8.12
Conflicting
Functional
Objectives

Functional objectives	Impact of objectives on...		
	Inventory	Customer service	Total costs
• High customer service	⬆	⬆	⬆
• Low transportation costs	⬆	⬇	⬇
• Low warehousing costs	⬇	⬇	⬇
• Reduce inventories	⬇	⬇	⬇
• Fast deliveries	⬆	⬆	⬆
• Reduced labor costs	⬆	⬇	⬇
• Desired results	⬇	⬆	⬇

Organizational Support

Figure 8.12, taken from a paper written by Jones and Riley, shows conflicting functional objectives and their impact on inventory, customer service, and total costs. This figure illustrates some inherent conflicts that need resolution in an integrated MPC system. These conflicts are particularly real when DRP is part of the overall MPC system. In many firms, minimization of transportation costs, for example, is a transportation department's objective. The resultant impact on other parts of the organization is often not clearly understood.

In a comprehensive MPC system with DRP, linkages across functional boundaries are encouraged; but organizational support and evaluation measures need to be established that will minimize suboptimization of overall enterprise goals. Many firms have implemented a **materials management** form of organization to help align responsibilities to the material flow needs. Materials management organizations are responsible for all aspects of materials, from purchasing to final distribution to the customers. Their responsibilities include determining what to make and when, when to take delivery of raw materials, how much to allocate to field locations, and how to relieve short-term materials problems.

As firms improve MPC systems either through more comprehensive approaches (e.g., DRP) or through such enhancements as JIT, emphasis shifts from material control to material velocity. Basic discipline and data integrity aren't abandoned—they're assumed. Time and responsiveness become the most important objectives. Implied is a need to reduce the organizational fragmentation that has built-in time delays. New organizational structures will increasingly be required, ones with overarching authority to dictate actions that provide rapid response to customer needs.

Figure 8.13 illustrates where DRP fits within the supply chain management concept, showing the many organizational entities that need to be coordinated. The ideas parallel those of materials management, but they focus on the process of building the products. Coordinating the chain in Figure 8.13 requires integrated information in DRP form and an organizational form, such as materials management.

FIGURE 8.13 **Supply Chain Management**

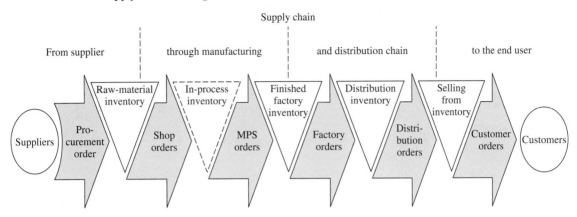

Key to implementing an MPC system with DRP, regardless of the organizational form, is developing planners. The titles can vary in different organizations. Planners establish firm planned orders, evaluate alternative means to solve short-term problems, coordinate problems that cross functional boundaries, and help evaluate trends. They are also responsible for checking feasibility of changes, monitoring data integrity, and assessing the impact of new situations.

Problem Solving

We have already discussed changing conditions due to uncertainty in demand and the techniques that help to deal with them. Other problems come from changing market conditions, product lines, or marketing plans. Examples are product substitutions, promotions, changes in warehouse locations or customer assignments, and controlling the age of stock. DRP records help us solve these problems. We'll describe three of these as illustrative: a sales promotion, closing a warehouse, and monitoring stock aging.

Figure 8.14 presents a sales promotion served by a warehouse. For simplicity, we consider only one product at a single warehouse and the product's packaging line. The process starts with modifying the demand forecast at the warehouse. In the example, the promotion is planned for weeks 5 through 8. The impact is estimated to double sales (from 20 to 40) during the first two weeks and to have a reduced impact during the next two weeks. Note the promotion "steals" from demand in weeks 9 and 10.

The safety stock has been left at five units for the promotion period, although it might have been increased. Stock for the sales promotion is planned for delivery in the weeks in which needed, although it also might have been planned for earlier delivery if there were a need to set up some special display area. The shipping quantity is in multiples of 20, representing a shipping carton or pallet load. Planned shipments are exploded to the packaging record. Using the firm planned orders, the planner has scheduled product packaging at a constant rate of output for the next five weeks (just under the capacity of the packaging line), building inventory in anticipation of the promotion.

FIGURE 8.14 **A Sales Promotion**

Warehouse		Period									
		1	2	3	4	5	6	7	8	9	10
Forecast requirements		20	20	20	20	40	40	30	30	10	10
In transit		20									
Projected available balance	27	27	7	7	7	7	7	17	7	17	7
Planned shipments			20	20	40	40	40	20	20		

Q = 20; lead time = 1; SS = 5.

Packaging		Period									
		1	2	3	4	5	6	7	8	9	10
Gross requirements		0	20	20	40	40	40	20	20		
Scheduled receipts											
Projected available balance	0	0	12	24	16	8	0	0	0		
Planned order release						20	20				
Firm planned orders		32	32	32	32	32					

Q = lot-for-lot; lead time = 1; SS = 0; planning fence: .3.
Note: Packaging capacity = 35 units/period.

The anticipation inventories are shown as remaining at the packaging facility, but they might be sent to the field if space is available or if a truck is on its way with available cargo space. The pattern of inventory buildup could be different, depending on the trade-off between level production and varying the production levels. The DRP records facilitate both planning the buildup and analyzing alternative ways to meet the need (or even arguing for a postponement if capacity is a problem).

Our second example deals with a warehouse closure. Firms often change distribution systems, so closing warehouses and changing shipping patterns are ongoing activities. In Figure 8.15, warehouse 1 is scheduled to close at the end of four weeks, and warehouse 2 is to start supplying the customers. Again, the process of managing the cutover starts with the forecasts. The requirements at warehouse 1 stop at the end of week 4 and are picked up by warehouse 2, reflecting the timing and quantities of the closedown and transfer.

In the example, warehouse 1 would normally have had a planned shipment for 60 units in week 3. The planner has overridden the planned order with a firm planned order for the exact need, reducing safety stock to zero. Note the system plans an order to restore the safety stock and, eventually, the planner will need to change the safety stock parameter to zero in order not to send the wrong signal to the master production scheduler.

As time goes on, the actual quantity needed for warehouse 1 may well be different, but there are two weeks before the exact determination must be made. The planner may decide

FIGURE 8.15

Warehouse Closure

Warehouse 1		Period						
		1	2	3	4	5	6	7
Forecast requirements		30	30	30	30	0	0	0
In transit		60						
Projected available balance	43	73	43	13	60	60	60	60
Planned shipments				60				
Firm planned shipments				17				

Q = 60; lead time = 1; SS = 10.

Warehouse 2		Period						
		1	2	3	4	5	6	7
Forecast requirements		100	100	100	100	130	130	130
In transit								
Projected available balance	207	107	207	107	207	77	147	217
Planned shipments						200	200	
Firm planned shipments		200		200				

Q = 200; lead time = 1; SS = 20.

to send even less to warehouse 1 because it might be easier to pick up some unsatisfied demand from warehouse 2 than to deal with the remnant inventories at warehouse 1. The point is DRP systems provide visibility for solving these problems. Even though the exact quantity to be sent to warehouse 1 won't be determined until week 3, the amount produced and made available to send to either warehouse will be correct, since planned shipments from both are exploded to the requirements at the central facility. The main questions are how to divide the available stock between the two facilities and how to manage the transition.

Our final example deals with controlling inventory of products whose shelf life is a concern. Certainly one aspect of this problem is to use strict first-in/first-out physical movement and to make this part of the training for warehouse personnel. The second way to deal effectively with shelf life problems is to identify those products that may be headed for a problem before it's too late. One way to do this is to use the DRP records and build in exception messages to flag potential shelf life problems.

If, for example, demand for a product at a location is dropping for some reason, the forecast should be reduced. This means any available inventory or in transit stock will cover a longer time period; as a result, the first planned shipment will be several periods in the future. This condition can be detected, calling for a review of the particular product's shelf life at this location. Perhaps it should be immediately shipped to another warehouse. This feature is incorporated in the actual system, to which we now turn our attention.

Company Example

Abbott Laboratories, Ltd., of Canada produces health-care products. Three lines (pharmaceuticals, hospital products, and infant nutrition products) are produced in three plants. About 750 end items are distributed through DCs (distribution centers) throughout Canada.

Abbott Laboratories uses DRP to manage field inventories. Detailed forecast data are entered into warehouse DRP records. These records are represented as the zero level of the bill of materials (BOM). Figure 8.16 illustrates these records for two locations: Vancouver and Montreal. Forecast data are entered as the requirements rows. The first 20 weeks are displayed in weekly time periods (buckets). Thereafter, monthly buckets are used for a total planning horizon of two years.

In the Montreal record, an entry of 120 in the week of 8/7 appears in a row labeled "Customer orders." This row allows the inclusion of specific advance order information. The information is not added to the gross requirements, however. It's there for detailed planning of shipments and to recognize advanced special orders.

Lead time in the Vancouver record is 35 days (five weeks) including safety lead time. DRP time-phased records are produced using these parameters. For example, projected on-hand balance at the end of week 9/4 for Vancouver is insufficient to meet the gross requirements of 9/11. The result is a planned order for a quantity of 24, five weeks earlier in the week of 8/7.

Figure 8.17 shows the DRP records for the central warehouse and for the bulk item used to make the end-item product B. Gross requirements for central are based on planned orders from all the DCs. For example, in the week of 8/7, the gross requirement of 1,908 consists of 24 from Vancouver, 1,872 from Montreal, and 12 from some other DC.

The batch size shown for the central warehouse in Figure 8.17 is 7,619—the number of product B units yielded from a batch of 4,000 in the unit of measure for the bulk product; that is, the 7,619 shown as a firm planned order in 9/11 becomes a gross requirement of 4,000 for bulk in that week.

The master production scheduler works with the DRP record for central. This person's job is to convert planned orders into firm planned orders, and to manage timing of the firm planned orders. For example, all orders at central are firm planned in Figure 8.17 until 12/31 in the last row. The last three orders (12/31, 2/25, and 4/21) are only planned orders. DRP logic can replan these as needed. Only the master production scheduler can move the firm planned orders that appear early in the record. The result is a stable MPS for the bulk production.

Figure 8.18 illustrates the information available for actual shipment planning. The requirements due to be shipped this week or in the next two weeks (also any past-due shipments) are summarized by distribution center and product type. This enables the planner to look at the current requirements or future planned shipments in making up carloads destined for a distribution center. Since the information is available in terms of cube, weight, and pallet load, the planner can use the most limited resource in making a shipment decision. This flexibility enables planners to efficiently use transportation resources to meet product needs.

The application of DRP at Abbott Laboratories resulted in benefits in many areas of the company. The product obsolescence costs were reduced, inventory turnover improved, and customer service increased. The logistics information also led to reductions in transportation and warehouse costs.

FIGURE 8.16 Abbott DRP Records for Vancouver and Montreal

Description	Size	um	Std Bactr	FC	BY	PL	IT	C	Scrap	Total Landed Costs	OP	Life	O-LT	P-LT	O-LT	QA-LT	T-LT	On Hand	OA Inventory	Allocated	Safety Stock
Product-B	200	BL	1872	A2		08		C	1.0			1095	14		0	0	14	2520.0	0.0	0.0	0.0

21-MONTREAL

	Past Due	7/24	7/31	08/07	08/14	08/21	08/28	09/04	09/11	09/18	09/25	10/02	10/09	10/16
CUSTOMER ORDERS				120										
GROSS REQUIREMENTS		601	601	601	601	576	556	556	556	578	633	633	633	633
SCHEDULED RECEIPTS	2520													
ON HAND		1919	1318	717	116	1412	856	300	1616	1038	405	1644	1011	378
FIRM PLANNED ORDERS														
PLANNED ORDERS				1872			1872			1872			1872	

MONTHLY

	10/23	10/30	11/06	11/13	11/20	11/27	12/04	01/01	01/29	02/26	03/26	04/23	05/21	06/18
CUSTOMER ORDERS														
GROSS REQUIREMENTS	777	801	801	801	633	507	2100	2386	2744	2167	2356	2404	2479	2212
SCHEDULED RECEIPTS														
ON HAND	1473	672	1743	942	309	1674	1446	932	60	1637	1153	621	14	1546
FIRM PLANNED ORDERS														
PLANNED ORDERS	1872		1872	1872		1872	1872	3744	1872	1872	3744	1872	1872	1872

	07/16	08/13	09/10	10/08	11/05	12/03	12/31	01/28	02/25	03/24	04/21	05/19	06/16	TOTAL
CUSTOMER ORDERS														
GROSS REQUIREMENTS	2418	2289	2400	2844	2742	2100	2323	2480	2285	2356	2280	2348	2944	62735
SCHEDULED RECEIPTS														
ON HAND	1000	583	55	955	85	1729	1278	670	257	1645	1237	761	1561	
FIRM PLANNED ORDERS														
PLANNED ORDERS	3744	1872	1872	3744	1872	1872	1872	3744	1872	1872	1872	3744	1872	61776

NOTES & COMMENTS

Comm list no.
List xyz

(continued)

FIGURE 8.16 (Concluded)

03-VANCOUVER

Description	Size	um	Std Bactr	FC	BY	PL	IT	C	Scrap	Total Landed Costs	OP	Life	O-LT	P-LT	O-LT	QA-LT	T-LT	On Hand	OA Inventory	Allocated	Safety Stock
Product-B	200		24			08	F	C	1.00	0.000		1095	35	0	0	0	35	36.0	0.0	0.0	0.0

	Past Due	7/24	7/31	08/07	08/14	08/21	08/28	09/04	09/11	09/18	09/25	10/02	10/09	10/16
CUSTOMER ORDERS															
GROSS REQUIREMENTS		5	5	5	5	5	5	5	5	5	5	5	5	5
SCHEDULED RECEIPTS															
ON HAND	36	31	26	21	16	11	6	1	20	15	10	5	5	19
FIRM PLANNED ORDERS								24						
PLANNED ORDERS												24		

MONTHLY

	10/23	10/30	11/06	11/13	11/20	11/27	12/04	01/01	01/29	02/26	03/26	04/23	05/21	06/18
CUSTOMER ORDERS														
GROSS REQUIREMENTS	7	7	7	7	5	4	17	21	23	20	20	20	20	20
SCHEDULED RECEIPTS														
ON HAND	12	5	22	15	10	6	13	16	17	21	1	5	9	13
FIRM PLANNED ORDERS														
PLANNED ORDERS	24	24	24	24	24	24	24	24	24	24	24	24	24	24

	07/16	08/13	09/10	10/08	11/05	12/03	12/31	01/28	02/25	03/24	04/21	05/19	06/16	TOTAL
CUSTOMER ORDERS														
GROSS REQUIREMENTS	20	20	20	24	23	17	20	20	20	20	20	20	26	533
SCHEDULED RECEIPTS														
ON HAND	17	21	1	1	2	9	13	17	21	1	1	9	7	
FIRM PLANNED ORDERS														
PLANNED ORDERS	24	24	24	24	24	24	24	24	24	24	24	24	24	504

NOTES & COMMENTS

Comm list no.
List xyz

Source: W. L. Berry, T. E. Vollmann, and D. C. Whybark, *Master Production Scheduling: Principles and Practice*. Falls Church, Va.: American Production and Inventory Control Society, 1979, p. 87.

FIGURE 8.17 Abbott DRP Records for Central and Bulk

Description	Size	um	Std Bactr	FC	BY	PL	IT	C	Scrap	Total Landed Costs	OP	Life	O-LT	P-LT	O-LT	QA-LT	T-LT	On Hand	OA Inventory	Allocated	Safety Stock
Product-B	200	BL	7619	A2	00	03	C	0	1.07			1095		12	0	11	23	5220.0	0.0	144.0	1000.0

01-CENTRAL

	Past Due	7/24	7/31	08/07	08/14	08/21	08/28	09/04	09/11	09/18	09/25	10/02	10/09	10/16
CUSTOMER ORDERS	0	0	0	0	0	0	0	0	0	0	0	0	0	0
GROSS REQUIREMENTS	204	12	12	1908	12	12	2916	156	36	1884	12	1104	1980	12
SCHEDULED RECEIPTS	0	0	0	7619	0	0	0	0	0	0	0	0	0	0
ON HAND	4872	4860	4848	10078	10066	10054	7138	6982	6946	5062	5050	3946	9104	9092
FIRM PLANNED ORDERS	0	0	0	0	0	0	0	0	7619	0	0	0	0	0
PLANNED ORDERS	0	0	0	0	0	0	0	0	0	0	0	0	0	0

MONTHLY

	10/23	10/30	11/06	11/13	11/20	11/27	12/04	01/01	01/29	02/26	03/26	04/23	05/21	06/18
CUSTOMER ORDERS	0	0	0	0	0	0	0	0	0	0	0	0	0	0
GROSS REQUIREMENTS	2952	3108	36	1884	96	1092	1944	4968	3108	3012	4968	3108	2076	3108
SCHEDULED RECEIPTS	0	0	0	0	0	0	0	0	0	0	0	0	0	0
ON HAND	6140	6128	6092	4208	4112	3020	8214	10384	7276	4264	6434	3326	8388	5280
FIRM PLANNED ORDERS	0	0	0	7619	7619	0	7619	0	7619	7619	0	7619	0	7619
PLANNED ORDERS	0	0	0	0	0	0	0	0	0	0	0	0	0	0

	07/16	08/13	09/10	10/08	11/05	12/03	12/31	01/28	02/25	03/24	04/21	05/19	06/16	TOTAL
CUSTOMER ORDERS	0	0	0	0	0	0	0	0	0	0	0	0	0	0
GROSS REQUIREMENTS	4740	3120	3108	4980	2052	3108	3012	4980	2964	2052	3108	4956	2808	87612
SCHEDULED RECEIPTS	0	0	0	0	0	0	0	0	0	0	0	0	0	7619
ON HAND	7678	4558	8588	10746	8694	5586	2574	4732	1768	6854	3746	5928	3120	0
FIRM PLANNED ORDERS	0	7619	7619	0	0	0	0	0	0	0	0	0	0	60952
PLANNED ORDERS	0	0	7619	0	0	0	7619	7619	0	7619	0	0	0	22857

NOTES & COMMENTS

Comm list no.
List xyz

(continued)

FIGURE 8.17 (Concluded)

Description	Size	um	Std Bactr	FC	BY	PL	IT	C	Scrap	Total Landed Costs	OP	Life	O-LT	P-LT	O-LT	QA-LT	T-LT	On Hand	OA Inventory	Allocated	Safety Stock
Product-B	200	L	4000			00	B	C	1.00		N						0	0	0	0	0

84-Bulk

	Past Due	7/24	7/31	08/07	08/14	08/21	08/28	09/04	09/11	09/18	09/25	10/02	10/09	10/16
CUSTOMER ORDERS														
GROSS REQUIREMENTS														
SCHEDULED RECEIPTS									4000					
ON HAND														
FIRM PLANNED ORDERS														
PLANNED ORDERS									4000					

MONTHLY

	10/23	10/30	11/06	11/13	11/20	11/27	12/04	01/01	01/29	02/26	03/26	04/23	05/21	06/18
CUSTOMER ORDERS														
GROSS REQUIREMENTS					4000		4000		4000	4000		4000		4000
SCHEDULED RECEIPTS														
ON HAND														
FIRM PLANNED ORDERS														
PLANNED ORDERS					4000		4000		4000	4000		4000		4000

	07/16	08/13	09/10	10/08	11/05	12/03	01/01	01/28	02/25	03/24	04/21	05/19	06/16	TOTAL
CUSTOMER ORDERS														
GROSS REQUIREMENTS		4000	4000		4000	4000		4000	4000	4000	4000			44000
SCHEDULED RECEIPTS														
ON HAND														
FIRM PLANNED ORDERS														
PLANNED ORDERS		4000	4000		4000	4000		4000	4000	4000	4000			44000

NOTES & COMMENTS

Comm list no.
List xyz

Source: W. L. Berry, T. E. Vollmann, and D. C. Whybark, *Master Production Scheduling: Principles and Practice.* Falls Church, Va.: American Production and Inventory Control Society, 1979, p. 88.

FIGURE 8.18 **Abbott Short-Term Shipping Information**

DC 21 - MONTREAL
DIVISION 2

LIST/SIZE	QUANTITY	PALLET	WEIGHT	CUBE	QUANTITY	PALLET	WEIGHT	CUBE
	---- PAST DUE ----				---- WEEK 1 ----			
XYZ-200	0	0.0	0.0	0.0	0	0.0	0.0	0.0
	WEEK 2				WEEK 3			
PRODUCT B	0	0.0	0.0	0.0	1872	2.0	3744.0	112.3

PRIORITY 96: 5076 AVAILABLE IN CENTRAL

DC 03 - VANCOUVER
XYZ-200

	QUANTITY	PALLET	WEIGHT	CUBE	QUANTITY	PALLET	WEIGHT	CUBE
	---- PAST DUE ----				---- WEEK 1 ----			
PRODUCT B	0	0.0	0.0	0.0	0	0.0	0.0	0.0
	WEEK 2				WEEK 3			
	0	0.0	0.0	0.0	24	0.0	48.0	1.4

PRIORITY 96: 5076 AVAILABLE IN CENTRAL

Source: W. L. Berry, T. E. Vollmann, and D. C. Whybark, *Master Production Scheduling: Principles and Practice.* Falls Church, Va.: American Production and Inventory Control Society, 1979, p. 90.

Concluding Principles

This chapter has presented a technique for bridging between successive stages in the supply chain. Some of these can be internal, such as factories to distribution centers, but the technique can also be used to make linkages across firms. The technique, distribution requirements planning (DRP), relates current field inventory availability (in distribution centers, warehouses, and customer locations), forecasts, and knowledge of demand to develop resupply plans and bring those to the master production scheduling and material planning modules of the MPC system. Moreover, DRP utilizes record formats and processing logic consistent with MRP. To effectively use DRP, we apply the following general principles:

- The top-level records for a DRP system should cover items in a location as close to the customer as possible (or even at the customer, if feasible).
- Local information on demand patterns should be incorporated into the DRP record at a warehouse and/or the customers' MPC system data should be used at a customer location.
- Data and performance measurement systems should be put in place to monitor forecast adjustments in the field.
- Matching supply to demand requires close control of supply as well as data on demand.
- Projections of future requirements should be used to decide inventory allocation in periods of short supply.
- Transparent records and consistent processing logic should be used to integrate the system.
- What-if analysis should be based on integrated records of the system.
- Uncertainty filters, like firm planned orders or error addback, should be available to the master production scheduler.
- The organization form should be consistent with the supply chain being managed.

References

Allen, W. B. "A Comparative Simulation of Central Inventory Control Policies for Positioning Safety Stock in a Multi-Echelon Distribution System," DBA dissertation, Indiana University, 1988.

Barash, Mark, and Donald H. Mitchell. "Account Based Forecasting at NABISCO Biscuit Company," *Journal of Business Forecasting Methods & Systems* 17, no. 2 (summer 1998), pp. 3, 4.

Bookbinder, J. H. "Replenishment Analysis in Distribution Requirements Planning," *Decision Sciences* 19, no. 3 (1988).

Bregman, R. L. "Enhanced Distribution Requirements Planning," *The Journal of Business Logistics* 11, no. 1 (1990), pp. 49–65.

Brown, R. G. *Materials Management Systems.* New York: Wiley InterScience, 1977.

Caridi, M., and R. Cigolini. "Improving Materials Management Effectiveness: A Step Towards Agile Enterprise," *International Journal of Physical Distribution & Logistics Management* 32, no. 7 (2002), p. 556.

Christopher, Martin. *Logistics and Supply Chain Management: Strategies for Reducing Cost and Improving Service,* 2nd ed. Englewood Cliffs, N.J.: Prentice Hall, 1998.

de Leeuw, Sander; Ad R. van Goor; and Rien Ploos van Amstel. "The Selection of Distribution Control Techniques," *International Journal of Logistics Management* 10, no. 1 (1999), pp. 97–113.

Feare, T. "Lilly—How They Buy," *CPI Purchasing,* February 1985, pp. 26–34.

Freund, B. C., and J. M. Freund. "Hands-on VMI," *APICS—The Performance Advantage,* March 2003, p. 34.

Ho, C. "An Examination of a Distribution Resource Planning Problem: DRP System Nervousness," *Journal of Business Logistics* 13, no. 2 (1992).

Huin, S. F.; L. H. S. Luong; and K. Abhary. "Internal Supply Chain Planning Determinants in Small and Medium-sized Manufacturers," *International Journal of Physical Distribution & Logistics Management* 32, no. 9/10 (2002), p. 771.

Jones, T. C., and D. W. Riley. "Using Inventory for Competitive Advantage through Supply Chain Management," *International Journal of Physical Distribution and Materials Management,* 1985, p. 16.

Kanet, John J., and Alan R. Cannon. "Implementing Supply Chain Management Lessons Learned at Becton Dickinson," *Production and Inventory Management Journal* 41, no. 2 (2nd quarter 2000), pp. 33–41.

Karnes, Carol L., and Larry R. Karnes. "A Case Study in Mass Customization," *Production and Inventory Management Journal,* 3rd quarter, p. 1.

Lavallee II, Raymond W. "Utilizing Forecast Information to Drive Solutia's Supply Chain," *Journal of Business Forecasting Methods & Systems* 17, no. 2 (summer 1998), pp. 7–14.

Lawrence, F. Barry. "Closing the Logistics Loop: A Tutorial," *Production and Inventory Management Journal* (1st quarter 1999), p. 43.

Lee, Young Hae, and Sook Han Kim. "Production-Distribution Planning in Supply Chain Considering Capacity Constraints," *Computers & Industrial Engineering* 43, no. 1–2 (July 2002), p. 169.

Mallya, Sudhir; Snehamay Banerjee; and William G. Bistline. "A Decision Support System for Production/Distribution Planning in Continuous Manufacturing," *Decision Sciences* 32, no. 3, pp. 545–557.

Martin, A. *Distribution Resource Planning.* New York: John Wiley & Sons, 1993.

Martin, André J. *DRP: Distribution Resource Planning: The Gateway to True Quick Response and Continuous Replenishment.* Oliver Wight, 1995.

Martin, A. "DRP, Another Resource Planning System," *Production and Inventory Management Review,* December 1982.

Masters, J. M.; G. M. Allenby; B. J. LaLonde; and A. Malz. "On the Adoption of DRP," *The Journal of Business Logistics* 13, no. 1 (1992).

Stenger, A. J., and J. L. Cavinato. "Adapting MRP to the Outbound Side—Distribution Requirements Planning," *Production and Inventory Management* (4th quarter 1979), pp. 1–14.

Timpe, Christian H., and Josef Kallrath. "Optimal Planning in Large Multi-site Production Networks," *European Journal of Operational Research* 126, no. 2 (October 16, 2000), p. 422.

Turner. J. R. "DRP: Theory and Reality." *1990 APICS Annual Conference Proceedings.*

van Donselaar, K. "Commonality and Safety Stocks," *Pre-Prints of the 4th International Working Seminar on Production Economics,* 1986, pp. 446–456.

Vaughn, O.; T. Perez; and R. Stemwedel. "Short Cycle Replenishment at 3M," *1990 APCS Annual Conference Proceedings.*

Wemmerlöv. U. "A Time-Phased Order Point System in Environments with and without Demand Uncertainty: A Comparative Analysis of Nonmonetary, Performance Variables," *International Journal of Production Research* 24, no. 2 (1986), pp. 343–358.

Yang, S. "Positioning Inventory in Distribution Systems with Stochastice Demand," Ph.D. dissertation, University of North Carolina at Chapel Hill, 1999.

Zmolek, J. "Global DRP: Using the MPS as a Coordinating Mechanism," *1990 APICS Annual Conference Proceedings.*

Discussion Questions

1. What is meant by the statement, "The real task of managing materials is matching supply to demand"?

2. Describe how DRP helps bridge the gap between the market and the factory.

3. What are some of the benefits a warehouse manager derives from improved resupply information?

4. Discuss the risks and benefits of local warehouse personnel modifying forecast data for field warehouses.

5. A consumer goods manufacturer uses a periodic review system to manage field inventories. This means, once a period, field inventory clerks check to see if inventory is below reorder point; if so they order an amount equal to the EOQ. The materials manager argues this is the same as using TPOP records. What's your opinion?

6. How can you monitor forecast data modifications by field personnel to ensure changes result in improvements over original computer forecasts?

7. What are the differences between the planned shipments, as indicated in Figure 8.3 and planned orders from MRP records?

8. How are the supply chain management concept and materials management similar? How do they differ?

9. The Abbott records in Figure 8.16 show a customer order for Montreal on 8/07. Why do you think this customer order isn't added to the forecast requirements ("Gross requirements" in their terminology) in the record?

Problems

1. Bob Stahl, the distribution manager at Forbes Industries, is considering using error addback for his DRP system. To evaluate its use, he compiled data for three periods on a sample product, the Scarlet Tiara. The initial DRP record is given below:

		Period			
	1	2	3	4	5
Forecast requirements	30	30	30	30	30
In transit	60				
Projected available balance	10	40	10	40	10	40
Planned shipments		60		60	

$Q = 60$; lead time $= 1$; SS $= 10$.

a. Develop the DRP records above for periods two through four given demands of 24, 38, and 27 in periods one, two, and three.

b. Complete the same records using the error addback method. What differences occur?

2. For the warehouse of Figure 8.8, suppose actual demands were 24, 16, and 18 in periods 1, 2, and 3, respectively. The initial DRP record is:

		Period			
	1	2	3	4	5
Forecast requirements	20	20	20	20	20
In transit	40				
Projected available balance	6	26	6	26	6	26
Planned shipments		40		40	

$Q = 40$; lead time $= 1$; SS $= 6$.

a. Create the other three DRP records as done in Figure 8.8. What problem is created in period 2? What can be done?

b. Does error addback work for this set of circumstances?

3. The Hazy Company maintains a West Coast distribution center (DC), which is supplied from the plant warehouse in the Midwest. It takes exactly one week to ship to the distribution center from the Midwest. One of its products has an ordering cost of $10 per order, inventory carrying cost of $1 per unit per week, and average weekly demand at the DC of 5 units (although it has fluctuated uniformly between 0 and 10 units per week in actuality). Over the years, the product's safety stock level has varied. There are currently (early Monday morning) nine units in inventory at the DC. The company is willing to risk a probability of stocking out of 0.10 in any order cycle.

a. If the company uses an economic order quantity, reorder point system, what should the order quantity and reorder point be?

b. If the company adapted DRP logic to this DC supply situation and decided to ship only on Mondays (to consolidate shipments), what would you suggest for the planned shipping pattern over the next 10 weeks? (Use a safety stock level of two units.)

c. If actual demand for the upcoming week were six units, what would the new shipping pattern be? (Assume any planned shipments in the current week are released.)

4. The Tasmanian Tire Company's distribution manager has supplied the following information pertaining to its product, the Super Taz Tire, which is stocked at the firm's field warehouse:

Average weekly demand = 35 units.

Current on-hand balance = 10 units.

In-transit order (due next week) = 70 units.

Economic shipping quantity = 70 units.

Shipping time = 1 week.

Safety stock = 0 units.

Complete the record for the field warehouse indicating the planned shipment schedule for the next eight weeks:

		Period							
		1	2	3	4	5	6	7	8
Forecast requirements									
In transit									
Projected available balance									
Planned shipments									

5. The XYZ Company's finance manager is currently studying projected inventory investment for product 101 at the central (plant) warehouse. Quantities of product 101 are shipped from the central warehouse to warehouses A and B, based on individual warehouse requirements. The product costs $100 per unit.

Using DRP parameters and inventory information for product 101 in Exhibit A, determine the planned order releases at the central warehouse. Construct a graph indicating projected inventory investment at warehouse A for this product at the beginning and end of each week over the next six-week period. Assume this product's demand is equally divided among the days of each week.

EXHIBIT A

Product 101

Product 101 Warehouse A		Week					
		1	2	3	4	5	6
Forecast requirements		20	20	20	20	20	20
In transit		15					
Projected available balance	10						
Planned shipments							

$Q = 40; LT = 1; SS = 0.$

Product 101 Warehouse B		Week					
		1	2	3	4	5	6
Forecast requirements		10	10	10	10	10	10
In transit							
Projected available balance	15						
Planned shipments							

$Q = 20; LT = 1; SS = 0.$

Product 101 Central Warehouse		Week					
		1	2	3	4	5	6
Gross requirements							
Scheduled receipts							
Projected available balance	60						
Planned order release							

$Q = $ lot-for-lot; $LT = 1; SS = 0.$

6. The distribution of Blues Brothers' Sunglasses is from the plant in Joliet to two warehouses and then to the customers. The distribution pattern is as follows:

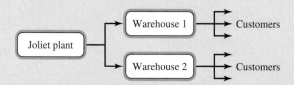

For the purpose of analysis, assume that each warehouse will sell exactly 40 cases of Blues Brothers' Sunglasses per week. Inventory carried either at the plant or at the warehouse locations costs 25 cents per week per case (based on Friday night inventory). The ordering cost is $15 per order at each facility, and it takes exactly one week to transport the product from the plant to either of the two warehouses or to produce the product. The beginning inventory at each warehouse is 40 units, and the beginning inventory at the Joliet plant is 140 units. No safety stock is planned at any location.

a. On the basis of a record of seven weeks, determine the inventory carrying cost plus setup cost per week at Joliet plus both warehouses managing the system with EOQ at all locations.

b. Determine the total inventory carrying cost and setup cost per week, using DRP to manage the system based on the same seven-week record.

7. The MVA Pet Food Company distributes one of its products, Gro-Pup, through warehouses in Seattle and Portland. A central warehouse at the St. Louis plant distributes Gro-Pup to these two warehouses in serving the Northwest regional market.

a. Develop a distribution schedule for the two warehouses and a production schedule for the plant for the next eight-week period, using the DRP worksheet in Exhibit B (page 294). (Note the sales forecast for this product is 20 units per week at the Seattle warehouse, and 43 units of the product are currently on hand. The shipment order quantity is 60 units, planned shipment lead time is one week, and there's no safety stock requirement. Similar information is included in Exhibit B for the other two facilities.) The product is packed in lots of 50 units at St. Louis. The packaging process takes two weeks.

b. Each Gro-Pup package requires one unit of packaging material. Develop a purchasing schedule for the packaging material assuming:

1. There are currently 25 units on hand.
2. An open order for 100 units is due to be received from the vendor next week.
3. The purchase order quantity equals 100 units.
4. Purchasing lead time is four weeks.

c. Update all four records as of the start of week 2, assuming the following transactions occurred during week 1:

	Receipts	Order Releases	Sales (Disbursements)	Inventory Adjustment	Open Order Scrap
Gro-Pup/Seattle	0	0	19	−3	0
Gro-Pup/Portland	15	15	20	+3	0
Gro-Pup/Plant	0	50	15	0	0
Gro-Pup/Packaging	90	100	50	+4	10

8. The Drip Producers are planning a promotion of one of its products, the Dead Drop. Dead Drops are distributed through only one of the warehouses. The promotion is to begin in period 4 and run through period 6. The sales forecast is normally 30 per period, but during the promotion the company expects sales to be 60 per period. This is shown below with other data.

	Period					
	1	2	3	4	5	6
Sales forecast	30	30	30	60	60	60

	Warehouse	Central
Ship/ord. quantity	40 units	Lot-for-lot
Current inventory	12 units	0 units
Lead time	1 period	1 period
Safety stock	10 units	0 units
Sched. rec./ship.	40 units in period 1	40 units in period 1

a. Develop the warehouse and central facility's records.

b. Suppose the central facility's capacity was limited to 50 units per period. How would you provide the material for the promotion in the field?

EXHIBIT B

Distribution Requirements Planning Worksheet

Gro-Pup Seattle Warehouse		Week 1	2	3	4	5	6	7	8
Forecast requirements		20	20	20	20	20	20	20	20
In transit									
Projected available balance	43								
Planned shipments									

Q = 60; LT = 1; SS = 0.

Gro-Pup Portland Warehouse		Week 1	2	3	4	5	6	7	8
Forecast requirements		10	10	10	10	10	10	10	10
In transit		15							
Projected available balance	2								
Planned shipments									

Q = 15; LT = 1; SS = 0.

Gro-Pup Plant Warehouse		Week 1	2	3	4	5	6	7	8
Gross requirements									
Scheduled receipts			50						
Projected available balance	30								
Planned order release									

Q = 50; LT = 2; SS = 0.

Gro-Pup Packaging Material		Week 1	2	3	4	5	6	7	8
Gross requirements									
Scheduled receipts		100							
Projected available balance	25								
Planned order release									

Q = 100; LT = 4; SS = 0.

9. Develop the records for the Cranstable Company's two warehouses and one central facility system using the following data. What happens if the central order quantity changes to 200?

	Warehouse 1	Warehouse 2	Central
Forecast requirements	20/period	30/period	
Ship/ord. quantity	48 units	60 units	100 units
Current inventory	23 units	12 units	0 units
Lead time	1 period	1 period	1 period
Safety stock	10 units	10 units	0 units
Sched. rec./ship.	48 units in period 1	60 units in period 1	None

10. The Cranstable Company was just getting into the swing of DRP when old Barnstable moved away from warehouse 1's region, never to be seen again by anyone at the company. (Barnstable's demand was lost to a competitor.) Now this wouldn't normally cause problems, but for Cranstable it meant sales were halved at warehouse 1. Using problem 9's data, what's the impact of Barnstable's departure?

11. The Cranky Tea Company performs sales forecasting on a national basis. Each month it prepares a sales forecast of monthly sales for the coming year for each of the firm's end products. At each of the firm's three distribution warehouses, distribution requirements planning records are maintained for the individual products. The national sales forecast for Constant Torment, the company's best selling product, is 4,000 units per four-week period. The sales of this product at each of the three warehouses are split as follows: 40 percent from warehouse A, 35 percent from warehouse B, and 25 percent from warehouse C. An analysis of the sales history of Constant Torment at warehouse C indicates weekly sales of this product are distributed as follows: 10 percent in week 1, 25 percent in week 2, 45 percent in week 3, and 20 percent in week 4 in a monthly period. Complete the following DRP record for Constant Torment at Warehouse C.

		Month							
		1				2			
		Week				Week			
Constant Torment / Warehouse C	1	2	3	4	1	2	3	4	
Forecast requirements									
In transit		260	445						
Projected available balance	105								
Planned shipments									

Q = LFL; SS = 0; LT = 3 weeks.

12. The Excello Corporation's distribution planner is concerned about the variability of transit times between the plant in Madison, Indiana, and the firm's distribution center in Atlanta. It's been decided to incorporate a one-week safety lead time into the DRP records for items stocked in the Atlanta distribution center. Complete the record for product X in the Atlanta distribution center.

Forecast: 200 units per week.

In transit: 410 units scheduled for receipt in week 1.

On-hand inventory: 15 units.

Order quantity: 600 units.

Lead time: 1 week.

Safety stock = 0.

Safety lead time = 1 week.

Product X	Week							
	1	2	3	4	5	6	7	8
Forecast requirements								
In transit								
Projected available balance								
Planned shipments								

13. The Allied Product Company's sales director has decided to close the firm's San Diego warehouse and open a new warehouse in Los Angeles. The San Diego warehouse is scheduled to close the end of week 4; the new warehouse in Los Angeles is scheduled to open for business at the start of week 5. Product B is currently stocked in the San Diego warehouse and will be stocked in the new Los Angeles warehouse. Sales forecast for product B is 100 units per week. Complete the following DRP records for product B, reflecting the change in the company's warehousing plans for the item and the implications for the plant.

Product B/San Diego Warehouse		Week							
		1	2	3	4	5	6	7	8
Forecast requirements									
In transit									
Projected available balance	205								
Planned shipments									

Q = LFL; SS = 10 units; LT = 2 weeks.

Product B/Los Angeles Warehouse		Week							
		1	2	3	4	5	6	7	8
Forecast requirements									
In transit									
Projected available balance									
Planned shipments									

Q = LFL; SS = 10 units; LT = 1 week.

Product B/Plant		Week							
		1	2	3	4	5	6	7	8
Gross requirements									
Scheduled receipts									
Projected available balance	300								
Planned order release									

Q = 200 units; SS = 15 units; LT = 3 weeks.

14. The Stasik Pharmaceutical Company's distribution planning manager is concerned about the rising cost of outdated inventory in the firm's distribution warehouses. Shelf life for the company's products shouldn't exceed four weeks. Government regulations require products in stock longer than four weeks to be scrapped. Devise an exception notice test that can be applied to the DRP records in the firm's distribution warehouses to direct the inventory planner's attention to items where excess inventory may exist. Apply this procedure to the record below to determine whether out-of-date inventory is likely to occur for product W.

Product W		Week							
		1	2	3	4	5	6	7	8
Forecast requirements		300	300	300	300	300	300	300	300
In transit			900						
Projected available balance	350	50	650	350	950	650	1250	950	1550
Firm planned orders			900		900		900		
Planned shipments									

Q = 900; SS = 50 units; LT = 2 weeks.

15. Product D is stocked only at the AMC Chemical Company's Dallas warehouse and at the company's plant warehouse in Akron. The sales director has forecast product sales from the Dallas warehouse to be 40 units per week. Product D is manufactured at the firm's Akron plant using 2 units of ingredient X per unit of product D.

   a. Complete the DRP records for product D at the Dallas warehouse and the plant warehouse as well as the MRP record for ingredient X using the following information. (Assume ingredient X is only used in product D.)

Product D/Dallas Warehouse		Week							
		1	2	3	4	5	6	7	8
Forecast requirements									
In transit									
Projected available balance	85								
Planned shipments									

Q = LFL; SS = 5 units; LT = 2 weeks.

Product D/Plant Warehouse		Week							
		1	2	3	4	5	6	7	8
Gross requirements									
Scheduled receipts		46							
Projected available balance	2								
Planned order release									

Q = LFL; SS = 8 units; LT = 1 week.

Ingredient X		Week							
		1	2	3	4	5	6	7	8
Gross requirements									
Scheduled receipts		320							
Projected available balance	4								
Planned order release									

Q = 320 units; SS = 2 units; LT = 4 weeks.

b. Actual sales for product D at the Dallas warehouse in week 1 were 48 units and all planned shipments/orders were released. Prepare DRP and MRP records as of the beginning of week 2. What actions should the master production scheduler take on the basis of this information?

Product D/Dallas Warehouse		Week							
		2	3	4	5	6	7	8	9
Forecast requirements									
In transit									
Projected available balance									
Planned shipments									

Q = LFL; SS = 5 units; LT = 2 weeks.

Product D/Plant Warehouse		Week							
		2	3	4	5	6	7	8	9
Gross requirements									
Scheduled receipts									
Projected available balance									
Planned order release									

Q = LFL; SS = 2 units; LT = 2 weeks.

Ingredient X	Week							
	2	3	4	5	6	7	8	9
Gross requirements								
Scheduled receipts								
Projected available balance								
Planned order release								

Q = 320 units; SS = 2 units; LT = 4 weeks.

c. Suppose product D's actual sales at the Dallas warehouse in week 2 were 31 units. Again, all planned shipments/orders were released and expedite actions taken. What action would the master scheduler take on the basis of this information? In this situation, what modifications to the master production schedule might be taken?

Product D/Dallas Warehouse		Week							
		3	4	5	6	7	8	9	10
Forecast requirements									
In transit									
Projected available balance	85								
Planned shipments									

Q = LFL; SS = 5 units; LT = 2 weeks.

Product D/Plant Warehouse		Week							
		3	4	5	6	7	8	9	10
Gross requirements									
Scheduled receipts									
Projected available balance	42								
Planned order release									

Q = LFL; SS = 2 units; LT = 2 weeks.

Ingredient X		Week							
		3	4	5	6	7	8	9	10
Gross requirements									
Scheduled receipts									
Projected available balance	4								
Planned order release									

Q = 320 units; SS = 2 units; LT = 4 weeks.

9

Just-in-Time

This chapter addresses just-in-time (JIT) approaches for manufacturing planning and control. JIT is a key building block for modern approaches to manufacturing planning and control (MPC), and is both a philosophy and a set of techniques. Moreover, the techniques go beyond traditional manufacturing planning and control systems. JIT changes manufacturing practices, which in turn affect MPC execution. JIT greatly reduces the complexity of detailed material planning, the need for shop-floor tracking, work-in-process inventories, and the transactions associated with shop-floor and purchasing systems. These gains come at the cost of more tightly coordinated manufacturing processes—both inside a company and with supplier firms that produce under JIT. The chapter concentrates on the MPC aspects of JIT but necessarily touches on broader aspects as well. It is organized around the following seven topics:

- *JIT in manufacturing planning and control:* What are JIT's key features and how do they impact MPC systems?
- *A JIT example:* How can the basic principles of JIT be illustrated in one simplified example?
- *JIT applications:* What are some concrete examples of JIT practice?
- *Nonrepetitive JIT:* How can JIT concepts be applied to the nonrepetitive manufacturing environment?
- *Joint-Firm JIT:* How is supplier-customer coordination supported with JIT?
- *JIT software:* What features of computer packages support JIT?
- *Managerial implications:* What changes are required to fully pursue the benefits of JIT?

JIT is one of two classic approaches to detailed material planning and control. Chapter 7 describes the other—material requirements planning (MRP). JIT techniques have the most influence on the "back-end" execution concepts in Chapter 11. Chapter 17 focuses on supply chain management—where the MPC systems need to be interfirm in their orientation. This is quite the case when JIT includes suppliers' firms. In addition, the integration of JIT and MRP, as well as the market requirements that drive MPC choices, are described in Chapter 13. Chapter 15 describes advanced concepts in JIT. More fundamentally, JIT influences will be referred to in many other chapters where the techniques used are essentially different when JIT is in place.

JIT in Manufacturing Planning and Control

Figure 9.1 shows how just-in-time programs relate to our manufacturing planning and control framework. The shaded area indicates the portions of MPC systems that are most affected by implementation of JIT. The primary application area is in back-end execution. However, JIT extends beyond manufacturing planning and control. JIT programs raise fundamental questions about manufacturing strategy and effectiveness. For this reason, we begin with a discussion of the major elements in a JIT program. Thereafter, we turn to the impact on the MPC system and the overhead cost savings from reduced MPC system transaction processing. The section closes by describing four fundamental JIT building blocks.

Major Elements of Just-in-Time

Many definitions have been put forward for just-in-time, and they have evolved over time. One popular definition of JIT is an approach to minimize waste in manufacturing. This focus is too broad: it helps to subdivide waste into time, energy, material, and errors. A useful common denominator running through this and other JIT definitions is a broad philosophy of pursuing zero inventories, zero transactions, and zero "disturbances" (*zero disturbances* means routine execution of schedules day in—day out).

The JIT literature is largely one of cases. The best-known JIT examples are from firms with high-volume repetitive manufacturing methods, such as the classic case of Toyota. The most important features of these applications have been the elimination of discrete manufacturing batches in favor of production rate goals, the reduction of work-in-process inventories, production schedules that level the capacity loads and keep them level, mixed

FIGURE 9.1
Manufacturing Planning and Control System and JIT

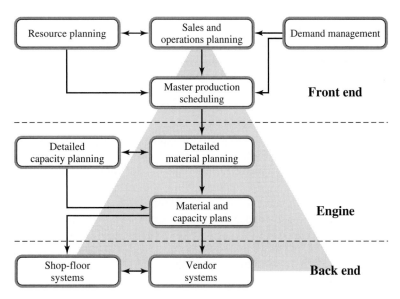

model master production schedules where all products are made more or less all the time, visual control systems where workers build the products and execute the schedule without paperwork or complex overhead support, and direct ties to vendors who deliver high-quality goods frequently. All of these have MPC implications.

Just-in-time objectives require physical system changes—and programs to make the changes. A prime example is setup time reduction and a drive toward constantly smaller lot sizes. This is necessary to make all of the products constantly. It's also consistent with reducing inventory levels. Setup times are typically reduced by applying common industrial engineering techniques to analyzing the setup process itself, often by workers themselves using a video camera. The results of setup time reduction have been impressive indeed. Changeovers of several hours have been reduced to less than 10 minutes. The goal now being achieved by many firms is expressed by Shigeo Shingo: SMED (single-minute exchange of dies, meaning all changeovers take place in less than 10 minutes).

Another physical program is improved quality through process improvements. Most JIT firms have programs of quality awareness and statistical process control. In a repetitive manufacturing system, any quality problem will result in a stoppage of the entire flow line, unless undesirable buffer inventories are held.

Quality improvement has taken many forms and is largely beyond our present scope. Two critical aspects for JIT are *TPM* and *poka-yoke*. TPM can stand for both total preventative maintenance and total productive maintenance. The goal is to apply the diligence of product quality improvement to equipment and process quality. Poka-yoke means foolproof operations. This is achieved by building checking operations into processes so that quality is evaluated as it's created. This also ensures low cost through finding defects at the time they're created. These quality programs have an impact on MPC system requirements and design.

Most JIT programs include continual improvement as a maxim for day-to-day operations. Every day, each worker should get better in some dimension, such as fewer defects, more output, or fewer stoppages. Continual improvement is achieved by making thousands of small improvements in methods and products in a never-ceasing quest for excellence. JIT best practice includes a strong degree of worker involvement and worker participation. In the words of a union official at the GM/Toyota (NUMMI) plant in Fremont, California, "This is the way work ought to be. [With JIT] this plant employs our hearts and minds, not just our backs."

JIT firms often group their equipment for cellular manufacturing: a group of machines manufactures a particular set of parts. The equipment layout minimizes travel distances and inventories between machines. Cells are typically U-shaped to increase worker interactions and reduce material handling. Cross-trained workers can run several machines. Cellular manufacturing makes "capacity" more flexible, so surges or mix changes are more readily handled. An extension of the cellular concept is the plant within a plant, where a portion of a factory focuses solely on one group of products.

In summary, a JIT orientation includes several action programs:

1. Reduction of setup times and lot sizes
2. A "no defects" goal in manufacturing
3. A focus on continual improvement

4. Worker involvement

5. Cellular manufacturing

Figure 9.2 lists the typical benefits gained in a JIT program.

JIT's Impact on Manufacturing Planning and Control

JIT influences all three areas of our MPC framework (front end, engine, and back end). JIT's primary contribution is in the back end, providing greatly streamlined execution on the shop floor and in purchasing. JIT can eliminate standard shop-floor reporting systems, reduce costs of detailed shop scheduling, significantly reduce work in process and lead times, and support better vendor scheduling.

However, JIT is not without influence on the front end and engine. In the detailed MRP planning of the engine, JIT reduces the number of part numbers planned and the number of levels in the bill of materials. Many part numbers formerly planned by MRP analysts can now be treated as "phantoms" (i.e., as part numbers still in the bill of materials but not transacted into and out of inventories). This means that instead of MPC being based on detailed operation steps to make individual parts, the planning is at the level of assemblies, using cross-trained workers and cellular manufacturing to eliminate the detailed planning. The result is often an order of magnitude reduction in the complexity of detailed material planning, with a concomitant reduction in planning personnel. Moreover, with planning/execution at the assembly level instead of with detailed operations and parts, the overall flow time from parts to finished goods is significantly reduced.

In the front end, JIT also gives rise to important changes. JIT production plans and master production schedules require relatively level capacity loading for smooth shop operations. In many cases, this is a rate-based MPS—that is, producing so many units per hour or day. This drive toward more stable, level, daily-mix schedules dictates many of the required JIT activities, such as setup time reduction. To the extent that lead times are sufficiently reduced, many firms that had to provide inventories in anticipation of customer orders (made-to-stock firms) now find themselves more like make-to-order or assemble-to-order companies, better able to respond to customer orders. This, in turn, can affect demand management.

FIGURE 9.2
JIT Benefits

Manufacturing throughput time reductions
Materials moved shorter distances
Less material movements in/out of storage
Reduced transactions
Simplified MPC systems
Reduced changeover times
Greater responsiveness to market demands
Inventory reductions
Labor cost reductions
More satisfied/cohesive workers
Better team working
Space reductions
Quality cost reductions
Quality improvements

In JIT execution, orders move through the factory so quickly that it's not necessary to track their progress with a complex production activity control system. A similar argument holds for purchased items. If they're converted into finished goods within hours or days of receipt, it's unnecessary to put them into stockrooms, pick them, and go through all the details normally associated with receipts from vendors. Instead, the JIT firm can simply pay the vendor for the purchased components in whatever products are completed each time period; there will be so little work-in-process inventory that it's not worth either party keeping track of it.

The concept of updating component inventory balances when finished items are received into stock is called **backflushing.** Instead of detailed work-in-process accounting systems based on shop-order transactions, some JIT firms just reduce component part inventory balances by exploding the bills of material for whatever has been delivered into finished goods. However, backflushing implies a very high level of data integrity.

JIT execution is focused on simplicity. The intent is to design manufacturing cells, products, and systems so goods flow through routinely. With problems of quality and disturbances largely eliminated, routine execution becomes just that: routine. Simple systems can be employed by shop people without detailed records or the need for extensive overhead staff support.

The Hidden Factory

A manufacturing firm comprises two "factories." One makes products and the other (the hidden factory) processes transactions on papers and computer systems. Over time, the former factory has been decreasing in cost, relative to the latter. A major driver for these costs is transactions. **Logistical transactions** include ordering, execution, and confirmation of materials moving from one location to another. Included are the costs of personnel in receiving, shipping, expediting, data entry, data processing, accounting, and error follow-up. Under JIT, the goal is to eliminate the vast majority of this work and the associated costs. Work orders that accompany each batch of material as it moves through the factory are eliminated. If the flow can be simplified, fast, and guaranteed, there is no need for paperwork.

Balancing transactions are largely associated with the planning that generates logistical transactions. Included are production control, purchasing, master scheduling, forecasting, and customer order processing/maintenance. In most companies, balancing transaction costs are 10 to 20 percent of the total manufacturing overhead costs. JIT again offers a significant opportunity to sharply reduce these costs. MRP planning can be cut by perhaps 75 to 90 percent in complexity. Improvements generated by vendor scheduling can also be extended. Vendor firms no longer need to process *their* sets of transactions.

Quality transactions extend far beyond what one normally thinks of as quality control. Included are identification and communication of specifications, certification that other transactions have taken place, and recording of backup data. Many of the costs of quality identified by Juran and others are largely associated with transactions. JIT, with closer coupling of production and consumption, has faster quality monitoring and response capability.

Still another category is **change transactions.** Included are engineering changes and all those that update MPC systems, such as routings, bills of materials, and specifications.

Engineering change transactions are some of the most expensive in the company. A typical engineering change might require a meeting of people from production control, line management, design engineering, manufacturing engineering, and purchasing. The change has to be approved, scheduled, and monitored for execution.

One way that firms attack the hidden factory is by finding ways to significantly reduce the number of transactions. Stability is another attack, and again JIT is important since it is based on stabilized operations. Still another attack on hidden factory transaction costs is through automation of transactions (as with bar coding), eliminating redundancies in data entry, and better data entry methods. But stability and transaction elimination should be pursued before turning to automation of transactions. JIT is clearly a key.

JIT Building Blocks in MPC

As Figure 9.3 shows, JIT links four fundamental building blocks: product design, process design, human/organizational elements, and manufacturing planning and control. JIT provides the connecting link for these four areas.

Critical activities in product design include quality, designing for manufacture in cells, and reducing the number of "real" levels in the bill of materials to as few as possible. By having no more than three real levels in the bill of materials, products have to go into inventory and out again, with MRP-based planning, only once or twice as they are produced.

Reducing bill of materials levels and process design are closely related. For fewer levels to be practical, the number of product conversion steps must be reduced through process design changes, often through cellular manufacturing. Equipment in cellular manufacturing is positioned (often in a U shape) to achieve rapid flow of production with minimal

FIGURE 9.3
Building Blocks for Just-in-Time

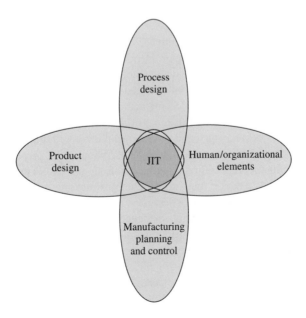

inventories. The object is to concentrate on material velocity. Jobs must flow through in short cycle times, so detailed tracking is unnecessary.

Bandwidth is an important notion in designing manufacturing processes. A wide bandwidth system has enough surge capacity to take on some variation in demand for the products as well as a fairly mixed set of products. The impact on MPC systems is the focus on inventory and throughput time reductions, where inventory is not built to level out capacity requirements. JIT systems are designed to be responsive to as large a set of demands as possible. Superior manufacturing processes support greater bandwidth. The objective is for MPC systems to schedule any product, right behind any other, with minimal disruption.

Human/organizational elements are another building block for JIT. One aspect of this is continual improvement, which implies cross training, process improvements, and whatever else is needed to enhance worker performance. The objective is continual learning and improvement. Human/organizational elements recognize that workers' range of capabilities and level of knowledge are often more important assets to the firm than equipment and facilities. Education is a continuing investment in the human asset base. As the asset base's capabilities grow, need for overhead support is reduced and overhead personnel can be redeployed to address other issues.

Linking human/organizational elements into the other activities has a significant effect on operation of the production process and MPC system. Bandwidth and the avoidance of building inventories to utilize direct labor mean surge capacity must be available. Implementing surge capacity with direct labor personnel means these people will not be fully utilized in direct production activities. In fact, the **whole person** concept is based on the premise of hiring *people,* not just their muscles. As a consequence, direct workers take on many tasks not usually associated with "direct labor." This work can be done in nonpeak production times. This includes equipment maintenance, education, process improvement, data entry, and scheduling. From a JIT standpoint, the human/organizational elements building block puts a greater emphasis on scheduling by workers and less on scheduling by a centralized staff function. The entire process is fostered by the inherent JIT push toward simplification. With no defects, zero inventories, no disturbances, and fast throughput, detailed scheduling is easier; moreover, any problems tend to be local in nature and amenable to solution on a decentralized basis. The whole person concept implies a shift from indirect labor to direct, where jobs are more widely defined.

The final building block in Figure 9.3 is the manufacturing planning and control system and its link to JIT. Applying JIT requires most of the critical MPC functions described in this book. It will always be necessary to do master production scheduling, production planning, capacity planning, and material requirements planning. If the bill of materials is reduced to two or three levels, detailed material planning and associated transaction costs can be cut significantly. If detailed tracking is done by direct laborers under the whole person concept, additional savings can be achieved.

We see then that JIT has the potential for changing the character of manufacturing in a company, since it reduces MPC transactions. JIT can significantly reduce the size of the "hidden factory" that produces papers and computer transactions instead of products. Figure 9.4 provides a more detailed listing of JIT's building blocks and objectives. Many of these will be described in the next section, which presents a detailed JIT example.

FIGURE 9.4
JIT Objectives and Building Blocks

Ultimate objectives:
- Zero inventory
- Zero lead time
- Zero failures
- Flow process
- Flexible manufacture
- Eliminate waste

Building blocks:
- Product design:
  Few bill of materials levels
  Manufacturability in production cells
  Achievable quality
  Appropriate quality
  Standard parts
  Modular design

- Process design:
  Setup/lot size reduction
  Quality improvement
  Manufacturing cells
  Limited work in process
  Production bandwidth
  No stockrooms
  Service enhancements

- Human/organizational elements:
  Cross training/job rotation
  Flexible labor
  Continual improvement
  Whole person
  Limited direct/indirect distinction
  Cost accounting/performance
    measurement
  Information system changes
  Leadership/project management

- Manufacturing planning and control:
  Pull systems
  Rapid flow times
  Small container sizes
  Paperless systems
  Visual systems
  Level loading
  MRP interface
  Close purchasing/vendor relationships
  JIT software
  Reduced production reporting/
    inventory transaction processing
  Hidden factory cost reductions

A JIT Example

In this section we develop a detailed but simple example to show how MPC approaches based on MRP would be modified to implement JIT and describe the necessary building blocks (Figure 9.4) to achieve this. The product is a 1-liter saucepan produced in four models by the Muth Pots and Pans Company. (See Figure 9.5.) The product's brochure sums up its importance: "If you ain't got a Muth, you ain't got a pot." We'll look at elements of a JIT program for the saucepan that range from leveling production to redesigning the product. Some of these elements have direct MPC relevance; others will affect MPC only indirectly.

Leveling the Production

We start the saucepan's JIT program by considering how to "level and stabilize" production. This means planning a level output of 1-liter saucepans with the full mix of models each day (or week or some other short interval). Full-mix production in a short interval provides less inventory buildup in each model. Moreover, the schedule can respond to actual customer order conditions more quickly. Level output implies "freezing" to stabilize production and related activities on the floor. Before seeing how this might be done, let's compare Muth's manufacturing situation with traditional MRP-based approaches.

FIGURE 9.5
The 151
One-Liter
Saucepan Line

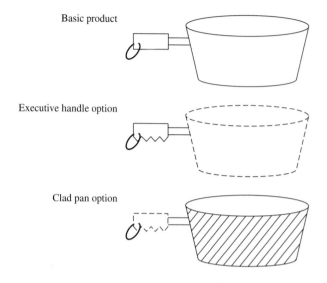

Basic product

Executive handle option

Clad pan option

FIGURE 9.6
Annual
Forecast Data

Completed Pan Model Number	Description of Model		Annual Forecast
	Handle	Metal	
151A	Basic	Sheet	200,000
151B	Basic	Clad	2,500
151C	Executive	Sheet	25,000
151D	Executive	Clad	100,000

Currently, Muth uses production planning to set the overall production rate, necessarily building inventories in anticipation of the Christmas season demand peak. The annual forecast for each of the four models is given in Figure 9.6. A master production schedule, for each of the four models, is exploded to produce a material requirements planning record for each of the 14 component part numbers shown on the part listing in Figure 9.7. Safety stock is carried for all components, and production is in the lot sizes indicated in Figure 9.7. Figure 9.8 gives lead times and routing data; lead times are computed on the basis of two days per operation, rounded up to the next whole week using five-day weeks. A typical MRP record is shown as Figure 9.9.

To plan for level production, the first step is converting the forecasts to the daily requirements for each model. Using a 250-day year, this conversion is shown in Figure 9.10. Note the difference between the current lot sizes and the daily requirements. Daily production will put pressure on process design to reduce setup times. Two other possible mixed-model master production schedules are shown in Figure 9.10, in addition to the one based on daily production batch sizes. The first shows quantities to be produced if hourly batches are to be made. The second shows an MPS with the minimum batch size of one for model 151B.

FIGURE 9.7 **Product Structure and Parts List**

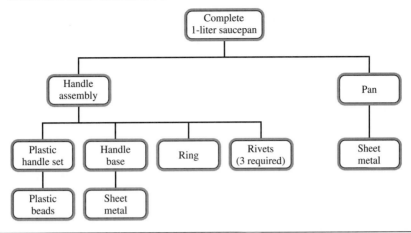

	Lot Size	Safety Stock	Finished Item Number			
			151A	151B	151C	151D
Models (end items)						
Complete pan 151A	8,000	5,000	X			
Complete pan 151B	900	1,000		X		
Complete pan 151C	3,000	3,000			X	
Complete pan 151D	6,000	5,000				X
Component part						
Regular pan 1936	14,000	10,000	X		X	
Clad pan 1937	8,000	6,000		X		X
Basic handle assembly 137	14,000	8,000	X	X		
Exec. handle assembly 138	8,000	5,000			X	X
Basic handle set 244	9,000	8,000	X	X		
Exec. handle set 245	9,000	8,000			X	X
Basic handle base 7731	14,000	8,000	X	X		
Exec. handle base 7735	12,000	5,000			X	X
Ring 353	24,000	15,000	X	X	X	X
Rivets 4164	100,000	50,000	X	X	X	X
Sheet metal 621	1 coil	1 coil	X		X	
Clad sheet 624	1 coil	1 coil		X		X
Handle sheet 685	1 coil	1 coil	X	X	X	X
Plastic beads 211	5 tons	1 ton	X	X	X	X

Pull System Introduction

A "pull" system exists when a work center is authorized to produce only when it has been signaled that there's a need for more parts in a downstream (user) department. This implies no work center is allowed to produce parts just to keep workers or equipment busy. It also means no work center is allowed to "push" material to a downstream work center. All movements and production are authorized by a signal from a downstream work center when it has a need

FIGURE 9.8 **Routing and Lead Time Data**

Department	Item	Routing	Lead Time
Final assembly	Complete pan	1. Spot weld	2 days
		2. Inspect	2 days
		3. Package	2 days
		Total = 6 days = 2 weeks	
Punch press	Pan	1. Blank and form	2 days
		2. Roll lip	2 days
		3. Test for flat	2 days
		4. Straighten	2 days
		5. Inspect	2 days
		Total = 10 days = 2 weeks	
Handle base	Handle base	1. Blank and form	2 days
		2. Inspect	2 days
		Total = 4 days = 1 week	
Handle assembly	Handle assembly	1. Rivet	2 days
		2. Inspect	2 days
		Total = 4 days = 1 week	
Injection molding	Plastic handle set	1. Mold	2 days
		2. Deburr	2 days
		3. Inspect	2 days
		Total = 6 days = 2 weeks	
	Purchased Items		
Purchasing	Sheet metal		⎧ Purchased
	Clad sheet metal		⎪ lead time
	Plastic beads		⎨ one week
	Ring		⎪ for all
	Rivets		⎩ items

FIGURE 9.9
MRP Record for Basic Handle Assembly (Part 137)

		Week									
		1	2	3	4	5	6	7	8	9	10
Gross requirements			8		8	3	8		8		8
Scheduled receipts											
Projected available balance	10	10	16	16	8	19	11	11	17	17	9
Planned order releases		14			14			14			

Q = 14; LT = 1; SS = 8.
All quantities are in thousands.

for component parts. Frequently, it's believed that the pull system creates the benefits in JIT. In fact, primary payoffs come from the discipline required to make the system work. Included are lot size reductions, limited work in process, fast throughput, and guaranteed quality.

Signals for communicating downstream work center demand vary widely. They include rolling a colored golf ball from a downstream work center to its supplying work center when the downstream center wants parts; yelling "Hey, we need some more"; sending an

FIGURE 9.10
Master Production Schedule Data*

	Model			
	151A	**151B**	**151C**	**151D**
Option configurations:				
Handle	Basic	Basic	Executive	Executive
Pan	Sheet	Clad	Sheet	Clad
Annual forecast (units)	200,000	2,500	25,000	100,000
Possible mixed model master production schedules:				
Daily batch MPS	800	10	100	400
Hourly batch MPS	100	1.25	12.5	50
Minimum batch MPS	80	1	10	40

*Data are based on a 250-day year and an eight-hour work day.

empty container back to be filled; and using cards (kanbans) to indicate more components are needed. A widely used technique is to paint a space on the floor that holds a specific number of parts. When the space is empty, the producing department is authorized to produce material to fill it. The consuming or using department takes material out of the space as it needs it; typically, this occurs only when the space authorizing that department's output is empty. For the Muth example, we'll use an empty container as the signal for more production; that is, whenever a using department empties a container, it sends the container back to the producing department. An empty container represents authorization to fill it up.

Given that Muth has committed to a level schedule where all models are made every day, the firm is almost ready to move into a pull mode of operation. Two additional issues need to be faced. First, there's the question of stability. For most pull systems, it's necessary to keep the schedule firm (frozen) for some reasonable time. This provides stability to the upstream work centers, as well as overall balance to the workflow. For Muth, assume the schedule is frozen for one month, with the daily batch quantities given in Figure 9.10 (1,310 pots per day).

The second issue is determining the container sizes to transport materials between work centers—a fairly complicated issue. It involves material handling considerations, container size commonality, congestion in the shop, proximity of work centers, and, of course, setup costs. For example, consider the container used between handle assembly and final assembly of the pots using the basic handle, part 137 (810 being used per day). The center is currently producing in lots of 14,000. We'll choose a container size that holds 100 pieces representing just under an eighth of a day's requirements. Note this choice puts a great deal of pressure on the handle assembly work center to reduce setup times.

Figure 9.11 shows the flow of work in Muth's new system for handle assembly to the final assembly line. Only two containers are used for part 137; while one is being used at the final assembly line, the other is being filled at handle assembly. This approach is very simple and is facilitated by the two departments being in close proximity. Figure 9.12 shows the factory layout. A worker from the final assembly line or a material handler can return empty containers. Any empty container is a signal to make a new batch of handles (i.e., fill it up). It's interesting to note the difference in average inventory that will be held in this system, compared with the former MRP methods and the lot size of 14,000. The system with a small container approaches "zero inventory," with an average inventory of about 100 units. Compare this to the inventories shown in the MRP record of Figure 9.8 (average inventory = 14,400).

FIGURE 9.11
Pull System for Muth Pots and Pans

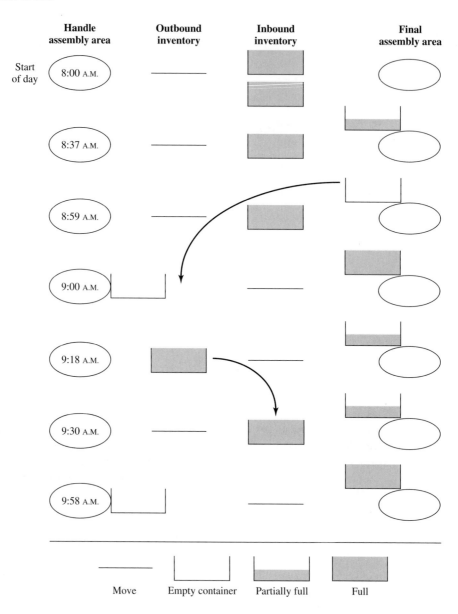

	Handle assembly area	Outbound inventory	Inbound inventory	Final assembly area

Start of day 8:00 A.M.

8:37 A.M.

8:59 A.M.

9:00 A.M.

9:18 A.M.

9:30 A.M.

9:58 A.M.

Move   Empty container   Partially full   Full

This pull system example has no buffer at either work center. It would be possible to add another container, which would allow greater flexibility in handle assembly, at the cost of extra inventory in the system. As it is, the final assembly area would use up a container in just under one hour. This means the system has to be responsive enough for the empty container to be returned to handle assembly and a batch made in this time frame. An extra container allows more time for responding to a make signal (an empty container) and also allows more flexibility in the supplying department. The extra inventory helps resolve problems—for example, when several production requests for different parts (containers) arrive at the same time.

FIGURE 9.12
Factory Layout

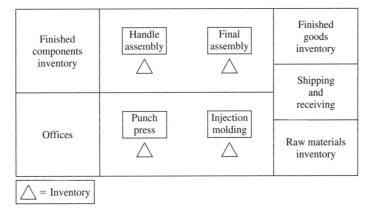

FIGURE 9.13
Redesigned
Handle Base

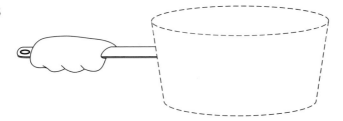

Product Design

To illustrate the implications for product design, consider the basic and executive handles for Muth's 1-liter saucepan shown in Figure 9.5. There are two differences between the handles: the grips and the ring placement. With some redesign of the plastic parts on the executive handle, the handle base becomes a common part and the ring placement is common between the two handle models; the methods for handle assembly could also be standardized. The only difference would be the choice of plastic handle parts. Such a redesigned handle base is shown in Figure 9.13.

In addition to the improvements this design change makes in handle subassembly, there are potential impacts in other areas as well. For example, handle bases would have one combined lot of production instead of two, with attendant reductions in inventory. It might now be possible to run the handle base area on a pull system as well, with containers passing between the handle base area and the handle subassembly area. Another advantage is a simplification in the bill of materials, a reduction in the number of parts that must be planned and controlled with MRP, and a concomitant reduction in the number of transactions that have to be processed.

Process Design

The product redesign, in turn, opens opportunities for process improvement. For example, it may now be possible to use the same equipment to attach both kinds of plastic handles to the handle base. Perhaps a cell can be formed, where handle bases are made and assembled as a unit. Figure 9.14 shows one way this might be accomplished, including an integration

FIGURE 9.14
Cellular
Manufacturing
of Handle
Assembly and
Final Assembly

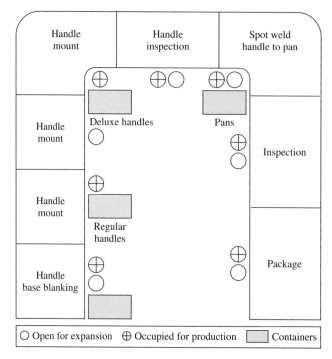

of the handle assembly cell and the final assembly line in a U-shaped layout. Note in this example that no significant inventories are anywhere on the line, and both handle base material and plastic handle parts are replenished with a pull system based on containers.

Figure 9.14 also illustrates the bandwidth concept. Several open stations along the line would permit adding personnel if volume were increased. Moreover, perhaps Muth would like to establish different production rates for certain times. For example, perhaps this pan might be manufactured in higher volumes near the Christmas season. What's needed is the capacity at the cell to move from one level of output to another. This added capacity probably means the dedicated equipment will not be highly utilized.

The cell is designed to permit variations in staffing to better respond to actual customer demands. If an unexpected surge in demand for executive handle pots comes through, the cellular approach will allow Muth to make the necessary changes faster—and to live with this kind of problem with smaller finished goods inventories. Over time, perhaps this cell can be further expanded in terms of bandwidth and flexibility to produce handles for other Muth products.

The value of quality improvement can be seen in Figure 9.14. The inspection station takes up valuable space that could be used for production. It adds cost to the product. If bad products are being culled by inspection, buffer stocks will be required to keep the final assembly line going. All of this is waste to be eliminated.

Bill of Materials Implications

The product redesign results in a streamlined bill of materials. The number of options from the customer's point of view has been maintained, but the number of parts required has

FIGURE 9.15
Simplified
Product
Structure

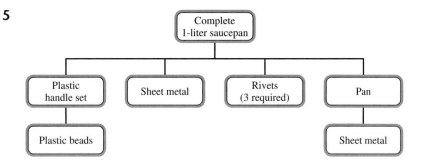

FIGURE 9.16   **MRP Record for Phantom (Part 137)**

		Week									
		1	2	3	4	5	6	7	8	9	10
Gross requirements		4,050	4,050	4,050	4,050	4,050	4,050	4,050	4050	4,050	4,050
Scheduled receipts											
Projected available bal.	15,000	10,950	6,900	2,850							
Planned order releases					1,200	4,050	4,050	4,050	4050	4,050	4,050

Q = lot for lot; LT = 0; SS = 0.

gone down (e.g., components have been reduced from 14 to 10). With the cellular layout shown in Figure 9.14, the handle base and handle assembly no longer exist as inventoriable items. They are "phantoms" that won't require direct planning and control with MRP. The product structure given as Figure 9.7 now will look like Figure 9.15.

Several observations can be made about Figure 9.15. One is that handle assemblies have ceased to exist as part of the product structure. If we wanted to maintain the handle assembly for engineering and other reasons, it could be treated as a phantom. Figure 9.16 shows what the MRP record would look like in this case. In Figure 9.16, there's some existing inventory to use up; phantom treatment allows this to occur, and will always use this inventory before making more.

Another observation is that pans *do* remain as inventoriable items. Elimination of these two part numbers and their associated inventories may well be the next goal for product and process redesign. Still another is to understand the magnitude of the reduction in transactions represented by the JIT approach illustrated in Figure 9.14. All MRP planning for the eliminated part numbers (or phantom treatment) is now gone. This affects MRP planning as well as stockrooms—and all other indirect labor associated with MRP control.

Finally, we need to consider the effect on lead times, the resultant ability to better respond to market conditions, the reductions in work-in-process inventories, and the greater velocity with which material moves through the factory. If the combined lead times are computed for the product structure in Figure 9.7 and lead time data in Figure 9.8, five weeks are required for the flow of raw materials into pots. The JIT approach cuts that to just over two weeks, which could be reduced even further.

JIT Applications

Toyota is the classic JIT company in that it has gone further than any other discrete manu-facturing firm in terms of truly making the production process into a continuous flow. Much of the basic terminology and philosophy of JIT have their origins at Toyota. A key issue in JIT at Toyota is understanding that automobile manufacturing is done in very large factories that are much more complex than our simplified example. Parts will flow from one work center to many others with intermediate storage, and flows into work centers will also come from many work centers with intermediate storage. The JIT systems at Toyota have to reflect this complexity. Before delving into the complexity, however, it's useful to first see how a **single-card kanban system** functions in a manufacturing environment with many work centers and intermediate storage.

Single-Card Kanban

Figure 9.17 depicts a factory with three work centers (A, B, and C) producing component parts, three work centers (X, Y, and Z) making assemblies, and an intermediate storage area for component parts. A single component (part 101) is fabricated in work center C and used by work centers Y and Z. To illustrate how the system works, suppose work center Z wishes to assemble a product requiring component 101. A box of part 101 would be moved from the storage area to work center Z. As the box was removed from storage, the accompanying kanban card would be removed from the box; shortly thereafter, the card would be placed

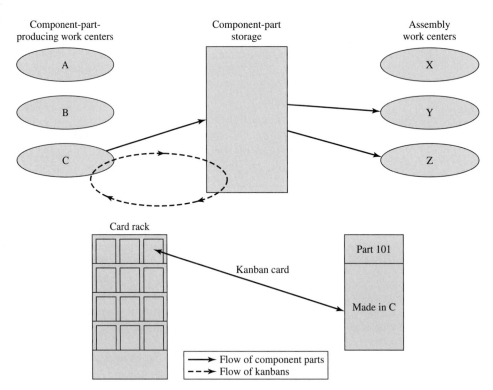

FIGURE 9.17
Single Kanban System

Component-part-producing work centers

Component-part storage

Assembly work centers

A

B

C

X

Y

Z

Card rack

Kanban card

Part 101

Made in C

→ Flow of component parts
--→ Flow of kanbans

in the card rack at work center C. The cards in the rack at any work center represents the authorized production for that work center.

The greater the number of kanban cards in the system, the larger the inventory, but also the greater the autonomy that can be attained between the component-producing work centers and the assembly work centers. Some priority system can be implemented in the component work centers, such as working on a first-come/first-served basis or imposing some time requirements (such as all cards delivered in the morning will be returned with filled containers in the afternoon of the same day and all afternoon cards will be delivered the next morning).

Toyota

The production system at Toyota is in many ways the most advanced JIT system in the world. Its results are seen on the highways of the world. By virtually any yardstick, Toyota is truly a great manufacturing company. For example, Toyota turns its inventories 10 times as fast as U.S. and European car manufacturers and about 50 percent faster than its Japanese competitors. It's also very competitive in price, quality, and delivery performance.

Figure 9.18 shows the Toyota production system and where JIT fits within the overall approach. To some extent, the role given to JIT in Figure 9.18 may appear less encompassing

FIGURE 9.18 Toyota's Production System

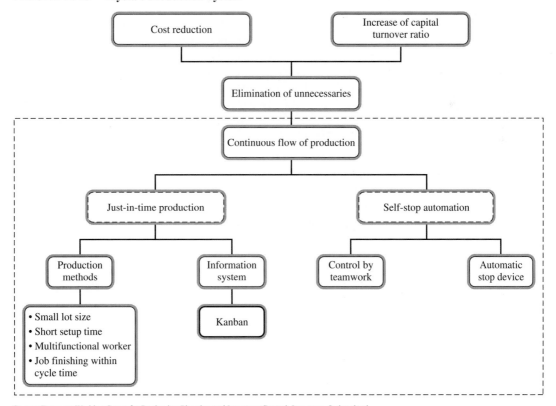

Source: European Working Group for Production Planning and Inventory Control, Lausanne, Switzerland.

than that just described. For example, the "elimination of unnecessaries" is seen as fundamental. All of the objectives and building blocks for JIT listed in Figure 9.4 are in basic agreement with those in Figure 9.18. The box for production methods is basically the same as process design in Figure 9.3. Included under this heading is the multifunctional worker, which matches with several aspects of the human/organizational element building block. Also included is "job finishing within cycle time"; this is consistent with the dominance of material flow velocity and the subservient role of direct labor utilization.

Toyota's Kanban System

The Toyota view of just-in-time production shown in Figure 9.18 includes "Information system" with "Kanban" below it. The information system encompasses the MPC activities necessary to support JIT execution. Kanban is the Toyota technique for controlling material flows. The situation at Toyota is much more complex than that illustrated in the single-card kanban example. Toyota has intermediate storage after production of components and additional intermediate storage in front of assembly work centers. This means the work flows from a producing work center into an inventory, then to another inventory, and then to the next work center. For this reason, Toyota uses a two-card kanban system, but the principles are the same as for the single kanban card system. The chain of dual kanban cards can extend all the way back to the suppliers. Several of Toyota's suppliers receive their authorizations to produce via kanban cards.

Figure 9.19 gives the formula used to calculate the number of kanban cards needed. In this formula, there's a factor for including safety stock, which Toyota says should be less than 10 percent. Using the formula, no safety stock, and a container size of 1, we can see the philosophy of the system. If a work center required eight units per day (one per hour) and it took one hour to make one unit, only one set of two kanban cards would be theoretically necessary; that is, just as a unit was finished, it would be needed at the subsequent operation.

The container sizes are kept small and standard. Toyota feels that no container should have more than 10 percent of a day's requirements. Since everything revolves around these containers and the flow of cards, a great deal of discipline is necessary. The following rules keep the system operating:

- Each container of parts must have a kanban card.
- The parts are always pulled. The using department must come to the providing department and not vice versa.
- No parts may be obtained without a conveyance kanban card.

FIGURE 9.19
Calculating the
Number of
Kanbans

$$Y = \frac{DL(1 + \alpha)}{a} \qquad (9.1)$$

where:

Y = number of kanban card sets
D = demand per unit of time
L = lead time
a = container capacity
α = policy variable (safety stock)

FIGURE 9.20
Toyota's View
of Inventory

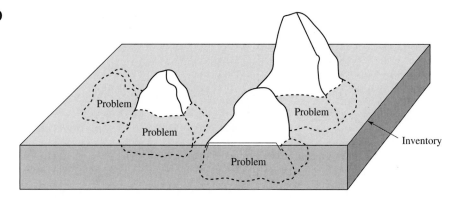

- All containers contain their standard quantities and only the standard container for the part can be used.
- No extra production is permitted. Production can only be started on receipt of a production kanban card.

These rules keep the shop floor under control. The execution effort is directed toward flawlessly following these rules. Execution is also directed toward continual improvement. In kanban terms, this means reducing the number of kanban cards and, thereby, reducing the level of work-in-process inventory. Reducing the number of cards is consistent with an overall view of inventory as undesirable. It's said at Toyota that inventory is like water that covers up problems that are like rocks. Figure 9.20 depicts this viewpoint. If the inventory is systematically reduced, problems are exposed—and attention can be directed to their solution. Problems obscured by inventory still remain.

Hewlett-Packard

Hewlett-Packard (HP) has been one of the more successful users of JIT in the United States. An interesting approach to JIT was implemented at its Medical Electronics Division in Waltham, Massachusetts. JIT was used for assembling two major patient-monitoring products called Pogo and Clover. Figure 9.21 shows the assembly area layout for these products. Clover was the older, more expensive product, with a larger number of customer-specified options. Pogo was designed as a lower-cost alternative with JIT manufacture in mind. The Clover assembly process was made up of four feeder subassemblies (A to D) and a final assembly and test area (E). Pogo was designed to be built in four successive assembly stations in a U shape with a test performed in each. A final test was performed at station V. Both Clover and Pogo went into a heat test area, shown at the top of Figure 9.21. The series of tests performed on Pogo at each station (I to IV) allowed HP to reduce the failure rate in heat testing more quickly than it did for Clover.

Both Clover and Pogo were supported by dedicated component stock areas. Each was also supported with a printed circuit board stock. In Pogo's case, 12 types of circuit boards were maintained, with a single-card kanban approach. They were supplied in lot sizes of four, with coded clothespins acting as the single kanban. On the other hand, the printed circuit boards for Clover were maintained with traditional MRP lot sizes. Both Pogo and Clover used a single-card kanban approach to pull kits of parts from the controlled stock areas.

FIGURE 9.21   **Hewlett-Packard Waltham Division Pogo/Clover Production U Stations**

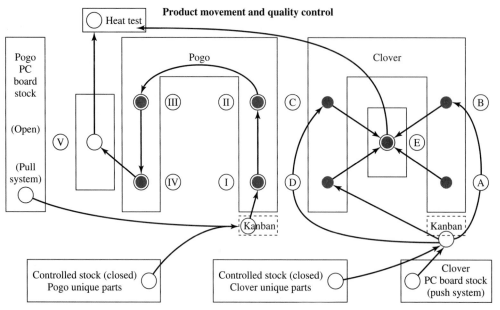

This JIT system was supported by several MRP-based computer systems. These company-wide systems were mainly used for component-part planning. As time went by, however, the semimonthly MRP explosion, weekly allocation quantities, and daily release against these allocation quantities became more cumbersome for JIT manufacturing. JIT operates in a very different time frame.

A more profound issue concerned HP's overall philosophy in adopting JIT. The primary emphasis was on stability. In Pogo, for example, the goal was to make 10 units per day, each and every day. This goal was achieved; then it became possible to get 10 good units between 8 A.M. and 1:30 P.M. on most days. To concentrate on stability, the Pogo assembly area was buffered on both ends. Extra supplies of component materials were held, as were extra finished goods inventories.

Once stability was achieved, relatively flawless output could be achieved with regularity. The continuous improvement attention then shifted to reducing buffers and increasing responsiveness. If the assembly area could produce 15 units on a particular day when necessary, the finished goods could be reduced. With flawless production, lower component inventories could also be attained. The JIT results were impressive. Total plant inventory fell from $56 million to $40 million in 15 months. Work-in-process inventory for the Pogo line was reduced from 50 units to 4, and the assembly floor space required decreased 65 percent. Quality increased substantially by the JIT approach, as well. But there were still new avenues for improvement. Included were further reductions in the printed circuit board inventories and tackling what appeared to be bottlenecks in circuit board production.

Nonrepetitive JIT

Many JIT principles for high-volume repetitive manufacturing apply in low-volume production environments as well. However, most low-volume manufacturers have balked at two basic problems: (1) the requirement of setting up high-volume flow lines dedicated to a few products and (2) level loading. However, merging of the two camps is taking place: even for the high-volume repetitive manufacturer, it's increasingly important to respond to customer pressures for greater flexibility in volume, product mix, and other service features. The lower-volume job shop manufacturers are in turn learning to adapt JIT concepts to their environments.

A Service-Enhanced View of Manufacturing

An examination of service operations provides insights into producing products faster with greater variety. Rapid response is critical, the number of possible product/service combinations continues to grow, end-item forecasting is more difficult, and large buffer inventories are unacceptable. One example was a repair facility for Palm Pilots and other electronics products, placed in the DHL (worldwide parcel shippers) facilities in Singapore. Using DHL's rapid product movements and tracking, a product could be picked up, repaired, and returned in two to three days, instead of supplying a replacement.

All of this argues for a JIT mode of manufacture—one whose objective is to be able to accept any customer order and turn it out right behind any other, with flexibility to handle surges in volume or mix changes, all done on a routine basis. Service industries provide an example. McDonald's can handle two busloads of Boy Scouts or an unexpected shift from Big Macs to fish sandwiches without resorting to some "panic mode" of operation. Fast-food operations provide still another example. Most have seen an evolution toward a broader product line (greater bandwidth). McDonald's no longer just serves hamburgers, for example. The objective is to increase market appeal while maintaining maximum responsiveness, minimal inventories, small lot sizes, and short lead times.

The traditional JIT view of level capacity must be adapted in nonrepetitive situations. Responsiveness to fickle demand requires a large bandwidth in terms of surge capacity. No one wants the fire department to be operated at high capacity utilization; immediate response is essential. Surge capacity must be in place in both equipment and labor. A different view of asset management and labor utilization is required. Fixed assets (both capital and people) will be less intensively utilized to increase material velocity and overall system responsiveness.

Flexible Systems

Leading-edge firms are coming to understand requirements for volume and product flexibility. Some have had experience in repetitive manufacturing applications of JIT and are now moving into nonrepetitive applications. An example is a telecommunications equipment manufacturer, which began JIT in its high-volume telephone handset operations. The firm had a limited number of high-selling models; in two years its inventory turns were tripled, work in process was reduced by 75 percent, failure rates in manufacturing were cut in half, and setup times fell 50 percent. Thereafter, the firm turned to its low-volume telecom systems plant, where more than 150 basic circuit boards were manufactured, and every end item was somewhat of a custom order. The company learned it needed to go back to the basics of JIT—product engineering, process engineering, and the whole person concept—to successfully implement JIT for its nonrepetitive products.

The firm developed cellular designs, began cellular manufacturing with great flexibility, and cross trained people with an emphasis on being able to handle volume surges in the telecom systems plant. MRP was still used for overall planning, but far fewer transactions were processed by the hidden factory of indirect labor. In the first six months, first pass yields improved 27 percent, work in process fell 31 percent, and manufacturing cells under JIT hit 100 percent of schedule. The people then helped out other parts of the company that were behind schedule!

Simplified Systems and Routine Execution

A major issue in any JIT firm, repetitive or nonrepetitive, is flow times. Work must flow through the factory so quickly that detailed tracking is not required. A related idea is responsiveness. In several JIT systems for nonrepetitive environments, the firm installed what might be called a **weekly wash.** In its simplest form, weekly wash means week 1's sales orders become week 2's production schedule.

As an example, Stanley Hardware in New Britain, Connecticut, was a make-to-stock firm for most items, but some were unique to particular customers. It applied JIT with the weekly wash concept to three different production areas. In each case, weekly sales for a particular week were determined on Friday, with resultant quantities manufactured the next week within some change parameters. In one case, the week-to-week variation in production could be plus or minus 20 percent. For a second product group, the swing was plus or minus 35 percent, and for a third group any adjustment could be handled. Because response times were shortened, customer service was enhanced.

The weekly wash approach to JIT for nonrepetitive manufacturing shifts the emphasis from scheduling material to scheduling time blocks. The focus is on what's scheduled in the next time frame, rather than on when we'll make product X. This focus is driven by the actual requirements, rather than a forecast of needs. It's as though we were scheduling a set of trains or buses. We don't hold the train until it's full, and we can always cram a few more people into a car, within reason. By scheduling trains on a relatively frequent basis, attempting to keep capacity as flexible as possible, and assigning "passengers" only to a time frame, responsiveness to actual demand can be increased, and detailed scheduling can be made more simple. A hospital administrator once expressed the idea well: We do not make people sick to fill the beds!

Joint-Firm JIT

JIT has been applied and misapplied by companies with their suppliers. Some firms simply ask the suppliers to buffer poor schedules. On the other hand, when done well, a joint JIT approach can lead to greater bottom-line results for both firms and increased competitiveness in the marketplace. It is critical to understand the need for joint efforts in JIT. For example, we are told by several automotive component suppliers that they are able to provide lower prices to Toyota than other firms, because Toyota is easy to do business with—the company makes a schedule and sticks to it. Others change their requirements often, with serious cost implications.

The Basics

The first prerequisite to joint-firm JIT is a scheduling system producing requirements that are reasonably certain. Without predictability, JIT for vendors is a case of the customers exporting the problems. Although this may work in the short run, in the long run it can't. We've seen a factory where JIT benefits were extolled, only to find a new paving project— for vendors' trucks. Inventory had moved from the warehouse to trailer trucks! Similar war stories abound about warehousing firms in Detroit that are needed to buffer suppliers as auto companies implement JIT.

Joint-firm JIT needs, to whatever extent possible, a stable schedule. This is consistent with level schedules for the repetitive manufacturer. To the extent that a firm makes the same products in the same quantities every day—without defects and without missing the schedule—a supplier firm's schedule is extremely simple. For the nonrepetitive manufacturer, the issue isn't leveling as much as it is avoiding surprises. The level schedule may be violated in nonrepetitive environments, but there is a greater need for coordinated information flows and, perhaps, larger buffer inventories. However, there's a major difference between a *stable* (albeit nonlevel) schedule and one that's simply uncertain. The only cure for the latter case is buffer inventories.

Certainty is a relative commodity. A vendor might be able to live fairly well with a schedule that's unpredictable on a daily basis but very predictable on a weekly basis. A weekly MRP-based total, with some kind of daily call-off of exact quantities, could be reasonably effective. In fact, some firms have developed "electronic kanbans" for this purpose. The notion of weekly wash could also be used; that is, an inventory equal to some maximum expected weekly usage could be maintained and replenished on a weekly basis. For high-value products, it might be worth it to go to some kind of twice-weekly wash, or to obtain better advance information from the customer via an e-based system.

Other "basics" for joint-firm JIT include all the objectives and building blocks discussed earlier in the chapter. A JIT basic uniquely associated with suppliers relates to pruning their number. Many companies have reduced their vendor base by as much as 90 percent to work on a truly cooperative basis with the remaining vendors. Hidden factory issues have to be considered in vendor relations as well. Some people feel the secret in joint-firm JIT is to connect MRP systems in the firms. This isn't a good idea. The focus must be on coordinated execution. A better approach might be to use blanket orders (or *no* orders), MRP for weekly quantities, agreed-upon safety stocks, or amounts by which the sum of daily quantities can exceed weekly totals, and e-based systems to determine the next day in-shipment. All this could be done without intervention of indirect labor personnel.

A telecom equipment manufacturer has such a system: Each day at about 4 P.M., an e-mail is sent to a vendor specifying how many of a particular expensive item to deliver the day after tomorrow. The units delivered never enter a stockroom or inventory record. They're delivered directly to the line without inspection and assembled that day. The vendor is paid on the basis of item deliveries into finished goods inventory. Stability is handled by providing the vendor weekly MRP projections, using time fences that define stability. Daily fluctuations reflect actual market conditions.

Tightly Coupled JIT Supply

Major suppliers to automobile manufacturers utilize JIT extensively. As an example, consider a seat supplier, such as Johnson Controls, and a manufacturer such as Volkswagen. In such a case, the two firms need to develop a form of synchronous manufacturing, operating almost as a single unit. The execution is driven by JIT. JIT execution between these two firms means that the automobile manufacturer will pass the exact build sequence (models, colors of seats, etc.) to the seat supplier, perhaps something like 30 hours in advance. The supplier needs to *build* the seats and deliver them in this time frame. Seats are not built to inventory at the supplier, and no seats are inventoried at the auto manufacturer. The seats are delivered directly to the assembly line, to match the sequence, so the assembly team simply takes the next seat, and installs it in the next car.

This synchronization allows for almost no transactions between the firms, with the supplier paid by backflushing completion of cars off the line. Inventory costs are avoided, as well as damage from multiple handling with minimal use of protective packaging. But achieving the synchronization on a continuous basis requires *flawless execution* in both firms. The auto manufacturing company cannot change the schedule or take a car off of the line for repairs, since this would change the seat installation sequence. The supplier must make each seat perfectly, since there is no stock of seats to replace one that is imperfect. The bottom line here is that this form of joint-firm JIT is highly productive. But it is rigidly connected and requires joint excellence in execution. It works well—for certain kinds of products.

Less Tightly Coupled JIT Supply

In the majority of cases, two firms will not couple their manufacturing activities as closely as those of a seat supplier to its automotive customer. The supplier will have multiple customers, only some of which will be supplied by JIT. Similarly, the customer has multiple suppliers, and not all of these will be expected to deliver directly to the line. An alternative solution is for the customer to pick up goods from vendors on some prearranged schedule. This is increasingly done for several reasons. The most obvious is the savings in transportation costs over having each vendor deliver independently. In some cases JIT has been called "just-in-traffic." A second reason relates to stability and predictability. If the customer picks up materials, some uncertainty inherent in vendor deliveries can be eliminated. Finally, pickup offers more chances to directly attack hidden factory costs. The customer can, for example, provide containers that hold the desired amounts and that will flow as kanbans through the plant. Savings in packaging materials as well as costs of unpacking are helpful to both parties. Items can also be placed on special racks inside the truck to minimize damage. Defective items can be returned easily for replacement without the usual costly return-to-vendor procedures and paperwork. Other paperwork can similarly be simplified when third parties aren't involved and when the loop is closed between problem and action in a short time frame.

Pickup can also be done in geographic areas beyond the factory. A Hewlett-Packard factory in Boise, Idaho, has key suppliers in Silicon Valley, California (about 600 miles away). Pickup from them is done by a trucking firm, with the entire shipment moved to Boise on a daily basis. New United Motor Manufacturing, Inc. (NUMMI) in Freemont, California, did the same thing with its Midwest suppliers: a Chicago-based trucking company collected trailer loads for daily piggyback shipments to California about 2,000 miles away. NUMMI started off holding a three-day safety stock of these parts but reduced it to one day after experience had been gained.

"JIT" Coordination through Hubs

A relatively new innovation that has JIT characteristics is the supply of materials through hubs. A hub is most easily seen as an inventory, placed close to the customer, and filled by the suppliers. The costs of carrying the inventories is born by the suppliers, and they are paid for their goods either as they leave the hub or as they are backflushed into finished goods at the customer. This form of supply is called **vendor-managed inventory (VMI).** VMI is well liked by customers, since it moves inventory carrying costs off their books and onto those of the suppliers. But the "no free lunch" principle applies: If the customer only exports its problems, and does not aid in the solution, the prices will have to be adjusted to make this work. Moreover, the firm with the lowest cost of capital in the chain is ideally suited to absorb inventory-carrying costs.

There is, however, a major potential saving in this relationship. When it is done well, the supplier should eliminate its own finished goods inventory, while the customer in turn also eliminates any inventories of these materials. All inventories are in the hub and are visible to both customer and supplier. The customer needs to take the responsibility for providing highly accurate information on its expected removals from inventory (i.e., its build schedules). This is typically provided via an e-based system. The supplier thus has *knowledge* of exact customer usage: no forecasts (guesses), and no surprise orders. The supplier also has the option of working in what we call the **uphill skier** mode, where it is the supplier's responsibility to supply, but in whatever ways it wishes (just as the uphill skier has the responsibility for not colliding with the downhill skier). Having a few customers who can be supplied with the uphill skier concept allows the supplier to use its capacities and logistics more effectively. For example, if a supplier knows the customer will take 55 units out of inventory 11 days from today, this provides a window for manufacturing and delivery, which is much less constraining than classic JIT coordination.

Lessons

The primary lesson to be learned in joint-firm JIT is to not shift the execution problems from the customer back to its suppliers: joint-firm JIT means *joint.* Many firms have made this mistake, demanding that their suppliers support them in closely coordinated execution—while the suppliers see the customer as "waking up in a new world every morning." Typically, when the consequences become known, the emphasis necessarily shifts to joint problem identification and solution, a focus on joint (chain) measures, the need for stabilized schedules, a true partnership, and help from the customers for the suppliers to implement JIT with *their* suppliers. The results for a manufacturer of office equipment were impressive: overcoming a 40 percent cost disadvantage, reducing its vendor base from 5,000 to 300, and winning several important awards for manufacturing excellence.

JIT Software

The MPC systems required to execute JIT are relatively straightforward. Most ERP systems include software that supports JIT execution. Figure 9.22 shows how this software typically functions.

FIGURE 9.22   **Block Diagram of JIT Software**

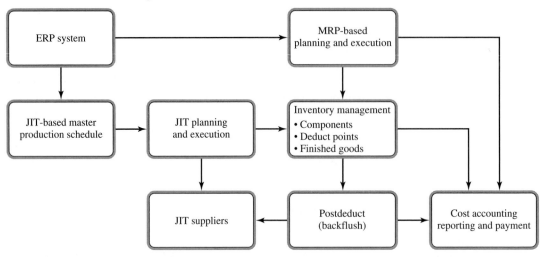

The MRP-JIT Separation

Figure 9.22 depicts the way JIT typically functions as a part of the overall MPC system. An ERP system, such as SAP, provides the overall platform and integration with other company systems. Figure 9.22 shows a split into those items that are to be planned/controlled with JIT and those that will utilize classic MRP-based systems. For the JIT products, it is necessary to first establish a master production schedule, which typically is rate based. This MPS is then passed to a JIT planning and execution subsystem that utilizes simplified bills of materials (phantoms) and cellular manufacturing. The detailed planning is also passed to JIT suppliers, typically with an e-based system providing the exact build sequence.

JIT Planning and Execution

JIT planning and execution is driven by a daily build schedule, supported by the JIT dictates of flawless execution, zero failures, no buffer inventories, cellular manufacturing, pull systems, cross-trained personnel, etc. JIT planning and execution also utilizes an inventory management subsystem for any components that are planned with MRP-based systems. This subsystem also keeps track of finished goods, any hub inventories, and **deduct points.** A deduct point is a stage in the manufacturing process where the inventories for certain parts are backflushed. That is, in some JIT systems, the backflushing is not held off until the goods are finally passed into finished goods inventory. The accounting is done in stages. This is most usually seen in early stages of JIT, when the flow times are longer and the yields less certain. The use of deduct points also helps in migrating from MRP-based planning to JIT-based planning/execution. In fact, a typical improvement is to decide when a deduct point can be eliminated, since a deduct step requires production reporting to indicate that product completion has reached this stage. Figure 9.22 also depicts an accounting/reporting subsystem to collect performance data and support supplier payments.

An Example

Let us illustrate how this software might work by returning to the HP case depicted in Figure 9.21. Concentrating on the Pogo product, let us assume that originally this product was built as five separate subassembly and test steps (I to V), going into inventory after each stage of assembly or test. For each discrete step, the prior assembly would be picked from inventory, along with the unique components associated with the particular subassembly stage. Withdrawals of subassemblies and component parts would be deducted from on-hand inventory balances as they occurred in classic MRP fashion.

Under JIT planning the entire flow might be considered one step from I to V; that is, the deduct point for inventory reductions would be when step V is completed (note that this only becomes feasible when steps I to V occur quickly). Completion of step V would be the only transaction needed through production reporting. When this occurs, a deduct list for all the components used in steps I to V would trigger inventory reporting through backflushing (in this case including the Pogo printed circuit board stocks and controlled stock area for unique Pogo parts). We also noted that HP controlled the PC boards for Pogo with a JIT system. This means that receipt of boards into this area would be a deduct point for PC components. It is worth noting that this approach could lead to serious problems if there is significant scrap in PC board manufacturing (i.e., usage would be under-reported, leading to unreliable inventory values).

Parts and bills of material in JIT systems are the equivalent of the usual product structure files in MRP, but they are defined according to deduct points. That is, the deduct point is like an assembly that is planned as one part and supported by cellular manufacturing to execute the manufacturing accordingly. As products are converted from MRP to JIT, it is necessary to reformat the data according to deduct points. In execution, it is imperative, in fact, to utilize the exact quantities of materials indicated by the deduct lists (flawless execution). As reengineering efforts allow deduct points to be eliminated, the data also need to be reformatted.

JIT Execution with SAP Software

Most ERP systems incorporate some means to accomplish JIT execution within their system structure. SAP, providing the most widely used ERP system, has the following approach to support JIT planning, as reported by Knolmayer et al.:

> The R/3 module supports the Kanban principle. Objects are cards, production supply areas, control cycles, and Kanban boards that provide an overview of the current status (e.g., full, empty, in progress, being transported) of the containers. The board visualizes bottlenecks and problems arising with material supply. The R/3 Kanban system allows external procurement, internal production, and supply from a warehouse. The initiating event for delivery of the material is a status change at the container; when the container status is altered from "full" to "empty," R/3 automatically generates replacement bookings. The status of the containers can be changed directly on the Kanban board, in an input mask, or by scanning a barcode printed on the card. When a receiver sets the status of a container to empty, a replacement element is created and the associated source is requested to supply the material. As soon as the status changes to "full," the arrival of the material is booked automatically with reference to the procurement element. A supplier can view the inventory levels of materials via the Internet and determine what quantities of the materials need to be provided. It can define a delivery due list and inform the customer by setting the status at "in progress."

Managerial Implications

The vision of JIT presented here is much broader than manufacturing planning and control. JIT is best seen as an integrated approach to achieving continued manufacturing excellence. A holistic view of JIT encompasses a set of programs, as well as a process where human resources are continually redeployed in better ways to serve company objectives in the marketplace. In the balance of this chapter, we feel compelled to speculate a bit on what this implies for manufacturing planning and control and related areas.

Information System Implications

Since JIT requires changes in the ways manufacturing is managed and executed, changes are required in the computer-based systems to support JIT manufacturing. The changes run counter to some classic IT systems in manufacturing. JIT calls for continuous improvement, reducing transactions, and eliminating the hidden factory. This implies an ongoing migration of MPC systems to support reengineered manufacturing processes. To the extent that JIT is for nonrepetitive manufacturing, personal computers are often used on the shop floor to support detailed scheduling. For joint-firm JIT planning and execution, the increasing use of e-based systems is taking place. In practice, there tends to be an evolution from simple buying and routine transaction processing to more coordinated work, including new product developments and other less structured activities. Many firms now are implementing extranets to support these objectives, where individual company pairings work on achieving increasingly unique benefits.

Manufacturing Planning and Control

JIT has profound implications for all detailed MPC activities. JIT (including its extensions into less tightly linked supply chains) offers the potential for eliminating or sharply reducing inventories, incoming quality control, receiving, kitting, paper processing associated with deliveries and shipments, detailed scheduling done by central staff, and all the detailed tracking associated with classic production activity control systems. It is important to understand these benefits as the MPC system is enhanced to embody JIT thinking. Many of them are well hidden.

It is never easy to change IT systems. Organizations have grown around them, cost accounting and other areas seem to require data generated by these systems, and many jobs are involved. However, the potential is real, and leading-edge companies are increasing their competitiveness through JIT and related concepts.

Scorekeeping

A firm adopting JIT in its fullest context will need to think carefully about reward systems and managerial scorekeeping. Traditional measurement systems focus attention on producing the products, using cost accounting systems that have changed little since the Industrial Revolution. These systems are from an era when direct labor was the major cost source. Now, in many companies, material costs dominate, with direct labor cost (using traditional definitions) continually decreasing in relative importance. Far too many manufacturing firms are hobbled by antiquated measures such as tons or other overall productivity measures. For example, a large ice cream manufacturer evaluates its factories on "liter-tons" produced. A 1-liter brick of ice cream has less gross margin than a particular ice cream bar—but 1-liter bricks are always put in inventory at year-end to make the numbers look good.

JIT thinking focuses on material velocity, which is consistent with inventory reduction and lead-time compression. Under JIT, we must be wary of how "costs" are measured and the resultant implications for decision making. The values of bandwidth, flexibility, responsiveness, and worker skill enhancement need to be recognized. None of these is incorporated in traditional accounting systems. The entire approach to capacity utilization needs to be rethought in JIT. Utilization of capital assets may not be as important as responsiveness and material velocity. Being able to take any customer order, even when vastly different from forecast, and doing so with short lead times with minimal use of "shock troops" is the goal. Improved responsiveness to marketplace needs will separate successful firms from the also-rans.

What all of this means for cost accounting is that many traditional views will need to be scrapped. For example, some companies have given up the cost category of direct labor. The distinction between direct and indirect isn't useful, and basing product costs on multiples of direct labor cost leads to more erroneous implications than some other scheme. The whole person concept leads to the conclusion that the labor pool is an asset to be enhanced. It also dictates using direct labor for activities not normally associated with direct labor. Trying to apportion labor into various categories is constraining. A final scorekeeping issue is the top-management challenge to create the organizational climate where the JIT/supply chain management journey can best take place. We see this journey is the best means for survival in the years ahead. Leadership will be required to guide manufacturing firms through the necessary changes.

Pros and Cons

There are situations where JIT will work well and ones where it won't. Many authorities believe JIT to be what every Japanese company strives for. In fact, many Japanese firms with complex product structures are now actively working to implement MRP-based systems. However, JIT's realm seems to be expanding. At one time JIT was thought to apply only to repetitive manufacturing with simple product structures and level schedules. Increasingly, companies are applying JIT concepts to nonrepetitive schedules; product complexity is being partially overcome with decentralized computing on the shop floor; make-to-order schedules are being adapted to JIT; and JIT is being applied to interfirm contexts.

Some companies ask if they need to install MRP before adopting JIT, since JIT implementation often means they must dismantle parts of the MRP-based system. Although it's conceptually possible to implement JIT without first implementing MRP, for firms that can benefit significantly from MRP, it's usually not done. Unless we can find some other way to develop the discipline of MRP, JIT operations are at great risk. In the discipline's absence, when JIT takes away the buffers, there will usually be costly disruptions of the manufacturing process, poor customer service, and panic responses to the symptoms rather than to the underlying problems.

Concluding Principles

This chapter is devoted to providing an understanding of JIT and how it fits into MPC systems. Our view of JIT encompasses more than MPC-related activities, but there's a significant overlap between JIT and our approach to MPC systems. In summarizing this chapter, we emphasize the following principles:

- Stabilizing and in some cases leveling the production schedules are prerequisites to effective JIT systems.
- Achieving very short lead times supports better customer service and responsiveness.
- Reducing hidden factory costs can be at least as important as reducing costs more usually attributed to factory operations.
- Implementing the whole person concept reduces distinctions between white- and blue-collar workers and taps all persons' skills for improving performance.
- Cost accounting and performance measurements need to reflect the shift in emphasis away from direct labor as the primary source of value added.
- To achieve JIT's benefits in nonrepetitive applications, some basic features of repetitive-based JIT must be modified.
- JIT is not incompatible with MRP-based systems. Firms can evolve toward JIT from MRP-based systems, adopting JIT as much or as little as they want, with an incremental approach.

References

Brown, J. S.; S. Durchslag; and J. Hagel III. "Loosening Up: How Process Networks Unlock the Power of Specialization," *McKinsey Quarterly,* no. 2 (2002).

Dixon, Lance. *JITII, Revolution in Buying and Selling.* Boston: Cahners, 1994.

Fine, C. H.: *Clockspeed: Winning Industry Control in the Age of Temporary Advantage.* Reading, Mass.: Perseus Books, 1998.

Hall, R. W. *Driving the Productivity Machine.* Falls Church, Va.: American Production and Inventory Control Society, 1981.

——. *Zero Inventories.* Homewood, Ill.: Dow Jones–Irwin, 1983.

Hall, R. W.; H. T. Johnson; and P. B. B. Turney. *Measuring Up: Charting Pathways to Manufacturing Excellence.* Homewood, Ill.: Business One Irwin, 1990.

Hammer, M., and S. Stanton. "How Process Enterprises Really Work," *Harvard Business Review,* November–December 1999, pp.108–118.

Hyer, N., and U. Wemmerlov. *Reorganizing the Factory: Competing through Cellular Manufacturing.* Portland, Ore.: Productivity Press, 2002.

Juran, J. M., and A. B. Godfrey. *Juran's Quality Handbook,* fifth edition. New York: McGraw-Hill, 1999.

Karmarkar, Uday S. "Getting Control of Just-in-Time." *Harvard Business Review,* September–October 1989.

Kern, G. M., and J. C. Wei. "Master Production Rescheduling Policy in Capacity Constrained Just-In-Time Make-To-Stock Environments," *Decision Sciences* 27, no. 2 (spring 1996), pp. 365–387.

Knolmayer, G.; P. Mertens; and A. Zeier. *Supply Chain Management Based on SAP Systems.* Berlin: Springer-Verlag, 2002.

Lummus, R. R. "A Simulation Analysis of Sequencing Alternatives for JIT Lines Using Kanbans," *Journal of Operations Management* 13, no. 3 (1995).

Miller, J. G., and T. E. Vollmann. "The Hidden Factory," *Harvard Business Review,* September–October 1985, pp. 141–150.

Monden, Yasuhiro. *Toyota Production System,* Norcroos, Ga.: Industrial Engineering and Management Press, 1983.

Nakane, J. R., and R. W. Hall. "Management Specs for Stockless Production," *Harvard Business Review,* May–June 1983, pp. 84–91.

Ohno, Taiichi. *Toyota Production System: Beyond Large-Scale Production.* Cambridge, Mass.: Productivity Press, 1988.

Schmenner, R. "Looking Ahead by Looking Back: Swift Even Flow in the History of Manufacturing," *Production and Operations Management* 10, no. 1 (2001), pp. 87–96.

Schonberger, R. *World-Class Manufacturing: The Next Decade,* New York: The Free Press, 1996.

Shingo, Shigeo. *A Revolution in Manufacturing: The SMED System.* Cambridge, Mass.: Productivity Press, 1985.

Wantuck, Kenneth A. *Just-In-Time for America: A Common Sense Production Strategy,* Ken Wantuck Associates, June 1989.

Wemmerlov, U., and D. J. Johnson. "Empirical Findings on Manufacturing Cell Design," *International Journal of Production Research,* no. 3 (2000), pp. 481–507.

Womack, J. P., and D. T. Jones. *Lean Thinking: Banish Waste and Create Wealth in Your Corporation,* New York: Simon & Schuster, 1996.

Voss, C. A., and L. Okazaki-Ward. "The Transfer and Adaptation of JIT-Manufacturing Practices by Japanese Companies in the U.K.," *Operations Management Review* 7, nos. 3 and 4 (1990).

Discussion Questions

1. Some people have argued that just-in-time is simply one more inventory control system. How do you think they could arrive at this conclusion?

2. Take a common system at a university—for example, registration. Describe what kinds of "waste" can be found. How might you reduce this waste?

3. "Surge" capacity is the ability to take on an extra number of customers or product requests. Tell how the following three facilities handle surges: a football stadium, a clothing store, and an accounting firm.

4. List several ways to signal the need for more material in a pull-type system. Distinguish between situations where the feeder departments are in close proximity and those where they're at some distance.

5. Some companies contend that they can never adopt JIT because their suppliers are located all over the country and distances are too great. What might you suggest to these firms?

6. "We just can't get anywhere on our JIT program. It's the suppliers' fault. We tell them every week what we want, but they still can't get it right. I've been over to their shops, and they have mountains of the wrong materials." What do you think is going on here?

7. One manager at a JIT seminar complained that he couldn't see what he would do with his workers if they finished their work before quitting time. How would you respond to this comment?

8. How do you go about creating the organizational climate for successful JIT? Where do you start?

Problems

1. Calculate the number of kanbans needed at the ABC Company for the following two products, produced in a factory that works eight hours per day, five days per week:

	Product 1	Product 2
Usage	300/week	150/day
Lead time	1 week	2 weeks
Container size	20 units	30 units
Safety stock	15 percent	0

2. Calculate the number of kanbans required for the following four components at the ABC Company in problem 1.

	Component			
	W	**X**	**Y**	**Z**
Daily usage	900	250	1,200	350
Lead time	2 hours	5 hours	1 hour	3 hours
Container size	25 units	40 units	50 units	20 units
Safety stock	25 percent	20 percent	15 percent	10 percent

3. The BCD Company has successfully implemented JIT internally, and now wishes to convert one of its main suppliers to JIT as well. As a test of feasibility, the firms have selected one item made by this supplier for BCD. The supplier currently manufactures and delivers this item in batches of 6,000, the price paid is $150/unit, and the average usage rate at BCD is 250 units per day. Under JIT, the kanban container size would be 100 units, 10 percent safety stock, and lead time of 2 weeks (10 days).

   a. What is the current investment in work-in-process inventory for this item at BCD (assume average inventory is Q/2)?

   b. What is the change in investment if the proposed JIT system is implemented?

   c. A consulting study indicates that under JIT and an additional investment of $100,000, the lead time could be reduced from 2 weeks to 1 week. Evaluate the feasibility of this investment.

4. The CDE Company buys 200 different capacitors from 25 suppliers, with most of the capacitors purchased with an individual purchase order. An analysis indicates that the annual number of purchase orders placed for capacitors is roughly 2,000, and a cost analysis estimates the cost to place an order as $30. Additional annual cost estimates for these items include:

Obsolescence	$ 20,000
Maintaining multiple vendors	10,000
Extra shipping costs	5,000
Expediting/shortages	5,000

   One of the suppliers has offered to provide all capacitors, in a racking system, which will be replenished weekly, where each week CDE only pays for what it has used. There will be no orders at all. The supplier offers to provide this service for $25,000 per year, plus the standard cost per item. What are the potential cost savings to CDE in this proposal?

5. The DEF Company produces three products using a mixed-model assembly line, which is operated 16 hours per day (2 shifts of 8 hours each) for 250 days per year. The annual demand forecasts for the products are as follows:

Products	Forecasts
1	20,000
2	10,000
3	5,000

   a. Determine a mixed-model master production schedule for a daily batch, based on the minimum batch size for each product.

b. Prepare a daily schedule indicating the number of each product to be produced each day.

c. Product 1 requires 2 units of component A and one unit of component B. If component A is manufactured internally at DEF, how many kanbans would be required for this component if the lead time is 2 days, the safety factor is 15 percent, and the container size is 25 units?

6. The EFG Company works an 8-hour/day, 250-day/year schedule, producing four models with the following annual demand forecasts:

Model	Forecast
I	500
II	1,500
III	4,500
IV	6,000

a. Determine a mixed-model minimum batch master production schedule for EFG, based on a daily batch and an hourly batch.

b. Construct a detailed mixed-model schedule for an eight-hour day using minimum batch sizes.

7. The FGH Company assembles nine products, working 8 hours/day, 250 days/year. All products are assembled in batches of 120 units, on a line with capacity of 360 units per hour. The forecasted demands for the nine products are as follows:

Product	Forecast
1	180,000
2	150,000
3	120,000
4	120,000
5	90,000
6	30,000
7	15,000
8	7,500
9	7,500

Develop a level-minimum-batch (120 units) scheduling cycle for the assembly line at FGH.

8. The GHI Company produces models W, X, Y, and Z on an assembly line that operates 250 eight-hour days per year. The demand forecasts are:

	Model			
	A	B	C	D
Annual forecast	1,000	3,000	7,000	9,000

a. Determine the mixed-model master production schedule for a daily batch and hourly batch with minimum batch sizes.

b. Determine the schedule of production for an eight-hour day using mixed-model minimum batch production.

9. The GHI Company makes air conditioners, in either the standard model or additionally with a special option it calls the "turbo-charger," using the following indented bill of materials. The air conditioners are assembled at a rate 600 per five-day week, and the turbo-charger is added to every fourth unit. Develop the ten-week MRP record for the turbo-charger, using a one-week lead time, no safety stock, a lot size of 800, and a starting inventory of 200.

   Air Conditioner

       Part no. 101 (1 required)

       Part no. 102 (1 required)

       Part no. 103 (1 required)

       Turbo-charger assembly ($\frac{1}{4}$ required)

       Coupling (1 required)

       Bracket (1 required)

       Alternator (1 required)

10. Continuing with problem 9, suppose the turbo-charger assembly was phantomed (i.e., the coupling, bracket, and alternator were assembled directly onto the air conditioner.

    a. What would the new bill of materials look like?

    b. Construct the phantom MRP record and compare it to that in problem 9. What are the differences?

    c. Construct the MRP record for the coupling (lot size = 200, safety stock = 20, 250 on hand, lead time = 2 weeks).

11. The air conditioner line is now to be run with JIT. In order to stabilize the planning for components, the GHI Company committed to producing exactly 125 units per each day in the week. Productivity on the air conditioner line started at a somewhat low level, but has been steadily increasing. At the outset, the four-person line could assemble 125 units per day, but it required 10.5 hours per day to do so (2.5 hours of overtime). After six weeks (3,600 units cumulative) the team could assemble 125 units with little or no overtime. Thereafter, the team followed a classic learning curve (90 percent) pattern. At about 7,000 units cumulative, the daily time requirement to assemble 150 units fell to 7.2 hours.

    a. What would be a good estimate of the cumulative average time for the first 3,600 units?

    b. How long will it be before the team can assemble 125 units in 6 to 6.5 hours?

    c. If after 30,000 units the team can assemble 125 units in 5.5 hours, what is the weekly "surge capacity" of the line? In particular, if there was a special promotion, how many units could be built in a week where the team worked 10 hours per day?

12. ZMW Motorwerks buys its car seats from Slippery Seats, Inc. Slippery puts 10 different fabrics on the same seats delivered to one of ZMW's assembly plants. Slippery sells and delivers each seat to ZMW in batches of 500, which ZMW orders when its inventory on a particular seat reaches 100 units—the expected use by ZMW during the two-week lead time (guaranteed as a maximum by Slippery). Every day, the particular 100 seats expected to be used the next day are removed from the inventory at ZMW and transported to the line where the seats are installed (at a rate of 10/hour during a 10-hour day (100/day, 250 days/year). As the cars pass through the seat section, the workers pick the right seat to go with the particular car. In the event that a seat is damaged, another of the same fabric is used (there is a safety stock of 5 seats in each fabric, which is replenished each day as needed). Slippery tries to maintain a finished goods inventory of one batch of each seat-fabric combination. This allows it to almost always be able to ship a batch of seats quickly when ordered by ZMW. The lead time required to make a batch of 500 seats is 3 weeks, and slippery has promised to deliver in 2 weeks at a maximum. The lead time is based on one week to make the frames, one week to order/receive the fabric, which is cut and

sewn in week 2, with the final seats assembled in week 3 (when all the other materials have been ordered and delivered). A new batch is started whenever an order is received, which will replenish the batch removed from inventory to fill the order.

a. What is the expected inventory level (average) of seats at ZMW?

b. What is the expected inventory level (finished goods) at Slippery?

c. What is the expected inventory level (work-in-process) at Slippery?

d. What are the hidden factory costs in both companies?

13. Returning to problem 12, Slippery sees its own operation as a type of kanban system. It has a batch of finished products in inventory, and whenever that is removed, this becomes the trigger to make another batch.

a. What are the fundamental differences between this approach and one based on a mixed-model daily schedule?

b. What is the average batch size for each product that would be run in the latter case?

c. What are the changes that would be required at ZMW?

d. What changes would be required at Slippery?

14. Slippery presently wraps each seat in plastic to protect it from damage and soiling during assembly/delivery. Assume that the plastic material costs $1, the labor to install it costs $2, and at the dealer it costs $3 to remove the plastic and dispose of it. Slippery is now telling ZMW that other auto manufacturers are able to train their assemblers to be more careful, thereby eliminating the plastic wrapping.

a. What would be the annual benefits of this change to Slippery?

b. What would be the annual benefits of this change to ZMW?

c. What would be the annual benefits of this change to the dealers?

d. How might the end customers benefit?

e. How might one resolve any conflicts between Slippery, ZMW, and the dealers over implementing this change?

15. Suppose ZMW provides the daily build schedule to Slippery, and Slippery delivers four times per day (every 2.5 hours), in the exact build sequence, when the inventory at ZMW is down to only 1 hour of stock.

a. What is the reduction in inventory at ZMW?

b. What is the potential reduction in inventory at Slippery if it *builds* to the schedule?

c. What other advantages are gained in the two firms?

d. What kind of information system is needed to support this JIT execution?

e. What else has to be implemented in both firms to make it a reality?

Capacity Planning and Utilization

In this chapter we discuss the role of capacity planning and utilization in MPC systems. We focus primarily on techniques for determining the capacity requirements implied by a production plan, master production schedule, or detailed material plans. One managerial problem is to match the capacity with the plans: either to provide sufficient capacity to execute plans, or to adjust plans to match capacity constraints. A second managerial problem with regard to capacity is to consciously consider the marketplace implications of faster throughput times for making products, at the expense of reduced capacity utilization. For example, JIT production results in very fast throughput times for manufacturing products, but typically some capacities are underutilized. Similarly, by scheduling the highest-priority jobs through all work centers—taking explicit account of available capacity—it is possible to complete these jobs in much shorter times than under more conventional MPC approaches. But this gain in speed for high priority jobs comes at the expense of lower priority job throughput times and some underutilization of capacity.

This chapter is organized around five topics:

- *The role of capacity planning in MPC systems:* How does it fit and how is capacity managed in various manufacturing environments?
- *Capacity planning and control techniques:* How can capacity requirements be estimated and capacity utilization controlled?
- *Scheduling capacity and materials simultaneously:* How can finite scheduling techniques be applied, and what are the costs/benefits of these techniques?
- *Management and capacity planning/utilization:* What are the critical managerial decisions required to plan/utilize capacity most effectively?
- *Example applications:* How are techniques for capacity planning applied and what are some best practices?

Some of the techniques developed in this chapter are closely analogous to approaches for demand management and operations planning as described in Chapters 2 and 3. Finite loading techniques and the theory of constraints are described here as forms of capacity planning to produce detailed schedules; these are described in further detail under production activity control in Chapter 11. Perhaps the major linkage between capacity planning and other MPC modules is with the master production schedule, the subject of Chapter 6.

The Role of Capacity Planning in MPC Systems

MPC is often seen as encompassing two major activities: planning/control of materials and planning/control of capacities. The two need to be coordinated for maximum benefits, on the basis of managerial perceptions of what is required in the marketplace. Capacity planning techniques have as their primary objective the estimation of capacity requirements, sufficiently far enough into the future to be able to meet those requirements. A second objective is execution: the capacity plans need to be executed flawlessly, with unpleasant surprises avoided. Insufficient capacity quickly leads to deteriorating delivery performance, escalating work-in-process inventories, and frustrated manufacturing personnel. On the other hand, excess capacity might be a needless expense that can be reduced. Even firms with advanced MPC systems have found times when their inability to provide adequate work center capacities has been a significant problem. On the other hand, there are firms that continually manage to increase output from what seems to be a fixed set of capacities. The bottom line difference can be substantial.

Hierarchy of Capacity Planning Decisions

Figure 10.1 relates capacity planning decisions to other MPC system modules. It depicts a scope of capacity planning starting from an overall plan of resource needs, and then moves to planning procedures to estimate the capacity implications of a particular master production

FIGURE 10.1
Capacity Planning in the MPC System

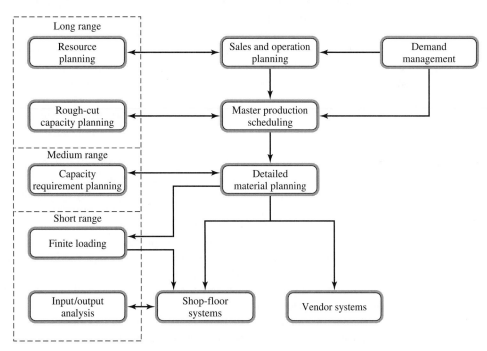

schedule. Thereafter the hierarchy depicts middle-range capacity planning, which evaluates the capacity implications of the detailed material plans, then to the short-range actual scheduling/capacity trade-offs, and finally to the evaluation of particular capacity plans.

These five levels of capacity planning range from large aggregate plans for long time periods to the detailed scheduling decisions as to which job to run next on a particular machine. In this chapter the focus is first on the several rough-cut capacity planning procedures. With this background, one can see how capacity requirements planning (CRP) systems are a logical extension, with a more detailed view of capacity needs. Understanding these systems allows one to appreciate the different approaches, with each providing a more exact estimate of capacity needs, but with a corresponding need for more information and system complexity. Thereafter, we can see how advanced production scheduling (APS) based on finite loading provide still another approach to the planning/management of capacity. Finally, Figure 10.1 shows input/output analysis as the last of the five levels of capacity planning. Here, the focus is on capacity management, in which capacity plans are continually compared with actual results.

Many authorities distinguish between long-, medium-, and short-range capacity planning horizons as indicated in Figure 10.1. This is a useful distinction, but the time dimension varies substantially from company to company. Moreover, in the last several years, the focus has shifted more to the short term, as firms operate with lower inventory levels and faster response times to customer needs. In this chapter, we will examine capacity planning/utilization decisions ranging from one day to a year or more in the future.

Links to Other MPC System Modules

System linkages for the capacity planning modules follow the basic hierarchy shown in Figure 10.1. **Resource planning** is directly linked to the sales and operations planning module. It's the most highly aggregated and longest-range capacity planning decision. Resource planning typically involves converting monthly, quarterly, or even annual data from the sales and operations plan into aggregate resources such as gross labor-hours, floor space, and machine-hours. This level of planning involves new capital expansion, bricks and mortar, machine tools, warehouse space, and so on, and requires a time horizon of months or years.

The master production schedule is the primary information source for **rough-cut capacity planning.** A particular master schedule's rough-cut capacity requirements can be estimated by several techniques: *capacity planning using overall planning factors (CPOF), capacity bills,* or *resource profiles.* These techniques provide information for modifying the resource levels or material plan to ensure execution of the master production schedule.

For firms using material requirements planning to prepare detailed material plans, a much more detailed capacity plan is possible with the **capacity requirements planning (CRP)** technique. To provide this detail, time-phased material plans produced by the MRP system form the basis for calculating time-phased capacity requirements. Data files used by the CRP technique include work in process, routing, scheduled receipts, and planned orders. Information provided by the CRP technique can be used to determine capacity needs for both key machine centers and labor skills, typically covering a planning horizon of several weeks to a year.

Resource planning, rough-cut capacity planning, and capacity requirements planning link with the sales and operations plan, master production schedule, and MRP systems, respectively. Linkages are shown as double-headed arrows for a specific reason. There must be a correspondence between capacity required to execute a given material plan and capacity made available to execute the plan. Without this correspondence, the plan will be either impossible to execute or inefficiently executed. We don't claim capacity must always be changed to meet material plans. In fact, whether this is worthwhile or whether plans should be changed to meet capacity is a managerial judgment. Capacity planning systems provide basic information to make that a *reasoned* judgment.

Finite loading in some ways is better seen as a shop scheduling process, and therefore part of production activity control (PAC), but it is also a capacity planning procedure. There are an increasing number of software systems provided by vendors, usually called **advanced production scheduling (APS)** techniques to do finite loading. The fundamental difference between the other capacity planning approaches and finite loading is that the former set does not consider any adjustment to plans because of planned capacity utilization. The latter starts with a specified capacity and schedules work through work centers only to the extent that capacity is available to do so. Moreover, by scheduling within exact capacity constraints, the APS systems allow work to flow through the necessary set of work centers more quickly. The jobs are scheduled with exact timing on all work centers—not merely in some general way, such as during a particular week.

Input/output analysis provides a method for monitoring the actual consumption of capacity during the execution of detailed material planning. It is necessarily linked to the shop floor execution systems, and supported by the database for production activity control (PAC). Input/output analysis can indicate the need to update capacity plans as actual shop performance deviates from plans, as well as the need to modify the planning factors used in the capacity planning systems.

This overview of capacity planning's scope sets the stage for the techniques the chapter discusses. The primary interaction among these techniques is hierarchical: long-range planning sets constraints on medium-range capacity planning, which in turn constrains detailed scheduling and execution on the shop floor.

Capacity Planning and Control Techniques

Here we describe four procedures for capacity planning. The first technique is *capacity planning using overall factors (CPOF).* The simplest of the four techniques, CPOF is based only on accounting data. The second, *capacity bills,* requires more detailed product information. The third, *resource profiles,* adds a further dimension—specific timing of capacity requirements. The first three procedures are rough-cut approaches and are applicable to firms with or without MRP systems. The fourth, *capacity requirements planning,* is used in conjunction with time-phased MRP records and shop-floor system records to calculate capacity required to produce both open shop orders (scheduled receipts) and planned orders. To describe the four planning techniques, we use a simple example. The example allows us to clearly see differences in approach, complexity, level of aggregation, data requirements, timing, and accuracy among the techniques.

Capacity Planning Using Overall Factors (CPOF)

Capacity planning using overall factors (CPOF), a relatively simple approach to rough-cut capacity planning, is typically done on a manual basis. Data inputs come from the master

FIGURE 10.2
Example
Problem Data

Master production schedule (in units):

							Period							
End Product	1	2	3	4	5	6	7	8	9	10	11	12	13	Total
A	33	33	33	40	40	40	30	30	30	37	37	37	37	457
B	17	17	17	13	13	13	25	25	25	27	27	27	27	273

Direct labor time per end product unit:

End Product	Total Direct Labor in Standard Hours/Unit
A	0.95 hours
B	1.85

FIGURE 10.3 **Estimated Capacity Requirements Using Overall Factors (in standard direct labor-hours)**

Work Center	Historical Percentage	Period													Total Hours
		1	2	3	4	5	6	7	8	9	10	11	12	13	
100	60.3	37.87	37.87	37.87	37.41	37.41	37.41	45.07	45.07	45.07	51.32	51.32	51.32	51.32	566.33
200	30.4	19.09	19.09	19.09	18.86	18.86	18.86	22.72	22.72	22.72	25.87	25.87	25.87	25.87	285.49
300	9.3	5.84	5.84	5.84	5.78	5.78	5.78	6.96	6.96	6.96	7.91	7.91	7.91	7.91	87.38
Total required capacity		62.80*	62.80	62.80	62.05	62.05	62.05	74.75	74.75	74.75	85.10	85.10	85.10	85.10	939.20

*62.80 = (0.95 × 33) + (1.85 × 17) for the standards in Figure 10.2.

production schedule (MPS), rather than from detailed material plans. This procedure is usually based on planning factors derived from standards or historical data for end products. When these planning factors are applied to the MPS data, overall labor or machine-hour capacity requirements can be estimated. This overall estimate is thereafter allocated to individual work centers on the basis of historical data on shop workloads. CPOF plans are usually stated in terms of weekly or monthly time periods and are revised as the firm changes the MPS.

The top portion of Figure 10.2 shows the MPS that will serve as the basis for our example that was developed by Berry, Schmitt, and Vollmann. This schedule specifies the quantities of two end products to be assembled during each time period. The first step of the CPOF procedure involves calculating capacity requirements of this schedule for the overall plant. The lower portion of Figure 10.2 shows direct labor standards, indicating the total direct labor-hours required for each end product. Assuming labor productivity of 100 percent of standard, the total direct labor-hour requirement for the first period is 62.80 hours, as shown in Figure 10.3.

The procedure's second step involves using historical ratios to allocate the total capacity required each period to individual work centers. Historical percentages of the total direct labor-hours worked in each of the three work centers the prior year were used to determine allocation ratios. These data could be derived from the company's accounting records. In the example, 60.3 percent, 30.4 percent, and 9.3 percent of the total direct labor-hours were worked in work centers 100, 200, and 300, respectively. These percentages are used to estimate anticipated direct labor requirements for each work center. The resulting work center capacity requirements are shown in Figure 10.3 for each period in the MPS.

The CPOF procedure, or variants of it, is found in a number of manufacturing firms. Data requirements are minimal (primarily accounting system data) and calculations are straightforward. As a result, CPOF approximations of capacity requirements at individual work centers are valid only to the extent that product mixes or historical divisions of work between work centers remain constant. This procedure's main advantages are ease of calculation and minimal data requirements. In many firms, data are readily available and computations can be done manually.

The CPOF procedure will work reasonably well for many manufacturing environments. For example, in a just-in-time (JIT) manufacturing company, the CPOF approach would allow the firm to make fairly good estimates of capacity needs under different planning scenarios. The inherent inaccuracies of CPOF will present fewer problems in a JIT environment where execution is fast, with virtually no work-in-process inventories to confound the analysis. This might be particularly useful for estimating the capacity needs for firms that supply a JIT manufacturing company.

Capacity Bills

The **capacity bill procedure** is a rough-cut method providing more-direct linkage between individual end products in the MPS and the capacity required for individual work centers. It takes into account any shifts in product mix. Consequently, it requires more data than the CPOF procedure. A bill of materials and routing data are required, and direct labor-hour or machine-hour data must be available for each operation.

To develop a bill of capacity for the example problem, we use the product structure data for A and B shown in Figure 10.4. We also need the routing and operation time standard data in the top portion of Figure 10.5 for assembling products A and B, as well as for manufacturing component items C, D, E, and F. The bill of capacity indicates total standard time required to produce one end product in each work center required in its manufacture. Calculations involve multiplying total-time-per-unit values by the usages indicated in the bill of materials. Summarizing the usage-adjusted unit time data by work center produces the bill of capacity for each of the two products in the lower portion of Figure 10.5. The bill of capacity can be constructed from engineering data, as we've done here; similar data might be available in a standard cost system. Some firms' alternative approach is to prepare the bill of capacity only for those work centers regarded as critical.

Once the bill of capacity for each end product is prepared, we can use the master production schedule to estimate capacity requirements at individual work centers. Figure 10.6 shows the determination of capacity requirements for our example. The resultant work center estimates differ substantially from the CPOF estimates in Figure 10.3. The differences reflect the period-to-period changes in product mix between the projected MPS and historical average figures. Estimates obtained from CPOF are based on an overall historical ratio of work between machine centers, whereas capacity bill estimates reflect the actual product mix planned for each period.

It's important to note that the total hours shown for the MPS (939.20) are the same in Figure 10.3 and Figure 10.6; the differences are in work center estimates for each time

FIGURE 10.4
Product Structure Data

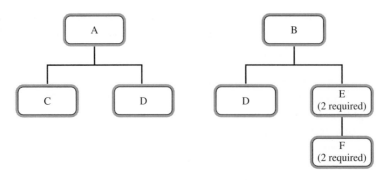

FIGURE 10.5   Routing and Standard Time Data

	Lot Sizes	Operation	Work Center	Standard Setup Hours	Standard Setup Hours per Unit	Standard Run Time Hours per Unit	Total Hours per Unit
End Products							
A	40	1 of 1	100	1.0	0.025*	0.025	0.05†
B	20	1 of 1	100	1.0	0.050	1.250	1.30
Components							
C	40	1 of 2	200	1.0	0.025	0.575	0.60
		2 of 2	300	1.0	0.025	0.175	0.20
D	60	1 of 1	200	2.0	0.033	0.067	0.10
E	100	1 of 1	200	2.0	0.020	0.080	0.10
F	100	1 of 1	200	2.0	0.020	0.0425	0.0625

	Bill of Capacity: End Product	
	A	**B**
Work Center	**Total Time/Unit**	**Total Time/Unit**
100	0.05	1.30
200	0.70‡	0.55§
300	0.20	0.00
Total time/unit	0.95	1.85

*0.025 = Setup time ÷ Lot size = 1.0/40.
†0.05 = Standard setup time per unit + Standard run time per unit = 0.025 + 0.025.
‡0.70 = 0.60 + 0.10 for one C and one D from Figure 10.4.
§0.55 = 0.10 + 2(0.10) + 4(0.0625) for one D, two E's, and four F's.

FIGURE 10.6   Capacity Requirements Using Capacity Bills

Work Center	Period													Total Hours	Projected Work Center Percentage
	1	2	3	4	5	6	7	8	9	10	11	12	13		
100	23.75*	23.75	23.75	18.90	18.90	18.90	34.00	34.00	34.00	36.95	36.95	36.95	36.95	377.75	40%
200	32.45	32.45	32.45	35.15	35.15	35.15	34.75	34.75	34.75	40.75	40.75	40.75	40.75	470.05	50%
300	6.60	6.60	6.60	8.00	8.00	8.00	6.00	6.00	6.00	7.40	7.40	7.40	7.40	91.40	10%
Total	62.80	62.80	62.80	62.05	62.05	62.05	74.75	74.75	74.75	85.10	85.10	85.10	85.10	939.20	100%

*23.75 = (33 × 0.05) + (17 × 1.30) from Figures 10.2 and 10.5.

period. These differences are far more important in firms that experience significant period-to-period mix variations than in those that have a relatively constant pattern of work.

Resource Profiles

Neither the CPOF nor the capacity bill procedure takes into account the specific timing of the projected workloads at individual work centers. In developing **resource profiles,** production lead time data are taken into account to provide time-phased projections of the capacity requirements for individual production facilities. Thus, resource profiles provide a somewhat more sophisticated approach to rough-cut capacity planning.

In any capacity planning technique, time periods for the capacity plan can be varied (e.g., weeks, months, quarters). However, when time periods are long relative to lead times, much of the time-phased information's value may be lost in aggregating the data. In many firms, this means time periods longer than one week will mask important changes in capacity requirements.

To apply the resource profile procedure to our example, we use the bills of material, routing, and time standard information in Figures 10.4 and 10.5. We must also add the production lead time for each end product and component part to our database. In this simplified example, we use a one-period lead time for assembling each end product and one period for each operation required to produce component parts. Since only one operation is required for producing components D, E, and F, lead time for producing these components is one time period each. For component C, however, lead time is two time periods: one for the operation in work center 200 and another for work center 300.

To use the resource profile procedure, we prepare a time-phased profile of the capacity requirements for each end item. Figure 10.7's operations setback charts show this time phasing for end products A and B. The chart for end product A indicates that the final assembly operation is to be completed during period 5. Production of components C and D must be completed in period 4 prior to the start of the final assembly. Since component C requires two time periods (one for each operation), it must be started one time period before component D (i.e., at the start of period 3). Other conventions are used to define time phasing, but in this example we assume the master production schedule specifies the number of units of each end product that must be completed by *the end* of the time period indicated. This implies *all* components must be completed by the end of the preceding period.

For convenience, we've shown the standard hours required for each operation for each product in Figure 10.7. This information is summarized by work center and time period in Figure 10.8, which also shows the capacity requirements the MPS quantities generated in time period 5 from Figure 10.2 (40 of end product A and 13 of end product B). The capacity requirements in Figure 10.8 are only for MPS quantities in period 5. MPS quantities for other periods can increase the capacity needed in each period. For example, Figure 10.8 shows that 7.9 hours of capacity are needed in period 4 at work center 200 to support the MPS for period 5. The MPS for period 6 requires another 27.25 hours from work center 200. This results in the total of 35.15 hours shown in Figure 10.9, which provides the overall capacity plan for the current MPS using the resource profile procedure.

Comparing the capacity plans produced by the capacity bills and the resource profile procedures (Figures 10.6 and 10.9), we see the impact of the time-phased capacity information. Total workload created by the master production schedule (939.2 hours) remains the same, as do the work center percentage allocations. But the period requirements for

**FIGURE 10.7
Operation
Setback Charts
for End
Products A
and B**

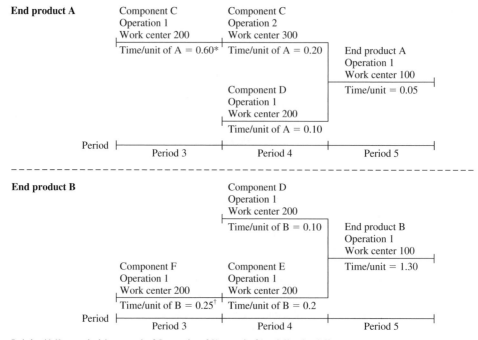

Period: *0.60 = standard time per unit of C × number of C's per unit of A = 0.60 × 1 = 0.60.
†0.25 = standard time per unit of component F × number of F's per unit of B = 0.0625 × 4 = 0.25.

work centers 200 and 300 projected by the two techniques vary somewhat. A capacity requirement of 8 hours was projected for work center 300 in time period 6 using capacity bills versus 6 hours using resource profiles, a difference of more than 30 percent. This change reflects the difference in the timing of resources required to produce the component parts, which is taken into account by the resource bill procedure.

Capacity Requirements Planning (CRP)

Capacity requirements planning (CRP) differs from the rough-cut planning procedures in four respects. First, CRP utilizes the time-phased material plan information produced by an MRP system. This includes consideration of all actual lot sizes, as well as lead times for both open shop orders (scheduled receipts) and orders planned for future release (planned orders). Second, the MRP system's gross-to-net feature takes into account production capacity already stored in the form of inventories of both components and assembled products. Third, the shop-floor control system accounts for the current status of all work-in-process in the shop, so only the capacity needed to *complete the remaining work* on open shop orders is considered in calculating required work center capacities. Fourth, CRP takes into account demand for service parts, other demands that may not be accounted for in the MPS, and any additional capacity that might be required by MRP planners reacting to scrap, item record errors, and so on. To accomplish this, the CRP procedure requires the same input information as the resource profile procedure (bills of material, routing, time standards, lead times) plus information on MRP-planned orders and the current status of open shop orders (MRP-scheduled receipts) at individual work centers.

FIGURE 10.8
Resource
Profiles by
Work Center

Time required during preceding periods for one end product assembled in period 5:

	Time Period		
	3	4	5
End product A			
Work center 100	0	0	0.05
Work center 200	0.60	0.10	0
Work center 300	0	0.20	0
End product B			
Work center 100	0	0	1.30
Work center 200	0.25	0.30	0

Time-phased capacity requirements generated from MPS for 40 As and 13 Bs in time period 5:

	Time Period		
	3	4	5
40 As			
Work center 100	0	0	2
Work center 200	24	4	0
Work center 300	0	8	0
13 Bs			
Work center 100	0	0	16.9
Work center 200	3.25	3.9	0
Work center 300	0	0	0
Total from period 5 MPS			
Work center 100	0	0	18.9
Work center 200	27.25	7.9	0
Work center 300	0	8.0	0

FIGURE 10.9 **Capacity Requirements Using Resource Profiles**

Work Center	Past Due*	Period													Work Total Hours	Center Percentage
		1	2	3	4	5	6	7	8	9	10	11	12	13		
100	0.00	23.75*	23.75	23.75	18.90	18.90	18.90	34.00	34.00	34.00	36.95	36.95	36.95	36.95	377.75	40%
200	56.50	32.45	35.65	35.15	35.15	32.15	34.75	34.75	39.45	40.75	40.75	40.75	11.80		470.05	50%
300	6.60	6.60	6.60	8.00	8.00	8.00	6.00	6.00	6.00	7.40	7.40	7.40	7.40		91.40	10%
Total	63.10	62.80	66.00	66.90	62.05	59.05	59.65	74.75	79.45	82.15	85.10	85.10	56.15	36.95	939.20	100%

*This work should be completed already for products to meet the master production schedule in periods 1 and 2. (If not, it's past due and will add to the capacity required in the upcoming periods)

As a medium-range capacity planning procedure, CRP exploits MRP information so as to calculate only the capacity required to complete the MPS. By calculating capacity requirements for actual open shop orders and planned orders in the MRP database, CRP accounts for the capacity already stored in the form of finished and work-in-process inventories. Since MRP data include timing of both these open and planned orders, the potential for improved accuracy in timing capacity requirements is realized. This accuracy is most important in the most immediate time periods. Rough-cut techniques can overstate required capacity by the amount of capacity represented in inventories. In Figure 10.9, for example, the past due or already completed portion of the capacity requirements is 63.1 hours— about a full time period's capacity. This work should already have been completed if we expect to meet the MPS in periods 1 and 2. CRP's potential benefits aren't without cost. A larger database is required, as well as a much larger computational effort.

The process of preparing a CRP projection is similar to that used for resource profiles. The major difference is that detailed MRP data establish exact order quantities and timing for calculating capacity required. The resultant capacity needs are summarized by time period and work center in a format similar to Figure 10.9. The CRP results would differ from those of the other techniques, primarily in the early periods, but would be a more accurate projection of work center capacity needs. Since calculations are based on all component parts and end products from the present time period through all periods included in the MRP records (the planning horizon), we can see the enormity of the CRP calculation requirements. Some firms have mitigated this cost by collecting data as the MRP explosion process is performed.

Figure 10.10 presents one of the MRP records that drive the CRP procedure for our example. To simplify the presentation, we show the MPS only for end product A and the MRP record for one of its components, component C. We've used these data to calculate capacity requirements for work center 300. These capacity requirements incorporate the influence of lot sizes, inventories, and scheduled receipts for component C. Since item C is processed at work center 300 during the second period of the two-period lead time, the planned order for 40 units due to be released in period 1 requires capacity in period 2 at work center 300.

FIGURE 10.10
CRP Example:
Detailed
Calculations

Product A *MPS*

	Period												
	1	2	3	4	5	6	7	8	9	10	11	12	13
Product A *MPS*	33	33	33	40	40	40	30	30	30	37	37	37	37

Component C
Lot size = 40
Lead time = 2

	Period												
	1	2	3	4	5	6	7	8	9	10	11	12	13
Gross requirements	33	33	33	40	40	40	30	30	30	37	37	37	37
Scheduled receipts		40											
Projected available balance 37	4	11	18	18	18	18	28	38	8	11	14	17	20
Planned order releases	40	40	40	40	40	40		40	40	40	40		

Work center 300 Capacity Requirements Using CRP

	Period												
	1	2	3	4	5	6	7	8	9	10	11	12	13
Hours of capacity* Total = 88	8	8	8	8	8	8	8	0	8	8	8	8	

*The eight hours of capacity required is derived from the scheduled receipt and planned order quantities of 40 units multiplied by the time to fabricate a unit of component C in machine center 300, 0.20 hours (see Figure 10.7).

Required capacity is calculated using the setup and run time data from Figure 10.5 for component C.

For a lot size of 40 units, total setup and run time in work center 300 is eight hours $[1.0 + (40 \times .175)]$. Each planned order for component C in Figure 10.10 requires eight hours of capacity at work center 300, one period later. Similarly, the scheduled receipt of 40 units due in period 2 requires eight hours of capacity in week 1. Note the eight hours of capacity required for the scheduled receipt may not, in fact, be required if this job has already been processed at work center 300 before the beginning of period 1. The shop order's actual status is required to make the analysis.

In comparing CRP to the other capacity planning procedures, we shouldn't expect total capacity requirements for the 13 periods or the period-by-period requirements to be the same. Comparing capacity requirements for work center 300 developed by the resource profile procedure (Figure 10.9) and CRP (Figure 10.10) indicates estimated total capacity requirements for the 13 periods are less using CRP than resource profiles (88 versus 91.4 hours) and vary considerably on a period-by-period basis. Differences are explained by the initial inventory and use of lot sizing. Any partially completed work-in-process would reduce the capacity requirements further.

Scheduling Capacity and Materials Simultaneously

Thus far in the chapter we have taken what has been the traditional view of capacity in MPC systems: one first plans the materials, and thereafter examines the capacity implications of those plans. The underlying assumption in all of this is that if one knows of capacity requirements in sufficient time, adjustments to capacity can be effected. The capacity planning techniques we have examined thus far all make this assumption: their major difference is only in sophistication of the plans produced.

Moreover, the material plans produced by classic MRP systems are based on batches of materials traveling between work centers for subsequent operations, then flowing through inventories in order to be subsequently processed/integrated into higher-level part numbers. The overall lead times associated with producing end products on this basis tend to be quite long as a multiple of actual manufacturing times, particularly when the products have many levels in the bill of materials. For many firms today this just will not do: they must respond to actual customer demands faster, without holding large inventories. This implies "smarter" scheduling, which must simultaneously reflect actual capacity conditions. Furthermore, those "capacity conditions" are tighter and tighter: in order to be profitable one must utilize capacities more effectively, and satisfy end customer demands faster with lower inventories. The bottom line is a need to simultaneously schedule both capacity and materials.

Finite Capacity Scheduling

Finite scheduling systems can first be seen as an extension of the approach used by capacity requirements planning (CRP) systems, with one major difference: CRP calculates only capacity needs—it makes no adjustments for infeasibility. If, for example, we take the capacity requirements data for work center 300 coming from Product A, as shown in Figure 10.10, these would be depicted in either a CRP or finite workload capacity profile as the top part of Figure 10.11. If similar capacity requirements were collected from *all* the MRP

FIGURE 10.11

Infinite versus Finite Loading (CRP Profile for Work Center 300)

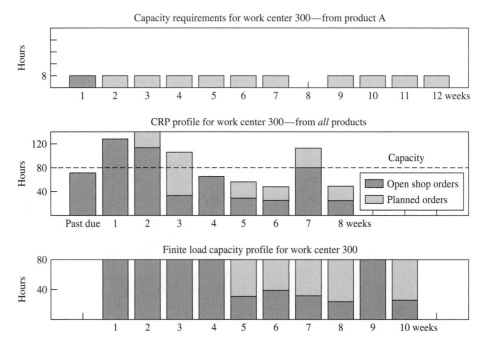

records, for all the jobs passing through work center 300, the CRP record might look like the middle portion of Figure 10.11 (here we have expanded the example to realistically include more products).

The bottom portion of Figure 10.11 shows the difference in the approach using finite scheduling. Here the capacity is scheduled only up to the 80-hour capacity limit. Thus the 75 hours of work shown as past due in the middle of Figure 10.11 would be scheduled in week 1 in the finite scheduling approach. Finite scheduling does not solve the undercapacity problem shown here. If capacity is not increased, only 80 hours of work can be completed in any week, regardless of the scheduling procedure. Finite scheduling will determine *which* jobs will be completed, according to how the jobs are scheduled—and there are various methods used to prioritize these decisions.

Finite scheduling systems simulate actual job order starting and stopping to produce a detailed schedule for each shop order and each machine center; that is, finite scheduling *loads* all jobs in all necessary work centers for the length of the planning horizon. For this reason, the terms *finite scheduling* and *finite loading* tend to be used interchangeably. The result of finite loading is a set of start and finish dates for each operation at each work center. Finite scheduling explicitly establishes a detailed schedule for each job through each work center based on work center capacities and the other scheduled jobs. Figure 10.1 depicts finite loading as a short-term capacity planning technique. Since it produces a detailed schedule of each work center, it tends to be most correct in the short term. That is, predictions of exact job schedules will be less valid in the longer term.

One output of finite scheduling is a simulation of how each machine center is to operate on a minute-by-minute basis for whatever time horizon is planned. For example, suppose we begin with work center 300 on Monday morning of week 1. A job is already in process and 150 pieces remain with a standard time of one minute per piece. This order consumes the first 150 minutes of capacity; if work starts at 8 A.M., the machine is loaded until 10:30 A.M. The finite scheduling system would pick the next job to schedule on this machine, and load it, taking account of setup time and run times. The process is repeated to simulate the entire day, then the next day, and so on.

Selection of the next job to schedule is not based just on those jobs physically waiting at the work center. Most finite scheduling systems look at jobs coming to the work center, when they will be completed at the prior work centers, and these jobs' priorities to decide whether to leave the work center idle and immediately available for the arrival of a particular job. Also, some systems allow for overlap operations, where a job can start at a downstream work center before all of it is complete at the upstream work center.

The approach we have just described, where a work center is scheduled, job by job, is called **vertical loading.** Its orientation is on planning/utilizing the capacity of a work center—independently. This is consistent with how most job shop scheduling research is conducted where the focus is on establishing relative job order priorities for deciding which job to schedule next in a work center. A different approach used in finite scheduling is **horizontal loading.** In this case the orientation is on entire shop orders. Here, the highest-priority shop order or job is scheduled in *all* of its work centers, then the job with the next highest priority, and so on. The horizontal loading approach is often in conflict with using the work centers to their highest capacity, since it will have more "holes" in the schedule than the vertical loading approach.

There is a temptation to see vertical loading as better than horizontal because of the capacity utilization. This is not the case. Horizontal loading will complete whole jobs faster than vertical loading. And it is whole jobs that are sold to the customers, not partial jobs, and it is harder to sell jobs that take long times to complete. It is far better to have 50 percent of the jobs completed than 90 percent that are not quite completed!

In addition to the horizontal-vertical distinction, there is also the issue of **front scheduling** versus **back scheduling.** The back scheduling approach starts with scheduling jobs backward from their due dates, whereas front scheduling starts with the current date scheduling into the future, where each job is completed as early as possible. If a back scheduling approach produces a past due start date for a shop order, this indicates infeasibility; similarly, if a front schedule does not produce jobs by the dates needed, it is also infeasible

Since any plan produced by any finite scheduling model is indeed a simulation, it is to be expected that errors will result. That is, the times used for the schedule are only estimates, and randomness will occur. This means that many times a job is expected to be at a work center and it is not complete at the prior center, raising the question as to whether to wait or choose another job. Furthermore, the further out the simulation model is extended, the greater the uncertainty in the expected results. If the finite schedule is prepared on Sunday night, schedules for Monday might be fairly good, while those for Tuesday will have to deal with the actual results achieved on Monday. The validity of the schedule will decay as the time horizon for scheduling is extended. One way to improve the scheduling is to reschedule more often. Even though today's computers are fast, redoing an entire finite schedule every time a job is completed is still too expensive for most firms.

Finite Scheduling with Product Structures: Using APS Systems

The complexity of scheduling increases if one wishes to schedule not only *component parts* but also *products* with part structures. Thus if we return to Figure 10.4, the real problem is in scheduling products A and B, not just in scheduling the components C, D, E, and F. Again if all the components are 90 percent completed, we cannot ship anything! The approach used by classic MRP systems is to take a long time to complete these jobs or else to have plenty of capacity available. With present imperatives on deliveries, inventories, and capacity investments, many firms are turning to finite loading systems that schedule the entire product as an entity. These systems are called **advanced production scheduling (APS)** systems, and several leading edge software companies provide them.

Essentially, APS systems use horizontal loading, and either front or back scheduling depending on whether the product is desired as soon as possible (front scheduling). But now the entire product structure is scheduled. Thus, for product A (see Figure 10.4), it is necessary to schedule A, C, and D. Let us illustrate the methodology, with back scheduling, for the 30-unit master schedule quantity shown for week 8 in Figure 10.2, the lot sizes for C and D (40 and 60) shown in Figure 10.5, and the assumptions that the MRP records are run without safety stock and that there would be no projected available balances to offset the calculations by the time week 8 is planned.

Figure 10.12 shows how the master production schedule and component MRP records would be depicted for this example. Note that the records show *only* the requirements for this particular MPS quantity (e.g., not including any requirements for component D to support end product B). Figure 10.13 shows the capacity requirements for the MPS (work center 100) as well as for work centers 300 and 200 that would be produced by the resultant APS back schedule. This figure is based on the two-shift capacity (80 hours per week) assumption

FIGURE 10.12
Data for APS Approach to End Product A

Master production schedule

MRP records for components C and D

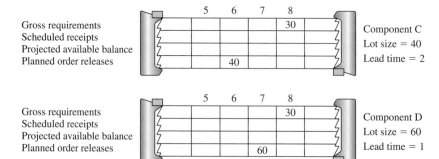

FIGURE 10.13
Back Schedules for the MPS and Work Centers 300 and 400

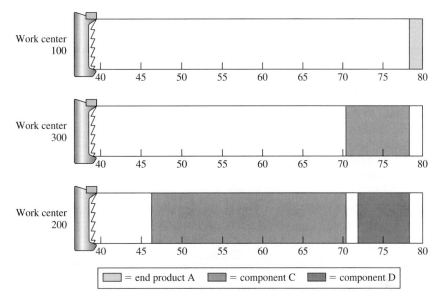

used in the other calculations for this example. For work center 100, the capacity requirement is 1.5 hours, based on the data in Figure 10.7 (0.05 hours per unit × 30). Component C requires 24 hours of capacity in work center 200 (0.6 hours per unit × 40), followed by 8 hours of capacity in work center 300 (0.2 hours per unit × 40). Also shown in Figure 10.13 is a capacity requirement of 6 hours for work center 200 (0.1 hours per unit × 60) in order to fabricate the batch of component D needed to support the MPS for end product A.

Figure 10.13 allows us to discuss some of the key issues raised by using APS systems. First, let us be clear on the major benefit: The entire schedule for the MPS quantity has been fulfilled in less than $\frac{1}{2}$ week (total elapsed time = 33.5 hours/80 = .41 weeks). This can be contrasted with an expected time of 3 weeks for standard MRP based approaches (86 percent lead time reduction). This implies a corresponding reduction in work-in-process inventories as well as a faster response to market conditions.

Executing the schedule planned in Figure 10.13 may make some people nervous. But it has been shown that this problem will absolutely not be made better by overstating the times used for the APS scheduling. Doing so puts in a *consistent* bias that degrades the planning process. The better approach is to focus on improving time estimates as much as possible (unbiased) and thereafter focus on flawless execution and recovery from any problems (work to the plan). More frequent rescheduling by the APS system allows errors to be reflected and compensated for in updated plans.

Figure 10.13 is simplified to show only the capacity requirements for one MPS quantity and its supporting components. In reality, the APS will schedule all MPS quantities, producing an overall capacity profile and detailed schedules for each work center. The *next* MPS quantity that is scheduled has to deal with the realities established by the prior schedules. That is, for example, if end product B is scheduled next in week 8, it will be backscheduled to complete at hour 78.5 in work center 100, and its needs for capacity in work center 200 can end only at hour 46.5. One might therefore ask if the scheduling of end product B should precede that of end product A. This is a complex issue. Sequential processing of MPS quantities in APS means that one needs to determine the priorities for scheduling these end products. We will come back to this issue.

Figure 10.13 shows a "hole" in the schedule for work center 200 between hours 70.5 and 72.5. An APS system would allow this capacity to be used for another job or work order, but only if the work order had a capacity requirement equal or less than 2 hours. That is, the criterion here is to respect the schedules for the *end products,* not to optimize work center utilizations. The hole also illustrates another choice: The capacity requirement for Component D has been back-scheduled from the time when it is needed to produce end product A. This will result in the lowest inventory levels. But it could start at time 70.5 (front-schedule it), but then it would be completed 2 hours before needed. Doing so provides more surety that the MPS can proceed as planned, since now only the schedule for component C might upset it, rather than the schedules for either component part.

Front-scheduling component D will increase the work-in-process inventory, since it is started in production earlier. But there is another issue here, similar to when you arrive with enough time to take an earlier plane though not having a ticket for that flight. For the airline, if there is a seat available on the earlier flight, it is in their interest to put you on the earlier flight—regardless of what the payment/ticket conditions are—since the seat is empty, and the one you will occupy on the subsequent flight might be sold to someone else. The same issue comes up in Figure 10.13. The front schedule allows the "hole" to be shifted later, when it has a much better chance to be used, since there is not presently any work scheduled beyond hour 80 in work center 200. Front scheduling of component D allows work on another shop order to begin at hour 78.5 instead of hour 80.

What all of this illustrates is that there are "many ways to skin the cat." APS systems typically provide the ability to look at the schedules visibly—to allow manual intervention—and thereafter to see the resultant effects throughout the company (work centers, shop orders, MPS, customer orders). The outputs from APS are often displayed as schedule boards (bar charts showing each shop order being processed over time in each work center). APS systems are also usually linked to spread sheet models to allow users to examine the implications of various choices/schedule changes.

Management and Capacity Planning/Utilization

Capacity planning is one side of the coin; capacity management is the other. Plans need to be executed, and this needs to be done effectively; moreover, well-developed demand management can provide conditions that are much more favorable to routine execution. For example, Toyota and several other Japanese auto manufacturers develop production plans with a stable rate of output (cars per day). Product mix variations are substantially less than those for other auto companies because they carefully manage the number and timing of option combinations. The result is execution systems that are simple, effective, and easy to operate with minimal inventories and fast throughput times. Capacity planning is straightforward and execution is more easily achieved, not only for the company itself but for its suppliers as well. That is, well-managed front-end planning can rationalize the entire supply chain.

Capacity Monitoring with Input/Output Control

One key capacity management issue concerns the match between planning and execution. This implies monitoring on a timely basis to see whether a workable capacity plan has been created and whether some form of corrective action is needed. The best-known approach to this issue is **input/output control,** where the work flowing through a work center is monitored: the planned work input and planned output are compared to the work actual input and output.

Input/Output Control

The capacity planning technique used delineates the planned input. Planned output results from managerial decision making to specify the capacity level; that is, planned output is based on staffing levels, hours of work, and so forth. In capacity-constrained work centers, planned output is based on the rate of capacity established by management. In non-capacity-constrained work centers, planned output is equal to planned input (allowing for some lead-time offset).

Capacity data in input/output control are usually expressed in hours. Input data are based on jobs' expected arrivals at a work center. For example, a CRP procedure would examine the status of all open shop orders (scheduled receipts), estimate how long they'll take (setup, run, wait, and move) at particular work centers, and thereby derive when they'll arrive at subsequent work centers. A finite loading system would do the same, albeit with better results. The approach would be repeated for all planned orders from the MRP database. The resultant set of expected arrivals of exact quantities would be multiplied by run time per unit from the routing file. This product would be added to setup time, also from the routing file. The sum is a planned input expressed in standard hours.

Actual input would use the same routing data, but for the *actual* arrivals of jobs in each time period as reported by the shop-floor control system. Actual output would again use the shop-floor control data for exact quantities completed in each time period, converted to standard hours with routing time data.

The only time data not based on the routing file are those for planned output. In this case, management has to plan the labor-hours to be expended in the work center. For example, if two people work 9 hours per day for five days, the result is 90 labor-hours per week. This value has to be reduced or inflated by an estimate of the relation of actual hours to standard hours. In our example, if people in this work center typically worked at 80 percent efficiency, then planned output is 72 hours.

A work center's actual output will deviate from planned output. Often deviations can be attributed to conditions at the work center itself, such as lower-than-expected productivity, breakdowns, absences, random variations, or poor product quality. But less-than-expected output can occur for reasons outside the work center's control, such as insufficient output from a preceding work center or improper releasing of planned orders. Either problem can lead to insufficient input or a "starved" work center. Another reason for a variation between actual input and planned input was shown by our capacity planning model comparisons— some models don't produce realistic plans!

Input/output analysis also monitors backlog. Backlog represents the cushion between input and output. Backlog decouples input from output, allowing work center operations to be less affected by variations in requirements. Arithmetically, it equals prior backlog plus or minus the difference between input and output. The planned backlog calculation is based

FIGURE 10.14

Sample Input/Output for Work Center 500* (as of the end of period 5)

		Week				
		1	2	3	4	5
Planned input		15	15	0	10	10
Actual input		14	13	5	9	17
Cumulative deviation		−1	−3	+2	+1	+8
Planned output		11	11	11	11	11
Actual output		8	10	9	11	9
Cumulative deviation		−3	−4	−6	−6	−8
Actual backlog	20	26	29	25	23	31

Desired backlog: 10 hours

*In standard labor-hours.

on planned input and planned output. Actual backlog uses actual input and output. The difference between planned backlog and actual backlog represents one measure of the total, or net, input/output deviations. Monitoring input, output, and backlog typically involves keeping track of cumulative deviations and comparing them with preset limits.

The input/output report in Figure 10.14 is for work center 500 shown in weekly time buckets with input and output measured in standard labor-hours. The report was prepared at the end of period 5, so the actual values are current week-by-week variations in planned input. These could result from actual planned orders and scheduled receipts; that is, for example, if the input were planned by CRP, planned inputs would be based on timings for planned orders, the status of scheduled receipts, and routing data. The *actual* input that arrives at work center 500 can vary for any of the causes just discussed.

Work center 500's planned output has been smoothed; that is, management decided to staff this work center to achieve a constant output of 11 hours per week. The results should be to absorb input variations with changes in the backlog level. Cumulative planned output for the five weeks (55 hours) is 5 hours more than cumulative planned input. This reflects a management decision to reduce backlog from the original level of 20 hours. The process of increasing capacity to reduce backlog recognizes explicitly that flows must be controlled to change backlog; backlog can't be changed in or of itself.

Figure 10.14 summarized the results after five weeks of actual operation. At the end of week 5, the situation requires managerial attention. The cumulative input deviation (+8 hours), cumulative output deviation (−8 hours), current backlog (31 hours), or all three could have exceeded the desired limits of control. In this example, the increased backlog is a combination of more-than-expected input and less-than-expected output.

One other aspect of monitoring backlog is important. In general, there's little point in releasing orders to a work center that already has an excessive backlog, except when the order to be released is of higher priority than any in the backlog. The idea is to not release work that can't be done, but to wait and release what's really needed. Oliver Wight summed this up as one of the principles of input/output control: "Never put into a manufacturing facility or to a vendor's facility more than you believe can be produced. Hold backlogs in production and inventory control." With today's APS system, a similar dictate results: concentrate on executing the most immediate schedule—exactly. The APS system will take care of the future schedules.

FIGURE 10.15
The Capacity
Bathtub

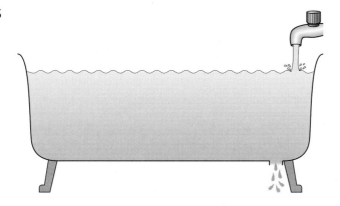

Figure 10.15 depicts a work center "bathtub" showing capacity in hydraulic terms. The input pipe's diameter represents the maximum flow (of work) into the tub. The valve represents MPC systems like MPS, MRP, and JIT, which determine **planned input** (flow of work) into the tub. Actual input could vary because of problems (like a corroded valve or problem at the water department) and can be monitored with input/output analysis. We can determine **required capacity** to accomplish the planned input to the work center with any of the capacity planning techniques. The output drain pipe takes completed work from the work center. Its diameter represents the work center's planned or **rated capacity,** which limits planned output. As with actual input, actual output may vary from the plan as well. It too can be monitored with input/output analysis. Sometimes planned output can't be achieved over time even when it's less than maximum capacity and there's a backlog to work on. When that occurs, realized output is called **demonstrated capacity.** The "water" in the tub is the **backlog** or **load,** which can also be monitored with input/output analysis.

Managing *Bottleneck* Capacity

Eliyahu Goldratt developed a key capacity management idea that he popularized more than 20 years ago in *The Goal.* Fundamentally, one needs to find the bottlenecks in any factory, and thereafter manage their capacities most effectively. Goldratt's maxim is that an hour of capacity lost in a bottleneck work center is an hour of capacity lost to the entire company—worth a fortune. But an hour of capacity gained in a nonbottleneck work center will only increase work-in-process inventory and confusion. Eli Goldratt has gone on to other things, but this fundamental concept remains at the base of his work. Today, he and his colleagues have generalized the ideas into what they refer to as "theory of constraints" (TOC). For the purposes of capacity planning and management, TOC teaches that the capacities of bottleneck work centers need to be planned and managed much more carefully than those of nonbottlenecks. In fact, Goldratt points out that for nonbottlenecks it may not be important to even have decent data. If sufficient capacity exists, execution of capacity plans is easy. Spend the time and energy on execution of what at first seems impossible.

Goldratt has many suggestions for how to execute the impossible. For example, why shouldn't bottleneck work centers run through lunch hours and coffee breaks—others can run these work centers while the primary personnel eat lunch and drink coffee. Alternative routing is another solution, and this is a good idea even when it "costs" much more. Usually the costs are calculated with unrealistic assumptions. Extra work done in an underutilized work center has no real cost, and if the bottleneck workload is thereby reduced, it is an excellent idea to do it.

The TOC approach to capacity planning is essentially to first determine the bottleneck work centers. This can be done with a rough-cut capacity planning model or with CRP. Where are the bottlenecks? Next, TOC would try to find the quick solutions for eliminating bottlenecks. Finally, scheduling will concentrate on best managing bottleneck capacity. Essentially, TOC will separate those jobs that pass through the bottlenecks from those that do not. Only the jobs or work orders requiring capacity in the bottleneck resource are finite scheduled, using horizontal loading and back scheduling for the most critical jobs.

If we return to the hole in the schedule of Figure 10.13, the TOC approach would definitely front-schedule component D for the reason described there: it is the schedule for component C that constrains the start of end product A. Do not let component D become a constraint to this overall product schedule. TOC treats this early schedule (front-loaded) as a buffer in order to reduce the possibility of missing the overall goal: Ship the end product!

TOC uses APS systems, but concentrates their attention on what is truly critical. For nonbottleneck work centers it is more than unimportant to utilize their capacity—it is fundamentally *wrong*. Increasing utilization of nonbottlenecks will result in more work being in the factory than necessary, yielding higher inventories and confusion. Nonbottleneck work will be done easily since there is basically no constraint to it. Restricting the use of APS systems to focus on the bottlenecks allows smart users to examine the best ways to "skin the cat."

The most critical capacity requirements need to be identified and thereafter utilized to maximum effectiveness. Capacity planning techniques can help with the former, but effective management is needed for the latter. Moreover, managerial policies can also create environments that are easier to execute—environments where capacities are utilized in a predictable and stable fashion.

Capacity Planning in the MPC System

To illustrate the importance of the interrelationships in designing and using the capacity planning system, let's consider the impact of production planning and resource planning decisions on shorter-term capacity planning decisions. To the extent that production planning and resource planning are done well, problems faced in capacity planning can be reduced, since appropriate resources have been provided. If, for example, the production plan specifies a very stable rate of output, then changes in the master production schedule (MPS) requiring capacity changes are minimal. If the material planning module functions effectively, the MPS will be converted into detailed component production plans with relatively few unexpected execution problems.

A quite different but equally important linkage that can affect capacity planning system design is the linkage with shop-floor execution systems. A key relationship exists in scheduling effective use of capacity. With sufficient capacity and efficient use of that capacity ensured by good shop-floor systems, we'll see few unpleasant surprises requiring capacity analysis and change. Effective shop-floor procedures utilize available capacity to process orders according to MRP system priorities, provide insight into potential capacity problems in the short range (a few hours to days), and respond to changes in material plans. Thus, effective systems reduce the necessary degree of detail and intensity of use of the capacity planning system. The result is a better match between actual input/output and planned input/output. Again, we see attention to the material planning side of the MPC system, in this case the shop-floor module, having an effect on the capacity planning side.

Choosing the Measure of Capacity

The choice of capacity measures is an important management issue. Alternatives run from machine-hours or labor-hours to physical or monetary units. The choice depends on the constraining resource and the firm's needs. In any manufacturing company, the "bundle of goods and services" provided to customers increasingly includes software, other knowledge work, after-sales service, and other customer services. In every case, providing these goods and services requires resources—"capacities" that must be planned, managed, and developed. Appropriate measures of capacity must be established and changed as evolution in the bundle of goods and services occurs.

Several current trends in manufacturing have a significant bearing on the choice of capacity measures. Each can have a major impact on what's important to measure in capacity. One important trend is considerable change in the concept of direct labor. Direct labor has been shrinking as a portion of overall manufacturing employment. Distinctions between direct and indirect labor are becoming less important. The ability to change labor capacity by hiring and firing (or even using overtime) has been reduced; notions of "lifetime employment" have further constrained this form of capacity adjustment.

Since one objective in JIT systems is continual improvement, the basis for labor capacity is constantly changing. This mandates control procedures for identifying and changing the planning factors as improvements take place.

Another important trend is decreased internal fabrication and increased emphasis on outside purchasing, i.e., outsourcing. This trend can alter the conception of what capacity requirements are important. Procurement analysis, incoming inspection, and engineering liaison may become the critical capacities to be managed, as well as planning and scheduling the capacities in vendor firms. In fact, one of the major benefits ascribed to major outsourcing companies such as Solectron and Flextronics is their ability to more flexibly respond to changing capacity needs.

For many firms engaged in fabrication, machine technology is changing rapidly. Flexible automation has greatly increased the range of parts that can be processed in a machine center. Future product mixes are likely to be much more variable than in the past, with a marked effect on the equipment capacity required. Moreover, as equipment becomes more expensive, it may be necessary to plan and control the capacity of key pieces of equipment at a detailed level.

To the extent that cellular technologies are adopted as part of JIT manufacturing, the unit of capacity may need to change. Usually the entire cell is coupled and has only as much capacity as its limiting resource. Often, the cell is labor limited, so the unit of capacity is labor-hours (continually adjusted for learning). Sometimes, however, the capacity measure needs to be solely associated with a single aspect of the cell. Also, when dissimilar items are added to the cell for manufacture, it's necessary to estimate each new item's capacity requirements in terms of individual processing steps.

The first task in choosing a capacity measure is to creatively identify resources that are critical and in short supply. Capacity control is too complicated to apply to all resources. The next step is to define the unit of measure. If the key resource is people, then labor-hours may be appropriate. In other instances, such measures as tons, gallons, number of molds, number of ovens, hours of machine time, square yards, linear feet, lines of code, customer calls, and cell hours have been used. In some cases, these are converted to some "equivalent" measure to accommodate a wider variety of products or resources.

After the resources and unit of measure have been determined, the next concern is to estimate available capacity. The primary issue here is theory versus practice. The engineer can provide theoretical capacity from the design specifications for a machine or from time studies of people. A subissue is whether to use "full" capacity or some fraction thereof (often 75 to 85 percent). A further issue is "plasticity" in capacity. For almost *any* resource, if it's *really* important, more output can be achieved. We've seen many performances that fall short of or exceed capacity calculations.

Choice of capacity measure follows directly from the objective of providing capacity to meet production plans. The appropriate measure of capacity most directly affects meeting these plans. The measure, therefore, should be appropriate to the critical limited resources and be based on what's achievable, with allowances for maintenance and other necessary activities. It must be possible to convert the bundle of products and services into capacity measurement terms. The results must be understood by those responsible, and they should be monitored.

Choice of a Specific Technique

In this chapter's discussion, the capacity planning techniques for converting a material plan into capacity requirements include three different methods for rough-cut capacity planning (CPOF, capacity bills, and resource profiles). We also examined capacity requirements planning, CRP, which is particularly useful for medium range planning. For the detailed day-to-day capacity planning APS systems can be valuable under some circumstances. The choice of method depends heavily on characteristics of the manufacturing environment.

The three rough-cut methods are most general, being applicable even in companies using just-in-time methods for shop-floor control. Rough-cut approaches can be useful in JIT operations to estimate the impact of changes in requirements called for by revisions to the master production schedule. For example, under level scheduling conditions, a change from a production rate of 480 units per day (one unit per minute) to 528 units per day (1.1 units per minute) might be needed. A rough-cut procedure could be used to examine the impact on each work center or manufacturing cell through which this volume would pass (including those of suppliers). Any indicated problems or bottleneck conditions could be addressed *before* the crisis hits. Similarly, a planned reduction in MPS could be evaluated to determine resources that might be freed to work on other tasks.

Rough-cut approaches do vary in accuracy, aggregation level, and ease of preparation. There's a general relationship between the amount of data and computational time required, and the quality and detail of the capacity requirements estimated. The issue is whether additional costs of supporting more complex procedures are justified by improved decision making and subsequent plant operations.

The capacity bills procedure has an advantage over capacity planning using overall factors (CPOF) because it explicitly recognizes product mix changes. This can be important in JIT operations, particularly where the level schedule is based on assumptions of product mix and where different products have different capacity requirements. On the other hand, if changes in mix are easily accommodated, and there are minimal differences in capacity requirements for different products, then CPOF's simplicity can be exploited. Under JIT operations, however, there's often little need to incorporate the added sophistication of the resource profile procedure. There simply won't be any added advantage to making lead time offsets in the planning process. Work is completed at virtually the same time as it's started.

Capacity requirements planning is only applicable in companies using time-phased MRP records for detailed material planning and shop-order-based shop scheduling systems. CRP is unnecessary under JIT operations anyway since minimal work-in-process levels mean there's no need to estimate the impact in capacity requirements of partially processed work. All orders start from "raw material" with virtually no amount of "capacity" stored in component inventories. Also, under JIT, there's no formal PAC procedure. There are no work orders. Thus, there are no status data on work orders.

Input/output control isn't usually an issue under JIT operations because attention has been shifted from planning to execution. As a result, actual input should equal actual output. Actual input becomes actual output with an insignificant delay. The backlog is effectively a constant zero. However, planned input can indeed vary from actual input and so can planned output vary from actual output. These variations should be achievable without violating the equality between actual input and actual output–with backlog remaining at zero. To the extent that plan-to-actual variations are possible, the result reflects the flexibility, or bandwidth, of the JIT unit.

Using the Capacity Plan

All the techniques we've described provide data on which a manager can base a decision. The broad choices are clear—if there's a mismatch between available capacity and required capacity, either the capacity or the material plan should be changed. If capacity is to be changed, the choices include overtime/undertime authorization, hiring/layoff, and increasing/ decreasing the number of machine tools or times in use. Capacity requirements can be changed by alternate routing, make-or-buy decisions, subcontracting, raw material substitutions, inventory changes, or revised customer promise dates.

Choice of capacity planning units can lead to more effective use of the system. Capacity units need not be work centers as defined for manufacturing, engineering, or routing purposes. They can be groupings of the key resources (human or capital) important in defining the factory's output levels. Many firms plan capacity solely for key machines (work centers) and gateway operations. These key areas can be managed in detail, while other areas fall under resource planning and the shop-floor control system.

Capacity planning choices dictate the diameter of the manufacturing pipeline. Only as much material can be produced as there's capacity for its production, *regardless of the material plan*. Not understanding the critical nature of managing capacity can lead a firm into production chaos and serious customer service problems. In the same vein, the relationship between flexibility and capacity must be discussed. You can't have perfectly balanced material and capacity plans *and* be able to easily produce emergency orders! We know one general manager who depicts his capacity as a pie. He has one slice for recurring business, one for spare parts production, one for downtime and maintenance, and a final specific slice for opportunity business. He manages to pay for this excess capacity by winning lucrative contracts that require rapid responses. He *does not add* that opportunity business to a capacity plan fully committed to the other aspects of his business.

Example Applications

We finish this chapter with three example applications of capacity planning/utilization. The first example, Montell USA, Inc., is a straightforward application of rough-cut capacity planning used to compare capacity plans with actual customer demands on an ongoing basis. The second example, Applicon, is tailored to the company's JIT manufacturing environment, allowing it to make systematic adjustments to the labor force. Finally, we see how the Manugistics APS software can be applied.

Capacity Planning at Montell USA, Inc.

Montell USA, Inc., manufactures plastic pellets used in injection molding machines. The pellets are made up of combinations of plastic material, coloring agents, and other chemicals. The company's primary customers use injection molding machines to make plastic components for the automotive industry. Montell currently utilizes a combination of two software packages in its manufacturing planning and control system. Front-end activities, like master production scheduling and demand management, are done with a system termed Picaso. MRP and back-end activities, like shop-floor control and vendor scheduling, are accomplished with an enterprise resource planning system provided by SAP. The Picaso system is used to produce the capacity planning reports for the company.

Montell prepares a rough-cut capacity plan from the master production schedule. It is a rolling plan, revised each month for the coming six months. It is prepared for each of the company's production lines, using a capacity measure of thousands of pounds of output. An example of part of a plan is given in Figure 10.16. For each of the next six months, two figures are shown for each production line: FINL and PLAN. The first of these, FINL, shows the booked customer orders for the month.

The second column for each month is the PLAN column. This gives the master production schedule quantity for each of the production lines. There are a few instances where booked orders exceed the planned capacity (e.g., months 12 and 01 for line B1). In some of these cases, management action (like overtime or a partial extra shift) may be needed to meet the requirements; in others, no action is needed because of the specific products being produced. To help determine where action should be taken, the rough-cut capacity plan is also detailed by specific product. An example showing part of the capacity plan detailed by product is provided in Figure 10.17. In this report the planners can see, for instance, the breakdown of specific products that sum up the quantities of 616 FINL and 561 PLAN for line G2 in month 12. The planners at Montell use this data to determine if changes need to be made in the MPS and/or in the commitments to customers.

Capacity Planning at Applicon

Applicon, a division of Schlumberger, designs and manufactures computer-aided engineering (CAE), computer-aided design (CAD), and computer-aided manufacturing (CAM) systems. Applicon implemented numerous JIT concepts and replaced some of its MRP system modules. Its dramatic results included a reduction in lead time (20 weeks to 4 days), an inventory reduction of over 75 percent, virtual elimination of obsolescence costs, little or no inspection, and a decline in MPC personnel (86 to 14).

FIGURE 10.16 **Part of Montell's Capacity Plan by Production Line**

Line	FINL 12*	PLAN 12	FINL 01	PLAN 01	FINL 02	PLAN 02	FINL 03	PLAN 03	FINL 04	PLAN 04	FINL 05	PLAN 05
B 1	2,327	1,685	2,610	2,598	2,758	2,530	2,818	2,862	2,763	2,621	508	2,842
BW-8	887	649	792	892	713	752	686	810	615	837	76	997
C 1	264	330	426	247	672	225	262	254	42	313	42	311
CK	180	162	190	159	180	116	52	201	132	134	0	159
CT-1	0	88	0	0	0	0	0	0	0	0	0	0
E 1	0	0	0	0	0	0	0	0	0	0	0	0
E 2	0	0	0	0	0	0	0	0	0	0	0	0
E 4	0	0	0	0	0	0	0	0	0	0	0	0
E 7	0	0	0	0	0	0	0	0	0	0	0	0
G 1	910	532	1,076	1,180	887	1,230	752	1,255	440	1,265	160	1,297
G 2	616	561	645	719	637	634	509	639	600	661	16	665
G 3	582	431	716	438	600	411	458	414	219	514	62	416
G 4	1,347	791	1,494	1,391	1,182	1,222	1,074	1,292	1,102	1,471	82	1,409
G 5	1,802	1,698	2,430	1,571	2,211	1,631	2,127	1,708	1,669	1,424	320	1,449

*Month 12.

FIGURE 10.17 **Part of Montell's Capacity Plan by Product and Line**

Line	Name	FINL 12	PLAN 12	FINL 01	PLAN 01	FINL 02	PLAN 02	FINL 03	PLAN 03	FINL 04	PLAN 04	FINL 05	PLAN 05
G 2	722-44-06 BB73F KZE	30	10	25	35	33	45	35	35	35	35	0	35
	722-44-07 BB73F DC4A	60	95	70	80	99	90	100	90	90	80	0	90
	722-44-08 BB73F YCD	90	100	10	110	10	110	10	110	0	110	0	110
	722-44-09 BB73F MDD	0	0	90	0	90	0	90	0	100	0	0	0
	722-46-01 BB73F DCC	15	20	10	50	15	20	15	25	15	50	0	25
	722-46-04 BB73F YCC	10	20	15	25	10	20	10	25	10	20	0	25
	840-43-05 EXP149628	0	0	0	0	0	0	0	0	0	0	0	0
	840-43-06 EXP149629	0	0	0	0	0	0	0	0	0	0	0	0
		616	561	645	719	637	634	509	639	600	661	16	665
G 3	102-64-08 RTA3184 6P	0	0	0	0	0	0	0	0	0	0	0	0
	102-64-13 RTA3184 JA	0	0	0	0	0	0	0	0	0	0	0	0
	105-02-01 RTA3363E B	0	0	0	0	0	0	0	0	0	0	0	0
	109-03-05 CL37BC BLA	0	0	0	0	0	0	0	0	0	0	0	0
	120-05-17 CA45GC PA7	0	0	0	0	0	0	0	0	0	0	0	0
	120-05-52 CA45GC SPN	17	36	25	0	25	0	25	0	25	0	0	0

Figure 10.18 shows an Applicon "Capacity Status Report." Applicon divided the factory into 17 capacity groupings (work centers) for planning purposes. It used actual customer orders as a monthly MPS to drive capacity planning. Capacity bills were used to convert the MPS into the present "load" over the next month (20 working days) in standard hours (the second column in Figure 10.18). The capacities in column 3 are based on a total workforce of 48 people (e.g., ALF-A had three workers who worked 8 hours per day for 20 days in the month = 480 standard hours). Work center OLD-P's zero capacity indicates no worker is presently assigned to this activity.

The fourth column reduces the capacity amounts by 30 percent (the desired rate of direct production activity for Applicon workers). The remaining time was used for "whole person" activities. That is, the company operated with the direct workers taking on many

FIGURE 10.18
Applicon
Capacity
Status Report

Work Center	Load (Std. Hours)	Capacity (Standard)	Capacity (Adj. Std.)	Capacity (Maximum)
ALF-A	70	480	336	528
ALF-T	5	80	56	88
HLT-A	438	800	560	880
HLT-T	85	160	112	176
MIS-A	270	800	560	880
MIS-T	14	80	56	88
MVX-A	399	1,120	784	1,232
MVX-T	79	80	56	88
OLD-P	81	0	0	0
PCB-A	52	160	112	176
PCB-H	44	160	112	176
PCB-I	124	320	224	352
PCB-M	441	480	336	520
PCB-P	408	960	672	1,056
PCB-T	918	1,680	1,176	1,848
PCB-V	123	160	112	176
PCB-W	56	160	112	176
Totals	3,634	7,680	5,376	8,440

20 total workdays included.

other tasks, such as design of work methods, new drawings, and database maintenance. On the average, Applicon expected that 30 percent of the time would be spent on this indirect work. This was *instead* of having a larger number of indirect workers. The last column provides a "maximum" capacity value based on 10 percent overtime. Applicon felt that it had the flexibility to operate easily between these two capacity levels. Where the volume was much higher or lower, they needed to make adjustments.

This report was run on June 12 for the next 20 days. Differences between "load" and the three capacities represented Applicon's ability to take on additional work in the next month. Large orders could be included into a trial run of the MPS to examine the orders' impact in terms of existing capacity availabilities. Total load (3,634 hours) represented 47 percent of standard capacity, 68 percent of adjusted capacity, and 43 percent of maximum capacity. Management reviewed these numbers carefully—particularly if possible large orders were under negotiation. It was relatively easy to make trial runs with those orders included to examine the impact of accepting the orders.

Of all the work centers in Figure 10.18, MVX-T appeared to be in the most trouble. However, this could easily be fixed. MVX-T only had one-half person allocated to it (80 hours/month). Reducing MVX-A (or some other work center) by one-half person and increasing MVX-T's capacity to one person for the month solved the problem. OLD-P similarly needed to have a person allocated to it.

This rough-cut capacity planning system serves Applicon well. Problems can be anticipated. JIT operations mean results are very current, with little or no bias because of work-in-process inventories. Results of the capacity planning are given to shop personnel, who make their own adjustments as they see fit, making allowances for absenteeism, particular workers' relative strengths, and other local conditions.

Capacity Planning with APS at a Consumer Products Company

A large European based consumer products company uses APS extensively in one of its factories. The APS software package is provided by Manugistics, and is called NetWORKS Scheduling. It is essentially a horizontal loading, back-scheduling system operating like the one illustrated in this chapter. It produces schedules for each work center that are similar to that of Figure 10.14. Figure 10.19 is a portion of a sample output report as generated by the APS software. Here we see a work center (packing line 250 ml. sauce), and the 10 pasta sauces that are scheduled for production over the next seven days. Each of the items shown is a 250-milliliter bottle of a particular end product. For each item there are two values shown: the planned production in each day, and the expected inventory in days of supply. By using days of supply, the system makes comparisons of inventory positions more transparent. To accomplish this, there is a linkage to a demand management system that allows the calculations for days of supply to reflect forecasts, actual orders, and provisions for special promotions.

Figure 10.19 seems to reflect ample capacity to meet demands at this company. There do not appear to be any shortages predicted in this plan, except perhaps for the third item (103), which might run out on 15/9. The match of production with capacity seems fairly close, with most production quantities scheduled to occur just when the days of supply approach zero. Thus, items 102, 105, and 107 are all scheduled the day after the days of supply is one day. It is only items 108 and 109 that seem to be scheduled earlier than necessary.

FIGURE 10.19
Sample APS Output—Pasta Sauce Line

Res: 250 ml. Sauce

Item	Description	10/9	11/9	12/9	13/9	14/9	15/9	16/9
101	250 ml.			6,600				
				5D	4D	3D	2D	1D
102	250 ml.						5,400	
		5D	4D	3D	2D	1D	8D	7D
103	250 ml.							5,100
		5D	4D	3D	2D	1D		3D
104	250 ml.	2,700						
		9D	8D	7D	6D	5D	4D	3D
105	250 ml.			7,200				
		2D	1D	12D	11D	10D	9D	8D
106	250 ml.	10,800						7,200
		6D	5D	4D	3D	2D	1D	3D
107	250 ml.						3,100	
		5D	4D	3D	2D	1D	4D	3D
108	250 ml.						1,800	
		12D	11D	10D	9D	8D	14D	13D
109	250 ml.						3,600	3,900
		6D	5D	4D	3D	2D	5D	9D
110	250 ml.			5,000				

One might look at Figure 10.19 and ask why item 103 is not scheduled a day earlier with item 108 moved one day later, in order to better balance the inventory days of supply across all items. The answer is that there are many reasons for scheduling decisions, and balanced inventory is only one of them. The Manugistics APS software package allows for many scheduling options. For example, the four items now scheduled for 15/9 might be scheduled as a group because they share a common setup. Another possibility is that they are all made from a common raw material. Perhaps this is the day that the company schedules all the pasta sauce made with mushrooms or some other common material.

The Manugistics APS software allows the schedulers at this consumer products company to evaluate output schedules like Figure 10.19 with graphical review. A user can view a schedule (it can be tailored with 14 different colors), changing schedule assignments by pointing/clicking. The schedules produced can be analyzed with a user-specified set of tools called "Troubleshooter," which alerts the user to any conditions he/she would like to flag. Particular assignments (schedules) can be frozen, which allows one to override whatever basic logic is used for making scheduling decisions. Thereafter, the APS model can be rerun to determine the shifts that result from these user imposed decisions. Changes in schedules also automatically generate the changes in setup/changeover costs if these are particularly relevant.

The APS software has been found to be quite versatile, allowing the company to use it in somewhat different kinds of manufacturing environments. For example, some packing lines necessarily need to complete all the jobs before the ends of days, while in other cases equipment can simply be turned off at night and back on in the morning, with work taking up where it has left off. The software also has helped coordinate scheduling of the packaging lines with scheduling of bulk products to be packed in multiple packages.

Concluding Principles

Clear principles for design and use of the capacity planning system emerge from this chapter:

- Capacity plans must be developed concurrently with material plans if the material plans are to be realized.
- The particular capacity planning technique(s) chosen must match the level of detail and actual company circumstances to permit making effective management decisions.
- Capacity planning can be simplified in a JIT environment.
- The better the resource and production planning process, the less difficult the capacity planning process.
- The better the shop-floor system, the less short-term capacity planning is required.
- The more detail in the capacity planning system, the more data and database maintenance are required.
- It's not always capacity that should change when capacity availability doesn't equal need.
- Capacity not only must be planned, but use of that capacity must also be monitored and controlled.
- Capacity planning techniques can be applied to selected key resources (which need not correspond to production work centers).
- The capacity measure should reflect realizable output from the key resources.

References

Berry, W. L.; T. Schmitt; and T. E. Vollmann. "Capacity Planning Techniques for Manufacturing Control Systems: Informational Requirements and Operational Features," *Journal of Operations Management* 3, no. 1 (November 1982).

_____. "An Analysis of Capacity Planning Procedures for a Material Requirements Planning System," *Decision Sciences* 15, no. 4 (fall 1984).

Blackstone, J. H. Jr. *Capacity Management*. Cincinnati: Southwestern, 1989.

Chakravarty, A., and H. K. Jain. "Distributed Computer Systems Capacity Planning and Capacity Loading," *Decision Sciences Journal* 21, no. 2 (spring 1990), pp. 253–262.

Fine, C. H. *Clockspeed Winning Industry Control in the Age of Temporary Advantage*. Reading: Perseus Books, 1998.

Goldratt, E. *Critical Chain*. Great Barrington, Mass.: North River Press, 1997.

Goldratt, E. M., and J. Cox. *The Goal: Process of Ongoing Improvement,* 2nd revised edition. Crofon-on-Hudson, NY: North River Press, 1992.

Hoover, W. E. Jr.; E. Eloranta; J. Holmstrom; and K. Huttunen. *Managing the Demand-Supply Chain*. New York: Wiley 2002, pp. 127–152.

Hyer, N., and U. Wemmerlov. *Reorganizing the Factory*. Portland: Productivity Press, 2002, pp. 311–368.

Karmarker, U. S. "Capacity Loading and Release Planning with Work-in-Progress (WIP) and Lead-times," *Journal of Manufacturing and Operations Management* 2, no. 2 (1989), pp. 105–123.

Knolmayer, G.; P. Mertens; and A. Zeier. *Supply Chain Management Based on SAP Systems*. Berlin: Springer, 2002, pp. 116–147.

Material and Capacity Planning Reprints. Falls Church, Va: APICS, 1993.

Metters, R., and V. A. Vargas. "A Comparison of Production Scheduling Policies on Costs, Service Levels, and Schedule Changes," *Production and Operations Management* 17, no. 3 (1999), pp. 76–91.

Matsuura, H; H. Taubone; and K. Katoka. "Comparisons between Simple Infinite Loading and Loading Considering a Workload Status under Uncertainty in Job Shop Operation Times," *International Journal of Production Economics* 40, no. I (1995).

Miller, T. *Hierarchical Operations and Supply Chain Planning*. London: Springer, 2001.

Vakharia, A. J.; D. A. Parmenter; and S. M. Sanchez, "The Operating Impact of Parts Commonality," *Journal of Operations Management* 14, no. 1 (1996).

Waller, D. L., *Operations Management*. London: Thompson, 2002, pp. 417–457.

Discussion Questions

1. Figure 10.1 shows a hierarchy of capacity planning and material planning processes. How does a better job of long-range planning affect the medium-range planning? Is the issue similar between production planning and master production scheduling?

2. Why does JIT execution require a less-intensive capacity planning approach?

3. What are the advantages and disadvantages of using CRP over rough-cut capacity planning?

4. What are the relative advantages of horizontal versus vertical loading?

5. How does input-output analysis provide a reality check on material and capacity planning processes?

6. Why is an hour of capacity lost in a bottleneck work center so valuable?

7. How might the Montell capacity plan (Figure 10.16) allow the company to determine if its revenue projections are on target?

8. What is the thinking behind Applicon's three different capacity values for its work centers?

9. In the Manugistics APS system, what would it mean if the days of supply were negative whenever a new batch of the products was scheduled? What would it mean if each time a new batch was scheduled, the days of supply was at 5D?

10. What are some examples of capacity planning in a University? What are good and poor practices?

Problems

1. A firm makes car seats for an automaker in two varieties: leather and fabric. The standard labor hours for these are 1.2 and 1.0 hours, respectively. The seats are made in two work centers, sewing and assembly, where the average percentage of work has been 55 percent for sewing and 45 percent for assembly. Given the following schedule for the next six weeks, calculate the labor hours needed in each of the two work centers:

Week	1	2	3	4	5	6
Leather	15	20	18	21	15	13
Fabric	65	60	62	59	65	67

(All quantities are in hundreds of units)

2. Returning to problem 1, what are the average labor hours needed over the six-week period, and how might the company handle deviations for the average? How might they staff their departments?

3. Returning again to problem 1, the leather requires incoming inspection for each car seat in order to be sure the colors match. The time required for this is five minutes per set of car seats. What are the expected capacity requirements for the inspection department over the next six weeks? Is there any way that this problem can usefully be combined with problem 1?

4. Returning to problem 3, what if inspection is done by the seat manufacturer in combination with assembly? How does this influence analysis of problem 1?

5. A metal fabricating company has the following master production schedule for one of its items (a frame), as well as the accompanying product structure.

	Week 1	Week 2	Week 3	Week 4
MPS	20	30	35	20

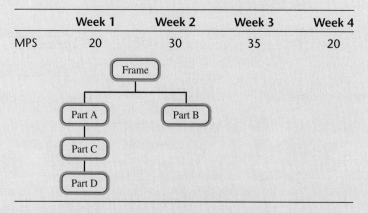

The resource profile for the frame is as follows:

Item	Work Center	Setup Hours	Run Hours/Unit	Lead Time
Frame	200	4	1.5	0 weeks
Part A	300	3	1.0	1 week
Part B	300	3	.8	1 week
Part C	400	2	1.2	2 weeks
Part D	500	2	1.0	1 weeks

Determine the capacity requirements for all work centers, assuming all usages are one, and that a new setup is required in each week at each work center.

6. A furniture manufacturer makes a bookcase from two end panels, four shelves, fasteners, and hangers. The end panels and shelves have the following data:

	End Panel		
Operation	Machine	Run Time	Setup Time
1	Saw	5 minutes	.6 hours
2	Planer	3 minutes	.3 hours
3	Router	4 minutes	.8 hours

	Shelf		
Operation	Machine	Run Time	Setup Time
1	Saw	4 minutes	.5 hours
2	Molder	5 minutes	1.3 hours
3	Router	5 minutes	.7 hours
4	Sander	1 minute	.1 hours

The master schedule for the next three weeks is 35, 50, and 40 bookcases, respectively. Each MPS quantity requires a setup.

a. What is the total number of hours required on each of the five machine centers for each week?

b. If each of the two parts is started into production one week (five days) before needed in assembly, and it takes one day per operation, generate the week-by-week load on the routing machine.

c. If in b the two parts arrive at the router on the same day, which would you process first? Why?

7. An office supply company makes notebooks with the following product structure:

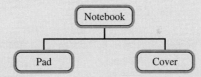

The company uses an MRP system, and has the following records for these three items.

Notebook		Week					
		1	2	3	4	5	6
Gross requirements		25	25	25	25	25	25
Scheduled receipts							
Projected available balance	30	5	0	0	0	0	0
Planned order releases		20	25	25	25	25	0

$Q = L4L, LT = 1, SS = 0.$

Pad		1	2	3	4	5	6
Gross requirements		20	25	25	25	25	0
Scheduled receipts		15					
Projected available balance	10	5	10	15	20	25	25
Planned order releases		30	30	30	30	0	0

$Q = 30, LT = 1, SS = 0.$

Cover		1	2	3	4	5	6
Gross requirements		20	25	25	25	25	0
Scheduled receipts		50					
Projected available balance	10	40	15	40	15	40	40
Planned order releases		50	0	50	0	0	0

Q = 50, LT = 2, SS = 0.

The notebooks are fabricated in the following work centers, listed with accompanying time requirements.

Operation	Work Center	Setup Time	Run Time
Notebook assembly	100	2 hours	10 minutes
Pad production	200	3 hours	5 minutes
Cover production	300	2 hours	9 minutes

Determine the weekly capacity requirements in each of the work centers. For the two scheduled receipts, assume that the setup is complete, and that in each case they are half complete.

8. Returning to Figures 10.12 and 10.13 and the supporting data, construct the APS back schedule that would be based on product B being horizontally loaded, not product A.

9. Continuing with problem 8, construct the APS back schedule for *both* products A and B, first with B given priority, then with A given priority.

10. Suppose the best customer asked for one unit of product B. How quickly could it be delivered if only enough component parts for one unit were made and assembled, and all existing work in the affected work centers was halted as necessary to make this unit?

11. Suppose that product B had a gross margin of $100/unit, while that of product A was $30. Which product should be the APS system schedule first? Why?

12. The following input-output data were gathered at the end of week 8 for a work center:

	Week							
	1	2	3	4	5	6	7	8
Planned input	60	60	60	60	60	60	60	60
Actual input	68	70	75	70	68	60	55	55
Planned output	65	65	65	65	65	65	65	65
Actual output	60	62	63	63	64	65	63	60

Beginning backlog = 50 hours.

a. Complete the input output document

b. What was the planned objective?

c. Was it met?

d. What recommendations would you make

13. A company with three product lines has estimated its weekly capacity requirements for four work centers as follows.

	Product Line		
Work Center	**A**	**B**	**C**
100	35 hours	28 hours	12 hours
200	25 hours	37 hours	56 hours
300	46 hours	35 hours	33 hours

a. How many workers (and duplicate machines) are needed in each work center if they are to work 40 hours per week?

b. What is the difference if the firm decides to work two shifts (80 hours per week)?

14. Suppose in the Montell example (Figure 10.16) a customer wanted to place the maximum order possible for the B1 line. What is the total quantity that could be provided in the next months (12, 01, and 02) with the current capacity? What might be done to improve the response?

15. Applicon has the following capacity bills for its popular items A and B.

A		B	
Work Center	**Hours/Unit**	**Work Center**	**Hours/Unit**
ALF-A	1.0	ALF-T	0.4
HLT-A	0.5	HLT-T	0.7
MIS-A	0.7	MIS-T	0.5
MVX-A	0.7	MVX-T	1.0
PCB-A	0.4	PCB-P	0.8
PCB-P	1.2	PCN-B	1.6

It is now June 15, and an important customer wishes to have 100 units of both A and B during the next month (20 working days). Analyze the effect of accepting this order. Assume there are adequate materials, and work center MVX-T has had its capacity increased to one full person (capacity now = 160). This was accomplished by reducing MVX-A to 6.5 persons, and no other orders have been booked since June 12. Use the capacity data and conditions of Figure 10.18 as the basis for your analysis.

11

Production Activity Control

This chapter concerns the execution of detailed material plans. It describes the planning and release of individual orders to both factory and outside vendors. Production activity control (PAC) also concerns, when necessary, detailed scheduling and control of individual jobs at work centers on the shop floor, as well as vendor scheduling. An effective production activity control system can ensure meeting the company's customer service goals. A PAC system can reduce work-in-process inventories and lead times as well as improve vendor performance. A key element of an effective PAC system is feedback on shop and suppliers' performance against plans. This loop-closing aspect provides signals for revising plans if necessary.

This chapter is organized around three topics:

- *A framework for production activity control:* How does PAC relate to other aspects of material planning and control, and how do just-in-time production of individual firm decisions affect PAC system design?
- *Production activity control techniques:* What basic concepts and models are used for shop-floor and vendor scheduling and control?
- *Production activity control examples:* How have PAC systems been designed and implemented in several different kinds of companies?

Chapter 11 is linked closely to Chapter 7 in that many PAC techniques are designed to execute the detailed material plans produced by material requirements planning (MRP) systems. Much of the detail order tracking of PAC is not required in a just-in-time (JIT) environment, so many of the appropriate JIT shop-floor systems are described in Chapter 9. Chapter 16 deals with advanced scheduling techniques. Chapter 17 treats supply chain linkages where vendor schedules are coordinated with customer schedules.

A Framework for Production Activity Control

Production activity control (PAC) concerns execution of material plans. It encompasses activities within the shaded areas of Figure 11.1. The box entitled "Shop-floor scheduling and control," which we refer to as shop-floor control, falls completely within PAC. Vendor

FIGURE 11.1
Production
Activity
Control in the
MPC System

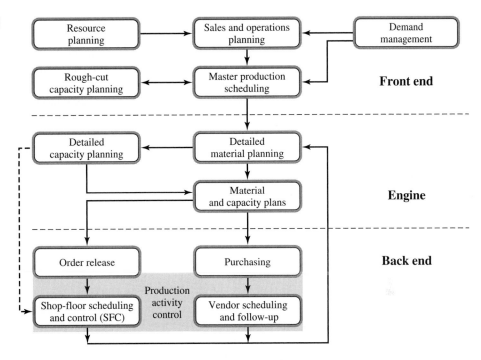

scheduling and follow-up is depicted as largely being part of production activity control, but not completely. Many firms, particularly those with JIT material control approaches, assign most vendor scheduling to PAC. Order release (which authorizes release of individual orders to the factory and provides accompanying documentation) is similarly becoming more a part of PAC. In purchasing, **procurement** is seen as a professional activity where information networks, relationships, terms, and conditions are established with vendor companies outside of PAC, while release of individual orders and follow-up activities are a part of PAC.

The extension of the definition of *production activity control* is accentuated by the growing use of computers on the shop floor as well as **electronic data interchange (EDI)** and Internet-based system linkages with vendors. As more and more traditional staff work is integrated into the basic manufacturing infrastructure, it will expand PAC as well.

MPC System Linkages

The primary connection between PAC and the rest of the MPC systems shown in Figure 11.1 comes from the box marked "Material and capacity plans." The capacity plan is especially critical to managing the detailed shop-floor flow of materials. In essence, the capacity provided represents resource availabilities for meeting material plans.

Capacity's importance for shop-floor control (SFC) is illustrated by considering two extremes. If insufficient capacity is provided, no SFC system will be able to decrease backlogs, improve delivery performance, or improve output. On the other hand, if more than enough capacity exists to meet peak loads, almost *any* SFC system will achieve material flow objectives. It's in cases with bottleneck areas and where effective utilization of capacity is important that we see the utility of good SFC systems.

A related issue is the extent to which good capacity planning is done. If the detailed capacity planning activity in Figure 11.1 provides sufficient capacity, with relatively level loading, shop-floor control is straightforward. On the other hand, if peaks and valleys in capacity requirements are passed down to the back end, execution becomes more complex and difficult. The same general issues apply to vendor follow-up systems: vendor capacity must be carefully planned to ensure effective execution. If one does not help vendors utilize capacity effectively, total system costs increase, which in the end must be borne by the end customers. Thus, several automobile suppliers report that Toyota is the easiest customer to work for since it maintains a much more level schedule, with fewer changes/surprises.

The material plan provides information to the SFC and vendor follow-up systems and sets performance objectives. The essential objective of both execution systems is to achieve the material plan—to provide the right part at the right time. This will result in being able to hit the master production schedule and to satisfy customer service objectives.

The Linkages between MRP and PAC

The shop-floor and vendor scheduling activities begin when an order is released. A critical information service provided by MRP is apprising the SFC systems of all changes in material plans. This means revising due dates and quantities for scheduled receipts so correct priorities can be maintained. The job thereafter might be likened to that of a duck hunter following a moving target. Control and follow-up systems must keep each order lined up with its due date—one that's moving—so overall MPC is supported.

Linkages between PAC and the engine aren't all one-way. There's important feedback from the shop-floor control and vendor follow-up systems to material and capacity planning. Feedback is of two types: status information and warning signals. Status information includes where things are, notification of operational completions, count verifications, order closeout and disposition, and accounting data. The warning signals help flag inadequacies in material and capacity plans: that is, will we be able to do what was planned?

Just-in-Time Effect on PAC

Shop-order-based systems are founded on the premises of job shop (now more frequently called *batch*) manufacturing, where parts are routed to different parts of the factory for processing steps, with relatively long lead times, high work-in-process inventories, and high utilization of work center capacities. JIT has none of these. Manufacturing takes place in facilities, often in cells, where jobs are easily kept track of; work is completed quickly; work-in-process inventory levels are insignificant; and work centers have surge capacity or else are level loaded. In either case, capacity utilization is not a key issue.

Formal systems for shop-floor control are largely unnecessary under JIT. Release of orders is still part of PAC, but the typical "shop order" with associated paperwork isn't maintained. Therefore, the PAC functions in Figure 11.1 are greatly simplified. Order release can be accomplished with kanbans or other pull system methodologies, and work-in-process inventories in the factory are severely limited. Detailed scheduling is also unnecessary since orders flow through cells in predictable ways so that workers know the sequence of conversion operations. Work is completed fast enough that "order scheduling" isn't required. Detailed scheduling of workers and equipment is similarly not an issue, since design of the JIT system itself determines schedules. There's no need for data collection or monitoring since JIT basically assumes only two kinds of inventories: raw materials and finished goods. Receipt of finished goods is used to "backflush" required raw materials from inventory. The JIT-based systems dramatically reduce the number of transactions to be processed, as well as the associated inventories and lead times.

Vendor scheduling under JIT can be a bit more complex than shop-floor control, but if the relationship with the vendors is good, differences are very small. Many firms use some form of electronic kanban to authorize work at the vendor factories, and excellent vendors don't build inventories in anticipation of orders from their customers. Well-run auto companies, for example, transmit an exact build schedule to their seat vendors several times a day, as actual cars are started. By the time these cars are ready for seats to be installed, seats will be delivered by the vendor in the exact sequence required. The seats are not pulled from inventory. They are built to order and delivered in the exact sequence to match the build schedule at the assembly plant. There is no need for transactions such as shipping or receiving documents. The seat manufacturer is paid on the basis of the build schedule; one just assumes that each car has the requisite seats!

The Company Environment

The primary PAC objective is managing the materials flow to meet MPC plans. In some firms, other objectives relate to efficient use of capacity, labor, machine tools, time, or materials. Under JIT and time-based competition, the objective is material velocity. A firm's particular set of objectives is critical to PAC design.

The choice of objectives for PAC reflects the firm's position vis-à-vis its competitors, customers, and vendors. It also reflects the company's fundamental goals and the constraints under which it operates. In many countries firms find changing capacity to be more difficult than in the United States. This viewpoint colors the view of PAC. Similarly, some firms have more complex products and/or process technologies than others. The result can be a difficult shop-floor management problem and a resultant difference in the appropriate PAC system. As a result PAC system design must be tailored to the particular firm's needs.

Production Activity Control Techniques

This section begins by describing basic concepts for production activity control under batch manufacturing with an MRP system. It covers basic shop floor concepts, including the elements of lead time, operation setback charts, and lead-time management. It then examines three approaches to shop-floor control. The first, **Gantt charts,** provides graphic understanding of the shop-floor control problem; moreover, Gantt chart models can be used in manual shop-floor control systems. The second approach is based on **priority sequencing rules** for jobs at a work center under MRP. The third approach to shop-floor control, **theory of constraints scheduling,** involves the preparation of an exact schedule of jobs for bottleneck work centers, and sequencing the nonbottleneck work centers by a priority sequencing rule. We next look at vendor scheduling where the concepts are applied to supplier operations.

Basic Shop-Floor Control Concepts

Figure 11.2, an example product structure for end item A, demonstrates basic concepts underlying shop-floor control techniques. One essential input to the SFC system is the routing and lead-time data for each product item. Figure 11.3 presents this for parts D and E of the example. The routing specifies each operation to be performed to make the part and which work center will perform the operation.

FIGURE 11.2
Example
Product
Structure
Diagram

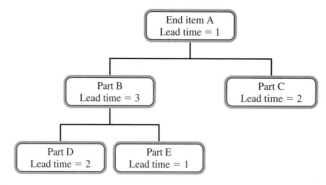

FIGURE 11.3
Routing Data
and Operation
Setback Chart

Operation	Work Center	Run Time	Setup Time	Move Time	Queue Time	Total Time	Rounded Time
Part D routing							
1	101	1.4	0.4	0.3	2.0	4.1	4.0
2	109	1.5	0.5	0.3	2.5	4.8	5.0
3	103	0.1	0.1	0.2	0.5	0.9	1.0
Total lead time (days) 10.0							
Part E routing							
1	101	0.3	0.1	0.2	0.5	1.1	1.0
2	107	0.2	0.1	0.3	0.5	1.1	1.0
3	103	0.3	0.2	0.1	1.5	2.1	2.0
4	109	0.1	0.1	0.1	0.5	0.9	1.0
Total lead time (days) 5.0							

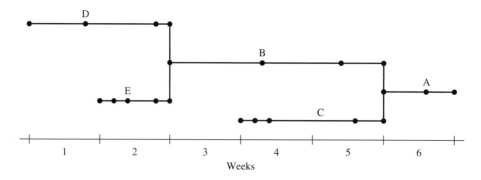

Production of part D, for example, requires three operations of 4, 5, and 1 days, respectively, for a total of 10 days, or two weeks. Part E requires four operations of 1, 1, 2, and 1 days, respectively, for a total of 5 days, or one week. The remaining lead times in Figure 11.2 are all derived the same way. Lead times used for MRP should match those in the routing file. If the MRP time for part E was set at two weeks instead of one week, orders would constantly be released one week early.

Lead times are typically made up of four elements:

Run time (operation or machine run time per piece × lot size).

Setup time (time to prepare the work center, independent of lot size).

Move time (delay waiting to be moved plus time spent moving from one work center to the next).

Queue time (time spent waiting to be processed at a work center, which depends on workload *and* schedule).

Queue time (the critical element) frequently accounts for 80 percent or more of total lead time; it's the element most capable of being managed. Reducing queue time means shorter lead time and, therefore, reduced work-in-process inventory. This reduction requires better scheduling.

The bottom of Figure 11.3 shows an **operation setback chart** based on each part's lead times. Here we clearly see the implications of incorrect MRP lead time. If the MRP lead time for part E isn't the one week calculated from the routing data, the part will be released either early or late to the shop. Neither of these is a desirable outcome. Note that Figure 11.3 shows that both parts D and E go through work center 101 for their first operation. The top of Figure 11.4 shows the partial schedule for work center 101, with parts D and E scheduled according to the timing in Figure 11.3.

The bottom of Figure 11.4 shows two alternative detailed schedules for part D in week 1 at work center 101. The shaded portion represents the 1.8 days of lead time required for

FIGURE 11.4
Work Center
101 Schedules

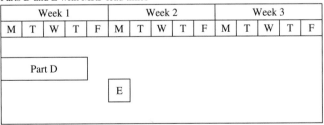

Parts D and E with MRP lead times

	Week 1					Week 2					Week 3			
M	T	W	T	F	M	T	W	T	F	M	T	W	T	F

Part D

E

Alternative detailed schedules for Part D
(The shaded area represents setup and run time only)

Monday	Tuesday	Wednesday	Thursday	
Part D				Early schedule
		Part D		Late schedule

setup and run time. The early schedule has part D loaded as soon as possible in the four days. The late schedule loads part D into the latest possible time at work center 101. The key differences between the top and bottom of Figure 11.4 are the timing of the setup and run times. The blank area in both schedules includes queue time. Queue time represents slack that permits the choice of alternative schedules—a form of flexibility. This slack can be removed by good SFC practice; that is, this schedule allows 4 full days to complete part D, when actual time on the machine is only 1.8 days. For the remaining 2.2 days, the part waits in a queue or is moving between work centers.

The shaded portion of the schedules shown at the bottom of Figure 11.4 contains no queue time. These schedules represent loading a particular job onto a particular work center for a particular time period. The two alternatives in the bottom of Figure 11.4 are different loadings; one typically chooses between alternative loadings to utilize the machine center effectively.

Lead-Time Management

Many people think of **lead time** as a constant, such as π. In fact, it's not a value to be measured as much as a parameter to be managed. Of the four elements of lead time (run, setup, move, and queue), the last two can be compressed with good PAC design and practice.

Lead time and work in process (WIP) are directly related. Moreover, some critical feedback linkages operate. The longer the lead time is perceived to be, the longer the time between the order launching date and due date. The longer this time, the more orders in the shop. The more orders in the shop, the longer the queue time (and WIP); we have a self-fulfilling prophecy.

Some WIP is needed at work centers where high utilization is important. However, a basic principle of MPC systems is to *substitute information for inventory.* The firm doesn't need to have jobs physically in front of machines. Orders can be held in a computer and converted to physical units only as needed. For many plants, setup and run time constitute only 10 to 20 percent of total lead time. The rest is slack that can be substantially cut.

One interesting question is how to manage lead time. This means changing database elements for both SFC and MRP. One alternative is to go through the database and systematically change all lead times. Reducing them could result in a transient condition of dry work centers at early gateway operations. This might be a reasonable price to pay for the resulting WIP reduction.

Changing lead-time data elements naturally leads to the question of how they're established in the first place. For most firms, lead-time data are usually an input from some functional area, such as production control. An alternative is to *calculate* lead time. When we think about changing lead times as part of a management process, and when we remember that SFC lead time must be in tune with MRP lead-time offset data, this approach has increasing appeal. One firm calculated lead times as follows:

1. Nonqueue time for each operation was set equal to setup plus run (time per piece × lot size) plus move times.
2. Nonqueue time was converted to days by dividing total hours by number of shifts per day, assuming seven productive hours per day.

3. Queue time was set equal to two days if the next work center routing was in another department, one day if it was in the department but a different work center, and zero days if it was on the same machine.

4. Lead time for the total order was the sum of the queue and nonqueue times. This time was calculated with an average order quantity, rounded to a weekly lead time, and used for MRP lead-time offsetting.

Selecting queue time is the critical element in this formula. Values were chosen by taking a sample of 50 parts and using different queue time estimates to yield lead times consistent with production control personnel opinions. The initial estimates were padded, but the company was not very concerned. Once the system was in operation, estimates for queue times were systematically reduced a bit at a time. The result was a managed approach to shorter lead times and reduced work in process.

Before leaving this discussion, let's look at one firm's results. David A. Waliszowski says a $25 million division of Hewlett-Packard reduced lead time 70 percent and increased customer service levels 80 percent. This amounted to a $1.7 million reduction in work-in-process inventory that was achieved in three months.

Gantt Charts

Gantt or **bar charts,** like those in Figure 11.4, show a schedule. The operation setback chart in Figure 11.3 is very similar. It too is a schedule for when to make each of the five parts based on lead times that include move and queue times.

One form of shop-floor control is to prepare operation setback charts similar to Figure 11.3 for each job, and use them with the kind of data in Figure 11.3 to prepare Gantt charts, such as those in Figure 11.4. The objective is to prepare a schedule for each machine center. This schedule can be based on the assumptions in either the top or bottom of Figure 11.4; that is, the schedule may or may not use lead times that include queue and move times.

The more usual practice is to prepare the detailed work center schedule *without* move and queue times. Many firms' systems do this. The typical approach is a **schedule board** with racks to hold pieces of paper. Each paper is a job and its length represents the setup plus run time required.

The primary problem with this kind of system is updating. Actual data must be captured and integrated into an ongoing replanning cycle. Moreover, a means to communicate with the shop floor is usually required since schedule boards typically reside in planning offices. However, with personal computers on the shop floor, some firms have in essence created a fairly dynamic version of the schedule board.

Priority Sequencing Rules

Priority sequencing rules determine which job to run next at a work center. To some extent, these rules can be seen as producing a loading of jobs onto individual machines, but usually only one job is committed at a time; that is, the job to run *next* is determined only near the time when the prior job has been completed. The priority (sequencing) rule is just what the name suggests: a *rule* for what job to process next.

Many different priority rules have been established. A fairly common one is to base priorities on the type of data in Figure 11.3. The lower half of that figure contains scheduled due dates for parts and operations. These due dates can be used as priorities. For example, a priority rule could be: the job to process next is the job with the earliest operation due date. An alternative is to next process the job with the earliest *part* due date. Four other commonly used sequencing rules are:

- *Order slack:* Sum the setup times and run times for all remaining operations, subtract this from the time remaining (now until the part due date), and call the remainder slack. The rule is to work on that job with the least slack. This rule addresses the problem of work remaining.

- *Slack per operation:* A variant of order slack is to divide the slack by the number of remaining operations, again taking next the job with the smallest value. The reasoning behind slack per operation is that it will be more difficult to complete jobs with more operations because they will have to be scheduled through more work centers.

- *Critical ratio:* A rule based on the following ratio:

$$\frac{\text{Time remaining}}{\text{Work remaining}}$$

For calculation, the rule is expressed as

$$\frac{\text{Due date} - \text{Present time}}{\text{Lead time remaining (including setup, run, move, and queue)}}$$

If the ratio is 1.0, the job is on time. A ratio below 1.0 indicates a behind-schedule job, while a ratio above 1.0 indicates an ahead-of-schedule condition. The rule is to always process that job with the smallest critical ratio next.

- *Shortest operation next:* This rule ignores all due date information as well as all information about work remaining. It simply says, take as the next job the one that can be completed in the shortest time at the work center. This rule maximizes the number of shop orders that go through a work center and minimizes the number waiting in queue.

In an MRP system, each shop order would be a scheduled receipt for the part. As such, the scheduled receipt has a due date. From this due date, operational due dates could be established by backing off expected operation times, if these data are needed to establish priority sequence. The great advantage of this computer-based system is that, whenever the due date for a scheduled receipt changes, operation due dates can be changed accordingly. These changes, in turn, lead to priority changes for shop-floor control, resulting in an execution system that works on the most-needed shop orders first. The objective is for high-priority jobs to move through the shop very quickly, while low-priority jobs are set aside. In this way, the shop-floor control system can indeed execute the dictates of the detailed material plan. In recent times, many companies have developed a preference for sequencing rules that are easy to understand. One straightforward approach is to develop operation start and operation due dates, and use them for determining priority sequence decisions. In a computer-based shop-floor control system, due dates wouldn't be printed on any shop paper that travels with the work-in-process inventory. The shop paper would show the routing or sequence of operations (static data), but no due dates. The changing (dynamic) due date information would be printed daily or be displayed on line in the form of a work center schedule or dispatch list. It's the dispatch list, not the traveling paper, that shows the priority sequence. The dispatch list can be updated as rapidly as transactions are processed to the MRP database.

Theory of Constraints (TOC) Systems

An increasing number of firms have been implementing a plant scheduling system that uses theory of constraints (TOC) concepts. Initially, TOC scheduling systems were viewed as a replacement of an integrated MPC system. In fact, TOC scheduling systems encompass the functions performed in the engine and back end of Figure 11.1, but combine these functions so that material and capacity are planned simultaneously. TOC systems accomplish many functions in the MPC framework, but not all.

Basic Concepts of TOC Systems

Most manufacturing firms have a very limited number of constraints. Any resource whose capacity is equal to or less than the required demand is referred to as a *bottleneck*. As a consequence the fundamental principle of TOC systems is that only those work centers (or other types of resources) that are bottlenecks are of critical concern in scheduling. This is because the bottleneck work centers limit the overall production output of a plant. Further output beyond the constraint of the bottleneck can be achieved only by improved utilization of the bottleneck facilities, using approaches such as reduced downtime, improved productivity, and reduced changeover times. The objective of TOC scheduling is to maximize throughput. Since throughput is limited by the bottleneck resources, all efforts are devoted to maximizing capacity utilization in these work centers. Therefore, TOC scheduling systems focus on the identification of bottleneck work centers, and the scheduling of these work centers.

The concept of a bottleneck has been generalized into "constraints," which include marketplace constraints. In fact, it is argued that the goal is to have company output constrained by the marketplace, not by constraints over which the firm has more control. Further, TOC adds some operational concepts for dealing with constraining situations. Constraints are explicitly identified, and they're buffered with inventory. Also, the constraint's importance is made clear to the entire factory. For example, bottleneck work centers are operated over coffee breaks and lunch, and are worked a maximum of overtime hours. Moreover, jobs are closely examined to find any that can be alternatively routed, even if the result is "excess cost" for the work so routed. The goal is always to break a constraint, or bottleneck condition, and thereafter identify the next constraint. Continuous improvement is an integral part of the theory of constraints philosophy. Moreover, the path for the improvement is directed by the theory, always following the constraints.

TOC Scheduling

The scheduling approach used in TOC systems is called **drum-buffer-rope.** The bottleneck work centers (constraints) are the drums, and are, therefore, used to control the workflow in a plant. Any resource whose capacity is more than the demand is called a *non drum*. The rope refers to "pull" scheduling at the nonbottleneck work centers. The purpose of the rope is to tie the production at each resource to the drum. Buffers exist at all of the bottleneck work centers, and the shipping dock, but not at nonbottleneck work centers. These buffers are used to protect the throughput of the bottleneck work centers from the inevitable minor fluctuations through the use of time buffers (WIP inventory) at a relatively few critical points in the plant. The basic concept is to move material as quickly as possible through nonbottleneck work centers until it reaches the bottleneck. The work at the bottleneck resources is scheduled for maximum efficiency. Thereafter, work again moves at maximum speed to the shipping dock (finished goods).

The diagram shown in Figure 11.5 outlines the basic TOC scheduling steps. TOC begins its process by combining data in the bill of materials file with data in the routing file. The result is a network, or extended tree diagram, where each part in the product structure also has its operational data attached directly. These data are then combined with the MPS to form the "product network." Figure 11.6 provides an example of a TOC product

FIGURE 11.5
TOC
Scheduling

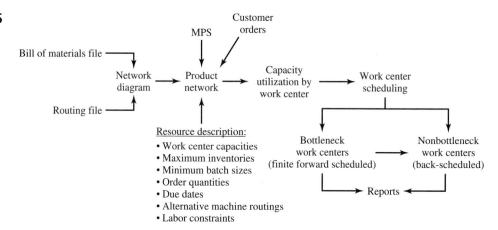

FIGURE 11.6
Sample
Product
Network

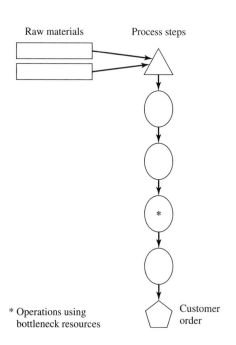

network. Here customer orders are linked to the final operation (such as the final assembly process), which, in turn, is linked to previous operations (such as the detailed fabrication steps for components), and then to raw materials. Additional data typically included in the TOC files are: capacities, maximum inventories, minimum batch quantities, order quantities, due dates, alternative machine routing, labor constraints, and other data typically used in finite scheduling models. In Figure 11.5, these data would be part of the "Resource description."

Next, the product network and resource descriptions are fed into a set of routines that identify the bottleneck resources. This routine combines the product network and resource information to form a TOC network of the bottleneck resources. To determine the bottleneck resources an initial analysis is prepared that provides reports indicating bottleneck resources. This involves using a rough-cut capacity planning routine that provides much of the information of other capacity planning procedures. Since the TOC product network includes both the parts and their routings, a pass through this network can result in an estimate of the capacity required at each work center. Lot sizes at this rough-cut stage are based on lot-for-lot rules. The resultant capacity needs, when divided by the number of weeks in the planning horizon, are the average capacity requirements for each resource. When divided by the resource capacities, the result is the average expected load.

As illustrated in Figure 11.7, the average loads on machine centers are sorted, and the most heavily loaded are studied by analysts. Typical questions include: Are the data correct? Are the time standards accurate? Can we easily increase capacity? Can we use alternative routings for some items? Any changes based on these questions result in another run to see if the bottleneck resources change. Those work centers in Figure 11.7 having a utilization exceeding 80 percent would be considered bottleneck work centers.

At this point the TOC product network is split into two portions, as shown in Figure 11.5. The left-hand portion incorporates all bottleneck resources and all succeeding operations, including market demand for end products with parts that have processing on the bottleneck resources. *This portion of the network is forward finite loaded.*

The right-hand portion includes all of the nonbottleneck resources. *This portion of the network is not forward finite loaded.* Operation start dates/times are, however, established by using the setup times, run times, and queue times for the nonbottleneck resource operations. An initial scheduling pass is made through the product network, and the raw material release dates are offset from customer order due dates by taking into account the processing and queue times for all part operations. In a second pass, however, due dates for any part operations that feed bottlenecks are based on those established by the TOC scheduling of bottlenecks. Schedules for these part operations are set so that material will be available in time for the first operation in the TOC network. This scheduling logic provides a dispatch list for the nonbottleneck resources.

One advantage of the TOC network split is that we can readily see where attention should be focused. Not only is bottleneck capacity utilized more intensively by finite scheduling of this small subset of work centers, but identifying bottlenecks allows us to target efforts in quality and production improvements on these resources.

Buffers

One issue with TOC is the assumption of certainty of the processing times. TOC buffers the schedules for critical operations at bottleneck operations by using both safety stock and

FIGURE 11.7 Capacity Utilization Chart (without Setups)

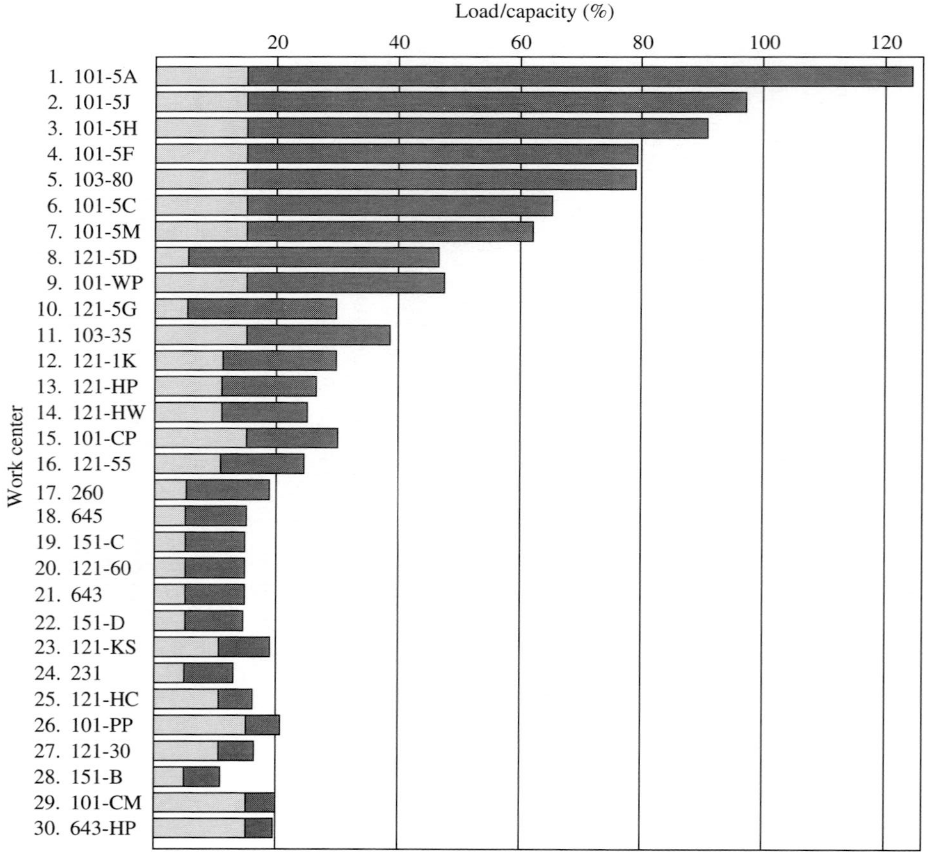

Load/capacity (%)

Work center	Load	Capacity (hours)
1. 101-5A	392.5	357.0
2. 101-5J	1233.5	1530.0
3. 101-5H	1066.6	1428.0
4. 101-5F	1371.8	2142.0
5. 103-80	677.3	1071.0
6. 101-5C	1057.3	2142.0
7. 101-5M	483.0	1020.0
8. 121-5D	599.7	1428.0
9. 101-WP	1058.8	3213.0
10. 121-5G	254.5	1020.0
11. 103-35	252.0	1071.0
12. 121-1K	203.8	1071.0
13. 121-HP	1704.0	10710.0
14. 121-HW	154.9	1071.0
15. 101-CP	154.3	1071.0
16. 121-55	96.6	714.0
17. 260	142.6	1071.0
18. 645	113.3	1071.0
19. 151-C	108.5	1071.0
20. 121-60	34.6	357.0
21. 643	101.9	1071.0
22. 151-D	95.5	1071.0
23. 121-KS	183.3	2142.0
24. 231	76.1	1071.0
25. 121-HC	62.0	1071.0
26. 101-PP	60.2	1071.0
27. 121-30	60.1	1071.0
28. 151-B	240.1	4284.0
29. 101-CM	108.6	2142.0
30. 643-HP	48.0	1071.0

Work center

Source: Company Records

safety lead time. In scheduling a sequence of jobs on the same machine, safety lead time can be introduced between subsequent orders. This provides a cushion against variations adversely affecting the flow of jobs through this machine.

To protect against having these variations affect subsequent bottleneck operations on the same job, safety lead time is employed. In this case, the start of the next bottleneck operation on the same job isn't scheduled immediately after the current operation is completed. A delay is introduced to perform the buffering here. (*Note:* there can be another job in process during the delay; its completion will affect the actual start date for the arriving job.) Each of these allowances means actual conditions will vary from the TOC schedule. While the schedule for bottleneck resources is clear, an important question for the supervisors at some point could easily be *which* job to run next at nonbottleneck resources. Such decisions can be made by using a priority sequencing rule.

To ensure there's always work at the bottleneck operation (to provide maximum output), there is safety lead time in front of these work centers. Thus, whenever one job is completed, another is ready to go on the bottleneck machine. Further, in order to protect the final assembly schedule against shortages that could severely cut output, a safety stock of nonbottleneck operation completed parts is held before final assembly. The idea is to not disrupt the flow of material from a bottleneck operation. Parts shortages that can be made up by going through nonbottleneck operations won't cut capacity.

Other management considerations also enter the TOC scheduling system to reduce the effect of uncertainty. These include making realistic schedules that meet material and capacity limitations. Considerations involving the appropriate level of work-in-process inventory, the capacity utilization attainable, degree of schedule protection, and batch size controls can all be applied to the TOC procedure. These help take into account the company culture as the TOC procedure is implemented.

TOC and Lot Sizing

TOC calculates different batch sizes throughout the plant, depending on whether a work center is a bottleneck. This has several MPC implications. In typical finite scheduling procedures, the batch size is fixed. Such isn't the case with TOC. It also follows that a batch size for one operation on a part could be different than for other operations on the same part. This implies special treatment will be required for any paperwork that travels with shop orders. In fact, TOC is designed to do order splitting at nonbottleneck resources. In usual practice, order splitting is done on backlogged (bottleneck) machines; in this situation TOC would do the opposite in order to reduce setup time and maximize output at the bottleneck resources.

The key to lot sizing in TOC is distinguishing between a *transfer* batch (that quantity that moves from operation to operation) and a *process* batch (the total lot size released to the shop). Any differences are held as work-in-process inventories in the shop. In essence, no operation can start until at least a transfer batch is built up behind it.

The transfer batches are predetermined integral fractions of the original order quantity (process batch). They provide a work center with the flexibility to start producing an order before it is completed at the previous work center. Such flexibility, frequently referred to as *lot splitting* and *overlap* or *line scheduling,* reduces order flow times and smooths work flow in the shop to yield better use of capacity. This flexibility also means the number of

FIGURE 11.8 TOC Example

Product	Customer Order Number	Order Quantity	Raw Material Specification Number	Processing Time (in Hours)				Requested Customer Shipping	
				First Machining, Operation 1	Heat Treating, Operation 2	Testing, Operation 3	Final Machining, Operation 4	Date	Hour
A	1XXX	100	124	3	6	1	4	Day 5	32
B	2XXX	10	101	2	4	1	2	Day 6	40
C	3XXX	50	88	4	6	1	4	Day 6	40

Notes: 1. Shop operates 8 hours each day.
2. All orders require 2 hours in shipping department.
3. All raw material is stocked and available.
4. An 8-hour buffer is maintained at the final machining work center.

units produced during a given work center setup, the *operation batch size,* can vary between a transfer batch and the original order quantity.

This lot-sizing concept can be applied by using any standard priority scheduling method (e.g., shortest processing time, critical ratio). When an order is completed under traditional priority scheduling rules, the highest-priority order in the queue is selected for processing next. Under this lot-sizing concept, a work center may contain transfer batches coming from many released orders. In this case, the queue is searched for transfer batches of the same part order that has just been completed at the work center in order to save setup time at a bottleneck resource. If such an item is available, it is processed next, regardless of priority; otherwise, the highest-priority transfer batch in the queue is selected and a new setup is made at the work center. If the queue is empty, the next batch to arrive at the work center is processed.

Managing the TOC Schedule

Managing the TOC schedule on a daily basis involves five basic steps that are illustrated by the example products shown in Figure 11.8. In this example, each product requires processing on four work centers: first machining, heat treating, testing, and final machining. The processing time (setup and run time) for each operation is shown in Figure 11.8. The first three operations are performed in a fabrication cell. Capacity is sufficient in this cell, so these are nonbottleneck operations. The fourth operation, final machining, is a bottleneck operation. Other data such as the customer order number, order quantity, and requested customer delivery date are included in Figure 11.8.

Scheduling the Drum

The first step is scheduling new orders on the bottleneck operations, referred to as the *drums.* This is accomplished by using the following logic:

- Calculate the earliest start time on the first constraint by adding the processing time before the constraint to the raw material lead time and the first constraint buffer time.
- Place the order after and as close as possible to the earliest start time on the constraint.
- Calculate the earliest start time on the next constraint (or the shipping date) by adding the processing time after the first constraint and the next buffer time to the completion time on the current constraint.

Product A in Figure 11.8 illustrates this logic. Note that in Figure 11.8 the processing time for the three operations before the first constraint (final machining) is 10 hours, the raw material lead time is zero (since this material is stocked), and the buffer time for the first constraint (final machining) is 8 hours. As a result, the earliest start time on the first constraint is in 18 hours, or at the end of hour 2 in day 3 (assuming the plant works one eight hour shift each day). Figure 11.9 shows a workload profile of the drum (the final machining work center), indicating that the last 4 hours of day 3 have not yet been scheduled. Therefore, the order for Product A is scheduled to start at the end of hour 4 and complete at the end of hour 8 on day 3.

Figure 11.10 shows a flow diagram of the process and indicates the key dates that are set by using the TOC scheduling logic. These include: the date/time that the order is scheduled to enter the final machining buffer, the date that the final machining operation starts, the date that the order is to enter the shipping buffer, and the customer delivery date. Figure 11.11 shows these dates/times for Product A. The raw material release for Product A is planned for the end of hour 2 on day 1, and this product is scheduled to enter the final machining buffer at the end of hour 12 (day 2, hour 4). This job is therefore expected to wait

FIGURE 11.9
Final Machining Work Load Profile

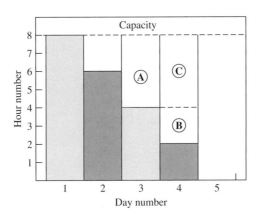

FIGURE 11.10
TOC Example: Plant Scheduling— Bottleneck Work Centers

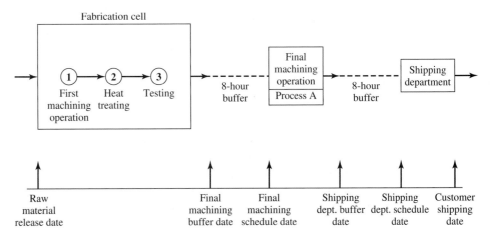

FIGURE 11.11 TOC Example—Plant Schedule

Product	Customer Order Number	Order Quantity	Raw Material Release	First Machining	Heat Treat	Test	Final Machining Buffer	Final Machining	Shipping Buffer	Shipping Department	Promised Scheduled Shipping Date	
											Hour	Day
A	1XXX	100	2	2	5	11	12	20	24	32	34	Day 5 Hour 2
B	2XXX	10	11	11	13	17	18	26	28	36	38	Day 5 Hour 6
C	3XXX	50	9	9	13	19	20	28	32	40	42	Day 6 Hour 2

Notes: 1. All times represent scheduled start times as of the end of the hour indicated.
   2. First machining, heat treat, and test are nonbottleneck work centers and are not finite capacity scheduled.
   3. Final machining and shipping are bottleneck work centers and are, therefore, finite capacity scheduled.

8 hours before processing at the bottleneck machining process. This ensures that errors in processing time estimates do not affect the 100 percent utilization of the bottleneck. Likewise, this order is scheduled to enter the shipping buffer at the end of hour 24 (day 3, hour 8) with shipment scheduled for the end of hour 34 (day 5, hour 2).

Orders are scheduled by using finite backward scheduling. This logic proceeds as follows:

- Subtract the shipping buffer and the processing time after the final constraint from the scheduled ship date. This provides the latest completion time.
- Place the order on the final constraint (drum) before and as close as possible to the latest completion time.
- Determine the start time on the final constraint by subtracting the processing time on the constraint from the completion time.
- Subtract the final constraint buffer time and the processing time back to the latest completion time of the previous constraint (or the raw material release time) from the final constraint start time.
- Once the material release is determined, the delivery schedule for the raw material can be determined.

Product C in Figure 11.8 illustrates this scheduling logic. The customer-requested shipping date for this order is the end of hour 8 on day 5 (or hour 40 in the example). Since no processing occurs on this order after the drum (final machining), the latest completion time can be determined by subtracting the shipping department time of 2 hours plus the shipping buffer of 8 hours from the scheduled shipping date of hour 40. This means that the latest completion time for the final machining operation is the end of hour 30, and that the order should enter the shipping buffer at that time. Since the drum is currently scheduled for the first four hours on day 4, product C can be scheduled from the end of hour 4 through 8 on day 4 (hours 28 through 32). The latest raw material release date can be determined for product C by subtracting both the processing time prior to the drum and the drum buffer time from the drum start time. In this case 11 hours of processing time and a drum buffer time of 8 hours is subtracted from the drum start time of the end of hour 28 to yield a raw material release time of the end of hour 9. The schedule for product C is also shown in Figure 11.11.

Exploiting the Drums

In scheduling the drums, product demand may exceed the available capacity at the drums. In this case it may be necessary to take steps to augment the capacity of the drum. This may involve offloading some of the orders scheduled on the drum to other machines that are nondrums, or outsourcing this work to suppliers. Other options would include working the drums through lunches and breaks, adding overtime, and increasing the batch sizes at the drum to minimize setup time. Batch sizes should, however, not be increased if this would result in delaying the scheduled shipment dates for customer orders. This is a good example of how lot splitting might be usefully employed. By dividing the batch into that which services customers and that which goes into inventory, the overall constraint utilization (selling the throughput) is maximized.

Material Release—Rope

In managing plant operations, raw material should not be released earlier than the scheduled TOC raw material release date. Releasing the raw material on these dates will minimize the WIP inventory and reduce the choice of orders to be run on the nonbottleneck operations.

Proactive Management of Buffers

Buffers are put in place for unforseen variations in production at the nonconstraint work centers. While the entire buffer time is scheduled for every order, it is not expected that every order will arrive at the drum on time. Therefore, the key to a successful implementation of TOC is the proactive management of the buffers. In many plants the management of the buffers is the responsibility of a shop-floor scheduling person designated as the *buffer coordinator.*

One way of accomplishing this is to divide the buffers in thirds. The first third is the **red zone.** The red zone includes the orders that are scheduled next on the constraint. The middle third is the **yellow zone,** and the final third is the **green zone,** which includes the orders that are the furthest out in the drum schedule.

The red zone should rarely have missing orders. Orders that are missing from the red zone represent an immediate danger to the drum schedule. If an order is missing from the red zone, the buffer coordinator should be working nonstop on getting this order to the machine. Management should be aware of the situation and actively working to assist the buffer coordinator to resolve the problem. If the red zone is always full, consideration should be given to reducing the buffer size. The larger the buffer size, the more money invested in WIP inventory. Therefore, buffers should be only large enough to ensure delivery performance to the drums.

The yellow zone will occasionally have missing orders. The buffer coordinator should be actively working to get these orders to the buffer as quickly as possible. Likewise, the green zone will regularly have orders missing. The buffer coordinator should know where these orders are, and verify that they should arrive at the buffer shortly.

Elevating the Drum

This is really a planning step. Once the shop floor is running smoothly, consideration should be given in the planning process to increasing the capacity at the drum. If the capacity is increased at the constraint, it is possible for the organization to grow the business.

TOC and the MPC Framework

Returning to Figure 11.1, we see that TOC can't uniquely be put in the front end, the engine, or the back end. It works in all three areas and does some things quite differently than when scheduling is done by other approaches. However, TOC uses most of the same data as other MPC applications. We still need a front end, engine, and back end (both shop-floor and vendor systems). For the firm with an operating MPC system, the basic database and closed-loop understanding exist. Implementing TOC as an enhancement seems to be a logical extension. TOC is another example of separating the vital few from the trivial many, and thereafter providing a mechanism to exploit this knowledge for better manufacturing planning/control. It allows a firm to simultaneously plan materials and capacities and to integrate important concepts from finite scheduling into the MPC system.

It's been argued TOC doesn't have the same needs for data accuracy that MRP scheduling has. This is partially correct, if you feel less accuracy is required for nonbottleneck parts and work centers. But going into the process of using TOC, you may not realize very well what these bottleneck operations are. Both TOC and MRP require detailed knowledge of product structures and processes. Databases, accurate transaction processing, and the right managerial commitment are required for both as well.

TOC Contributions

Now we can identify clearly one of TOC's primary contributions. When finite scheduling through bottleneck resources is complete, the result is a doable master production schedule. For this reason, TOC is sometimes considered to be a "front-end" system (i.e., a master production scheduling technique). We see it less as an MPS technique than an enhancement to the MPS. TOC conceivably can take any MPS as input and determine the extent to which it is doable.

This means TOC makes an explicit computer-based analysis of the feedback from engine (and back end) to the front end—an important enhancement to MRP systems. It means a valid MPS is generated—one the firm has a strong chance of achieving—that is based on the capacity parameters used in the scheduling.

A secondary contribution at this stage comes from the way TOC schedules the nonbottleneck resources. The easiest way to see this is to assume (as is often the case in practice) there are no bottlenecks. In that case, TOC schedules are based on MRP logic. The difference is that TOC in this case will change batch sizes (reducing them) to the point where some resources almost become bottlenecks. The result is less WIP, reduced lead time, greater material velocity, and a move toward "zero inventory" manufacturing. TOC does much of this by overlapping schedules, using unequal batch sizes for transferring and processing.

TOC's third important contribution is to virtually eliminate the fundamental issue of conflicting priorities between MRP and finite scheduling. With finite scheduling of only a small fraction of the work centers priority conflict issues should largely disappear. Moreover, computational time required to do finite scheduling should be dramatically cut by dealing only with a subset of orders and work centers/resources.

In operation as a shop-floor control technique, TOC has a few other differences from usual practice. A fundamental tenet in TOC is that an hour lost in a bottleneck resource is an hour lost to the entire factory's output, while an hour lost in a nonbottleneck resource has no real cost. This means capacity utilization of bottleneck resources is important. TOC increases utilization by using WIP buffers in front of bottlenecks, and where output from a bottleneck joins with some other parts. TOC also runs large batch sizes at bottleneck operations, thereby reducing relative time spent in setup downtime.

In practice, the variable lot size issue has two major implications. First, lead times should be shorter: smaller batches will move faster through nonbottleneck work centers. Second (and less felicitous), procedures have to be developed to split/join batches as they go through production.

Implementation Issues

A major paradigm shift is required in order to obtain the benefits of TOC scheduling. Management needs to recognize that the plant culture needs to change from one of keeping people busy and equipment fully loaded to one of maximizing throughput at the critical resources—the bottleneck. This means that under TOC, as with JIT, it's quite all right to not work if there's no work to do at nonbottleneck resources. In fact, working (by the usual definition) in this situation will cause problems. If people at the nonbottleneck work on orders that are not needed to maximize flow through the bottleneck work centers, the net result of their work will be to simply increase WIP and cause confusion for scheduling at other work centers. Understanding the basic concepts is critical in obtaining the benefits of TOC scheduling.

TOC presents further difficulties in implementation. Companies also need sound basic systems, education, top-management support, and a willingness to unlearn some ingrained habits. One firm we know of has been working for several years to implement finite scheduling, without great success, because it has strong pressures to fully utilize all direct labor-hours. In this case, the fundamental principles of TOC have not been accepted.

Vendor Scheduling and Follow-up

The **vendor-scheduling** and **follow-up** aspects of PAC are the direct analog of the shop-floor scheduling and control systems. There are some important differences, however. From the vendor's perspective, each customer is usually only one of a number of demand sources. Customer demands are managed in the vendor's plant with its MPC system. The MPC relationship is largely through information exchanged between vendor and customer, often from the back-end activities of the customer directly to the vendor's MPC system.

From the customer's standpoint, the objectives of vendor scheduling are the same as those for internal work center scheduling: keep the orders lined up with the correct due dates from the material plan. This means the vendor must have a continually updated set of relative priority data. A typical approach to providing this information is a weekly updated report reflecting the current set of circumstances in the customer's plant and, sometimes, the final customer requirements that dictate them. Increasingly, computer-to-computer communication is used to transmit this information.

Since the vendor follow-up system is often concerned with changes to the schedule and keeping priorities correct, there must be limits to the amount of change the vendor will be asked to accommodate. Contractual agreements with the vendor typically define the types and degree of changes that can be made, time frames for making changes, additional elements of flexibility required, and so on. In addition, the agreement specifies procedures for transmitting needs to the vendor plus the units in which the vendor's capacity is planned and controlled. This sets the stage for vendor PAC including order release, scheduling, and follow-up.

The Internet and Vendor Scheduling

The Internet provides several ways in which manufacturing companies and their vendors can share information for the purpose of improving the timing and reliability of supplier deliveries. For manufacturing companies the use of information technology can provide improvements such as quicker delivery response to customers, improved delivery reliability, and reductions in operating costs involving both purchasing staff costs and inventory. These improvements have also had an important effect on the national economy. Rapid response times are a result of technological advances. Increased use of real-time information, such as computerized order tracking, enables business to know when demand is shifting and to instantly change output schedules, workshifts, inventory levels, and capital spending plans. Like increased productivity and greater labor flexibility, quick reflexes became a key characteristic of the U.S. economy.

Websites and E-Mail

Increasingly, companies are creating websites to provide a routine way of communicating with vendors. These websites include forward planning information such as listings of open purchase orders (scheduled receipts from MRP), planned future purchase orders from MRP records, and vendor requirements stated in terms of capacity, as well as information on accounts payable status for completed vendor shipments and vendor report cards indicating on-time delivery, shipment quantity shortfalls, and quality performance. Websites are also important sources of historical information on item usage that is helpful to vendors in improving their sales forecasting methods. Furthermore, companies are increasingly sharing engineering information with their vendors through their websites. Websites now contain product management data that includes product specifications and part drawings. Sharing such information electronically enables vendors to access up-to-date information that contains the latest engineering designs and change notices. Sharing this type of information reduces costs on the part of both manufacturers and their vendors, since both are working with the same latest information on product designs.

Another important area of electronic information sharing between manufacturers and their vendors involves the routine use of e-mail to communicate schedule changes, new orders, and order revisions/cancellations. The use of e-mail eliminates much of the more expensive communication with vendors, involving phone calls, letters, and fax documents. E-mail reduces the time and effort of buyers and planner-schedulers in purchasing and customer service coordinators at vendors, thereby improving productivity in both companies. Further, e-mail updates on schedule changes in open orders enables both parties to know the current status and availability of specific items. Accurate order status information enables manufacturers to better plan their operations, and leads to improved delivery reliability on customer orders.

Implementation Issues

While the use of e-mail is gaining widespread usage in improving customer/vendor communications, the use of websites appears to be more limited under certain operating conditions. First, companies that are able to make real progress with vendors in developing JIT supply programs have little need to communicate open orders to vendors on websites. The JIT delivery of goods eliminates the need to develop future plans and schedules for vendor items using MRP. The JIT delivery of vendor items is less expensive, involves shorter lead times, and provides less exposure to a purchasing commitment on the part of the manufacturer. However, other website items such as historical data on item usage and vendor report cards may still have value.

A second reason that limits the use of websites to communicate future plans and orders to vendors involves the stability of the manufacturer's MPS. Companies that face major changes in the MPS on a routine basis can pass a high degree of schedule uncertainty to the vendors through the communication of open orders and future planned orders on their websites. This can create considerable confusion at the vendors. Further, companies with poor inventory accuracy can also pass highly uncertain schedules to their suppliers. Therefore, vendors need to assess the quality and the value of the information provided by the customer websites in planning and scheduling their operations. Simply making effective use of the historical data provided on a customer's website to improve the supplier's sales forecasting methods may yield better plans.

Finally, in some cases issues of confidentially and information security can be reasons for not sharing planning and scheduling information with suppliers on websites. Clearly, some of these concerns can be reduced through careful attention to system security, and avoiding the sharing of sensitive information about costs and prices. In many companies production order quantities and production volumes are considered less sensitive information.

Some of the limitations of using websites to communicate open and planned order information to vendors have to do with economic conditions. During times of economic downturn and recession, companies typically do not have full order books and often take orders in less than normal lead time in order to maintain operations. Under these conditions the MPS can be very unstable, producing less valuable planning information for the vendors. However, when economic conditions improve, and economic expansion is underway, company order backlogs increase and lead times often lengthen. In these conditions, when the production and supplier lead times are long, and the MPS is stable, open and future planned order information on the websites can often provide more stable information to suppliers.

Production Activity Control Examples

This section applies production activity control techniques in three quite different examples. The first example covers Tosoh SMD, Inc. This company has implemented a TOC finite loading system for shop-floor control. Special alloy products for the computer industry are processed in manufacturing cells that include machining, heat treating, and testing operations. The company produces products on a make-to-order basis for companies that often face highly cyclical demand. As a result, resulting capacity requirements vary widely at individual work centers. The firm employs a technically based, highly paid workforce that is not easily expanded or contracted.

The second example is vendor scheduling at Liebert. Here MRP-based planning is extended into vendor follow-up with excellent results. Finally, PAC procurement practice using electronic data interchange (EDI) is examined at the Caterpillar Tractor Company.

TOC Scheduling at TOSOH

TOSOH is a manufacturer of special alloy materials for computer manufacturing firms. The products are custom designed to meet the specifications of the customer's production process and product design. The product unit selling price ranges from $500 to $6,000. The annual sales are $100 million, with 80 percent of the sales volume going to 10 customers.

Products are manufactured on a make-to-order basis with approximately 500 open shop orders at any given time. Each product passes through 10 to 20 operations, and there are four focused factory operations within the main plant, each of which has about 10 work centers. Each product is manufactured from a special metal alloy, and the master database contains approximately 1,500 end-product items. The bill of material has two levels: product items and raw materials.

Before installing the TOC system, the plant used a manual scheduling system that was based on very rough estimates of process setup and run times. While bills of material and product routings existed, these were poorly maintained. There was no clear measure of plant capacity nor an ability to forecast the upcoming capacity constraints.

The company chose to implement TOC to achieve several business objectives. The foremost objective was to deliver product faster and more reliably in a market characterized by life cycles approximating 6 to 12 months a relatively short time. The company also wanted to maximize the throughput of the factory and to achieve a better utilization of the expensive machine tools and heat-treatment facilities. The company felt that the TOC system would enable manufacturing to minimize batch sizes, reducing cycle time and WIP inventory while improving responsiveness to customers. Finally, because of the short product life cycle, and the costs of product obsolescence, the company wanted to reduce the investment in finished goods inventory.

The TOC project began with a one-year manual pilot implementation of the TOC system. Subsequently, the TOC software was purchased, the manufacturing database was developed, and the software was tested. An example of the TOC schedules at TOSOH, using product item 3596C-13-108-501 is illustrated. This item is being manufactured for shop order RWO502, which has a due date of 10/16/XX. The process routing for this item is shown in Figure 11.12. Note that *only* operation 500 on this order is performed on a drum work center.

Portions of the schedule at all of the work centers in the example are shown in Figure 11.13a. Figure 11.13a shows the schedule for shop order RW0502 for the five work centers preceding the drum (work center 101-5M). The material release date of 9/19/XX in Figure 11.13a is back-scheduled from the drum schedule, and all of the operations in between (operations 100 through 400) are run on a first-in, first-out basis, using process and delay time data. A portion of the drum schedule for work center 101-5M is shown in Figure 11.13b. Shop order RWO502 is scheduled to start at 10:20 A.M. on 10/11/XX and to be completed 2 hours and 15 minutes later. (The setup time of 45 minutes and the run time of

FIGURE 11.12
Process
Routing,
Product Item
3596C-13-
108-501

Operation Number	Work Center	Work Center Status
100	101-KS	Nonconstraint
200	101-WP	Nonconstraint
300	101-5C	Nonconstraint
400	101-80	Nonconstraint
500	101-5M	Constraint
600	101-CM	Nonconstraint
700	255-XRF	Nonconstraint
800	260	Nonconstraint
900	231	Nonconstraint
1000	Stores	Nonconstraint

1 hour and 30 minutes is shown in the upper portion of Figure 11.13b.) Likewise, all of the nonconstraint operations following the drum (600 through 1000) are expected to be complete by the order due date (10/16/XX), using first-in, first-out scheduling priorities. The TOC schedule for this product allows a buffer of 56 hours for the drum (operation 500), and a buffer of 72 hours for the shipping dock buffer. These are shown in the "buffer plan" columns of Figures 11.13a and b.

The company learned several lessons during implementation. First, the culture needed to change in order to achieve the benefits of TOC scheduling. The importance of educating all of the manufacturing personnel on the basic concepts of TOC scheduling became clear. Other changes included the elimination of traditional cost accounting performance measures relating to productivity, efficiency, product cost, etc. Manufacturing people needed to understand that it is all right for the nondrum work centers to be idle. Further, this training needed to be performed on a company wide basis for the system to be totally effective.

Second, in using TOC the company needed to emphasize the elimination of obstacles to the flow of materials through the plant. In addition to the physical constraints, these obstacles included such items as paperwork, procedural roadblocks, and work rules. This effort involved ensuring raw material availability, instilling a sense of urgency in people regarding the TOC schedule, achieving a high level of process reliability, and reducing waste in time and materials. Both TOC scheduling and the focus on process improvement at TOSOH have produced important achievements in operating performance. This includes a sales revenue increase of 14 percent, a 38 percent improvement in delivery reliability, a 14 percent reduction in customer lead times, a doubling of the overall inventory turns, and a 50 percent reduction in the reserve for obsolete inventory. These results were achieved over a four-year period.

Vendor Scheduling at Liebert

Liebert is the world's leading supplier of computer support systems and the largest supplier of precision air-conditioning and power-protection systems worldwide. At Liebert the procurement group is responsible for strategic sourcing efforts, while the materials control

FIGURE 11.13a Plant Schedule

Analyst ID: JB

Release on: 9/19/XX

Part ID	Work Order ID	Qty	Work Center ID	Order ID	Line No.	Order Due Date Target	Order Due Date Projected	Product ID	Customer ID	Buffer Planned	Buffer Remaining
3596C-13-108-501	RWO502	1.00	101-KS	C10402	18	10/16/XX	10/16/XX	3596C-13-108-501	7138568-4	56	103
4028H-13-108-501	RWO500	10.00	101-KS	01090062	2	10/8/XX	10/8/XX	4028H-13-108-501	7011585-1	56	114

Part ID	Job Step	Qty	Work Order ID	Setup Time	Run Time	Start Date	Buffer Plan	Buffer Remain	Order ID	Target Date	Proj. Date	Product ID
Priority list for work center 101-KS—KASTO SAWS (2)				*Calendar: Default*								
3596C-13-108-501	100.00	1.00	RWO502	00:15	00:01	09/19/XX	56	103	C10402	10/16/XX	10/16/XX	3596C-13-108-501
Priority list for work center 101-WP—WISCONSIN COLD				*Calendar: Default*								
3596C-13-108-501	200.00	1.00	RWO502	00:30	12:00	09/19/XX	56	103	C10402	10/16/XX	10/16/XX	3596C-13-108-501
Priority list for work center 101-SC—MAZAK II & III PLANAR				*Calendar: 10 hour*								
3596C-13-108-501	300.00	1.00	RWO502	00:30	00:45	09/19/XX	56	108	C10402	10/16/XX	10/16/XX	3596C-13-108-501
Priority list for work center 101-80—OUTSIDE WELD				*Calendar: Default*								
3596C-13-108-501	400.00	1.00	RWO502	01:00	168:0	09/19/XX	56	116	C10402	10/16/XX	10/16/XX	3596C-13-108-501
3596C-13-108-501	400.00	1.00	RWO508	01:00	168:0	10/03/XX	56	221	C10402	10/30/XX	10/30/XX	3596C-13-108-501
3596C-13-108-501	400.00	1.00	RWO519	01:00	168:0	10/17/XX	56	431	C10402	11/13/XX	11/13/XX	3596C-13-108-501
3596C-13-108-501	400.00	1.00	RWO527	01:00	168:0	10/31/XX	56	536	C10402	11/27/XX	11/27/XX	3596C-13-108-501

FIGURE 11.13b Drum Schedule: Grouped By Unit

| Work Center: 101-5M : AMAT CELL | | | | | | | | Unit: 1 | | | | Calendar: 14 Hour | |

Part ID	Job Step	Qty	Qty Finished	Work Order	Setup	Duration	Start Time	Actual Start	Order ID	Target Data	Proj. Data	Product ID	Customer ID
Start date: 10/11/XX													
3596C-13-108-501	500.00	1.00	0.00	RW0502	00:45	01:30	10:20		C10402	10/16/XX	10/16/XX	3596C-13-108-501	7138568-4
Start date: 10/18/XX													
3596C-13-108-501	500.00	1.00	0.00	RW0508	00:45	01:30	10:20		C10402	10/30/XX	10/30/XX	3596C-13-108-501	7138568-4
Start date: 11/08/XX													
3596C-13-108-501	500.00	1.00	0.00	RW0519	00:45	01:30	10:20		C10402	11/13/XX	11/13/XX	3596C-13-108-501	7138568-4
Start date: 11/15/XX													
3596C-13-108-501	500.00	1.00	0.00	RW0527	00:45	01:30	10:20		C10402	11/27/XX	11/27/XX	3596C-13-108-501	7138568-4

Part ID	Job Step	Qty	Work Order ID	Setup Time	Run Time	Start Date	Buffer Plan	Buffer Remain	Order ID	Target Date	Proj. Date	Product ID
Priority list for work center 101-CM—CMM (2)												
Calendar: Default												
3596C-13-108-501	600.00	1.00	RW0502	00:00	00:00	10/11/XX	72	357	C10402	10/16/XX	10/16/XX	3596C-13-108-501
3596C-13-108-501	600.00	1.00	RW01139	00:00	00:00	10/18/XX	72	462	C10402	10/30/XX	10/30/XX	3596C-13-108-501
3596C-13-108-501	600.00	1.00	RW01375	00:00	00:00	11/08/XX	72	672	C10402	11/13/XX	11/13/XX	3596C-13-108-501
Priority list for work center 255—XRF												
Calendar: Default												
3596C-13-108-501	700.00	1.00	RW0502	00:00	00:00	10/11/XX	72	357	C10402	10/16/XX	10/16/XX	3596C-13-108-501
3596C-13-108-501	700.00	1.00	RW01139	00:00	00:00	10/18/XX	72	462	C10402	10/30/XX	10/30/XX	3596C-13-108-501
3596C-13-108-501	700.00	1.00	RW01375	00:00	00:00	11/08/XX	72	672	C10402	11/13/XX	11/13/XX	3596C-13-108-501
Priority list for work center 260—CLEAN/PACK/SHIP C/P												
Calendar: Default												
3596C-13-108-501	800.00	1.00	RW0502	00:00	00:00	10/11/XX	72	357	C10402	10/16/XX	10/16/XX	3596C-13-108-501
3596C-13-108-501	800.00	1.00	RW01139	00:00	00:00	10/18/XX	72	462	C10402	10/30/XX	10/30/XX	3596C-13-108-501
3596C-13-108-501	800.00	1.00	RW01375	00:00	00:00	11/08/XX	72	672	C10402	11/13/XX	11/13/XX	3596C-13-108-501
Priority list for work center 231—INSP MEDIA/PM												
Calendar: Default												
3596C-13-108-501	900.00	1.00	RW0502	00:10	00:03	10/11/XX	72	357	C10402	10/16/XX	10/16/XX	3596C-13-108-501
3596C-13-108-501	900.00	1.00	RW01139	00:10	00:03	10/18/XX	72	462	C10402	10/30/XX	10/30/XX	3596C-13-108-501
3596C-13-108-501	900.00	1.00	RW01375	00:10	00:03	11/08/XX	72	672	C10402	11/13/XX	11/13/XX	3596C-13-108-501
Priority list for work center STORES—KITTED												
Calendar: Default												
3596C-13-108-501	1,000.00	1.00	RW0502	00:00	00:00	10/11/XX	72	357	C10402	10/16/XX	10/16/XX	3596C-13-108-501
37000-13-950-100	300.00	1.00	130313	00:00	00:00	10/17/XX	56	418	C10402	11/13/XX	11/13/XX	3596C-13-108-501
3596C-13-108-501	1,000.00	1.00	RW01139	00:00	00:00	10/18/XX	72	462	C10402	10/30/XX	10/30/XX	3596C-13-108-501
37000-13-950-100	200.00	1.00	RW01411	00:00	00:00	10/31/XX	56	523	C10402	11/27/XX	11/27/XX	3596C-13-108-501
3596C-13-108-501	1,000.00	1.00	RW01375	00:00	00:00	11/08/XX	72	672	C10402	11/13/XX	11/13/XX	3596C-13-108-501

group manages the operational functions that include order release and vendor scheduling functions for suppliers. Although Liebert uses MRP II to plan and schedule end product, component, and purchased items, it continues to currently introduce JIT into both its manufacturing and vendor operations.

Liebert utilizes an e-procurement system that issues purchase orders to suppliers and provides each supplier with access to computer files that contain a listing of all open purchase orders, forecast information, and usage history data on the items supplied by the individual vendor. Figure 11.14 shows a sample open purchase order report that can be accessed on the Internet by a supplier. Each vendor can obtain a listing of all of the open purchase orders that have been placed with that company by Liebert. This information includes the due date, the ship-to location, and status update notes that can be routinely accessed by both Liebert and supplier personnel.

As shown in Figure 11.15, suppliers can also download to a spreadsheet forecast information for each of the items that are supplied by the company to Liebert. This information contains actual released orders (scheduled receipts) over the item's vendor lead time, and forecast (planned orders) information up to one year beyond the vendor's lead time. In addition, a supplier can also download historical usage information on the items supplied to Liebert by the vendor. This is shown in Figure 11.16. The "Netable" column in this figure indicates the on-hand inventory for the individual items at Liebert, and the "Wgt Mth Use" column indicates the average historical usage for each item. Further, Liebert's suppliers can download a supplier performance report indicating their performance over the past year. An example of this report is shown in Figure 11.17. It includes quality, cost, and delivery metrics.

Currently, about 50 percent of Liebert's suppliers are linked to the e-procurement system. Because of the important overhead savings involved in Liebert's procurement and material control groups, the company is planning to extend this system to all of its vendors. In addition, Liebert has incorporated accounts payable status information into this system to provide easy access to the payment status of supplier invoices.

Liebert is also expanding its efforts with suppliers to implement JIT deliveries of low-value items such as hardware. Since a kanban signal will be used to initiate the replenishment of a JIT vendor item, issuing and tracking of individual purchase orders in the e-procurement system (Figure 11.14) will no longer be required. On delivery, a manual transaction will initiate an invoice payment request. However, the forecast and historical sales information shown in Figures 11.15 and 11.16 will continue to be available to suppliers on the e-procurement system.

Vendor Scheduling at Caterpillar

As the number of purchased components increases, many firms routinely use electronic data interchange (EDI) to communicate with their suppliers on a routine basis. Caterpillar Tractor Company illustrates use of EDI in PAC. Nearly 400 of the firm's domestic and offshore supplier locations are connected by EDI using standards developed by the Automotive Industry Action Group (AIAG). Each supplier is assigned an electronic mailbox on the network. Suppliers retrieve information from their mailboxes and can forward information though the mailboxes to Caterpillar. By adopting AIAG, the "mail" is read in a language common to computers of Caterpillar and its vendors.

FIGURE 11.14 Review and Reschedule Purchase Orders

Liebert® KEEPING BUSINESS IN BUSINESS®

eProcurement Home | Phone Book | Liebert Facilities | Procurement News | View/Download Documents | Part Look-up
Choose Supplier # | Open Purchase Orders | Historical Usage | Forecasted Usage | Your Preferences | Feedback | Log Off

SUPPLIER SELECTED:

submit   preview changes

☐ check this box to include yourself on the 'SUBMIT' audit e-mailing (for your records)

Row	Pls Cnfrm	PO Number	Line/Sch	Liebert Part #/ Supplier Part #	Ord Qty	Bal Due	Ship To:	Request Date			Due on Liebert Dock Date	Evaluation Date	Status note	Contact e-mail Phone
1	☐	P00694893 view	001/Y1		1	1	Q	10	16	Y1	10/16/Y1	10/16/Y1		E-mail
2	☐	P23606412 view	003/Y1		1	1	K	10	20	Y1	10/20/Y1	10/20/Y1		E-mail
3	☐	P23606519 view	001/Y1		1	1	K	10	29	Y1	10/29/Y1	10/29/Y1		E-mail
4	☐	P23606587 view	001/Y1		1	1	K	10	29	Y1	10/29/Y1	10/29/Y1		E-mail
5	☐	P00694886 view	001/Y1		1	1	Q	11	05	Y1	11/05/Y1	11/05/Y1		E-mail
6	☐	P23606622 view	001/Y1		2	2	K	11	05	Y1	11/05/Y1	11/05/Y1		E-mail
7	☐	P00694895 view	001/Y1		2	2	Q	11	06	Y1	11/06/Y1	11/06/Y1		E-mail
8	☐	P00694899 view	001/Y1		1	1	Q	11	26	Y1	11/26/Y1	11/26/Y1		E-mail
9	☐	P23606416 view	001/Y1		2	2	K	01	07	Y2	01/07/Y2	01/07/Y2		E-mail

FIGURE 11.15 Forecasted Inventory Usage as of 10/28/Y1

Liebert KEEPING BUSINESS IN BUSINESS

SUPPLIER SELECTED:

Download Forecast Data

Plant	Liebert Part. / Vendor Part.	Net-able	Non-Net-able	Type	Past Due	10/28	11/04	11/11	11/18	11/25	12/02	12/09	12/16	12/23	12/30	01/06	01/13	01/20 02/16	02/17 03/16	03/17 04/13	04/14 05/11	05/12 06/08	06/09 07/06	07/07 08/03	08/04 08/31	09/01 09/28	09/29 10/26
001		2304	0	Frcast	0	0	0	0	0	0	0	0	0	0	0	0	0	432	720	1152	864	720	864	864	720	864	0
				Orders	0	0	0	0	0	0	0	0	0	0	0	0	0	0	0	0	0	0	0	0	0	0	0
001		563	0	Frcast	0	0	0	0	0	144	288	0	288	0	0	144	0	432	288	720	288	432	432	432	288	432	0
				Orders	0	0	0	200	200	70	200	200	210	0	0	144	0	0	0	0	0	0	0	0	0	0	0
001		225	330	Frcast	0	0	0	0	0	144	0	0	288	0	0	0	0	342	156	226	156	160	160	156	156	148	0
				Orders	0	40	0	0	0	0	0	0	0	0	0	0	0	0	0	0	0	0	0	0	0	0	0
001		57	64	Frcast	0	40	0	0	0	0	27	35	70	0	70	0	35	141	140	210	140	140	140	140	140	140	0
				Orders	47	0	35	0	0	25	0	0	0	0	0	0	35	0	0	0	0	0	0	0	0	0	0
001		60	3	Frcast	0	0	0	0	0	0	60	500	0	0	0	0	0	407	420	660	352	0	656	0	352	320	0
				Orders	0	0	115	240	0	0	0	0	0	0	0	0	0	0	0	0	0	0	0	0	0	0	0
001		585	0	Frcast	0	0	0	0	0	0	60	0	0	0	0	0	0	0	0	0	0	20	65	72	0	90	0
				Orders	0	0	0	0	0	0	0	0	0	0	0	0	0	0	0	0	0	0	0	0	0	0	0
012		328	4	Frcast	0	0	0	0	300	300	0	0	400	0	0	300	100	700	700	800	900	500	800	500	500	700	600
				Orders	0	0	0	0	0	0	0	0	0	0	0	0	0	0	0	0	0	0	0	0	0	0	0
012		156	0	Frcast	0	0	0	0	100	0	100	0	0	100	0	200	100	200	200	200	300	200	300	300	200	300	200
				Orders	0	0	0	0	0	0	0	0	0	0	0	0	0	0	0	0	0	0	0	0	0	0	0
001		159	0	Frcast	0	0	0	0	0	0	0	0	0	12	12	0	12	56	102	114	180	144	114	120	144	0	0
				Orders	0	0	0	200	0	0	0	0	0	0	0	0	0	0	0	0	0	0	0	0	0	0	0
001		0	0	Frcast	0	0	0	0	0	0	0	0	0	0	0	0	0	0	0	0	0	0	0	0	0	0	0
				Orders	0	0	0	110	110	0	0	0	0	0	0	0	0	0	0	0	0	0	0	0	0	0	0
001		547	39	Frcast	0	0	0	157	0	0	0	0	93	290	190	190	0	222	614	700	700	700	0	0	0	0	0
				Orders	0	0	0	157	266	266	380	0	0	0	0	0	0	0	0	0	0	0	0	0	0	0	0
001		0	1	Frcast	0	0	0	31	0	0	0	0	206	0	0	142	450	457	614	700	700	700	0	0	0	0	0
				Orders	0	0	0	0	0	0	0	0	0	0	0	0	0	0	0	0	0	0	0	0	0	0	0
012		79	8	Frcast	131	62	0	0	0	0	0	0	206	128	0	142	0	0	244	258	442	256	256	32	256	232	0
				Orders	131	62	82	62	128	0	64	64	0	0	0	0	0	190	0	0	0	0	0	0	0	0	0
012		2300	1	Frcast	0	0	0	0	0	0	0	0	0	0	0	0	0	0	0	0	0	0	0	0	0	0	0
				Orders	0	0	0	0	0	0	0	0	0	0	0	0	0	0	0	0	0	0	0	0	0	0	0
001		69	0	Frcast	0	0	0	0	0	0	0	0	0	0	0	0	0	0	0	0	0	0	0	0	0	0	0
				Orders	0	0	0	0	0	0	0	64	0	128	0	0	0	0	0	0	0	0	0	0	0	0	0
001		921	2	Frcast	0	0	0	0	357	0	0	280	344	266	284	322	282	1241	1282	1716	1264	1001	678	779	761	795	0
				Orders	0	0	0	271	357	0	0	0	0	0	0	0	0	0	0	0	0	0	0	0	0	0	0
012		658	0	Frcast	0	0	0	0	0	0	0	0	0	0	0	80	0	240	349	368	330	202	256	0	202	252	202
				Orders	0	0	0	0	0	0	0	0	0	0	0	0	0	0	0	0	0	0	0	0	0	0	0
001		456	1	Frcast	0	0	0	480	480	0	0	480	0	480	480	0	0	480	960	960	480	960	480	960	480	480	0
				Orders	0	0	0	480	0	0	0	0	0	0	0	0	0	0	0	0	0	0	0	0	0	0	0

Liebert Part. / Vendor Part. Z↓A↑ A↑Z↓ ; Liebert Part. / Vendor Part. Z↓A↑ A↑Z↓

FIGURE 11.16 Historical Usage

Liebert® KEEPING BUSINESS IN BUSINESS®

eProcurement Home | Phone Book | Liebert Facilities | Procurement News | View/Download Documents | Part Look-up
Choose Supplier # | Open Purchase Orders | Historical Usage | Forecasted Usage | Your Preferences | Feedback | Log Off

SUPPLIER SELECTED:

Download Historical Data

Usage is from all supplier sources

Plant	Liebert Part. A–Z Z–A / Vendor Part. A–Z Z–A	Net-able	Wgt Mth Use	Hgh Mth Use	11/Y1	10/Y1	09/Y1	08/Y1	07/Y1	06/Y1	05/Y1	04/Y1	03/Y1	02/Y1	01/Y1	12/Y0	11/Y0
001		2304	457.7	1322	269	145	645	646	593	1005	699	864	991	797	709	672	1322
001		563	332	1214	242	465	343	218	480	409	333	1214	366	811	975	997	759
001		225	99.1	144	88	68	89	144	58	116	96	132	62	91	57	1	3
001		57	112.2	179	117	85	179	71	74	85	109	92	103	40	157	32	14
001		60	423.5	882	365	82	882	326	394	308	253	413	509	0	0	0	0
001		585	49.9	70	46	43	70	38	28	31	25	14	13	8	1	11	0
012		328	632.2	941	547	576	702	647	646	740	525	517	622	941	789	804	750
012		156	151.6	296	154	140	163	151	179	168	153	200	203	296	233	222	285
001		159	536.1	2505	261	86	582	1032	2505	700	0	0	0	0	0	0	0
001		0	44	440	440	0	0	0	0	0	0	0	0	0	0	0	0
001		547	532.2	589	288	510	579	589	456	530	199	0	0	0	0	0	0
001		0	14.6	143	143	1	0	0	0	0	0	0	0	0	0	0	0
001		79	258.1	331	196	266	331	198	0	0	0	0	0	2	0	0	0
001		2300	97	872	49	128	76	103	90	90	75	155	208	633	823	527	872
012		69	3.6	20	0	10	0	2	0	0	10	20	0	0	0	0	0
001		921	967	3000	889	898	1053	976	1075	1902	1522	2617	3000	2776	2388	2486	2545
012		658	240.5	544	179	192	231	319	269	279	533	509	544	190	4	38	19
001		456	621.3	2830	624	558	643	662	880	1062	1121	2696	1966	2230	2830	2216	2296

FIGURE 11.17   **Supplier Performance**

Liebert

SUPPLIER NAME

SUPPLIER PERFORMANCE REPORT   **SUPPLIER: ORG**   **CODE**

MONTH	DELIVERY	%	#	QTY FAILED	QTY RECVD.	PPM	COST RED	AVG LT	LT PCT	SHORT AGES	AVG DAYS OUT	SPEND
Jul/Y0	LATE	37.5%	15	57	4,417	12,905	$0	22	0.00	0	0	$70,016.00
	EARLY	17.5%	7									
	ONTIME	45.0%	18									
Aug/Y0	LATE	20.6%	7	0	4,026	0	$0	22	0.00	0	0	$39,057.00
	EARLY	5.9%	2									
	ONTIME	73.5%	25									
Sep/Y0	LATE	16.1%	5	18	3,670	4,905	$0	22	0.00	0	0	$89,512.00
	EARLY	6.5%	2									
	ONTIME	77.4%	24									
Oct/Y0	LATE	29.2%	14	18	5,444	3,306	$0	22	0.00	1	2	$46,310.00
	EARLY	16.7%	8									
	ONTIME	54.2%	26									
Nov/Y0	LATE	31.6%	6	37	2,292	16,143	$0	22	0.00	0	0	$53,311.00
	EARLY	31.6%	6									
	ONTIME	36.8%	7									
Dec/Y0	LATE	33.3%	6	34	2,793	12,173	$0	22	0.00	0	0	$74,238.00
	EARLY	0.0%	0									
	ONTIME	66.7%	12									
Jan/Y1	LATE	12.5%	1	2	2,103	951	$0	21	0.00	0	0	$56,402.00
	EARLY	0.0%	0									
	ONTIME	87.5%	7									
Feb/Y1	LATE	5.0%	1	3	1,016	2,953	$0	22	0.00	0	0	$14,253.00
	EARLY	0.0%	0									
	ONTIME	95.0%	19									
Mar/Y1	LATE	3.0%	1	19	2,966	6,406	$0	22	0.00	0	0	$29,261.00
	EARLY	9.1%	3									
	ONTIME	87.9%	29									
Apr/Y1	LATE	9.7%	3	0	5,248	0	$55,031	22	33.00	0	0	$14,550.00
	EARLY	0.0%	0									
	ONTIME	90.3%	28									
May/Y1	LATE	0.0%	0	15	2,429	6,175	$0	23	0.00	0	0	$18,142.00
	EARLY	0.0%	0									
	ONTIME	100.0%	16									
Jun/Y1	LATE	13.0%	3	101	2,621	38,535	$76,741	26	0.00	0	0	$56,990.00
	EARLY	0.0%	0									
	ONTIME	87.0%	20									

Tuesday, July 17, Y1

MONTH: **06/Y1**   Page 1

Caterpillar's EDI network for suppliers and purchasers electronically exchanging data is called "Speed." Although Caterpillar has been building the Speed network for several years, it began as an outgrowth of the company's existing MPC systems. The company recognized the need to add effective electronic communications with the outside suppliers to facilitate JIT. The company viewed the Speed network's advantages to be applicable to both Caterpillar and its vendors. Direct benefits include:

- Reducing transaction time to a few hours, compared with processing through the mail.
- Quicker response to changes for revised material requirements.
- Reduced paper-handling expenses.
- Fewer errors involving transmitting information.

Concluding Principles

We see the following principles emerging from this chapter:

- Production activity control system design must be in concert with the firm's needs.
- Vendor capacities should be planned and scheduled with as much diligence as are internal capacities.
- Lead times are to be managed.
- Feedback from PAC should provide early warning and status information to other MPC modules.
- E-based systems can dramatically improve customer/vendor communication, reducing lead time and overhead cost.
- TOC scheduling provides improved performance by focusing on the constraining resources.
- TOC implementation requires a change in plant culture in order to obtain the full benefits of this approach.
- Adapting standards for communication is a prerequisite to global EDI.
- Traditional priority rules can play a role in nonbottleneck scheduling.
- Stability in the manufacturing loads and capacity planned facilitates shop-floor execution.

References

Arnold, J. R. T., and S. N. Chapman. *Introduction to Materials Management*, 4th ed. Columbus, Ohio: Prentice Hall, 2001, pp. 141–175 and pp. 396–427.

Atwater, J. B., and S. S. Chakravorty. "A Study of the Utilization of Capacity Constrained Resources in Drum-Buffer-Rope Systems," *Production and Operations Management* 11, no. 2 (summer 2002), pp. 259–273.

"APS/Finite Scheduling Software Comparison," *APICS—The Performance Advantage*, September 2001, pp. 48–53.

Bihun, T. A. "Electronic Data Interchange: The Future," *American Production and Inventory Control Society 1990 Annual Conference Proceedings,* pp. 605–609.

Carter, J. R., and L. D. Fredendall. "The Dollars and Sense of Electronic Data Interchange," *Production and Inventory Management Journal* 31, no. 2 (2nd quarter 1990), pp. 22–26.

Chakravorty, S. S. "Improving a V-Plant Operation: A Window Manufacturing Case Study," *Production and Inventory Management Journal* 43, no. 3 (3rd quarter 2000), pp. 37–42.

Christy, D. P., and J. J. Kanet. "Open Order Rescheduling in Job Shops with Demand Uncertainty: A Simulation Study," *Decision Sciences* 19, no. 4 (fall 1988), pp. 801–818.

Davis, D. J., and Vincent A. Mabert. "Order Dispatching and Labor Assignment in Cellular Manufacturing Systems," *Decision Sciences Journal* 31, no. 4 (fall 2000), pp. 745–771.

Fogarty, D. W.; J. H. Blackstone, Jr.; and T. R. Hoffmann. *Production & Inventory Management,* 2nd ed. Cincinnati: Southwestern, 1991.

Frazier, G. V., and P. M. Reyes. "Applying Synchronous Manufacturing Concepts to Improve Production Performance in High Tech Manufacturing," *Production and Inventory Management Journal* 43, no. 3 (3rd quarter 2000), pp. 60–65.

Goldratt, E. M., and J. Cox. *The Goal,* New York: North River Press, 1984.

Greenstein, Irwin. "Caterpillar Erects Paperless Network," *Management Information Systems Week,* January 20, 1986.

Hyer, N. L., and Karen A. Brown. "The Discipline of Real Cells," *Journal of Operations Management* 17, no. 5 (August 1999), pp. 557–574.

Jensen, E. B.; P. R. Philipoom; and M. K. Malhotra. "Evaluation of Scheduling Rules with Commensurate Customer Priorities in Job Shops," *Journal of Operations Management* 13, no. 3 (1995).

McCollum, Benjamin D. "How Changing Purchasing Can Change Your Business," *Production and Inventory Management Journal* 44, no. 2 (2nd quarter 2001).

Melnyk, S. A.; P. L. Carter; D. M. Dilts; and D. M. Lyth. *Shop Floor Control.* Homewood, Ill.: Dow Jones–Irwin, 1985.

———. *Production Activity Control.* Homewood, Ill.: Dow Jones–Irwin, 1987.

Melnyk, S. A.; S. Ghosh; and G. L. Ragatz. "Tooling Constraints and Shop Floor Scheduling: A Simulation Study," *Journal of Operations Management* 8, no. 2 (April 1989), pp. 69–89.

Philipoom, P.; R. E. Markland; and T. D. Fry. "Sequencing Rules, Progress Milestones and Product Structure in a Multistage Job Shop," *Journal of Operations Management* 8, no. 3 (August 1989), pp. 209–29.

Plenert, G., and B. Kirchmier. *Finite Capacity Scheduling.* New York: Oliver Wight Publications, John Wiley & Sons, 2000.

Production Activity Control Reprints. Falls Church, Va.: American Production and Inventory Control Society, 1993.

Production Flows at Timken Steel, I2 Technologies, Web: www.i2.com, 1999.

Sabuncuoglu, I., and H. Y. Karapinar. "A Load-Based and Due-Date-Oriented Approach to Order Review/Release in Job Shops," *Decision Sciences Journal* 31, no. 2 (spring 2000), pp. 413–447.

Scherer, E., ed. *Shop Floor Control—A Systems Perspective.* Berlin: Springer Verlag, October 15, 1998.

Schorr, J. E. *Purchasing in the 21st Century: A Guide to State-of-the-Art Techniques and Strategies.* New York: John Wiley & Sons, 1995.

Schragenheim, E., and B. Ronen. "Drum-buffer-rope Shop Floor Control," *Production and Inventory Management Journal* 31, no. 3 (1990), pp. 18–22.

Simons, Jacob B., and Wendell P. Simpson III. "An Exposition of Multiple Constraint Scheduling as Implemented in the Goal System (Formerly Disaster ™), *Production and Operations Management* 6, no. 1 (spring 1997).

Smunt, T. L., and Charles A. Watts. "Improving Operations Planning with Learning Curves: Overcoming the Pitfalls of 'Messy' Shop Floor Data," *Journal of Operations Management* 21, no. 1 (January 2003), pp. 93–107.

Spearman, M. L. "On the Theory of Constraints and The Goal System," *Production and Operations Management* 6, no. 1 (1997), pp. 28–33.

Taylor, S. G., and S. F. Bolander. *Process Flow Scheduling,* APICS, 1994.

Umble, M., and M. L. Srikanth. *Synchronous Manufacturing*, Spectrum Publishing, 1995.

Umble, M., E. Umble, and L. Von Deylen. "Integrating Enterprise Resources Planning and Theory of Constraints: A Case Study," *Production and Inventory Management Journal* 42, no. 2 (2nd quarter 2001), pp. 43–48.

Waliszowski, David A. "Lead Time Reduction in Multi Flow Job Shops," *APICS Annual Conference Proceedings,* 1975.

Wassweiler, W. L. "Fundamentals of Shop Floor Control," *APICS Conference Proceedings,* 1980, pp. 352–354.

Discussion Questions

1. Suppose an average of 20 students per year were in your major and the number of graduates varied between 15 and 30 each year. One required course, open to both juniors and seniors, is offered once a year and has a capacity of 20 students. What system would you use to assign students to that course? Would it make any difference if the course capacity was 40 students or 10 students per year?

2. What kind of warning signals would you like fed back from PAC to the MRP system?

3. Lead times have sometimes been called "rubbery." What accounts for this concept of elasticity in lead times?

4. In the list of priority rules, there is no first-come/first-served (FCFS) rule, yet most banks, cafeterias, and theater ticket booths use this rule in waiting on patrons. Why isn't it a suggested rule for the shop floor?

5. What are the differences in how bottleneck and nonbottleneck work centers are scheduled under TOC? Why are these differences desirable?

6. Why should buffers be located in front of bottleneck work centers under TOC scheduling? How should the size of these buffers be determined?

7. How would you determine how much discretion to give the foreman in combining and reprioritizing jobs?

8. What benefits might be gained by having clerks in a retail store use a wand to read tags on items?

9. Discuss the merits of separating the daily transaction people (schedulers) from the buyers in the purchasing organization.

Problems

1. Tom's Sailboard manufactures custom wind surfers in Seattle. The incoming orders follow different routes through the shop, but all orders must stop at each of the three work centers (WCs) in the plant. The following table contains information regarding the four jobs that arrive over five days and need to be scheduled at the company. It is currently November 10 and Tom works a seven-day week.

Order	Arrival Date	Job/WC Routing	Processing Time (Days)		
			WC 1	WC 2	WC 3
(B)iff	Nov. 10	1-3-2	1	3	1
(G)riff	Nov. 10	2-3-1	2	2	2
(H)erbie	Nov. 12	3-2-1	3	1	2
(K)erri	Nov. 14	2-1-3	1	3	1

Assume that the material for all orders is ready for processing as soon as the orders arrive and that a first-come/first-served sequencing rule is used at all work centers. All three work centers are idle as work begins on orders B and G on November 10.

a. Construct a Gantt chart depicting the processing and idle times for the three work centers for these four jobs.

b. How many days does each job wait in queue for processing at work center 2?

2. The production manager at the Knox Machine Company is preparing a production schedule for one of the fabrication shop's machines, the P&W grinder. He has collected the following information on jobs currently waiting to be processed at this machine. (There are no other jobs and the machine is empty.)

Job	Machine Processing Time, Days*	Date Job Arrived at this Machine	Job Due Date
A	4	6-23	8-15
B	1	6-24	9-10
C	5	7-01	8-01
D	2	6-19	8-17

*Note: This is the final operation for each of these jobs.

a. The production manager has heard about three dispatching rules: the shortest operation next rule, the first-come/first-served rule, and the earliest due date rule. In what sequence would these jobs be processed at the P&W grinder if each rule were applied?

b. If it's now the morning of July 10 and the shortest operation next rule is used, when would each of the four jobs start and be completed on the P&W grinder? (Express your schedule in terms of the calendar dates involved, assuming that there are seven working days each week.)

3. Jobs A, B, and C are waiting to be started on machine center X and then be completed on machine center Y. The following information pertains to the jobs and work centers.

Job	Hours Allowed for Machine Center X	Hours Allowed for Machine Center Y	Day When Due
A	36	20	10
B	96	24	17
C	60	28	25

Machine center X and machine center Y have 40 hours of capacity per weekday. Two days are allowed to move jobs between machine centers.

a. If these jobs are rescheduled by earliest due date, can they be completed on time?

b. Can they be completed on time using the critical ratio technique?

c. Can the jobs be completed on time (using the earliest due date or critical ratio technique) if 20 hours of overtime are run in work center X each week?

d. Can the jobs be completed on time (using the earliest due date or critical ratio technique) if only one day is required between operations?

4. The customer for job B in problem 3 has agreed to take half the order on day 17 and the rest on day 28. Use earliest due date rule to schedule the four jobs (A, Bl, B2, C). Can they be completed on time, assuming no extra setup time is required for splitting job B?

5. Ms. Mona Hull is in charge of a project to build a 50-foot yacht for a wealthy industrialist from Jasper, Indiana. The yacht is scheduled to compete in the famous Lake Lemon Cup Race. Eight weeks remain for constructing the yacht. Assume that each week consists of 5 workdays, for a total lead time of 40 days. The work required to complete the yacht comprises 10 operations, 4 days for each.

   a. On Tuesday morning of week 3, 3 of the 10 operations had been completed and the yacht was waiting for the fourth operation. What's the critical ratio priority?

   b. What's the critical ratio priority if only 2 of the 10 operations are completed by Tuesday morning of week 3?

6. Big Dan's Machine Shop is considering the use of a priority scheduling rule in the fabrication shop and must decide whether to use: (1) critical ratio (CR), (2) earliest due date (EDD), (3) shortest operation next (SON), or (4) order slack. The current shop status of the company is given below:

Order Number	Total Remaining Manufacturing Time	Time Remaining until Due Date	Current Operation Processing Time
1	15	12	8
2	12	15	5
3	10	14	4
4	15	18	3
5	20	19	6

   a. Using the four sequencing rules, compute the scheduling priority for each order given in the table above.

   b. What order should be run first under each of these scheduling rules?

7. Marucheck's makeshift manufacturing facility had three departments: shaping, pickling, and packing. Marucheck's orders averaged 100 pieces each. Each of the three shaping machines required one hour setup, but could run a piece in one minute. The pickling department lowered baskets of pieces into brine tanks and subjected them to low-voltage current, a heating and cooling, and a rinse. The whole process took four hours for any number of baskets or pieces. The only brine tank could hold four baskets, each of which could contain 50 pieces. (Baskets were loaded while another load was in the tank.) Each piece was inspected and wrapped in bubble pack in the packing department. Each of the four people in the department could do this at the rate of 25 pieces per hour. Marucheck had heard of optimized production technology (OPT) and wanted to identify the bottleneck department. Which is it?

8. The Ace Machine Company is considering using a priority scheduling rule in its fabrication shop and must decide whether to use: (1) the critical ratio rule, (2) the order slack rule, (3) the shortest operation next rule, or (4) the slack per operation rule. Exhibit A shows the company's current inventory and shop status.

   a. State the formula for calculating the priority index for each of sequencing rules given previously.

   b. Compute the scheduling priority for each order in Exhibit A, four sequencing rules.

EXHIBIT A

Order Number	Manufacturing Lead Time Remaining	Time Remaining Until Due Date	Current Operation Processing Time	Number of Operations Remaining	Total Processing Time Remaining
1	15	7	2	3	8
2	15	11	3	4	8
3	20	−2	5	2	8
4	15	−5	4	3	8
5	15	3	1	12	8

Note: Time is measured in days. Manufacturing lead-time remaining includes both the machine processing time and the length of time orders spend moving and waiting to be processed in a machine queue. Current operation processing time (as well as total processing time remaining) includes no move or queue times.

	Big Mess	No Problem
Customer order 1	Part A: setup 5, run 10 Part B: setup 2, run 5	Part C: setup 1, run 2
Customer order 2	Part A: setup 5, run 3	Part D: setup 2, run 2
Customer order 3	Part B: setup 2, run 5	Part C: setup 1, run 3

9. The Optima Shop has two work centers: Big Mess and No Problem. The Monday list of orders to be filled this week shows the total setup and total run time requirements (in hours) at the two centers.

   Joe Biggs, the scheduler of Optima, said his first criterion is to minimize setups, and the second is to prioritize customer orders in numerical order.

   a. How should he schedule part production in the two centers? (Please illustrate using a Gantt chart.)

   b. Can customer delivery promises be met without overtime if capacity is 40 hours in each work center?

   c. How does the answer to part b change if only one person is assigned to do the setup in *both* work centers?

   d. Is the schedule consistent with the OPT philosophy?

10. The XYZ Company uses MRP to plan and schedule plant operations. The plant operates five days per week with no overtime, and all orders are due at 8 A.M. Monday of the week required. It's now 8 A.M. Monday of week 1, all machines are currently idle, and the production manager has been given the information in Exhibit B.

    a. Assuming that the shortest operation next rule is used to schedule orders in the shop, how should the open orders (scheduled receipts) for items A, B, and C be sequenced at their current operations? What are the implications of this schedule?

    b. Assuming that the critical ratio rule is used to schedule orders in the shop, how should the open orders for items A, B, and C be sequenced at their current operations? What are the implications of this schedule?

    c. Suppose that 32 additional units of item B have just been found in the stockroom as a result of a cycle count. What actions are required on the part of the MRP planner?

11. The Ace Tool Company is considering implementing the transfer batches in scheduling the firm's fabrication shop. The production manager selected an example order to use in evaluating benefits and potential costs of this scheduling approach. A transfer batch size of 100 units was suggested for this item. The example order is for a quantity of 1,000 units and has the

EXHIBIT B
System Data

MRP System Data

Item A

		Week							
		1	2	3	4	5	6	7	8
Gross requirements		3	16	8	11	5	18	4	2
Scheduled receipts			30						
Projected available balance	10	7	21	13	2	27	9	5	3
Planned order release			30						

Q = 30; LT = 2; SS = 0.

Item B

		Week							
		1	2	3	4	5	6	7	8
Gross requirements		2	5	12	4	18	2	7	10
Scheduled receipts				30					
Projected available balance	12	10	5	23	19	1	29	22	12
Planned order release			30						

Q = 30; LT = 4; SS = 0.

Item C

		Week							
		1	2	3	4	5	6	7	8
Gross requirements		14	4	12	7	8	3	17	2
Scheduled receipts			20						
Projected available balance	17	3	19	7	0	12	9	12	10
Planned order release		20		20					

Q = 20; LT = 4; SS = 0.

Shop-Floor Control System Data

Item	Routing					Current Operation Number
A	Operation number	1	2	3	4	3 (machine 2)
	Machine number	4	6	2	3	
	Processing time*	1	1	1	1	
B	Operation number	1	2	3	4	2 (machine 2)
	Machine number	4	2	6	1	
	Processing time*	4	2	5	3	
C	Operation number	1	2	3	4	4 (machine 2)
	Machine number	6	3	1	2	
	Processing time*	3	4	6	1.5	

*In days. For computing lead times, assume that there are 1.5 days of move and queue time associated with each operation, including time to complete paperwork after the last operation.

following routing data:

Operation	Work Center	Setup Time	Run Time/Unit
2	1	40 minutes	2.4 minutes/unit
2	2	20 minutes	1.44 minutes/unit

a. Assuming a single-shift, 8-hour day, 5-day week for work centers 1 and 2, prepare a Gantt chart showing the earliest start- and finish-time schedule for this order under a conventional scheduling approach where all items in the order are processed at one time. Do the same when transfer batches are used. What are the earliest start and finish times for each transfer batch at work center 2, assuming none of the transfer batches are processed together to save setup time?

b. What's the difference in the order-completion times under the two scheduling approaches in part a above?

c. What are the benefits and potential costs of this scheduling approach?

12. This morning, Pete Jones, integrated circuit buyer at Flatbush Products, Inc., received the following purchased part MRP record:

		Week											
Circuit 101		1	2	3	4	5	6	7	8	9	10	11	12
Gross requirements		50									50	50	50
Scheduled receipts													
Projected available balance	65												
Planned order releases													

Q = 50; LT = 3; SS = 2.

a. Complete the circuit 101 MRP record.

b. Pete noted that the vendor for circuit 101 recently indicated its plant has limited production capacity available. At most, this supplier can provide 50 units per four-week period. Pete wondered what action, if any, needs to be taken on this item as a result of this capacity limitation.

13. To remain competitive, Ed's Sheet Metal must reduce manufacturing lead time for a product that typically sells in lots of 800 units. The product goes through two operations in different departments. The company wants to evaluate the value of using a transfer batch between operations. Its idea is to split the order at the first operation and transfer an amount to the second operation to get it started while the rest of the order is finished at the first operation. The setup of operation 2 can start as soon as parts arrive, but not sooner. Other data are:

Order size	800 units
Operation 1 processing time	6 minutes/unit
Operation 2 processing time	8 minutes/unit
Transfer time from operation 1 to 2	20 minutes
Setup time for operation 1	1.0 hours
Setup time for operation 2	1.5 hours

a. What is the *minimum* transfer batch that assures that operation 2 has no idle time?

b. How much would manufacturing lead time be reduced by using the transfer batch instead of the full order of 800 units?

14. On a busy day in June, the Framkrantz Factory had five jobs lined up for processing at machine center 1. Each job went to machine center 2 after finishing at machine center 1. After that they had different routings through the factory. It's now shop day 83 and due dates have been established for each job. Machine time includes setup time, but it takes one day to move between centers and two days of queue time at each center (including Finish).

Shop Day = 83	Machine Center Sequence for the Jobs and Days of Machine Time Required						
Job	1	2	3	4	5	Finish	Due Date
A	1	4				X	102
B	3	2	8			X	123
C	3	8		2		X	104
D	6	2	1		2	X	98
E	4	1		8	3	X	110

a. Use a spreadsheet program to calculate the priorities for each job using the critical ratio rule.

b. All jobs were at machine 2 by the morning of shop day 96. (Job A took 2 days instead of 1 and Job D took 1 day instead of 6 on machine 1.) Unfortunately, there was a long job on machine 2 and none of the five jobs had started yet. What would their priorities be for machine 2?

c. What would priorities be if Job N's due date were 96?

15. Shown below is the MRP record for part no. 483. The current shop day is 100 (with five-day weeks); it's now Monday of week 1. Open orders (scheduled receipts) are due Mondays (shop days 100, 105, 1, 10, etc.) of the week for which they're scheduled. The shop floor has just reported that the batch of 40 on shop order number 32 has just finished at machine center A43 and is waiting to be moved to C06. It takes one day to move between machine centers (or to I02, the inventory location) and one day of queue time at the machine centers. (The inventory location doesn't require the queue time, but one day of "machine time" is shown for clearing the paper work.) Part number 483's routing and status are also given below.

Part No. 483		Week					
		1	2	3	4	5	6
Gross requirements		14	4	10	20	3	10
Scheduled receipts			40*				
Projected available balance	20	6	42	32	12	9	39
Planned order releases					40		

Q = 40; LT = 2; SS = 5.
*Shop order no. 32.

Part No. 483

Routing (machine center):	A12	B17	A43	C06	I02
Machine time (days)	4	1	1	1	1
Status shop order 32:	Done	Done	Done		

a. Use a spreadsheet to replicate the MRP record and calculate the critical ratio for part no. 483. Should the planner take any action?

b. What would the priorities be if the inventory were 23 instead of 20? What action should be taken now?

c. What if inventory were 17 instead of 20?

16. Consider the following data for three jobs processed in the boring machine center for Conway Manufacturing.

Job	Setup Time (Minutes)	Run Time/Unit (Minutes)	Batch Size
A	15	0.05	200
B	10	0.15	100
C	20	0.10	200

Queue data for the boring machine center:

Job	Arrival Time	Job	Arrival Time	Job	Arrival Time
A	8:24	B	8:40	B	9:12
B	8:28	C	8:42	C	9:14
C	8:31	C	8:44	A	9:18
A	8:34	A	8:57	B	9:21
B	8:39	A	9:03	B	9:31

a. If the boring machine center used a first-come/first-served rule to schedule jobs, how long would it take to process the queue? (Assume no other jobs arrive, all jobs in queue are for one batch each, and job B has just been completed.)

b. How long would it take to process all jobs in the queue, using the transfer batch logic?

17. Howie's Handicraft needs your advice on the production schedule for its Hallowe'en product line. Analyze the information for the three-station four-product line, given below:

Product	Estimated Weekly Sales, (Units)	Selling Price, ($)	Material Cost, ($)	Process Time Work Station* 1	2	3
Witches	60	35	15	10	10	40
Goblins	50	40	15	10	15	40
Ghosts	40	45	20	10	10	20
Ghouls	30	50	20	15	20	20

*The times for workstations 1, 2, and 3 are in minutes per unit. Capacity at each workstation is 2,400 minutes/week and operating expenses are $2,000/week.

a. What is the bottleneck workstation? What schedule of products at this work station maximized the profit to Howie?

b. What is the total profit from the schedule in question a above?

18. The Marlborough Manufacturing Company in New Zealand was considering embarking on a program of rationalizing its vendor base. It had heard of the benefits of doing so, but was unsure where to start. To begin the process, it recorded the total New Zealand dollar (NZD) purchases in the last year and the number of orders that it placed with each firm in a sample of 20 suppliers. The data are shown below.

Company	NZD	Orders/Year
Axel	321,760	7
Backer	55,122	2
Booker	186,242	3
Century	16,088	4
Farmic	80,440	22
First	48,262	3
Gentry	1,850,120	10
Grist	40,220	1
Hooker	64,532	2
Hume	63,253	6
Jacobs	965,283	8
Kelvin	8,124	2
Kolst	1,367,484	5
Kume	57,305	4
Locket	563,087	1
Neive	7,944	1
Whist	2,171,886	3
Wolf	31,523	3
Young	17,053	6
Zydec	121,555	2

a. Develop a Pareto diagram of the purchases in this sample. For which suppliers should Marlborough focus its efforts in building relationships?

b. For which might it consider making some deletions?

c. What other questions does the sample information raise about the purchasing policies of the company?

12

Advanced Concepts in Sales and Operations Planning

This chapter deals with modeling procedures for establishing the overall, or aggregate, production and inventory portion of the sales and operations plan, and the disaggregation of that plan. Given a set of product demands stated in some common denominator, the basic issue is what levels of resources should be provided in each period. Resources include items such as production capacity, employment levels, and inventory investment. A long history of academic research has addressed aggregate production planning models. Today, powerful and easily accessible tools are available for solving these models. This is important because as firms implement MPC systems, there's a natural evolution toward questions of overall production planning that provide direction to the other MPC system modules. This chapter provides a basic understanding of these models together with an introduction to how problems formulated with these models can be solved using a spreadsheet. This chapter is organized around five topics:

- *Mathematical programming approaches:* How can aggregate production planning problems be solved using mathematical programming techniques?
- *Other approaches:* What other techniques have been developed for aggregate planning and how do they differ from math programming models?
- *Disaggregation:* How are aggregate production plans disaggregated into the specific products and quantities needed for a master production schedule?
- *Company example: Lawn King, Inc.:* How can mathematical programming approaches be used to develop an actual production plan, and what information does it provide for the company?
- *Applications potential:* How widely used are the advanced concepts in sales and operations planning, and what's the prognosis for the future?

Chapter 12 is linked to Chapter 3, which describes basic sales and operations planning approaches. There are also linkages to Chapter 6 on master production scheduling and to Chapter 10 on capacity planning. It's the sales and operations plan that constrains the master production schedule in a hierarchical view of manufacturing planning and control. Capacity planning procedures can be used to determine the feasibility of an MPS.

Mathematical Programming Approaches

In this section, we present an overview of some mathematical programming models that have been suggested for the aggregate production planning problem. The academic literature has long been concerned with developing formal decision models for this problem. We start by formulating the problem as a linear programming model. This approach is relatively straightforward but is necessarily limited to cases where there are linear relationships in the input data. Thereafter, we describe a mixed integer programming approach for preparing aggregate production plans on a product line basis.

These approaches are already substantially more sophisticated than the practice found in most firms. More common are spreadsheet programs used to explore alternative production plans. Using forecasts of demand and factors relating to employment, productivity, overtime, and inventory levels, a series of what-if analyses helps to formulate production plans and evaluate alternative scenarios. Level and chase strategies are developed to bracket the options, and alternatives are evaluated against the resultant benchmarks. Although spreadsheet programs do not provide the optimal solutions reached by the models discussed in this chapter, they do help firms better understand the inherent trade-offs and provide a focal point for important dialogue among the functional areas of the firm.

Linear Programming

There are many linear programming formulations for the aggregate production planning problem. The objective is typically to find the lowest-cost plan, considering when to hire and fire, how much inventory to hold, when to use overtime and undertime, and so on, while always meeting the sales forecast. One formulation, based on measuring aggregate sales and inventories in terms of direct labor hours, follows:

Minimize:

$$\sum_{t=1}^{m}(C_H H_t + C_F F_t + C_R X_t + C_O O_t + C_I I_t + C_U U_t)$$

subject to:

1. Inventory constraint:

$$I_{t-1} + X_t + O_t - I_t = D_t$$

$$I_t \geq B_t$$

2. Regular time production constraint:

$$X_t - A_{1t} W_t + U_t = 0$$

3. Overtime production constraint:

$$O_t - A_{2t} W_t + S_t = 0$$

4. Workforce level change constraints:

$$W_t - W_{t-1} - H_t + F_t = 0$$

5. Initializing constraints:

$$W_O = A_3$$

$$I_O = A_4$$

$$W_m = A_5$$

where:

C_H = The cost of hiring an employee.

C_F = The cost of firing an employee.

C_R = The cost per labor-hour of regular time production.

C_O = The cost per labor-hour of overtime production.

C_I = The cost per month of carrying one labor-hour of work.

C_U = The cost per labor-hour of idle regular time production.

H_t = The number of employees hired in month t.

F_t = The number of employees fired in month t.

X_t = The regular time production hours scheduled in month t.

O_t = The overtime production hours scheduled in month t.

I_t = The hours stored in inventory at the end of month t.

U_t = The number of idle time regular production hours in month t.

D_t = The hours of production to be sold in month t.

B_t = The minimum number of hours to be stored in inventory in month t.

A_{1t} = The maximum number of regular time hours to be worked per employee per month.

W_t = The number of people employed in month t.

A_{2t} = The maximum number of overtime hours to be worked per employee per month.

S_t = The number of unused overtime hours per month per employee.

A_3 = The initial employment level.

A_4 = The initial inventory level.

A_5 = The desired number of employees in month m (the last month in the planning horizon).

m = The number of months in the planning horizon.

Similar models have been successfully formulated for several variations of the production planning problem. In general, however, few real-world aggregate production planning decisions appear to be compatible with the linear assumptions. Some plans require discrete steps such as adding a second shift. For many companies, the unit cost of hiring or firing large numbers of employees is much larger than that associated with small labor force changes. Moreover, economies of scale aren't taken into account by linear programming formulations. Let's now turn to another approach, which partially overcomes the linear assumption limitations.

Mixed Integer Programming

The linear programming model provides a means of preparing low-cost aggregate plans for overall workforce, production, and inventory levels. However, in some firms, aggregate plans are prepared on a product family basis. Product families are defined as groupings of products that share common manufacturing facilities and setup times. In this case, overall production, workforce, and inventory plans for the company are essentially the summation of the plans for individual product lines. Mixed integer programming provides one method for determining the number of units to be produced in each product family. Chung and Krajewski describe a model for accomplishing this:

Minimize:

$$\sum_{i=1}^{n}\sum_{t=1}^{m}(C_{si}\sigma(X_{it}) + C_{mi}X_{it} + C_{Ii}I_{it}) + \sum_{t=1}^{m}(C_H H_t + C_F F_t + C_O O_t + A_{1t}C_R W_t)$$

subject to:

1. Inventory constraint:

$$I_{i,t-1} - I_{it} + X_{it} = D_{it} \qquad \text{(for } I = 1, \ldots, n \text{ and } T = 1, \ldots, m)$$

2. Production and setup time constraint:

$$A_{it}W_t + O_t - \sum_{i=1}^{n}X_{it} - \sum_{i=1}^{n}\beta_i\sigma(X_{it}) \geq 0 \qquad \text{(for } t = 1, \ldots, m)$$

3. Workforce level change constraint:

$$W_t - W_{t-1} - H_t + F_t = 0 \qquad \text{(for } t = 1, \ldots, m)$$

4. Overtime constraint:

$$O_t - A_{2t}W_t \leq 0 \qquad \text{(for } t = 1, \ldots, m)$$

5. Setup constraint:

$$-Q_i\sigma(X_{it}) + X_{it} \leq 0 \qquad \text{(for } t = 1, \ldots, m \text{ and } I = 1, \ldots, n)$$

6. Binary constraint for setups:

$$\sum(X_{it}) = \begin{cases} 1 & \text{if } X_{it} > 0 \\ 0 & \text{if } X_{it} = 0 \end{cases}$$

7. Nonnegativity constraints:

$$X_{it}, I_{it}, H_t, F_t, O_t, W_t \geq 0$$

where:

X_{it} = Production in hours of product family i scheduled in month t.

I_{it} = The hours of product family i stored in inventory in month t.

D_{it} = The hours of product family i demanded in month t.

H_t = The number of employees hired in month t.

F_t = The number of employees fired in month t.

O_t = Overtime production hours in month t.

W_t = Number of people employed on regular time in month t.

$\sigma(X_{it})$ = Binary setup variable for product family i in month t.

C_{si} = Setup cost of product family i.

C_{Ii} = Inventory carrying cost per month of one labor-hour of work for product family i.

C_{mi} = Materials cost per hour of production of family i.

C_H = Hiring cost per employee.

C_F = Firing cost per employee.

C_O = Overtime cost per employee hour.

C_R = Regular time workforce cost per employee hour.

A_{1t} = The maximum number of regular-time hours to be worked per employee in month t.

β_i = Setup time for product family i.

A_{2t} = Maximum number of overtime hours per employee in month t.

Q_i = A large number used to ensure the effects of binary setup variables; that is,

$$Q_i \geq \sum_{t=1}^{m} D_{it}$$

n = Number of product families.

m = Number of months in the planning horizon.

The objective function and constraints in this model are similar to those in the linear programming model. The main difference is in the addition of product family setups in constraints 5 and 6. This model assumes all the setups for a product family occur in the month in which the end product is to be completed. Constraint 5 is a surrogate constraint for the binary variables used in constraint 6. This constraint forces $\sigma(X_{it})$ to be nonzero when $X_{it} > 0$ since Q_i is defined as at least the total demand for a product family over the planning horizon.

Additional constraints should be added to the model to specify the initial conditions at the start of the planning horizon; that is, constraints specifying beginning inventory for the product family, I_{io}, and workforce level in the previous month, W_o, are required. Likewise, constraints specifying workforce level at the end of the planning horizon, and minimum required closing inventory balance at the end of each month in the planning horizon, may be added.

Other Approaches

Several other models have been formulated for solving the aggregate production planning problem. In this section, we briefly describe two of them. The first is a classic academic work based on linear and quadratic cost assumptions. Another approach uses direct search methods that allow for more general cost expressions.

The Linear Decision Rule

The linear decision rule model (LDR) for aggregate production planning was developed by Holt, Modigliani, Muth, and Simon in the 1950s. The primary application was in a paint producing company.

The major difference between the LDR model and linear programming models is the approach to cost input data. The four cost elements considered in LDR are regular payroll cost, hire/fire cost, overtime/undertime cost, and inventory/backlog cost. The regular payroll cost is simply a linear function of the number of workers employed. For the other three cost elements, however, a quadratic cost function is used. For example, the hire/fire cost is defined as:

$$64.3(W_t - W_{t-1})^2$$

where:

W_t = The workforce to be established for the tth month.

W_{t-1} = The prior month's workforce.

64.3 = Analytically derived coefficient for best fitting the squared differences in workforce levels to actual operating costs results.

Figure 12.1 is an example quadratic hire/fire cost function, along with the presumed actual cost data. The presumed actual cost data only approximate the quadratic function. However, in some ways, the implication that each hire or fire decision results in ever-increasing unit costs is consistent with many managerial opinions. The total cost function for the paint company was made up of the four cost elements. The problem is to minimize the total cost function. Since cost data are linear and quadratic, we can derive the solution to the problem by calculus. The result is a set of two decision rules specifying the production output rate and the workforce level in each month.

LDR was implemented at the paint company. Several years later, John Gordon visited the company and described the results:

> After considerable study and investigation it became apparent that although top management thought the rules were being used to determine aggregate production and workforce, a more intuitive and long-standing system was in fact being used. The production control clerk

FIGURE 12.1
LDR Quadratic Cost Function for Workforce Changes

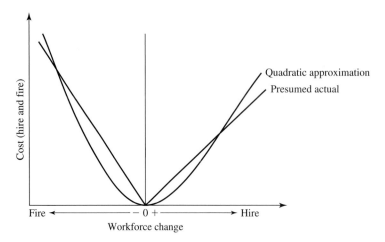

whose responsibility it was to calculate the production and workforce sizes, as well as convert these into item orders, was doing just that and posting the results in the form of job tickets on the production control board. When the foremen came into the production control office for a job ticket, they surveyed the available tickets for one that agreed with their intuitive feeling or judgment. If they found one, they took it but if they did not, they simply wrote out a ticket which corresponded with their feeling. During the period in which the rules were in effect, it turned out that about 50 percent of the tickets were used and the others ignored. Management, however, had the feeling that the rules were being used except in the odd case when judgment indicated that they should be overruled. At a later date, the calculations associated with the rules were centralized with the installation of a data-processing center. The personnel in the center became concerned when their reports indicated that many of the production orders that they had issued were ignored. Consequently, and with the compliance of higher management, they instituted a reporting system that fed back to the plant management and to the foremen a cumulative listing of outstanding production orders. After a short time, the length of this cumulative list began to diminish until it all but vanished. But in the meantime, the inventory of finished goods associated with this plant rose steadily to alarming proportions, especially in some obsolete items. Further investigation revealed that although the rules were indicating the size of the workforce, no action was ever taken to reduce the workforce because it was against the policy of the company. This meant that the workforce rule was indicating a reduction in the workforce: the production rule, attempting to minimize costs given the present workforce level but anticipating layoff, called for some production for the excess workforce. The rules are interactive, but in this case the interaction had been eliminated.

The moral to the story seems clear: Without auditing, never assume the real world matches the model. In fact, any system that's not readily understood by the users is more subject to overrides than one where the logic is transparent. This is a classic example of the informal system supplanting the formal system.

Search Decision Rules

As we've noted, linear programming models are limited by the linear cost assumptions. Similarly, LDR is restricted to linear and quadratic costs. The search decision rule (SDR) methodology helps overcome these restrictions. SDR approaches allow us to state cost data inputs in very general terms. The only requirement is that a computer program be constructed that will unambiguously evaluate any production plan's cost. The procedure then searches among alternative plans (in a guided fashion) for the plan of minimum cost. Unlike linear programming and LDR, there's no guarantee of mathematical optimality with SDR. However, the increased realism in input data provides the potential for solving a problem more in line with managerial perceptions.

Several researchers have worked with search procedures for the aggregate production planning problem. Taubert compared SDR with LDR for the paint company problem. He found SDR results were very close to those obtained by LDR. The technique has been applied in a number of companies. The versatility of the underlying approach provided makes it especially attractive for real-world applications.

Disaggregation

Thus far, we've considered only establishing an overall plan of production. This plan must necessarily be disaggregated into specific products and detailed production actions. Moreover, the aggregate production planning problem, as formulated up to now, has been based on a single facility (although it's conceivable a facility subscript could be used in the linear programming model). For many firms, the problem of determining which facility will produce which products, in which quantities, is an important prerequisite to planning at each facility. In this section, we first consider an approach to disaggregation that closely parallels the managerial organization for making these decisions. We then turn to a mathematical programming model for determining the MPS within each product family (the product family planning having been done earlier with mixed integer programming).

The Disaggregation Problem

One issue receiving increased attention is converting overall aggregate production plans into detailed MPS plans; that is, managers must make day-to-day decisions on a product and unit basis rather than on the overall output level. The concept of disaggregation facilitates this process and avoids mismatches between plan and execution. In essence, disaggregation considers overall production planning as well as consistent lower-level capacity decisions. It recognizes that aggregate decisions constrain the disaggregated actions. It therefore is concerned with breaking down the total or aggregate plan into plans for subunits of product.

Disaggregation is an important topic. There has been some growth in both theory and practice, but the number of applications to date is limited. The disaggregation frame of reference is to maintain a match between the production plan and the master production schedule. The aggregate production plan must be the sum of the production called for by the detailed master production schedule (MPS). At issue is how to keep the two in concert. Some recent research offers potential help, but there's much to be done.

Hierarchical Production Planning

Hierarchical production planning is one approach to aggregate capacity analysis that is based upon disaggregation concepts and can accommodate multiple facilities. The approach

FIGURE 12.2
Hierarchical Planning Schema

Source: G. R. Bitran, E. A. Haas, and A. C. Hax, "Hierarchical Production Planning: A Two-Stage System," *Operations Research,* March–April 1982, pp. 232–251.

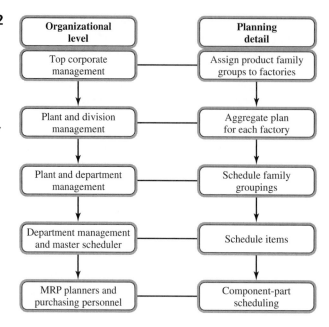

incorporates a philosophy of matching product aggregations to decision-making levels in the organization. Thus, the approach is not a single mathematical model but utilizes a series of models, where they can be formulated. Since the disaggregation follows organization lines, managerial input is possible at each stage. Figure 12.2 shows a schema of the approach.

A group of researchers (Bitran, Haas, Hax, Meal, and others) has been developing hierarchical production planning (HPP) over several years. Some of the work has involved mathematical contributions, while other work has increased the depth or breadth of application (incorporating distribution centers or levels of detail in a factory). All work, however, is based on some fundamental principles.

One principle has been mentioned already: disaggregation should follow organizational lines. Another principle is that at the aggregation level it is only necessary to provide information appropriate to the decision. Thus, we don't need to use detailed part information for the plant assignment decisions. Finally, it's necessary to schedule only for the lead time needed to change decisions. That means detailed plans can be made for periods as short as the manufacturing lead times.

The process of planning follows Figure 12.2's schema. It first involves specifying which products to produce in which factories. Products are combined in logical family groupings to facilitate aggregation, assignment to factories, and modeling processes. Assignment to factories is based on minimizing capital investment cost, manufacturing cost, and transportation cost.

Once the assignment to factories has been done and managerial inputs incorporated, an aggregate production plan is made for each plant. The procedure for determining the aggregate production plan could be any of those discussed previously. The aggregate plan specifies production levels, inventory levels, overtime, and so on for the plant. This plan is constrained by the specific products and volumes assigned to the plant.

The next step in the disaggregation calls for scheduling family groupings within the factory. The schedule is constrained by the aggregate production plan and takes into account any inventories that may exist for the group. The intention at this stage is to realize the economies of producing a family grouping together. Production lots (or share of the aggregate capacity) for the groups are determined and sequenced. If no major economies are achieved by scheduling the group as a unit, the procedure can move directly to the scheduling of individual items, the next stage in Figure 12.2.

Determining the individual item schedule is analogous to making a master production schedule. In the HPP schema, the MPS is constrained by the previously scheduled family groupings and may cover a shorter planning horizon. In some instances, we can use mathematical models to establish schedules. In all cases, items are scheduled within the capacity allocated for their family group. Detailed part and component scheduling can be done with MRP logic, order launching and inventory systems, or even mathematical modeling.

A recent extension to the basic HPP model is the use of variable planning periods rather than the fixed planning period of 20 days used in the Bitran, Haas, and Hax approach. Oden develops a recursive algorithm to predict the length of the planning period that minimizes the annual sum of setup and inventory holding costs. Oden's model produces consistently lower production costs (overtime, setup, inventory holding) than those of the fixed period approach.

Disaggregation through Mathematical Programming

A disaggregation model by Chung and Krajewski illustrates how the aggregate production plan for each family, determined by their mixed integer programming model, can be disaggregated into a detailed master production schedule specifying lot size and timing for individual end products. Since family production and inventory levels have been established by the aggregate plan, the master production schedule must adhere to targets set by the aggregate plan. To do this the formulation includes resource requirements and limitations from the aggregate plan as constraints. The model uses information from the aggregate plan for each family, including setup time (β_i), setup status $[\sigma(X_{it})]$, production level (X_{it}), and inventory level (I_{it}). Also used are overtime (O_t), workforce level (W_t), and regular time availability (A_{1t}) for each month. The formulation of the disaggregaton model follows:

Minimize:

$$\sum_{i=1}^{n}\sum_{k\in Ki}\sum_{t'\in Nt} b_i^k B_{it'}^k + \sum_{t=1}^{m}\left(w^{3-}d_t^3 + w^{3+}d_t^{3+}\right)$$

$$+ \sum_{i=1}^{n}\sum_{t=1}^{m}\left(w_i^{1-}d_{it}^{1-} + w_i^{1+}d_{it}^{1+} + w_i^{2-}d_{it}^{2-} + w_i^{2+}d_{it}^{2+}\right)$$

subject to:

1. Inventory constraint:

$$I_{i,t'-1}^k - I_{it'}^k + X_{it'}^k + B_{it'}^k - B_{i,t'-1}^k = D_{it'}^k$$

$$(\text{for } i = 1, \ldots, n; k \in K_i; t' \in N_t; \text{ and } t = 1, \ldots, m)$$

2. Regular time and overtime production constraint:

$$\sum_{i=1}^{n} \sum_{k \in Ki} \sum_{m'=1}^{Li} \sum_{j=1}^{J} \left(r_{im'j}^{k} X_{i,t'+Li-m'}^{k} \right) + d_{t'}^{o-} - d_{t'}^{o+}$$

$$= \left(\frac{1}{4} \right) \left[A_{1t} W_{t} - \sum_{i=1}^{n} \beta_{i} \sigma(X_{it}) \right] \qquad \text{(for } t' \in N_{t} \text{ and } t = 1, \ldots, m \text{)}$$

3. Overtime deviation constraint:

$$\sum_{t' \in Nt} d_{t'}^{o+} + d_{t}^{3-} - d_{t}^{3+} = O_{t} \qquad \text{(for } t = 1, \ldots, m \text{)}$$

4. Regular time deviation constraint:

$$\sum_{k \in K_i} \sum_{t' \in N_t} X_{it'}^{k} + d_{it}^{1-} - d_{it}^{1+} = X_{it} \qquad \text{(for } i = 1, \ldots, n \text{ and } t = 1, \ldots, m \text{)}$$

5. Inventory deviation constraint:

$$\sum_{k \in K_i} \sum_{t' \in N_t} I_{it'}^{k} + d_{it}^{2-} - d_{it}^{2+} = I_{it} \qquad \begin{array}{l} \text{(for } i = 1, \ldots, n; t = 1, \ldots, m; \\ \text{and} \quad t' = 4(t-1)+1, \ldots, 4(t-1)+4 \text{)} \end{array}$$

6. Nonnegativity constraints:

$$X_{it'}^{k}, I_{it'}^{k}, B_{it'}^{k}, d_{t'}^{0-}, d_{t'}^{0+}, d_{it}^{2-}, d_{it}^{2+}, d_{it}^{3-}, d_{it}^{3+}, d_{t}^{1-}, d_{t}^{1+} \geq 0$$

where:

$X_{it'}^{k}$ = The production hours of end item k of product family i in week t'.

$I_{it'}^{k}$ = The hours of end item k of product family i at the end of week t'.

b_{i}^{k} = Cost to backorder one hour of production of end item k of product family i.

$B_{it'}^{k}$ = Backorder hours of end item k of product family i in week t'.

$D_{it'}^{k}$ = Hours of end item k of product family i demanded in week t'.

$d_{t'}^{0-}$ = Undertime in week t'; that is, the number of planned regular time hours not used in week t'.

$d_{t'}^{0+}$ = Overtime hours used in week t'.

d_{t}^{3-} = Negative deviation from the planned overtime level in month t.

d_{t}^{3+} = Positive deviation from the planned overtime level in month t.

d_{it}^{1-} = Negative deviation from the planned aggregate production level of product family i in month t.

d_{it}^{1+} = Positive deviation from the planned aggregate production level of product family i in month t.

d_{it}^{2-} = Negative deviation from the planned inventory of product family i at the end of month t.

d_{it}^{2+} = Positive deviation from the planned inventory of product family i at the end of month t.

$w_i^{1-}, w_i^{1+}, w_i^{2-}, w_i^{2+}, w^{3-}, w^{3+},$ = Weights (costs) assigned to the deviation variables.

$r_{im'j}^{k}$ = Proportion of total production labor-hours required for processing item k of product family i at operation or work center j in week m' (the week since production started on k) assuming at most one operation for each item at each work center j.

L_i = Production lead time for items in product family i.

n = Number of product families.

m = Production planning horizon length.

J = Number of work centers.

K_i = Set of end items within product family i.

N_t = Set of time-phased weeks, (t')'s, in month t. This example uses monthly time buckets for aggregate plans and uses weekly time buckets for the time-phased master production schedule. It's assumed there are 4 weeks in each month: that is, month 1 ($t = 1$) has $t' = 1, 2, 3, 4$; and month 2 ($t = 2$) has $t' = 5, 6, 7, 8$; and so on.

The first constraint represents production and inventory relationships from week to week with the back-order position for the individual product lines included. The second constraint defines the labor-hour requirements. The right-hand side value in this constraint is obtained from the aggregate plan solution, and it equals the regular labor-hours planned for the month, excluding hours consumed for setups for product families. The value of $\frac{1}{4}$ is used to translate the monthly (t) figures into weekly (time-phased t') values, assuming there are four weeks in every month. Therefore, this constraint specifies the total employee hours at all work centers that produce items in the product families (including the under- and overtime adjustments) should equal overall employee capacity planned to be available each week (t').

The third, fourth, and fifth constraints use deviations to force the overtime, family production quantities, and closing inventory values to correspond to monthly goals set by the aggregate production plan; that is, O_t, X_{it}, and I_{it}, respectively. Weights placed on the deviations in the objective function control these deviations' magnitude and frequency.

The initial end-item inventories and workforce conditions must be included in the master production scheduling model. The beginning inventories of the end items within a product family must sum to the beginning inventory for the product family used in the aggregate planning model; that is:

$$\sum_{k \in K_i} I_{i,o}^k = I = I_{i,o}$$

Also, the lead time (L_i) for each product family must be considered in solving the master production scheduling model. For example, if a four-week production lead time is used for a product family, including one week for the end item and three weeks for the components,

FIGURE 12.3

A Schematic Diagram of a Sequential Production Planning Process

Source: C. Chung and Lee J. Krajewski, "Planning Horizons for Master Production Scheduling," *Journal of Operations Management,* August 1984.

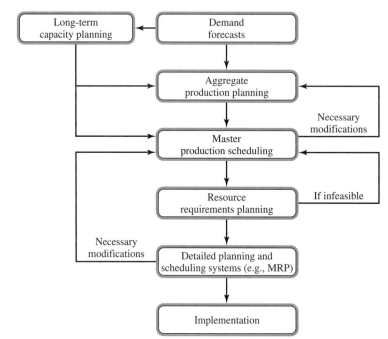

then only the master schedule for week 4 and beyond can be changed. Components for weeks 1 to 3 must have been produced in the previous month. Therefore these items' resource requirements must be netted from resource capacities given for the first month in the second constraint. Likewise, demands for weeks 1 to 4 in the master production schedule must also be netted from the planned production in weeks 1 to 3.

Figure 12.3 presents a schematic that shows the relationship of the aggregate planning and the master production scheduling models to other MPC activities. This diagram indicates the sequential nature of the solution process. It begins with long-term capacity planning and demand forecasting. Then aggregate planning for each family is done. Factor values for X_{it}, I_{it}, $\sigma(X_{it})$, W_t, and O_t are then passed to the master production scheduling model, which sometimes requires modifications to the aggregate production planning results. Thereafter, the master scheduling model's outputs are examined for feasibility in terms of resource requirements and then are passed to the company's detailed planning and scheduling systems. These include material requirements planning (MRP) and capacity planning, which are driven from the MPS. The detailed plans are integrated as well as possible, with the cycle repeated each month.

This approach represents one method for disaggregating overall production plans into detailed master production schedules.

Company Example: Lawn King, Inc.

In this section we present an application of advanced production planning models. The example is based on a case in Roger Schroeder's operations management textbook. The case, Lawn King, Inc., has been refocused to demonstrate the role of production planning models

FIGURE 12.4
Profit and Loss
Statement
($000)

Year	Last Year	This Year
Sales	$11,611	$14,462
Cost of goods sold		
Material	6,430	8,005
Direct labor	2,100	2,595
Depreciation	743	962
Overhead	256	431
Total CGS	9,439	11,993
G&A expense	270	314
Selling expense	140	197
Total expenses	9,849	12,504
Pretax profit	1,762	1,958

in the sales and operations planning process. Included are the ways a company might estimate the necessary parameters, the additional information that might be generated in a sales and operations planning meeting, and the construction and use of the model. We start with a description of the company and its products, then turn to the development of the planning model, and close with how the model might be used in a sales and operations planning meeting.

Company Background

Lawn King, Inc. (disguised name) is a medium-sized producer of lawn mower equipment. The company makes four lines of gas-powered lawn mowers: an 18-inch push mower, a 20-inch push mower, a 20-inch self-propelled mower, and a 22-inch deluxe self-propelled mower. Lawn care products in general, of course, face a seasonal demand and have historically been sensitive to overall economic conditions. Lawn King, Inc. enjoys a positive reputation for product quality and customer service in the industry, so, despite the recent economic downturn, it has been able to show sales growth and profitability in the last few years. Moreover, the sales team expects a significant recovery in the economy and is very optimistic about sales for the next year. Sales, costs and profits for the last two years are shown in Figure 12.4.

The only cloud over the rosy expectations for sales growth next year was the occurrence of some product shortages last year. These shortages occurred even though manufacturing used overtime to try to keep up with demand. It was the first time that the firm had ever needed to put any of its products on backorder, and even though the backorders were filled quickly, there was still some concern that its reputation for good customer service could be negatively impacted. This concern persuaded Lawn King's management to consider more formal planning processes to help meet the increased demand.

Deciding on a Planning Model

Up to this year, Lawn King's annual planning had been quite informal. The process consisted of gathering forecast information and establishing budgets for the fiscal year (from September 1 to August 31). Once the budgets were established, external events (big customer order or a cancellation or adverse weather pattern) would trigger informal meetings where plans would be adjusted, reduced time or overtime would be authorized, and other adjustments would be made. In discussions about preparing for next year's selling season, there was general agreement that backorders should be avoided if possible, and that more formalized meetings during the year might be helpful. Management also agreed that it would be worthwhile to evaluate a formal planning model as part of the budgeting process and as the basis for the subsequent meetings.

Though there was general agreement to proceed with the development of a planning model, there was little agreement on what approach to take, whether to hire a consultant, how extensive the model should be, and other details of the approach. During one meeting, the marketing manager, plant manager, and the managing director agreed to start simply, use internal resources (not a consultant), and not use unfamiliar technology. With this in mind, all members of management were charged to consult with their colleagues in trade associations, their classmates from school, people in their departments, and professors who they felt might be useful.

The results of these discussions turned up remarkably similar results. Most of the advice the managers received reinforced their decision to start simply. Many of their contacts recommended an aggregate production-planning model formulated as a linear program. Several of the managers were familiar with linear programming, and if the time increments were monthly, it could tie in with the more formal meetings the company was planning. Another advantage was that the model could be formulated using spreadsheet technology (such as Excel), which all of the management team currently used for some of their own management tasks. Moreover, there were several people in the company who were familiar with Excel's advanced capabilities.

The managing director and plant manager had already used Excel to estimate the results of different staffing levels and inventory policies, so they had some experience with simple production planning models. Some of the managers had studied linear programming in college and others were familiar with the use of such models to find solutions to complex problems and provide what-if capability. The end result was an agreement to focus on aggregate production planning, to determine staffing levels, to provide sufficient inventory to avoid backorders, to develop an in-house linear programming model of the process, and to assign a young engineer to assist in the model development and subsequent analysis.

The Linear Programming Model

The linear programming model the managers developed can determine aggregate inventory levels, direct labor staffing levels, and production rates for each month of the year. The objective function minimizes direct payroll, overtime, hiring and layoff, and relevant inventory costs. The model also incorporated the desired inventory level for each month and direct labor force at the end of the year. The model is shown below:

Minimize:

$$\sum_t (C_H H_t + C_F F_t + C_R W_t + C_O O_t + C_I I_t)$$

subject to:

1. Inventory constraint:

$$I_{t-1} + P_t + O_t - D_t = I_t$$

2. Regular time production constraint:

$$P_t \le A_1 W_t$$

3. Overtime production constraint:

$$O_t \le A_2 W_t$$

4. Workforce level change constraint:

$$W_{t-1} + H_t - F_t = W_t$$

5. Initializing constraints:

$$W_0 = A3$$
$$I_0 = A4$$
$$W_m = A5$$
$$I_t = A6$$

where:

C_H = The cost of hiring an employee.

C_F = The cost of firing an employee.

C_R = The cost per month of an employee on regular time.

C_O = The cost per unit of production on overtime.

C_I = The cost per month of carrying one unit of inventory.

H_t = The number of employees hired in month t.

F_t = The number of employees fired in month t.

P_t = The number of units produced on regular time in month t.

O_t = The number of units produced on overtime in month t.

W_t = The number of people employed in month t.

I_t = The number of units stored in inventory at the end of month t.

D_t = The number of units of demand in month t.

A_1 = The number of units that one employee can produce in one month on regular time.

A_2 = The maximum number of units that one employee can produce in one month on overtime.

A_3 = The initial inventory level.

A_4 = The initial workforce level.

A_5 = The desired workforce level at the end of the planning horizon.

A_6 = The desired inventory level at the end of each month

m = The number of months in the planning horizon.

Developing the Planning Parameters

In the early stages of the development of the model, management decided to use the actual sales data for the current year. This would give them a known base and might also provide some insights into what they might have done differently to avoid the shortages they incurred during the last year. In addition to the sales data, they needed estimates of the other parameters for the linear programming planning model.

Lawn King fabricates metal frames and other metal parts for its lawn mowers in its own machine shop. Much of the parts fabrication is coordinated with the assembly schedule, but some inventory is kept in order to support schedule changes, overtime, and other unanticipated events. In addition to fabrication, it purchases parts and components including engines, bolts, paint, wheels, and sheet steel directly from vendors. In the current year, approximately $8 million in parts and supplies were purchased and an inventory of $1 million in purchased parts was held to supply the machine shop and the assembly line. When a particular mower is running on the assembly line, the purchased and fabricated parts for that model are moved to the assembly line.

The workforce strategy of Lawn King might be described as a one-shift level-workforce strategy with overtime used as needed. At the time the model was being developed in the current year, a total of 93 employees worked at the plant. These employees included 52 workers on the assembly line, 6 floaters, 20 workers in the machine shop, 10 maintenance workers, and 5 office staff. Even though the employment level of the direct workforce (assembly and machine shop workers) may be varied over the course of a year, the company tried to keep it as level as possible. The company is not able to do this exactly due to turnover and short-run production requirements. There is, however, very little turnover for the office staff and the maintenance group. Overtime is used when regular time cannot meet production requirements (as was the case in the current year).

The plant is unionized, and relations between the union and the company have always been good. The company had access to good direct labor skills and provided a comprehensive training program. It estimated the total training cost in the current year was $42,000. Using this and other factors (overhead, personnel, screening, and so forth) the personnel officer estimated it cost $800 to hire a new employee. The company relied mostly on turnover to reduce the direct labor but did have some experience with layoffs. The personnel officer estimated that the cost to lay off an employee was $1,500, including the severance costs and supplemental unemployment benefits that are required.

The six floaters are kept on the workforce to fill in for people who are absent, especially on Mondays and Fridays. They also help train the new employees when they are not needed for direct production work and often perform some administrative tasks. There was some discussion about how to treat the floaters in the planning model. To be conservative, the decision was to not consider them as producing employees. This would compensate for absences, new employee training, and the time they spent in administrative tasks. This meant that, even though there are 78 direct employees, only 72 would be considered as production employees.

Since the model was an aggregate planning model, an "average" aggregate product was to be used, so an average cost of direct labor and labor productivity were needed as parameters in the model. A beginning assembly-line worker was paid $7.15 per hour plus $2.90 an hour in benefits. The maintenance and machine-shop employees earned an average of $12 per hour (including benefits). To simplify the model, the machine-shop and assembly activities were combined and the average labor cost per direct worker was calculated to be $1,828 per month, using a 12-month planning horizon. The actual production data for the current year is shown in Figure 12.5. The average productivity for the assembly and machine shop workers combined was 83 end-product units per month per employee on regular time. Due to union restrictions, a maximum of 17 units could be produced per month per employee (on four eight-hour Saturdays) at this productivity rate. Based on this information, the labor cost per unit on regular time for the combined assembly and machine shop units was $22.03, and the overtime labor cost per unit was $33.04.

FIGURE 12.5
Monthly Production During the Current Year (units)

	18"	20"	20" SP	22" SP	Total Units	Overtime Units*
September	3,000	3,100	—	—	6,100	—
October	—	—	3,400	3,500	6,900	—
November	3,000	3,800	—	—	6,800	—
December	—	—	4,400	3,750	8,150	1,000
January	4,000	4,100	—	—	8,100	1,500
February	—	—	4,400	3,500	7,900	1,620
March	3,000	3,000	2,000	—	8,000	1,240
April	—	—	2,000	4,500	6,500	—
May	3,000	2,000	2,000	—	7,000	—
June	1,000	—	2,000	3,000	6,000	—
July	2,000	3,000	2,000	—	7,000	—
August	2,000	2,000	—	2,000	6,000	—
Total	21,000	21,000	22,200	20,250	84,450	

*Number of units produced on overtime (included in the total units).

FIGURE 12.6
Beginning Inventory, Monthly Sales, and Ending Inventory in the Current Year

	18"	20"	20" SP	22" SP
Beginning Inventory	4,120	3,140	6,250	3,100
September	210	400	180	110
October	600	510	500	300
November	1,010	970	860	785
December	1,200	1,420	1,030	930
January	1,430	1,680	1,120	1,120
February	2,140	2,210	2,180	1,850
March	4,870	5,100	4,560	3,210
April	5,120	4,850	5,130	3,875
May	3,210	3,310	2,980	2,650
June	1,400	1,500	1,320	800
July	710	950	680	1,010
August	400	600	660	960
Total	22,300	23,500	21,200	17,600
End inventory	2,820	640	7,250	5,750

The beginning inventory, monthly sales and closing inventory for the current year are shown in Figure 12.6. The sales vary considerably from month to month with the strong sales season occurring from February through May. Not only are the sales highly seasonal, but total sales are dependent on a number of other factors, such as the weather and the economy. Thus, there is considerable uncertainty in addition to the seasonal variation. This can result in overall changes in volume and variations in the mix of models sold. An indication of the variation between expectations and actual sales can be seen in Figure 12.7, which provides the forecast and actual values for the last two years and next year's forecast.

Finished goods inventory was used to buffer against the uncertainties, to decouple production and sales, and to accommodate the cycle between models on the assembly line. When Lawn King was out of stock, any sales were backordered and filled from the next available production run. In an effort to avoid the backorders that were incurred last year, management decided to establish a planned minimum inventory of 2,000 units for each month.

FIGURE 12.7
Annual Sales Data in Units

	Last Year Forecast	Last Year Actual	This Year Forecast	This Year Actual	Next Year Forecast
18"	30,000	25,300	23,000	22,300	24,000
20"	11,900	15,680	20,300	23,500	35,500
20" SP	15,600	14,200	20,400	21,200	31,500
22" SP	10,500	14,320	21,300	17,600	19,000
Total	68,000	69,500	85,000	84,600	110,000

FIGURE 12.8
Actual Total Sales, Production, Employment, Inventory, and Overtime for the Current Year

Month	Actual Sales	Total Actual Production	Ending Inventory	Workforce	Overtime Production*
August			16,610	84	
September	900	6,100	21,810	73	
October	1,910	6,900	26,800	83	
November	3,625	6,800	29,975	82	
December	4,580	8,150	33,545	92	1,000
January	5,350	8,100	36,295	88	1,500
February	8,380	7,900	35,815	85	1,620
March	17,740	8,000	26,075	88	1,240
April	18,975	6,500	13,600	78	
May	12,150	7,000	8,450	84	
June	5,020	6,000	9,430	72	
July	3,350	7,000	13,080	84	
August	2,620	6,000	16,460	72	
Total	84,600	84,450			

*Included in the total actual production figures.

The determination of the cost of carrying inventory required estimates from nearly all of the management. The controller said that the cost of capital was on the order of 10 percent. The direct cost of storage (space, light, wages, etc.) was estimated to be about 4 percent of the amount invested, and design changes meant that there was some obsolescence which was estimated to be about 3 percent of the inventory investment. Thus a total of 17 percent of inventory value was to be used for the carrying cost per year for inventory. The average unit produced in the current year had $94.62 in material costs. The current year mix of regular and overtime resulted in $30.67 in direct labor costs. Thus, the average inventory carrying cost was estimated at $1.77/unit/month [($94.62 + $30.67) × (.17/12) = $1.77].

The actual sales, starting conditions, and ending conditions were the only other data needed for the planning model. The actual monthly sales for the individual product has been totaled to provide the total aggregate sales for the company during the current year selling season, which is shown in Figure 12.8. Also shown are the beginning aggregate inventory level and the beginning employment level of 84 direct workers. In addition, Figure 12.8 provides the closing aggregate inventory level and the actual direct workforce of 72 people. Using this data, the planning model could be run to determine the improvement in operating costs that could be obtained with the LP model. Once this was accomplished, additional work could be initiated to apply the model to the forecasts for next year's selling season so that these improvements could be obtained in the coming year.

Figure 12.8 also provides the data to determine a cost base against which to compare the results of the planning model. This figure shows the aggregate sales, production, inventory, workforce, and overtime production actually achieved in the current year. By applying the planning cost parameters to this data a cost basis can be developed for comparison with the LP model results. When the planning costs are applied to the actual current year's results, the total annual cost is $2,562,925. This includes: regular-time costs of $1,793,268, inventory carrying costs of $480,263, overtime costs of $177,094, firing costs of $79,500, and hiring costs of $32,800.

Solving the Linear Programming Model and Understanding the Results

The LP model was used to evaluate the actual operating performance for the current year's season. A summary of the planning assumptions and the cost parameters used in developing the model are provided in Figure 12.9. These parameters were used along with the actual sales figures to produce the LP results shown in Figure 12.10 for the current year's selling season. Overall, the LP model produced savings of $207,432, or 8.1% of the production planning related costs for actual operations.

FIGURE 12.9
LP Model Planning Assumptions and Cost Parameters

Regular-time cost/employee/month	$1828
Overtime cost/unit	$33.04
Inventory carrying cost/unit/month	$1.77
Hiring cost/employee	$800
Firing cost/employee	$1500
Regular-time productivity (units/month/employee)	83
Maximum overtime units/month	17
Ending inventory must be at least 2,000 units	
The August (current year) inventory is equal to 16,460 units	
The August (current year) employment level is 72	

FIGURE 12.10   LP Model Optimal Results for the Current Year's Selling Season

Month	Sales	Regular Production	Overtime Production	Workforce	Ending Inventory	Number Hired	Number Fired
September	900	6,972	—	84	22,682	—	—
October	1,910	6,972	—	84	27,744	—	—
November	3,625	6,972	—	84	31,091	—	—
December	4,580	6,972	—	84	33,483	—	—
January	5,350	6,972	—	84	35,105	—	—
February	8,380	7,221	—	87	33,946	3	—
March	17,740	7,221	—	87	23,427	—	—
April	18,975	7,221	—	87	11,673	—	—
May	12,150	7,221	—	87	6,744	—	—
June	5,020	7,221	—	87	8,945	—	—
July	3,350	7,221	—	87	12,816	—	—
August	2,620	5,976	—	72	16,460	—	15

In reviewing the differences between the LP model result in Figure 12.10 and the actual operating results shown in Figure 12.8 several conclusions can be drawn. First, substantial overtime was incurred by the plant to meet the actual sales demand. Overall, the employment-related costs of regular time and overtime totaled $1,970,362 for actual operations. Using the LP model, the total employment-related costs equaled $1,863,108, saving $107,254. The main difference is that while substantial overtime was used in actual operations ($177,094), the LP model used regular-time production capacity instead of overtime to produce nearly all of the product units.

Second, the employment level was adjusted each month, hiring and firing employees as required to meet the actual sales demand. This resulted in $112,300 in hiring and firing costs. In contrast, the LP model made small adjustments in the employment level in February and August, maintaining a relatively constant workforce throughout the year because of the magnitude of the hiring and firing costs. Thus, $87,400 was saved in hiring and firing costs.

Third, the LP model was also able to provide a small reduction in finished goods inventory and still meet the inventory goals of the company. This amounted to a reduction of $12,778 in total.

Many of the cost improvements are related to implementing an overall sales and operations plan as opposed to reacting to monthly variations in sales and customer backorders. Reducing the level of system nervousness produces a better balance of costs in managing operations. Clearly, the overall cost of operations is affected by the planning assumptions regarding the employment level and the ending inventory targets at the end of seasonal cycle (in this case ending figures for August of the current year). Different assumptions regarding the appropriate level for employment and inventory can change the overall cost of operations. These assumptions are heavily influenced by executive judgments regarding the sales forecast for the next year and the level of safety stock inventory needed to achieve the level of customer service required by the market. Such judgments are discussed and agreed on by senior executives in the company's sales and operations meetings.

Sales and Operations Planning Issues

After the results of the LP model and the comparisons to actual operating performance were available, a formal meeting of the senior managers of Lawn King was scheduled in a planning retreat. The purpose was to look at what adjustments should be made to the parameters as the basis for starting next year's planning. Although not called a sales and operations planning meeting, that is precisely what the company was doing. Here are some of the key points and perspectives brought out during the meeting.

1. *Marketing manager:* The company's best customers are complaining about back orders during the peak selling season. A few have threatened to drop the Lawn King product line if they don't get better service next year. It is important to produce not only enough product, but also to produce the right models to service the customer demand. We need to determine the right amount of inventory to avoid shortages on individual products when we have peaks in demand.

2. *Plant manager:* Three months ago the marketing and sales group predicted sales of 98,000 units for the next year. Now the forecast has been raised by 12 percent to 110,000 units. It is difficult to do a reasonable job of production planning when the target is always moving. The plant is already operating at full capacity, and the additional units in the new

forecast can't be made with one shift. A new shift might have to be added to accommodate the higher forecast. It is important to be sure these sales forecasts are realistic before hiring an entire second shift.

3. *General manager:* We have to be responsive to changing market conditions. We cannot permit the same stockout situation we experienced last year.

4. *Controller:* We must find a way to reduce costs. Last year we carried too much inventory, which required a great deal of capital. At 17 percent carrying cost, we cannot afford to build up as much inventory again next year.

5. *Personnel officer:* If we reduce our inventories by more nearly chasing demand, the labor force will fluctuate from month to month and our hiring and layoff costs will increase. These include the severance costs and supplemental unemployment benefits that are paid.

The sales and operations planning issues raised by the executives at Lawn King can be resolved using a planning model, such as a spreadsheet model or an LP model, and planning meetings can be focused on decision making by senior executive regarding the important trade-off issues between the various functions in the company. The development of the sales and operations plan can help in stimulating discussion between the executives in a company so that a consensus can be reached regarding the operating plans to be pursued by the company. It is critical to note that the sales and operations plan serves as the basis for other detailed plans and schedules in manufacturing, and provides the capacity available for responding to sales throughout the year. Business issues such as the amount of inventory investment necessary to ensure that customer demand is met, the timing and amount of investment in manufacturing capacity that is appropriate, and the acceptable level of employment costs that must be provided for in the sales and operations plan need to be resolved in order to be competitive in the market place.

Using Microsoft Excel Solver

The sales and operations planning problem at Lawn King can be addressed using the "Solver" tool in Microsoft Excel. Figure 12.11 shows a spreadsheet design to solve the problem. The table, starting on row 9, is the aggregate plan. The decision variables are in cells D10:D21 (regular production), E10:E21 (overtime production), H10:H21 (workers hired), and I10:I21 (workers fired). As given in the first constraint set of the model, ending inventory in each month is calculated as:

$$\text{Beginning inventory} + \text{Regular production} + \text{Overtime} - \text{Forecast demand}$$

The ending inventory for a month is the beginning inventory for the next month. Similarly, the workforce level for a month is:

$$\text{Previous month workforce level} + \text{Hires} - \text{Fires}$$

These are often called *balance equations* by those familiar with setting up linear programming models.

Maximum regular time production is calculated by taking the workforce level (C10:C21) and multiplying by the number of units produced by a regular-time employee per month (cell G7, 83 units). Overtime production is calculated in the same way, using the overtime maximum units per employee (G8, 17 units). These maximum levels are needed for setting up constraints that limit regular and overtime production.

FIGURE 12.11   Excel Lawn King Spreadsheet

	A	B	C	D	E	F	G	H	I	J	K	L
	Microsoft Excel - lawnking optimal.xls											
	File Edit View Insert Format Tools Data Window Help											
	G10		ƒ× =B10+D10+E10-F10									
1	Lawn - Optimal Solution				Costs:							
2					Cost/Employee/Month		$1,828					
3					Inventory Cost/Unit/Mon		$1.77					
4	Beginning Workforce =		84		OT Cost/Unit		$33.04					
5	August Workforce =		72		Hire Cost/Employee		$800					
6	Beginning Inventory =		16,610		Fire Cost/Employee		$1,500					
7	Ending Inventory Minimum =		2,000		Reg.Time Unit/Mo/Emp		83					
8	August Ending Inventory =		16,460		OT Max Units/Month		17					
9	Month	Beginning Inventory	Workforce	Reg. Production	Overtime	Sales	Ending Invent.	#Hired	#Fired	Max Reg Production	Max OT Production	Total Production
10	September	16,610	84	6,972	0	900	22,682	0	0	6,972	1,428	6,972
11	October	22,682	84	6,972	0	1,910	27,744	0	0	6,972	1,428	6,972
12	November	27,744	84	6,972	0	3,625	31,091	0	0	6,972	1,428	6,972
13	December	31,091	84	6,972	0	4,580	33,483	0	0	6,972	1,428	6,972
14	January	33,483	84	6,972	0	5,350	35,105	0	0	6,972	1,428	6,972
15	February	35,105	87	7,221	0	8,380	33,946	3	0	7,221	1,479	7,221
16	March	33,946	87	7,221	0	17,740	23,427	0	0	7,221	1,479	7,221
17	April	23,427	87	7,221	0	18,975	11,673	0	0	7,221	1,479	7,221
18	May	11,673	87	7,221	0	12,150	6,744	0	0	7,221	1,479	7,221
19	June	6,744	87	7,221	0	5,020	8,945	0	0	7,221	1,479	7,221
20	July	8,945	87	7,221	0	3,350	12,816	0	0	7,221	1,479	7,221
21	August	12,816	72	5,976	288	2,620	16,460	0	15	5,976	1,224	6,264
22												
23	Total Cost Model											
24		Hiring Cost	Firing Cost	Workf. Cost-RT	Overtime Cost	Invent. Cost	Total Cost					
25		$2,400	$22,500	$1,853,592	$9,516	$467,485	$2,355,493					
26												

Lawn King — Ready — NUM

Solutions are evaluated by calculating the total cost of the solution. Hiring cost is the sum of the number of employees hired during the year [SUM(H10:H21)] multiplied by $800 (G5). Firing cost is the number of employees fired during the year [SUM(I10:I21)] multiplied by $1,500 (G6). Workforce regular time cost is the number of regular time employees over the year [SUM(C10:C21)] multiplied by $1,828 (G2). Overtime cost is the number of units produced during overtime [SUM(E10:E21)] multiplied by overtime cost per unit (G4, $33.04). Inventory cost is the sum of the ending inventory levels [SUM(G10:G21)] multiplied by inventory cost per unit per month (G3, $1.77). The total cost is calculated by summing these individual costs [G25, SUM(B25:F25)].

Constraints and other parameters needed to solve this problem with Excel are specified in the Excel Parameters form (see Figure 12.12). This form is accessed through Tools then Solver menu options. First, the target cell is set to G25 and Equal To: is set to Min. This tells Solver to minimize the value calculated in cell G25 (i.e., total cost).

Next, By Changing Cells specifies the decision variables in the model. The Solver can change the values in two blocks of cells, D10:E21 and H10:I21. D10:E21 is where regular and overtime production is put into the model. H10:I21 is the block of cells for hiring and firing numbers. By specifying these cells in By Changing Cells, we are telling to program to determine the minimum cost solution by varying the values in these cells.

Next the remaining constraints need to be specified. Six constraints need to be specified. The first constraint forces the August workforce level to 72 employees (C21 = C5). The

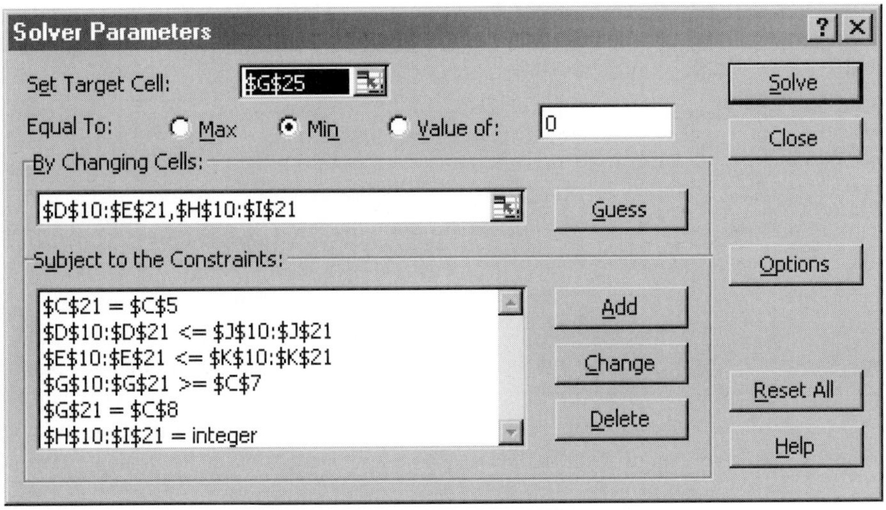

FIGURE 12.12
Solver Parameters

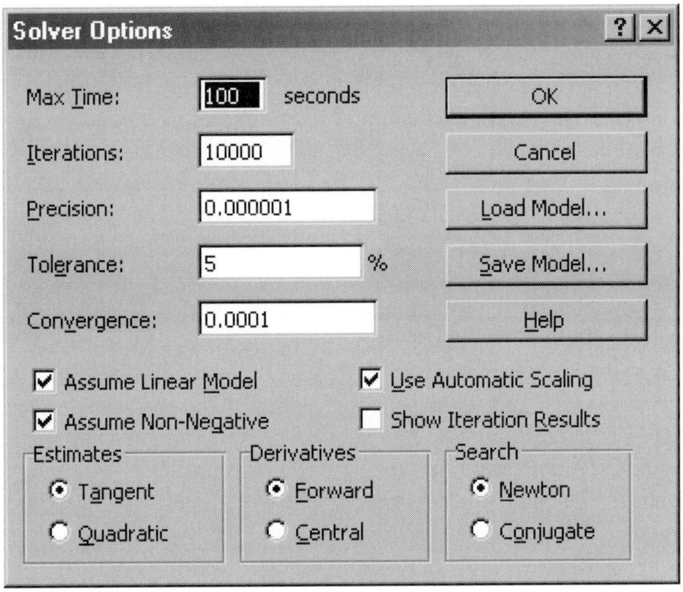

FIGURE 12.13
Solver Options

second requires regular-time production to be less than the maximum regular-time production (D10:D21 ≤ J10:J21). The third states that overtime production must be less than maximum overtime production (E10:E21 ≤ K10:K21). Next, we need monthly ending inventory levels to always be equal to or greater than 2,000 units (G10:G21 ≥ 2000). The fifth constraint forces ending inventory equal to 16,460 units (G21 = C8). Finally, the last constraint requires an integer number of employees.

Additional options need to be set through the Options button. Figure 12.13 shows this form. It is important that Assume Linear Model and Assume Non-Negative be checked on this form. Clicking OK returns to the Solver Parameters form. The problem can now be solved optimally by clicking on the Solve button. The optimal solution is given in Figure 12.11.

Applications Potential

The application of advanced sales and operations planning techniques has not been extensive. The linear decision rule model (LDR) is more than 30 years old, but has seen very limited application. Linear programming models have been more widely used, but generally for firms with relatively homogenous output measures and simple product structures, such as oil refineries and feed mixing plants. Hierarchical production planning, which is relatively new and parallels the managerial organization, has had few applications. Most interest in modeling techniques has been academic. Firms treating the aggregate production planning problem often combine approaches with long-range planning and budgeting cycles using simplified tabular or graphic methods. We see three key reasons for the lack of demonstrated applications of the theory.

The first reason is few firms actually make aggregate decisions in the way implied by the models. For most firms, the aggregate plans are merely the sum of several lower-level decisions. Among these decisions are output rates for particular factories, product lines, or even work centers. Management guidance on some overall or aggregate basis tends to be of a general nature, instead of providing a fixed set of constraints within which a process of disaggregation can unambiguously proceed. A related issue is the assumption of homogeneity. Some uniform measure of output makes more sense in a paint factory than in a multiproduct, multiplant firm. Also, there are great differences among workers. Analytical models treat them as equivalent.

A second reason for lack of application may be managerial understanding. It's difficult for many managers to understand quantitative models' analytic underpinnings. Our experience has shown the logic must be transparent to gain wide acceptance. This seems to be particularly true for aggregate planning models.

A final element inhibiting the expanded application of formal approaches is the data requirements. Often real-world data do not correspond to model assumptions. In other cases, data required do not exist. This is an area where databases like those developed for the manufacturing planning and control (MPC) system can help. We devote the next section to these important issues.

Data Issues

A high-quality database for manufacturing, especially if it's linked to the cost accounting and financial analysis system, can help greatly in gathering data for aggregate capacity analysis. Even so, many problems remain. Looking just at the data requirements for the models raises several issues.

Although of limited applicability in some countries (or companies), one of the most difficult issues is how to estimate hiring and firing costs. Clearly, the most important aspects of these costs are not part of the accounting records. In determining hiring costs, the more easily estimated components are recruiting, interviewing, and training. More difficult estimations are length of time to become fully effective, time to reach required quality levels, and ability to assimilate into the firm's social environment. Firing costs can be extremely difficult to assess, particularly in terms of the influence on morale. In most of the methods presented, we treated both hiring and firing costs as linear, with no constraints on the number of persons who could be hired or fired in a time period. In some examples, resulting labor force changes simply might not be possible. Moreover, costs of small adjustments are almost surely different from costs of large adjustments. A somewhat similar problem relates to overtime/undertime costs. Overtime in modest amounts represents a useful means for dealing with short-term capacity problems. However, to go from a 40-hour workweek to a 60-hour workweek is quite severe. Experience indicates there's a reduction in hourly productivity when people work that many hours. The situation is aggravated when the number of weeks worked on overtime increases. Moreover, the ability to vary the workweek at will is clearly very limited. Undertime costs are difficult to measure, especially in terms of long-term influence on worker morale, turnover, and loss of skill.

Inventory carrying costs might be linear over fairly wide ranges, but could change as capital resources are strained or new opportunities are developed. The percentage rate used to represent inventory carrying costs is presumed to include more than the interest charges from bank loans and direct storage costs. Risks of obsolescence, physical deterioration, and having the wrong items in finished goods also have to be considered. Again we raise the issue of finding a single aggregate output measure. Many firms rather cavalierly convert sales dollars to labor-hours to get such a measure. The assumptions are that all sales dollars are equal, any labor-hour can be used to make any sales dollar, and any inventory is, in fact, useful to meet any marketplace demand. In fact, an overall single homogenous capacity measure often isn't a meaningful concept in many firms. For example, the company with several different product lines, particularly if one product is highly labor intensive and another is capital intensive, will have difficulty finding a uniform capacity measure.

The Future

We feel guarded optimism about use of advanced sales and operations planning methods. As more and more firms implement MPC systems and continue to improve them, the applicability of more formal production planning becomes clear. This is typically first manifested in basic production planning where a monthly production plan is determined by a top-management group. As this process is refined, there's a natural tendency to consider formal models to support the effort. The trade-offs are better understood, as are costs to the firm.

Another reason for growing use of advanced planning models comes from better managerial understanding of underlying methodologies. Most business school students now learn linear programming and other mathematical methods.

Finally, MPC systems in the years ahead will necessarily focus on fast response. High clerical costs of a detailed MPC system with many levels of planning will fall as more firms migrate toward just-in-time (JIT) systems. However, the front-end sales and operations planning for these JIT systems remains critically important. Concepts like level schedules, flow rates, and close matching of manufacturing to the market all need effective production planning.

In summary, we feel many firms will be increasingly interested in advanced sales and operations planning methods. However, implementing these systems will remain difficult. Lessons learned from application to application indicate we have a long way to go before well-established guidelines emerge.

Concluding Principles

This chapter has reviewed formal approaches to sales and operations planning. We stress the following principles:

- The match between the real world and the model should be as close as possible to make it easier to build the credibility necessary to use the model.

- Relatively homogeneous product lines or portions of lines allow for a closer match between model and reality.

- Hierarchical approaches should be applied by management to match the production planning and disaggregation process to the appropriate organizational entities.

- Investing in training, enhancing data, improving basic MPC practices, and determining clear objectives must all be done before the full potential for using advanced techniques can be realized.

- Management must realize that significant efforts in model formulation, understanding, testing, and explanation are all important to successful applications.

- Advanced techniques must be built on a foundation of good basic practice. Modeling a mess doesn't make it better.

- Spreadsheet-based models offer a better choice for use by current executives.

References

Bechtold, Stephen E., and Larry W. Jacobs. "Subcontracting, Coordination, Flexibility, and Production Smoothing in Aggregate Planning." *Management Science* 36, no. 11 (November 1990), pp. 352–363.

Bitran, G. R.; E. A. Haas; and A. C. Hax. "Hierarchical Production Planning: A Two-Stage System." *Operations Research,* March-April 1982, pp. 232–251.

Chung, C., and L. J. Krajewski. "Planning Horizons for Master Production Scheduling." *Journal of Operations Management,* August 1984, pp. 389–406.

Connell, B. C.; E. E. Adam, Jr.; and A. N. Moore. "Aggregate Planning in Health Care Foodservice Systems with Varying Technologies." *Journal of Operations Management* 5 no. 1 (1985).

De Matta, R., and M. Guignard. "The Performance of Rolling Production Schedules." *IIE Transactions* 27 (1995).

Gelders, L. G., and L. N. Van Wassenhove. "Hierarchical Integration in Production Planning: Theory and Practice." *Journal of Operations Management* 3, no. 1 (1982).

Gordon, J. R. M. "A Multi-Model Analysis of an Aggregate Scheduling Decision." PhD Dissertation. Sloan School of Management MIT, 1966.

Holt, C. C.; F. Modigliani; J. F. Muth; and H. A. Simon. *Planning Production, Inventories, and Workforce.* New York: Prentice Hall, 1960, p. 16.

Holt, J. A. "A Heuristic Method for Aggregate Planning: Production Decision Framework." *Journal of Operations Management* 2, no. 1 (October 1981), pp. 43–51.

Lee, W. B.; E. Steinberg; and B. M. Khumawala. "Aggregate versus Dissaggregate Production Planning: A Simulated Experiment Using LDR and MRP." *International Journal of Production Research* 21, no. 6 (1983), pp. 797–811.

Leong, G. Keong; Michael Oliff; and Robert E. Markland. "Improved Hierarchical Production Planning." *Journal of Operations Management* 8, no. 2 (April 1989), pp. 90–114.

Martin, C. H.; D. C. Dent; and J. C. Eckhart. "Integrated Production, Distribution, and Inventory Planning at Libbey-Owens-Ford." *Interfaces* 23, no. 3 (1993).

Meal, H. L., and D. C. Whybark. "Material Requirements Planning in Hierarchical Planning Systems." *International Journal of Production and Operations Management* 25, no. 7 (1987), pp. 947–956.

Oden, Howard W. "Hierarchical Production Planning with Variable Planning Periods." DBA dissertation, Boston University, 1986.

Schroeder, Roger G. *Operations Management: Contemporary Concepts and Cases,* 2nd ed. Chicago: McGraw-Hill/Irwin, 2004.

Taubert, W. H. "A Search Decision Rule for the Aggregate Scheduling Problem."*Management Science* 14, no. 6 (February 1968).

Tersine, R. J.; W. W. Fisher; and J. S. Morris. "Varying Lot Sizes as an Alternative to Undertime and Days Off in Aggregate Scheduling." *International Journal of Production Research* 24, no. 1 (1986), pp. 97–106.

Vickery, S. K., and R. E. Markland. "Integer Goal Programming for Multistage Lot Sizing: Experimentation and Implementation." *Journal of Operations Management* 5, no. 2 (1985).

Discussion Questions

1. What is the least certain of the data inputs to sales and operations planning models? What can be done about this uncertainty?

2. What does a mixed integer programming formulation add over a linear programming approach?

3. What concerns should managers have about using sales and operations planning models?

4. How does the hierarchical approach match actual managerial practice?

5. Why have there been only limited documented successes of model applications to MPC activities?

6. In the disaggregation process, errors in the product mixes can occur. How do these creep in?

7. Why must we have effective MPC systems in place before we can anticipate adoption of advanced sales and operations planning concepts?

Problems

1. The Seymore Bicycle Manufacturing Company of Boise, Idaho, has developed the following demand forecast for next year's bicycle:

Quarter	Sales
1	5,000
2	10,000
3	8,000
4	2,000

On January 1, there are 1,000 units in inventory. The firm has prepared the following data:

Hiring cost per employee = $200.
Firing cost per employee = $400.
Beginning workforce = 60 employees.
Inventory carrying cost = $2 per unit per quarter of ending inventory.
Stockout cost = $5 per unit.
Regular payroll = $1,200 per employee per quarter.
Overtime cost = $2 per unit, limited to 40 units per employee per quarter.
Each employee can produce 100 units per quarter on regular time.
Demand not satisfied in any quarter is lost.

Using linear programming:

a. How much will Seymore produce during each quarter?

b. What's the total budget Seymore's plan will require for the next year?

2. Kosar Manufacturing has collected the following information on one of its major products. (Use a spreadsheet to model (a) and (b) below.)

Most efficient production rate = 2,100 units per period.
Production change costs = $15 per unit of change (from 2,100 units/period).

Inventory costs = $5 per unit per period (on closing inventory balance).
Backorder costs = $10 per unit to carry demand into next period.
Beginning inventory = 350 units.

Period	Demand (Units)
I	3,000
II	2,250
III	2,000
IV	2,700

a. Using the preceding demand schedule, calculate a level production schedule that yields zero inventory at the end of period IV.

b. Calculate the total costs associated with the production schedule in part a.

3. The Kew Toy Company's production manager wonders whether to produce at a level production rate or a rate that matches sales each quarter. His analysis of company operations yields the following information:

Beginning employment level = 10 employees.
Beginning inventory = 0
Hiring cost = $10 per employee.
Firing cost = $5 per employee.
Production per employee = 10 units per quarter.
Inventory carrying costs = $1 per unit per quarter (on ending inventory).
Target inventory at the end of the fourth quarter = 0.
Target employment level at the end of the fourth quarter equals the planned.

Employment level specified by the plan under consideration.

Quarter	Sales Forecast (Units)
1	50
2	80
3	120
4	150

a. Which of the two policies would result in the lowest annual cost?

b. What's the total annual cost of the policy adopted in part 1?

c. What production rate should he use each quarter?

d. Formulate this problem so it can be solved using linear programming.

4. Mischief Company had been experimenting with various sales and operations plans. As the firm started to lay out plans for next year, management decided to use a four-month planning horizon to reduce computation cost. The firm's basic data were:

Employment level for this December = 20 people.
Demand forecast for January of next year = 200.
Demand forecast for February of next year = 220.
Demand forecast for March of next year = 200.

Demand forecast for April of next year = 220.
Inventory level planned for the end of this December = 0.
Back orders aren't allowed in the plan.
Desired April ending inventory = 0.
Regular time per month = $2,000 per worker-month.
Production = 10 units/person/month.
Overtime premium = 50 percent of regular time.
Overtime limit = 25 percent of regular time per person per month.
Inventory carrying cost = $150/month/unit (on the average per month).
Hiring (or firing) cost = $2,000 per person.

Use a spreadsheet model to compare the cost of a fixed employment production plan (i.e., 20 people) that uses overtime to meet demand to a level production plan that uses no overtime to meet production.

5. Consider the following information for the Fairmount Company:

Production change cost = $20/unit of change (from a base of 4,000 units).
Most efficient production rate = 4,000 units per period.
Maximum amount of production capacity = 4,600 units per period.
Inventory costs = $4/unit per period on the ending inventory.
Shortage costs = $15/unit per period.
Subcontracting costs = $18/unit (maximum of 1,000 units per period).
Beginning inventory = 1,200 units.

Period	Demand (Units)
1	6,000
2	4,500
3	6,000
4	5,100

a. As production manager of Fairmount, you're in charge of meeting the preceding demand schedule for periods 1 through 4. President Shea specifies that you keep your production plan level for all four months. In addition, Shea limits the total amount of production per month to 4,600 units. Also, since the market Fairmount competes in is very competitive, planned stockouts are not allowed. Therefore, you must decide if and when to subcontract. Maximum amount of subcontracting available in any one period is 1,000 units. Ending inventory at the end of period 4 should be zero. Use a spreadsheet to determine your plan's cost.

b. Assuming the same facts as in part a, except that no subcontracting is allowed, could you follow a pure chase strategy and still meet demand? Why or why not?

6. On December 31, the ABC Company forecast its next year's sales to be:

Quarter	Sales Forecast
1	9,000 units
2	12,000
3	16,000
4	12,000
	49,000

Currently, the firm has 12 employees, each producing up to 1,000 units per quarter and earning $2,000 per quarter. The firm estimates its inventory carrying cost to be $2 per unit of ending inventory per quarter and its hiring or layoff costs to be $1,600 per employee. The firm could increase production by working overtime, but overtime work is limited to 25 percent of the regular production rate (or 250 units per employee per quarter). Overtime work is paid at the rate of 1.5 times the regular pay rate. Unused regular time costs the firm $4.16 per hour. (Assume there are 60 eight-hour days per quarter.) The company currently has an inventory of 1,000 units and wishes to have an ending inventory of 1,000 units at the end of the year. The company does not plan to incur inventory shortages.

a. Develop the total incremental cost expression of this problem.

b. Formulate this problem for solution, using linear programming.

c. What's the total incremental cost of a production plan that assumes a constant production rate (include both regular and overtime production) and level workforce (assume 12 workers) each quarter?

d. Compare the cost of the production plan in c to one based on a production rate equal to sales in each quarter. Which has the lowest cost?

7. The production manager at the Boston Paint Company is preparing production and inventory plans for next year. The production manager has the following data concerning the firm:

Quarter	Sales Forecast
1	3,000 units
2	1,800
3	2,400
4	3,500

Current inventory level = 300 units.
Current employment level = 600 people.
Production rate last quarter = 2,400 units (4 units/employee/quarter).
Inventory carrying cost = $20/unit/quarter (on ending inventory).
Hiring cost = $200/employee hired.
Layoff cost = $200/employee laid off.
Regular time production cost per unit = $320/unit.
Cost of overtime = $60/unit.
Desired closing inventory level = 100 units (minimum).

The production manager sees no equipment capacity limitations during the next two years. Employees are hired or laid off only at the beginning of each quarter.

a. Formulate a linear programming production planning model for this company, in sufficient detail so the production manager can solve it to determine the production plan.

b. After considering your recommendations, suppose the production manager revises his estimate of: (1) hiring and layoff costs and (2) overtime and idle time costs. The new costs are:

Cost of changing the employment level (Y_1):

$$Y_1 = \$200(Y_n - Y_{n-1})^2$$

Cost of producing on overtime or permitting idle time (Y_2):

$$Y_2 = \$60(S_n - AX_n)^2$$

where:

X_n = The number of people employed in quarter n.

$S_n =$ The planned production rate in quarter n.

$A =$ The number of units produced per employee per quarter.

Given this new information, how would you change your recommendations to the production manager regarding the formulation of a production planning model?

8. The Pickwick Company's production director and marketing director are currently negotiating next year's production and sales plans. The marketing director confidently forecasts a major sales increase as follows:

	Quarter			
	1	**2**	**3**	**4**
Sales forecast (in units)	950	1,200	1,420	1,630

a. Assume that the beginning inventory is 200 units and the target ending inventory for the fourth quarter is 200 units. What production each quarter will provide a level production plan?

b. If average variable cost per unit for items produced by Pickwick is $500, what will be the monetary value of the finished-goods inventory at the end of the second quarter if it uses a level production plan?

c. If average variable labor cost per unit for the items produced by Pickwick is $200 and average wage rate is $5 per hour, what's the quarterly labor budget in hours and in dollars for a level production plan?

9. The Columbia Manufacturing Company's sales manager has prepared the following sales forecast for next year:

Sales Forecast (in Units)

	Quarter			
Product Family	**1**	**2**	**3**	**4**
A	250	350	500	125
B	150	225	360	75

The production manager has supplied the following data:

Product Family A:

Two direct labor-hours per unit of product.
Setup cost equals $700 per changeover from B.
Setup time equals eight direct labor-hours per changeover.
Inventory carrying cost per quarter equals $1.50 per one direct labor-hour of work left in inventory at the end of the quarter.
Materials cost equals $70 per direct labor-hour of production.
The beginning inventory equals zero.

Product Family B:

One direct labor-hour per unit of product.
Setup cost equals $600 per changeover from A.
Setup time equals 10 direct labor-hours per changeover.
Inventory carrying cost per quarter equals $1 per one direct labor-hour of work left in inventory at the end of the quarter.

Materials cost equals $50 per direct labor-hour of production.
The beginning inventory equals zero.

In Addition, these Factors Apply:

Hiring cost per employee equals $1,500.
Firing cost per employee equals $500.
Overtime cost per direct labor-hour equals $15.
Regular time cost per direct labor-hour equals $10.
The maximum number of regular time hours to be worked per employee per quarter
equals 520.
Employees may not work more than 25 percent of the regular time hours on overtime
each quarter.

a. Formulate this problem for solution using mixed integer programming.
b. Why is linear programming not appropriate for solving this production planning problem?

10. The Columbia Manufacturing Company's production planning manager (in problem 9) has completed work on the firm's production plan for the coming year and is now preparing the master
production schedule for the next two weeks, indicating the lot size and timing for the firm's individual products. Selected data concerning Product Family A's production plan for the next two
weeks are as follows:

Item	Plan for Next Two Weeks
Production level	38 direct labor-hours during the 2 weeks
Closing inventory	5 direct labor-hours
Overtime hours	0
Family setup made	Yes

Additional Information:

Product Family A has two end products. (75 percent of the demand is for product 1;
the remainder is for product 2.)
The plant consists of a single machining center and each end product is processed in
one operation on the machining center.
Cost to back order one hour of production of either end product is $100.
Production lead time for each end product is zero.

a. Formulate the solution using linear programming. Assume that a weight of 1.0 is assigned to
each deviation variable.
b. What are the advantages and limitations of solving the master production scheduling problem separately from the production planning problem?

11. The sales manager at the Universal Manufacturing Company has prepared the following sales
forecast (in units) for next year:

Product Family	Quarter			
	1	**2**	**3**	**4**
A	3,500	6,000	4,000	1,300
B	1,200	2,000	2,800	3,600

The production manager has supplied the following data:

Product Family A:

Three direct labor-hours are needed per unit of product.
Setup cost equals $3,000 per changeover from product family B.
Setup time equals 16 direct labor-hours per changeover.
Inventory carrying cost per quarter equals $.50 per direct labor-hour of work in inventory at the end of the quarter.
Materials cost equals $130 per direct labor-hour of production.
Beginning inventory equals zero.

Product Family B:

Two direct labor-hours are needed per unit of product.
Setup cost equals $1,800 per changeover from A.
Setup time equals 24 direct labor-hours per changeover.
Inventory carrying cost per quarter equals $.33 per one direct labor-hour of work left in inventory at the end of the quarter.
Materials cost equals $105 per direct labor-hour of production.
Beginning inventory equals zero.

Additional Information:

Hiring cost per employee equals $2,000.
Firing cost per employee equals $1,500.
Overtime cost per direct labor-hour equals $18.
Regular time cost per direct labor-hour equals $12.
The maximum number of regular time hours to be worked per employee per quarter equals 600.

a. Formulate this problem for solution using mixed integer programming.
b. Why is linear programming not appropriate for solving this production planning problem?

12. The production planning manager at the Universal Manufacturing Company (in problem 11) has completed the firm's production plan for the coming year. He's now preparing the master production schedule for the next two weeks, indicating the lot size and timing for the firm's individual products. Selected data on the production plan for the next two weeks for product family B is as follows:

Item	Plan for Next Two Weeks
Production level	370 direct labor-hours during the 2 weeks
Closing inventory	25 direct labor-hours
Overtime hours	0
Family setup made	Yes

Additional Information:

There are two end products in product family B. (Sixty percent of the demand is for product 1; the remainder is for product 2.)

The plant consists of a single machining center and each end product is processed in one operation on the machining center.

The cost to back order one hour of production of either end product is $50.
Product lead time for each end product is zero.

    a. Prepare a master production schedule for the next two weeks that conforms to the production plan.

    b. What is the cost of labor, material, and inventory for this master production schedule?

13. The executives at Lawn King are developing a sales and operations plan for the 2004 season. Using the cost parameters and the operating assumptions provided in this chapter, please formulate and solve an LP model to specify an optimal plan for 2004.

14. Please prepare a sensitivity analysis on the optimal solution reached in Problem 13. What is the impact on the solution of independent changes in:

    a. the Hiring and Firing costs?

    b. the Inventory Carrying Cost?

    c. the target ending inventory on August 31, 2004?

13

Strategy and MPC System Design

This chapter concerns two integration issues in designing manufacturing planning and control (MPC) systems. The first is linking the design of a firm's MPC system with its corporate strategy for competing in the marketplace. As the investment in an MPC system is large, getting it correct is critical to short- and long-term prosperity. Many companies make costly mistakes when their MPC system doesn't support their basic mission in the marketplace. The second issue concerns integrating manufacturing requirements planning (MRP) and just-in-time (JIT) in existing or new MPC systems. The chapter centers around four topics:

- *MPC design options:* What are critical alternatives in designing an MPC system to meet a firm's evolving needs?
- *Choosing the options:* How should the options be selected to best support the corporate strategy and to fit with production process design?
- *The choices in practice:* How have manufacturing firms with different competitive missions gone about designing their MPC systems?
- *Integrating MRP and JIT:* How can these different approaches be linked in a company's MPC system?
- *Extending MPC Integration to Suppliers and Customers:* How can MPC applications be integrated across the supply chain to improve competitiveness?

Integrated MPC design issues are connected to nearly every chapter in this book, especially Chapters 7 and 9 (the basic chapters on MRP and JIT) and Chapters 14 and 15 (on MRP and JIT's advanced features). Chapter 18's coverage of operational issues concerning MPC system implementation in organizations complements the strategic view of Chapter 13.

MPC Design Options

A wide range of alternatives are available in designing MPC systems. These include such basic approaches as MRP, MRPII, JIT, OPT (optimized production technology), periodic control systems, and finite scheduling systems. Moreover, there are a wide variety of options

FIGURE 13.1
Basic MPC System

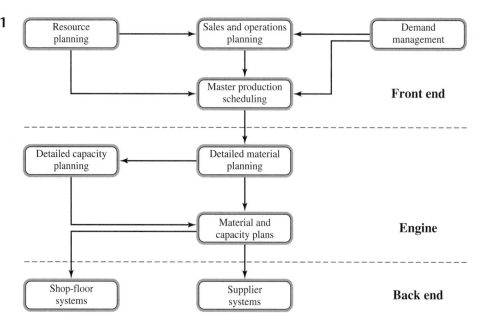

for designing the individual modules of the MPC system shown in Figure 13.1. The next three sections illustrate the variety of options for master production scheduling, detailed material planning, and back-end activities.

Master Production Scheduling Options

Several different approaches can be taken to designing the master production schedule: *make-to-order (MTO), assemble-to-order (ATO),* and *make-to-stock (MTS).* Figure 13.2 shows the major differences between these alternatives. A **make-to-order** approach to master production scheduling is typical when the product is custom-built to individual customer specifications. In this case the MPC system needs to encompass preproduction engineering design activities as well as manufacturing and supplier operations. For MTO, the customer order represents the unit of control in the MPS; the backlog of customer orders forms part of the overall lead time for the product. Overall, the order backlog is a critical measure for estimating material and capacity requirements. Customer order promising is based on the backlog plus estimates for each design, procurement, and manufacturing step for a particular job. Planning bills of material are extensively utilized to estimate times and to prioritize design efforts on the "critical path." There's an inherently large degree of uncertainty associated with the time requirements, since each order requires a unique approach.

An **assemble-to-order** approach is typically used when overall manufacturing lead time exceeds that desired by the customer, where the variety and cost of end products preclude investment in finished-goods inventory, and where engineering design has created modules or options that can be combined in many ways to satisfy unique customer requirements. Here component (or product option) inventory is held to reduce overall manufacturing lead time, and end products are assembled to meet the scheduled delivery dates for individual customer orders. As Figure 13.2 shows, a key control point is the final assembly schedule (FAS), which converts "average" products into unique products in response to actual customer orders.

FIGURE 13.2   Features of Master Production Scheduling Approaches

	Master Scheduling Approach		
	MTO	ATO	MTS
Basis for planning and control			
Control point	Order backlog	FAS	Forecast
MPS unit	Customer orders	Options	End items
Product level	End product	End to intermediate product	End product
MPS features			
Customer order promising	High requirement	⟶	Low requirement
Need to monitor forecast accuracy	Low requirement	⟶	High requirement
Use of planning bills	Yes	Yes	No
Need to cope with design and process uncertainty	High	⟶	Low
Basis of delivery to customer	Make to customer order on time	Make to customer order on time	Make-to-stock replenishment order or to customer call-off schedule

Planning bills of material are based on average products and on optional features. The planning bills reflect how the product is sold, rather than how it's manufactured. They are often used to simplify data requirements in preparing and maintaining the master production schedule. The uncertainty underlying an ATO business is fundamentally one of product mix, rather than one of product volume. The MPS and FAS are designed to hold off commitment to unique product configurations until the last possible moment and yet to offer wide configuration choices to customers.

Under **make-to-stock (MTS),** the MPS is stated in end items, and these end products are produced to forecast demand; customer orders are filled directly from stock in order to provide short delivery lead times for standardized products. While customer order promising records are not normally required, we must provide procedures for monitoring demand forecasts' accuracy since manufacturing plans are mostly based on forecast information. This means the type of uncertainty inherent in the MTS environment is one of forecasting errors; the manufacturing function needs to recognize errors on a timely basis and to make corrective responses.

Detailed Material Planning Options

We can accomplish detailed material planning in several ways. Two popular alternatives are *time-phased* and *rate-based material planning.* Use of these approaches depends importantly in the production process's design characteristics. Figure 13.3 shows key differences between these approaches.

Time-phased planning for individual product components is typically carried out with material requirements planning approaches. The production process design is usually based on **batch manufacturing** and materials are also purchased in batch orders. Preparation of time-phased plans requires a manufacturing database that includes information on: MPS

FIGURE 13.3 Features of Detailed Material Planning Approaches

	Material Planning Approach	
	Time-Phased	**Rate-Based**
Basis for planning and control		
Control point	Shop/purchase orders	Planning bills
Control unit	Batches	Kanbans
Product level	Material explosion of time-phased net requirements for product components	Material explosion of rate-based requirements for product components
Material planning features		
Fixed schedules	No	Yes
Use of WIP to aid planning	High	Low
Updating	Daily/weekly	Weekly/monthly
Inventory netting	Performed	None
Lead-time offsetting	Performed	None
Lot sizing	Performed	None
Safety stock/safety lead time	Considered	Not considered
Container size	Not considered	Considered
Bill of material	Many levels	Single level

quantities stated in bill of material terminology to determine gross requirements; on-hand inventory balances and open shop (or purchase) orders to determine net requirements; production lead times, supplier lead times, and safety stocks to determine order release dates; and lot size formulas to determine order quantities. Under MRP, plans are typically updated on a periodic (daily or weekly) basis to develop priorities for scheduling manufacturing and supplier operations.

As Figure 13.3 indicates, time-phased material planning is based on explosion of requirements, where shop and purchase orders are created for batches of components. The schedule for any work center varies depending on the batches that arrive at that work center; work in process is kept at high levels to effectively utilize work center capacities. Planning is carried out on a level-by-level basis corresponding to the levels in the bill of materials (BOM), with material going into and out of inventory at each level. Detailed planning is required for each level in the BOM, and lead time offsetting is utilized at each level.

A different approach is taken to detailed material planning under **rate-based planning.** Examples of firms using rate-based planning include repetitive manufacturing, assembly lines, just-in-time, and other flow systems. The primary intent in rate-based scheduling is to establish rates of production for each part in the factory. Realizing these rates allows the company to move material through the manufacturing system without stopping, in the shortest time possible. Typically, single-level planning bill of material information is used to convert rate-based master production schedules into material plans that specify the appropriate daily or hourly flow rates for individual component items. Planning of intermediate items in the bill of materials is not usually required, because the number of intermediate-level items is too small to be of concern. Because of MPS stability, high rates of material flow, negligible work-in-process inventory levels, short manufacturing lead times, and a relatively small variety of final products in the MPS, we don't need detailed status information on work-in-process items. This reduces the manufacturing database's size, the number of transactions, and the number of material planning personnel in comparison with time-phased detailed material planning.

Shop-Floor System Options

A wide variety of manual and computer-based shop-floor scheduling systems exist. The two basic approaches (material planning driven by MRP and material planning driven by JIT) depend greatly on the manufacturing process's characteristics. Figure 13.4 distinguishes between these approaches.

The MRP-based approach supports batch manufacturing operations where shop orders are released against a schedule developed by the material planning function, based on lead times for component and subassembly items largely comprised of queue or waiting time. The shop-floor scheduling system's objective is to coordinate the sequencing of orders at individual work centers with customer delivery requirements. A large manufacturing database requiring a substantial volume of shop transactions is needed to provide control reports for order tracking, dispatching, and work center monitoring.

FIGURE 13.4 **Features of Shop-Floor System Approaches**

	Shop-Floor System Approach	
	MRP	**JIT**
Basis for planning and control		
Control basis	Work center capacity utilization	Overall product flow times
Unit of control	Shop orders	Kanban cards or containers
Product level	Individual operations scheduled at each work center	Production on an as-required basis to replenish downstream stocks that support end-item requirements
Shop-floor system features		
Control of material flow	Work center dispatching rules	Initiated by downstream kanban cards
Sequencing procedure	Due-date-oriented dispatching rule	Not an issue
Order tracking	Shop-floor transactions by operation and stocking point	None (paperless system)
Monitoring and feedback	Input/output and shop load reports	Focus on overall result
Order completion	Shop order close-out in stockroom	None
Achieving delivery reliability	Batch order status reports	Through flow of material
Lot size	Large	Small
Work in process and safety stock	Large	Negligible

In MRP-based shop-floor systems, one objective is to utilize each work center's capacity effectively. The form of manufacturing is based on relatively large batches of each component and significant work-in-process inventories to support independence among the work centers. This shop-floor approach is based on scheduling shop orders that dictate the set of detailed steps or operations necessary to make each component part. The flow of materials is controlled with dispatching rules establishing the order in which all jobs in a particular work center are to be processed. The primary criterion in establishing this order are the due dates for the parts, which are continually reestablished through MRP planning. Shop orders are tracked as they progress through the factory by processing detailed transactions of work at every work center. Shop orders are opened as part of MRP planning, and they're closed out as components are received into a stockroom. Problems are highlighted through input/output analysis and shop load reports.

In JIT-based shop-floor scheduling systems, the approach is based on minimal flow times for the entire product. That is, the emphasis is on end items, with the scheduling of individual operations, and even component parts, in a subservient position. Cellular manufacturing techniques are typically employed, where detailed scheduling is accomplished as part of the basic manufacturing task. Kanban cards, containers, and other signals of downstream need for components serve as the authorization to produce, typically in small lot sizes. The sequencing procedure isn't an issue because work is only started on an as-needed basis, with little or no competition for work center capacity. Similarly, order tracking is nonexistent since work in process is minimal, and material moves through the factory quickly enough to negate the need for tracking. The only close-out is of finished items. Often the close-out transaction generates a computer-based "back flush" of the requisite component parts. The very short queue times, small lot sizes, and relatively narrow product range in JIT can result in a paperless shop-floor scheduling system. The manufacturing database requirements, volume of shop transactions, and number of shop scheduling personnel are minimal.

Many authorities have attempted to use the terms *push* and *pull* to distinguish between MRP-based and JIT-based shop-floor systems. The argument is, under JIT, when a customer "pulls" some product out of inventory it pulls some replacement inventory from the factory, which pulls some parts from the shops, which pulls some materials from the store rooms, and so on. On the other hand, MRP-based systems "push" components into the factory, then into inventory, then back into manufacturing, and so on. We find this terminology to be not very helpful. It has spawned debates over whether MRP is a push or pull system, whether kanbans are a part of a pull system when the company is make-to-stock with inventory, or if a JIT system is push-based when the need for an end item is exploded into raw materials that are then sent through the factory without any kanban type of replenishment. These debates simply aren't very helpful. The distinction we believe is useful pertains to whether individual work centers are allowed to utilize capacity ("to keep busy") without being driven by a specific end-item schedule. Increasingly, JIT is being utilized in nonrepetitive environments, where specific product configurations are moved through manufacturing in short lead times without tracking or other transactions and capacity utilization is a result, not an objective.

The key distinction we're trying to make is these two approaches' characteristics must match the manufacturing process and infrastructure in which they operate. Activities in the MRP-based systems are triggered by processes authorizing production quantities, routings, due dates, and so forth. JIT-based systems produce in response to downstream use of the item, which may be work center by work center or may be in response to demand for the overall end item. For systems installed to date, relatively constant demands are required for the JIT-based approach to function.

Choosing the Options

There's a temptation to view some MPC design options as a continuum where movement toward JIT is "good." This isn't the correct conclusion. We must match MPC system design with the ongoing needs of a company's market, the task in manufacturing, and the manufacturing process. An MPC system represents a major investment in a business, and as such it must be designed to support the firm's competitive strategy. The framework for accomplishing this was developed by Berry and Hill. Let's turn to how this matching takes place.

Market Requirements

Figure 13.5 shows how MPC system design is influenced by a company's market requirements and the resultant manufacturing task. Figure 13.5 labels these last two factors "business specifications." The point is these determine, from a business point of view, what has to be done in manufacturing to serve the chosen markets. Then technical requirements are defined. This involves the interaction of the manufacturing task, MPC system, and manufacturing process. Each of these three areas needs to be carefully considered before the choices can be made in the approaches in master production scheduling, detailed material planning, and shop-floor scheduling. Moreover, the three areas must be seen as constantly changing: new customer requirements, new process technology, and new strategic goals in manufacturing. Any of these can mandate a change in the MPC system design.

Figure 13.5 also shows the MPC system design as influenced by the desired MPC system and existing MPC system. In some cases, improvements can be made by investing in the evolution of the existing system design. In other cases, we need to start afresh.

The first step in the development of market requirements is to review the customers and market segments targeted by the business, their present needs with regard to the company's products and services, competitors' products and services, and existing sales growth

FIGURE 13.5
MPC System
Design Choices

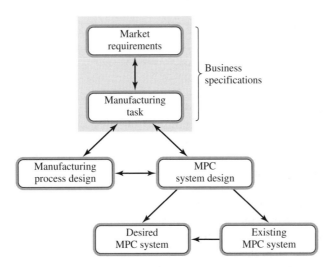

opportunities. Many companies face dynamic markets where customer requirements and global competition are changing dramatically. We must continuously review market requirements and adapt marketing strategies to exploit opportunities. For example, many companies increasingly see the need to enhance their products with services to help their customers solve problems. *Market focus, customer prosperity,* and *delighting the customer* are common phrases. But if these phrases are to be more than hype, we must redefine the manufacturing task to create the desired results. Thereafter, we may have to redesign the MPC system as well as the manufacturing process. To illustrate, the manufacturing organization in a packaging materials firm supplying the food industry suddenly had to deliver products in small quantities on a twice weekly basis to support its major customer's new JIT program. Neither the production process nor the MPC system was designed to support the changed business requirements. More fundamentally, the firm's manufacturing strategy had to be revised to support this kind of customer requirement.

The Manufacturing Task

The next step in choosing MPC system design options is to develop a statement of the manufacturing task that's consistent with (and that supports) the marketing strategy. If the company decides to satisfy customers on a just-in-time basis, this has to be reflected in the manufacturing task. Similarly, if quality is now the way to win orders, it too must be reflected in changed manufacturing values, process investments, improvements in the quality support function, and revised manufacturing performance measurements. If the targeted customers are moving toward more highly customized products, again, this needs to be captured in the manufacturing task.

Hill points out that stating the manufacturing task for the business is critical to ensuring that manufacturing capabilities are developed to support the different targeted market segments. Developing the manufacturing task involves characterizing the markets targeted by the company in terms of the requirements they place on manufacturing as described by Hill's manufacturing strategy framework. Such requirements may, for example, include volume and delivery flexibility, low-cost production, critical product quality specifications, and other manufacturing-related capabilities—whatever is required to win orders in different market segments.

A clear statement of the manufacturing task enables management to recognize that major changes may be required in the design of both production processes and the MPC system. Figure 13.5 shows this by the two-headed arrows linking the manufacturing task to the design of both manufacturing processes and MPC systems.

Manufacturing Process Design

Most firms have large investments in production processes, employee capabilities, and other elements of infrastructure in manufacturing. As a consequence they tend to change shortly over time. This establishes the manufacturing capabilities of a company according to Hill's process choice framework.

The arrow linking manufacturing process design and MPC design indicates the interdependency between MPC option choices and manufacturing process features. For example, installing a JIT process with cellular manufacturing and short production lead times means rate-based detailed material planning approaches may be much more appropriate than time-phased approaches.

A more subtle example of manufacturing process design impacting MPC system design occurs in the case of quality improvement programs. Many companies use complex scheduling procedures because the firms suffer from poor quality and the resultant unpleasant surprises. Quality is usually improved through investments in better manufacturing processes. Where quality is enhanced significantly, there are fewer surprises, the company is better able to execute routine plans, and MPC systems can be more straightforward.

Finally, in some cases there are simultaneous changes in marketplace requirements, manufacturing processes, and manufacturing task definitions. For example, computer manufacturers at one time faced a very long lead time to make a computer; they achieved customization by individual wiring and other hardware features. New computers were "announced" in the marketplace long before they were available for shipment, customers would place orders just to get their place in the queue of orders, and the MPC system had to manage a fictitious backlog of orders. Moreover, each order's configuration would constantly change and delivery dates would be extended or canceled. The net result was a very complex set of requirements for the MPC system. Now computers are relatively easy to make, most customization is done with software, and orders are rapidly shipped. Moreover, computers per se are becoming a commodity; IBM and other companies increasingly view their manufacturing strategy as solving problems for their customers. The resultant changes in end "products"—and the processes that produce them—dictate a completely different set of design requirements for the MPC system.

MPC System Design

Because of the magnitude of the investment in MPC systems and the time required to implement MPC system changes, we must recognize differences between desired and existing MPC system options and features. Figure 13.5 shows this by the lines connecting MPC system design with desired and existing MPC systems. A company currently using time-phased MRP records while installing a JIT process with cellular manufacturing might continue to use MRP records with some modifications until necessary investment funds and management time were available to make the MPC system changes required to implement rate-based material planning. Although the marketing strategy, manufacturing task, manufacturing process, and MPC system design specifications might have been agreed upon within the business, the opportunity to move to implementation might not yet have occurred.

This example illustrates another integration issue—consistent MPC option choices. We need to have the right choice (and consistency) in the MPS approach, the detailed material planning approach, and the shop-floor system approach. This issue frequently arises during JIT implementation in a company using MRP for detailed material planning in which batch and line production processes are appropriate for different parts of the business. Therefore, issues of how to link JIT and MRP options in MPC system design and how to maintain *one* MPC system are often difficult. Our experience indicates attention paid to marketplace requirements and to how these requirements may be changing helps you determine the dominant choices among the MPC options.

Master Production Scheduling Options

In Figure 13.6 the three MPS approaches are related to key aspects of marketplace requirements and to aspects of the manufacturing task and manufacturing process. A make-to-order (MTO) master scheduling approach supports products of wide variety and custom design,

FIGURE 13.6 Linking Market Requirements and Manufacturing Strategy to Design of the MPS Approach

Strategic Variables			Master Scheduling Approach		
			MTO	ATO	MTS
Market requirements	Product	Design	Custom	⟶	Standard
		Variety	Wide	⟶	Predetermined and narrow
	Individual product volume per period		Low	⟶	High
	Delivery	Speed	Through overlapping schedules	Through reducing process lead time	Through eliminating process lead time
		Reliability	Difficult	⟶	Straight-forward
Manufacturing	Process choice		Low-volume batch	⟶	High-volume batch/line
	Managing fluctuations in sales volume		Through order backlog	Through WIP or finished goods inventory	Through finished goods inventory

frequently involving the development of engineering specifications. They're typically produced in low unit volumes, where delivery speed is achieved through overlapping schedules for design and manufacture of the various elements comprising the customer order. Delivery reliability is somewhat difficult to guarantee, since products are customized to meet individual customer needs. This approach is frequently used to support markets characterized by high levels of product change and new product introductions, and where the firm's competitive advantage is in providing product technology requirements in line with the customer's delivery and quality requirements. Since the manufacturing task often involves providing a broad range of production capabilities, the process choice supports low-volume batch manufacturing. One key aspect of the manufacturing task is how to respond to fluctuations in sales volumes. These are typically managed through adjustments in the level of the customer order backlog.

An assemble-to-order (ATO) master scheduling approach represents an intermediate position. Products of both standard and special design are produced, and variety is accommodated by customer selection from a wide series of standardized product options. The unit production volumes are relatively high at the option level, and customer responsiveness in regard to delivery speed is enhanced by lead time reductions and short time frames for frozen final assembly schedules. Delivery reliability is well accommodated as long as overall volumes are kept within planning parameters. That is, the ATO environment is designed to be relatively accommodative of changes in product mix.

Typically, ATO manufacturing is done in batches, with more and more firms using cellular approaches for popular options and families of similar parts. Stocking components, intermediate subassemblies, or product option items can shorten customer lead time to that of the final assembly process, thereby improving delivery speed and reliability in markets where fluctuations in sales volumes are hard to anticipate.

The make-to-stock (MTS) master scheduling approach supports products of standard design produced in high unit volumes in narrow product variety for which short customer delivery lead times are critical. Delivery speed is enhanced by reducing process lead times, frequently by adopting flow-based manufacturing methods. Reliability of production schedules is relatively straightforward.

The process choice is usually line manufacturing or high-volume batch manufacturing. While an investment in finished-goods inventory can provide short, reliable delivery lead times to customers, and can buffer fluctuations in sales, it can also enable us to stabilize production levels, thereby permitting important cost improvements in manufacturing. Since products are often produced on high-volume batch or line processes, schedule stability is often critical, especially in price-sensitive markets.

Material Planning Options

Figure 13.7 relates the two detailed material planning approaches to key aspects of marketplace requirements and to aspects of manufacturing task and manufacturing process. Time-phased detailed material planning is appropriate for custom products produced in wide variety and low volumes. It also facilitates schedule changes and revisions in

FIGURE 13.7   Linking Market Requirements and Manufacturing Strategy to the Design of the Detailed Material Planning Approach

Strategic Variables			Detailed Material Planning Approach	
			Time Phased	Rate Based
Market requirements	Product	Design	Custom	Standard
		Variety	Wide	Narrow
	Individual product volume per period		Low	High
	Ability to cope with changes in product mix		High potential	Limited
	Delivery	Speed	Through scheduling/ excess capacity	Through inventory
		Schedule changes	Difficult	Straightforward
Manufacturing	Process choice		Batch	Line
	Source of cost reduction	Overhead	No	Yes
		Inventory	No	Yes
		Capacity utilization	Yes	No

customer delivery dates as well as changes in product mix. Delivery speed is enhanced through better scheduling, based on relative priorities. This approach can be applied in markets characterized by a high rate of new product introductions, rapid shifts in product technology, and custom-engineered products by using planning bill of material techniques.

Time-phased planning is often associated with batch manufacturing and is supported by relatively high overhead and work-in-process inventory costs due to the necessary planning staff and extensive transaction processing. This planning approach can result in higher capacity utilization and is often favored in manufacturing facilities employing expensive equipment.

Rate-based material planning is appropriate for a relatively narrow range of standard products, with stable product designs produced in high volume. Rate-based detailed material planning is much more limited in its ability to cope with changes in product mix. The limited product line permits straightforward changes in the schedule as long as they're within the product design specifications. Enhancements in customer delivery speed are typically accommodated with finished-goods inventories.

These marketplace requirements are normally best supported in manufacturing by production line processes. Use of rate-based material planning and line production processes yields an opportunity to cut work-in-process inventory and overhead costs, providing important support for price-sensitive markets. On the other hand, rate-based material planning doesn't support intensive utilization of capacities in the same way as time-phased approaches.

Shop-Floor System Options

In Figure 13.8 the two shop-floor system approaches are related to key aspects of marketplace requirements and to aspects of manufacturing task and manufacturing process. The MRP-based approach to shop-floor scheduling is appropriate when a wide variety of custom products is produced in low unit volumes. Changes in demand are accommodated relatively easily; volume changes are supported by overtime operations in critical work centers, and product mix change is an inherent characteristic. This approach supports markets characterized by rapid changes in product technology, high rates of new product introduction, and substantial changes in product design.

Low-volume batch or jobbing processes involve use of the MRP-based shop-floor scheduling system approach. These processes have significant changeover costs and numerous manufacturing steps, requiring a complex shop-floor scheduling system that's centrally driven, thereby limiting the reduction of overhead and inventory-related costs.

JIT-based approaches for shop-floor scheduling provide important support for standard products produced in limited variety and high volume. Such products are best supported by high-volume batch or line production processes that are able to provide short customer lead times. Accommodation of changes in product volume is limited because of the cost of production schedule and capacity changes; this increases the need for schedule stability. Delivery speed is enhanced by short manufacturing throughput times and often by finished-goods inventories.

The emphasis on inventory reduction and the simplicity of shop-floor control procedures under the JIT approach provide the potential for significant cuts in overhead and inventory-related costs, providing important support for price-sensitive markets.

FIGURE 13.8 **Linking Market Requirements and Manufacturing Strategy to the Design of the Shop-Floor System Approach**

Strategic Variables			Shop-Floor System Approach	
			MRP Based	**JIT Based**
Market requirements	Product	Design	Custom	Standard
		Variety	Wide	Narrow
	Individual product volume per period		Low	High
	Accom- modating demand changes	Total volume	Easy/incremental	Difficult/stepped
		Product mix	High	Low
	Delivery	Speed	Achieved by schedule change	Achieved through finished goods inventory
		Schedule changes	More difficult	Less difficult
Manufacturing	Process choice		Low-volume batch	High-volume batch/line
	Changeover cost		High	Low
	Organizational control		Centralized	Decentralized (shop-floor based)
	Work in process		High	Low
	Source of cost reduction	Overheads	Low	High
		Inventory	Low	High

The Choices in Practice

Achieving a close fit between marketplace requirements, the manufacturing task and process, and the MPC system design gives a firm important competitive advantages. In this section we briefly describe marketing and manufacturing strategies of three companies (Moog, Inc., Space Products Division; Kawasaki, U.S.A.; and Applicon, Division of Schlumberger) and how they've designed their MPC systems. Figure 13.9 shows the three MPC systems' overall design. Moog uses MTO and ATO approaches to master production scheduling, a time-phased approach to detailed material planning, and an MRP-based shop-floor system. Kawasaki uses MTS master production scheduling, rate-based material planning, and JIT shop-floor scheduling. Applicon uses ATO master production scheduling, both MRP and rate-based scheduling for material planning, and a JIT-based shop-floor system.

FIGURE 13.9
Linking
Business
Characteristics
to the Design of
MPC Systems

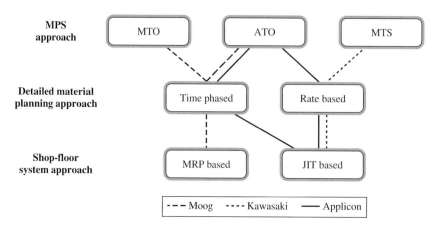

Moog and Kawasaki represent examples of stable MPC system designs to support the requirements of a single market. Applicon, however, provides an example of an MPC system that changed in response to shifting market requirements and process design changes. Let's now see the overall pattern of decisions in each firm concerning the influence of marketing and manufacturing strategy on MPC system design, and see how the resultant systems support their businesses.

Moog, Inc., Space Products Division

This firm produces high-quality hydraulic systems of advanced design for the aerospace industry. These products cover a wide range of design types and represent a critical element in the overall production lead times for its aerospace customers. The company designs and produces the initial order for new products as well as follow-on orders. Thus, engineering design and advanced product features are key factors in obtaining sales. Other important factors that qualify the firm to compete in this market include delivery reliability, reputation for quality, and price. Figure 13.10 summarizes characteristics of the market served by Moog along with key elements of its manufacturing strategy.

The manufacturing task involves providing a broad range of equipment and employee capabilities to make high-precision, custom-designed products in low unit volumes. Substantial uncertainty exists with regard to production process yields and time estimates to produce initial orders. In addition, design changes contribute to process uncertainty. Labor cost is a significant portion of product cost since highly skilled employees and a wide variety of precision equipment are keys to the production process. Major investments have been made in numerical control (NC) and computerized numerical control (CNC) equipment as well as machining centers in a batch manufacturing process.

All manufacturing planning and control system functions in Figure 13.1 are performed at Moog. Both make-to-order and assemble-to-order master production scheduling approaches are used. The MPS is stated in terms of actual, anticipated, and forecast customer orders with substantial emphasis on customer order promising and capacity planning activities. The master production schedule uses this information to determine requirements for component material. Time-phased material requirements planning records are used to coordinate scheduling of manufactured and purchased components, and these records are used to prepare shop load forecasts for individual departments and work centers.

FIGURE 13.10 Moog, Inc., Space Products Division

Market Characteristics	Manufacturing Strategy				
	Manufacturing		Manufacturing Planning and Control System		
	Task	Features	Master Production Scheduling	Detailed Material Planning	Shop-Floor Systems
Customized products Wide product range Low volume per product Make-to-customer specifications Initial pilot orders Future repeat (blanket) orders Key customer requirements: Design capability Delivery speed Market qualifiers: Delivery reliability Quality Price	Reducing process lead time Manufacturing to engineering specifications and quality standards Delivery reliability critical	Batch manufacturing Long process routings High-precision work Accommodate delivery and design changes with reliable deliveries Labor cost equals 60% Control of actual costs against budget Scrap and rework: First orders Repeat orders First order processing uncertainties (process unknown, time estimates) Process and product uncertainties	Make-to-order/ assemble-to-order from: Customer orders Anticipated orders Forecast orders Used for rough-cut capacity planning due to long lead time impact on delivery Customer order promising	Time-phased material planning Material is particular to customer orders High obsolescence risk Extra materials needed for scrapped items Trade-off: shorter lead time versus raw material inventory	MRP-based systems Priority scheduling of shop orders System supported by dispatching and production controller personnel Capacity requirements planning by work center Order tracking and status information

At Moog the MRP-based approach is used for shop-floor scheduling and vendor scheduling. An advanced computer-based MRPII system provides priority scheduling information for sequencing and dispatching shop orders at individual work centers. The shop-floor system supports the batch manufacturing of products under high levels of process uncertainty. A variety of production reports assist supervisors in the detailed tracking of open shop orders, reporting order status, and evaluating work center performance.

Kawasaki, U.S.A.

Kawasaki produces six different types of motorcycles as well as motorized water skis at its U.S. plant. About 100 different end-product items are manufactured for shipment to the firm's distribution centers. Although demand for products is highly seasonal, workload at the plant is stabilized by permitting fluctuations in the finished-goods inventory carried at the distribution centers. The company frequently introduces new product designs that represent styling changes in the product. The key elements in gaining sales are price, product

FIGURE 13.11   **Kawasaki, U.S.A.**

| Market Characteristics | Manufacturing Strategy | | | | |
| | Manufacturing | | Manufacturing Planning and Control System | | |
	Task	Features	Master Production Scheduling	Detailed Material Planning	Shop-Floor Systems
Narrow product range Standard products High volume per product Seasonal demand Sales from finished-goods inventory at distributors Introduction of new products Changing product mix Key customer requirements: Price Delivery speed (through finished-goods inventory in distribution divisions) Market qualifiers: Quality Delivery reliability Basic design and peripheral design changes	Provide a low-cost manufacturing support capability Support the marketing activity with high delivery speed through finished-goods inventory	High-volume batch and line production process Short setup times Small batch size Low-cost manufacturing Low labor cost High material cost Low inventories (raw material, components, and WIP) Low overheads (low MPC costs)	Make-to-stock Manufacture to forecast Level production Three-month frozen planning horizon Manufacture to replenish distribution inventories	Rate-based material planning	JIT-based systems Kanban containers JIT flow of material Low raw material, component, and WIP inventory

styling, and product performance. Factors qualifying the firm to compete in the market are quality and delivery speed. Figure 13.11 summarizes characteristics of the market served by Kawasaki along with key elements of its manufacturing strategy.

Manufacturing's task is to produce standardized products in high volume at low cost. Since material costs are significant, major emphasis is placed on reducing plant inventories using just-in-time manufacturing methods. The production process is characterized by short setup times and small production batches using production line and high-volume batch processes. Standardized assembly operations and repetitive employee tasks characterize the production process.

All the manufacturing planning and control functions in Figure 13.1 are performed at Kawasaki; a make-to-stock master production scheduling approach is used. Customer orders for end products are filled from the finished-goods inventory held by the company's distribution division. The MPS is based on forecast information, and mixed model assembly is used in performing final assembly operations. Substantial emphasis is placed on leveling the master production schedule and freezing it over a three-month planning horizon.

A rate-based material planning approach utilizes a simple planning bill of materials to schedule the rates of flow for manufactured and purchased components. A JIT shop scheduling system using kanban containers controls the flow of material between work centers. The JIT system supports low-cost manufacturing with small plant inventory levels and high-volume material flows. Very few personnel and minimal transactions are required in planning and controlling production activities.

Applicon

This firm designs and manufactures computer-aided engineering (CAE), design (CAD), and manufacturing (CAM) systems for the electronics and mechanical design markets. High-end products include systems for highly sophisticated customers in a variety of analytical engineering applications. Low-end systems use Applicon software, Sun and Tektronics workstations, and DEC VAX processors for applications in robotics and numerical control machines.

The mechanical design market represents the firm's major growth area. In this market, unlike the electronics market, the price-to-performance ratio is a critical issue to price-sensitive CAD/CAM customers. In addition, the ability to respond rapidly to changes in technology and frequent design changes is also critical. Figure 13.12 summarizes characteristics of the market served by Applicon along with key elements of the old manufacturing strategy (i.e., the one employed by the company before the process change).

The manufacturing task for the mechanical design market involves producing high-quality products having a wide range of optional features in small volumes at low cost in short customer lead times while accommodating rapid engineering changes. As Figure 13.12 shows, the previous manufacturing approach was to produce products using a batch manufacturing process where the plant was organized into functional groupings of machines, and production was planned and controlled using an MRPII system to fill customer orders directly from finished-goods inventory. Long production lead times under this strategy led to poor competitive performance. The inability to make changes in product designs didn't allow the firm to keep up with major changes in product technology; large work-in-process and finished-goods inventories created substantial write-offs of obsolete inventory; poor customer service in product delivery resulted with high manufacturing costs.

As a consequence the company changed its manufacturing strategy, investing in a JIT production process having straight line flows of material with closely coupled manufacturing cells dedicated to individual product families and short changeover times. Four cells are dedicated to the final assembly of four different product model families, while the fifth cell produces printed circuit boards (PCBs) for the final assembly cells. Thanks to this process, overall manufacturing lead time fell from 75 to 5 days, work-in-process and finished-goods inventories declined significantly, and product quality improved greatly. Likewise, the MPC system design was changed to include an assemble-to-order MPS because of the short manufacturing lead time, a new MRP material planning approach that takes into account JIT plant operations, and a JIT-based shop scheduling approach. Figure 13.13 describes the new manufacturing approach.

FIGURE 13.12 **Applicon's Old Manufacturing Strategy**

| Market Characteristics* | Manufacturing | | Manufacturing Planning and Control System | | |
	Task*	Features	Master Production Scheduling	Detailed Material Planning	Shop-Floor Systems
Customized products Wide product range Major design changes occurring monthly Quick response required to changes in product technology Need to reflect both price sensitivity and the price/performance ratio for a sophisticated customer base High product quality requirements Delivery responsiveness is critical.	Low-cost manufacturing Short production lead times High product quality Rapid engineering change capability	Batch manufacturing General-purpose equipment Functional plant layout 4–5-month manufacturing lead time Long design change cycle High rate of inventory obsolescence 85% plug and play rate in final inspection Excessive rework costs 160 actual production operators in the manufacturing areas 20 weeks of work-in-process inventory Product family mix change flexibility	Make-to-stock MPS High levels of finished-goods inventory Monthly MPS is created for each end product, using an annual build plan	Conventional MRP system Stockroom kitting of assemblies prior to release of work orders at each stage in the process MPS is exploded into time-phased work orders for components and subassemblies using bill of materials, inventory data, and monthly time periods.	Large shop-floor order quantities typically representing one month's usage Work is scheduled on the shop floor using a priority control system for work orders. Large numbers of shop-floor and inventory transactions are processed to maintain data integrity in the MRP system. Large overhead costs are incurred to support the MPC system, as illustrated by 83 people employed in the materials management area.

*The market characteristics and manufacturing task are common to the old and new strategies.

The Driver Is the Marketplace

It might be tempting to believe the evolution in MPC system design is always toward JIT-based systems. In fact, that's not the case. Several major Japanese companies that have used JIT approaches now are trying to integrate MRP into their MPC designs. Why? Because they're entering markets where MRP approaches make sense. More and more Japanese firms are moving out of standardized product markets and into more customized areas, where MRP planning supports wider product variety. The resultant systems will almost surely be hybrids where some JIT methodologies prevail, but the benefits of MRP planning are needed as well. The bottom line is, marketplace dictates define the manufacturing task, the process, and MPC design.

FIGURE 13.13 **Applicon's New Manufacturing Strategy**

Market Characteristics*	Manufacturing Strategy				
	Manufacturing		Manufacturing Planning and Control System		
	Task*	Features	Master Production Scheduling	Detailed Material Planning	Shop-Floor Systems
Customized products Wide product range Major design changes occurring monthly Quick response required to changes in product technology Need to reflect both price sensitivity and the price/performance ratio for a sophisticated customer base High product quality requirements Delivery responsiveness is critical.	Low-cost manufacturing Short production lead times High product quality Rapid engineering change capability	Straight-line flows of material Manufacturing cells dedicated to particular product families Short setup times Short manufacturing lead times (one week) Short design change cycles Low work-in-process and finished-goods inventories Low flexibility to product family mix changes	An assemble-to-order MPS is stated in top-level item terms and is coded by major model number. The company plans using forecast information in the MPS, but builds product only to customer orders using a final assembly schedule. Customer order promising is a key activity. Available-to-promise records are used. Customer orders are used to convert the weekly production plan into specific daily requirements.	MPS uses monthly time periods covering five future months to plan and order purchased materials using family bills of material, MRP records, and bill of material explosion techniques. No stockrooms since material is located in the manufacturing cells MPC system is run weekly providing planning information to planners and buyers, and capacity planning information to plant work cells. Only two inventory transactions are recorded—from suppliers into the stock bins, and out of stock bins as finished products are shipped from the plant.	Work orders are not scheduled for internally manufactured items. Material is pulled through the production process using JIT methods. Delivery of 70% of supplier items directly onto the shop floor Customer orders, referred to as build cards, provide the basis for scheduling work cells and for pulling material through the plant.

*The market characteristics and manufacturing task are common to the old and new strategies.

Integrating MRP and JIT

As was clear with the Applicon example, there are many ways that MRP and JIT are combined and substantial need to do so. Here we discuss needs to integrate these approaches, physical changes that support the integration, and techniques for integration.

The Need to Integrate

In the majority of the cases, the need for integration arises in companies that have an installed MRP system and are in the process of implementing some aspect of JIT. The pressure of meeting world class standards, the use of global benchmarking, and intimidating competition have all brought home the necessity of major changes in how manufacturing is done. The response to these concerns in the best of companies has been to implement aspects of JIT.

Often these JIT programs seem in conflict with the MRP system the firm may have in place. As lead times shrink and material velocity increases, the limiting activity can turn out to be transaction processing. Increased demand can compound the problem.

As an example, a European consumer electronics company significantly cut production time required to make a major high-volume component in response to increased demand. Product design changes and process capability improvements were both used to reduce setup and run times. Lot sizes were reduced, but lead times were not significantly reduced. The combination of smaller lot sizes and increasing volume simply meant there were substantially more open orders on the floor being tracked by the MRP system, moving into and out of inventory, and being accounted for during the process. These "hidden factory" activities were limiting the improvements possible from the other activities.

When changes take place on the factory floor, MPC system change may be a required response. These changes can come from internal actions like implementing a JIT program or from external requirements that change the manufacturing task. In either case the need for a change in production activity control systems may be clear; the direction is most often from shop-order–based systems to kanban or other simple signals. A typical response is backflushing component usages at all levels triggered by receipt of completed items into finished-goods inventory.

Physical Changes That Support Integration

One of the first requirements to support the JIT approaches in the factory is to reduce the inventory transaction volume. Cutting the number of times a lot has to be logged into and out of an inventory location not only reduces transactions but enables material to move to the next operation more quickly. This clearly helps increase the velocity and reduce lead times. Physically, this may mean making some changes in how lots get moved from department to department and how the need for the move gets signaled, but the major improvements are in making physical changes to the production process, such as the introduction of cellular manufacturing.

Cellular manufacturing supports integrating MRP and JIT approaches. The cell allows us to accomplish several routing steps as if they were a single step and allows the shop floor to be scheduled at the level of part numbers instead of the level of routing steps. More encompassing cellular manufacturing approaches permit the cell to be planned and controlled at the level of assemblies instead of at the part number level. One key objective is to reduce the need for inventory accounting and the other hidden factory transactions. Control of the cell is straightforward and doesn't need the detailed tracking necessary when parts move all over the factory.

The choice of where to implement cellular manufacturing is important since we can create islands of velocity, like the islands of automation prevalent in the early installations of some computer-integrated manufacturing schemes. These islands might be quite successful on their own, but not be well integrated into the system as a whole. Increasingly, we've found firms in this position needing to make more than cosmetic changes to their overall MPC system.

Some Techniques for Integrating MRP and JIT

Whenever there's a combination of MRP and JIT in the shop, we need to move back and forth between the systems. A JIT cell in the middle of a process under MRP control must communicate with the MRP system. There must be a handoff from MRP to JIT at the start of the JIT process and a transfer back to MRP at the end.

One way of supporting this need is to create phantom bills for activities under JIT control. Material requirements planning records can be used to plan raw material requirements, with movement through the factory done with JIT approaches (no shop orders or tracking). The phantom bill would ignore the creation of the detailed parts and assemblies performed under JIT scheduling, while the MRP system would pick up the completed part or assembly as a part number on the bill of materials at completion.

Strategy for Combining MRP and JIT

We're often asked if you need to go through the agony of implementing MRP if thereafter the goal is to dismantle parts of it to use JIT. A typical question is, "Why can't we just go to JIT in the first place?"

For a long time our response was that conceptually JIT could be implemented in a company with no formal MPC system, but it was difficult. First, you need the discipline of a system where execution according to a schedule was part of the basic factory culture. The usual problems of month-end surges in output, inadequate data integrity, pulling dollars instead of products, and panic conditions must be eliminated before you could implement a system with virtually no buffers. Even MRP has small buffering. JIT, by design, "exposes the rocks" as a basic philosophy. Without the underlying discipline, the steady-state condition would be rocks showing; the factory would be shut down much of the time until JIT discipline was achieved. Maintaining commitment to a JIT philosophy under these circumstances would be difficult.

Now, however, we believe a more balanced view toward MRP/JIT integration is required. We need to realize JIT encompasses much more than MPC. You can start to work on cellular manufacturing approaches at a fairly early point, either concomitant with JIT implementation or not. The result can be progress toward manufacturing excellence on more than one front.

Similarly, improved quality is a fundamental underpinning to JIT. One does not need to wait to get started on the quality improvement process. As quality is improved, the "surprises" in MPC are reduced, and more simple systems suffice.

Finally, it's important not to leave this discussion with the impression that every company is evolving from MRP toward JIT. In Japan, many firms are now going in the opposite direction, because the markets in which they wish to compete dictate a manufacturing task, process design, and MPC system that are consistent. In general, these companies are moving away from high-volume standardized goods (such as consumer electronics) to customized higher-value-added products (such as machine tools). We see the key point in all this in Figure 13.5.: Market choices dictate many manufacturing choices, including MPC system design.

Extending MPC Integration to Customers and Suppliers

The examples in this chapter illustrate the need to redesign MPC systems to respond to shifts in market requirements. In today's competitive marketplace environment, evolution is occurring at a rapid pace. As a result, one major change in leading edge companies is that of introducing the strategy of achieving much closer integration in MPC systems between customers and suppliers. Here, the focus is on optimizing the overall supply chain operations, rather than just the operations within a firm. The idea is that a set of firms operating *jointly* within a supply chain can become more competitive in meeting marketplace requirements.

TelTech

The strategy of MPC integration between companies in a supply chain can be illustrated using TelTech's operations. This company sells telecom equipment to telephone systems operators such as Vodaphone and Orange and the public telephone companies in many other countries. The entry of new telephone system operators, deregulation, and the growth in mobile/wireless applications have fundamentally changed the competitive landscape in this industry, requiring much faster customer response times.

TelTech's MPC systems have become more complex on the supplier side. The company needs to work with a much larger number of suppliers, since there is now an increased variety of product options offered to customers. These product options change rapidly, so reducing product obsolescence is a high priority. Further, there is a growing use of vendor-managed inventory (VMI) by TelTech's suppliers. The suppliers provide inventories of purchased items at TelTech that are paid for only when consumed by TelTech. Making this work requires that purchased part inventories are visible to both TelTech and its suppliers, and that TelTech's production plans are passed to the suppliers and continually updated. New methods for generating invoices and making payments electronically are required to support the changes in working with suppliers.

TelTech also works with third-party logistics providers that transport TelTech's products to its customers as well as from the suppliers. This collaboration has enabled the company to think in terms of the total delivered/installed cost of the system, including transportation, inventory, obsolescence, delayed delivery, delayed telecom system startup, and telecom system downtime. Increasingly, TelTech has become more of a systems integrator, providing customized products and taking over the complexity in making system installations previously faced by their customers.

On the customer side, TelTech has begun taking over total turnkey system implementation of countrywide mobile telecom systems. In order to manage the uncertain customer demands in such projects, TelTech has established country warehouses that can configure final site orders from the country warehouse inventory. Since this has proven to be an expensive solution, incurring significant inventory holding and obsolescence costs, TelTech has begun shifting to a more rapid response from regional and factory warehouses and running more factory operations on an assemble-to-order basis.

Customer-Supplier MPC Integration at TelTech

The TelTech example also illustrates how MPC approaches can be improved across firms in a supply chain context to reduce response times to customers. At TelTech the linkages with customers and suppliers have focused on finding the best ways to gain intelligence on actual site telecom installation conditions so that rapid response can be made in delivering product to customers.

An analysis of the actual site ordering processes in one of TelTech's key customers indicated that there are significant administrative delays. Customer orders were seen as official documents, needing to be signed by two different executives. This often required several days before the two signatures could be obtained. Customer orders were passed from the customer to the TelTech country marketing personnel and then on to the TelTech factory. This also typically caused another one to two days of delay. Finally, the receipt of the customer order at the factory necessitated "untangling" the product options, making certain that the product could, in fact, be built and confirming this information with the customer. The net result was that orders typically took 10 to 20 days to move from the decision to order to the actual customer order being entered into the master production schedule. The factory could assemble the customer order in one day, and it could be shipped to the customer site in five days by inexpensive transport.

The MPC solution to this lengthy process was the development of an online MPC system that supported product configuration management. The configuration of the customer order could take place before the order was issued. It could then be built and shipped, often arriving in the country before the customer order was, in fact, issued. This MPC system enhancement would allow any potential order to be screened for availability of component items and permit substitution when material was unavailable.

The TelTech example illustrates how our traditional view of MPC system design needs to be expanded to consider MPC system improvements that span the operations of customers, plants, and suppliers throughout the supply chain. In this way, the development of manufacturing strategy to support market requirements can include investments in MPC system architecture within an integrated supply chain context.

| **Concluding Principles** | This chapter focused on two major strategy issues in designing MPC systems: how to link the design of MPC systems to a firm's corporate strategy and the requirements of its market, and how to integrate MRP and JIT approaches in designing MPC systems. The following principles summarize the major points: |

- Since investment in MPC systems is large, its design must support the firm's competitive strategy.
- A wide range of options are available in designing MPC systems, and the choices must be governed by the company's competitive needs.
- Business as well as technical specifications need to be considered in designing an MPC system.
- MPC system design should begin with an analysis of the market requirements to support the firm's competitive strategy.
- Understanding the manufacturing task is critical in developing the production process design, the MPC system design, and the other elements of the manufacturing infrastructure.
- The manufacturing process's particular features need to be considered in choosing among the options in MPC system design.
- MRP and JIT approaches can be effectively integrated in designing MPC systems.
- MPC system integration is increasingly concerned with interfirm MPC system design.
- Improved company performance and overall supply chain performance can result from matching MPC system design to the firm's competitive strategy.

References

Belt, B. "MRP and KANBAN—A Possible Synergy?" *Production and Inventory Management Journal* 28, no. 1 (1987), pp. 71–80.

Berry, W. L., and T. J. Hill. "Linking Systems to Strategy." *International Journal of Operations and Production Management* 12, no. 10 (1922).

Berry, W. L.; J. E. Klompmaker; and T. Hill. "Aligning Marketing and Manufacturing Strategy," *International Journal of Production Research* 37, no. 16 (1999).

Das, A., and Ram Narasimhan, "Process-Technology Fit and Its Implications for Manufacturing Performance," *Journal of Operations Management* 19, no. 5 (November 2000), pp. 521–540.

Duray, R.; Peter T. Ward; Glenn W. Milligan; and William L. Berry. "Approaches to Mass Customization: Configurations and Empirical Validation," *Journal of Operations Management* 18, no. 6 (November 2000), pp. 605–625.

Fakhoury, E. A. F., and T. E. Vollmann. "Applicon Case Study." Boston: Boston University, School of Management, 1987.

Flynn, B. B.; Roger G. Schroeder; and E. James Flynn. "World Class Manufacturing: An Investigation of Hayes and Wheelwright's Foundation," *Journal of Operations Management* 17, no. 3 (March 1999), pp. 249–269.

Giffi, Co.; A. V. Roth; and G. M. Seal. *Competing in World Class Manufacturing.* Homewood, IL.: Irwin, 1990.

Hall, Robert W. "Kawasaki, U.S.A., Transferring Japanese Productivity Methods to the U.S.A." Case Study 08002. Falls Church, Va.: American Production and Inventory Control Society, 1982.

Hill, T. J. *Manufacturing Strategy: Text and Cases,* 3rd ed. Homewood, IL.: Richard D. Irwin, 2000, Chaps. 2 and 10 and the Sherpin Case.

Hill, T. J.; W. L. Berry; and J. E. Klompmaker. "Customer Driven Manufacturing." *International Journal of Operations and Production Management* 15, no. 3 (1994).

Karmarkar, U. S. "Alternatives for Batch Manufacturing Control," Working Paper no. QM8613. Rochester, N.Y.: Graduate School of Management, University of Rochester, 1986.

———. "Integrating MRP with Kanban/Pull Systems." Working Paper no. QM8615. Rochester, N.Y.: Graduate School of Management, University of Rochester, 1986.

———. "Push, Pull, and Hybrid Control Schemes." *Tijdschrift Voor Economic En Management* 26 (1991).

———. "Beyond MRPII: Evolution to a New Standard." Working Paper Series no. CMOM 89-1. Rochester, N.Y.: University of Rochester, 1989.

———. "Getting Control of Just-in-Time." *Harvard Business Review,* September–October 1989.

Kotha, S., and Paul M. Swamidass. "Strategy, Advanced Manufacturing Technology and Performance: Empirical Evidence from U.S. Manufacturing Firms," *Journal of Operations Management* 18, no. 3 (April 2000), pp. 257–277.

Leong, G. K.; D. L. Snyder; and Peter T. Ward. "Research in the Process and Content of Manufacturing Strategy," *Omega* 18, no 2 (1990), pp. 109–122.

Louis, R. S. "MRPIII: Material Acquisition System." *Production and Inventory Management,* July 1991, pp. 26–27.

Melnyk, S. A., and P. L. Carter. "Moog Inc., Space Products Division," *Shop Floor Control Principles, Practices, and Case Studies.* Falls Church, Va.: American Production and Inventory Control Society, 1987.

Mukherjee, A. Will Mitchell and F. Brian Talbot. "The Impact of New Manufacturing Requirements on Production Line Productivity and Quality at a Focused Factory," *Journal of Operations Management* 18, no. 2 (February 2000), pp. 139–168.

Olhager, Jan. "Long-Term Capacity Management: Linking the Perspectives from Manufacturing Strategy and Sales and Operations Planning," *International Journal of Production Economics* 69, no. 2 (2001), p. 215.

Pyke, D. F., and M. A. Cohen. "Push and Pull in Manufacturing and Distribution Systems," *Journal of Operations Management* 9, no. 1 (January 1990).

Rondeau, P. J.; Mark A. Vonderembse; and T. S. Ragu-Nathan. "Exploring Work System Practices For Time-Based Manufacturers; Their Impact on Competitive Capabilities," *Journal of Operations Management* 18, no. 5 (August 2000), pp. 509–529.

Safizaeh, H.; L. Ritzman; and D. Mallick. "Revisiting Alternative Theoretical Paradigms in Manufacturing Strategy," *Production and Operations Management* 9, no. 2 (2000), pp. 111–127.

Stalk, G., Jr., and T. M. Hout. *Competing against Time.* New York: Free Press, 1990.

Tracy, M.; Mark A. Vonderembse; and Jeen-Su Lim. "Manufacturing Technology and Strategy Formulation: Keys to Enhancing Competitiveness and Improving Performance," *Journal of Operations Management* 17, no. 4 (June 1999), pp. 411–428.

Van Dierdonck, R. J. M., and J. G. Miller. "Designing Production Planning and Control Systems." *Journal of Operations Management* 4, no. 1 (1980), pp. 37–46.

Ward, P. T.; J. K. McCreery; L. P. Ritzman; and D. Sharma. "Competitive Priorities in Operations Management," *Decision Sciences Journal* 29, no. 4 (fall 1998), pp. 1035–1046.

Westbrook, Roy. "Priority Management: New Theory For Operations Management," *International Journal of Operations and Production Management* 14, no. 6 (1994).

Zhang, O.; Mark A. Vonderembse; and Jeen-Su Lim. "Manufacturing Flexibility: Defining and Analyzing Relationships Among Competence, Capability, and Customer Satisfaction," *Journal of Operations Management* 21, no. 2 (March 2003), pp. 173–191.

Discussion Questions

1. It has been suggested that in a make-to-order company, order backlog is inventory carried by the customer. What does this statement mean?

2. Why do you suppose the terms *push* and *pull* came to be used for MRP and JIT systems?

3. What key features of the manufacturing task impact the design of the MPC system?

4. Some manufacturing executives have raised the question "Which is better, MRP or JIT?" How would you respond to this question?

5. What approaches other than finished goods inventory provide short lead times to the customers?

6. Henry Ford was said to have specified "any color as long as it's black." Today's automobiles come in literally billions of end-item combinations. What are the implications of this change in market requirements on MPC system design?

7. What changes in market requirements at Applicon dictated a new production process and MPC approach?

8. What kind of changes in the products produced and markets served would enable Moog to adopt make-to-stock master production scheduling?

9. Why is discipline required for both JIT and MRP?

Problems

1. Worldwide Batteries, Inc., sells industrial batteries to both OEM and replacement market customers. About 80 end products are classified as high-volume products, 200 as medium-volume products, and 170 as low-volume products. The vice president of marketing and sales has provided the following description for two market segments that reflect the general characteristics of all market segments currently targeted by the company:

   - Replacement batteries for indoor material handling equipment for which 60 percent of the sales volume is for deliveries desired by the customers in 7 days or less (high-volume items), 30 percent is for delivery within 14 days (medium-volume items), and 10 percent is for delivery within 30 days (low-volume items). Key factors in gaining sales orders in this segment are competitive prices and delivery speed.

   - Replacement batteries for outdoor transportation equipment applications which involve low-volume product items. Customers expect delivery within two weeks. The key factors in winning orders in this segment are competitive prices and delivery reliability.

Recently, the company has implemented a kanban system for controlling the material for manufacturing component parts for batteries. The lead time for final assembly of battery components into end products, battery charging, and transport to the customers is seven days. High- and medium-volume purchased components (used in the final assembly operation) are provided by suppliers on a JIT delivery basis with a guaranteed five-day delivery lead time. Low-volume purchased components (also used in the final assembly operation) require a four-week delivery lead time for the suppliers.

Specify the MPC system design requirements for the company's markets using the framework shown in Figures 13.10, 13.11, and 13.12. Refer to Figures 13.2, 13.3, 13.4, 13.6, 13.7, and 13.8 for MPC design details.

2. Currently, the Cambridge Plastics Company sells industrial packaging materials to two different market segments:

- Injection-molded plastic bottles sold to soft-drink bottlers in very high volume with significant seasonal variations in sales. The customers provide call-off schedules indicating their product requirements over the next six months, specifying the delivery quantities each week. Key factors in winning this business are the ability to meet large changes in the weekly quantities and the ability to provide a major capacity increase for the increased demand during the peak summer selling season.

- Custom-molded plastic bottles sold in wide variety and low volume to manufacturers of cosmetic, pharmaceutical, and agricultural chemical products. These are produced to specific customer orders, with the key factors in winning orders in this business being competitive prices and delivery reliability.

The soft-drink bottles are produced using high-volume processes dedicated to the production of specific products, while the custom products are produced using low-volume batch processes. In both cases the tracking of actual versus planned production is very important in ensuring that the current quantities of products are delivered against the customer orders.

Specify the MPC system design requirements for the company's markets using the framework shown in Figures 13.10, 13.11, and 13.12. Refer to Figures 13.2, 13.3, 13.4, 13.6, 13.7, and 13.8 for MPC design details.

3. The Oakmont Inc. is a make-to-stock firm. A typical part for one of the firm's products has the following data:

> Manufacturing lead time (LT) = 8 weeks.
>
> Forecast = 50 per week.
>
> Mean absolute deviation (MAD) of forecast errors = 8.
>
> Safety stock = 95 percent service level ($2.056 \times \text{MAD} \times 1.25 \times \sqrt{\text{LT}}$).

A cellular manufacturing approach will reduce a typical part's manufacturing lead time to two weeks.

a. What's the reduction in safety stock?

b. The cell can manufacture 40 percent of the parts (the present total safety stock investment is $200,000). If you assume a lead time reduction from eight weeks to two weeks for these parts, what's the overall reduction in safety stock investment?

c. An engineer believes redesign of the cell can increase the percentage of parts produced therein from 40 percent to 60 percent. How much safety stock investment reduction comes from the redesign?

4. The cell in problem 3 is designed with a capacity of 800 units per day. A new product design uses many common parts; the result is a cell scheduled with a one-day lead time and an overall shift to assemble-to-order manufacturing. Customers are happy to receive one-day deliveries. Overall demand for parts made in the cell is 500 units per day, with a standard deviation of 75 units. The

500 units are typically completed in approximately five working hours. Thereafter, workers in the cell perform equipment maintenance, schedule production, and manage quality.

    a. What happens to the service level provided to customers?

    b. What happens to safety stock inventory levels?

5. Dixon Plastics has 100 customers. It produces make-to-order products using time-phased material planning and an MRP-based shop-floor system. Amdur Electronics, one of its larger customers, accounts for 20 percent of total sales. It promises to double its volume with Dixon within two years and to communicate its detailed planning to Dixon via electronic data exchange (EDI). The plans would be frozen for the next week, subject to ±15 percent in weeks 2 through 6, and open to revision after six weeks. Any raw material purchased by Dixon to meet requirements in the next six weeks would be guaranteed against obsolescence by Amdur Electronics.

    a. What changes in MPC design options would Dixon require if total manufacturing lead time was one day?

    b. What if the total manufacturing lead time is six weeks?

6. Consider the following three MRP records. Product A comprises two part Bs. One part B requires one part C.

		Week							
Product A		**1**	**2**	**3**	**4**	**5**	**6**	**7**	**8**
Gross requirements		10	20	0	40	20	10	0	20
Scheduled receipts									
Proj. avail. balance	15	5	15	15	5	15	5	5	15
Planned order release		30		30	30			30	

$Q = 30, SS = 5, LT = 1.$

		Week							
Part B		**1**	**2**	**3**	**4**	**5**	**6**	**7**	**8**
Gross requirements		60		60	60			60	
Scheduled receipts			100						
Proj. avail. balance	75	15	115	55	95	95	95	35	35
Planned order release			100						

$Q = 100, SS = 0, LT = 2.$

		Week							
Part C		**1**	**2**	**3**	**4**	**5**	**6**	**7**	**8**
Gross requirements			100						
Scheduled receipts									
Proj. avail. balance	0	0	0	0	0	0	0	0	0
Planned order release		100							

$Q = LFL, SS = Q, LT = 1.$

a. What transactions are required to keep the shop on schedule?

b. Assume it takes one week for MRP processing for each level in the bill of materials. What's product A's total lead time?

c. If everything went according to plan in week 1, what would the records look like in week 2? (Assume a new requirement for 20 units of product A in week 9.) What transactions took place in week 1 and/or must take place in week 2 to keep the shop on schedule?

d. Suppose product A is to be built in a cell (lead time is one week), and parts B and C are to be made into phantom items. What happens to transaction counts and total lead time?

7. Product X is made from one unit of part Y, which in turn is made from one unit of Z, which is made from raw material R. Consider the following set of records:

Product X		Week				
		1	2	3	4	5
Gross requirements		50	50	50	50	50
Scheduled receipts		50				
Proj. avail. balance	10	10	10	10	10	10
Planned order release		50	50	50	50	

Q = LFL, SS = 10, LT = 1.

Part Y		Week				
		1	2	3	4	5
Gross requirements		50	50	50	50	
Scheduled receipts						
Proj. avail. balance	52	2	52	2	52	0
Planned order release		100		100		

Q = 100, SS = 0, LT = 1.

Part Z		Week				
		1	2	3	4	5
Gross requirements		100		100		
Scheduled receipts						
Proj. avail. balance	100	0	0	0	0	0
Planned order release			100			

Q = LFL, SS = 0, LT = 1.

	Week				
Raw Material R	1	2	3	4	5
Gross requirements		100			
Scheduled receipts					
Proj. avail. balance	0	0	0	0	0	0
Planned order release	100				

Q = LFL, SS = 0, LT = 1.

a. How many transactions (order launches, inventory receipts, and disbursements) are indicated in the records as shown above for product X and parts Y, Z, and R?

b. How would the records look if parts Y and Z are made into phantom items? Assume the raw material (LT = 1, Q = LFL) is still delivered to inventory before being released directly to the line that produces product X. Assume the lead time is still one week for product X. How many transactions are implied now?

8. Melnick Mines uses a special type of hardened crusher ball for preparing the ore. Purchasing the balls is managed with time-phased material planning. The following records are for two successive weeks:

	Week							
Part: Crusher Ball	1	2	3	4	5	6	7	8
Gross requirements	25	25	25	25	25	25	25	25
Scheduled receipts			80					
Proj. avail. balance	20	−5	50	25	80	55	30	85	60
Planned order release	80			80				

Q = 80, SS = 20, LT = 3.

	Week							
Part: Crusher Ball	2	3	4	5	6	7	8	9
Gross requirements	25	25	25	25	25	25	25	25
Scheduled receipts			80					
Proj. avail. balance	70	45	20	75	50	25	80	55	30
Planned order release			80					

Q = 80, SS = 20, LT = 3.

a. What transactions made during week 1 would result in the record as of week 2 (assuming no scrap losses)?

b. How would this set of transactions be changed if rate-based scheduling and JIT-based shop-floor control were implemented at the vendor with lead time one day?

9. Falcon Sports Inc. makes a line of jet skis in a make-to-stock environment. There are eight different end items (catalog numbers) in the jet ski product line. The skis vary according to horsepower (10 or 12), seating capacity (single or dual), and starting mechanism (manual or automatic). The company owner, Freddie Falcon, is adding two new colors to the jet ski line (orange and purple) in addition to their current color (teal). The company currently holds 25 units of safety stock for each jet ski model. Manufacturing lead time is two weeks.

   a. How much will the safety stock increase by offering the two new colors?

   b. Freddie says the safety stock of 25 units per model is not enough, given all the product variations, so he plans to limit the number of end items available. Freddie decides that orange and purple jet skis will be available only in the 12-horsepower model and teal is only available in the 10-horsepower model. He wants to use a total of 600 units of safety stock and spread it across the limited end items. How much safety stock would there be for each end item under this plan?

10. Falcon Sports Inc. (from problem 9) has decided to switch to an assemble-to-order manufacturing environment and hold 40 units of safety stock for each option. Assembly lead time is two hours.

   a. What is the total safety stock under this plan?

   b. What would the safety stock per option be if there were 600 units of safety stock in total?

11. The Ronsi Rist Watch Company, producers of famous brand watches, expanded its product line from 20 to 50 models. Each model requires approximately 100 units of safety stock to provide the customer service levels the company wants from make-to-stock operations. A small engineering change in watch design and new layout in the factory made it possible to shift to an assemble-to-order approach. Each model is assembled using one item from each of five options (12 face plates, 2 movements, 4 bands, 4 cases, and 2 kits of mounting hardware). The company was disappointed to learn it took about 100 units of safety stock for each option to provide the desired customer service levels, even though it could assemble virtually any order in a matter of hours. The marketing manager said, "Since we still need about 100 units of safety stock for each item, we should go back to our familiar make-to-stock system, which is much easier for my order entry clerks to handle." Do you agree?

12. In an attempt to react to a shifting market, the Isandar Wedge Company reengineered its product line for rate-based manufacturing. Previously, the company competed on product variety, custom tailoring products to meet customer needs on a make-to-order basis. The redesign allows customers to make their own adjustments and enables the company to produce a smaller number of end products to stock, thereby providing immediate delivery.

   a. Current inventory for an example product is zero, but the firm wants to build up 100 units of safety stock over the next four weeks. Average demand for the product is expected to be 25 units per week. From week 5 on, the company wants to produce at the demand rate. What should the master production schedule be for this product for the next six weeks.?

   b. Isandar now believes the 100-unit safety stock is excessive. Standard deviation of demand per week is 10 units, so a safety stock of 30 provides a service level above 99 percent. If the company is starting with 100 units of safety stock, what MPS results in a safety stock of 30 units in 5 weeks?

13. The Leone Company used to make designer underwear in red, white, and blue to stock. In response to many customer requests, it now offers them with or without three colors of exotic decals (black, green, and orange) and with or without four colors of sequins (white, brown, black, and gold). If 10 units of safety stock are kept for each end item, measure the increase in safety stock from the new product offerings. Customers require next-day delivery. Manufacturing lead time is one week.

14. If the Leone Company in problem 13 switches to an assemble-to-order manufacturing option and holds 20 units of safety stock in each option, what's the overall safety stock (in total number of parts)? Assembly lead time is one hour.

15. As part of the final assembly process, Leone (problems 13 and 14) decides to dye underwear to particular colors and replace decals with silk screening. They invest in the dye and silk screen capacity before checking on the reduction in the safety stock. Assembly lead time increases to two hours. What are the safety stock requirements, given that they hold no limits on safety stock per option? Does their ability to offer a full product line change?

14

Advanced Concepts in Material Requirements Planning

This chapter concerns some advanced issues in material requirements planning (MRP). Some concepts and conventions discussed here can improve well-functioning basic systems. Most concepts are of a "fine-tuning" nature and can provide additional benefits to the company.

We feel the first, most important phase in MRP is to install the system, make it part of an ongoing managerial process, get users trained in the use of MRP, understand the critical linkages with other areas, achieve high levels of data integrity, and link MRP with other modules of the front end, engine, and back end of manufacturing planning and control (MPC) systems. Having achieved this first phase, many firms then turn to the advanced issues discussed in this chapter.

Chapter 14 is organized around three topics:

- *Determining manufacturing order quantities:* What are the basic trade-offs in lot sizing in the MRP environment, and what techniques are useful?
- *Buffering concepts:* What are the types of uncertainties in MRP, and how can we buffer against these uncertainties?
- *Nervousness:* Why are MRP systems subject to nervousness, and how do firms deal with system nervousness?

Chapter 14 is linked with Chapter 7 in that this chapter presupposes understanding of MRP systems, record processing, the MRP database, and so on. Chapter 14 is also linked to Chapter 5, which treats several inventory concepts (lot sizing, buffering, and service levels). The focus here is on the dependent demand (MRP) environment, whereas Chapter 5, largely deals with systems for independent demand. Additional buffering concepts appear in Chapter 6 (master production scheduling) and Chapter 2 (demand management).

Determining Manufacturing Order Quantities

The MRP system converts the master production schedule into a time-phased schedule for all intermediate assemblies and component parts. Detailed schedules consist of two parts: scheduled receipts (open orders) and planned orders. Each scheduled receipt's quantity and timing (due date) have been determined prior to release to the shop. We determine quantities and timings for planned orders via MRP logic using the inventory position, the gross requirements data, and specific procedures for making the decisions.

A number of quantity-determination (lot-sizing) procedures have been developed for determining order quantities in MRP systems, ranging from **ordering as required (lot-for-lot),** to simple decision rules, and finally to extensive optimizing procedures. This section describes four such lot-sizing procedures using a problem developed by W. L. Berry.

The primary consideration in the development of lot-sizing procedures for MRP is the nature of the net requirements data. The demand dependency relationship from the product structures and the time-phased gross requirements mean the net requirements for an item might appear as illustrated in Figure 14.1. First, it's important to note that the requirements do *not* reflect the key independent demand assumption of a constant uniform demand. Second, the requirements are *discrete,* since they're stated on a period-by-period basis (time-phased), rather than as a rate (e.g., an average of so much per month or year). Finally, the requirements can be *lumpy;* that is, they can vary substantially from period to period and even have periods with no requirements.

MRP lot-sizing procedures are designed specifically for the discrete demand case. One problem in selecting a procedure is that reductions in inventory-related costs can generally be achieved only by using increasingly complex procedures. Such procedures require more computations in making lot-sizing determinations. A second problem concerns local optimization. The lot-sizing procedure used for one part in an MRP system has a direct impact on the gross requirements data passed to its component parts. The use of procedures other than lot-for-lot tends to increase gross requirements data lumpiness further down in the product structure.

The manufacturing lot-size problem is basically one of converting requirements into a series of replenishment orders. If we consider this problem on a local level—that is, only in terms of the one part and not its components—the problem involves determining how to group time-phased requirements data into a schedule of replenishment orders that minimizes the combined costs of placing manufacturing orders and carrying inventory.

Since MRP systems normally replan on a daily or weekly basis, timing affects the assumptions commonly made in using MRP lot-sizing procedures. These assumptions are as follows. First, since we aggregate component requirements by time period for planning purposes, we assume all requirements for each period must be available at the beginning of

FIGURE 14.1   **Example Problem: Weekly Net Requirements Schedule**

Week number	1	2	3	4	5	6	7	8	9	10	11	12
Requirements	10	10	15	20	70	180	250	270	230	40	0	10

Ordering cost = C_p = $300 per order.
Inventory carrying cost = C_H = $2 per unit per week.
Average requirements = $\bar{D}$ = 92.1

the period. Second, we assume all requirements for future periods must be met and can't be back ordered. Third, since the system is operated on a periodic basis, we assume ordering decisions occur at regular time intervals (e.g., daily or weekly). Fourth, we assume the requirements are properly offset for manufacturing lead times. Finally, we assume component requirements are satisfied at a uniform rate during each period. Therefore, we use average inventory level in computing inventory carrying costs.

In the following sections, we'll illustrate the results from applying four different ordering procedures to the example data in Figure 14.1. This example will illustrate how these procedures vary in their assumptions and how much they utilize available data in making lot-sizing decisions.

Economic Order Quantities (EOQ)

Because of its simplicity, people often use the **economic order quantity (EOQ)** formula as a decision rule for placing orders in a requirements planning system. As the following example shows, however, the EOQ model frequently must be modified in requirements planning system applications. Since we base the EOQ on the assumption of constant uniform demand, the resulting total cost expression won't necessarily be valid for requirements planning applications.

Figure 14.2 shows the results of ordering material in economic lot sizes for the example data. In this example the EOQ formula used average weekly demand of 92.1 units for the entire requirements schedule to compute the economic lot size. Note, too, order quantities are shown when received, and average inventory for each period was used in computing the inventory carrying cost.

This example illustrates several problems with using economic lot sizes. When the requirements aren't equal from period to period, as is often the case in MRP, fixed EOQ lot sizes result in a mismatch between order quantities and requirements values. This can mean excess inventory must be carried forward from week to week. As an example, 41 units are carried over into week 6 when a new order is received.

In addition, we must increase the order quantity in those periods where the requirements exceed the economic lot size plus the amount of inventory carried over into the period. An example occurs in week 7. This modification is clearly preferable to the alternative of placing orders earlier to meet demand in such periods, since this would only increase inventory

FIGURE 14.2   **Economic Order Quantity Example**

Week number	1	2	3	4	5	6	7	8	9	10	11	12
Requirements	10	10	15	20	70	180	250	270	230	40	0	10
Order quantity	166					166	223	270	230	166		
Beginning inventory	166	156	146	131	111	207	250	270	230	166	126	126
Ending inventory	156	146	131	111	41	27	0	0	0	126	126	116

Ordering cost	$1,800
Inventory carrying cost	3,065
Total cost	$4,865

$$\text{(Economic lot size} = \sqrt{2C_P \bar{D}/C_H} = \sqrt{2(300)(92.1)/2} = 166)$$

carrying costs. Likewise, the alternative of placing multiple orders in a given period would needlessly increase the ordering cost.

Finally, use of the average weekly requirements figure in computing economic lot size ignores much of the other information in the requirements schedule. This information concerns magnitude of demand. For instance, there appear to be two levels of component demand in this example. The first covers weeks 1 to 4 and 10 to 12; the second covers weeks 5 to 9. We could compute an economic lot size for each of these time intervals and place orders accordingly. This proposal, however, would be difficult to implement because determining different demand levels requires a very complex decision rule.

Periodic Order Quantities (POQ)

One way to reduce the high inventory carrying cost associated with fixed lot sizes is to use the EOQ formula to compute an economic **time between orders (TBO).** We do this by dividing the EOQ by the mean demand rate. In the preceding example, the economic time interval is approximately two weeks ($166/92.1 = 1.8$). The procedure then calls for ordering *exactly* the requirements for a two-week interval. This is termed the **periodic order quantity (POQ).** Applying this procedure to the data in our example (Figure 14.1) produces Figure 14.3. The result is the same number of orders as the EOQ produces, but with lot sizes ranging from 20 to 520 units. Consequently, inventory carrying cost has been reduced by 30 percent, thereby improving the total cost of the 12-week requirements schedule by 19 percent in comparison with the preceding EOQ result.

Although the POQ procedure improves inventory cost performance by allowing lot sizes to vary, like the EOQ procedure it too ignores much of the information in the requirements schedule. Replenishment orders are constrained to occur at fixed time intervals, thereby ruling out the possibility of combining orders during periods of light product demand (e.g., during weeks 1 through 4 in the example). If, for example, orders placed in weeks 1 and 3 were combined and a single order were placed in week 1 for 55 units, combined costs can be further reduced by $160, or 4 percent.

Part Period Balancing (PPB)

The **part period balancing (PPB)** procedure uses all the information provided by the requirements schedule. In determining an order's lot size, this procedure tries to equate the total costs of placing orders and carrying inventory. We illustrate this point by considering the alternative lot-size choices available at the beginning of week 1. These include placing

FIGURE 14.3 **Periodic Order Quantity Example**

Week number	1	2	3	4	5	6	7	8	9	10	11	12
Requirements	10	10	15	20	70	180	250	270	230	40	0	10
Order quantity	20		35		250		520		270			10
Beginning inventory	20	10	35	20	250	180	520	270	270	40	0	10
Ending inventory	10	0	20	0	180	0	270	0	40	0	0	0

Ordering cost	$1,800
Inventory carrying cost	2,145
Total cost	$3,945

an order covering the requirements for:

1. Week 1 only.
2. Weeks 1 and 2.
3. Weeks 1, 2, and 3.
4. Weeks 1, 2, 3, and 4.
5. Weeks 1, 2, 3, 4, and 5, etc.

Inventory carrying costs for these five alternatives are shown below. We base these calculations on average inventory per period, hence the 1/2 (average for one week), 3/2 (one week plus the average for the second week), and so on.

1. $(\$2) \cdot [(1/2) \cdot 10] = \$10.$
2. $(\$2) \cdot [(1/2) \cdot 10] + [(3/2) \cdot 10] = \$40$
3. $(\$2) \cdot [(1/2) \cdot 10] + [(3/2) \cdot 10] + [(5/2) \cdot 15] = \$115.$
4. $(\$2) \cdot [(1/2) \cdot 10] + [(3/2) \cdot 10] + [(5/2) \cdot 15] + [(7/2) \cdot 20] = \$255.$
5. $(\$2) \cdot [(1/2) \cdot 10] + [(3/2) \cdot 10] + [(5/2) \cdot 15] + [(7/2) \cdot 20] + [(9/2) \cdot 70] = \$885.$

In this case, the inventory carrying cost for alternative 4 (ordering 55 units to cover demand for the first four weeks) most nearly approximates the $300 ordering cost; that is, alternative 4 "balances" the cost of carrying inventory with the ordering cost. Therefore, we should place an order at the beginning of the first week and the next ordering decision need not be made until the beginning of week 5.

When we apply this procedure to all the example data, we get the result in Figure 14.4. As seen, total inventory cost falls almost $500—it's 13 percent lower than the cost obtained with the periodic order quantity procedure. The PPB procedure permits both lot size and time between orders to vary. Thus, for example, in periods of low requirements, it yields smaller lot sizes and longer time intervals between orders than occur in high demand periods. This results in lower inventory-related costs.

Despite the fact that PPB utilizes all available information, it won't always yield the minimum-cost ordering plan. Although this procedure can produce low-cost plans, it may miss the minimum cost, since it doesn't evaluate all possibilities for ordering material to satisfy demand in each week of the requirements schedule.

Wagner-Whitin Algorithm

One optimizing procedure for determining the minimum-cost ordering plan for a time-phased requirements schedule is the **Wagner-Whitin (WW)** algorithm. Basically, this

FIGURE 14.4   **Part Period Balancing Example**

Week number	1	2	3	4	5	6	7	8	9	10	11	12
Requirements	10	10	15	20	70	180	250	270	230	40	0	10
Order quantity	55				70	180	250	270	270			10
Beginning inventory	55	45	35	20	70	180	250	270	270	40	0	10
Ending inventory	45	35	20	0	0	0	0	0	40	0	0	0

Ordering cost	$2,100
Inventory carrying cost	1,385
Total cost	$3,485

FIGURE 14.5 **Wagner-Whitin Example**

Week number	1	2	3	4	5	6	7	8	9	10	11	12
Requirements	10	10	15	20	70	180	250	270	230	40	0	10
Order quantity	55				70	180	250	270	280			
Beginning inventory	55	45	35	20	70	180	250	270	280	50	10	10
Ending inventory	45	35	20	0	0	0	0	0	50	10	10	0

Ordering cost	$1,800
Inventory carrying cost	1,445
Total cost	$3,245

procedure evaluates all possible ways of ordering material to meet demand in each week of the requirements schedule, using dynamic programming. We won't attempt to describe the computational aspects of the Wagner-Whitin algorithm in the space available here. Rather, we'll note the difference in performance between this procedure and the part period balancing procedure.

Figure 14.5 shows the results of applying the Wagner-Whitin algorithm to the example. Total inventory cost is reduced by $240, or 7 percent, compared with the ordering plan produced by the part period balancing procedure in Figure 11.4. The difference between these two plans occurs in the lot size ordered in week 9. The part period balancing procedure didn't consider the combined cost of placing orders in both weeks 9 and 12. By spending an additional $60 to carry 10 units of inventory forward from week 9 to 12, we avoid the $300 ordering cost in week 12. In this case, we can save $240 in total cost. The increased number of ordering alternatives considered, however, clearly increases the computations needed in making ordering decisions.

Simulation Experiments

The example problem we've used to illustrate these procedures is for only one product item, without regard for *its* components, with no rolling through time, and with only a fixed number of weeks of requirements. To better understand lot-sizing procedures' performance, we should compare them in circumstances more closely related to company dynamics. Many simulation experiments do exactly that.

Figure 14.6 presents summary experimental results. The first experiment (performed by Wemmerlöv and Whybark) in this figure is for a single level (i.e., one MRP record) with no uncertainty. PPB, POQ, and EOQ are compared to Wagner-Whitin. PPB produces results about 6 percent more costly, POQ about 11 percent, and EOQ over 30 percent greater than Wagner-Whitin. These differences may be more important than the magnitudes indicate. Total cost savings of 6 percent may not be trivial.

Moving down to the third experiment (performed by B. J. McLaren), we see results for a multilevel situation, again with no uncertainty. In this case, the comparison isn't against Wagner-Whitin, but against a dynamic programming procedure that produces close to optimal results in a multilevel environment. The key finding in this experiment is that the results are roughly the same as in the first comparisons, although POQ does a little worse and PPB a little better than in the first experiment.

Perhaps the most interesting result in Figure 14.6 comes from comparing the first and third experiments to the *second* experiment. The second experiment (performed by Wemmerlöv

FIGURE 14.6
Summary
Experimental
Results

	Procedure			
	Wagner-Whitin	**PPB**	**POQ**	**EOQ**
Experiment 1: Percent over Wagner-Whitin cost; Single level, no uncertainty	0	5.74	10.72	33.87
Experiment 2: Percent over Wagner-Whitin cost; Single level, uncertainty	0	−.67	2.58	.19
Experiment 3: Percent over nearly optimal procedure; Multilevel, no uncertainty	.77	6.92	16.91	—
Computing time	.30	.10	.08	—

and Whybark) is for a single-level procedure, but *with* uncertainty expressed in the gross requirements data. The results here are quite mixed. Note PPB does *better* than Wagner-Whitin, and both POQ and EOQ are within 3 percent of Wagner-Whitin.

The conditions modeled in the second experiment replicate conditions likely to be found in actual industrial situations. Moreover, other studies show as uncertainty grows increasingly larger, it becomes very hard to distinguish between lot-sizing procedures' performance. What's more, while there were statistically significant differences among procedures in the first experiment, there were none in the second.

The message is clear. Lot-sizing enhancements to an MRP system should only be done *after* major uncertainties have been removed from the system: that is, *after* data integrity is in place, other MPC system modules are working, stability is present at the MPS level, and so on. If the MPC isn't performing effectively, that's the place to start, *not* with lot-sizing procedures.

Buffering Concepts

In this section we deal with another advanced concept in MRP, the use of buffering mechanisms to protect against uncertainties. We, however, make the same proviso as for lot sizing: Buffering is not the way to make up for a poorly operating MRP system. First things must come first.

Categories of Uncertainty

Two basic sources of uncertainty affect an MRP system: demand and supply uncertainty. These are further separated into two types: quantity uncertainty and timing uncertainty. The combination of sources and types provides the four categories of uncertainty illustrated in Figures 14.7 and 14.8.

Demand timing uncertainty is illustrated in Figure 14.8 by timing changes in the requirements from period to period. For example, the projected requirements for 372 units in period 7 actually occurred in period 4. This shift might result from a change in the promise date to a customer or from a change in a planned order for a higher-level item on which this item is used.

Supply timing uncertainty can arise from variations in vendor lead times or shop flow times. Thus, once an order is released, the exact timing of its arrival is uncertain. In Figure 14.8, for example, a receipt scheduled for period 3 actually arrived in period 1. Note

FIGURE 14.7

Categories of
Uncertainty in
MRP Systems

	Sources	
Types	**Demand**	**Supply**
Timing	Requirements shift from one period to another	Orders not received when due
Quantity	Requirements for more or less than planned	Orders received for more or less than planned

FIGURE 14.8   **Examples of the Four Categories of Uncertainty**

	Periods									
	1	**2**	**3**	**4**	**5**	**6**	**7**	**8**	**9**	**10**
Demand timing:										
Projected requirements	0	0	0	0	0	0	372	130	0	255
Actual requirements	0	0	0	372	130	0	146	255	143	0
Supply timing:										
Planned receipts	0	0	502	0	0	403	0	0	144	0
Actual receipts	502	0	0	0	0	403	0	0	144	0
Demand quantity:										
Projected requirements	85	122	42	190	83	48	41	46	108	207
Actual requirements	103	77	0	101	124	15	0	100	80	226
Supply quantity:										
Planned receipts	0	161	0	271	51	0	81	109	0	327
Actual receipts	0	158	0	277	50	0	77	113	0	321

in this case the uncertainty isn't over the order's amount but over its timing. The entire order may be late or early.

Demand quantity uncertainty is manifest when the amount of a requirement varies, perhaps randomly, about some mean value. This might occur when the master production schedule is increased or decreased to reflect changes in customer orders or the demand forecast. It can also occur when there are changes on higher-level items on which this item is used, or when there are variations in inventory levels. In Figure 14.8, period 1's projected requirements of 85 actually turned out to be 103 units of usage.

Supply quantity uncertainty typically arises when there are shortages of lower-level material, when production lots incur scrap losses, or when production overruns occur. Figure 14.8 illustrates this category of uncertainty, where actual quantity received varied around planned receipts.

Safety Stock and Safety Lead Time

There are two basic ways to buffer uncertainty in an MRP system. One is to specify a quantity of safety stock in much the same manner as with statistical inventory control techniques. The second method, safety lead time, plans order releases earlier than indicated by the requirements plan and schedules their receipt earlier than the required due date. Both

FIGURE 14.9
Safety Stock and Safety Lead Time Buffering

Order quantity = 50 units
Lead time = 2 periods

No Buffering Used		Period 1	2	3	4	5
Gross requirements		20	40	20	0	30
Scheduled receipts			50			
Projected available balance	40	20	30	10	10	30
Planned order released				50		

Safety Stock = 20 Units		1	2	3	4	5
Gross requirements		20	40	20	0	30
Scheduled receipts			50			
Projected available balance	40	20	30	60	60	30
Planned order releases		50				

Safety Lead Time = 1 Period		1	2	3	4	5
Gross requirements		20	40	20	0	30
Scheduled receipts			50			
Projected available balance	40	20	30	10	60	30
Planned order releases			50			

approaches produce an increase in inventory levels to provide a buffer against uncertainty, but the techniques operate quite differently, as Figure 14.9 shows.

The first case in Figure 14.9 uses no buffering. A net requirement occurs in period 5, and a planned order is created in period 3 to cover it. The second case specifies a safety stock of 20 units. This means the safety stock level will be broken in period 3 unless an order arrives. The MRP logic thus creates a planned order in period 1 to prevent this condition. The final case in Figure 14.9 illustrates use of safety lead time. This example includes a safety lead time of one period. The net result is the planned order being created in period 2 with a due date of period 4.

Most MRP software packages can easily accommodate safety stock, since we can determine planned orders simply by subtracting the safety stock from the initial inventory balance when determining the projected available balance. Safety lead time is a bit more difficult. We can't achieve it by simply inflating the lead time by the amount of the safety lead time. In our example, this approach wouldn't produce the result shown as the last case in Figure 14.9. The due date for the order would be period 5, instead of period 4. Thus, we must change the planned due date as well as the planned release date.

Both safety stock and safety lead time illustrate the fundamental problem with all MRP buffering techniques: They lie to the system. The *real* need date for the planned order shown in Figure 14.9 is period 5. If the *real* lead time is two periods, the *real* launch date should be period 3. Putting in buffers can lead to behavioral problems in the shop, since the resulting schedules don't tell the truth. An informal system may be created to tell people what's really needed. This, in turn, might lead to larger buffers. There's a critical need to communicate the reasoning behind the use of safety stock and safety lead times, and to create a working MPC system that minimizes the need for buffers.

Safety Stock and Safety Lead Time Performance Comparisons

Simulation experiments (performed by Whybark and Williams) reveal a preference for using either safety stock or safety lead time, depending on the category of uncertainty to be buffered. These results show a distinct preference for using safety lead time in all cases where demand or supply *timing* uncertainty exists. Likewise, the experiments show a strong preference for using safety stock in all cases where there's uncertainty in either the demand or supply *quantity*.

Figures 14.10 and 14.11 show typical results from these experiments. Figure 14.10 compares safety stock and safety lead time for simulated situations similar to Figure 14.8's top two examples. The horizontal axis shows the average inventory held, and the vertical axis depicts the service level in percentage terms; that is, the horizontal axis is based on the

FIGURE 14.10

Experimental Results: Average Inventory versus Service Level with Timing Uncertainty

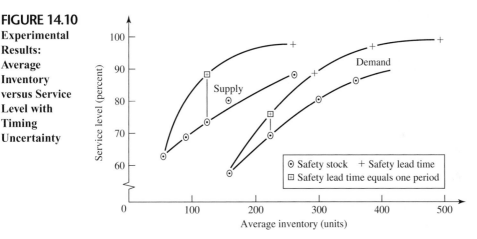

FIGURE 14.11

Experimental Results: Average Inventory versus Service Level with Quantity Uncertainty

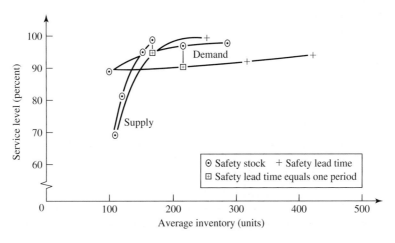

period-by-period actual inventory values in the simulation, and the vertical axis is based on the frequency with which actual requirements were met from inventory.

For both the supply and the demand timing uncertainty cases, Figure 14.10 shows a strong preference for safety lead time buffering. For any given level of inventory, a higher service level can be achieved with safety lead time than with safety stock. For any given level of service, safety lead time can provide the level with a smaller inventory investment.

Figure 14.11 shows the comparison for uncertainty in quantities. This simulated situation is similar to Figure 14.8's bottom two examples. The results are a bit more difficult to see, since the graphs for supply and demand uncertainty overlap. Nevertheless, the results are again clear. For any given level of inventory investment, higher service levels are achieved by use of safety stocks than by use of safety lead times. This result is true for situations involving quantity uncertainty in both demand and supply.

The results of the experiments provide general guidelines for choosing between the two buffering techniques. Under conditions of uncertainty in timing, safety lead time is the preferred technique, while safety stock is preferred under conditions of quantity uncertainty. The experimental conclusions didn't change with the source of the uncertainty (demand or supply), lot-sizing technique, lead time, average demand level, uncertainty level, or lumpiness in the gross requirements data. The experiments also indicate that, as lumpiness and uncertainty levels increase, so does the importance of making the correct choice between safety stock and safety lead time.

These guidelines have important practical implications. Supply timing uncertainty and demand quantity uncertainty are the two categories with the largest differences in service levels. An obvious instance of supply timing uncertainty is in vendor lead times. Orders from vendors are subject to timing uncertainty due to variability in both production and transportation times.

These experiments strongly support the use of safety lead time for purchased parts experiencing this type of uncertainty. Demand quantity uncertainty often appears in an MRP system for parts subject to service part demand. Another cause of demand quantity uncertainty is when an end product can be made from very different options or features. The experimental results support using safety stock for buffering against these uncertainties.

Scrap Allowances

A concept closely tied to buffering is use of scrap allowances in calculating the lot size to start into production to reach some desired lot size going into the stockroom. It's a fairly straightforward procedure to use any lot-sizing procedure to determine the lot size and then adjust the result to take into account the scrap allowance. One issue that arises is whether the quantity shown on the shop paper (and as a scheduled receipt) should be the *starting* quantity or the *expected finished* quantity. Practice suggests using the former. This requires, however, that each actual occurrence of scrap be transacted and reflected in updated plans.

The overall issue of the scrap allowance is clearly related to the use of safety stocks for quantity uncertainty buffering. One or both of these techniques could be used in a particular situation. The point is, if scrap losses occur, they must be planned for and buffered. It also means this may be an area where tight control can lead to performance improvements.

Other Buffering Mechanisms

Before we end our discussion of uncertainty, it's useful to consider some additional alternatives for dealing with uncertainty. First, rather than live with uncertainty, an alternative is to reduce it to an absolute minimum. In fact, that's one of the major objectives of MPC systems.

For example, increasing demand forecasts' accuracy and developing effective procedures for translating demand for products into master schedules reduces the uncertainty transmitted to the MRP system. Freezing the master schedule for some time period achieves the same result. Developing an effective priority system for moving parts and components through the shop reduces the uncertainty in lead times. Responsive shop-floor control systems can achieve better due date performance, thereby reducing uncertainty. Procedures that improve the accuracy of the data in the MRP system reduce uncertainty regarding on-hand inventory levels. Aspects of JIT manufacturing reduce lead time, improve quality, and decrease uncertainty, providing the same benefits. Other activities could be mentioned, but all focus on the reduction of the amount of uncertainty that needs to be accommodated in an MRP system.

Another way to deal with uncertainty in an MRP system is to provide for slack in the production system in one way or another. Production slack is created by having additional time, labor, machine capacity, and so on over what's specifically needed to produce the planned amount of product. This extra production capacity could be used to produce an oversized lot to allow for that lot's shrinkages through the process. We also could use slack to allow for production of unplanned lots or for additional activities to speed production through the shop. Thus, providing additional capacity in the shop allows us to accommodate greater quantities than planned in a given time period or to expedite jobs through the shop. We must understand, however, that slack costs money, but if the people can be put to good use when production is not needed, the "costs" can become investments.

Nervousness

This chapter so far has described several enhancements to MRP systems. However, we should recognize some lot-sizing procedures can contribute to the problem of "nervousness" (i.e., instability) in the MRP plans. In this section, we discuss the problem of nervousness in MRP systems and guidelines for reducing its magnitude.

Sources of MRP System Nervousness

MRP system nervousness, a term first coined by Daniel Steele, is defined as significant changes in MRP plans, which occur even with only minor changes in higher-level MRP records or the master production schedule. Changes can involve the quantity or timing of planned orders or scheduled receipts. Figure 14.12 illustrates just such a case. Here, a reduction of one unit in the master schedule in week 2 produced a significant change in the planned orders for item A. This change had an even more profound impact on component part B. It's hard to imagine a *reduction* at the MPS level could create a past-due condition, but that's precisely what Figure 14.12 shows—how the change caused by a relatively minor shift in the master schedule is amplified by use of the periodic order quantity (POQ) lot-sizing procedure.

There are a number of ways relatively minor changes in the MRP system can create nervousness and instability in the MRP plans. These include planned orders released prematurely or in an unplanned quantity, unplanned demand (as for spare parts or engineering requirements), and shifts in MRP parameter values, such as safety stock, safety lead time, or planned lead-time values. Nervousness created by such changes is most damaging in MRP systems with many levels in the product structure. Furthermore, use of some lot-sizing techniques, such as POQ, can amplify system nervousness at lower levels in the product structure, as Figure 14.12 shows.

FIGURE 14.12
MRP System
Nervousness
Example

Before reducing second-week requirements by one unit:
Item A
POQ = 5 weeks
Lead time = 2 weeks

Week		1	2	3	4	5	6	7	8
Gross requirements		2	24	3	5	1	3	4	50
Scheduled receipts									
Projected available balance	28	26	2	13	8	7	4	0	0
Planned order releases		14					50		

Component B
POQ = 5 weeks
Lead time = 4 weeks

Week		1	2	3	4	5	6	7	8
Gross requirements		14					50		
Scheduled receipts		14							
Projected available balance	2	2	2	2	2	2	0	0	0
Planned order releases			48						

After second-week requirement change:
Item A
POQ = 5 weeks
Lead time = 2 weeks

Week		1	2	3	4	5	6	7	8
Gross requirements		2	(23)	3	5	1	3	4	50
Scheduled receipts									
Projected available balance	28	26	3	0	58	57	54	50	0
Planned order releases			63						

Component B
POQ = 5 weeks
Lead time = 4 weeks

Week		1	2	3	4	5	6	7	8
Gross requirements			63						
Scheduled receipts		14							
Projected available balance	2	16	−47						
Planned order releases	(47)								

Past due

Reducing MRP System Nervousness

There are several ways to reduce nervousness in MRP systems. First, it's important to reduce causes of changes to the MRP plan. It's important to introduce stability into the master schedule through such devices as freezing and time fences. Similarly, it's important to reduce the incidence of unplanned demands by incorporating spare parts forecasts into MRP record gross requirements. Furthermore, it's necessary to follow the MRP plan with regard to the timing and quantity of planned order releases. Finally, it's important to control the introduction of parameter changes, such as changes in safety stock levels or planned lead times. All of these actions help dampen the small adjustments that can trigger MRP system nervousness.

A second guideline for reducing MRP system nervousness involves selective use of lot-sizing procedures; that is, if nervousness still exists after reducing the preceding causes, we might use different lot-sizing procedures at different product structure levels. One approach is to use fixed order quantities at the top level, using either fixed order quantities or lot-for-lot at intermediate levels, and using period order quantities at the bottom level. Since the fixed order quantity procedure passes along only order timing changes (and not changes in order quantity), this procedure tends to dampen lot-size–induced nervousness. Clearly, fixed order quantity values need to be monitored, since changes in the level of requirements may tend to make such quantities uneconomical over time.

A third guideline for reducing nervousness involves using firm planned orders in MRP (or in MPS) records. Firm planned orders tend to stabilize requirements for lower-level items. The offsetting cost, however, is the necessary maintenance of firm planned orders by MRP planners.

These guidelines provide methods for reducing nervousness in MRP plans. There's a distinction, however, between nervousness in the MRP *plans* and nervousness in the *execution* of MRP system plans. Nervousness in the execution of the plans can also influence behavior. If system users see the plans changing, they may make arbitrary or defensive decisions. This can further aggravate changes in plans.

One way to deal with the execution issue is simply to pass updated information to system users less often. This suggestion argues against the use of net change MRP systems, or at least against publishing every change. An alternative is simply to have more intelligent users. A well-trained user responding to the problem in Figure 14.12 might, through bottom-up replanning, change the lot sizes to eliminate the problem. However, Figure 14.12 does indicate this isn't an easy problem to detect. Many aspects are counterintuitive. The fact still is, more intelligent users will make more intelligent execution decisions. User education may still be the best investment!

Concluding Principles	Chapter 14 describes several advanced concepts and conventions in MRP systems. Many ideas are of research interest, but all have practical implications too. Certain kinds of enhancements can be made in a well-operating MRP system, if made by knowledgeable professionals and if implemented with knowledgeable users. The following principles are critical to successful implementation:

- MRP enhancements should be done *after* a basic MPC system is in place.
- Discrete lot-sizing procedures for manufacturing can reduce inventory-associated costs. The complexity should not outweigh the savings, however. |

- Safety stocks should be used when the uncertainty is of the quantity category.
- Safety lead times should be used when uncertainty is of the timing category.
- MRP system nervousness can result from lot-sizing rules, parameter changes, and other causes. The MPC professional should take appropriate precautions to dampen the amplitude and impact.
- Uncertainty needs to be reduced (flawless execution) before implementing complex procedures.
- MRP system enhancements should follow the development of ever more intelligent users.

References

Axsater, Sven. "Evaluation of Lot Sizing Techniques," *International Journal of Production Research* 24, no. 1 (1986), pp. 51–57.

Baker, K. R. "Lot Sizing Procedures and a Standard Data Set: A Reconciliation," *Journal of Manufacturing and Operations Management* 2, no. 3 (1989), pp. 199–221.

Benton, W. C., and D. C. Whybark. "Material Requirements Planning (MRP) and Purchase Discounts," *Journal of Operations Management*, February 1982, pp. 137–143.

Berry, W. L. "Lot Sizing Procedures for Requirements Planning Systems: A Framework for Analysis," *Production and Inventory Management* 13, no. 2 (2nd quarter 1972), pp. 19–33.

Blackburn, J. D.; D. H. Kropp; and R. A. Millen. "A Comparison of Strategies to Dampen Nervousness in MRP Systems," *Management Science* 32, no. 4 (April 1986).

Bobko, P. R., and D. C. Whybark. "The Coefficient of Variation as a Factor in MRP Research," *Decision Sciences* 16, no. 4 (fall 1985).

Callarman, T. F., and D. C. Whybark. "Determining Purchase Quantities for MRP Requirements," *Journal of Purchasing and Materials Management* 17, no. 3 (fall 1981), pp. 25–30.

Callarman, T. F., and R. S. Hamrin. "A Comparison of Dynamic Lot Sizing Rules for Use in a Single Stage MRP System with Demand Uncertainty," *International Journal of Operations and Production Management* 4, no. 2 (1984), pp. 39–48.

Carlson, R. C., and C. A. Yano. "Safety Stocks in MRP-Systems with Emergency Setups for Components," *Management Science* 32, no. 4 (April 1986).

Chalmet, L. C.; M. De Bodt; and L. Van Wassenhove. "The Effect of Engineering Changes and Demand Uncertainty on MRP Lot Sizing: A Case Study," *International Journal of Production Research* 23, no. 2 (1985), pp. 233–251.

Christoph, Orinda Byrd. "McLaren's Order Moment Lot-Sizing Technique in Multiple Discounts," *Production and Inventory Management Journal* 30, no. 2 (2nd quarter 1989), pp. 44–47.

Christoph, O. B., and R. Lawrence LaForge. "The Performance of MRP Purchase Lot-Size Procedures under Actual Multiple Purchase Discount Conditions," *Decision Sciences Journal* 20, no. 2 (spring 1989), pp. 348–358.

Coleman, B. J., and M. A. McKnew. "An Improved Heuristic for Multilevel Lot Sizing in Material Requirements Planning," *Decision Sciences Journal* 22, no. 1 (winter 1991), pp. 136–156.

Collier, D. A. "A Comparison of MRP Lot-Sizing Methods Considering Capacity Change Costs," *Journal of Operations Management* 1, no. 1 (1980).

Dixon, P. S., and E. A. Silver. "A Heuristic Solution Procedure for the Multi-Item, Single Level, Limited Capacity, Lot-Sizing Problem," *Journal of Operations Management* 2, no. 1 (1981).

De Bodt, M. A., and L. N. Van Wassenhove. "Cost Increases Due to Demand Uncertainty in MRP Lot Sizing," *Decision Sciences* 14, no. 3 (July 1983).

Dolinsky, L. R.; T. E. Vollmann; and M. J. Maggard. "Adjusting Replenishment Orders to Reflect Learning in a Material Requirements Planning Environment," *Management Science* 36, no. 12 (December 1990).

Gaimon, C. "Optimal Inventory, Backlogging, and Machine Loading in a Serial Multistage, Multi-Period Production Environment," *International Journal of Production Research* 24, no. 2 (May–June 1986).

Gardiner, S. C., and J. H. Blackstone. "The Effects of Lot Sizing and Dispatching on Customer Service in an MRP Environment," *Journal of Operations Management* 11, no. 2 (1993).

Heady, R. B., and Z. Zhu. "An Improved Implementation of the Wagner-Whitin Algorithm," *Production and Operations Management* 3, no. 1 (1994).

Inderfurth, K. "Nervousness in Inventory Control: Analytical Results," *OR Spektrum* 16 (1994), pp. 113–123.

Inderfurth, Karl, and Ton de Kok. "Nervousness in Inventory Management: Comparison of Basic Control Rules," *European Journal of Operational Research* 103, no. 1 (November 16, 1997), pp. 55–82.

Jesse, Jr., R. R., and J. H. Blackstone, Jr. "A Note on Using the Lot-Sizing Index for Comparing Discrete Lot-Sizing Techniques," *Journal of Operations Management* 5, no. 4 (1986).

Kadipasaoglu, S. N., and V. Sridharan. "Alternative Approach for Reducing Schedule Instability in Multistage Manufacturing under Demand Uncertainty," *Journal of Operations Management* 13, (1995), pp. 193–211.

Karmarkar, U.S. "Lot Sizes, Lead Times and In-Process Inventories," *Management Science* 33, no. 3 (1987).

Kropp, D. H.; R. C. Carlson; and J. V. Jucker. "Heuristic Lot-Sizing Approaches for Dealing with MRP System Nervousness," *Decision Sciences* 14, no. 2 (April 1983).

Lambrecht, M. C.; J. A. Muckstadt; and R. Luyten. "Protective Stocks in Multi-Stage Production Systems," *International Journal of Production Research* 22, no. 6 (1984), pp. 1001–1025.

McClelland, Marilyn K., and Harvey M. Wagner. "Location of Inventories in an MRP Environment," *Decision Sciences Journal* 19, no. 3 (summer 1988), pp. 535–553.

McKnew, M. A.; C. Seydam; and B. J. Coleman. "An Efficient Zero-One Formulation of the Multi-level Lot-Sizing Problem," *Decision Sciences Journal* 22, no. 2 (spring 1991), pp. 280–295.

McLaren, B. J. "A Study of Multiple Level Lot Sizing Techniques for Material Requirements Planning Systems." Ph.D. dissertation, Purdue University, 1977.

Melnyk, S. A., and C. J. Piper. "Leadtime Errors in MRP: The Lot-Sizing Effect," *International Journal of Production Research* 23, no. 2 (1985), pp. 253–264.

Narasimhan, R., and S. A. Melnyk. "Assessing the Transient Impact of Lot Sizing Rules Following MRP Implementation," *International Journal of Production Research* 22, no. 5 (1984), pp. 759–772.

New, C., and J. Mapes. "MRP with High Uncertain Yield Losses," *Journal of Operations Management* 4, no. 4 (1984).

Prentis, Eric L., and Basheer M. Khumawala. "Efficient Heuristics for MRP Lot Sizing with Variable Production/Purchasing Costs," *Decision Sciences Journal* 20, no. 3 (summer 1989), pp. 439–450.

Raturi, Amitabh S., and Arthur V. Hill. "An Experimental Analysis of Capacity-Sensitive Setup Parameters for MRP Lot-Sizing," *Decision Sciences Journal* 19, no. 4 (fall 1988), pp. 782–800.

Ritzman, L. P., and B. E. King. "The Relative Significance of Forecast Errors in Multi-Stage Manufacturing," *Journal of Operations Management* 11, no. 1 (1993).

St. John, R. "The Cost of Inflated Planned Lead Times in MRP Systems," *Journal of Operations Management* 5, no. 2 (1985).

Schmitt, T. G. "Resolving Uncertainty in Manufacturing Systems," *Journal of Operations Management* 4, no. 4 (1984).

Smith-Daniels, D. E., and N. J. Aquilano. "Constrained Resource Project Scheduling Subject to Material Constraints," *Journal of Operations Management* 4, no. 4 (1984).

Steele, Daniel C. "The Nervous MRP System: How to Do Battle," *Production and Inventory Management* (fourth quarter 1975), pp. 83–89.

Steinberg, E., and A. Napier. "Optimal Multilevel Lot Sizing for Requirements Planning Systems," *Management Science* 26, no. 12 (December 1980), pp. 1258–1272.

Tang, Ou. *Planning and Replanning Within the Material Requirements Planning Environment: A Transform Approach,* Department of Production Economics, Linköping Institute of Technology, Linköping, Sweden, 2000.

Veral, E. A., and R. L. LaForge. "The Performance of a Simple Incremental Lot-Sizing Rule in a Multilevel Inventory Environment," *Decision Sciences* 16, no. 1 (winter 1985).

Veral, Emre A., and R. Lawrence LaForge. "The Integration of Cost and Capacity Considerations in Material Requirements Systems," *Decision Sciences Journal* 21, no. 3 (summer 1990), pp. 507–520.

Verganti, R. "Order Overplanning with Uncertain Lumpy Demand: A Simplified Theory," *International Journal of Production Research* 35, no. 12 (December 1997), pp. 3229–3249.

Vickery, S. K., and R. E. Markland. "Multi-Stage Lot Sizing in a Serial Production System," *International Journal of Production Research* 24, no. 3 (1986), pp. 517–534.

Wacker, John G. "A Theory of Material Requirements Planning (MRP): An Empirical Methodology to Reduce Uncertainty in MRP Systems," *International Journal of Production Research* 23, no. 4 (1985), pp. 807–824.

Wagner, H. M., and T. M. Whitin. "Dynamic Version of the Economic Lot Size Model." *Management Science,* October 1958, pp. 89–96.

Wassweiler, W. "Tool Requirements Planning." *American Production and Inventory Control Society 1990 Annual Conference Proceedings,* pp. 451–453.

Wemmerlöv, Urban. "The Behavior of Lot-Sizing Procedures in the Presence of Forecast Errors," *Journal of Operations Management* 8, no. 1 (January 1989), pp. 37–47.

Wemmerlöv, U., and D. C. Whybark. "Lot Sizing under Uncertainty in a Rolling Schedule Environment," *International Journal of Production Research* 22, no. 3 (1984), pp. 467–84.

Whybark, D. C., and J. G. Williams. "Material Requirements Planning under Uncertainty," *Decision Sciences* 7, no. 4 (October 1976).

Yano, C. A., and R. Carlson. "Interaction between Frequency of Rescheduling and the Role of Safety Stock in Material Requirements Planning Systems," *International Journal of Production Research* 11 (1987), pp. 185–205.

Discussion Questions

1. Some practitioners complain discrete lot-sizing procedures (e.g., POQ, PPB) aggravate system nervousness because of changing lot quantities. What do they mean?

2. Reviewing Figure 14.6 and using your own powers of intuition, what do you think would happen to the difference in costs between lot-sizing procedures as uncertainty gets larger and larger? What about the absolute cost values?

3. How could the lot-sizing procedures be modified to consider quantity discounts that might occur in a purchasing situation?

4. Why is it necessary to change both the release date and the due date for safety lead time?

5. What are some of the difficulties with introducing "organizational slack" as a method of buffering against uncertainty?

6. One suggestion for reducing execution nervousness is to give the status information only at the time of need. Thus, the only time a foreman would need to determine job priorities would be when he or she was choosing the next job to put on a machine. Give pros and cons of this suggestion.

Problems

1. Consider the following information about an end-product item:

   Ordering cost = $45/order.

   Average usage = 12 units/week.

   Inventory carrying cost = $1/unit/week.

a. How many orders should we place per year (52 weeks) to replenish inventory of the item based on average weekly demand?

b. Given the following time-phased net requirements from an MRP record for this item, determine the sequence of planned orders using economic order quantity and periodic order quantity procedures. Assume lead time equals zero and current on-hand inventory equals zero. Calculate the inventory carrying cost on the basis of weekly ending inventory values. Which procedure produces the lowest total cost for the eight-week period?

	Week							
	1	2	3	4	5	6	7	8
Requirements	15	2	10	12	6	0	14	9

2. A final assembly (A) requires one week to assemble and has a component part (B) requiring two weeks to fabricate. Three units of final assembly A and four units of part B are currently on hand. The gross requirements for assembly A for the next 10 weeks are as follows (one part B is used on each A):

	Week									
	1	2	3	4	5	6	7	8	9	10
Requirements	1	4	2	8	1	0	6	2	1	3

a. What are the planned order releases for part B using lot-for-lot lot sizing for both parts A and B?

b. What are the planned order releases for part B using POQ = 2 for both parts A and B?

3. A company has estimated net requirements for a particular part as follows:

	Month											
	1	2	3	4	5	6	7	8	9	10	11	12
Requirements	100	10	15	20	70	250	250	250	250	40	0	100

Ordering cost associated with this part is $300. Estimated inventory carrying cost is $2 per unit per month calculated on average inventory. Currently no parts are available in inventory. The company wishes to know when and how much to order over the next 12 months.

a. Apply the economic order quantity and the part period balancing procedures to solve this problem.

b. What important assumptions are involved in each of the approaches used in part a?

4. The Thrifty Computer Company is trying to decide which of several lot-sizing procedures to use for its MRP system. The following information pertains to one of the typical component parts:

Setup cost = $100/order.

Inventory cost = $1.50/unit/week.

Current inventory balance = 0 units.

	Week							
	1	2	3	4	5	6	7	8
Demand forecast	65	45	35	10	115	25	85	20

a. Apply the EOQ, (only integer multiples of the EOQ can be ordered), POQ, and PPB lot-sizing procedures and show the total cost resulting from each procedure. Calculate inventory carrying costs on the basis of average inventory values. Assume orders are received into the beginning inventory.

b. Indicate advantages and disadvantages of using each procedure suggested in part a.

5. Apply the part period balancing (PPB) lot-sizing procedure to the following 12 periods of requirements data, indicating order receipts' size and period. Assume order costs are $100/order placed and inventory carrying cost is $1/unit/period. Calculate the inventory carrying costs on the basis of *ending* inventory values.

	Period											
	1	2	3	4	5	6	7	8	9	10	11	12
Requirements	70	30	35	60	60	25	35	70	45	70	80	55

6. Use the requirements data from problem 5 and order costs of $100/order, inventory carrying cost of $1/unit/period, and a unit cost of $50 in lots of less than 100 and $45 for lots of 100 or more, and inventory carrying costs calculated on the basis of *ending* inventory values to apply the least unit cost (LUC) procedure.

7. Ellen Farr is responsible for purchasing forgings and castings for Farr Machine Corporation's raw material stockroom. Ellen's job is to purchase a sufficient number of castings and forgings to meet weekly demand for these items by the firm's fabrication shop in producing machined parts. She's interested in low cost and whether to take the discount offered. Forecast weekly requirements for one item (the input shaft forging) and cost information for this item are as follows:

	Week								
	1	2	3	4	5	6	7	8	9
Forecast	44	2	10	42	46	2	30	10	4

Ordering cost = $50.

Inventory carrying cost = $5/unit/week.

Item price = $100/unit ($95/unit if orders are issued for 80 units or more).

Calculate the orders Ellen would place using the least unit cost and the least period cost procedures. Find total cost of each solution procedure, assuming inventory carrying cost is based on the average inventory.

8. The Fisher Products Company produces a line of children's parlor games. The production process includes two departments: fabrication and assembly. The fabrication shop produces game parts, such as plastic pieces, game markers, and special indicators. The company maintains inventories both of the raw material needed to produce the game parts and of finished game parts themselves. The assembly department consists of a single assembly line that collates and packages all parlor

EXHIBIT A

Material
Requirements
Planning
Worksheet

End Products	Week Number							
	1	2	3	4	5	6	7	8
Game A master schedule	21	0	0	21	20	0	15	0
Game B master schedule	2	2	9	0	6	3	0	9

Toy Cup		1	2	3	4	5	6	7	8
Gross requirements									
Scheduled receipts*									
Projected available balance	44								
Planned order release									

Plastic Molding Material		1	2	3	4	5	6	7	8
Gross requirements									
Scheduled receipts*		90							
Projected available balance	20								
Planned order release									

*Received at the beginning of each week.

games in Fisher's product line to meet incoming customer orders. The company maintains no inventory of finished products (games) but produces only to customer order.

Each week the assembly foreman schedules the assembly line and supervises withdrawal of game parts from the stockroom that are needed on the assembly line to meet the production schedule. Sometimes several games are assembled during a single week. Since the company uses MRP to plan and control production of games and game parts, the assembly foreman prepares a master production schedule for a period covering eight weeks into the future. Exhibit A shows his master schedule with two end products (games A and B).

a. A component (game part) called the toy cup is used in producing the two parlor games (A and B). Two units of the toy cup are needed to produce one unit of game A, and one unit of the toy cup is required to produce one unit of game B. Assuming the toy cup planned lead time is one week, current on-hand inventory is 44 units, and there are no scheduled receipts, complete the MRP record for the toy cup in Exhibit A. Use the periodic order quantity ordering policy for lot sizing. Ordering cost for the toy cup is $9/order; inventory carrying cost is $.10/unit/week.

b. After completing the toy cup's MRP record in part a, complete the MRP record in Exhibit A for the plastic molding material needed to produce the toy cup. Two ounces of the plastic molding material are needed to produce one toy cup, planned lead time for the plastic material is one week, 20 ounces of plastic material are currently on hand, a scheduled receipt for 90 ounces of plastic material is due in week 1 from the supplier, and the periodic ordering policy is used for this item. Ordering cost is $5/order; inventory carrying cost is $.04 per ounce per week.

c. Fisher's assembly foreman has just handed you the MRP records for the toy cup and plastic molding material in Exhibit B. These MRP records contain a different master schedule, changed on-hand inventory values, and a new scheduled receipt value. Also, planned lead time for both items is now two weeks. Complete the new MRP records for both items, assuming the part period balancing ordering policy is used for the toy cup and plastic material.

EXHIBIT B

**Material
Requirements
Planning
Worksheet**

End Products		Week Number							
		1	2	3	4	5	6	7	8
Game A master schedule			22		21	15			
Game B master schedule		9	1	7	7	3	10	1	2

Toy Cup		1	2	3	4	5	6	7	8
Gross requirements (2 units/game A) (1 unit/game B)									
Scheduled receipts*									
Projected available balance	55								
Planned order release (Lead time = 2 weeks)									

Plastic Molding Material		1	2	3	4	5	6	7	8
Gross requirements (2 oz./toy cup)									
Scheduled receipts*		166							
Projected available balance	10								
Planned order release (Lead time = 2 weeks)									

*Received at the beginning of each week.

   d. What problem(s), if any, are apparent after you've completed the MRP records in Exhibit B? What are the MRP planner's alternative courses of action in resolving the problem(s)? What specific course of action should be taken? Why?

9. Chambers Inc. is considering using the PBB lot-sizing approach, but first they want to compare it to their current lot-sizing method (EOQ). They have selected a sample component for the comparison, and its requirements are given below. Ordering cost is $27 per order, and carrying cost is $.25 per unit per period. (Use average inventory.)

	Period							
	1	2	3	4	5	6	7	8
Requirements	51	14	59	93	44	12	67	60

10. The Silver brothers (Ed, Quick, and Hiho) had their very own factory. Ed was the general manager, and Quick produced the finished product from a part Hiho made. Here are selected data for the finished product and part. Requirements for the finished product for the next few periods appear as well.

	Quick	Hiho
Order quantity (EOQ)	40	100
Safety stock	5	0
Lead time	1	1
Current inventory	7	12
Scheduled receipt in period 1	40	0

			Period				
1	**2**	**3**	**4**	**5**	**6**	**7**	**8**
Requirements	23	13	36	12	21	8	34	23

a. Using a spreadsheet, develop MRP records for Quick and Hiho. What are the planned order releases for Hiho's part?

b. Devise a different ordering plan for Quick and Hiho that has the same number of orders as the solution in part a but reduces inventory levels *and* has the same amount of closing inventory (period 8) as the original plan.

11. Develop a spreadsheet to calculate LUC. Purchased part usage averages 20 units per period, ordering cost is $5 per order, carrying cost is $.20 per unit per period, and purchase price is $1. Use these requirements:

			Period			
	1	**2**	**3**	**4**	**5**	**6**
Requirements	10	18	30	35	10	16

a. What is the ordering pattern?

12. The XYZ Company's production manager is investigating causes of nervousness in the firm's MRP system. His study has produced MRP schedules for item A as of the start of weeks 1, 2, 3, and 4.

LT = 0.

SS = 0.

Q calculated using the Wagner-Whitin algorithm.

Ordering cost = $400/order.

Inventory carrying cost = $1/unit/week.

		Week			
Item A		**1**	**2**	**3**	**4**
Gross requirements		177	261	207	309
Scheduled receipts					
Projected available balance	0	261	0	309	0
Planned order release		438		516	

Item A		Week			
		2	3	4	5
Gross requirements		261	207	309	64
Scheduled receipts					
Projected available balance	261	0	373	64	0
Planned order release			580		

Item A		Week			
		3	4	5	6
Gross requirements		207	309	64	182
Scheduled receipts					
Projected available balance	0	0	246	182	0
Planned order release		207	555		

Item A		Week			
		4	5	6	7
Gross requirements		309	64	182	0
Scheduled receipts					
Projected available balance	0	246	182	0	0
Planned order release		555			

a. Assume we need one unit of raw material item B to produce one unit of product item A. Calculate gross requirements for item B covering a four-week planning horizon as of the start of weeks 1, 2, 3, and 4. Compare gross requirements for item B for each week as they're calculated at the start of weeks 1, 2, 3, and 4. What differences do you observe in item B's gross requirements from week to week?

b. If there are no changes to either item A's gross requirements or beginning inventory over the four-week interval, how do you explain changes in the gross requirements for item B observed in part a? How do you explain this situation to the production manager? What impact would such changes in gross requirements for item B have on supplier relations if B is a purchased part?

13. The following MRP record is for an item purchased from the K. C. Jones company, a supplier to Ajax Diesel. The purchase quantity is 45 units. The history on K. C. Jones's delivery lead time shows an average lead time of three weeks. Sometimes orders from K. C. Jones show up a week late. Complete the following MRP record so that shortages do not occur even if K. C. Jones is late by one week.

		Week							
		1	2	3	4	5	6	7	8
Gross requirements		33	12	23	37	26	3	8	31
Scheduled receipts		45							
Projected available balance	60								
Planned order release									

14. The following MRP record is for an item purchased from Cannonball Adderly, another supplier for Ajax Diesel. This sample part requires a two-week lead time. The percent defective for purchased lots of this item averages 17 percent and has been as large as 27 percent. Defective items are removed and returned to the vendor when found. Construct an MRP record to protect against inventory shortages using a fixed order quantity. An economic order quantity of 30 units has been calculated for this item.

		Week							
		1	2	3	4	5	6	7	8
Gross requirements		12	0	27	8	34	3	23	29
Scheduled receipts									
Projected available balance	21								
Planned order release									

15. Atlas Wrench Company was having problems with the sensitivity of its MRP system. The following records are typical of its planning system. The two records are for the Z Wrench and for one of its components, the Z Shaft. There is one Z Shaft used in each Z Wrench.

		Week					
Z Wrench		1	2	3	4	5	6
Gross requirements		2	20	5	1	3	45
Scheduled receipts							
Projected available balance	26	24	4	4	3	0	0
Planned order release		5			45		

POQ = 3 weeks; LT = 2 weeks; SS = 0.

		Week					
Z Shaft		1	2	3	4	5	6
Gross requirements		5			45		
Scheduled receipts		5					
Projected available balance	3	3	3	3	0	0	0
Planned order release		45					

POQ = 3 weeks; LT = 3 weeks; SS = 0.

a. What happens if the gross requirement for the Z Wrench in week 2 drops to 19? Are there any problems?

b. How can Atlas Wrench deal with situations like the one that occurs above?

15

Advanced Concepts in Just-in-Time

As just-in-time (JIT) has grown in importance for coordinating material flows in manufacturing supply chains, research on both the philosophy of JIT and associated techniques has increased. Much of this research is focused on the broader aspects of the JIT approach—the general management concepts related to elimination of waste in all its forms. In this chapter, although we present a broad framework for JIT research, we focus on topics directly related to manufacturing planning and control. This is not to diminish the importance of the other work, but simply to keep our focus from becoming too broad. As research on and implementation of JIT concepts continue, our knowledge increases and the frontiers of that knowledge expand. In the world of JIT, we can already see the research agenda moving to problems of combining JIT with other techniques integrating JIT with ERP systems, and expanding the scope to incorporate issues of intercompany coordination along the supply chain. We have organized the chapter around the following five topics:

- *A JIT research framework:* What are the key areas of research in JIT and which of these relate to manufacturing planning and control?
- *Scheduling:* How does the need for mixed model schedules and schedule stability affect the master production schedule?
- *Supply chain coordination:* How should decisions concerning the scheduling of incoming shipments be determined?
- *Production floor management:* How should the number of kanbans be determined and to what extent do operating conditions affect the determination?
- *JIT performance and operating conditions:* How do factors such as demand uncertainty, process time variance, and the number of kanbans affect operating performance?

Chapter 15 is closely linked to Chapter 9, which describes basic JIT methods, and Chapter 11, which discusses the design of scheduling systems under JIT. Chapter 5 provides the basic inventory theory for independent-demand environments, while Chapter 17 discusses supply chain management. Chapter 4, on ERP, and Chapter 13, on MPC systems and strategy, both provide additional material on system integration.

A JIT Research Framework

There are many aspects to a JIT manufacturing system. Before considering those that affect design of manufacturing planning and control systems, we'll describe a framework that shows how they relate to key manufacturing functions and to other functions in a company. The framework has been developed by Sakakibara, Flynn, and Schroeder in conjunction with their measurement research on JIT. As background they conducted a comprehensive review of the published literature on JIT and visited 12 plants in the United States (7 Japanese-owned and 5 U.S.-owned) that had implemented JIT.

In their literature review and field research, Sakakibara, Flynn, and Schroeder found substantial agreement between academics and practitioners on 16 core JIT components (shown in the center of Figure 15.1): setup time reduction, small lot size, JIT delivery from suppliers, supplier quality level, multifunction workers, small-group problem solving, training, daily schedule adherence, repetitive master schedule, preventive maintenance, equipment layout, product design simplicity, kanban (if applicable), pull system (if applicable), material requirements planning (MRP) adaptation to JIT, and accounting adaptation to JIT.

Figure 15.1 indicates the linkage between these core JIT components and other functions and activities in companies. As an example, there's a two-way link between JIT and human resource management. Here the core JIT component of multifunction workers is directly linked to the human resource management concerns with recruiting and selection, training, and other variables. Sakakibara, Flynn, and Schroeder note that in one plant over 600 applicants were interviewed for 20 positions. The company screened the applicants to find employees willing to work as team members, and to be trained to handle many different tasks.

The framework in Figure 15.2 groups the 16 core JIT components into 6 key manufacturing activities: production-floor management, scheduling, process and product design, workforce management, supplier management, and information system. This grouping provides a clear indication of JIT's impact on the design of manufacturing planning and control (MPC) systems. Eight of Figure 15.2's 16 core components affect MPC system design, as seen in the figure's shaded areas. We believe Figure 15.2's framework is useful in indicating those areas where JIT research is needed in the design of MPC systems. Accordingly, we've organized the recent JIT research findings described in this chapter to match many elements in this framework.

Scheduling

This section deals with advanced research relating to two aspects of the master production scheduling activity in JIT: the determination of mixed model schedules for end-product items and the problem of stabilizing the final assembly schedule.

Scheduling Mixed Model Assembly Lines under JIT

Mixed model assembly lines provide the flexibility to produce a wide range of end products in small lots, enabling the company to hold small inventories of finished products but

FIGURE 15.1
**Components of
a Just-in-Time
Manufacturing
System**

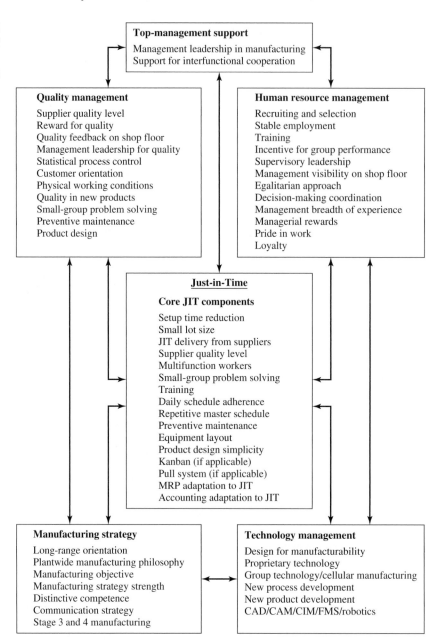

Top-management support

Management leadership in manufacturing
Support for interfunctional cooperation

Quality management

Supplier quality level
Reward for quality
Quality feedback on shop floor
Management leadership for quality
Statistical process control
Customer orientation
Physical working conditions
Quality in new products
Small-group problem solving
Preventive maintenance
Product design

Human resource management

Recruiting and selection
Stable employment
Training
Incentive for group performance
Supervisory leadership
Management visibility on shop floor
Egalitarian approach
Decision-making coordination
Management breadth of experience
Managerial rewards
Pride in work
Loyalty

Just-in-Time

Core JIT components

Setup time reduction
Small lot size
JIT delivery from suppliers
Supplier quality level
Multifunction workers
Small-group problem solving
Training
Daily schedule adherence
Repetitive master schedule
Preventive maintenance
Equipment layout
Product design simplicity
Kanban (if applicable)
Pull system (if applicable)
MRP adaptation to JIT
Accounting adaptation to JIT

Manufacturing strategy

Long-range orientation
Plantwide manufacturing philosophy
Manufacturing objective
Manufacturing strategy strength
Distinctive competence
Communication strategy
Stage 3 and 4 manufacturing

Technology management

Design for manufacturability
Proprietary technology
Group technology/cellular manufacturing
New process development
New product development
CAD/CAM/CIM/FMS/robotics

still provide short customer delivery times. Use of mixed model assembly involves the traditional problems of assembly line design (i.e., determining the line cycle time, the number and sequence of stations on the line, and balancing the line). The mixed model approach also involves determining the sequence in which products will be scheduled for assembly so a level work load is maintained at each station on the line and line cycle time isn't exceeded.

FIGURE 15.2 **Core Just-in-Time Manufacturing Framework**

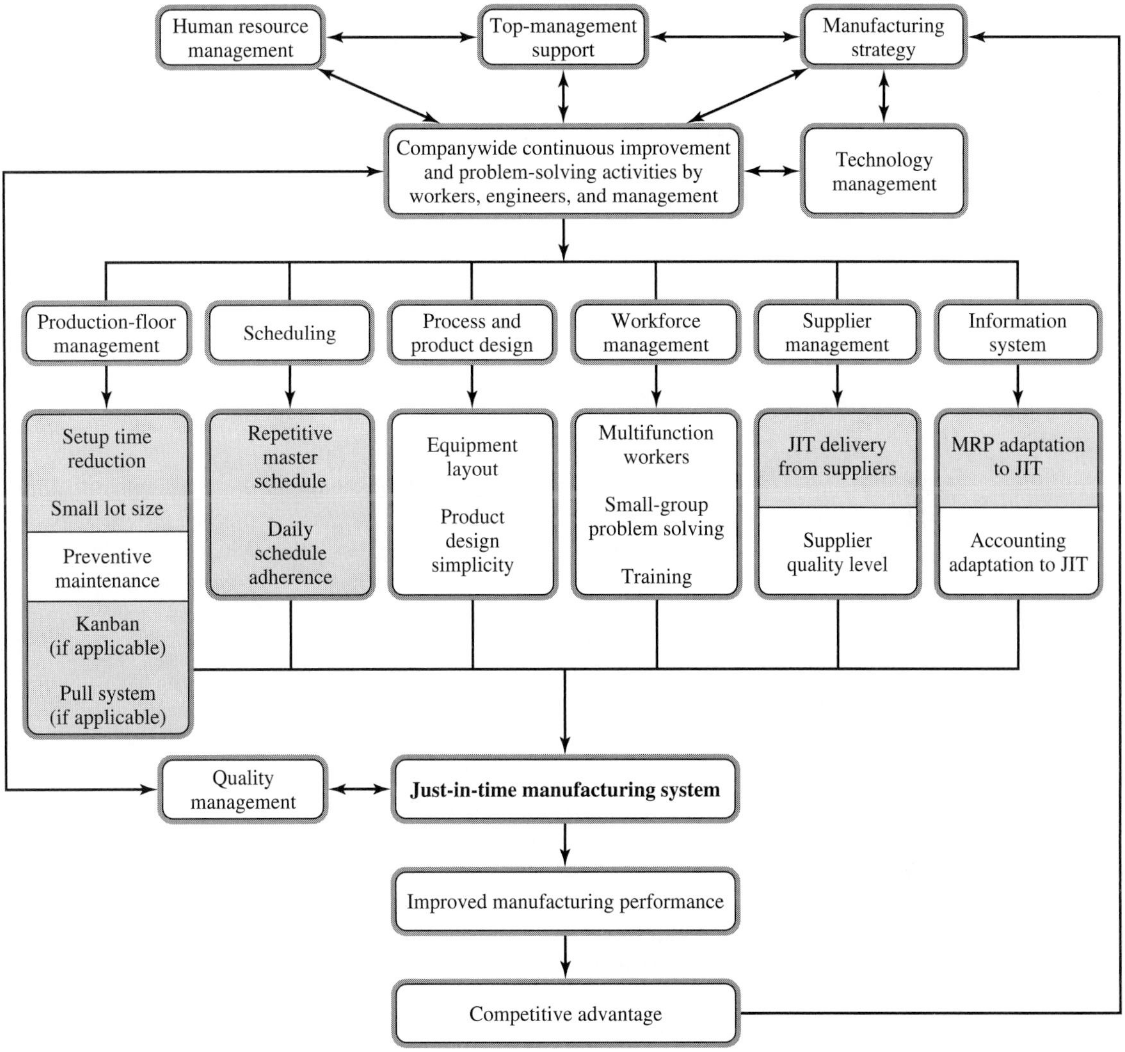

An objective, under JIT, is to have a fairly constant usage rate for each component going into final assembly to facilitate the use of kanban or other JIT shop-floor systems. This means sequencing the assembly of finished products in the mixed model line to provide a fairly constant rate of use for each component. While producing end products in small lots with level model scheduling will, itself, reduce variation in component part demand, variations in component part requirements can still occur because some components are only needed for some end products or because of variations in the number required for others.

Monden reports methods for the mixed model scheduling of final assembly lines that minimize the variation in usage for individual component parts (i.e., leveling or

FIGURE 15.3
**Example
Products and
Component
Requirements**

End Product (i)	1	2	3
Planned production quantity Q_i	2	3	5

End ＼ Component Product (i) ＼ i	1	2	3	4
1	1	0	1	1
2	1	1	0	1
3	0	1	1	0

balancing the component part schedule). These methods, used by Toyota, enable the "consumption speed" for each part used in a mixed model line to be kept as constant as possible.

The example in Figure 15.3 will be used to illustrate the use of the Monden heuristic. In the example three end products are assembled from four component parts. A total of 10 end products (2 of end product 1, 3 of end product 2, and 5 of end product 3) are planned for assembly. A total of 5 units of component 1 (8 of component 2, 7 of component 3, and 5 of component 4) will be used to produce these 10 end products. The average use rate per assembly is, therefore, 0.5 (5/10) units of component 1. For component 2 the average use rate is 0.8, for component 3 it is 0.7, and for component 4 it is 0.5. An ideal schedule would have the actual use rate of each component (as assemblies are completed) match the average use rate closely.

The objective of the Monden procedure is to construct an assembly schedule that comes as close to that ideal as possible. It begins by choosing the first end product to be scheduled and then decides the second to be assembled and so forth until the end. The heuristic chooses the next end product to be assembled that will make the actual use rate of the components most closely match their average use rates. Consider what would happen to component 1, for example, if all five of end product 3 are scheduled for assembly before either end product 1 or 2. In this case, no component 1 will be used until the sixth end product is assembled. At the end of the fifth assembly, component 1 will be 2.5 units behind its average use rate of 0.5 component 1 per end product. Beginning with unit six, component 1's actual use rate will catch up with its average use rate and will be even at the end of the end of the sequence. If the assembly of end products 1 and 2 had been interspersed among the product 3 units, the deviation from the average usage for component 1 would not have been so great.

For each decision (which end product to schedule next) each possible end product is evaluated. The squared deviations of the actual component usage from the average use rates for each component are summed and compared for each possible end product. The end product with the lowest sum is selected for assembly next. This minimization of squared deviations makes the situation of ignoring component 1 until the sixth unit very "expensive." (Monden actually uses the square root of the sum of the squares as the criterion, but it is equivalent to minimizing the sum of the squares.) The calculation at each step is made by using Equation (15.1).

$$D_{Ki} = \sqrt{\sum_{j=1}^{\beta} \left(\frac{K N_j}{Q} - X_{j,K-1} - b_{ij} \right)^2} \qquad (15.1)$$

where:

D_{Ki} = The deviation to be minimized for sequence number K and for end product i.

β = The number of different components required.

K = The schedule sequence number of the current end product.

N_j = The total number of component j required in the entire final assembly sequence.

Q = The total number of end products to be assembled in the final assembly sequence.

$X_{j,K-1}$ = The cumulative number of component j actually used through assembly sequence $K - 1$.

b_{ij} = The number of component j required to make one unit of end product i.

The final assembly sequence for this example is built by applying the heuristic (Equation 15.1) to select each end product in the sequence. The first end product in sequence number one ($K = 1$) is selected by computing D_{Ki} for each end product and selecting the minimum D_{Ki} as follows:

$$D_{1,1} = \sqrt{\left(\frac{1 \times 5}{10} - 0 - 1 \right)^2 + \left(\frac{1 \times 8}{10} - 0 - 0 \right)^2 + \left(\frac{1 \times 7}{10} - 0 - 1 \right)^2 + \left(\frac{1 \times 5}{10} - 0 - 1 \right)^2}$$
$$= 1.11. \qquad (15.2)$$

$$D_{1,2} = \sqrt{\left(\frac{1 \times 5}{10} - 0 - 1 \right)^2 + \left(\frac{1 \times 8}{10} - 0 - 1 \right)^2 + \left(\frac{1 \times 7}{10} - 0 - 0 \right)^2 + \left(\frac{1 \times 5}{10} - 0 - 1 \right)^2}$$
$$= 1.01. \qquad (15.3)$$

$$D_{1,3} = \sqrt{\left(\frac{1 \times 5}{10} - 0 - 0 \right)^2 + \left(\frac{1 \times 8}{10} - 0 - 1 \right)^2 + \left(\frac{1 \times 7}{10} - 0 - 1 \right)^2 + \left(\frac{1 \times 5}{10} - 0 - 0 \right)^2}$$
$$= 0.79. \qquad (15.4)$$

In this case, end product 3 is selected since it has the minimum D_{Ki} ratio of .79. Next, the actual cumulative usage for each component item (X_{jK}) is updated using the $X_{jK} = X_{j,K-1} + b_{ij}$. These computations as well as the D_{Ki} values are shown on the right-hand side of Figure 15.4.

FIGURE 15.4 Final Assembly Sequence

K	D_{K1}	D_{K2}	D_{K3}	Sequence of End Products (i)	X_{1K}	X_{2K}	X_{3K}	X_{4K}
1	1.11	1.01	.79†	3	0	1	1	0
2	0.85	0.57†	1.59	3 2	1	2	1	1
3	0.82†	1.44	0.93	3 2 1	2	2	2	2
4	1.87	1.64	0.28†	3 2 1 3	2	3	3	2
5	1.32	0.87†	0.87	3 2 1 3 2	3	4	3	3
6	1.64	1.87	0.28†	3 2 1 3 2 3	3	5	4	3
7	0.93	1.21	0.82†	3 2 1 3 2 3 3	3	6	5	3
8	0.57†	0.85	1.59	3 2 1 3 2 3 3 1	4	6	6	4
9	1.56	0.77†	1.01	3 2 1 3 2 3 3 1 2	5	7	6	5
10	—	—	0†	3 2 1 3 2 3 3 1 2 3	5	8	7	5

†Indicates smallest deviation D_{Ki}.

The second end product to be scheduled in the sequence ($K = 2$) is selected after new values of D_{Ki} are computed:

$$D_{2,1} = \sqrt{\left(\frac{2 \times 5}{10} - 0 - 1\right)^2 + \left(\frac{2 \times 8}{10} - 1 - 0\right)^2 + \left(\frac{2 \times 7}{10} - 1 - 1\right)^2 + \left(\frac{2 \times 5}{10} - 0 - 1\right)^2}$$
$$= 0.85. \tag{15.5}$$

$$D_{2,2} = \sqrt{\left(\frac{2 \times 5}{10} - 0 - 1\right)^2 + \left(\frac{2 \times 8}{10} - 1 - 1\right)^2 + \left(\frac{2 \times 7}{10} - 1 - 0\right)^2 + \left(\frac{2 \times 5}{10} - 0 - 1\right)^2}$$
$$= 0.57. \tag{15.6}$$

$$D_{2,3} = \sqrt{\left(\frac{2 \times 5}{10} - 0 - 0\right)^2 + \left(\frac{2 \times 8}{10} - 1 - 1\right)^2 + \left(\frac{2 \times 7}{10} - 1 - 1\right)^2 + \left(\frac{2 \times 5}{10} - 0 - 0\right)^2}$$
$$= 1.59. \tag{15.7}$$

Since end product 2 has the smallest D_{Ki} value, it's placed second in the assembly sequence. Again, the actual cumulative component usage values (X_{jK}) are updated as is shown in the right-hand side of Figure 15.4. The overall solution for the final assembly line sequence is shown as the last line in Figure 15.4. This solution produces the actual usage values for components shown in Figure 15.5.

Figure 15.5 shows the average usage for each component (as a dashed line) and the actual component usage as a function of the assembly sequence. For example, end product 3 is first in the assembly sequence and it does not use component 1. Therefore, there is no component usage shown on the graph (the upper left corner of Figure 15.5) but there is one unit of component 2 used, as seen on its graph (the upper right corner). One unit of component 1 is used for sequence number 2, which is the assembly of end product 2. Another unit of component 1 is used at sequence number 3, which is the assembly of end product 1. Next assembled is end product 3, and so no additional use of component 1 is shown for the

FIGURE 15.5
Assembly
Sequence
Numbers
versus
Component
Usage

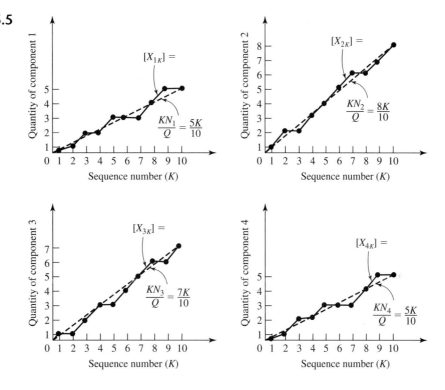

fourth assembly unit. You can see that, for this example, the actual usage for all components tracks closely to their average usages.

In situations where the number of end products and components is large, this approach could be applied by scheduling short periods such as an hour instead of a day. Additional research on mixed model assembly scheduling is required. Such research can provide important benefits in stabilizing factory schedules for component operations under JIT.

Schedule Stability in Implementing JIT

Stabilizing the manufacturing schedule is an important objective under JIT, especially when customer demand is erratic and unpredictable. Chapman reports a general model for maintaining final assembly schedule stability while implementing JIT. This approach is particularly applicable in make-to-stock environments where finished-goods inventories can be used to buffer final customer demand uncertainty.

Many companies cite a stable production environment as necessary to concentrate resources toward simplifying shop-floor systems, setup time reduction, product quality programs, process improvements, and machine maintenance. All these process modifications support shorter production lead times, reduced lead time variation, and increased product flexibility. However, without a stable production environment, manufacturing resources tend to be devoted to reacting to constant schedule changes instead of achieving process improvements.

Chapman indicates one solution is to create an inventory barrier between the company and its customers to absorb demand fluctuations while the internal JIT activity takes place.

This "wall" of inventory would enable the company to establish a stable schedule covering the manufacturing lead time to allow allocation of resources toward JIT improvement activities. This inventory is temporary and should be reduced as JIT is implemented. There are two key questions concerning this implementation strategy:

- How does the organization determine how much inventory is enough?
- How does the organization eventually eliminate the temporary buffer?

Chapman recommends using statistics on demand and manufacturing lead time to determine the approximate size of the downstream inventories necessary to stabilize manufacturing schedules. This isolates manufacturing from demand fluctuations when finished-goods inventory is used as the barrier. Lot size is calculated using the economic order quantity (EOQ) formula. The average inventory required is calculated as:

$$\text{Average inventory} = \text{EOQ}/2 + S \qquad\qquad \textbf{(15.8)}$$

where:

$S = \text{Safety stock} = z\sqrt{\bar{L}\sigma_D^2 + \bar{D}^2\sigma_L^2}.$

$\bar{D} = \text{Average demand per day.}$

$\bar{L} = \text{Average manufacturing lead time in days.}$

$\sigma_L = \text{Standard deviation of manufacturing lead time.}$

$\sigma_D = \text{Standard deviation in demand per day.}$

$z = \text{Number of standard deviation of demand during lead time required to provide the stockout probability desired during a replenishment cycle.}$

Proper implementation of JIT should reduce both $\bar{L}$ and σ_L, thereby reducing the average inventory calculated in Equation (15.8). The methods for achieving these improvements include reduced setup times, improved yields, and smaller queues, which provide shorter manufacturing lead times, more predictable manufacturing lead times, and increased facility flexibility. In addition, a shorter manufacturing lead time implies that the period over which the schedule must be stabilized is reduced. Since requirements for the near future can generally be forecast with much better accuracy than those for the more distant future, these changes enhance our ability to meet customer demand. All these improvements should combine to reduce lot size and safety stock, thereby reducing the "wall" of inventory.

Supply Chain Coordination

The use of JIT as a principle of organization and a coordinating mechanism in supply chain management has been increasing. One critical area of supply chain coordination in the JIT environment involves developing suppliers to support JIT delivery. An aspect of JIT delivery that is sometimes problematical is that of scheduling transportation. In some cases, this is left to third-party providers; in others the supplier provides the transportation. When small frequent deliveries are required, supplier transportation economies or third-party schedules may make them difficult to achieve. Hill and Vollmann argue that customer pickup from suppliers may be a better alternative for achieving the JIT aims. Moreover, when a manufacturer manages its own inbound deliveries, it benefits from more timely information on delays, reduced transportation costs and, most important, reduced uncertainty in deliveries.

In a JIT company, by definition, very small buffers exist between vendors and factory. In the best of circumstances, vendors deliver directly to points of use several times per day. In such companies we'd expect vendor deliveries to be scheduled only hours or days before they're needed on the factory floor. The exact timing depends on the manufacturer's confidence in its vendor's delivery performance. It's important to note in any true JIT firm, a stockout has very high costs, typically shutting down an entire line or factory. Hill and Vollmann report the experience of some JIT companies that still have substantial safety lead times used to protect against inventory shortages and other firms with hidden buffers. They therefore argue that the JIT firm should give serious consideration to assuming responsibility for inbound transportation because of reduced delivery uncertainty and reduced transportation costs.

Hill and Vollmann present a formulation of the "JIT vendor pickup problem" and propose a scheduling heuristic. This problem is stated as follows:

> For a given number of vehicles with limited capacity find a one-week vendor pickup schedule that will minimize the total inventory carrying, travel, and setup costs subject to the constraint that the manufacturer does not run out of any item from any vendor.

A multistep heuristic scheduling algorithm is proposed to provide solutions to this problem. These steps include:

1. Determining the number of pickups per week for each vendor.
2. Assigning these pickups to each day of the week.
3. Developing an initial vehicle schedule for each vehicle for each day.
4. Applying three improvement heuristics to improve the schedules as much as possible.

Since the heuristic does not construct the vehicle schedule until after the number and day of the vendor pickups are decided, a key feature of the method involves determining an upper and a lower bound on the travel time to and from each vendor (Vendor $= 1, 2 \ldots k$).

The upper and lower bounds on the travel time to each vendor are determined in the following manner. The upper bound, $dt\max(k)$, is assumed to be simply the time to visit the vendor and return to the manufacturer's plant, and not visit any other vendor. If $t(0, k)$ represents the travel time from the manufacturer's plant (0) to vendor k, then the complete trip takes $[t(0, k) + t(k, 0)]$ hours. The example shown in Figures 15.6 and 15.7 illustrates this calculation. Using the data shown in Figure 15.7, the round-trip travel time from the plant to vendor 3 is four hours.

The lower bound on the travel time, $dt\min(k)$, to and from a vendor is assumed to be the travel time from the vendor closest to vendor k plus the time to travel from vendor k to the next-closest vendor. If j is the closest vendor and l is the next-closest vendor to vendor k, then the lower bound on the travel time is $[t(j, k) + t(k, l)]$. In the data shown in Figure 15.7, the nearest vendor to vendor 3 is vendor 6, and the next-closest is vendor 2. Therefore, the minimum travel time to vendor 3 is determined to be three hours.

Having calculated upper and lower bounds on the travel time to each vendor, the heuristic is then able to calculate upper and lower bounds on the number of pickups to be scheduled each week for each vendor. This information is needed to construct the actual

FIGURE 15.6
Example JIT
Pickup
Problem Map

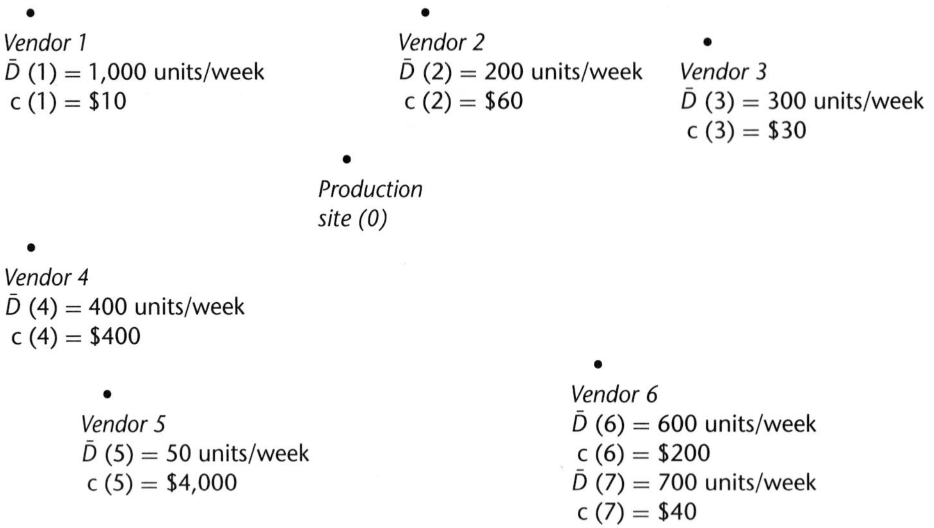

•

Vendor 1
$\bar{D}(1) = 1{,}000$ units/week
$c(1) = \$10$

•

Vendor 2
$\bar{D}(2) = 200$ units/week
$c(2) = \$60$

•

Vendor 3
$\bar{D}(3) = 300$ units/week
$c(3) = \$30$

•

Production
site (0)

•

Vendor 4
$\bar{D}(4) = 400$ units/week
$c(4) = \$400$

•

Vendor 5
$\bar{D}(5) = 50$ units/week
$c(5) = \$4{,}000$

•

Vendor 6
$\bar{D}(6) = 600$ units/week
$c(6) = \$200$
$\bar{D}(7) = 700$ units/week
$c(7) = \$40$

Note: Each dot (•) represents a location on the map.

FIGURE 15.7
JIT Pickup
Problem:
Travel Time
Matrix (Times
in Decimal
Hours)

		To Vendor						
		0	1	2	3	4	5	6
From vendor	0	0.0	1.6	0.6	2.0	1.7	1.6	1.5
	1	1.6	0.0	1.9	3.5	0.7	1.3	3.1
	2	0.6	1.9	0.0	1.6	2.2	2.2	1.6
	3	2.0	3.5	1.6	0.0	3.7	3.6	1.4
	4	1.7	0.7	2.2	3.7	0.0	0.7	3.1
	5	1.6	1.3	2.2	3.6	0.7	0.0	2.7
	6	1.5	3.1	1.6	1.4	3.1	2.7	0.0

vehicle schedule. Bounds on the number of pickups are calculated using the expression for the minimum-cost number of pickups, $n(k)$, shown in Equation (15.9):*

$$n(k) = \left[\left[.5C_r \, \Sigma_{i \in P(k)} D(i)c(i)\right] / \left[\Sigma_{i \in P(k)} \; C_P(i) + \text{VVC } dt(k)\right]\right]^{0.5} \textbf{(15.9)}$$

*Notes:
1. With $n(k)$ pickups at vendor k at even intervals, the average quantity picked up is $\bar{D}(i)/n(k)$, and the average lot size inventory is $.5 \, \bar{D}(i)/n(k)$ units.
2. The demand $\bar{D}(i)$ rates are assumed to be constant.
3. All items sourced from each vendor are picked up upon each stop to the vendor.
4. The preceding formulation is similar to the periodic review inventory model where setup cost is $\Sigma C_p(i) + \text{VVC } dt(k)$ and weekly demand is $\Sigma \bar{D}(i)$ where we sum all over $i \in P(k)$.

where:

$n(k)$ = Number of stops to vendor k per week.

C_r = Inventory carrying cost (percent of unit cost/week).

$D(i)$ = Weekly demand (usage) rate at the customer for item i.

$c(i)$ = Unit cost for item i.

$C_P(i)$ = Setup cost required to pick up item i.

VVC = Variable vehicle cost (\$/hour of travel time).

$dt(k)$ = Additional travel time to make a pickup at vendor k.

An upper bound for the number of pickups each week for a vendor, $n\max(k)$, is calculated by substituting the lower bound on the travel time to the vendor, $dt\min(k)$, for the $dt(k)$ term in Equation (15.9). Likewise, a lower bound for the number of pickups each week for a vendor, $n\min(k)$, is calculated by substituting the upper bound on the travel time to the vendor, $dt\max(k)$, for the $dt(k)$ term in Equation (15.9). Once these bounds have been calculated, the heuristic assigns pickups for a vendor to a particular day(s) of the week. Next the actual vehicle schedule for making the pickups is constructed.

The authors make two key assumptions in using their heuristic algorithm. First, they assume that each time a vendor pickup is scheduled, all of the items purchased from that vendor are included in the pickup. Second, they calculate total weekly costs using an equation similar to that used in an inventory model. This cost equation is shown in Equation (15.10):

$$TWC = \text{Inventory carrying cost} + \text{setup cost} + \text{travel cost}$$
$$= \Sigma_k\left[.5C_r\ \Sigma_{i \in P(k)}D(i)c(i)\right]/n(k) + \left[\Sigma_{i \in P(k)}\ C_p n(k) + (\text{VVC})\,(\text{TT})\right]$$

(15.10)

where:

$P(k)$ = Set of all items to be picked up from vendor k. If item i is sourced at vendor k, we denote this as $i \in P(k)$.

TT = Total travel time per week.

The flowchart shown in Figure 15.8 lists the eight steps in the Hill and Vollmann heuristic. Step 1 begins by initializing the variables in the algorithm. Step 2 calculates the upper and lower bounds on the travel time to each vendor, $dt\max(k)$ and $dt\min(k)$, and then calculates the upper and lower bounds on the number of pickups per week for each vendor, $n\max(k)$ and $n\min(k)$. In Step 3, a parametric range for the minimum-cost number of pickups to be made weekly at each vendor, $n(k)$, is used to generate a range of schedules by defining $n(k)$ as equaling $n\min(k) + \text{alpha}[n\max(k) - n\min(k)]$. When alpha is zero, the number of pickups at each vendor is at the lower bound $n\min(k)$. Conversely, when alpha is one, the number of pickups at each vendor is at the upper bound $n\max(k)$. Next, Step 4 assigns the $n(k)$ pickups determined in Step 3 to the five days of the week. It's important to assign pickups evenly over the week to minimize inventory carrying costs. This step is also shown in Figure 15.8.

FIGURE 15.8
Hill and Vollmann's Algorithm Flow Chart

Step 1:	Read input data. Number of vehicles, $\bar{D}(i)$, $c(i)$, C_r, VVC, $P(k)$, $t(k, l)$.

Step 2:	Initialize.
	Set alpha to zero.
	Calculate:
	   dtmax(k)
	   dtmin(k)
	   nmax(k)
	   nmin(k)

Step 3:	Calculate $n(k)$ for all k. $n(k) = nmin(k) + alpha\,[nmax(k) - nmax(k)]$
Step 4:	Assign the $n(k)$ pickups to days of the week. If $n(k) \geq 5$, then assign pickups to each day of the week and set $n(k)$ to $n(k) - 5$. If $n(k) = 4$, then assign pickups to Monday, Tuesday, Thursday, and Friday. If $n(k) = 3$, then assign pickups to Monday, Wednesday, and Friday. If $n(k) = 2$, then assign pickups to Tuesday and Thursday. If $n(k) = 1$, then assign a pickup to Wednesday.
Step 5:	Apply the Clarke-Wright heuristic to develop initial vehicle schedules for each day.
Step 6:	Apply improvement heuristics.
Step 7:	If this is the lowest-cost schedule so far, save this schedule as the best schedule.
Step 8:	Alpha = alpha + .1. If alpha $\leq$ 1, go to Step 3. Otherwise stop and report the best schedule.

Step 5 takes a "first cut" at scheduling the vehicles on each day to efficiently make the pickups, using the Clarke-Wright "travel time saved" heuristic. This procedure allows for constraints on the vehicle capacities (weight and volume) as well as on the maximum route length and travel time per day. If the Clarke-Wright heuristic is unable to find a feasible schedule for a day because of the preceding constraints, the pickup with the lowest marginal economic value is reassigned to the next day, and the heuristic is retried. $V(k)$, the marginal economic value for a pickup at vendor k, may be estimated using Equation (15.11).

$$V(k) = .5C_r \Sigma_{i \in P(k)}\,[\bar{D}(i)c(i)/n(k)^2 + C_P(i)] + dt(k)\ \text{VVC} \qquad \textbf{(15.11)}$$

where $dt(k)$ equals $nmin(k) + alpha\,[nmax(k) - nmin(k)]$.

Step 6 attempts to improve the schedule constructed in Step 5 by applying three iterative improvement heuristics: the exchange heuristic, the insertion heuristic, and the deletion heuristic. The exchange heuristic tests all pairwise exchanges of all vendors in the schedule (within a route, between routes on the same day, or between routes on different days) to find the exchange that will most reduce total incremental cost. At every iteration of the heuristic the best exchange is found and made. The exchange heuristic is continued until no further exchanges will result in a lower total incremental cost schedule. The insertion and deletion heuristics are applied in a similar manner to find the best opportunity to improve total incremental cost. If any improvement is found, the best improvement is made in the schedule and then the heuristic is run again. The three heuristics are applied repetitively in sequence until no further improvement can be made.

If the current schedule has the lowest total incremental cost so far, this schedule is saved in Step 7. Otherwise, the alpha value is increased by 0.1 in Step 8 and the algorithm returns to Step 3. When the algorithm reaches an alpha value of 1.0, the algorithm stops and reports the best schedule found.

Figures 15.6, 15.7 and 15.9 show and example JIT pickup problem illustrating the Hill and Vollmann procedure. In this example the objective is to find a schedule for the manufacturer's one vehicle given setup cost is zero, the cost of carrying inventory per week is 1 percent of the inventory investment, and variable vehicle cost is $12 per hour per vehicle. Figures 15.10 and 15.11 detail a solution resulting from an alpha setting of 0.

In using this model, the set of vendors considered for JIT pickups must be predefined. Vendors more than one day away cannot be incorporated into daily routes for JIT pickup. Likewise, vendors that already provide inexpensive and reliable service may also be excluded. The question of whether a vendor can provide less expensive delivery is largely a matter of which firm can run the most effective distribution system given the set of vendors for the manufacturer and the set of customers for the vendor.

FIGURE 15.9 **Example JIT Pickup Problem: Minimum and Maximum Number of Stops per Week**

Vendor k	Item i	Demand $\bar{D}(i)$	Cost $c(i)$	Travel Times		Number of Stops	
				dtmin(k)	dtmax(k)	nmin(k)	nmax(k)
1	1	1,000	$ 10	2.0	3.2	1.1	1.4
2	2	200	$ 60	1.3	1.3	2.0	2.0
3	3	300	$ 300	3.0	4.1	1.0	1.1
4	4	400	$ 400	1.4	3.4	4.4	6.9
5	5	50	$4,000	2.0	3.2	5.1	6.5
6	6	600	$ 200	2.9	3.1	4.5	4.6
6	7	700	$ 40	—	—	—	—

FIGURE 15.10
Example JIT Pickup Problem: Day Assignments (Alpha = 0)

Vendor Schedule		Truck Schedule	
Vendor	Visited on Days	Day	Stops at Vendors
1	W	M	4, 5, 6
2	T, TH	T	2, 4, 5, 6
3	W	W	1, 3, 5, 6
4	M, T, TH, F	TH	2, 4, 5, 6
5	M, T, W, TH, F	F	4, 5, 6
6	M, T, W, TH, F		

FIGURE 15.11
Example JIT
Pickup
Problem: Final
Schedule
(Alpha = 0)

Day	Sequence	Travel Time
Monday	0–4–5–6–0	6.90 hours
Tuesday	0–2–6–5–4–0	7.30 hours
Wednesday	0–1–5–6–3–0	9.00 hours
Thursday	0–2–6–5–4–0	7.30 hours
Friday	0–4–5–6–0	6.90 hours

Total travel time per week = 37.40 hours.
Total travel cost per week = $448.80.

Item	Average Inventory (Units)	Average Inventory Investment	Average Carrying Cost
1	570.24	$ 5,702.28	$ 57.02
2	66.86	$ 4,011.43	$ 40.11
3	171.07	$ 5,132.14	$ 51.32
4	78.43	$31,373.69	$313.74
5	7.94	$31,765.14	$317.65
6	95.26	$19,052.68	$190.53
7	111.11	$ 4,444.30	$ 44.44

Total carrying cost per week = $1,014.81.
Total increment cost per week = $1,463.61.

Comments:
1. Each of the above schedules starts at 8 A.M.
2. This schedule is for alpha equal to zero. If the algorithm were completed, it would generate similar schedules for alpha equal to .1, .2, . . . , 1.0. The algorithm would then report the "best" schedule (lowest total incremental cost schedule).
3. In this example we allowed overtime for the driver on Wednesday.
4. Carrying cost is assessed on the average inventory assuming a five-day work week with a single eight-hour shift per day. In other words, carrying cost is affected by inventory levels during the nights and weekends as well as during the workday.

Production Floor Management

Another group of core JIT components from Figure 15.2 that has a major impact on MPC systems is production floor management. In this section we discuss the results of research concerned with setup time reduction, small lot size production, and kanbans. We also report work that assesses the impact of different plant factors, such as the variability of demand rates and processing times, on the production floor management components and, subsequently, on production performance.

Setup Time Reduction

Setup time reduction is a key aspect of JIT since it supports reductions in manufacturing lead times and inventories. It also enables small lot sizes and kanban systems for material flow—achieving major improvements in production floor management. To date, however, little research has been reported concerning the impact of setup reduction programs on plant performance. Hahn, Bragg, and Shin have posed three questions for managers regarding implementing setup reduction programs:

- What are the direct costs and benefits associated with setup time, and how should they be measured?
- Under what conditions is setup time reduction most effective?
- How does setup reduction compare to other alternatives such as overtime and capacity expansion?

In pursuing these questions, Hahn, Bragg, and Shin considered the situation when demand exceeds the production capacity at an operation. They noted that under these conditions, much of the previous inventory model research focused on increasing order quantities by reducing setup frequencies to meet capacity limitations, as opposed to investigating the possible increase of available capacity to allow increased setup frequency or investigating reducing the time required per setup. On the basis of this observation, they developed a decision model to evaluate the setup time reduction and increased capacity alternatives in a way that allows for reductions in both order quantities and inventory levels in capacity-constrained situations.

Figures 15.12 and 15.13 illustrate Hahn, Bragg, and Shin's decision model to evaluate the effectiveness of setup time reduction activities. Three different joint lot-sizing models' solutions are compared. The IS (independent solution) model does not consider capacity as a limiting factor, and lot sizing is simply based on setup and inventory holding cost trade-offs. The model for the IS approach is

$$N^* = \sqrt{\frac{\Sigma_j C_{Hj} A_j \left(1 - \frac{d_j}{p_j}\right)}{2\Sigma_j C_{pj}}} = \frac{A_j}{Q_j^*} \qquad (15.12)$$

$$\text{TIC}^* = \sqrt{2\Sigma_j C_{Pj} \Sigma_j C_{Hj} A_j \left(1 - \frac{d_j}{p}\right)} \qquad (15.13)$$

$$\text{TIC} = \Sigma_j \left\{ \left(C_{Pj} \times \frac{A_j}{Q_j}\right) + \left[C_{Hj}\left(1 - \frac{d_j}{p_j}\right)\right] \times \frac{Q_j}{2} \right\} \qquad (15.14)$$

FIGURE 15.12
Example Problem of Setup Time Reduction

Product	Annual Demand A_j	Setup Time S_j	Processing Time/Unit P_j	Inventory Holding Costs/Unit/Year
A_1	18,000	10 hours	.025 hours	$ 75.00
A_2	34,000	10 hours	.025 hours	87.50
A_3	36,000	10 hours	.025 hours	100.00
A_4	13,500	10 hours	.025 hours	62.50
A_5	25,000	10 hours	.025 hours	62.50
Total	126,500	50 hours		

Annual inventory holding costs = 25% of unit costs.
Production capacity = 16 hours/day × 250 working days = 4,000 hours.
Setup cost = 10 hours × 5 workers × $10/hour = $500/setup. (This assumes setup cost is solely a function of setup time.)
Additional capacity cost = $75.00/hour.
Setup time reduction = $1,000/hour of setup time reduced.
Regular capacity cost = $50/hour (for 4,000 hours per year).

FIGURE 15.13
Comparison of Different Solution Methods for Capacity Constrained Situation

	Independent Solution (IS)	Sugimori et al., Pinto and Mabert (CC)	Optimum Solution
Time between cycles	6.09 days	14.92 days	7.46 days
Number of orders/year	41.04 orders	16.75 orders	33.51 orders
Setup hours	2,052.00 hours	837.50 hours	1,675.50 hours
Processing time	3,162.50 hours	3,162.50 hours	3,162.50 hours
Total capacity requirements	5,214.50 hours	4,000.00 hours	4,838.00 hours
Inventory holding costs	$102,600	$251,360	$125,680
Capacity increase costs[†]	91,087	-0-	62,840
Total relevant costs	$193,687	$251,360	$188,520
Cost of existing capacity	$200,000	$200,000	$200,000
Total costs	$393,687	$451,360	$388,520

[†]The IS solution assumes there are no capacity limits. If we assess the cost of $75 per hour for additional capacity, the cost will increase to $91,087.

where:

N^* = Optimal number of order cycles.

Q_j = Order quantity in units for item j.

TIC = Total incremental costs per year.

C_{Hj} = Inventory carrying cost per unit per year for item j.

C_{Pj} = Setup costs per order for item j.

d_j = Daily demand rate in units for item j.

p_j = Daily production rate in units for item j.

A_j = Demand per year in units for item j.

The CC (common cycle) model described by Sugimori et al., as well as Pinto and Mabert, takes into account capacity limitations, but does so by increasing order quantities and reducing setup frequencies to meet the capacity limitations. The CC model is

$$T^* = \frac{\Sigma_j S_j}{W - \Sigma_j A_j P_j} \tag{15.15}$$

and

$$Q_j^* = TA_j \tag{15.16}$$

Where:

W = Available capacity in hours.

S_j = Setup time per order for item j (in hours).

P_j = Processing time per unit for item j (in hours).

T^* = Length of the processing cycle time (a fraction of a period) or $1/N^*$.

In contrast, the Hahn, Bragg, and Shin optimum solution model determines the order quantities by considering whether it's better to increase available capacity to allow increased setup frequency, or to reduce the time required per setup. This approach represents a new direction in inventory model research.

In this example the capacity limitation is 4,000 hours, and the IS model exceeds this capacity by 1,214.5 hours. Hahn, Bragg, and Shin have added the assumptions that capacity can be expanded at a cost of $75 per hour (150 percent of the current cost rate of $50 per hour) and that setup time can be decreased at a cost of $1,000 per setup hour eliminated. Using their model, three steps are required to determine whether the setup time reduction or the capacity expansion alternative is best.

Step 1. Determine the optimum level of capacity given the capacity increase cost ($H = \$75$) and current setup times:

$$W^* = \Sigma_j A_j P_j + \sqrt{\frac{\Sigma_j S_j \Sigma_j C_{Hj} A_j \left(1 - \frac{d_j}{p_j}\right)}{2H}} = 3,162.5 + 1,675.5 \quad \textbf{(15.17)}$$

$$= 4,838 \text{ hours.}$$

Step 2. Compute the savings rate per hour of setup time reduction (SR) made possible by shorter setup times:

$$\text{SR} = \frac{\Sigma_j C_{Hj} A_j \left(1 - \frac{d_j}{p_j}\right)}{2(W - \Sigma_j A_j P_j)} = \$5,026. \quad \textbf{(15.18)}$$

Step 3a. If cost of the setup time reduction ($1,000 per setup hour in this example) is greater than the hourly savings rate (SR), setup time shouldn't be reduced.

Step 3b. If cost of the setup time reduction is less than the savings rate—as is the case in the example ($1,000 < \$5,026$)—then the ideal condition is to eliminate the setup time entirely. (However, in reality it may be difficult to eliminate the setup time completely.)

Figure 15.13 shows the results of applying the IS, CC, and Hahn, Bragg, and Shin models. The total relevant cost of the IS solution ($193,673) includes the cost of the additional 1,214.5 hours required to implement the smaller lot sizes at the higher setup frequency and the inventory holding costs. The total relevant cost of the CC model solution ($251,360) reflects the larger inventory carrying cost associated with the reduced setup frequency and larger order quantities because of the capacity constraint.

The total relevant cost of the Hahn, Bragg, and Shin model ($188,520) reflects the fact that when the option of increasing the capacity at $75 per hour is added to the CC model, a different lot-sizing solution results and some additional capacity is desirable (i.e., 838 hours) given the change in economic trade-offs in the model. This new capacity level is determined in Step 1 of the Hahn, Bragg, and Shin model. Steps 2 and 3 of their model indicate in this example savings can be obtained by reducing setup times at the rate of $1,000 per reduced setup hour. For example, if setup time were reduced from 10 to 5 hours per setup (i.e., from 50 to 25 hours for all five products each cycle), then total setup hours per year could be reduced from 1,675.5 to 838. This would eliminate the additional capacity cost of $62,840 since the 4,000 hours of regular capacity would be sufficient. This would require setup reduction costs of $25,000.

As a result of an analysis of the implications of their decision model, Hahn, Bragg, and Shin develop several propositions concerning setup time reduction activities. These include:

- The general effectiveness of setup time reduction as an alternative to increasing capacity improves as the ratio of total setup requirements to total capacity requirements increases. Therefore, setup time reduction is most effective when a large portion of available capacity is dedicated to setup operations.

- The incremental effectiveness of setup time reduction as an alternative to increasing capacity accelerates as a further reduction is made. Therefore, in order to assess the true impact of setup time reduction on the capacity alternative, the maximum extent of setup time reduction must be considered.

The importance of this research is to provide a more fundamental understanding of the impact of setup time reduction activities on plant performance. Further research in this area should provide managers with guidelines indicating those products and processes where implementing setup time reduction programs under JIT can provide maximum benefits.

Determining the Optimal Number of Kanbans

In many firms the focus on setup time reduction and small lot production leads directly to implementing simple shop-floor scheduling systems. Rapid transit through the shop means low work-in-process inventory where each operation in the process can be triggered by usage at the next operation, and a kanban card (or other signal) can be used to authorize additional production. The number of circulating kanban cards is important in the system's operation. Too many kanban cards produce excess work-in-process inventory, while too few lead to production-floor disturbances.

When the demand rate is constant for each period over the planning horizon, the number of kanban cards can be determined using the Toyota formula:

Number of kanban cards $=$

$$\frac{\text{Demand rate} \times \text{Lead time} \times [1 + \text{Policy variable (i.e., safety stock)}]}{\text{Container size}} \quad \textbf{(15.19)}$$

However, when the demand rate is permitted to vary between periods over the planning horizon, further analysis is required. Bitran and Chang have proposed several mathematical models to determine the optimal number of kanban cards for each period when the demand rate varies. Their approach is deterministic and involves multiple time periods and multiple work centers. For some special cases the linear integer model can be transformed into a linear program (LP), requiring $2NT$ constraints (N is the number of work centers and T is the number of time periods) with $NT + T$ variables.

Because of the size and complexity of the optimization approaches, Moeeni and Chang propose two heuristics for determining the number of kanban cards. These heuristics can be applied manually, producing solutions that appear to be close to the LP solutions for those problems that can be solved by LP, and close to the LP approximations to the integer programming problem when LP won't work. These heuristics are based on the following assumptions:

- Each work center in the production process produces only one type of product.
- Demand must be met with no back orders.

- Production lead time is zero for all operations.
- Kanban lead time is 1 (i.e., a kanban card returned to a work center at time t can be used to initiate production at time $t + 1$).
- There are no limitations on capacity.
- There is a single inventory point between any two consecutive work centers so that each kanban card is circulated for an individual item.

In addition, a feasible solution to the problem will satisfy the following constraints:

$$W_{t-1}^1 + X_t^1 \geq D_t \text{ for all } t, \tag{15.20}$$

$$W_{t-1}^j + X_t^j \geq X_t^n \text{ for all } n, t, \text{ and } j \in P(n), \tag{15.21}$$

$$U_t^n \geq X_t^n \text{ for all } n, \text{ and} \tag{15.22}$$

$$U_t^n + W_{t-1}^n = U_o^n + W_o^n \text{ for all } n \text{ and } t \tag{15.23}$$

where:

$n =$ Work center index; $n \in \{1, \ldots N\}$. Note that $n = 1$ corresponds to the last work center in the production sequence.

$t =$ Time index; $t \in \{0, 1, \ldots T\}$. A relatively short time period (e.g., one hour or one-half shift) is typically used.

$P(n) =$ Set of immediately preceding work center(s) to work center n.

$U_t^n =$ Number of kanban cards waiting to initiate production at the beginning of time t at work center n. Note that U_o^n is the number of kanban cards injected into work center n at the start of the planning horizon.

$W_t^n =$ Number of kanban cards for completed work at work center n at the end of time t. The number of kanban cards for completed work in work center n at the beginning of the planning horizon W_o^n is the starting inventory.

$X_t^n =$ Number of kanban cards that actually initiate production in work center n at time t.

$D_t =$ Demand for final product in terms of an integral number of kanban card orders.

The first constraint ensures that demands are met each period while the second constraint requires production at any work center not to exceed the amount of product supplied by its immediately preceding work centers. The third constraint limits production at any work center to the number of kanbans available at this point. The fourth constraint states the total number of kanban cards for each work center must be constant over the planning horizon, that is, $U_o^n + W_o^n$.

Heuristic 1

Although not formally stated, this heuristic's objective is to minimize costs associated with work-in-process inventory. The solution process begins with values for demand (D_t) and the number of kanban cards for completed work (W_o^n), and determines values for the number of kanban cards ready to initiate production at each work center at the start of period 1 (U_o^n). (Note that $S(n)$ is the set of immediately succeeding work center(s) of work center n.)

There are two steps in this heuristic:

Step 1. Set $U_o^1 = \text{Max}_t \{D_t\} - W_o^1$. (15.24)

Step 2. Set $U_o^n = U_o^{s(n)} + W_o^{s(n)} - W_o^n$, $N = 2, 3, \ldots N$. (15.25)

The example in Figure 15.14 is a production process with four work centers where production starts at work center 4 and moves through work centers 3 and 2 to the final operation at work center 1. There are five periods in the planning horizon with the following demand rates and starting inventory levels:

Given this information, the heuristic determines the number of kanbans to be injected into the system at the beginning of the planning horizon (U_o^n):

Step 1. $U_0^1 = \text{Max}\{4, 14, 20, 5, 12\} - 0 = 20$. (15.26)

Step 2. $U_0^2 = 20 + 0 - 5 = 15$. (15.27)

$U_0^3 = 15 + 5 - 0 = 20$. (15.28)

$U_0^4 = 20 + 0 - 2 = 18$. (15.29)

FIGURE 15.14
Solution to Example Problem Using Heuristic 1

		Period 1	Period 2	Period 3	Period 4	Period 5
Demand	U_o^n	4	15	20	5	12
Work center 1	20					
Beg. inv.		0	16	5	0	15
Prod.		20	4	15	20	5
End. inv.		16	5	0	15	8
Work center 2	15					
Beg. inv.		5	0	16	5	0
Prod.		15	20	4	15	20
End. inv.		0	16	5	0	15
Work center 3	20					
Beg. inv.		0	5	0	16	5
Prod.		20	15	20	4	15
End. inv.		5	0	16	5	0
Work center 4	18					
Beg. inv.		2	0	5	0	16
Prod.		18	20	15	20	4
End. inv.		0	5	0	16	5

Demand Rates	Starting Inventory
$D_1 = 4$	$W_0^1 = 0$
$D_2 = 15$	$W_0^2 = 5$
$D_3 = 20$	$W_0^3 = 0$
$D_4 = 5$	$W_0^4 = 2$
$D_5 = 12$	

Column 2 of Figure 15.14 shows this solution along with the starting values for the kanban cards waiting to initiate production (W_o^n) and the demand rates for each period (D_t). The figure also simulates the production process over the five periods, indicating the beginning and ending inventories as well as the production at each work center each period.

Heuristic 2

While heuristic 1 produces a feasible solution, improved solutions can be obtained by using a different heuristic. The second heuristic works on reducing the number of kanban cards at the work centers upstream from the final work center (1) by applying the following steps:

Step 1: Set $U_0^1 = $ Max $\{D_t\} - W_0^1$. For the preceding example,

$$U_0^1 = \text{Max}_t \{D_t\} - W_0^1 = 20 - 0 = 20.$$

Step 2: Divide the planning horizon into F smaller subplanning horizons such that every subproblem contains a time-ordered, nondecreasing demand. For example, if $F = 2$ in the preceding example, the planning horizon can be divided into $\{4, 15, 20\}$ and $\{5, 12\}$.

Step 3: For every subproblem find the average demand ($\bar{D}^n$) and the second largest demand ($\hat{D}^n$). Set $\hat{D}^n = 0$ for subproblems with only one element, and round any noninteger average demand up to the next integer. For the preceding example, the $\{\bar{D}^n, \hat{D}^n\}$ values are $\{13, 15\}$ and $\{9, 5\}$.

Step 4: Compute $U^* = $ Max$_n$ $\{\bar{D}^n, \hat{D}^n\}$. For the example,
$$U^* = \text{Max} \{(13, 15), (9, 5)\} = 15.$$

Step 5: Compute $U_o^k = U^* - W_o^k, k \in P(1)$. For the example, $U_o^2 = 15 - 5 = 10$.

Step 6: Compute $U_o^n = U_o^{s(n)} + W_o^{s(n)} - W_o^n$, for all n without a designated number of kanbans. For the example, $U_o^3 = 10 + 5 - 0 = 15$ and $U_o^4 = 15 + 0 - 2 = 13$.

This solution is shown in Figure 15.15, whose information is similar to Figure 15.14's. Note that this solution requires fewer kanbans and there are no shortages (back orders) in any period, so we have a feasible solution again.

Experimental Results

Moeeni and Chang report experimental results that compare the performance of heuristic 2 against the linear programming approximation Bitran and Chang proposed. These procedures were compared on the basis of the cost of work-in-process inventory for all work centers, using the percentage increase of the objective function value: (heuristic $-$ LP)/LP. Figure 15.16's results indicate the heuristic's performance relative to the LP method improves rapidly as variability in demand is decreased. Moeeni and Chang also investigated the impact of planning horizon length on the heuristic's performance. Figure 15.16 shows that the changes in planning horizon length don't seem to affect this heuristic's performance. These results indicate that the development of heuristic methods for determining the number of kanbans when demand varies from period to period looks very promising, but their performance may well be sensitive to differences in operating conditions. The next section discusses these differences further.

FIGURE 15.15
Solution to Example Problem Using Heuristic 2

		Period 1	Period 2	Period 3	Period 4	Period 5
Demand	U_o^n	4	15	20	5	12
Work center 1	20					
Beg. inv.		0	11	5	0	10
Prod.		15	9	15	15	10
End. inv.		11	5	0	10	8
Work center 2	10					
Beg. inv.		5	0	6	0	0
Prod.		10	15	9	15	15
End. inv.		0	6	0	0	5
Work center 3	15					
Beg. inv.		0	5	0	6	0
Prod.		15	10	15	9	15
End. inv.		5	0	6	0	0
Work center 4	13					
Beg. inv.		2	0	5	0	6
Prod.		13	15	10	15	9
End. inv.		0	5	0	6	0

FIGURE 15.16
Comparison of Heuristic and Linear Programming Solutions

Planning Horizon (Number of Periods)	Demand Variability			
	$U(0,300^\dagger)$	$U(150,300)$	$U(225,300)$	Mean
5	.125[‡]	.028	.003	.052
10	.039	.004	.000	.014
15	.164	.034	.005	.068
20	.144	.048	.019	.070
Mean	.118	.029	.007	.051

[†]The uniform distribution was used for demand $U(x, y)$ where x, y represents the demand range.
[‡]Average of the percent increase in work-in-process inventory cost for the heuristic over the programming procedure for five randomly generated problems.

JIT Performance and Operating Conditions

Research on various aspects of JIT indicates production performance may be affected by the operating conditions under which JIT is implemented. Substantial differences in such conditions exist between plants. For example, firms that have made progress in areas such as stabilizing the MPS, developing highly skilled multifunction employees, standardizing machine processing times, reducing setup times, and eliminating variation may achieve better results overall. Therefore, other managers may be concerned with determining to what extent JIT performance is sensitive to such factors, and what guidelines exist for determining what factors should receive major attention in implementing JIT. Several recent research efforts have examined these issues, using simulation analysis.

Variability in Operating Conditions

Huang, Rees, and Taylor report the results of a Q-Gert model that simulates a kanban-based MPC system with three production lines, each having between one and three work centers. They examined three factors' effects on JIT performance: variable processing times, variable master production schedules, and imbalances between different production work centers.

Figure 15.17 shows the effect of variation in the machine processing times on the mean (μ) and standard deviation (σ) of four measures of operating performance: overtime, preproduction activity inventory at the final assembly work center, postproduction activity inventory at the same work center, and end-of-day production at the final assembly work center. Clearly, increases in processing time variability have a major effect on overtime, postproduction inventory, and end-of-day production performance, but not on preproduction inventory. The impact of increased processing time variance on mean overtime is nearly linear, as Figure 15.18 shows. Figure 15.19 shows the effect of additional kanbans on overtime requirements. Adding a second kanban reduces the impact of processing time variation on overtime requirements. But additional kanbans after the second have little effect on overtime requirements.

In a second set of experiments, Huang, Rees, and Taylor evaluate the effect of uncertainty in the demand rate on the plant. While very little data is reported on these experiments, they do indicate overtime and end-of-day production increase substantially. Changes in the other measures weren't nearly as dramatic. In a final set of experiments, Huang, Rees, and Taylor tested the impact of variance in both machine processing times and demand rate. These results appear in Figure 15.20. Again end-of-day production variance and overtime are up sharply, while all other values are similar to those we see in Figure 15.17.

FIGURE 15.17   Impact of Variability in Processing Times on JIT Performance

Processing Time Distribution	Overtime (Minutes)		Preproduction Activity Inventory at Operation 1		Post-Production Activity Inventory at Operation 1		End-of-day Production (before Overtime) at Operation 1	
	μ	σ	μ	σ	μ	σ	μ	σ
Constant								
1 kanban	.00	.00	300.00	.00	.00	.00	1,000.00	.00
2 kanbans	.00	.00	600.00	.00	10.00	30.00	1,000.00	.00
Exponential								
1 kanban	32.80	19.39	233.90	95.10	9.82	29.76	982.74	37.84
2 kanbans	12.07	18.22	549.91	90.66	20.67	53.32	985.75	35.78
Normal ($\sigma = 4.8$)								
1 kanban	29.93	9.49	258.54	85.86	5.73	23.23	950.41	50.07
2 kanbans	19.58	8.91	572.49	69.45	15.82	44.48	952.05	50.03
Normal ($\sigma = 24$)								
1 kanban	160.04	43.87	219.68	92.66	12.25	32.79	817.53	80.99
2 kanbans	110.07	42.22	508.04	133.52	36.45	31.59	904.11	96.99

FIGURE 15.18

The Effect on Overtime of Increasing Uncertainty

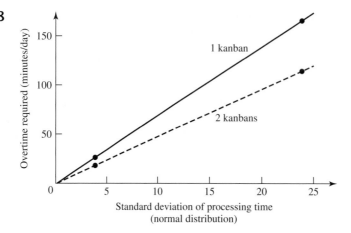

FIGURE 15.19

The Effect on Overtime of Increasing the Number of Kanbans

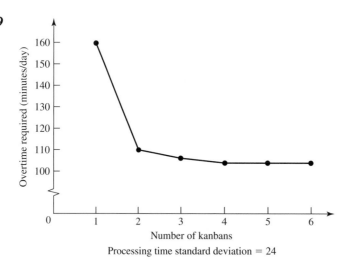

These results reveal the favorable performance impact that standardizing machine processing times has under JIT. They also indicate the impact of schedule instability on production performance under JIT through the demand uncertainty experiments. The results also point to the need for further research in this area.

Lot Size

Shen's simulation research addressed another element of operating conditions that can impact JIT performance: lot size. In this case a Slam model is used to analyze a two–work-center kanban production process. The objective of Shen's research is to determine the effect of changes in production lot size on manufacturing performance in terms of unfilled demand and finished-goods inventory. One experiment simply varied lot size; the results appear in Figure 15.21. Here smaller lot sizes required a higher portion of the

FIGURE 15.20 **Impact of Uncertainty in Demand and Processing Times on JIT Performance**

Distribution	Overtime (Minutes)		Preproduction Activity Inventory at Operation 1		Post-Production Activity Inventory at Operation 1		End-of-day Production (before Overtime) at Operation 1	
	μ	σ	μ	σ	μ	σ	μ	σ
Constant								
1 kanban	.00	.00	300.00	.00	.00	.00	1,000.00	.00
2 kanbans	.00	.00	600.00	.00	10.00	30.00	1,000.00	.00
Exponential								
1 kanban	3.06	91.75	233.04	95.68	10.29	30.38	873.97	98.10
2 kanbans	−14.96	87.88	551.18	89.55	21.67	54.26	877.26	104.58
Normal ($\sigma = 4.8$)								
1 kanban	29.50	53.55	259.39	85.31	5.62	23.03	924.66	59.26
2 kanbans	18.99	52.93	570.64	72.67	16.18	45.23	929.59	61.13
Normal ($\sigma = 24$)								
1 kanban	227.32	302.21	221.37	93.86	16.32	39.96	731.55	185.39
2 kanbans	178.73	288.59	510.20	131.25	51.59	76.73	787.61	221.87

FIGURE 15.21
Impact of Lot Size on JIT Performance

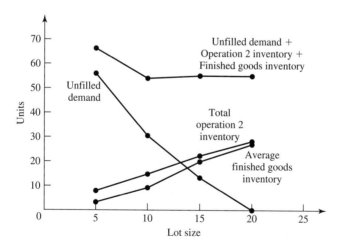

production capacity when the setup time doesn't change. The results indicate an unfavorable trade-off between reduced lot size and unfilled demand, although inventories (and cycle stock) drop. Further analysis of Shen's results in Figure 15.22 shows the interaction between lot size, setup time, and unfilled demand. When setup times were reduced in Shen's experiments by 20 percent, 40 percent, and 60 percent, unfilled demand also fell, indicating the importance of a setup reduction time program in releasing capacity for more timely production.

FIGURE 15.22
Effect of Setup Time Reduction on Manufacturing Performance

Setup Reduction	Lot Size	Unfilled Demand	Total Operation 2 Inventory	Average Finished-Goods Inventory
0%	5	55	8	3
	10	30	15	8
	15	13	22	20
	20	0	28	27
20%	5	49	8	4
	10	24	15	11
	15	10	21	20
	20	0	28	31
40%	5	40	7	4
	10	17	14	12
	15	1	21	24
	20	0	28	34
60%	5	29	7	4
	10	7	14	13
	15	0	21	27
	20	0	29	35

Comparing MPC System Approaches

Simulation research by Krajewski, King, Ritzman, and Wong indicates while kanban systems do indeed perform well under certain operating conditions, so do other MPC systems approaches like material requirements planning (MRP) and reorder point (ROP). As a result of their research they argue that the operating conditions themselves are the key to major improvements in manufacturing performance. Thus, they argue the key to improved performance is "shaping the production environment" through factors such as reduced setup times and lot sizes, improved product yield rates, and increased employee flexibility.

Krajewski et al. developed a discrete-event simulator capable of modeling nearly any batch manufacturing plant. Their simulator was developed over an eight-year period with the help of plant managers representing diverse manufacturing environments in a major U.S. corporation. This model's results, incorporating up to 250 inventory items and 250 work centers, were validated using the panel of plant managers.

The robustness of the JIT production system using kanbans was tested under a wide variety of plant-floor conditions. Figure 15.23 shows these experiments' results. Three clusters of operating condition factors indicate statistically significant differences in operating performance: inventory, process, and product structure. Analysis of the inventory cluster shows kanban performance (measured in terms of inventory investment) is highly sensitive to lot sizes and setup times. Like Shen's work, this underscores the importance of reduced setup times and lot sizes. Furthermore, customer service (past due demand) performance is very sensitive to changes in process factors such as scrap rates, low worker flexibility, and high equipment failure; but these factors have little effect on inventory performance.

Changes in product structure affect kanban performance in reverse directions for inventory and customer service. Inventory performance improves with pyramid product structures, shallow bills of materials, and low commonality of parts, while customer service improves when an inverted pyramid structure is used with deep bills of materials

FIGURE 15.23
Kanban System Performance

Factor Operating Conditions	Setting	Inventory (Weeks of Supply)	Past Due Demand (% Orders)
Customer influence (CI)	High	1.95	48.3
	Low	1.89	48.2
	Relative difference[†]	3%	0%
Vendor influence (VI)	High	2.06	46.5
	Low	1.78	51.9
	Relative difference	15%	−11%
Buffer mechanisms (BM)	High	2.06	46.8
	Low	1.78	49.7
	Relative difference	15%	−6%
Product structure (PS)	High	2.14	38.8
	Low	1.71	57.7
	Relative difference	23%[‡]	−39%[‡]
Facility design (FD)	High	2.14	43.6
	Low	1.70	52.9
	Relative difference	23%	−19%
Process (P)	High	1.91	56.2
	Low	1.93	40.3
	Relative difference	−1%	33%[‡]
Inventory (I)	High	2.95	50.8
	Low	0.89	45.7
	Relative difference	107%[§]	11%
Averages	High	2.17	47.3
	Low	1.67	49.5
	Relative difference	26%	−5%

[†]Relative differences are the differences between the results from the high and low settings divided by the average performance for all kanban experiments. Effects on weekly labor requirements aren't shown. The PS and I clusters were significant at the 0.01 level, while all other clusters weren't statistically significant. Changing the PS factor changes work content by definition. The I cluster had a 34 percent impact on labor because of the added labor requirements for long setup times at the high setting.
[‡]Statistically significant at the 0.05 level. The Biomedical Package P Series (1977) was used for the fractional factorial analysis of variance. The eight interaction terms were pooled (none were statistically significant) to create the error term.
[§]Statistically significant at the 0.01 level.

and high part commonality. When the pyramid structure is used, kanban tends to reduce inventories at the end-item level, exposing the plant to problems in master production scheduling due to forecast errors. Likewise, the inverted pyramid structure leads to larger component lot sizes and inventories making the plant less sensitive to market uncertainties experienced with the pyramid structure.

These results suggest the importance of the inventory, process, and product structure factors in implementing JIT systems. Indeed, a second set of simulation experiments reported by Krajewski et al. further underscores the importance of shaping the production environment by improving operating conditions. The second set of experiments compares a kanban system's performance with that of the reorder point system (ROP). The objective is to determine how much of the performance improvement is attributable to the kanban system as opposed to the operating conditions under which it was applied.

The kanban system in these experiments differs from the ROP system in that kanban has more frequent reviews of inventory positions, stages material on the shop floor, doesn't

FIGURE 15.24
Comparison of the Kanban and Reorder Point Approaches

Experimental Setting	Labor Requirements (Hours per Week)	Inventory (Weeks of Supply)	Past Due Demand (Weeks of Supply)
Shop 1:			
Kanban	21,888	4.12	0.17
Daily ROP	21,925	3.80	1.02
Shop 2:			
Kanban	6,563	14.68	0.67
Daily ROP	6,583	11.65	1.18
Weekly ROP	4,562	16.18	0.05

Source: L. J. Krajewski, B. E. King, L. P. Ritzman, and D. S. Wong, "Kanban, MRP and Shaping the Production Environment," *Management Science* 33, no. 1 (January 1987).

adjust lot sizes for yield losses, and uses the first-in-system/first-served dispatching rule. The simulation results, shown in Figure 15.24, for two shop configurations, indicate the kanban system and ROP systems are similar in performance. Differences in inventory and customer service exist because two kanbans were used in the kanban system experiments to assure reasonable customer service performance. This provides additional safety stock not afforded the ROP systems. Allowing this added stock would have made the performance results even closer.

The authors conclude the reason the kanban system appears attractive is not the system itself. ROP systems perform just as well. The reason is the kanban system is simply a convenient way to implement a small lot production strategy and to expose operating conditions that need improvement. Thus, the key to improved performance is to shape the production environment.

In the work of Hurley and Whybark, another approach to improvements was tested. In most of the comparisons of JIT to alternative MPC system approaches, the kanbans tested signaled the replenishment of material that has just been used. Hurley and Whybark evaluated kanbans that took into account customer order information and signaled the production of material in anticipation of a future customer need. As might be expected, these "anticipation" kanbans provided better product availability than the replenishment kanbans. The key to the improvements was making use of the information on customer requirements that was available to the company.

Concluding Principles

This chapter presents some of the research on a broad range of topics that were identified by Sakakibara et al. as important to both academics and practitioners. The choice of work presented was driven by the need to maintain a focus on the aspects of JIT that affect the MPC design. Thus, we looked at topics from the areas of production floor management, scheduling, and supply chain coordination (supplier management). All of these have JIT core components that have implication for MPC system design and performance. We draw the following principles from the work:

- The sequence of models in a mixed model final assembly schedule must be carefully planned to achieve stability in component production.

- The number of kanban cards that are released must be closely managed to achieve inventory reductions without factory disruptions.
- Improved supply chain coordination, including reduced raw-material stocks and transportation costs, can result from undertaking inbound transportation scheduling.
- Setup time reduction programs should be implemented to enable small-lot production.
- The proportion of setup time to total capacity should be considered in determining the attractiveness of setup time reduction programs.
- Small-lot production must be undertaken to achieve advantages associated with kanban MPC methods.
- Making use of information on customer requirements can lead to improved performance, even when kanban cards are used.
- MPC professionals must realize that improving operating conditions can be more important than changing the features of the MPC system to achieve improved manufacturing performance.

References

Alles; Michael; Amin Amershi; Srikant Datar; and Ratna Sarkar. "Information and Incentive Effects of Inventory in JIT Production," *Management Science* 46, no. 12 (December 2000), pp. 1528–1544.

Amasaka, Kakuro. "New JIT: A New Management Technology Principle at Toyota," *International Journal of Production Economics* 80, no. 2 (November 21, 2002), pp. 135–144.

Axsater, Sven, and Rosling Kaj. "Ranking of Generalised Multi-Stage KANBAN Policies," *European Journal of Operational Research* 113, no. 3 (March 16, 1999), pp. 560–567.

Berkleg, B. "A Review of the Kanban Production Control Research Literature," *Production and Operations Management* 1, no. 4 (1992).

Bitran, G. R., and L. Chang, "Mathematical Programming Approach to Deterministic Kanban Systems," *Management Science* 33, no. 4 (April 1987), pp. 427–421.

Bolander, Steven F., and Sam G. Taylor. "Scheduling Techniques: A Comparison of Logic," *Production and Inventory Management Journal* 41, no. 1 (1st quarter 2000), pp. 1–5.

Bowman, R. Alan. "Job Release Control Using a Cyclic Schedule," *Production and Operations Management* 11, no. 2 (summer 2002), pp. 274–287.

Brox, James A., and Christina Fader. "Assessing the Impact of JIT Using Economic Theory," *Journal of Operations Management* 15, no. 4 (November 1997), pp. 371–388.

Chapman, S. N. "Schedule Stability and the Implementation of Just-in-Time," *Production and Inventory Management* 31, no. 3 (3rd quarter 1990), pp. 66–70.

Chausse, Sylvain; Sylvain Landry; Federico Pasin; and Sylvie Fortier. "Anatomy of a Kanban: A Case Study," *Production and Inventory Management Journal* 9, no. 4 (4th quarter 2000), p. 11.

Co, Henry C., and Moosa Sharafali. "Overplanning Factor in Toyota's Formula for Computing the Number of Kanban," *IIE Transactions* 29, no. 5 (May 1997), pp. 409–415.

Deleersnyder, J.; T. J. Hodgson; H. Muller; and P. J. O'Grady. "Kanban Controlled Pull Systems: An Analytic Approach." *Management Science* 35, no. 9 (September 1989), pp. 1079–1091.

Duplaga, E. A.; C. K. Hahn; and C. A. Watts. "Evaluating Capacity Change and Setup Time Reduction in a Capacity-Constrained, Joint Lot Sizing Situation." *International Journal of Production Research* 34, no. 7 (July 1996).

Fullerton, R. R., and Cheryl S. McWatters. "The Production Performance Benefits from JIT Implementation," *Journal of Operations Management* 19, no. 1 (January 2001), pp. 81–96.

Hahn, C. K.; D. J. Bragg; and D. Shin. "Impact of the Setup Variable on Capacity and Inventory Decisions." *Academy of Management Review* 13, no. I (1988), pp. 91–103.

Hill, A. V., and T. E. Vollmann. "Reducing Vendor Delivery Uncertainties in a JIT Environment," *Journal of Operations Management* 6 (1986), pp. 381–392.

Huang, P. Y; P. L. Rees; and B. W. Taylor. "A Simulation Analysis of the Japanese JIT Technique for a Multiple, Multistage Production System." *Decision Sciences* 14 (1983), pp. 326–344.

Hurley, Simon F., and D. Clay Whybark. "Comparing JIT Approaches in a Manufacturing Cell," *Production and Inventory Management Journal* 40, no. 2 (2nd quarter 1999), pp. 32–37.

Karmarkar, U. S., and S. Kekre. "Batching Policy in Kanban Systems," *Journal of Manufacturing Systems* 8, no. 4 (1989).

Kaynak, Hale. "The Relationship between Just-in-Time Purchasing Techniques and Firm Performance," *IEEE Transactions on Engineering Management* 49, no. 3 (August 2002), p. 205.

Kelle, Peter; Faisal Al-khateeb; and Pam Anders Miller. "Partnership and Negotiation Support by Joint Optimal Ordering/Setup Policies for JIT," *International Journal of Production Economics* 81/82 (January 11, 2003), pp. 431–441.

Kovalyov, Mikhail Y.; Wieslaw Kubiak; and Julian Scott Yeomans. "A Computational Analysis of Balanced JIT Optimization Algorithms," *INFOR* 39, no. 3, part 2 (August 2001).

Krajewski, L. J.; B. E. King; L. P. Ritzman; and D. S. Wong. "Kanban, MRP and Shaping the Production Environment," *Management Science* 33, no. 1 (January 1987), pp. 39–57.

Kubiak, W., and S. Sethi. "A Note on 'Level Schedules for Mixed Model Assembly Lines in Just-in-Time Production Systems,'" *Management Science* 37, no. 1 (January 1991), pp. 121–122.

Liping, Cheng, and Fong-Yuen Ding. "Modifying Mixed-Model Assembly Line Sequencing Methods to Consider Weighted Variations for Just-in-Time Production Systems," *IIE Transactions* 28, no. 11 (November 1996), pp. 919–927.

Miltenburg, G. J. "Level Schedules for Mixed-Model Assembly Lines in Just-in-Time Production Systems," *Management Science* 35, no. 2 (February 1989), pp. 192–207.

Mitra, D., and I. Mitrani. "Analysis of a Kanban Discipline for Cell Coordination in Production Lines," *Management Science* 36, no. 12 (December 1990), pp. 1548–1566.

Moeeni, F., and Y. Chang. "An Approximate Solution to Deterministic Kanban Systems," *Decision Sciences* 21, no. 3 (summer 1990), pp. 608–625.

Monden, Y. *Toyota Production System,* 2nd ed. Norcross, Ga.: Institute of Industrial Engineers Press, 1993.

Narasimhan, R., and S. A. Melnyk. "Setup Time Reduction and Capacity Management: A Marginal Cost Approach," *Production and Inventory Management* 31, no. 4 (4th quarter 1990), pp. 55–59.

Petroff, John N. *Handbook of MRP II/JIT Integration and Implementation.* Englewood Cliffs, N.J.: Prentice Hall, 1993.

Pinto, P., and V. Mabert. "A Joint Lot-Sizing Rule for a Fixed Labor Cost Situation," *Decision Sciences* 17 (1986), pp. 139–150.

Sakakibara, S.; B. B. Flynn; and R. G. Schroeder. "A Framework and Measurement Instrument for Just-in-Time Manufacturing." *Production and Operations Management Journal* 2, no. 3 (1993).

Samaddar, Subhashish. "The Effect of Setup Time Reduction on Its Variance," *Omega* 29, no. 3 (June 2001), pp. 243–247.

Shen, H. N. "Simulation of a Two Stage Kanban System Using Slam," Working Paper CMOM 87-03. Rochester, N.Y.: Graduate School of Business Administration, University of Rochester, 1987.

Steele, D. C.; W. L. Berry; and S. T. Chapman. "Planning and Control in Multi-Cell Manufacturing," *Decision Sciences Journal* 26, no. 1 (1995).

Steiner, George, and Yeomans, Julian Scott. "Optimal Level Schedules in Mixed-Model, Multilevel JIT Assembly Systems with Pegging," *European Journal of Operational Research* 95, no. 1 (November 22, 1996), pp. 38–53.

Sugimori, Y.; K. Kusunoki; F. Cho; and S. Uchikawa. "Toyota Production System and Kanban System-Materialization of Just-in-Time and Respect-for-Human System," *International Journal of Production Research* 151 (1977), pp. 553–564.

White, Richard E., and Victor Prybutok. "The Relationship between JIT Practices and Type of Production System," *Omega* 29, no. 2 (April 2001), pp. 113–124.

Yang, Po-Chung, and Hui-Ming Wee. "An Integrated Multi-Lot Size Production Inventory Model for Deteriorating Items," *Computers & Operations Research* 30, no. 5 (April 2003), pp. 671–682.

Discussion Questions

1. Figure 15.1 implies manufacturing strategy is part of the JIT program and is linked to quality, technology, and JIT core components. Do you agree?

2. The Monden (Toyota) heuristic for level schedule determination uses squared penalties for deviations from average requirements for component manufacturing. What other approaches might be suggested?

3. Chapman suggests using a "wall of inventory" to provide level schedules and insulation for manufacturing while implementing JIT improvements. What will it take to get this to work and assure the improvements get translated into reducing the wall?

4. "Today's kanban research is the modern equivalent of yesterday's economic order quantity research." Do you agree?

5. There's considerable evidence that getting correct operating conditions is more important than the choice between MRP, kanban, or reorder point methods in the material planning and control system. How general do you believe this situation to be?

Problems

1. TMI, Inc., produces electronics equipment for the telephone industry. At one plant a single assembly line produces memory circuits for cellular telephones using a mixed model scheduling approach. Component operations at this plant have recently been converted to a JIT material flow operation. The company wants to reduce demand variation at the component manufacturing stations using the Toyota approach. TMI has provided the following data for two end products, 1 and 2 (which use differing quantities of two components, A and B):

End Product	1	2
Planned quantity/shift	2	3

End Product	Component Item Usage/End Product	
	A	B
1	4	1
2	1	2

a. In what sequence should the five units (two of end product 1 and three of end product 2) be run on the final assembly line to minimize demand variation at the A and B component manufacturing station?

b. Graph cumulative versus average usage for components A and B.

2. Killjoy Electrical produces surge protectors for the computer industry. On one of the assembly lines in its plant Killjoy produces two end-product models of surge protectors. The data shown

below are for the two products and their components.

End Product	1	2
Planned quantity	3	2

End Product	Component Item Usage/End Product		
	W	X	Y
1	1	1	0
2	0	1	1

Component operations at Killjoy have been recently converted to JIT operation. Use the Toyota approach to reduce demand variation at the component manufacturing stations.

3. The Bridgerock Tire Company is planning to install JIT in its passenger tire plant. Bridgerock plans to continue to hold finished-goods inventory until the new system is functioning properly. The following data have been collected for one of its popular models, the Slush Tire:

   Average daily customer demand = 40 units/day.

   Daily demand standard deviation = 2.25 units.

   Manufacturing lead time = 30 days.

   Manufacturing lead time standard deviation = 1.25 days.

   Finished-goods inventory carrying cost = 30 percent of item cost/year (365 days).

   Item cost = $50.

   Currently, the Slush Tire's average setup cost is $300 (20 hours at $15 per hour). The company plan is to reduce average manufacturing lead time to 2 days, the lead time standard deviation to 0.2 days, and the setup cost to $2.50 (10 minutes at $15 per hour).

   a. Calculate the Slush Tire's economic order quantity for current and planned operations.

   b. Assuming that the company plans to hold sufficient safety stock to permit a .05 stock-out probability per order cycle for the current and planned operations, calculate the safety stock for both current and proposed operating conditions.

   c. What will the average finished-goods investment be for both current and planned operating conditions?

4. During the past several months the Hanson Manufacturing Company has experienced an increased number of line shutdowns because of unreliable deliveries of incoming purchased parts from its JIT suppliers. As a result the company is considering a decision to manage the transportation of incoming purchased parts from three of its suppliers. The company has developed the following data concerning purchased items A, B, and C:

Item	Vendor	Average Weekly Usage	Item Cost*
A	1	8,000 units	$50/unit
B	2	3,000	80/unit
C	3	40,000	20/unit

*This value is adjusted for a transportation rebate given to Hanson if it picks up the item at the vendor's plant.

Notes: 1. Inventory carrying cost/week = 0.4% of item cost

2. Truck setup cost = $60/item picked up

3. Variable vehicle cost = $100/hour

Transportation Time (in Hours)

From Vendor	To Vendor			To Plant
	1	2	3	
1	—	.1	.1	.85
2	.1	—	.1	1
3	.1	.1	—	.4
From plant	.85	1	.4	—

a. Calculate the minimum and maximum travel times using the Hill and Vollmann method for each item and vendor.

b. Calculate the upper and lower bounds on the number of stops per week for each item and vendor.

5. Vendors 1, 2, and 3 at the Hanson Manufacturing Company have agreed to give the firm a 10 percent rebate on the price of items A, B, and C if Hanson takes over transporting the items from the vendor's plant to Hanson's plant. The following data have been provided:

Item	Vendor	Current Price/Unit	New Price/Unit
A	1	$55.55	$50
B	2	88.88	80
C	3	22.22	20

a. Using the preceding data and the data in problem 4, compute the combined weekly cost of purchasing and carrying inventory for items A, B, and C when vendors deliver the items to Hanson once a week.

b. Assuming Hanson picks up items A, B, and C from the vendor once a week, compute the weekly total incremental cost (TWC) of this alternative using the TWC equation in the Hill and Vollmann method. In this case one truck picks up the three items in one run, starting at the Hanson plant and visiting vendors 3, 2, and 1 (in that order) prior to returning to the plant.

c. What recommendations would you make to Hanson?

6. Given the following information:

Item	Annual Demand (in Units)	Setup Time (in Hours)	Processing Time/Unit	Inventory Carrying Cost/Unit/Year	Unit Cost	Daily Demand Rate (in Units)	Daily Production Rate (in Units)
R	54,000	8	1 min./unit	$2.50	$10.00	216	480
S	27,000	6	2 min./unit	$3.00	$12.00	108	240

Notes: 1. Setup cost = [(Item setup time) ($40) + $400 per item in setup waste].
2. Assume 250 days per year and an eight-hour work shift per day.

    a. Compute the optimal number (N^*) of times per year to produce items R and S using the IS model and assuming both items are run in each processing cycle.

    b. Compute optimal order quantities for items R and S using the IS model.

    c. Compute total incremental cost per year (TIC^*) using the IS model.

    d. How many hours per year of capacity are required to use this solution?

7. Using the data in problem 6 and the following information:

    Production capacity/year = 1,850 hours (since 150 hours per year are required for maintenance).

    a. Compute the optimal processing cycle (T^*) to produce items R and S using the CC model and assuming both items are produced in each cycle.

    b. Compute the optimal order quantities for items R and S using the CC model.

    c. Compute TIC per year using the CC model.

    d. How many hours per year of capacity are required to use this solution?

8. Using the data in problems 6 and 7 and the following information:

    Overtime capacity hours (exceeding 1,850) cost $60/hour.

    Setup time can be reduced at a cost of $600 per setup hour reduced.

    a. Compute the optimum level of capacity (W^*) using the Hahn, Bragg, and Shin model.

    b. Compute the savings rate per hour of setup time reduction (SR) and determine whether a setup time reduction program should be implemented using the Hahn, Bragg, and Shin model.

9. Using the Hahn, Bragg, and Shin model and the data from problems 6 through 8:

    a. Compute the optimal order quantity for items R and S.

    b. Compute the total incremental cost per year for items R and S using the Hahn, Bragg, and Shin model.

    c. How many capacity hours per year are required to implement the Hahn, Bragg, and Shin solution?

    d. By what percentage would the setup times for items R and S need to be reduced in order to implement the Hahn, Bragg, and Shin solution with 1,850 hours per year of capacity? What would this reduction cost?

10. Complete the following table for the IC, CC, and Hahn, Bragg, and Shin model solutions computed in problems 6 through 9, assuming 1,850 hours per year of capacity for each case.

	IS	CC	Hahn, Bragg, and Shin
Inventory carrying cost/year	___	___	___
Setup cost/year	___	___	___
Extra capacity cost/year	___	___	___
Total cost/year	___	___	___

11. Given the following information, please determine the number of kanban cards required:

    Demand rate = 100 units/hour (constant)

    Lead time = 2 hours

    Safety factor = .05

    Container size = 50 units

12. The XYZ Electronics Company recently implemented JIT in its manufacturing plant and its major vendors. However, requirements for the subassemblies used in the final assembly operation vary considerably throughout each day. The following example shows this variation for one subassembly item.

	Hour #							
	1	2	3	4	5	6	7	8
Hourly subassembly A requirements (in terms of kanbans)	2	18	10	25	5	15	4	6

The subassembly is produced in two steps at work centers 102 and 103 as follows:

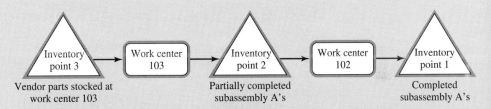

Inventory point 3	Work center 103	Inventory point 2	Work center 102	Inventory point 1
Vendor parts stocked at work center 103		Partially completed subassembly A's		Completed subassembly A's

Assume there are now six kanbans of completed subassembly A's at inventory point 1 and two kanbans for partially completed subassembly A's at inventory point 2. Apply Moeeni and Chang heuristic 1 to determine the total number of kanbans at work centers 102 and 103.

13. Complete an eight-hour simulation in the following table using the solution obtained in problem 12. Use a spreadsheet program for performing the simulation.

		Hour							
		1	2	3	4	5	6	7	8
Work center 102	Demand (in kanbans)								
	Beginning inventory								
	Production								
	Ending inventory								
Work center 103	Beginning inventory								
	Production								
	Ending inventory								

14. Using the data in problem 12, please apply Moeeni and Chang heuristic 2 to determine the number of kanbans at work centers 102 and 103.

15. Complete the following eight-hour simulation using the solution determined with heuristic 2 in problem 14. Use a spreadsheet program for the simulation. What differences do you observe between the number of kanbans in the solutions to problems 12 and 14? Explain these differences.

		Hour							
		1	2	3	4	5	6	7	8
Work center 102	Demand (in kanbans)								
	Beginning inventory								
	Production								
	Ending inventory								
Work center 103	Beginning inventory								
	Production								
	Ending inventory								

16

Advanced Concepts in Scheduling

This chapter addresses advanced issues in scheduling, with primary emphasis on detailed scheduling of individual jobs through work centers in a shop. The intent is to provide direction for the firm that has a working MPC system in place and wishes to enhance the shop-floor systems.

The approaches in this chapter presume effective front-end, engine, and back-end systems are in place. Chapter 16 provides an application perspective to research in scheduling. It's completely beyond our scope to even summarize the vast amount of research on this topic. Rather, our interest here is to focus on some basic concepts and results, relate them to some of the newer manufacturing approaches, and show how you might apply results in certain operating situations.

Chapter 16 centers around three topics:

- *Basic scheduling research:* What are the fundamental scheduling research problems and what are the practical implications of scheduling results that have been consistently verified in the research?

- *Advanced research findings:* What findings from advanced research seem to be particularly helpful in assigning jobs or labor to machines? What are the critical scheduling issues in cellular manufacturing?

- *Multiple constraint scheduling.* How can the theory of constraints (TOC) scheduling be extended to multiple constraining resources?

Chapter 16 is most closely linked to Chapters 9 and 11, which describe just-in-time and basic shop-floor systems and their place within an overall MPC system framework. Constraint scheduling is introduced in Chapter 11. There are also indirect links to Chapters 6 for master production scheduling and 10 for capacity planning.

Basic Scheduling Research

We can define a schedule as a plan with reference to the sequence of time allocated for and operation necessary to complete an item. This definition lets us think of a schedule that has a series of sequential steps, or a routing. The entire sequence of operations, the necessary sequential constraints, the time estimates for each operation, and the required resource capacities for each operation are inputs to developing the detailed plan or schedule.

The One-Machine Case

Research on single-machine scheduling has been largely based on the static problem of how to best schedule a fixed set of jobs through a single machine, when all jobs are available at the start of the scheduling period. It's further assumed setup times are independent of the sequence.

If the objective is to *minimize total time* to run the entire set of jobs (i.e., the minimum make-span), it doesn't matter in which order jobs are run. In this case, the make-span equals the sum of all setup and run times for any sequence of jobs. However, if the objective is to *minimize the average time* each job spends at the machine (setup plus run plus waiting times), then we can show this will be accomplished by sequencing jobs in ascending order according to their total processing time (setup plus run time). As an example, if three jobs with individual processing times of one, five, and eight hours, respectively, are scheduled, *total time* required to run the *entire* batch under any sequence is 14 hours. If we process jobs in ascending order, the average time that each job spends in the system is $(1 + 6 + 14) \div 3 = 7$ hours. However, if we process jobs in the reverse order, average time in the system is $(8 + 13 + 14) \div 3 = 11.67$ hours.

This result has an important consequence. Average time in the system will always be minimized by selecting the next job for processing that has the shortest processing time at the current operation. This rule for sequencing jobs at a work center (called **shortest processing time,** or **SPT**) provides excellent results when we use the average time in system criterion.

SPT also performs well on the criterion of *minimizing the average number of jobs in the system.* As we've noted previously, work-in-process inventory levels and average flow time are directly related measures. If we increase or reduce one, the other changes in the same direction. Analytical work shows that the SPT rule again provides superior performance when the work-in-process criterion is applied in the single-machine case.

When the criterion is to *minimize the average job lateness,* again SPT is the best rule for sequencing jobs for the single-machine case. To introduce the lateness criterion, we first must establish due dates for the jobs. Lateness measures both positive and negative deviations from the due date. An interesting aspect of scheduling research is, no matter what procedure we use to establish due dates, SPT will minimize *average job lateness.*

The one-machine scheduling research is very useful in gaining insights into scheduling rules' behavior under particular criteria. The most important conclusion we can draw from the single-machine research is the SPT rule represents the best way to pick the next job to run, if the objective is to minimize average time per job, to minimize average number of jobs in the system, or to minimize average job lateness. However, if the objective is to minimize either the maximum lateness of any job or the lateness variance, then jobs should run in due date sequence.

The Two-Machine Case

Developing scheduling procedures for the two-machine case is somewhat more complex than for single-machine systems. In the two-machine case, we must schedule both machines to best satisfy whatever criterion is selected. Moreover, we have to consider job routings. We assume each job always goes from a particular machine to another machine. For analytically based research, we make additional assumptions, such as those for the one-machine case. For example, all jobs are available at the start of the schedule, and setup times are independent.

A set of rules has been developed to minimize the make-span in the two-machine case. Note while the minimum make-span doesn't depend on job sequencing in the one-machine case, this isn't true in the two-machine case. Additionally, if total time to run the entire batch of jobs is to be minimized, this doesn't ensure either the average time each job spends in the system or the average number of jobs in the system will also be minimized.

The following scheduling rules to minimize make-span in a flow shop were developed by Johnson:

Select the job with the minimum processing time on either machine 1 or machine 2. If this time is associated with machine 1, schedule this job first. If it's for machine 2, schedule this job last in the series of jobs to be run. Remove this job from further consideration.

Select the job with the next smallest processing time and proceed as above (if for machine 1, schedule it next; if for machine 2, as near to last as possible). Any ties can be broken randomly.

Continue this process until all of the jobs have been scheduled.

The intuitive logic behind this rule is the minimum time to complete the set of jobs has to be the larger of the sum of all run times at the first machine plus the smallest run time at the second machine, or the sum of all run times at the second machine plus the smallest run time at the first machine.

We can also apply these rules to larger flow shop scheduling problems. For example, Campbell, Dudek, and Smith (CDS) have developed an efficient heuristic. This procedure uses the Johnson algorithm to solve a series of two-machine approximations to the actual problem having M machines using the following rules:

Solve the first problem considering only machine 1 and M, ignoring the intervening $M - 2$ machines.

Solve the second problem by pooling the first two machines (1 and 2) and the last two machines ($M - 1$ and M) to form two dummy machines. Processing time at the first dummy machine is the sum of the processing time on machines 1 and 2 for each order. Processing time at the second dummy machine is the sum of the processing time at machines $M - 1$ and M for each order.

Continue in this manner until $M - 1$ problems are solved. In the final problem, the first dummy machine contains machines 1 through $M - 1$, and the second dummy machine contains machines 2 through M.

Compute the make-span for each problem solved and select the best sequence.

Additional procedures using branch and bound algorithms and integer-programming methods have been developed to solve static flow shop three-machine scheduling problems using the minimum make-span criterion. However, the solutions are generally feasible only for very small problems. Currently, heuristic methods such as the Campbell, Dudek, and Smith algorithm are the only means of solving larger-scale flow shop scheduling problems.

We can make several important observations from these research efforts. First, the size of problems we can treat with analytical methods is small and of limited applicability for the "real world." Second, computer time required to solve scheduling problems with analytical methods grows exponentially with the number of jobs and/or machines to be scheduled. Third, the performance measure, minimizing the make span, isn't the same as minimizing average time in the system or average number of jobs in the system. Moreover, any of these criteria aren't necessarily related to the job lateness criterion. Fourth, static scheduling assumptions (beginning with all machines idle and all jobs available, and ending with all jobs processed and all machines idle) clearly influence the results. Fifth, the machine processing times reflect no randomness, which could reduce the techniques' applicability. Finally, on the positive side, it's important to note the two-machine scheduling rules utilize the shortest processing time logic. The SPT application in the two-machine case isn't exactly the same as it was in the single-machine case, but it's clearly an essential element in producing the desired scheduling performance in both problem situations.

Dispatching Approaches

Applying dispatching approaches to scheduling problems allows us to relax some of the limiting constraints just mentioned. In particular, dispatching approaches deal with the dynamic problem, rather than the static problem. Randomness in interarrival and service times are considered, and steady state results are provided for average flow time, average work-in-process, expected work center utilization, and average waiting time.

Dispatching involves the use of logic rules that guide the prioritizing of jobs at a workstation. These rules are referred to as *sequencing rules.* Sequencing rules range from simple local rules, such as SPT, to more complex rules that consider due dates, shop congestion, and other criteria.

To examine realistic, multiple-machine, dynamic scheduling situations, we often use simulation models. With simulation, we can examine various rules' performance against several criteria. We can expand the size of problems studied (work centers and jobs), consider effects of startup and ending conditions, and accommodate any kind of product structure, interarrival time patterns, or shop capacity. Simulation studies address such primary research questions as: Which dispatching approach for sequencing jobs at work centers performs best? For which criteria? Are some classes of rules better than others for some classes of criteria or classes of problems?

Sequencing Rules

Figure 16.1 illustrates a typical scheduling environment for a complex job shop. At any time, if a set of n jobs is to be scheduled on m machines, there are $(n!)^m$ possible ways to schedule the jobs, and the schedule could change with the addition of new jobs. For any problem involving more than a few machines or a few jobs, the computational complexity of finding the best schedule is beyond even a modern computer's capacity.

Figure 16.1 shows complex routings. For example, after processing at work center A, we may send jobs for further processing to work centers B, D, or F. Similarly, some jobs are completed after being processed at work center A and go directly to finished component inventories. Also note a job might flow from work center A to work center D and then back to A.

Figure 16.1 depicts a sequencing rule between each queue and its associated work center. This indicates a rule exists for choosing the next job in the queue for processing. The

FIGURE 16.1   **The Scheduling Environment**

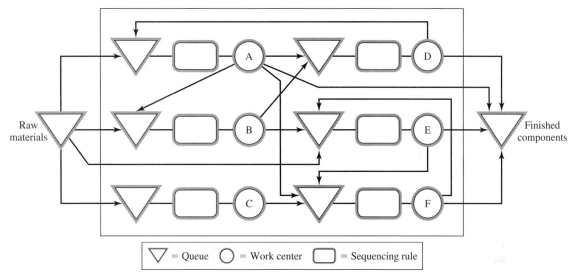

question of interest is which sequencing rule will achieve good performance against some scheduling criterion.

A large number of sequencing rules have appeared in research and in practice. Each could be used in scheduling jobs. Here are some well-known rules with their desirable properties:

R (random). Pick any job in the queue with equal probability. This rule is often used as a benchmark for other rules.

FCFS (first come/first served). This rule is sometimes deemed to be "fair" in that jobs are processed in the order they arrive at the work center.

SPT (shortest processing time). As noted, this rule tends to reduce work-in-process inventory, average job completion (flow) time, and average job lateness.

EDD (earliest due date). This rule seems to work well for criteria associated with job lateness.

CR (critical ratio). This rule is widely used in practice. Calculate the priority index using (due date–now)/(lead time remaining).

LWR (least work remaining). This rule is an extension of SPT in that it considers *all* processing time remaining until the job is completed.

FOR (fewest operations remaining). Another SPT variant that considers the number of successive operations.

ST (slack time). A variant of EDD that subtracts the sum of setup and processing times from time remaining until the due date. The resulting value is called "slack." Jobs are run in order of the smallest amount of slack.

ST/O (slack time per operation). A variant of ST that divides the slack time by the number of remaining operations, again sequencing jobs in order of the smallest value first.

NQ (next queue). A different kind of rule. NQ is based on machine utilization. The idea is to consider queues at each of the succeeding work centers to which the jobs will go and to select the job for processing that's going to the smallest queue (measured either in hours or perhaps in jobs).

LSU (least setup). Still another rule is to pick the job that minimizes changeover time on the machine. In this way, capacity utilization is maximized. Note this rule explicitly recognizes dependencies between setup times and job sequence.

This list isn't exhaustive. Many other rules, variants of these rules, and combinations of these rules have been studied. In some cases, use of one rule under certain conditions and use of another under other conditions has been studied.

One issue Figure 16.1 highlights is whether we should use the same rule at each work center. We might, for example, build a case for using SPT at the "gateway" work centers and using some due date–oriented rules for downstream centers. Or perhaps selection of a rule should depend on queue size or how much work is ahead of or behind schedule.

Another issue in selecting sequencing rules is their usage cost. Some rules (such as random, first come/first serve, shortest processing time, earliest due date, and fewest operations remaining) are easy to implement, since they don't require other information than that related to the job itself. Other rules (such as the critical ratio, least work remaining, slack time, and slack time per operation rules) require more complex information plus time-dependent calculations. The next queue and least setup rules require even more information, involving the congestion at other work centers, or a changeover cost matrix for all jobs currently at a work center.

Extensive research has addressed the performance of the different sequencing rules listed above. Conway, Maxwell, and Miller tested 39 different sequencing rules, using the same set of 10,000 jobs. Figure 16.2 reports their results for two criteria: average time in the system and variance of the time in system. Recall that the average time in the system is directly related to work-in-process inventory and average number of jobs in the system. The results in Figure 16.2 clearly show the SPT rule performs quite well for this set of criteria.

There is, however, a concern in using SPT. It can allow some jobs with long processing times to wait in queue for a substantial time, causing severe due-date problems for a few jobs. However, since the SPT rules can complete the average job in a relatively short time compared with other rules, overall lateness performance might be much less severe than we might think.

Other research efforts have tried to combine SPT with other sequencing rules to obtain most of SPT's benefits without the large time in system variance. One approach has been to alternate SPT with FCFS to "clean out the work centers" at periodic intervals. A combination rule can be very effective in reducing this negative attribute of SPT.

FIGURE 16.2
Simulation Results for Various Sequencing Rules

Sequencing Rule	Average Time in System	Variance of Time in System
SPT	34.0	2,318
EDD	63.7	6,780
ST/O	66.1	5,460
FCFS	74.4	5,739
R	74.7	10,822

Advanced Research Findings

This section covers several additional research studies we feel are particularly relevant to MPC practice. These studies focus on determination of lead times (management of due dates) for manufactured items and determination of labor assignments in manufacturing operations. In each case, we think important practical issues are raised and the practicing professional can use the available, though perhaps tentative, conclusions.

Due Date Setting Procedures

An important issue in scheduling manufacturing orders is establishing order release and due dates. Many firms assign setting such dates to manufacturing; it's frequently the subject of intense negotiations between manufacturing and marketing personnel. Often, due dates must be set at the time of order receipt or when bidding for an order. An effective MPC system can help by providing appropriate information regarding material availability, capacity, and resource requirements for individual jobs. As an example, we normally assign due dates for make-to-order products based on raw material and equipment capacity availabilities. Likewise, we set order release and due dates for manufactured components in MRP systems by determining length of the planned lead time for such items. Therefore, establishing lead time offsets and due dates is a vital and ongoing function in a manufacturing system. A well-functioning shop-floor control system based on good sequencing rules will help us achieve these due dates.

Early research by Baker and Bertrand provided some useful insights for setting due dates for a job shop. Specifically, they set due dates for orders by adding an estimate of the manufacturing time to the date the order is received. Their three methods for establishing the estimate of manufacturing time are:

CON: A *constant* time allowance for manufacturing all jobs; that is, the same lead time is added to all jobs at receipt date to calculate the due date.

SLK: A time allowance that provides an equal (constant) waiting time or *slack* for all jobs; that is, the due date is set equal to the receipt date plus the sum of all processing times, plus a fixed additional slack time.

TWK: A time for waiting that has slack proportional to a job's *total work content;* that is, lead time to be added to the receipt date is a multiple of the sum of all processing times.

Each procedure has a single parameter (the constant time, the slack time, or the multiple) to be determined. Other informational needs are similar to those of shop-floor scheduling problems. The first procedure is easy to implement in many firms since shop-floor system database requirements are minimal. The other two procedures, however, require an estimate of a job's processing time to set the due date.

Experiments testing the three due date setting rules involved a single-machine system using the shortest processing time sequencing rule. They were conducted under a wide variety of operating conditions: 80 percent to 99 percent machine utilization, a variety of jobs, 20 replications, and use of both exponentially and normally distributed processing times. The exponentially distributed processing times gave a much greater degree of variability in achieved lead times (coefficient of variation, $c_v = 1.0$) than the normally distributed processing time ($c_v = .25$). Two releasing rules were used as well. The random release rule

FIGURE 16.3 Simulation Results for Manufacturing Lead Time Estimating Procedures

Treatment	Mean Number of Jobs	Utilization	Mean Manufacturing Lead Time			Frequency Best*		
			TWK	SLK	CON	TWK	SLK	CON
Exponential times, random release	4.00	0.80	4.43	9.04	10.14	20	0	0
	5.67	0.85	5.63	10.37	11.39	20	0	0
	9.00	0.90	6.20	11.79	12.76	20	0	0
Exponential times, controlled release	4.00		5.26	4.53	8.79	3	17	0
	5.67		6.51	6.23	10.09	7	13	0
	9.00		8.28	9.51	13.49	17	3	0
Normal times, random release	4.28	0.90	7.20	7.70	7.72	16	2	2
	9.59	0.95	10.06	10.70	10.75	16	2	2
	52.09	0.99	10.44	10.99	11.07	20	0	0
Normal times, controlled release	4.28		6.65	5.31	5.90	0	20	0
	9.59		12.35	10.61	11.18	0	20	0
	52.09		48.53	53.10	53.64	20	0	0

*Number of times in the 20 replications that each procedure performed the best (i.e., produced the lowest mean manufacturing lead time).

meant orders were issued to the shop as soon as received. The "controlled" release rule meant jobs were released when work-in-process inventory levels fell below a "trigger point." The trigger point was chosen to provide a specified average number of jobs in the shop.

The evaluative criterion was "due date tightness." Here we presume tight due dates (or short lead times) are strategically more desirable than loose due dates. Tight due dates provide a competitive advantage by permitting the firm to offer an improved level of customer service, as well as achieve lower costs through reductions in work-in-process inventory. The experiments' approach was to set each of the three parameters so that *no* late deliveries occurred; that is, the parameters were chosen so the longest lead time is just sufficient. Thereafter, actual lead times are observed in the simulation. The preferred procedure is the one that achieves the smallest mean lead time.

The results indicate the SLK and TWK procedures set tighter due dates than the CON procedure. As Figure 16.3 shows, these two procedures provided as much as a 50 percent reduction in lead time required for manufacturing (in comparison with the CON procedure) under exponentially distributed processing times. Much smaller differences were noted when normally distributed processing times were used. Furthermore, there was a clear preference for the TWK procedure (as opposed to the SLK procedure) when random work releasing was used. In using controlled work releasing, preference shifts to the TWK procedure at higher levels of machine utilization.

While considerable research has been done since this early work, the important message that calculating lead times on the basis of total work content is best still prevails. In the next section, we consider the important question of whether a due date should be changed after the order has been released to the shop.

Dynamic Due Dates

Determining due dates for orders when they are released to the shop is only one aspect of managing due dates in scheduling. A second aspect concerns maintaining *valid* due dates as orders progress through the manufacturing process and as new orders are added. The need for due date maintenance arises from the manufacturing environment's dynamic nature. Management actions (such as master production schedule changes, planned lead time adjustments, and bill of materials modifications) can create the need to reschedule manufacturing orders and to revise priorities given to the shop. Likewise, variations in shop conditions (such as unexpected scrap and unplanned transactions) can also create the need to revise job due dates.

Many firms' systems and procedures result in changes in open order due dates. This practice is called *dynamic due date maintenance.* The primary argument for this practice is the shop should use accurate and timely information in dispatching jobs to machines to provide a high level of customer service. In spite of its widespread use, controversy surrounds the advisability of implementing dynamic due date maintenance systems. Some suggest dynamic due dates can have an adverse impact on scheduling performance because of system "nervousness." Steele, for example, argues a job shop can function effectively only if open order priorities are stable enough to generate some coherent action on the shop floor. He defines a scheduling system with *unstable* open order priorities as a nervous scheduling system, which can lead to shop floor distrust and overriding formal priorities. A second behavioral argument against dynamic due date maintenance is the volume of rescheduling messages might so inundate the production planner that he or she can't process the necessary changes in a timely fashion.

In such cases, the production planner may simply stop trying to perform an impossible task; the shop could lose faith in the priority system and revert to using an "informal" system; or ill-chosen or misleading rescheduling messages may be communicated to the shop. Any or all of these responses may cause the shop and inventory system performance to deteriorate.

Penlesky conducted an important experiment to better understand when dynamic due dates might be attractive and when they are not attractive. He evaluated the use of several dynamic due date procedures as well as the use of simple procedures for selectively implementing a few of the many due date changes that would normally be implemented (filtering procedures). In particular, the study concerned determining what types of job-related information are important to consider in formulating open order rescheduling procedures and evaluating rescheduling's impact on manufacturing performance in MRP systems.

He considered three different filters for making rescheduling decisions: ability, magnitude, and horizon filters. The ability filter's purpose is to assure only attainable due date adjustments are passed along to the shop. In using this procedure:

1. All *rescheduling out* actions (when the new due date is later than the previous due date) are implemented.
2. Implementing *reschedule-in* actions depends on one of three conditions:
   a. If the machine setup and processing time remaining is less than the time until the new due date, the new due date is implemented.
   b. If the machine setup and processing time remaining is less than the time until the old due date but greater than the time until the new date, the due date is set to the present time plus the machine setup and processing time to complete the order.
   c. If the machine setup and processing time remaining exceeds the time allowed until the old due date, no change is made to the old due date.

The magnitude and horizon filters consider different information. These procedures are designed to filter out trivial due date adjustments by means of a *threshold* value. In the magnitude procedure, if the absolute value of the difference between the new and the old

FIGURE 16.4 **Percentage Improvements in Service and Inventory Levels Using Dynamic Due Dates***

Periodic Order Quantity	Planned Lead Time	Performance Measure	Low Master Schedule Uncertainty		High Master Schedule Uncertainty	
			Low Machine Utilization	High Machine Utilization	Low Machine Utilization	High Machine Utilization
Small	Low	Experiment number	1	2	3	4
		Customer service level	3.4	—	15.2	—
		Total inventory level	—	—	10.5	—
	High	Experiment number	5	6	7	8
		Customer service level	.5	9.3	4.8	31.8
		Total inventory level	—	5.1	—	8.3
Large	Low	Experiment number	9	10	11	12
		Customer service level	4.3	—	14.3	—
		Total inventory level	—	—	8.0	—
	High	Experiment number	13	14	15	16
		Customer service level	2.5	—	6.2	—
		Total inventory level	—	—	—	—

*[(Static − Dynamic) ÷ Static] × 100; calculated only in those cases where there was a statistically significant difference in the performance measure between the two procedures.

due dates exceeds a threshold value (T_m), the due date is changed. Similarly, the horizon procedure is designed to filter out due date changes too far out in the planning horizon to be of immediate concern to the production planner. Only if the old due date falls within the period of interest (T_H) is the new due date implemented. By setting parameter values for T_m and T_H, the number of rescheduling changes to be implemented can be adjusted. The procedures will implement all changes when $T_m = 0$ and $T_H = \infty$, providing full dynamic procedures. Static dates result when $T_m = \infty$ and $T_H = 0$.

Simulation experiments were used to investigate the effect of incorporating dynamic due date information in the sequencing rules and use of filtering procedures. These experiments were conducted using a make-to-stock job shop simulator, with both component manufacturing and assembly operations, controlled by an MRP system. Procedures were tested under differing values of machine utilization, uncertainty in the master production schedule, length of planned lead times, and size of production order quantities. The three measures of effectiveness used were end-product customer service level, combined work-in-process and finished item inventory level, and number of rescheduling changes implemented.

Figure 16.4 indicates performance gains from dynamic due dates depend on shop operating conditions. These results indicate that under certain operating conditions, dynamic due date information improves customer service and total inventory level. We can draw another important conclusion from Figure 16.4's results. Dynamic due dates can reduce total inventory level while *simultaneously* improving customer service (e.g., in experiments 3, 6, 8, and 11).

Figure 16.5 compares the filtering procedures' performance for experiment number 8 of Figure 16.4. We can make two observations regarding these results. First, there's no significant difference in performance between the filtering procedures and the dynamic due date procedure without filtering. All rescheduling procedures significantly improve performance

FIGURE 16.5
Results of
Applying the
Filtering
Procedures

Procedure	Filter Level*	Customer Service Level		Total Inventory Level	
		Mean	Standard Deviation	Mean	Standard Deviation
Static due dates	0	.651	.084	14,357	895
Ability filter	100	.871	.048	12,990	412
Magnitude filter	53	.873	.041	12,873	919
Horizon filter	45	.831	.055	13,190	958
Dynamic due dates without filtering	100	.858	.049	13,161	999

Note: Data from experiment 8 of Figure 13.5.
*Percent of indicated reschedules that were implemented.

over the static procedures. Second, magnitude and horizon filters provide comparable performance to the dynamic rescheduling procedure—but with far fewer rescheduling actions implemented. Therefore, it would seem dynamic rescheduling's benefits can be achieved by *selectively* implementing rescheduling actions. By filtering rescheduling messages, we can reduce information processing costs and adverse behavioral effects of system nervousness without an adverse effect on operating performance.

Labor-Limited Systems

The scheduling research results presented so far are useful when sequencing rules represent the principal means of controlling work flow in a plant. In many firms, besides assigning jobs to work centers, there's a need to make labor assignment decisions. Labor assignment decisions are important in controlling work flow when labor capacity is a critical resource in completing work. This can occur even when only one particular labor skill is the bottleneck resource. In such instances, the system is said to be labor-limited.

Labor limitations provide an additional dimension to shop-floor scheduling that's important for many JIT and cellular manufacturing situations. The controllable cost is labor, and the primary scheduling job is assigning labor to machine centers. Good labor scheduling practice enables us to vary labor capacity at work centers to better match day-to-day fluctuations in work loads. To the extent there's flexibility in assigning people to work centers, we can improve manufacturing performance (e.g., reduced flow times, better customer service, and decreased work-in-process inventory). However, the degree of flexibility in making labor assignments depends on such factors as amount of cross-training in the workforce, use of temporary labor, favorable employee work rules, and costs of shifting people between work centers.

In a classic study, Nelson has provided a comprehensive framework for control of work flow in labor-limited systems. It lists three major elements for controlling work flow in scheduling:

1. Determining which job to do next at a work center (dispatching).
2. Determining when a person is available for transfer to another work center (degree of central control).
3. Determining the work center to which an available person is to be assigned (work center selection).

Various decision rules, using information similar to that used in making dispatching decisions, have been suggested for making the latter two decisions. The decision rules Nelson suggested for determining a person's availability for transfer utilize a central control parameter, d, that varies between 0 and 1. When $d = 1$, the person is always available for reassignment to another work center. When $d = 0$, the person can't be reassigned as long as jobs are waiting in the queue at the person's current work center assignment. We can control the proportion of scheduling decisions in which a person is available for transfer by adjusting d's value between 0 and 1.

Fryer suggests two different approaches to transfer availability. One considers time; the other considers the queue. The time approach suggests the person must be idle for t or more minutes before a transfer can be made. The queue approach suggests making a transfer only when the person's work center queue has fewer than q jobs waiting for processing. Labor flexibility is increased by decreasing the value of t or increasing the value of q.

The third decision in the framework, deciding to which work center a person should be assigned, can be made using decision rules that resemble sequencing rules. We can determine priorities for assigning labor to unattended work centers on the basis of which work center has as its next job to process:

1. The job that was first at the current work center, first-come/first-served (FCFS).
2. The job that was first in the shop, first-in-system/first-served (FISFS).
3. The shortest job (SPT).
4. The most jobs in the queue.

We combine these decision rules with decision rules for making dispatching and labor availability decisions to control the work flow. Random assignment was used as a baseline for comparison.

Simulation experiments have been conducted to evaluate the performance of the different work flow control rules suggested for labor-limited systems. These studies generally measure improvement in the job flow time performance. An interesting general finding is, while changes in sequencing rules involve a trade-off between the mean and variance in job flow times, changes in labor assignment rules often reduce both measures simultaneously. Figure 16.6 shows these results.

Experiments involving the labor flexibility factor d also show the importance of labor flexibility in a shop. A change between no labor flexibility ($d = 1$) and complete labor flexibility ($d = 0$) resulted in 12 percent and 39 percent reductions in the mean and variance of job flow times, respectively.

Research on labor assignment rules demonstrates the importance of cross-training and labor assignment flexibility. Moreover, it indicates that both labor and job dispatching can have a major impact in controlling work flow through a shop. With an operating shop-floor control system in place, further performance improvements might come from better design of labor assignments and from operational changes that permit greater flexibility in labor assignments.

Group Scheduling and Transfer Batches

The theory of constraints (TOC) scheduling approach described in Chapter 11 uses different batch sizes, depending on whether a work center is a bottleneck. This idea has led to research

FIGURE 16.6 Time and Number of Jobs in System

Size of Labor Force	Statistic Queue Discipline		Mean Time and Mean Number in System*			Variance of Time in System			Variance of Number in System		
			FCFS	FISFS	SPT	FCFS	FISFS	SPT	FCFS	FISFS	SPT
4	Machine limited		17.7	17.7	9.4	488	295	612	201	205	24
3	Labor assignment rule	0	11.0	11.0	7.0	200	125	295	76	80	17
		1	10.2			173			54		
		2		10.5			102			63	
		3			6.6			343			15
		4	10.1	10.1	6.4	169	97	281	50	53	11
2	Labor assignment rule	0	8.7	8.7	6.2	158	147	186	65	67	23
		1	8.7			153			49		
		2		8.7			147			67	
		3			5.0			285			10
		4	8.7	8.8	5.1	154	89	293	46	48	9
1	Labor assignment rule	0	8.3	8.3	5.5	157	174	176	74	69	24
		1	8.3			149			48		
		2		8.3			174			69	
		3			4.2			296			9
		4	8.3	8.3	4.4	150	174	298	45	69	8

Note: Labor assignment rules:
  0 = Random labor assignment to a work center.
  1 = FCFS labor assignment to a work center.
  2 = FISFS labor assignment to a work center.
  3 = SPT labor assignment to a work center.
  4 = Most jobs in queue labor assignment to a work center.
*Parameters so chosen that the mean time and the mean number in the system were equal.

efforts that study combining shop scheduling decisions with lot sizes. Jacobs and Bragg have developed the **repetitive lots concept,** and through simulation studies show that major improvements in the average flow time for manufactured lots and work-in-process inventory can be made by using conventional priority scheduling procedures and transfer batches for shop production.

Jacobs and Bragg permit the *original order quantities* released to the shop for manufacturing to be split into smaller *transfer batches* that can flow immediately to the next operation prior to the operation's completion at its current work center. The transfer batches are predetermined integral fractions of the original order quantity. They provide a work center with the flexibility to start producing an order before it is completed at the previous work center. Such flexibility, frequently referred to as "lot-splitting" and "overlap or line scheduling," reduces order flow times, improves machine utilization, cuts setup times, and smoothes work flow in the shop to yield better use of capacity. This flexibility also means the number of units produced during a given work center setup, *operation batch size,* can vary between a transfer batch and the original order quantity.

Figure 16.7 illustrates the repetitive lots concept and its effect on order flow time. Using fixed operation batch sizes of 1,000 (equal to the original order quantity) in Part A, the

FIGURE 16.7

A Comparison of Fixed versus Variable Operation and Transfer Batch Sizes for a Single Job

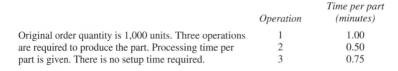

	Operation	Time per part (minutes)
Original order quantity is 1,000 units. Three operations are required to produce the part. Processing time per part is given. There is no setup time required.	1	1.00
	2	0.50
	3	0.75

A. Fixed operation batch size = 1,000
Transfer batch size = 1,000

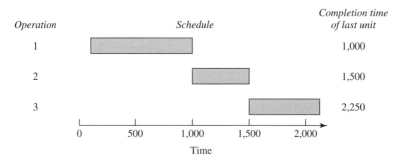

B. Variable operation batch size
Transfer batch size = 100

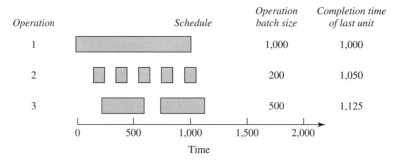

order is completed at hour 2,250. In Part B, while the original order quantity is used at operation 1, a transfer batch size of 100 is used to permit processing the order simultaneously at operations 2 and 3 for completion by hour 1,125. In this case, the operation batch sizes for work centers 2 and 3 are 200 and 500, respectively. Although Figure 16.7 doesn't consider the fact that other jobs may be competing for the resources each operation uses, the simulation took this into account when assessing the potential benefit of the repetitive lots concept.

The repetitive lots concept can be applied by using any standard priority sequencing rule (e.g., shortest processing time, critical ratio). When an order is completed under traditional priority sequencing rules, the highest-priority order in the queue is selected for processing next. Under the repetitive lots concept, a work center may contain transfer batches coming from many released orders. In this case, the queue is searched for transfer batches of the same item that has just been completed at the work center. If such an item is available, it's processed next, regardless of priority; otherwise, the highest-priority transfer batch in the queue is selected and a new setup is made at the work center. If the queue contains no transfer batches, the next batch to arrive at the work center is processed. This idea of first searching the queue of jobs for work that does not require a new setup is often referred to as **part family scheduling.**

Jacobs and Bragg report simulation results in which the repetitive lots concept is tested using a model of a shop with 10 work centers. The original order quantity for released orders was varied from 120 to 400 in these experiments, and two different transfer batch sizes (50 and 10) were used. A 38 percent average improvement in the mean order flow time was observed when a transfer batch size of 50 was used; a 44 percent average improvement was obtained with a transfer batch size of 10. Total setup time at the work centers fell 23 to 27 percent when transfer batches were used in conjunction with small original order quantities (120 to 200) for the released setup times. While the repetitive lot concept may raise material handling costs and make tracking orders in a shop more complex, it appears to be a promising approach for improving manufacturing performance. High-volume manufacturers with limited product lines having numerous operations appear to benefit most from the reduced order flow times, lower levels of work-in-process inventory, and potential gains in customer service provided by using the repetitive lots concept.

Scheduling Manned Cellular Manufacturing Systems

Both static and dynamic scheduling approaches have been applied to scheduling flow shop cells. Some of this work uses analytical methods for solving static scheduling problems developed by Johnson and Campbell, Dudek, and Smith, which we described earlier in this chapter. These methods assume all jobs to be scheduled are available at the first machine in the cell at the beginning of the scheduling period. Work has also been reported on development of dynamic scheduling approaches for flow shop cells. Here, orders arrive at random time intervals for processing in a manufacturing cell. Wemmerlöv provides a survey of this research. An important part of this effort has been directed toward developing and testing sequencing heuristics similar to those this chapter earlier described for application to dynamic flow shop scheduling problems. In this section we describe a study that tests scheduling rules for a manufacturing cell dedicated to producing certain part families.

Wemmerlöv and Vakharia report dynamic scheduling heuristics for a five-stage flow shop cell, with a queue of orders in front of each stage. Each stage in this cell has one machine, and all orders have the same routing through the cell. This cell processes as many as six part families, with individual part orders arriving at random time intervals according to a Poisson process. Upon arrival at the cell, each part order is assigned a due date based on the total work content (TWK) to be performed in the cell on the order. Total work content includes combined values of the part family setup time and processing time at each stage in the cell.

Simulation studies were conducted to evaluate different scheduling rules, using a computer model of the manufacturing cell. A scheduling rule is used to sequence orders at the first stage in the cell: this same sequence is maintained at all of the remaining stages in the cell. The four scheduling rules evaluated were:

FCFS: First come/first served.

SLACK: Slack time.

CDS: Campbell, Dudek, and Smith's procedure.

NEH: Nawaz, Enscore, and Ham's procedure.

The first two rules are job shop sequencing rules and are used to maintain a priority sequence of orders in the queue at the first stage in the line. The second two rules are static scheduling rules, which were applied periodically in these experiments to develop a priority sequence of orders in the queue at the first stage of the line.

While the CDS rule was used as described earlier in this chapter, the NEH rule uses a different sequencing procedure. This heuristic starts with a partial sequence (it could be just one job) of jobs in queue at the first stage. We compute the make-span for a new job inserted in all positions without disturbing the order of the previous, partial sequence. We keep it in the position that gives the lowest make-span, and we evaluate another job until all available jobs have been considered.

In an effort to minimize setup time at each stage in the cell, a variation of each of the four rules was developed. The variation simply partitions the queue of orders at the first stage in the line according to a part family. The sequence in which we process orders within each part family grouping and the sequence in which we process part families are both established. For example, the FCFS rule processes that family having the oldest order first. After all orders in that family are processed, the part family having the next oldest order is processed next. This variation is similar to the repetitive lots concept described in the last section, the only difference being that transfer batches are not used.

The family versions for the SLACK, CDS, and NEH rules are more complex. For the SLACK rule, we partition orders in the queue at the first stage into those orders having negative and positive slack. For those orders having negative slack, we first process the family having the order with the most negative slack. After we've processed all orders in this family in the order of their slack time priority, we then apply the rule to determine the next part family to process. For orders having a positive slack priority, the next part family we process is that family having the largest sum of the combined setup and processing time for all stages in the cell. Once we've selected the next part family to be processed, orders within that family are processed in order according to the smallest sum of the combined setup and processing time for all stages in the line.

The family versions of the CDS and the NEH rules also develop a sequence for the families represented in the order set, and then a sequence for the jobs in each family. These procedures proceed by first collapsing the five-stage scheduling problem into a series of two-stage scheduling problems, and then use a procedure similar to the Johnson algorithm to solve each two-stage problem. The solution with the minimum make-span is used both to sequence the part family to be processed next and to establish order sequence within each part family.

Wemmerlöv and Vakharia report simulation experiments that evaluate performance of these rules considering the following measures of performance: average order flow time and lateness, total number of early orders, total number of late orders, total number of family setups, and total number of operations processed. Several factors were varied in these experiments, including: number of part families, ratio of family setup time to order processing time, and cell utilization level.

Simulation results indicate family-oriented versions of the sequencing rules consistently outperform other rules, and the difference in performance increases as the ratio of the setup to processing time increases. However, these results are quite sensitive to number of part families processed by a cell. When a small number of part families was processed (e.g., 3), family versions of the FCFS and the SLACK rules outperformed other rules. However, when the cell processed a larger number of part families (e.g., 6), the FCFS(Family) rule produced the best due date performance while the CDS(Family) rule produced a smaller average flow time. In analyzing simulation results, differences between the FCFS(Family) and the CDS(Family) rules are apparently quite small. Therefore when administrative costs of using the CDS(Family) rule are considered, it may be advantageous to use the simpler FCFS(Family) rule.

In selecting a scheduling rule for a manufacturing cell, these results indicate the value of using a sequencing rule that works toward reducing setup time in the cell. The resulting increase in effective capacity in the cell provides an important improvement in scheduling performance. Also the FCFS(Family) is very effective, especially when we consider costs of administering the shop-floor control system. However, if a cell is designed to produce a larger number of part families than the number considered in these experiments, we should consider the CDS(Family) rule.

Multiple-Constraint Scheduling

When the production system contains a single constraining resource, the TOC approach is relatively straightforward. But what if multiple constraint operations must be scheduled for the same job? This situation can arise either when a production system contains more than one bottleneck resource or when a job requires more than one operation (multiple passes) at the same bottleneck resource. Originally it was thought that drum-buffer-rope scheduling could not be used in such situations. However, in this section we will show how Simons and Simpson extend the basic TOC ideas to the multiple constraint scenario.

Buffers between Constraint Operations: Rods

When a production system contains only a single resource that has been identified as a constraint, all timing decisions are derived from a schedule constructed specifically for that resource. Each job's release time is computed by subtracting a constant lead time from the time that job is scheduled to begin work at the constraint resource. The amount of lead time is determined by management and is designated as the size of the constraint buffer. This lead time accommodates operations required prior to the constraint.

However, the problem becomes far more complex when more than one constraint operation is required. Consider initially the case where a job is processed by a constraint resource, moves on to be processed by some nonconstraints, and then returns to the original constraint resource for a different operation.

The notion of a *rod* is introduced in response to this problem. A rod serves the purpose of ensuring that nonconstraint operations following one constraint operation have sufficient time for completion prior to a subsequent constraint operation. In the case of operations on the same constraint, the rod is referred to as a *batch rod* since it provides the required time between two process batches in the constraint's schedule. When the constraint operations involve multiple constraints, the rods are referred to as *time rods* since they indicate the specific point in time at which one constraint's operation must be complete to conform to the time called for in another constraint's schedule.

The duration of a rod (i.e., the rod length) may be arbitrarily set at one-half the constraint's normal buffer size. The rod's placement in the constraint schedule is a function of two factors: transfer batch size and the relative magnitude of the per unit processing time in the two constraint operations being spaced apart. Ideally, transfer batches would consist of single units, since that would permit subsequent processing to begin as soon as possible.

When the processing time per unit is *smallest* for the earlier constraint operation, the rod is placed between the scheduled completion of the *first* unit on the first constraint operation and the scheduled start of processing of the *first* unit on the second constraint operation. This situation is illustrated in Figure 16.8. Since the processing time per unit is smaller on the earlier constraint operation, this ensures that all units will be processed at least as far ahead as the rod length before they are scheduled to be processed in the second constraint operation.

By contrast, when the processing time per unit is *largest* for the earlier constraint operation, the rod is placed between the scheduled completion of the *last* unit on the first constraint operation and the scheduled start of processing of the *last* unit on the second constraint operation. (See Figure 16.9.) By using the *last* unit in this case, the two processes are separated sufficiently for *all* units.

Multiple-Constraint Scheduling Algorithm

The algorithm described below is derived directly from the first three TOC focusing steps of identifying the constraint, exploiting the constraint, and subordinating to the constraint. Initially, the customer market is assumed to be the only constraint, i.e. no internal resource constraints are assumed. The job order schedule is then used for rough-cut capacity planning to determine the sufficiency of each resource's capacity, using daily time buckets. Internal constraints are identified as resources with insufficient capacity to achieve customer due dates for the effective planning horizon. Exploitation of a constraint is

FIGURE 16.8
Batch Rod (Smaller Time per Part on Earlier Operation)

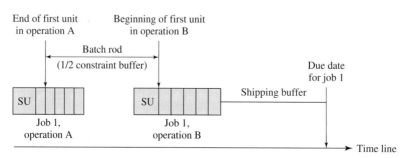

FIGURE 16.9
Batch Rod (Larger Time per Part on Earlier Operation)

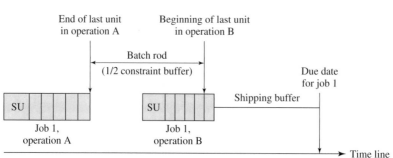

achieved by creating a finite schedule for the operations required of that resource. Subordination involves a return to rough-cut capacity planning for nonconstraint resources, this time in consideration of the operation due dates specified in the constraint schedule. The subordination process may reveal the existence of additional constraints, which triggers a return to the exploitation step (the scheduling of constraints).

Step 1. Compute effective horizon = planning horizon + shipping buffer.

Step 2. Subordinate all resources to the market.
   a. Working backward in time from the end of the effective horizon, calculate daily loads for each resource to achieve all job due dates, assuming jobs are backward scheduled.
   b. Identify resource constraints via first-day load (FDL) peaks.
   c. If no resource constraints are identified, go to Step 7.

Stpe 3. Build drum schedule for primary constraint resource.
   a. Build *ruins* (a Gantt chart that ignores capacity) using operation finish time = job due date − shipping buffer and including any batch rods required because of multiple-constraint operations for the same job.
   b. Accomplish a backward pass to level the ruins consistent with available capacity of constraint resource.
   c. If batches are scheduled in the past, accomplish a forward pass to achieve feasibility. (*Note:* At this stage, the user is given the opportunity to specify actions that would further exploit the constraint, e.g., combining batches to avoid setups or offloading operations to other resources or to subcontractors).
   d. Fix drum schedule in time and reconcile constraint batch times with order due dates.

Step 4. Subordinate nonconstraint resources to the market and the drum schedule(s).
   a. Reaccomplish backward rough-cut capacity check for nonconstraint resources (as in Step 2a) to satisfy both job due dates and constraint operation due dates.
   b. Identify additional constraints by the presence of either FDL peaks or red lane peaks.
   c. If no additional constraints are identified, go to Step 7.

Step 5. Build schedule for additional drum.
   a. Build drum schedule as in Steps 3a to d, but consider time rods from any fixed-constraint schedules, as well as batch rods for the additional constraint.
   b. Identify drum violations (infeasibility due to overlaps of the additional drum's schedule with time rods for other existing constraint schedules). (*Note:* At this point, the user again has the opportunity to manipulate the schedule, this time to resolve drum violations.)
   c. If no drum violations exist, go to Step 4.

Step 6. Drum loop.
   a. Rebuild the first fixed-constraint schedule, shifting batches later by the amount of the drum violation.
   b. Unfix (eliminate) all additional constraint schedules.
   c. Go to Step 4.

Step 7. Stop. Implement drum schedules.

Step 1 expands the planning horizon to incorporate the shipping buffer. By adding the shipping buffer to the horizon, we ensure planning is accomplished for jobs whose constraint processing must be completed during our intended scheduling horizon so that the shipping buffer prior to their order due dates are not "eaten into." Step 2 is an attempt to determine whether the customer orders can be met without treating any resources as internal constraints. At this stage, only the customer due dates themselves are being treated as constraints. If all resources have sufficient capacity to support the due dates, then no constraint schedules will be necessary (other than the shipping schedule itself).

Step 2a works as follows. Beginning with the latest due date, each job's operational requirements are subtracted from the remaining capacity of each affected resource. If a resource's capacity for that day is exceeded, the required load is moved back a day and all preceding operations will be checked using this earlier date. When resources have excessive loads, the workload will be pushed backward until the load on the first day is greater than available capacity. Such a condition is referred to as a first-day load (FDL) peak and reveals the presence of a constraint resource. If more than one resource has an FDL peak, the one with the largest peak is normally chosen for Step 3.

The term "ruins" in Step 3a can best be visualized in Gantt chart form. Figure 16.10 shows a simple illustration of the ruins for a single constraint resource with two jobs to process. Each job requires two operations on the constraint resource with the need to visit other (nonconstraint) resources in between the two constraint operations. Each job is situated on the time line such that the processing of its final operation would be completed exactly one shipping buffer's length of time before the job due date. Since each job requires multiple operations on the same resource, batch rods are used in lieu of the due date and shipping buffer to determine placement of the earlier operations on the time line.

In Step 3b, the constraint schedule is made capacity-feasible by working backward, left-shifting operations as required to permit operations to "drop down" on the Gantt chart consistent with the number of machines available. (See Figure 16.11.) The net result will be that the operations will remain sequenced in order of the ideal completion times first shown

FIGURE 16.10
Ruins for a Single Constraint with Two Jobs (James and Mediate, 1993)

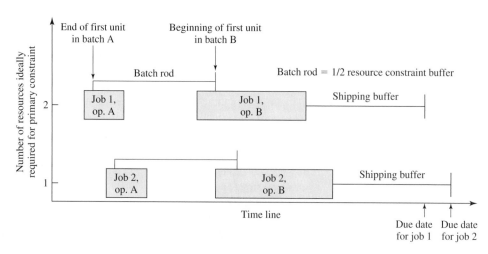

FIGURE 16.11
Schedule for Batches after Backward Pass

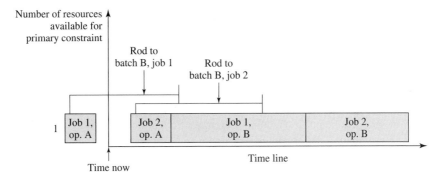

FIGURE 16.12
Drum Schedule after Forward Pass

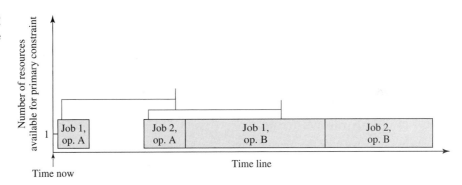

in the ruins, but will be spread out over a longer period of time. Since the left-shifting operation has moved operations earlier in time, it is likely that this backward pass will result in some operations being scheduled to occur in the past. This infeasibility is resolved by the forward pass of Step 3c, which shifts the entire schedule as far right as necessary to avoid work being scheduled in the past. (See Figure 16.12.) Since this will likely cause some jobs to have less than the desired shipping buffer or to exceed their customer due dates outright, Step 3d includes an opportunity to revise promised order dates.

Having created a schedule for the constraint resource (exploiting the constraint), the algorithm revisits the notion of subordination in Step 4. Step 4a differs from Step 2a in that the dates on which workload is allocated to the nonconstraints are now determined by both the original job due dates *and* the operation "due dates" required to support the constraint schedule. Therefore, nonconstraint operations that occur *subsequent* to the constraint operations are evaluated for capacity in time to achieve the overall job due date, while those that must occur *prior to* a constraint operation are evaluated for capacity in time to meet the schedule of the constraint. Infeasibility in the former case is referred to as a red lane (RL) peak, while infeasibility in the latter case retains the FDL peak designation used in Step 2.

If Step 4b identifies any additional constraints, the most heavily loaded one is now scheduled in Step 5. The logic of Step 5 is similar to that of Step 3. However, the schedule to be built for the additional constraint (Step 5a) must also be supportive of the schedule built in Step 3 for the primary constraint resource. This is accomplished by the use of time rods, which are placed on the time line where necessary to ensure that sufficient buffer time is provided between the two constraint schedules. A drum violation (Step 5b) occurs whenever the time rods generated by the primary drum schedule are too restrictive to permit the generation of a feasible schedule for the additional constraint.

If no drum violations are encountered, the algorithm returns (Step 5c) to Step 4 and rechecks the nonconstraint capacities. However, a drum violation (Step 5b) necessitates the drum loop in Step 6. A drum loop is no more than the rebuilding of the schedule for the primary constraint, during which constraint operations are shifted later in the schedule by the amount of the drum violation to avoid the detected infeasibility. Since the primary constraint is being rescheduled with more time allowed to do the work, it is now possible that previously identified additional constraints may no longer have excessive workloads. To check this possibility, all additional constraint schedules are discarded (Step 6b) and subordination is reaccomplished (Step 6c).

Since iteration among Steps 4 to 6 could occur multiple times, different resources may alternately gain and lose designation as constraints. The end result is that constraint schedules will be produced for one or more resources and all remaining resources will have been determined to have sufficient capacity during the scheduling horizon to support the constraint schedules. However, the original due dates may not be achieved by the final constraint schedule(s). Therefore, schedulers may consider rerunning the algorithm after combining jobs to avoid setups or changing due dates for lower-priority jobs.

Example Multiple Constraint Scheduling Problem

The example shop receives orders for a single product type with proposed due dates. Each order is for a batch of 100 units. Each batch is processed using the sequence of operations shown in the table. We will use the notation J1 (A) to designate the operation performed by resource A on Job J1. Since resource B performs two operations on each job, they will be differentiated as J1 (B1) and J1 (B2).

	Operations	Resource	Hours per Batch
Raw materials	(A)	A	8
	(B1)	B	8
	(C)	C	8
Finished products	(B2)	B	8
	(D)	D	8

There is one unit of each resource type and production occurs eight hours each day, Monday through Friday. The shipping and constraint buffer sizes have been established as eight and sixteen hours, respectively. The shop uses a transfer batch size of one unit (i.e. each unit can be moved to the next operation without waiting for completion of the entire batch). No setup time is required for any of the operations and raw materials are always available for each job. There is no work in process currently in the shop, so any jobs scheduled will have to be initiated "from scratch."

Step 1. Compute effective horizon: planning horizon plus shipping buffer.

The scheduler desires to produce a schedule for the coming week, beginning on Monday morning. Only two jobs call for completion during the planning horizon plus eight hours (one shipping buffer). Job J1 is due at hour 28 (the middle of the day on Thursday) and job J2 is due at hour 32 (the end of the day on Thursday).

Step 2a. Working backward in time from the end of the effective horizon, calculate daily loads for each resource to achieve all due dates, assuming jobs are backward scheduled.

Resource		Mon	Tue	Wed	Thu	Fri
A	J1 (A)		J2 (A)			
B	J1 (B1)	J1 (B2)	J2 (B1)	J2 (B2)		
C		J1 (C)		J2 (C)		
D			J1 (D)	J2 (D)		

Step 2b. Identify resource constraints via first-day load (FDL) peaks.

Both resources A and B would have to have completed work in the past, which they have not done. Since B has the heavier total load, we choose to select it as our primary constraint.

Step 3a. Build ruins for the primary constraint.

We place an 8-hour batch rod (BR) between the start of the first operation, e.g., J1 (B1), and the start of the second operation, e.g., J1 (B2), on each job.

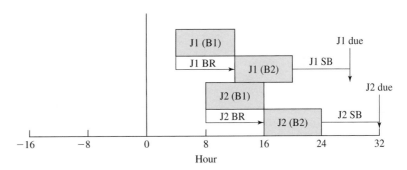

Step 3b. Accomplish a backward pass to level the ruins consistent with available capacity.

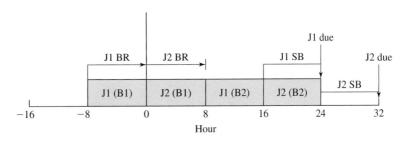

Step 3c. If batches are scheduled in the past, accomplish a forward pass to achieve feasibility.

Since operation J1 (B1) is scheduled in the past, the entire sequence is right shifted.

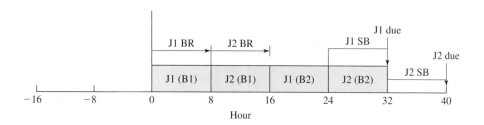

Step 3d. Fix drum schedule in time and reconcile constraint batch times with order due dates.

Based on the drum we've just created, job J1 would be completed by the constraint at hour 24. Adding the 8-hour shipping buffer, the job should not be promised to the customer until hour 32. Similarly, job J2's due date would need to be changed to hour 40.

Step 4a. Reaccomplish capacity check for nonconstraint resources considering both job due dates and constraint operation due dates.

Resource D's operations are checked for capacity according to the revised job due dates. However, the operations for resources A and C are checked for capacity one constraint buffer (16 hours) prior to when the jobs must be processed by resource B according to its schedule (although the operations on resource C will not be scheduled any earlier than the preceding B operation allows).

Resource			Mon	Tue	Wed	Thu
A	J1 (A)	J2 (A)				
B			J1 (B1)	J2 (B1)	J1 (B2)	J2 (B2)
C			J1 (C)	J2 (C)		
D					J1 (D)	J2 (D)

Step 4b. Identify additional constraints.

Resource A would not be able to support B's drum (schedule), so it will also need to be treated as a constraint.

Step 4c. If no additional constraints are identified, go to Step 7.

Since A has been identified as a secondary constraint, we proceed to Step 5.

Step 5a. Build schedule for additional drum, considering time rods from previous drums.

Two time rods (TRs) will need to be considered in building a drum for resource A. Operation J1 (A) should not be scheduled to start less than eight hours prior to the start of J1 (B1) (currently scheduled for hour 0) and J2 (A) should not start less than eight hours prior to J2 (B1) (currently scheduled for hour 8).

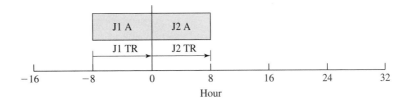

Step 5b. Identify drum violations.

Since we cannot schedule work in the past, we would need to push operation J1 (A) forward by eight hours, which pushes J1 (B) forward by the same amount.

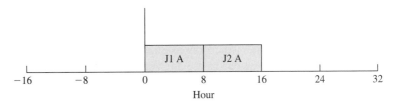

However, this violates both of the time rods between the operations on resource A and those on operation B. Therefore, we have a drum violation by an amount of eight hours.

Step 5c. If no drum violations exist, go to Step 4.

Since a violation does exist, we proceed to Step 6.

Step 6a. Rebuild the earlier constraint schedule, shifting batches by the amount of the drum violation.

Since our violation was for eight hours and affected both operations J1 (B1) and J2 (B1), we rebuild resource B's drum with the requirement (via time rods) that J1 (B1) not start before hour 8 and that J2 (B1) not start before hour 16.

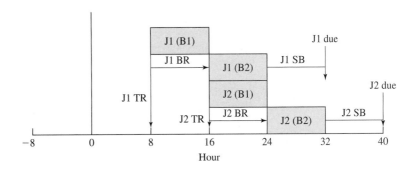

After leveling the ruins and right shifting to honor the time rods at hours 8 and 16, we have:

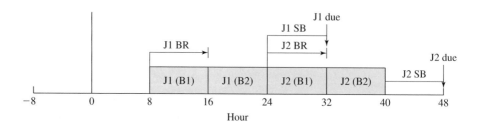

On the basis of the revised B drum, J1's due date could remain unchanged at hour 32, but J2's due date would slip from 40 to 48.

Step 6b. Unfix (eliminate) all additional constraint schedules.

Since we are unaware how the revision of B's drum would affect other constraint schedules, we return resource A to an undetermined status and delete its drum.

Step 6c. Go to Step 4.

Step 4a. Reaccomplish capacity check for nonconstraint resources considering both job due dates and constraint operation due dates.

Resource		Mon	Tue	Wed	Thu	Fri
A	J1 (A)		J2 (A)			
B			J1 (B1)	J1 (B2)	J2 (B1)	J2 (B2)
C			J1 (C)		J2 (C)	
D				J1 (D)		J2 (D)

According to the revised drum schedule and, as before, taking into account the requirement for constraint buffers prior to operations scheduled for resource B, we find these daily capacity loads:

Step 4b. Identify additional constraints.

If treated as a nonconstraint resource, A would still not be able to support B's drum, since it would have to accomplish processing of job J1 prior to time zero.

Step 4c. If no additional constraints are identified, go to Step 7.

Since A has been identified as a secondary constraint, we proceed to Step 5.

Step 5a. Build schedule for additional drum, considering time rods from previous drums.

As before, we build a drum for A in consideration of 8-hour time rods between its operations and the first operation for each job on resource B. Note that the placement of A operations is different this time because B's operations have been slipped.

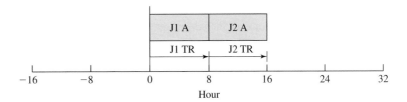

Step 5b. Identify drum violations.

> This time, we have no violations. Although it was necessary to reidentify A as a secondary constraint, the lesser requirement of the time rod (8 hours) versus a full constraint buffer (16 hours) makes A's constraint schedule feasible.

Step 5c. If no drum violations exist, go to Step 4.

Step 4a. Reaccomplish capacity check for nonconstraint resources considering both job due dates and constraint operation due dates.

Resource	Mon	Tue	Wed	Thu	Fri
A	J1 (A)	J2 (A)			
B		J1 (B1)	J1 (B2)	J2 (B1)	J2 (B2)
C		J1 (C)		J2 (C)	
D			J1 (D)		J2 (D)

> On the basis of the drums for both A and B and, as before, taking into account the requirement for constraint buffers prior to operations scheduled for resource B, we find these capacity loads:

Step 4b. Identify additional constraints.

> This time, no additional constraints are identified.

Step 4c. If no additional constraints are identified, go to Step 7.

Step 7. Stop. Implement drum schedules.

> In this case, we will have two such schedules: one for A and one for B. In this simple example, the schedule for A may seem unnecessary since it has such a light load. However, it must be remembered that nonconstraint resources in a DBR system are only loosely controlled. The constraint schedule for A helps ensure that work on J1 (A) will begin promptly at time zero, since there is only an 8-hour buffer decoupling it from J1 (B1).

Concluding Principles

Over the past 50 years, shop scheduling has been a popular area for research. Many of the procedures that have been developed are specialized applications, therefore their general applicability is limited. The following are concluding principles derived from the procedures described in this chapter:

- It is important to determine the objective(s) to be achieved in scheduling before selecting a scheduling approach since different approaches provide different results.

- The shortest processing time sequencing rule can produce effective performance and should be considered as a standard in designing shop-floor systems.

- Flexibility is introduced in scheduling through alternative routing, adjustments in labor assignments, the use of transfer batches, and overlap scheduling. Great improvements in manufacturing performance can be gained through scheduling flexibility.
- Setting and managing due dates is an important scheduling activity.
- Due date filtering procedures should be used to diminish shop-floor nervousness.
- The theory of constraint approach to scheduling can be used even when there is more than a single resource constraint.

References

Baker, K. R., and J. W. M. Bertrand. "A Comparison of Due Date Selection Rules," *AIIE Transactions* 13, no. 2 (June 1981).

Blocher, J. D.; D. Chhajed; and M. Leung. "Customer Order Scheduling in a General Job Shop Environment," *Decision Sciences* 29, no. 4 (fall 1998), pp. 951–981.

Campbell, H. G.; R. A. Dudek; and M. L. Smith. "A Heuristic Algorithm for the n-Job m-Machine Sequencing Problem," *Management Science* 16, no. 10 (June 1970).

Conway, R. W.; W. L. Maxwell; and L. W. Miller. *Theory of Scheduling.* Dover Publications, 2003.

Fryer, J. S. "Labor Flexibility in Multiechelon Dual-Constraint Job Shops," *Management Science* 20, no. 7 (March 1974).

Goldratt, E. M., and J. Cox. *The Goal.* New York: North River Press, 1984.

Jacobs, F. R., and D. J. Bragg. "Repetitive Lots: Flow-Time Reductions through Sequencing and Dynamic Batch Sizing," *Decision Sciences* 19, no. 2 (spring 1988), pp. 281–294.

James, S. W., and B. A. Mediate, Jr. "Benchmark Production Scheduling Problems for Job Shops with Interactive Constraints," MS thesis, Graduate School of Logistics and Acquisition Management, Air Force Institute of Technology, 1993.

Johnson, S. M. "Optimal Two- and Three-Stage Production Schedules with Setup Time Included," *Naval Research Logistics Quarterly* 1 (1954), pp. 61–68.

Mohan, R. P., and L. P. Ritzman. "Planned Lead Times in Multistage Systems," *Decision Sciences* 29, no. 1 (winter 1998), pp. 163–191.

Nelson, R. T. "Labor and Machine Limited Production Systems," *Management Science* 13, no. 9 (May 1967).

Penlesky, R. J. "Open Order Rescheduling Heuristics for MRP Systems in Manufacturing Firms." Ph.D. dissertation. Indiana University, 1982.

Penlesky, R. J.; W. L. Berry; and U. Wemmerlöv. "Open Order Due Date Maintenance in MRP Systems," *Management Science* 35, no. 5 (May 1989).

Rohleder, T. R., and G. Scudder. "A Comparison of Order Release and Dispatch Rules for the Dynamic Weighted Early/Late Problem," *Production and Operations Management* 2, no. 3 (1993).

Ruben, R. A., and F. Mahmoodi. "Lot Splitting in Unbalanced Production Systems," *Decision Sciences* 29, no. 4 (fall 1998), pp. 921–949.

Schragenheim, E., and B. Ronen. "Drum-Buffer-Rope Shop Floor Control," *Production and Inventory Management Journal* 31 (3rd quarter 1990), pp. 18–23.

Simons, J. B., Jr., and W. P. Simpson III. "An Exposition of Multiple Constraint Scheduling as Implemented in The Goal System (Formerly Disaster™)," *Production and Operations Management* 6 (spring 1997), pp. 3–22.

Steele, D. C. "The Nervous MRP System: How to Do Battle," *Production and Inventory Management* 16 (4th quarter 1975).

Tsubone, H.; S. Masahiko; T. Uetake; and M. Ohba. "A Comparison between Basic Cyclic Scheduling and Variable Cyclic Scheduling in a Two-Stage Hybrid Flow Shop," *Decision Sciences* 31, no. 1 (winter 2000), pp. 197–222.

Vargas, V. A., and R. Metters. "Adapting Lot-Sizing Techniques to Stochastic Demand through Production Scheduling Policy," *IIE Transactions* 28 (1996), pp. 141–148.

Wemmerlöv, U. *Production Planning and Control Procedures for Cellular Manufacturing: Concepts and Practice.* Falls Church, VA: American Production and Inventory Control Society, 1987.

Wemmerlöv, U., and A. J. Vakharia. "Job and Family Scheduling a Flow Line Manufacturing Cell: A Simulation Study." *IIE Transactions* (December 1991).

Webster, S., and F. R. Jacobs. "Scheduling a Flexible Machining System with Dynamic Tool Management," *Production and Operations Management* 2, no. 1 (1993).

Discussion Questions

1. Why is rescheduling so important in production planning and control?
2. What kinds of performance measures would apply to "scheduling" at a college?
3. Provide some examples of static and dynamic scheduling problems.
4. What sequencing rule do you use to do your homework?
5. What is the purpose of a rod in multiple constraint scheduling?
6. What is the difference between a time rod and a batch rod?
7. How does the multiple constraint scheduling algorithm first identify a resource as a constraint?
8. What is a drum violation?
9. Why may a resource that is initially identified as a constraint ultimately *not* be a constraint when the multiple constraint scheduling algorithm is completed?

Problems

1. The Pohl Pool Company has seven jobs waiting to be processed through its liner department. Each job's estimated processing times and due dates are as follows:

Job	Processing Time (Days)	Due Date (Days from Now)
A	4	8
B	13	37
C	6	8
D	3	7
E	11	39
F	9	21
G	8	16

a. Using the shortest processing time scheduling rule, in what order would the jobs be completed? Processing can start immediately.
b. What is the average completion time (in days) of the sequence calculated in question a?
c. What is the average job lateness (in days) of the sequence calculated in question a?

2. The Thompson Toilet Company has the following information on five jobs waiting to be processed in the bowl-molding work center. Processing can start immediately.

Job	Remaining Processing Time (Days)	Due Date (Days from Now)	Remaining Number of Operations
B	4	8	4
O	8	7	3
W	12	24	4
L	7	7	2
S	9	4	2

a. If the slack per operation scheduling rule is used, in what order would the jobs be started?
b. What is the average job lateness (in days) of the sequence calculated in question a?
c. What is the average number of jobs in the system using the sequence in question a?

3. The Hyer-Than-Ever Kite Manufacturing Emporium must schedule the latest set of work orders through its frame-making department. Kites begin at frame making and then proceed through one, two, or three other departments, depending on the ordered kite's sophistication. It is 8 A.M. Monday morning. Processing can start immediately. There is one operation per department. Shop scheduler Joan Weber faces the following set of orders listed in order of arrival (Assume no other jobs will arrive at the frame-making department until the five already there have been started.):

Kite Order	Frame-Making Time (Days)	Total Processing Time (Days)	Total Number of Operations	Kite Due Date (Days from Now)
A	10	20	4	25
B	12	18	2	15
C	7	12	2	16
D	5	12	3	17
E	8	10	2	12

a. Using the order data, evaluate the first-come/first-served sequencing rule:

  1. In what sequence should the frame making department process the jobs?
  2. What will be the average completion time in frame making?
  3. What will be the average number of jobs in the frame-making department?

b. Using the order data, evaluate the earliest due date sequencing rule:

  1. In what sequence should the frame making department process the jobs?
  2. Which specific jobs, if any, will be late in leaving frame making?
  3. What will the average job lateness be in the frame-making department?

c. Using the order data, evaluate the shortest processing time sequencing rule:

  1. In what sequence should the frame-making department process jobs?
  2. On what days will order E be in process in frame making?
  3. What will the average job lateness be in the frame-making department?

d. While Joan debated which rule to use, she received the following memo from Diane Britenbach, the president:

  Effective this morning, all departmental job sequencing should be performed using the slack time per operation rule. This should improve scheduling performance throughout the plant.

  1. In what sequence should the frame-making department process the jobs if it uses the slack time per operation rule and considers due dates to be final due dates?
  2. On what day will frame making complete order D?
  3. What is the average completion time for this sequence in the frame-making department?

4. Prepare a two-machine schedule using the Johnson procedure for jobs A through D. The processing time per job (in days) is shown below:

	Machine	
Job	I	II
A	4	3
B	1	7
C	8	2
D	8	5

a. In what sequence should jobs be processed?

b. Construct a Gantt chart of the schedule for both machines.

c. Construct a Gantt chart, assuming there's no buffer storage between machines (e.g., machine I can't start a new job until machine II has started the old job).

5. Dave Grubbs of Grubbs Auto Body has five cars waiting for Economy Detailing. An Economy Detailing consists of a wash and then a hand wax. Cars cannot be waxed until they are washed.

	Wash (Hours)	Wax (Hours)
(J)aguar	3	5
(C)adillac	5	3
(F)ord	1	2
(H)onda	2	1
(L)exus	4	4

a. What schedule produces the shortest time span in which these orders can be completed?

b. How many hours does it take to complete the five orders?

c. For the schedule in question a, how many hours is the waxing task idle?

d. When will Dave finish the Cadillac?

e. What is the average order completion time?

6. Flash Fasttrack (associate dean of janitorial services at Wombat University) must schedule the regular maintenance by his janitorial engineers. There are two crews: sweeping crew and waxing crew. Union rules prohibit sweepers from waxing and waxers from sweeping. A building's floors must first be swept before they can be waxed. Flash must schedule the order in which maintenance crews will visit each of Wombat U's six buildings. He wished to minimize the sequence's total completion time. Times required to sweep and wax each building are as follows:

Building	Sweeping Time (Hours)	Waxing Time (Hours)
Astronomy	18	10
Biology	8	9
Chemistry	26	13
Drama	15	16
English	17	20
Foreign language	12	17

a. Schedule the crews through the buildings.

b. When will the waxing crew start and stop work in the chemistry building?

c. During the schedule, for how much time are sweepers and waxers available for other activities?

7. Currently, Bart Simpson, the sales manager at Baxter Boards, Inc. (a manufacturer of custom-made skateboards), promises eight-week delivery time for all customer orders. The production manager is under pressure from top management to improve the firm's performance against quoted delivery dates. In his review of alternative procedures for making customer delivery date

promises, he provides the following data on representative orders:

Order	Total Processing Time (in Weeks)
1	3
2	5
3	8

a. Determine delivery time to be quoted on these orders, if the TWK (total work content) procedure is used. (Assume average time from order receipt to customer delivery is eight weeks.)

b. Determine delivery time to be quoted on these orders if the SLK (slack) procedure is used. (Assume average time from order receipt to customer delivery is eight weeks.)

c. Suppose the production manager knows the overall flow time for order #3 has averaged 10 weeks in the past, and the flow time standard deviation for this order is 1 week. How would this information influence your recommendation of a delivery date setting procedure in this situation?

8. A single test operator staffs the SCM Corporation's three testing machines in its quality control lab. Only one machine is run at a time. SCM uses two scheduling rules: one for sequencing jobs at individual machines and another for assigning labor to machines. As of 8 A.M. this morning (on day 10), jobs waiting to be processed at each of the three machines are as follows:

	Job	Due Date*	Processing Time†	Arrival Date*
Test Machine A	1	12	1	9
	5	18	6	8
Test Machine B	2	14	3	6
	3	16	4	7
	6	14	6	6
Test Machine C	4	13	4	5

* = Day number.
† = In days.

a. Assuming SCM uses the shortest processing time rule to sequence orders at each testing machine, determine to which machine the test operator should be assigned and which job will be processed when each of the following labor assignment decision rules are used (assume the operator has just completed his or her last job):

1. The shortest job.

2. The job that has been in the laboratory the longest.

3. The most jobs in the queue.

b. Suppose SCM uses the slack time rule to sequence jobs at each testing machine. To which machine should the test operator be assigned and which job will be processed when each of the following labor assignment decision rules are used? (Again it's 8 A.M. and the test operator is available for assignment.)

1. The shortest job.

2. The job that has been in the laboratory the longest.

3. The most jobs in the queue.

c. Would you recommend any other labor assignment decision rule under the conditions in question b above?

9. The materials manager at the Excello Grinding Wheel Company is concerned about the high volume of rescheduling exception messages his firm's MRP planners have to cope with each week. He's considering implementing one of several possible rescheduling filters (e.g., the Ability, Magnitude, or Horizon heuristic) and has provided the following example MRP record to illustrate such procedures' use:

		Week Number									
Item A		**1**	**2**	**3**	**4**	**5**	**6**	**7**	**8**	**9**	**10**
Gross requirements		16	20	15	20	2	27	1	15	8	10
Scheduled receipts			30		30		30				
Projected available balance	12	−4	6	−9	1	−1	2	1	16	8	28
Planned order release		30		30							

Q = 30; LT = 7; SS = 0.

a. Assume total setup plus run times remaining on the three scheduled receipts in weeks 2, 4, and 6 are 2 weeks, 3.4 weeks (three weeks plus two days), and 4 weeks, respectively. What rescheduling exception messages would the Ability heuristic make?

b. Assume total setup plus run times remaining on the three scheduled receipts in weeks 2, 4, and 6, are 0.4 weeks (two days), 1 week, and 2 weeks, respectively. What rescheduling exception messages would the Ability heuristic make?

c. Assume $T_m = 1$. What rescheduling exception messages would the Magnitude heuristic make?

d. Assume $T_H = 2$. What rescheduling exception messages would the Horizon heuristic make?

e. Assume $T_m = 0$. What rescheduling exception messages would the Magnitude heuristic make?

f. Assume $T_m = \infty$. What rescheduling exception messages would the Magnitude heuristic make?

g. Suppose a rescheduling exception message calls for moving the 30 units in week 6 to week 8. Would this message be produced in $T_m = 1$?

10. The Ace Tool Company is considering implementing the repetitive lot concept in scheduling the firm's fabrication shop. The production manager selected an example order to use in evaluating benefits and potential costs of this scheduling approach. A transfer batch size of 100 units was suggested for this item. The example order is for a quantity of 1,000 units and has the following routing data:

Operation	Work Center	Setup Time	Run Time/Unit
1	1	40 minutes	2.4 minutes/unit
2	2	20 minutes	1.44 minutes/unit

a. Assuming a single-shift, eight-hour day, five-day week for work centers 1 and 2, prepare a Gantt chart showing the earliest start- and finish-time schedule for this order under a conventional scheduling approach where all items in the order are processed at one time. Do the same when the repetitive lot concept is used. What are the earliest start and finish times for each transfer batch at work center 2, assuming none of the transfer batches are processed together to save setup time?

b. What's the difference in the order-completion times under the two scheduling approaches in part a above?

c. What are the benefits and potential costs of this scheduling approach?

11. To remain competitive, Ed's Sheet Metal must reduce manufacturing lead time for a product that typically sells in lots of 800 units. The product goes through two operations in different departments. The company wants to evaluate the value of using a transfer batch between operations. The idea is to split the order at the first operation and transfer an amount to the second operation to get it started while the rest of the order is finished at the first operation. The setup of operation 2 can start as soon as parts arrive, but not sooner. Other data are:

Order size	= 800 units
Operation 1 processing time	= 6 minutes/unit
Operation 2 processing time	= 8 minutes/unit
Transfer time from operation 1 to 2	= 20 minutes
Setup time for operation 1	= 1.0 hours
Setup time for operation 2	= 1.5 hours

a. What is the *minimum* transfer batch that assures that operation 2 has no idle time?

b. How much would manufacturing lead time be reduced by using the transfer batch instead of the full order of 800 units?

12. Calculate completion times for part B of Figure 16.7. Assume there are no other jobs in the shop and each operation will know when a transfer batch will reach it. There doesn't need to be a complete operation batch available to start work at any of the three operations but, once started, the operation batch must be completely processed without waiting for additional transfer batches (i.e., no idle time during an operation batch's run).

13. Consider the following data for three jobs processed in the boring machine center for Conway Manufacturing.

Job	Setup Time (Minutes)	Run Time/ Unit (Minutes)	Batch Size
A	15	.05	200
B	10	.15	100
C	20	.10	200

Queue data for the boring machine center:

Job	Arrival Time	Job	Arrival Time	Job	Arrival Time
A	8:24	B	8:40	B	9:12
B	8:28	C	8:42	C	9:14
C	8:31	C	8:44	A	9:18
A	8:34	A	8:57	B	9:21
B	8:39	A	9:03	B	9:31

a. If the boring machine center used a first-come/first-served rule to schedule jobs, how long would it take to process the queue? (Assume no other jobs arrive, all jobs in queue are for one batch each, and a job B has just been completed.)

b. How long would it take to process all jobs in the queue using a repetitive lot logic?

14. Dave Grubbs of Grubbs Auto Body also offers a Deluxe Detailing service. The Deluxe Detailing consists of washing, buffing, and then hand waxing the customer's automobile (the steps must be done in this order). When Dave offered Deluxe Detailing to the customers in problem 5, they all decided to get the Deluxe service.

	Wash (Hours)	Buff (Hours)	Wax (Hours)
(J)aguar	3	4	5
(C)adillac	5	3	3
(F)ord	1	8	2
(H)onda	2	6	1
(L)exus	4	5	4

a. Prepare a schedule for Dave, using the Campbell, Dudek, and Smith (CDS) heuristic.

b. In what sequence should Dave process the jobs to minimize the make-span? Follow the same processing sequence at each step of the process.

c. Construct a Gantt chart of the best sequence schedule for all three steps of the processes.

15. The Philip Company has the following processing time data for machines 1, 2, 3, and 4. Routing for each job begins at machine 1 and ends at machine 4:

	Processing Time (in Hours)			
Job	Machine 1	Machine 2	Machine 3	Machine 4
A	6	2	4	2
B	1	8	7	5
C	5	7	2	3
D	4	4	1	6

a. Prepare a schedule for a four-machine manufacturing cell using the Campbell, Dudek, and Smith heuristic.

b. In what sequence should Philip process the jobs to minimize make-span? Follow the same processing sequence at each machine in the cell.

c. Construct a Gantt chart of the best sequence schedule for all four machines.

16. The Arnold Company has the following processing time data for the three-machine manufacturing cell. Each job's routing begins at machine 1 and ends at machine 3:

	Processing Time (in Hours)		
Job	Machine 1	Machine 2	Machine 3
A	1	7	3
B	4	2	8
C	2	9	2

a. A partial schedule, sequencing job A first and job B second, has already been prepared below. Use the NEH procedure that minimizes the make-span to determine the sequence through all three machines in the cell for jobs A, B, and C.

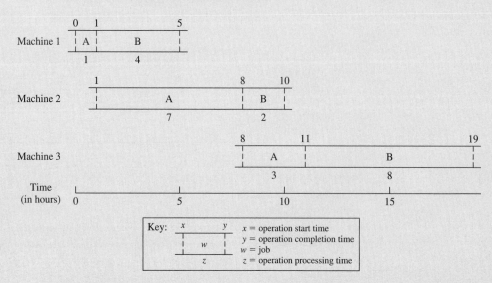

b. A partial schedule, sequencing job B first and job A second, has already been prepared below. Using the NEH procedure, determine the sequence through all three machines in the cell for jobs A, B, and C that minimizes the make-span. How does this schedule compare with that in part a of this problem?

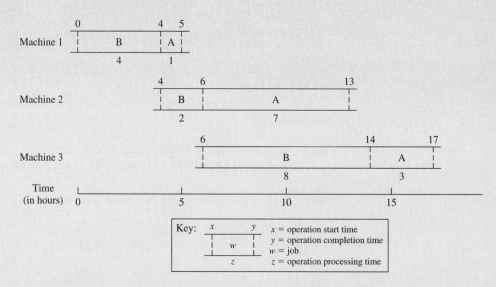

17. Prepare a schedule for a four-machine manufacturing cell using the Slack Time procedure and the following processing time data for the cell. Routing for each job begins at machine 1 and ends at machine 4. Assume the machines are currently set up for family C and no setup can be done until a job arrives at a machine.

Job	Family	Processing Time (in Hours)				Hours Until Due Date
		Machine 1	Machine 2	Machine 3	Machine 4	
1	A	2	3	9	2	30
2	B	5	4	2	7	31
3	A	1	6	4	1	24
4	B	4	7	9	8	48

The due date for each order is set using the TWK rule; in this case TWK equals total processing plus setup time plus an allowance for queuing. Setup time is one hour when a change from one family to another is made and zero if another job of the same family is processed.

a. Using the conventional version of the Slack Time procedure, determine the sequence for processing jobs 1 through 4 at machine 1 (and through the remaining machines).

b. Using the Family version of the Slack Time procedure, determine the sequence for processing jobs 1 through 4 at machine 1 (and through the remaining machines).

18. A firm has installed a manufacturing cell containing five machines to process cylindrical parts in three different part families: A, B, and C. Though parts within each part family are similar in design, work can be routed through this cell in a variety of ways. Orders typically begin processing at either machine 1 or machine 2, and can be further processed at any or all of the remaining three machines. Therefore, a queue of orders exists at each of the five machines, and sequencing decisions are made at each machine in the cell.

Two decisions are made in sequencing orders at each machine. At the time an order is completed at a machine, the supervisor decides which part family to process next. Once she has selected the part family to process next, she uses the slack time rule to decide which order within the part family to process next. Exhibit A shows a dispatching report for machine 2 in this cell. This machine has just completed an order in part family A.

a. Which order should be processed next at machine 2 if the ECON procedure is used to select the part family to process next?

b. Which order should be processed next at machine 2 if the WORK procedure is used to select the part family to process next?

c. Which order should be processed next at machine 2 if the AVE procedure is used to select the part family to process next?

19. A particular job (consisting of 20 units) must have two different operations accomplished by a constraint resource. The first constraint operation has a setup time of 15 minutes and requires 10 minutes of processing time per unit. The second constraint operation has a setup time of 20 minutes and requires 5 minutes of processing time per unit. Describe precisely where a batch rod should be inserted between these operations and why.

Use the following information for problems 20 through 22:

Eagle Chemicals produces a variety of industrial chemicals, using two proprietary chemical processes. Most jobs consist of chemicals flowing through the first process (A1), then through the second process (B), and then back through the first process (A2). Although the chemicals flow continuously within each process, the processes are not connected to each other, so it is possible for a job to be held as work in process between stages of production. In addition, setups may be done externally, so no production time is lost due to setups. Eagle operates 24 hours per day, seven days per week, and plans its production for one week (168 hours) at a time. To ensure jobs are not completed late, the company builds its production plans using an 8-hour shipping buffer for each job. The company has just completed the current week's production and now wants to

EXHIBIT A
Machine 2
Dispatching
Report

Shop Order Number	Item Part Number	Operation Setup Time*	Processing Time†	Part Family	Order Due Date‡	Total Processing Time Remaining§
10-1234	5678	1	6.2	A	12	2
10-1240	1082	1	4.3	A	10	4
10-1241	1141	1	5.1	A	7	8
10-1231	1271	1	1.8	B	14	15
10-1229	4252	1	2.3	B	8	6
10-1215	8110	1	0.9	B	10	14
10-1251	1354	1	1.7	B	3	6
10-1249	1278	1	13.2	C	4	1
10-1225	7910	1	3.4	C	9	3
10-1242	6250	1	4.1	C	4	1
10-1260	5140	1	2.8	C	12	4
10-1261	6280	1	3.1	C	15	10
10-1042	1011	1	8.1	C	13	3

*In hours assuming a change in part family is required; otherwise setup time is zero.
†In hours.
‡Number of manufacturing days until the order due date.
§In manufacturing days.

plan for the following three jobs that they hope to complete next week. (All times are expressed as hours.)

	Processing Times			
Jobs	Process A1	Process B	Process A2	Due
J1	30	45	30	120
J2	30	30	30	144
J3	30	45	15	168

20. If the multiple constraint scheduling algorithm was applied to the data above, which resource(s), if any, would be identified as having first-day load (FDL) peaks?

21. Assuming that resource A has initially been identified as the primary constraint, build its drum schedule. Also, indicate which (if any) due dates will need to be changed. If you need to use any batch rods, use a duration (rod length) of 45 hours.

22. Complete the multiple-constraint scheduling algorithm on the data above and show what schedules would be produced. (The previous use of a 45-hour batch rod would normally suggest that we would attempt to use a 90-hour constraint buffer. However, that will not be possible for process B, since it lies between the two constraint operations, which may be separated only by a batch rod. The good news is that since this is a continuous process, it will be possible to feed the output of process A1 directly to process B, so that work can begin on process B almost immediately after it begins on process A1. Therefore, just plan to accomplish the work on Resource B as early as possible, given the scheduled start times of process A1.)

17

Supply Chain Management

In this chapter we shift our approach to manufacturing planning and control systems from a primary focus on intrafirm integration to one of interfirm integration. Today's MPC frontier is beyond ERP and related systems that coordinate flows of materials and information to optimize performance within one company. Supply chain management has the objective of coordinating these flows *across* companies, recognizing that major improvements are gained in the overall coordination.

Many improvements in company operations have been achieved with MRP/ERP and other factory and business-unit-focused systems. But now the major opportunities lie in more global improvements: MPC systems that achieve synergies through integration across business units—and with suppliers and customers. Examples include rationalization of the total company supplier base, reducing overall supply chain inventories, decreasing chain lead/response times, cutting chain obsolescence costs, reducing time to market, responding faster to marketplace realities, synchronizing cross-firm scheduling, and reducing the "hidden factory" of the chain—by eliminating transactions between firms.

Finally, as was the case for JIT, supply chain management extends the interfirm focus beyond MPC. At the end of the day "world-class supply chains" will deliver the best value/cost solutions to final customers, and set the standards for competitive conditions. But let us be clear on one overriding issue: Achieving supply chain results requires detailed MPC systems. One needs to go beyond the current hype of supply chain partnerships. Making a partnership *function* requires the MPC systems that coordinate the joint working in both companies—the customer and the supplier.

This chapter is organized around three topics:

- *Supply chain management and MPC systems:* What is supply chain management, and what are the implications for MPC systems? That is, what is the shift in emphasis when MPC design focuses on *interfirm* management? What are the problems to be solved and the opportunities for improvement?

- *Supply chain optimization—Examples and supporting MPC systems:* What are some illuminating examples of supply chain management—good and bad—that allow us to see the new MPC system requirements?

- *Enhancements to basic MPC systems:* What are the modifications needed in the classic ERP/JIT-based approaches to manufacturing planning and control systems, and what are the new e-based MPC approaches that support single partner (dyad) supply chain management systems?

This chapter has links to several others, most notably Chapters 1, 4, 8, 9, 10, 13, 18, and 19. Chapter 1 paints our current picture of the latest thinking on MPC systems, which includes an introduction to supply chain thinking. Chapter 4 focuses on ERP and its integration viewpoint; we now need to see where supply chain thinking is (and is not) consistent with this viewpoint. Chapter 8 uses distribution requirements planning to coordinate MPC activity across organizational units. Chapter 9 is devoted to JIT, which is often extended to link firms in a coordinated way, but this is not the only way to achieve the linkage. Chapter 10 includes discussion of capacity management across firms, which is one critical issue in supply chain management. Chapter 18 deals with implementation of MPC systems and examines the differences when the MPC systems focus on cross-organizational (supply chain) optimization. This is particularly important in the implementation of dyad-based MPC systems. Chapter 19 is devoted to the next frontier in manufacturing planning and control; supply chain management is clearly a new frontier for MPC systems. We are only at the beginning stages of supply chain management, about where we were with MRP-based systems 20 years ago.

Supply Chain Management and MPC Systems

Supply chain management represents a major shift in classic MPC thinking. There has been a continuous evolution in MPC approaches, as a more integrated approach to company operations has developed. Thus we have moved from fairly simplified tools for inventory control to the cross-functional integration imbedded in ERP systems. But this evolution has primarily focused on improvements (and further integration) *inside* the firm. Supply chain management has as its focus improvements in two or more units—i.e., an interfirm focus.

Figure 17.1 depicts a customer and a supplier, each operating with our general model for MPC systems. The assumption is that each has been successful, and now uses an ERP system to integrate its business activities. But the connections *between* the two firms are not well developed. Perhaps it is only the vendor systems at the customer [driven by production activity control (PAC)] linking with demand management at the supplier. But there is a potential hierarchy of linkages that might be exploited for common good (i.e., more effective response to the end marketplace). Some of these might be:

Customer		Supplier
PAC vendor systems	$\rightarrow$	Demand management
Material and capacity planning	$\rightarrow$	Material and capacity planning
Capacity planning	$\rightarrow$	Capacity planning
Master production scheduling	$\rightarrow$	Master production scheduling
Sales and operations planning	$\rightarrow$	Sales and operations planning
Resource planning	$\rightarrow$	Resource planning

FIGURE 17.1 Supply Chain Management

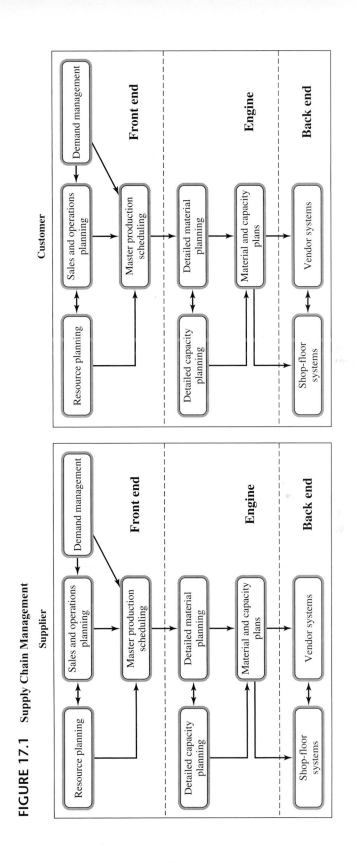

These joint efforts are indeed possible, but they require a great deal of work, as well as dedication by the senior managers in both the customer and the supplier. Moreover, several absolutes of classic MPC thinking are still appropriate: We need to create formal systems to replace informal approaches. *Flawless execution* is the ante to play any game in supply chain management; that is, both firms need to operate with as close to zero defects as possible, production schedules need to be met, the planning horizons in both firms need to be long enough for them to be coordinated, the firms need to operate with minimal buffer inventories, the information linkages need to be in place, and recovery systems need to be in place. Murphy's law dictates that things will go wrong—but thereafter the issue is how quickly they can be fixed. Finally, it is imperative that *both* partners execute flawlessly: the chain is as strong as its weakest link and if either partner makes a mistake, the performance of the chain will suffer.

People need to learn new ways of working and unlearn old habits. We will need new business process reengineering and new information systems. In essence the focus shifts from the classic "lean manufacturing" approach to the "lean supply chain." It is imperative that discussions of supply chain be anchored in key MPC principles. Supply chain management cannot be an abstract concept or some slogan. It *must* encompass the systems and other detailed infrastructure to work in actuality. In all MPC systems, the routine things must be done routinely.

New MPC Linkages

Supply chain management implies a transformation in physical flows, coordination, and MPC systems across company boundaries. The business and its supporting MPC systems are organized less by function, more by cross-company process, and even by customer or customer segment. We need MPC systems that support this shift in organizational emphasis. Figure 17.2 illustrates the problem. In two companies, both are using ERP based MPC systems; each firm focuses on intrafirm integration/optimization, where both firms have

FIGURE 17.2   **Up-Over-Down Processes**

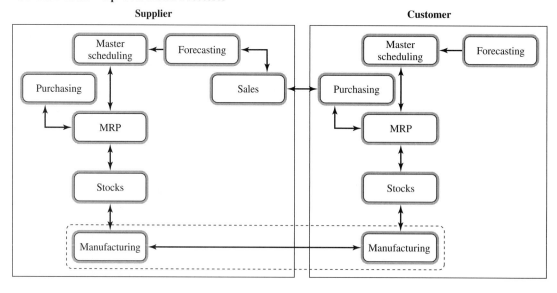

classical functional organizations. But if we look at the two firms together, we see a highly complex set of interactions that will yield long response times, high chain inventories, and potential amplifications in the responses made to requirements. Figure 17.2 shows the customer passing forecasts to its MPS, which generates MRP records based on inventory stocks, which support detailed manufacturing activities. This system is connected to its supplier through a purchasing activity that interacts with the sales function of the supplier firm. The supplier firm follows an ERP-based MPC system similar to that of the customer.

When there is a problem in manufacturing at the customer site (Murphy strikes), what is the response time—i.e., how long does it take to go "up over and down" using traditional MPC systems passing through various functional groups in both firms until the problem is solved, with more parts manufactured at the supplier and delivered? The answer in most cases is weeks. What we need is represented by the arrow in the bottom of Figure 17.2: e-based MPC systems using the Internet that connect the customer manufacturing with its supplier partner, in which the response is in hours or days, not weeks.

It is useful to note that the e-based systems depicted in Figure 17.2 are Web- or Internet-based, which is quite different from the older electronic data interchange (EDI) systems. The latter systems essentially automate existing transaction processes. In the case of Figure 17.2, EDI systems would process the classic up-over-and-down transactions through the functional hierarchy with greater speed. But best practice e-based systems provide visibility of the actual customer situation to the supplier. Moreover, these systems support communications between the customer and supplier for what is the best *joint* way to respond to the situation. This MPC system typically does not utilize orders and other obsolete transactions of classic MPC systems. Instead, the supplier has downstream visibility, allowing it to see problems that must be solved through its actions. It does so without formal ordering by its customer partner. An e-based business-to-business (B2B) system can significantly reduce the total inventories carried by both firms. With the classic MPC systems the supplier carries what it regards as finished items, while the customer carries the same goods as raw materials. Moreover, the requirements at the supplier are based on forecasts and orders (anticipating or guessing what the customers might want and reacting to their orders—which might be surprises). We will see how the e-based system can provide detailed *knowledge* of the customer's plans. Moreover, the time to respond to these plans is greatly shortened, which again allows buffer inventories to be reduced.

Figure 17.2 illustrates still another issue. Perhaps the problem in customer manufacturing involves one or two parts, but the order quantity in its traditional MPC systems is 100 and the manufacturing quantity at the supplier is 500! In the e-based MPC system we pass *exact* information between the partners to solve those problems that directly affect end customers. The e-based system allows the supplier leeway in choosing how much to make and when to deliver it. The exact needs of the customer over time are continually passed back to the supplier, which can decide how it wishes to fulfill them—one big order, several small ones, delivering early, whatever. This allows the supplier to optimize its use of capacity and logistics. The only constraint is that the supplier accept responsibility for supporting the customer and they jointly respond to problems. The customer does not care if the supplier delivers early, since suppliers are paid as supplier parts are converted into finished goods by the customer using **vendor-managed inventory** (VMI).

Figure 17.3 shows the new MPC systems in an overall supply chain context. Here two companies, A and B, are supplied by four different suppliers, which in turn are supplied by

FIGURE 17.3
**Supply-
Demand Chain
Network**

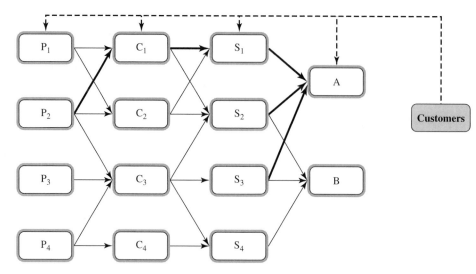

four component manufacturers, with four small part manufacturers even further up the
supply chain. Figure 17.3 shows a multitude of possible connections among these firms,
but also several strong connections, as indicated by the heavier arrows. Company A uses an
e-based system such as described above with its three main suppliers (S_1, S_2, S_3), so each
of them can respond to the exact issues and conditions of the manufacturing floor at company A. Company B, on the other hand uses the classic one-to-one functional approaches
(up-over-down) in dealing with its supply base. There can be little doubt as to which company will have the more competitive supply chain. Moreover, Figure 17.3 also shows heavy
arrows from C_1 to S_1 and from P_2. This overall chain should be more competitive than alternative chains such as P_3 to C_3 to S_4 to B. That is, the first supply chain will be much more
able to respond quickly to the market, it will operate with far less total chain inventory, and
it will be less subject to amplified signals. Moreover, supplier S_2 will learn more working
with company A than B; S_2 will choose to invest time working with its smartest customer,
the one with superior interfirm MPC systems.

Figure 17.3 illustrates one more important concept for supply chain management. The
really great benefits are achieved by MPC designs that are linked on the basis of fulfilling
the ultimate customer needs and working back, rather than starting with the suppliers and
working forward. That is, the term **demand chain** is really more appropriate than supply
chain. The ultimate customer needs should be understood as well as possible by all players
in the chain, with the bundles of goods and services provided by each player having one
overriding goal: maximizing the value/cost to the final customers. This implies coordinated MPC systems that cross organizations and continual reengineering of the joint company MPC systems to improve overall chain value/cost. Supply chain optimization also
recognizes that improvements will often incur extra efforts/costs in one link of the chain,
while achieving the benefits in another. If the benefits are achieved in the same place as the
improvement efforts, most firms are smart enough to take advantage of them. A winning
chain, however, requires nonparochial thinking, open discussions of opportunities, joint
efforts, chain measures of performance, and sharing of benefits.

Finally, true supply chain partnerships are few not many. Most of the arrows depicted in Figure 17.3 are *not* shown with heavy lines. Instead, most of the relationships are of the arms-length variety. Partnerships need to be of mutual interest, and require significant investments of money, energy, and time on the part of the key players in both firms to *implement* cross-firm MPC systems.

Strategic Thinking

Lean manufacturing involves a set of tools/techniques, but it also embodies a strategy: how to dramatically improve the marketplace response while simultaneously achieving a major improvement in cost structure. Lean supply chain embodies a similar goal. Design of a firm's supply chain needs to be seen as strategic, and subsequent operation of that chain will determine success or failure of the company. Supply chain management design is too important to relegate to some minor status or to pass off as an information systems issue. Continual enhancement of the supply chain is one of the best avenues for achieving competitive advantage. Michael Dell put it nicely once:

> If I have 11 days of inventory and my competitor has 80, and Intel comes out with a new chip, I am going to be in the market 69 days sooner.

But how does Dell only hold 11 days of inventory? Dell has virtually no finished goods inventory. Customer orders are assembled and shipped within a day or two of receipt. There is almost no work in process, since the customer orders are fed directly to suppliers who deliver the necessary components within hours. *But* there is another question: Does Dell provide the information to its suppliers in a way that allows them to design and operate excellent MPC systems? That is, at some point the real issue is the total chain performance and total chain inventory:

> A Cisco executive proudly described how the company had achieved $75 million annual savings through its "Virtual Enterprise" supply chain, which connects first-tier suppliers directly to Cisco's fulfillment process. But—oops! Cisco soon thereafter took a $2.5 billion write-down for obsolete inventory, almost all of which was held by its supplier partners!

Cisco also saw its total market capitalization drop to a fraction of its former value about that time. This cannot be totally blamed on supply chain problems, but these certainly played a key role. Let's see how this can happen.

The Bullwhip Effect

For Dell to maintain a true 11-day inventory level, it is essential that information it feeds back to its suppliers is as unbiased as possible. As long as the information is real customer orders and not overoptimistic forecasts of what the customers *might* order, the information is unbiased. The Cisco $2.5 billion write-off was largely due to overoptimistic plans on the part of Cisco that created excessive inventory levels at their suppliers. This is a classic problem with very high growth companies. The fear of inventory shortages leads to overstated needs. As long as the company does grow—even though not quite as fast—the overstated demand problems tend to wash out. But when one experiences a dip in demand, the upsteam amplification (bullwhip effect) can be huge. Thus a key need for MPC systems is one consistent set of numbers passing between supply chain partners, with no extra "windage." Moreover, partners need to be eternally vigilant to detect signs of major disruption.

FIGURE 17.4 Bullwhip Effect

Sales	Beginning Inventory	Ending Inventory	Supplier Orders	Supplier Beginning Inventory	Supplier Ending Inventory	Part Orders
50	100	50	50	100	50	50
55	100	45	65	100	35	95
61	110	49	73	130	57	89
67	122	55	79	146	67	91
74	134	60	88	158	70	106
67	148	81	53	176	123	−17
60	134	74	46	106	60	32
54	120	66	42	92	50	34
49	108	59	39	84	45	39
44	98	54	34	78	44	24

Let us examine how the Dell and Cisco situations might come to pass, and how the MPC systems need to support a supply chain perspective. Figure 17.4 presents a simplified example. Here is a product with sales growing at 10 percent per period for five periods, and then shrinking by 10 percent for five more periods. Let us assume that the company selling this product has a beginning inventory target of two periods of the most recent period sales. Its supplier has exactly the same policy. For simplicity, orders and deliveries are made in the period needed. For example, in period 2 the sales of 55 units result in ending inventory of 45, which is thereafter corrected by an order and delivery of 65 units to bring the period 3 beginning inventory to its desired level of 110 (2 × 55).

Figure 17.4 clearly shows the bullwhip effect. The sales go up 24 percent (50 to 74), and thereafter go down 30 percent (74 to 44). Orders to the supplier go up by 76 percent (50 to 88), and then down by 61 percent (88 to 34). Even more dramatically, orders from the supplier manufacturing for component parts go up by 112 percent (50 to 106) and then down by 100 percent (106 to −17). It is important to note that although this example is focused on inventory effects, similar problems would be extant in manufacturing capacity requirements, response times, and obsolescence (e.g., Cisco).

This example is more real than one might believe. We have seen examples where suppliers have been shut down completely for many weeks when the orders at the end of the supply chain are reduced only slightly. Moreover, this is almost certainly the sort of problem encountered at Cisco. Figure 17.4 does not capture the full story. In reality there are time lags and classic MPC ordering policies that accentuate the problems! Let's take a look at a real (but necessarily more complex) example.

The top half of Figure 17.5 depicts a process to produce and deliver a new tape drive product. As can be seen there are five steps or stages in the process to create the product and get it to the customer. A different firm, each in a different location, provides each step. The bottom half of Figure 17.5 shows the nomalized sales and production based on end-item sales. That is, the end-item sales are set at 100 percent, with the other production values in the supply chain set as percentages of the end-item sales As can be seen, the cumulative sales through distribution are set at 100. That is, the total sales from the beginning of this product launch until the time of the analysis is set to 100 percent. The cumulative

FIGURE 17.5   **Process for Production and Corresponding Sales/Inventories**

Process for tape drive production

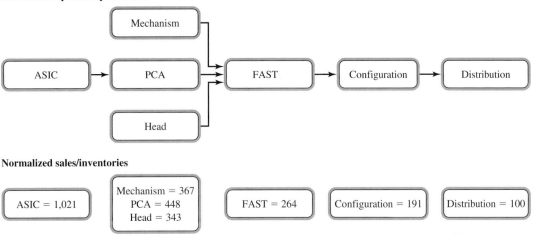

Normalized sales/inventories

production at the configuration stage (where the product is configured to several end models) is 191 (that is, although 100 percent of the product has moved through distribution—i.e., has been sold—91 percent more has been configured into final product specifications and resides somewhere in the supply chain between configuration and sales). At the final assembly and test (FAST) stage, the corresponding cumulative production is 264. At the next upstream stage, we have the three components that are assembled in FAST. For the mechanism the cumulative production is 367, for the printed circuit assembly (PCA) it is 448, and for the head the result is 343. Going still one stage further back, the application-specific integrated circuit (ASIC) has a cumulative production of 1,021. That is, the total ASIC inventory held in the chain is more than 10 times the total sales! But we will see that this is less a result of poor thinking at any one point in the chain than of a lack of overall chain thinking/coordination. In essence, each firm in the chain is operating independently, according to what it sees as its customer demands. If we start with the configuration stage, we see that 91 percent more items have been built than sold. Given that this item comes in several varieties and the company wishes to provide good customer service, "perhaps" this overbuild can be explained. If we next turn to FAST, it has built 264/191 = 138 (38 percent more than needed by its downstream supply chain link). This could be anywhere between the two firms, but it is in fact less of a buildup than at configuration. Indeed, perhaps configuration is screaming for more units from FAST. Ratios for mechanism, PCA, and head to FAST are 139, 169, and 129, respectively, while that of the ASIC to PCA is a whopping 228. But downstream overordering and optimistic forecasting might explain these results.

This is clearly the classic bullwhip effect. Corey Billington and his colleagues at Hewlett-Packard have done some studies to indicate that this effect—on average—tends to inflate or amplify the changes in demand at one stage by about 1.7 at the preceding stage. This implies that total chain amplification is $(1.7)^n$, where n = number of nodes or stages in the supply chain. Applying this logic to Figure 17.5 would yield estimated levels of about

170 for configuration, 290 for FAST, 490 for mechanism/PCA/head, and 840 for the ASIC. These estimates are reasonably consistent with Billington's estimate.

The key question becomes: How can the bullwhip effect be ameliorated? Unfortunately, there are those who believe that one needs to provide only the actual sales information (i.e. 100 in this case) to all levels in the chain. Such is not the case, and we have seen several examples where firms have unsuccessfully tried this approach. The stages shown in Figure 17.5 are independent companies, each responding to what it sees as *its* demands, which are the downstream orders/requirements. FAST has to build at least 191 units for configuration to respond to an uncertain market, in several product varieties. Moreover, there are necessarily in-transit inventories and lag times for transporting materials from stage to stage.

One way out of the problem is illustrated nicely by the growing use of electronic manufacturing service (EMS) firms by major electronics companies. For example, Hewlett-Packard uses Flextronics to make printers in Hungary (and other low-wage-cost locations). Flextronics has developed state-of-the-art plastic injection molding competencies; it can start with plastic raw materials and *deliver* the complete printers to the final customers in only a few days, thereby minimizing chain inventories and being very responsive to actual market conditions. There *is no* opportunity to create a bullwhip effect; the entire chain operates as if it were one integrated unit.

Thus, one solution to the bullwhip problem is to operate the supply chain as one stage. That is, an effective way to attack the $(1.7)^n$ problem is to reduce n. Continuing with the example in Figure 17.5, if an EMS firm built the mechanism, PCA, and head, and at the same time assembled them (the FAST process), then by the $(1.7)^n$ rule the cumulative production at FAST will be 290, while for ASIC it should be 490, a reduction of more than 50 percent.

The benefit of reducing n in the $(1.7)^n$ rule in the upstream supply chain steps (e.g., plastic parts) is also now being achieved by combining downstream steps. That is, EMS firms are extending their MPC systems to manage the downstream logistics from their operations as well. Printers can be delivered from Hungary to final customers in Europe, without field warehouses, within the same time frames as if they came from field warehouses.

Orchestration

Orchestration of a supply chain implies more than coordination and integrated MPC design. In addition to these ideas, one also faces an issue of power. *Who* will take the lead in making which decisions? Who will be the "orchestrator," and who will be the "orchestratee"? How is this going to be decided, how will orchestration be achieved, how will it evolve, and who will drive the evolution? Unfortunately, in far too many cases this is a power game. This is not right; there are natural points for orchestration, and we will show how they should change over time, such as in different phases of the product life cycle. MPC execution in a supply chain context has to be linked across firms and operate fast and efficiently. We must reduce time for endless coordination meetings or suboptimization as individual firms feather their own nests at the cost of the total chain. In fact, improving response times, inventories, and amplification is enhanced through orchestration that reduces or eliminates formal decision-making activities. It is imperative that chain metrics be developed, agreed upon by firms in the chain; thereafter, the most logical player orchestrates to optimize chain measures. In far too many cases, work across firms requires time-consuming joint decision

FIGURE 17.6
Supply Chain
Evolution

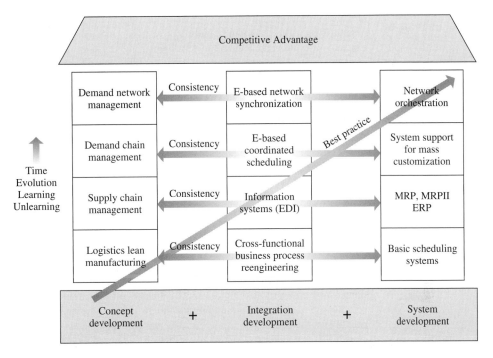

making at particular points, which leads to meetings that can be scheduled only with long lead times. This is particularly so when the firms are working on new product development/introduction.

Orchestration is closely related to the stage of development/integration/coordination in a supply chain. The approach needs to match the objectives of the players, their level of commitment to joint actions, and the MPC systems that support the activity. Figure 17.6 depicts a four-stage process of supply chain evolution, with each stage having a concept development, an integration development, and a system development. Figure 17.6 shows an arrow connecting these three developments, one that notes the need for consistency between the three development efforts in each stage. In the first (intrafirm) stage, the fundamental concept is the desire to achieve improved logistics and lean manufacturing. This requires an integration that focuses on business processes that cross functional lines of authority inside the company. Basic scheduling systems support this stage of supply chain development. Orchestration requires cross-functional integration, and optimizing the resultant processes, often at the expense of traditional functional metrics.

In a specialty chemicals company the efforts were focused on how to coordinate fulfillment of customer promises. The company wished to be able to more quickly respond to customer requests, with greater flexibility, while at the same time significantly reducing its buffer inventories. Orchestration was achieved by empowering a logistics group to coordinate customer order fulfillment. This required MPC systems that linked organizational units in sales, customer order servicing, manufacturing scheduling, and vendor coordination. The customer request became the central driving force; Its processing needed to be handled as one step, instead of what was formerly multiple steps in distinct functional areas (equivalent to reducing n in the $(1.7)^n$ rule). It also necessitated "unlearning" in the functional areas. For example, sales was now focused on developing customer solutions, with routine execution of customer orders handled by logistics. However, although orchestration here in stage 1 is cross-functional, it is largely not cross-organizational.

The second stage shown in Figure 17.6 raises the focus to a first level of interfirm coordination, which we here call supply chain management. The reach includes linkages outside the company, and information systems to support better integration with suppliers. Included is electronic data interchange (EDI), which allows suppliers to receive information from electronic processing of transactions from MRP-, MPPII-, ERP-, and DRP-based systems at the customer. Here the objective is to extend the internal planning generated by classic MPC systems to the suppliers (largely on a one-to-one basis), reducing chain inventories, while also reducing transaction costs and increasing the speed of communication.

> Skanska, a Swedish construction company, was able to set up a consortium with 10 major suppliers and a third-party logistics provider to jointly coordinate their transportation requirements, including all inbound shipments to Skanska building sites, and all outbound shipments for most of the 10 suppliers. The linkage was based on EDI communication of building site plans to the key suppliers and to the logistics provider, which orchestrated deliveries to the construction sites. Skanska was able to reduce its inbound transportation costs by 45 percent, and all of the other firms also achieved major improvements. One of the firms in the consortium, Rockwool, was able to leverage the learning from this smart partnership; Rockwool generated major new business by expanding use of the logistics provider and EDI based MPC systems to sister firms and new customers. The fundamental concept here is to develop detailed internal plans, thereafter execute them flawlessly, and routinely communicate updated plans—electronically—to the suppliers that need to provide the materials.

Orchestration depicted in the second stage is still mostly within the individual companies but now the overall supply chain activity is coordinated, with the focus in each firm on flawlessly executing its ERP-based plans. Orchestration in the supplier companies is largely left to them, but if the connection is one based on JIT-style cooperation, then the orchestration by the customer firm is more intense. Now EDI might be used for conveying the real-time final assembly schedule, as well as the master production schedule for longer-term planning purposes. This second stage again shows an arrow of consistency. This implies the need for consistency between the concept, the integration, and the system, as well as the consistency required to change the orchestration from the first stage to one that supports the second stage.

The concept depicted in the third stage in Figure 17.6 is called "demand chain management." The integration development is e-based coordinated scheduling, and system development is focused on supporting mass customization. The e-based coordinated scheduling can take on several forms, from the classic JIT linkages between supplier and customer, to ones where the customer needs are completely visible to the supplier, and perhaps a third party logistics provider, which have significant flexibility in responding—as long as customer plans are supported. We will examine the mass customization dictates in more detail later in this chapter. Fundamentally implied is the need to jointly cater to more exact needs of customer segments or even individual customers, but to do so easily (routinely). This is well illustrated by the Dell model. Customers can choose from a vast set of end-item configurations, but it is all done quickly with minimal chain inventories. In order to make this a reality, the integration among companies (with suppliers and customers) has to be e-based. This implies a one-to-many relationship, with differing forms of orchestration and rules between the company and its suppliers, depending on the degree of interfirm integration of MPC systems.

> The issue here is well illustrated by a major mobile phone manufacturer that sells both to end consumers and to service providers. The company's MPC philosophy is defined as "plan for capacity, execute to order." This is a firm that is increasingly in make-to-order format, planning the overall capacity needed and creating exact end products only when it has actual orders. The orchestration of the entire supply chain is e-based in order to achieve the end-to-end visibility/linkages, as well as to pass the exact execution requirements to all of the key suppliers on a timely basis. The focal point for the orchestration is the end customers and their precise requirements. The firm has its operations focused on rapidly fulfilling end customer demands with minimal inventories; moreover, the entire chain inventory levels need to be kept low, particularly when new models are being introduced, to reduce chain obsolescence costs. The work of the supplier partners needs to be closely coordinated, while for suppliers of lesser importance the orchestration (and MPC systems) can be more arm's length.

The last stage depicted in Figure 17.6 describes the orchestration of a network of firms. There are few really good examples in existence. The concept can be illustrated by returning to Figures 17.3 and 17.5. In Figure 17.3 we noted the potential advantages gained in responsiveness, inventories, and amplification reduction through joint design of MPC systems that optimize the chain. But in fact it is actually network optimization that is needed. Figure 17.5 shows that a focus on linking one firm in the chain with only its immediate customer can lead to the bullwhip effect. E-based synchronization of the network requires Web-based systems allowing visibility to the upstream chain providers of *all* downstream chain requirements, not just those of its most immediate customer. Moreover, the e-based systems should be able to provide all downstream players complete information on upstream production plans, execution of those plans, and all chain inventories. The final link in the chain (e.g., company A in Figure 17.3) needs to look carefully at the overall network performance; all imperfections will, in the end, reflect in the cost structure and in the ability to delight their customers! A large telecom manufacturer has this kind of visibility for many of its key upstream suppliers. Real-time information on production and quality is tracked in EMS factories such as Solectron. These data are incorporated into a Web-based system that allows the telecom manufacturer to monitor actual detailed production of its products—in supplier factories—and see potential problems.

Network optimization can be enhanced by use of **hubs** between the stages in the chain. A hub can be seen as a physical warehouse, or in fact a virtual warehouse where a third party distribution provider takes possession of the goods but can keep them anywhere—including on trucks! The use of hubs is particularly useful in the case of a finished goods manufacturer such as Dell or an EMS and its immediate suppliers. All inventories are best placed in one place, near the point of use (the finished goods manufacturer or EMS). Having finished goods inventories at the suppliers as well as at the EMS will aggravate the bullwhip effect, and impede joint efforts to develop MPC orchestration of joint work.

Returning to Figure 17.3, the connection between say S_1 and A, or S_1 and C_1, with a classic MPC approach would be to hold finished stock at S_1 and the same incoming stock at A, and similar stocks between C_1 and S_1. This is not only duplication of stocks. The incoming stocks can be used to solve stock shortages that occur for whatever reasons, while the finished stocks do not serve this purpose. It makes sense to not keep finished stocks at a supplier unless there are multiple customers to be served. Hubs are increasingly being used for this purpose, usually run by third-party logistics providers who manage flows of goods into and out of the hub, and provide security for the goods and clear transactions/processes when title passes. Use of hubs requires new MPC connections, often provided by hub operators. More important, hub use requires a change in mind set and a focus on overall chain costs and benefits.

Finally, depicted in Figure 17.6 are the notions of evolution over time and the need for continuous learning—as well as the need to *unlearn* many things. As a firm develops its supply chain initiatives it will need to adopt new ways of working supported by new detailed MPC systems. This implies learning new things as well as unlearning some old things. There will be major changes in the ways people work, and the goals to be achieved. Supply chain management needs to be seen as not some zero-sum game to be played with customers or suppliers. All firms can win if—and only if—the resultant supply chain is planned and controlled by MPC systems better than those in the other chains that compete for the same end consumers.

Supply Chain Optimization—Examples and Supporting MPC Systems

In this section we show some examples of supply chain opportunities, and the new MPC systems that are needed to achieve the desired results.

There was once a famous American criminal named Willy Sutton who when asked why he robbed banks replied "Because that is where the money is." The money today is in cross-company MPC design and implementation. It is increasing the value/cost ratio for the chain, not just for one company. Moreover, it is both numerator and denominator that need to be improved; this is not an either/or question. In focusing on the numerator, we will see how we need to now expand our set of objectives for supply chain management beyond the classical MPC measures. Moreover, we will see in this series of examples how the interactions between supply chain partners continues to take on an expanded improvement agenda. Finally, we will examine the detailed changes in MPC systems required to turn the promise into reality.

Suboptimal MPC Design in a Paint Supply Chain

Chain cost reduction can yield great improvements, but one does need a chain focus (and chain-based MPC systems):

> We once examined a chain of four firms consisting of a steel manufacturer, a can producer, a paint-making company, and a retailer of the paints. All four firms were losing money, each was trying to lower costs, but each was doing so by attempting to shift cost to another player in the chain. But analysis indicated that the overall chain held *40 weeks* of inventory! Moreover, final customers were interested in innovations, which take 40 weeks to reach the market and were not perceived as valuable by any of the four members independently.

Let us examine how independent (intrafirm) MPC design and execution exacerbated this problem:

- The retailer had one central warehouse to serve 100 stores. It utilized an EOQ/ROP system, and ABC analysis for products. It had experienced a steady growth in stock keeping units (SKUs) and increasing inventories of "dogs" (low-selling items). The approach to cost reduction was to demand shorter delivery lead times and lower lot sizes from the paint manufacturer, and make these adjustments in the values of their EOQ/ROP system. Lower lot sizes imply higher transaction costs plus greater exposure to stock outs.
- The paint manufacturer utilized an MRPII system. Lower-volume, more frequent orders from the retailer did not change overall forecast volumes. The MRP system used the same lot sizes (based on changeover costs), but shipping and order servicing costs were increased. The response was to also attempt to lower inventories, demanding shorter delivery lead times and batch sizes that more closely matched the manufacturing lot sizes.
- The can manufacturer also used MRP-based systems. The lower lot sizes delivered to the paint manufacturer resulted in larger inventories. The can manufacturer also faced increasing product variety, changing customer demands, and higher transaction costs. Its approach was to decouple can manufacturing from can painting, holding more unpainted cans and less painted, and paint to order when possible. Finally, it pushed the steel company to provide steel on a **vendor-managed inventory** (VMI) basis ("in order to get it off our books").
- The steel manufacturing firm also used MRP-based MPC systems. Fulfilling the VMI request now caused it to have higher inventories and complex transaction processing (how/when to invoice for the VMI at the customer site). The company was experimenting with smaller runs, but this made shop scheduling much more difficult.

An analysis of this problem led to an interfirm MPC design that would probably work: Send back exact inventory status and end-item sales at retail daily to the paint and can manufacturers. Jointly schedule these two firms so that cans are quickly painted, the exact quantity of paint is prepared at the same time to exactly fill the batch of cans, cans that arrive at the paint company one day are filled and shipped the following day, there are no "orders" from the retailer, and paint is maintained at retail under VMI conditions. The response times with this scenario could be less than one week, there would be no inventories at the paint manufacturer, no inventories of painted cans at the can manufacturer, and inventories at retail would reflect the economics of batch sizes in can/paint production. Moreover, the time it would take to introduce a new product would be greatly reduced, plant capacities could be better utilized, and the hidden factory costs of transactions would also be cut significantly. This could be a great win-win situation, but, alas, it was not possible to optimize the overall network, because there was not a trusting relationship among the four players, nor a willingness to renegotiate prices to achieve the overall objective. The costs to be borne by the various parties do not reflect immediate savings in their domains (this is particularly so for the paint manufacturer, which in essence assumes the cost of inventory at retail).

An Interfirm MPC Example for Coordinated Packaging

Let us now see how a totally different MPC approach can be developed—one that optimizes the overall supply chain. Figure 17.7 depicts a real but slightly disguised situation. Here two companies, "Alpha Food Products" and "Beta Packaging," work jointly. We

FIGURE 17.7
Linked Planning Processes Example: The Souper Soup Package

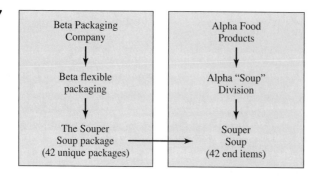

concentrate on one product group, "Souper Soup," which is sold in 42 end varieties (the actual product is not soup, but it too is sold in 42 end varieties). Each end item has a unique package created by Beta that protects the product in a special way. Figure 17.8 depicts an ABC analysis of the 42 items (slightly altered to facilitate subsequent calculations). As can be seen, 8 items represent 70 percent of the total sales (A's), 14 account for 20 percent (B's), and the remaining 20 account for the last 10 percent (C's).

Beta manufactures a special flexible package fabricated from three layers of plastic film. One layer is polyethylene (PE) that Beta makes, while the other two are purchased. The three films are laminated, then printed with the special product descriptions and thereafter delivered to Alpha. Figure 17.9 provides the process analysis, with the various inventories and the MPC systems utilized. Total order-to-delivery time was eight weeks. Alpha wanted an annual price reduction of 15 percent, and suggested that Beta achieve this by implementing JIT, providing packaging to Alpha on a VMI basis. Beta reduced printing lot sizes by one-half, putting them closer to a make-to-order basis. But this approach by the two firms is again wrong-headed; it is focused on intrafirm improvements at Beta, not on MPC approaches that optimize the supply chain. The "end-to-end" solution is shown in Figure 17.10, where scheduling of the entire chain is synchronized. Now, the Beta laminating process is directly linked to the Alpha build process, with *no* intermediate inventory. The two purchased films are bought on a VMI basis. Printing is done *before* laminating, which means that the investment in product specific inventory is now only for one film layer instead of three.

The major MPC innovation is the synchronization of the schedules. Alpha builds on a fixed schedule: A's items are made every week, B's every second week, and C's every fourth week. Alpha sets its schedule for week 2 on Monday of week 1. Beta laminates to this schedule during week 1, and delivers to Alpha before the start of week 2. The scheduling algorithm at Alpha is quite simple, and transparent to Beta. Every week, Alpha executes a fixed schedule of 20 products: the eight A items, one-half of the 17 B's, and one-quarter of the 20 C's. At the same time, Beta is laminating the packaging materials for the following week's schedule at Alpha. The schedule development for Alpha is straightforward:

- A items = 2 × forecasted weekly sales − present inventory + safety stock
- B items = 3 × forecasted weekly sales − present inventory + safety stock
- C items = 5 × forecasted weekly sales − present inventory + safety stock
- All quantities could be rounded to "rolls" of printed material
- Adjustments could be made to smooth overall capacity

FIGURE 17.8
Linked
Planning
Processes
Example: ABC
Analysis

Package	Estimated weekly sales
1	100
2	86
3	85
4	85
5	83
6	81
7	80
8	80

$\Sigma = 700$ (packages 1–8)

Package	Estimated weekly sales
9	20
10	18
11	18
12	18
13	17
14	16
15	14
16	13
17	13
18	13
19	10
20	10
21	10
22	10

$\Sigma = 200$ (packages 9–22)

Package	Estimated weekly sales
23	6
24	6
25	6
26	6
27	6
28	6
29	6
30	6
31	5
32	5
33	5
34	5
35	5
36	5
37	5
38	4
39	4
40	3
41	3
42	3

$\Sigma = 100$ (packages 23–42)

The benefits in the overall chain are inventory reductions, less scrap and obsolescence, better capacity utilization, fewer stockouts, production efficiencies, reduced ordering and other transaction costs, simplified purchasing/selling, fewer rush orders, and a much more predictable working environment. These do, however, require significant joint efforts.

Interfirm Reengineering Drives MPC Design for Airline Catering

The key lessons to be derived from the paint/cans and soup/packages examples is that one can make major improvements only by cross-firm integration efforts, supported by appropriate

FIGURE 17.9 **Linked Planning Processes Example: Process Analysis**

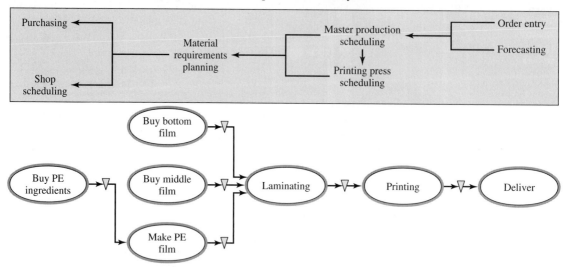

Total lead time (order to deliver) = 8 weeks
Printing lot size *was* 100, now cut to 50
Customer requests 15% price reduction per year, suggests JIT, VMI

FIGURE 17.10 **Linked Planning Processes Example: End-to-End Solution**

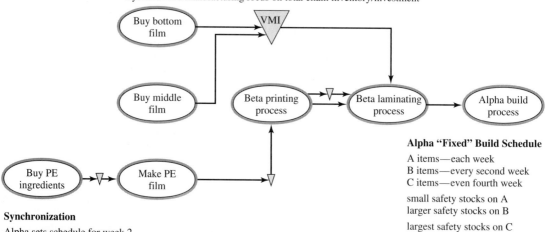

Synchronization

Alpha sets schedule for week 2
on Monday of week 1.

Beta laminates to schedule
during week 1. No inventory
between Beta and Alpha.

MPC systems and flawless execution. Continuous improvements on an intrafirm basis are always an important objective in any company. But the payoffs here need to be seen as limited. It is interfirm supply chain enhancements that will provide transformative improvements. Costs need to be taken out of the chain, not pushed from one player to the next. Costs are taken out through joint business process reengineering on new ways of doing business, with supporting MPC systems. But the approach needs to not be parochial. Often chain costs are reduced by actions that add costs to one player, with the benefits achieved by another. Appropriate price adjustments need to support true win-win.

Another best practice in supply chain reengineering is demonstrated with Gate Gourmet, one of the largest airline catering firms. Here one can see the focus as encompassing more than improved materials flow: The objective is how to make life more pleasant (and profitable) for your customers. This is the way to dominate the industry, but doing so requires design and implementation of MPC systems to accomplish whatever is necessary. Instead of the classic airline practice—specifying meals, receiving price quotations, and thereafter ordering meals from particular catering units—Gate Gourmet reengineered the processes and MPC systems to work effectively with its customers.

> For the airlines, Gate Gourmet makes it very easy to do business, taking over work from the airlines that Gate Gourmet can do much more effectively. For example, it is Gate Gourmet that decides on menus, on the basis of whatever can be purchased most effectively to provide best value/cost to the airline passengers. The MPC systems are similarly designed with a customer focus. All billing comes directly from the customer's passenger manifests. That is, the number of meals billed on a particular flight comes directly from the airline passenger record for that flight. There is little "forecasting," since Gate Gourmet knows which flights leave each city at specified times each day. Moreover, the actual "make-to-order" adjustments are easily handled, since passengers on all flights out of Boston on Tuesday (on all airlines catered by Gate Gourmet) eat chicken. There are no extra transactions for the customer firms and no need to check invoices since all billing is based on existing customer records. Moreover, the secret to the success of Gate Gourmet is that it recognizes that its core competency has to be logistics (moving boxes on and off airplanes) and the MPC systems to support logistics, rather than cooking (airline food quality has to be only "good enough"). The boxes can contain almost anything—newspapers, duty free goods, etc. The underlying MPC systems and approaches are the same for all customers and all boxes. Exact airline customer needs are passed electronically from customer records, with no bullwhip effect, and are executed in what amounts to a make-to-order environment. The customer needs are based only on passenger numbers. Airlines do not specify meals, except for nonstandard meals such as Kosher or vegetarian (but again exact choice is up to Gate Gourmet). The process and invoicing have been simplified so that the variable portion of catering costs depends only on exact passenger counts.

There is another key lesson in this example. Once Gate Gourmet worked out how to do this with one airline customer, it was relatively straightforward to do so with others. That is, the MPC systems are modular and adaptive to multiple locations, customers, and situations. The only critical interface is in passing passenger manifests to Gate Gourmet. Once these data are captured, the same MPC systems are used for routine execution. Each new airline customer is easier to serve, since most catering ingredients can be the same (e.g., all business class passengers on flights leaving Los Angeles tomorrow eat beef).

Gate Gourmet went on to work backward in its supply chain, applying the same kind of "easy to do business with" (minimum transactions) approach:

Gate Gourmet has made a contract with Diversy-Lever, a supplier of cleaning supplies, where all cleaning supplies (dishwashing soap, floor cleaner, etc.) are provided to all Gate Gourmet locations worldwide. There are no invoices, no orders, or other low-value-adding transactions. Diversy-Lever is paid a fixed price per year as a percentage of Gate Gourmet sales. The MPC is quite simple. Execution is achieved by a periodic visit by Diversy-Lever to a Gate Gourmet location, leaving enough material that the location does not run out before the next visit (a min-max system). Diversy-Lever keeps simple records of overall usage of each material at each location to identify best/poor usage practices. Emphasis at Diversy-Lever has shifted from selling more soap to helping Gate Gourmet use just the right amount. This illustrates supply chain optimization: Before Diversy-Lever was happy to see its customers waste cleaning products! The partnership has been such a good arrangement, that Diversy-Lever now provides this bundle of goods and services to other customers, such as fast food chains. The company leveraged what it learned from a smart customer.

Gate Gourmet has been a "smart partner" for both its customers and its suppliers. We also see that Diversy-Lever has been able to leverage the learning gained by working with this smart partner. This means that when Gate Gourmet has another new idea, it is likely to find enthusiastic participation from Diversy-Lever. The customer that is able to attract the best suppliers to work closely with will achieve a competitive advantage. One does not develop loyal suppliers only by good prices and large contracts: learning, competency development, networking relationships, joint improvement projects, MPC system development, and other infrastructure elements are critical to a supplier that wishes to be the best. Smart suppliers will be attracted to smart customers!

Nokia's Superior MPC Systems for Supply Chain Management

Inventory costs are a basic indicator of supply chain practice and are directly related to competitive stature. Figure 17.11 provides an interesting comparison of six similar firms. The *y* axis is inventory days of supply, and the *x* axis is time. At the bottom is Dell, running along at about 10 days of supply. Next is Compaq at about 30, more or less, then Nokia, which has come down from about 70 days to the low 40s. Then we see Cisco going along

FIGURE 17.11
Inventory Days of Supply (DOS)

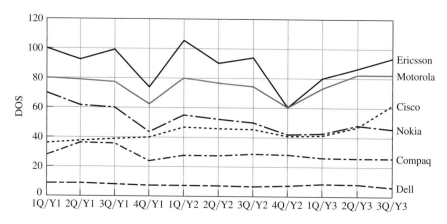

at about 40 with a major move up in the last two quarters. Then we see Motorola starting at about 80 days coming down to 60 but then going back up again. Finally, we see Ericsson starting at about 100 days, coming down but fluctuating greatly. A specialist in this industry tells us that 10 days of inventory is equal to 1 percentage point return on sales to the bottom line. The basic calculation for this rule of thumb is the following:

- Inventory carrying cost = 2% per month
- Obsolescence cost = 1% per month
- Component price reductions = 2% per month
- Total inventory holding cost = 5% per month (2% + 1% + 2%)
- Material cost = 60% of sales price
- Therefore holding cost = 3% of sales price per month (5% × 60%)
- Therefore 10 days of inventory = 1% of sales (assuming 30 days in a month)

Applying this rule of thumb to the data in Figure 17.11 means that Nokia can earn 3 percent more than its competitors Ericsson and Motorola. Additionally, if Nokia gained 2 percent by coming down 20 days, it can be expected that Ericsson and Motorola lost more than that amount by going up, because they will face even greater obsolescence costs. Finally, Figure 17.11 shows only the inventories at these firms. The true comparison should be the *chain* inventories, including those of the major suppliers for the firms. In fact, during this period, the suppliers for Cisco in particular were experiencing very large inventory buildups (and the bullwhip effect). But now let us focus our attention on comparing the MPC systems in the three Telecom firms.

The first question to answer is why Ericsson and Motorola experienced these problems while Nokia does not appear to have done so. A large part of the answer lies in better MPC systems for the Nokia supply chain, coupled with better execution. If the MPC systems between the firms are poorly connected one will get the bullwhip effect. Nokia experienced it in 1995 and learned its lesson. At that time the company was growing rapidly, and problems in overstating needs to suppliers were solved by growth. But when this growth moderated, Nokia was in trouble, since it simultaneously had high inventories of the wrong parts and high inventories of the wrong finished goods. All of these inventories were decreasing in value, while the company could not take advantage of decreasing electronic part prices, since it held inventories of those components.

The solution was for Nokia to transform its MPC systems and approaches from a functional base to one based on supply chain management. The top half of Figure 17.12 shows the new thinking. As can be seen, the scope of Nokia's supply chain management extends to new technology sourcing, product program materials management, and purchasing. This also can be seen as encompassing research and advanced development, concurrent engineering, and product engineering/global logistics. The focus is on MPC systems that plan and schedule existing products. Further, it is essential that each new product generation be brought to market with a predictable pattern, where Nokia can determine when its new product designs will obsolete their old ones. MPC systems have to include project planning and management of new product designs, product launches, ramp-ups, steady-state operations, and end-of-life phaseouts. The MPC systems include basic ERP systems, but they are more inclusive in scope and work practices. To make the top half of Figure 17.12 operational, five teams were formed that focus on particular component groups (electronics, electromechanical, mechanical,

FIGURE 17.12

Nokia Supply Chain Management Structure

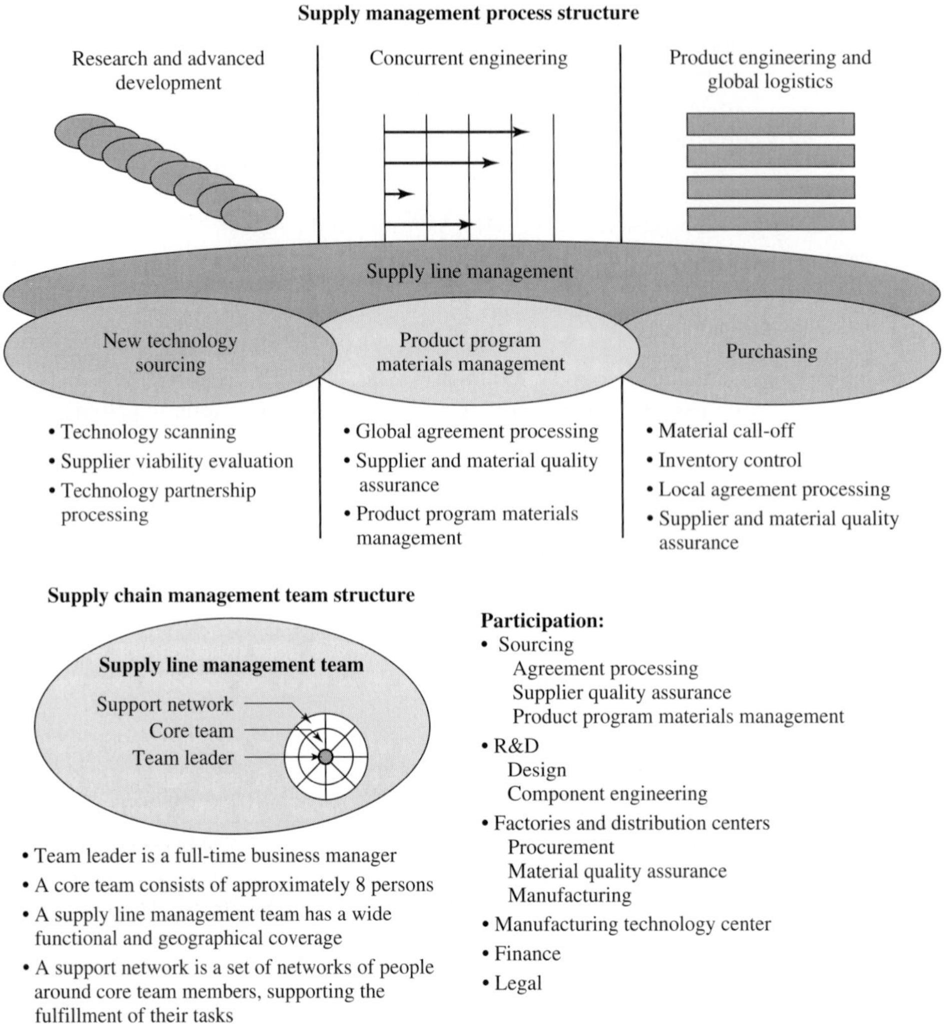

Supply management process structure

Research and advanced development

Concurrent engineering

Product engineering and global logistics

Supply line management

New technology sourcing

Product program materials management

Purchasing

- Technology scanning
- Supplier viability evaluation
- Technology partnership processing

- Global agreement processing
- Supplier and material quality assurance
- Product program materials management

- Material call-off
- Inventory control
- Local agreement processing
- Supplier and material quality assurance

Supply chain management team structure

Supply line management team

Support network
Core team
Team leader

- Team leader is a full-time business manager
- A core team consists of approximately 8 persons
- A supply line management team has a wide functional and geographical coverage
- A support network is a set of networks of people around core team members, supporting the fulfillment of their tasks

Participation:
- Sourcing
  Agreement processing
  Supplier quality assurance
  Product program materials management
- R&D
  Design
  Component engineering
- Factories and distribution centers
  Procurement
  Material quality assurance
  Manufacturing
- Manufacturing technology center
- Finance
- Legal

accessories, and investments). The bottom half of Figure 17.12 shows the team structure for each of these supply chain management teams. Each product, going through its life cycle, can be managed by planning/coordinating its needs by these supply line management teams.

The supply chain management teams are highly cognizant of what is happening in the detailed operations of their key suppliers. This comes back to flawless execution. Nokia must have flawless execution by its suppliers. A critical example is in fact illustrated by the problems shown for Motorola and Ericsson in Figure 17.11. The extra inventories made these firms less responsive to problems in their supplier firms. A significant illustration was a time when a Philips chip plant in the United States experienced a fire that disrupted production of a key mobile phone component. Nokia knew of the problem almost immediately (MPC systems need to provide detailed information on execution—in the chain!). Nokia went immediately to Philips with a plan for how to compensate. Philips agreed to the plan,

FIGURE 17.13

The Nokia 3 × 3 Transformation Model

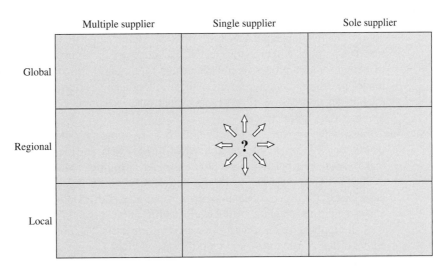

Nokia sailed through the problem, while other mobile phone companies became aware of the issue only when their orders were not fulfilled. One must have MPC systems and practices that do *more* than good routine execution; key problems need to be escalated to executives who can act, but do so on the basis of solid MPC information and requirements.

Figure 17.13 is a model that Nokia uses to categorize the nine potential relationships it might have with each of its suppliers. Every supplier can be categorized as a multiple supplier, a single supplier, or a sole supplier. Moreover, the suppliers can also be categorized as global, regional, or local. The difference between single supplier and sole supplier is whether Nokia has a choice. That is, a sole supplier is the only one that can provide the item. A single supplier also uniquely provides the item, but it is Nokia's choice; another supplier could be found.

The critical lesson in Figure 17.13 is that any time Nokia (along with a supplier) moves from one of the nine boxes to another, it creates a transformation of the supply chain, MPC systems, and orchestration that requires significant changes in *both* firms (neither can just do the same things better). When Nokia asked a Finnish supplier to supply all of its European needs, this was more than an increase in business. Both firms needed to redesign their MPC systems and processes to integrate the needs/demands of all European factories to coordinate logistics, order handling, etc. The supplier needed visibility into detailed planning systems in each of the Nokia factories to be supported. Nokia, on the other side, needed to be sure that the planning methods used in each of those factories were consistent in design and execution so that requirements data could indeed be aggregated across plants. As long as the supplier remained in the "multiple column," Nokia also needed to determine *which* specific plant requirement data to pass to this supplier. Information linkages were continually evolving, from classic purchase orders to EDI and then to e-based connections.

A shift from multiple suppliers to a single supplier implies an even greater commitment, since this firm is now the only source of the particular item. The implication is that the two firms move more closely together, with partnership seen by both as desirable. This implies a set of shared values and objectives—continuous improvement and perhaps **early supplier involvement** (ESI) for new products. Now, the joint work—and MPC systems—need to focus on joint new product development, utilizing the competencies of both supplier and customer. Making an explicit choice to shift from multiple to single puts both firms on notice: The relationship needs to be different. Doing better things jointly becomes imperative. The partners will probably need to exchange personnel for some extended time period to reengineer joint processes and supporting MPC approaches. For example, orders may no longer be required, with joint inventories in the chain systematically reduced. But as the relationship moves toward a single, global one, execution excellence—in both firms— becomes even more critical.

Finally, for any firm, categorizing each of its suppliers (and customers!) in this 3×3 matrix forces it to make choices as to which to work with, and the kinds of MPC linkages that make sense with particular supplier/customer categories. Making this thinking explicit implies an improved ability to develop and share best MPC practices with supply chain partners. That is, the firm can examine performance across all suppliers or customers in a particular category, and encourage joint work on MPC improvements. But it is not possible to work with all suppliers (or customers) on some uniform basis. The improvement agenda is different for different categories, and for different suppliers. Conscious choices are required.

MPC Enhancements to Support Outsourcing

As firms such as Nokia and Hewlett-Packard grow, there is an increasing need to expand the horizons of supply chain thinking (and supporting MPC systems), working on a diverse set of topical issues. Outsourcing is one major area, since it naturally leads to one company taking over activities formerly done by another, and these activities encompass more than routine materials planning. Outsourcing to the electronic manufacturing services (EMS) companies provides a prime example. Increasingly, they are becoming much more than providers of basic products. In the interaction between an EMS company and an OEM, we see four distinct phases that need to be understood (see Figure 17.14):

1. The first phase is new product development. Here the joint focus with the outsourcing EMS partner needs to be on product design with the best market appeal. This implies

FIGURE 17.14   Different Phases of the Product Life Cycle Require Different Approaches

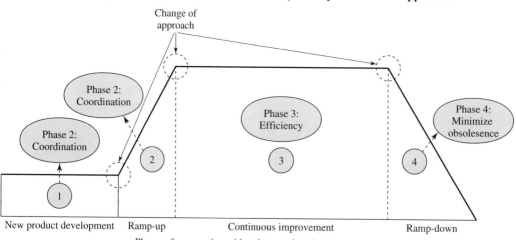

MPC system linkages to support **design for manufacturing** (DFM), early supplier involvement (ESI), use of the best competencies in both firms, and speed. This implies a project-based interaction between the customer and the EMS, supported by project MPC systems that drive toward a clearly articulated end point.

2. At that point, new product development definitively passes to the ramp-up phase. This now requires a new interaction, a revised cast of characters, and highly adaptive MPC systems that focus on providing the right amount of materials in this very uncertain environment. In this phase it is often the case that the two firms need to work very closely together, since some required components are provided by one and some by the other. The goal now is to come to market as quickly as possible, with a flawless product. Mistakes here can be tremendously costly, and the best efforts of both firms are required. Any necessary design modifications need to be implemented quickly, with minimal obsolescence, and the capacity needs to be adjusted to whatever the market requires. It is here that the EMS firms bring a major competency to the benefit of the chain.

3. The third phase is continuous improvement of the chain, often now based on taking cost out of the chain. Included are implementing better logistics, shifting manufacturing to a lower-wage area, improving design, developing better processes, reducing inventories, etc. Again, the cast of characters needed to do this is different, and the chain-based MPC systems to support it are different as well. The major change in MPC emphasis is for the EMS firm to take over the vast majority of the detailed MPC execution and orchestration. Here a key goal is to run with a very lean supply chain that maximizes the inventory turnover rate.

4. Finally we enter the ramp-down phase. Here good (and different) work is essential. Joint MPC systems need to be fine tuned, with coordination of all chain inventories. The MPC systems also need to be coordinated with key customers to establish final closeout dates, with downstream inventories managed so that downstream chain stages experience minimal obsolescence as well.

Best practice throughout this cycle requires that the partners in the chain have a shared understanding of their different roles in each of the phases. Being clear as to what they are, how to work in the differing circumstances, and to whom batons are to be passed is critical. The joint MPC system support has to match the needs of each phase. To the extent that the partners can develop a clear set of phases such as those described above, it should be possible to continually improve, learning from each product development. Application of EMS best practices supports these efforts. For example, if several stages in this supply chain are colocated it will be possible to create the total product as if it were a single step rather than a series of independent stages to be individually optimized.

MPC Systems to Support Quality in Complex Supply Chains

Partnering in supply chain management is increasingly concerned with better product design, rapid time to market, and subsequent smooth flows of materials through the network and out to the customers. But one very challenging issue comes from the need to monitor quality and provide traceability in complex supply chains. For this reason, best practice quality management is being integrated into MPC systems. It is not enough to only schedule the manufacture and distribution of products; it is increasingly important that the MPC systems ensure that products are manufactured to the right standards with the right-quality ingredients. Moreover, MPC systems need to keep track of where those products are in the distribution chain, and support the proper response when a quality problem occurs. This is particularly critical for food companies, and today's more complex supply chains exacerbate the problem.

> Some years ago, Nestlé was a firm that had many factories in different countries, largely manufacturing for local consumption. That is—by and large—the ingredients were grown, the products were manufactured, and they were sold to the trade, purchased, and consumed in the same country. Moreover, Nestlé did most of the manufacturing steps itself. In today's world, a much more regional approach is used, with a complex supply chain. Soy beans might be purchased in South America, processed into oil by a subcontractor, made into some intermediate product in France, processed further in Germany, sold to a wholesaler in The Netherlands, retailed in Saudi Arabia, purchased by a person returning to the Philippines, and consumed there. MPC systems are a key part of making all this possible. But at any point in this complex supply chain some problem could arise because of mishandling, heat, etc. If a person becomes ill from eating this product, it is imperative to find the cause quickly and forestall others who might be at a similar risk. The MPC systems need to support this effort. For some products such as those sold through duty-free shops, they might be transported long distances before being consumed—and one's assumptions about the product use might be incorrect. An interesting case in point was Nestlé sales in duty-free shops. One would normally think this outlet would be for selling chocolate, but in fact Nestlé found that large sales of powdered milk were possible in some duty-free shops. This was particularly the case for airports where Philippine maids were returning home. The milk was a good value and appreciated by relatives in the Philippines. Nestlé packaged the product in large tins, only to find empty tins in the airport washrooms, where passengers had put the milk into plastic bags, easier to carry. Nestlé worried about contamination from used plastic bags as well as exposure to other contaminants, so the package was changed to strong plastic bags (sealed).
>
> There are many other examples of complex traceability issues, such as how to trace products removed from full pallets, and food service sales to both well-run customers (e.g., Disneyland) as well as street vendors. In each of these supply chains, the MPC systems at Nestlé need to work jointly with those of suppliers and customers. Some of these firms have good MPC systems support, but others have almost nothing. Nestle continually searches for foolproof product solutions and better quality throughout the entire chain.

A related MPC issue of quality in the supply chain is how to reduce inspection and other transaction costs. Reducing the total chain cost needs to be the goal, recognizing that earliest prevention is usually the least expensive measure. Quality systems also need to be integrated across firms, and these are usually combined with classic MPC systems, which collect information on product creation steps. This is the natural point to also collect quality information. For some industries such as mobile phones, final product quality in use can be highly dependent upon the age of certain components. Electronic components, surface mounted on circuit boards, are held by a paste that fails more often when components are older, with greater oxidation on their connecting surfaces. This is more serious for mobile phones, which are constantly jostled, than for desktop computers. The supply chain must provide fresh components, and the MPC systems need to *know* the components are fresh. Freshness is directly related to inventories/time in the total chain: Lower inventories = fresher components!

> Making all this real implies complex MPC systems that support the levels of tracability required. Flextronics has what at first glance seems an overly complex production activity control (PAC) system that can be applied to its box assembly processes. It has bar-code readers at each station, where specific components are linked to serial-numbered end

products. Moreover, the system will not process an assembly step if the prior step has not been recorded as complete. The data are recorded in real time and incorporated in a system that can be monitored by Flextronics' customers. This kind of system could be extended to the suppliers of Flextronics to create chain tracability (e.g., to ensure the fresh components required by Nokia), it could allow joint work on quality improvement (e.g., joint 6-sigma efforts on linked products/processes), and it could also be extended downstream to customers in various ways (e.g., to Flextronics' customers in particular instances).

Enhancements to Basic MPC Systems

Supply chain management requires important modifications in some classic MPC systems. Many systems that make sense for intrafirm integration do not work as well—and sometimes not at all—for interfirm integration. We start by considering some basic MPC design issues, and then turn to the enhancements and changes needed for the classic ERP-based system. Thereafter we turn to enhancements of JIT-oriented supply chains. Finally, we consider a new set of ideas related to developing specific linkages between supply chain partner pairs, that is, in dyads.

MPC Design Issues

Best-practice supply chains require much more than good will, cooperative spirit, and shared objectives. At the end of the day, true supply chain partnerships need to function as one integral unit; that is, virtual integration is the goal. This can be achieved only through new business linkages supported by integrated MPC system design. Let us briefly overview some of the key MPC system issues.

For a company such as Hewlett-Packard that is increasingly outsourcing more and more of its manufacturing and distribution, there is an important need to periodically examine with its outsourcing partners whether they have the right strategic focus for their MPC integration (and orchestration). With Hewlett-Packard concentrating on new product design and marketing, does it, for example, make sense for customer data to flow directly from the marketplace to an electronic manufacturing services (EMS) supplier like Flextronics? When might it be smart for the supplier to assume final distribution, what are the MPC requirements, and how do both firms come to understand the necessary shift in orchestration?

> This is a complex set of questions. To some extent, the lessons of Gate Gourmet are useful: Why not let the EMS supplier do as much as possible and only pass summary information to its OEM customer? In this case the classic detailed MPC processes and orchestration would reside with the EMS firm, with the OEM having little knowledge of how the detailed execution works. But applying the kinds of MPC systems such as that used for production activity control at Flextronics could allow an OEM customer to have as much access to details as the customer chooses. Following this logic implies a great amount of trust/confidence between the supply chain partners.

A more general MPC issue concerns the right time to shift the focus for orchestration from a customer to a supplier—and what does this in fact mean? The supplier has to adapt its MPC systems to support this shift. But thereafter it will be the supplier, not the customer, that is driving the change in orchestration, and the customer needs to become comfortable with this shift. The best practicing EMS firms are developing superior systems for component supplier linkages, since the EMS firms are the major customer to these component suppliers, who are increasingly concentrating their volumes on a reduced number of "customers." In these cases the EMS can do a superior job of integrating detailed MPC systems with the component suppliers. But the EMS customers need to become comfortable with the idea of not purchasing their basic components and giving up some (but not all) of their relationships with the component suppliers.

This orchestration might be different for new product development linkages, and for particularly critical components in a product. OEM firms often wish to work with both an EMS company for manufacture of its products as well as with key component suppliers as design partners in early supplier involvement. But this in turn requires good ways to pass the baton from the early supplier involvement suppliers to the EMS for detailed manufacturing. Moreover, it is important to understand that at some point the relationships and interests shift from new product development to ramp-up and steady-state manufacturing. These shifts imply a different focus for orchestration.

Several of the examples in this chapter raise another critical issue for integrated MPC design. Many companies wish to concentrate their purchasing power and integrate with a small set of suppliers. This is particularly so in the regional buying programs of firms such as Nestlé and Unilever. The key issue is rationalization of the components based on *standardizing the components used.* In most companies this is a real problem, since different business units design their products according to their own particular engineering tradition, working with suppliers that are well known to them. For integrated MPC design, the things purchased must be standardized. If Unilever wishes to buy all its packages for the Magnum ice cream bar from one supplier it first needs to harmonize package design, with multilingual descriptions, of a standard size and materials—which well may necessitate standardization of packaging equipment and manufacturing practices as well. But Unilever also needs to standardize its MPC linkages so that standardized signals can be passed to a supplier and can be readily integrated with its own MPC systems and multiple-factory manufacturing.

This is not as easy as it seems. Multinational firms usually have individualized MPC systems operating, and the resultant set of needs must be consolidated in order to work effectively with the supplying firm. It might sound like this just involves combining outputs from MRP systems (which in itself may not be as easy as it seems). But more than combining is required. In one large electronics company we know, one division had an MRP system that truly reflected its needs (it told the truth), while another overstated its needs. As long as the systems worked separately, a smart supplier knew how to interpret the demands. Combining these demands would be a disaster. This firm worked two years to bring both divisions to truthful MRP systems.

A similar set of standardization issues arose for Skanska, the large Swedish construction company. It was necessary to develop standardized approaches to buildings (e.g., standardize elevator design, working with Kone, the Finnish elevator manufacturer). But this was not the end of it. Of more fundamental importance was the need to standardize building site planning and scheduling systems (project planning). Only with consistent MPC approaches for all building projects can Skanska pull together the MPC data in the right form for its suppliers to routinely execute.

The Gate Gourmet example illustrates another side to the standardization issue. By designing its MPC systems to link with the existing systems of its customers, Gate Gourmet becomes "easy to do business with." The customer systems will be different, so the standardization/integration task necessarily falls to Gate Gourmet, not to its customers.

The principle here is to take over the complexity so that the other party does not need to do so. This principle implies that the company that takes on the complexity will orchestrate and achieve "lock on" to the others in the chain. We make it easy for our customers by taking over the difficulties ourselves.

Enhancing ERP Systems

It is important to understand that MRP and the subsequent systems (MRPII, ERP) support particular methods for manufacturing. The classic manufacturing company was arranged in a functional layout, with large batches of parts moving from operation to operation. Completed parts were put in inventory and thereafter pulled to make subassemblies and final assemblies. The entire process was long, with actual work times being a small fraction of total time. Manufacturing has since evolved through cellular approaches and JIT, dramatically reducing times and batch sizes. But doing so required new approaches to the physical flow of materials and coordination through new MPC systems. Although ERP has been a major advance, it is still based on the same underlying model for manufacturing and the integration is based on classic functional definitions in the firm. That is, ERP is functionally oriented in its basic design and it is usually implemented in classic functional terms.

> A good example of the problems with a classical functional approach to MPC was illustrated at Heineken when its largest customer, Albert Heijn, asked the company to deliver beer each day, in quantities based exactly on the previous day's shipments from the Albert Heijn warehouse to its stores. Heineken at the time used four days to replenish this customer. But this lead time was largely composed of time to pass information between functional units at Heineken. An order was received in an order entry department on day 1 and then processed in an overnight batch-processing system. This made it visible to the manufacturing function on day 2, which scheduled the order and again processed the decision in an overnight batch-processing system. On day 3 it was visible in the transportation department, which scheduled shipment for day four.

At Albert Heijn, all stores are equipped with checkout terminals to yield point-of-sale (POS) data. These data are thereafter used to plan replenishment shipments to each of the stores (taking into account full cases, allocation in shortages, promotions, etc.). The summation of all store replenishment shipments is then passed to Heineken and other key suppliers, with the objective to exactly replace the replenishment shipments. These requirements may be modified for promotions, holidays, or other special events, but the basic principle is to *not* modify the data—to not create the bullwhip effect.

Running the batch-processing systems at Heineken more frequently cannot solve the problem. Up-over-and-down processing through functional groupings needed to be replaced with MPC systems that focused on the *processes*—order fulfillment based on linked systems with the customers. It was also necessary to reengineer the *work* so that it too was organized to support the process rather than the function. This required new skills, new organizational forms, and new metrics. The MPC systems no longer need to pass orders through a formal order entry department. In the same way that Gate Gourmet just executes against the passenger manifest, Heineken now just executes against the combined store replenishment shipments. This needs to be done more quickly and easily. It is now a daily activity rather than a periodic activity.

Making the kinds of changes needed in this new supplier-customer relationship is not easy. Sales people have been encouraged for their entire careers to push more stock on customers. Their methods of selling were often personal and informal. Now, there is no need for this kind of selling. In fact, Albert Heijn asked Heineken to not send sales people to them any more (fire these people and give us the cost savings!). In a similar vein, Heineken and Albert Heijn need to redesign their transactions. If deliveries are to be daily instead of weekly, there will be a fivefold increase in orders, shipment documents, invoices, etc. unless the approach is changed. The changes are often difficult to sell to accountants and others interested in controls. Moreover, there will need to be changes in classic IT systems that are based on the detailed transactions and matching of steps.

Turning now to the MPC system linkages, we again need to raise some words of caution. There is currently an idea floating around that the way to integrate supply chain partners is to simply connect their ERP systems. We would not advise doing so without very careful study. The problems we illustrated in Figure 17.2 with a shortage of one or two resulting in a vastly amplified quantity upstream are all too real. Any readers who have played what is called "the beer game" are well familiar with this phenomenon. Figure 17.15 shows the problem. The top record is from an ERP system of a customer, and the lower is that of the supplier. As can be seen, the safety stock requirement and lot sizing policy in the top record trigger a gross requirement for 50 units in period 1 at the supplier. This record generates a past due requirement for 200 units, none of which are needed for the customer until period 6 or until period 8 for the customer's customer. Worse yet, the same requirement would occur in the supplier record if *no* requirements were shown after period 1. In fact, we know of a supplier whose MRP system generated replenishment orders (that were fulfilled) for parts that were being phased out because of an end-of-life product.

It is also useful to consider what would happen in linked ERP systems if one of the partners changed planning parameters, such as lead times. If the customer extended its lead

FIGURE 17.15   ERP Amplification

		1	2	3	4	5	6	7	8	9	10	11	12	13
Gross requirements		10	10	10	10	10	10	10	10	10	10	10	10	10
Scheduled receipts														
Projected available balance	25	15	55	45	35	25	15	55	45	35	25	15	55	45
Planned orders		50					50					50		

Lead time = 1
$\quad$ Q = 50
$\quad$ SS = 10

		1	2	3	4	5	6	7	8	9	10	11	12	13
Gross requirements		50					50					50		
Scheduled receipts														
Projected available balance	55	205	205	205	205	205	155	155	155	155	155	105	105	105
Planned orders	200*													

*Past due
Lead time = 2
$\quad$ Q = 200
$\quad$ SS = 10

time by one week, it would immediately create a plan to fill at least one week of pipeline inventory upstream, but the bullwhip effect would almost surely inflate the demand in the chain. This example also shows how if inventories are to be managed down, this activity needs to be carefully coordinated, since the result will take corresponding capacity requirements out of the upstream providers.

> A great example again comes from the Heineken–Albert Heijn new supply chain. After this was operating, Heineken found it had a huge inventory of empty returnable beer bottles and didn't need to buy more for a long time. Beer was now either in tanks at the factory or in bellies of beer drinkers—not in bottles!

Joint MPC design supports joint problem perception/solution. In the first edition of this text, we introduced the concept of "demand management," where instead of only thinking about forecasts, one also needs to consider orders—and customer orders are seen as consuming the forecast. The top portion of Figure 17.16 shows this concept. The forecast establishes the long-run needs for the MPC system, with all the problems of forecast errors. In the short run, MPC planning is focused on executing exact customer orders. Many firms try to implement lean manufacturing approaches in order to make to order, for example, by pushing the customer order zone out in time and eliminating guessing (i.e., reducing the extent to which MPC systems are based on forecasts).

The bottom portion of Figure 17.16 moves us into today's world of supply chain management. In this figure very little of the planning is based on forecasts. Most is based on

FIGURE 17.16
Substitute Knowledge for Forecasting

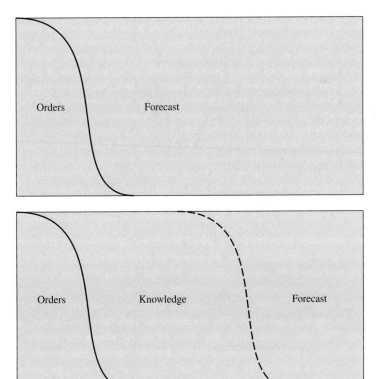

either actual orders or *knowledge!* If one *knows* exactly what the customers need with specific timings, one does not need to forecast (guess) or wait for them to order! In fact, "ordering" is not a good use of either partner's time. Today's MPC systems can be designed to pass customer planning information directly to suppliers and let them ship as they please, with no orders and the customer paying as it uses the materials. The supplier needs to support the schedule of the customer. The customer needs to be "smart," e.g., support flawless execution of plans, but if so, the plans become the minimal replenishment requirements for the suppliers. Let us now see how this is more than JIT.

Enhancing JIT-Based Systems

JIT can clearly be extended to interfirm operations, and doing so requires cross-firm MPC integration. But interfirm JIT also creates rigidities that need to be understood. Classic JIT systems require physical inventories that are kept to very tight limits. These are used to trigger production in closely linked production systems that provide a relatively uniform flow between adjacent operations. In many intrafirm JIT applications, this requirement is not overly demanding and the savings in cost and time justify the rigidities. But in interfirm JIT, costs can be quite high unless the flow of goods matches well with the economics of transportation and the schedules in the two firms can similarly be matched. This is indeed the case for a company building car seats for an automobile manufacturer, where seats are built in car assembly sequence, and delivered directly to the line. However, if this degree of coordination is impractical or the subsequent chain cost saving is not the case, JIT coordination—in uneconomic shipment sizes—is not the appropriate MPC choice.

> This can be nicely illustrated by returning to the Super Soup example. Instead of using a weekly schedule to connect Alpha and Beta, it is clearly possible to do so on a daily basis, in a quasi-JIT fashion. The classic JIT approach (advocated by Alpha) would be for Beta to have a kanban quantity of each product available at Alpha in whatever production batch size Alpha determines. However, this would result in higher chain inventories, since 42 batches would always be on hand, and Beta would be expected to replenish any batch quickly. Since Beta might find it uneconomical to produce in these batch sizes, it might also hold finished stocks of packaging materials rather than hold only printed polyethylene film (note that this is again Beta's problem, not Alpha's). An enhanced JIT approach would be to again schedule Alpha as before on a weekly basis, but then break this schedule down into daily quantities. Beta could run its laminating schedule to support the daily build schedule at Alpha, printing today what will be built tomorrow. This would indeed reduce chain inventories and potentially create other efficiencies. But it would put new constraints on Beta—and on the logistics to serve Alpha. This might not pay off from an overall supply chain viewpoint.

One approach to overcoming small batch transportation in JIT systems is to pass the transportation responsibility to the customer with linked MPC systems that support coordinated pickups from many suppliers. Another is to allow the supplier greater leeway in shipments as long as the customer does not run out, with the supplier using vendor-managed inventory (VMI). In this case the supplier can better coordinate its capacity usage as well as logistics activities. The fundamental idea here is what we call **the uphill skier** concept. The idea comes from the rules of skiing where the person uphill assumes the responsibility to avoid collisions with the downhill skiers. The downhill skier does not need to continually watch out for uphill skiers. Essentially, if one can pass knowledge to one's key suppliers, they can be responsible for supporting the schedule in any way they like. But they *must* dependably support the schedule. But providing them the flexibility to operate in this way means the supplier can work with this customer in a much different way; instead of exactly supporting a customer's exact demands, the customer is now one that can be supported with greater flexibility on the part of the supplier.

> A cement company in South America received orders from ready-mix concrete firms on a daily basis, often arriving about 5 P.M. for delivery before 7 A.M. the following morning. The orders were based on specific concrete orders for that day's delivery, with the objective to not carry any excess cement inventory. The ready-mix firms wished to make concrete, sell it, and receive payment before paying for cement. Fulfilling the resultant set of customer orders was difficult for the supplier, requiring extra transportation vehicles, overtime pay, and high-cost shipments. By placing silos at a few "smart customers," the cement firm could fill these at will, always filling a truck that was passing in that general area. The customers no longer need to order, and sufficient cement is always available. Silos have meters to bill the ready-mix firms as they use cement—with no orders. This form of VMI has proved highly useful. The cement exists in any case. It is the logistics costs that can be reduced.

It does not require many such customers to allow a supplier to do a much better job of optimizing use of manufacturing and transportation assets. But it does require flawless execution by both the supplier and the customer, supported by new MPC systems and mutual trust—and a product that can indeed be inventoried at little extra cost. This is not an option for car seats. The MPC system enhancements to support the uphill skier concept need to include a means to communicate and continually update the customer build schedule to the supplier. This could be done simply as in the case of the cement manufacturer, but in most cases more complex product structures require e-based systems to pass along (and update) the exact planning requirements of many more items. Changes to the schedule need to be jointly monitored; stability and flawless execution at the customer site—at least in the short run—support the objectives. That is, customer plans need to be executed and not changed dramatically unless there are sufficient stocks to allow it. New MPC links include a means to identify actual usages at the customer site and accompanying payment methods. Here new thinking and agreements are needed to perhaps utilize backflushing not constrained by classic invoicing-payment schemes. Backflushing refers to the idea of recognizing component usage when finished goods are produced. For example, every automobile produced can be assumed to contain one and only one radiator; thus, the radiator manufacturer can be paid on the basis of completed automobiles, as long as there is very little scrap of radiators. Backflushing eliminates a great deal of transaction processing associated with the classic processes (e.g., invoices that exactly match deliveries of radiators to the automobile manufacturer). Often, since the customer never owns the inventory until it is used, the customer might agree to pay immediately on use. Trust is important to make all of this work, and the supplier has to feel comfortable with the physical protection of what is still its property.

> Returning to the example in Figure 17.15 illustrates the potential. The problems we observed with crudely linked ERP systems could be somewhat ameliorated if the two firms changed their MPC systems to use lot-for-lot quantities and no safety stocks. Doing so increases the number of orders from the supplier and the number of batches manufactured at the supplier. In essence this approach links the two firms in a JIT relationship, with the classic problems of implementing JIT. Allowing the supplier to operate in uphill skier form reduces the constraints, and with the use of a hub, the advantages might be easier to achieve, since a third-party logistics provider can help implement the necessary changes in all companies. These changes will be less than if the firms did this on their own: It is the third-party logistics provider who takes on the complications, making life easier for both the supplier and the customer.

Although the classic JIT system is a Toyota-like environment with level production, minimal inventories, multiple daily deliveries, and linked production planning across companies, the Heineken/Albert Heijn connection is also a form of JIT. It is called "today for tomorrow," with the outflow from the warehouse today being the inflow tomorrow. But this approach can also include demand expectations that are not based on extrapolation. In some cases improved information exchange is based on events that can be anticipated by the customer.

Many of the major retailers, in their relations with key suppliers, maintain minimal inventories, which the suppliers are expected to replenish regularly, often on a daily basis. Wal-Mart has this relationship with key suppliers. In effect this is also a form of JIT. The problem for suppliers, however, is that the periodic quantity shipped will vary, depending on actual sales at the retail stores. If the fluctuation is minimal then it raises no significant problem. But often the fluctuation is large, and best-practice supply chain management is to pass *anticipated* fluctuations back to the supplier—even if only approximate—as soon as they are known. Wal-Mart, for example, will tell one of its suppliers such as Philips Consumer Electronics that it is planning a sale for some competing product as soon as it knows. Thus, if a Sony television set is to be put on sale in six weeks, Wal-Mart will tell Philips of this plan, so that Philips can expect a drop in demand for its competing model during the sale period. This allows Philips to reduce production *before* it ends up with large inventories. Philips cannot anticipate this demand by using standard forecasting methodologies. If Wal-Mart does not pass this information to Philips, costs in the overall chain will increase. Someone will end up paying these costs. Wal-Mart recognizes the need to reduce this chain cost, but more important, it has the MPC systems in place to help reduce it. Best-practice supply chain management MPC includes communication across firms about *future* requirements, even when only approximate. Wal-Mart has worked hard to become an attractive customer to its major suppliers. As such, it has been able to convince those suppliers to work jointly in development of state-of-the-art MPC systems for supply chain management.

Dyad-Based MPC Systems

A JIT system based on a specific relationship between two firms is a dyad, which can be defined as "a critical supply chain relationship between two firms that is designed to achieve a significant joint benefit."

As one focuses on developing multiple supply chain relationships, with several suppliers and customers, there is a natural tendency to see the process as one where ERP systems are expanded in scope to include a much larger group and focus for optimization. But an alternative—most surely a better alternative—is to focus on development of multiple dyads, each designed to optimize the unique objectives of that dyad. Thus, the dyad approach is designed to support mass customization. The multiple dyad approach is fundamentally different from that building on ERP and greater integration. It is essentially a new paradigm.

Let us start by examining dyad relationships within a large company. If we take the example of Unilever or Nestlé, we see these companies dividing their organizations into selling units and sourcing units. The selling units are based geographically, focused on the unique tastes of certain consumer groups as well as on the way food products are marketed in the region. Thus, Nestlé sells corn-flavored ice cream in China, and roadside markets in Africa require very different selling approaches than hypermarkets in France. The selling units are provided products from sourcing units, which increasingly are not colocated with selling units. Moreover, concentration in sourcing units (factory closures) and the growing use of outsourcing imply continual change in the match between sourcing units and selling

FIGURE 17.17
Sourcing Units and Selling Units

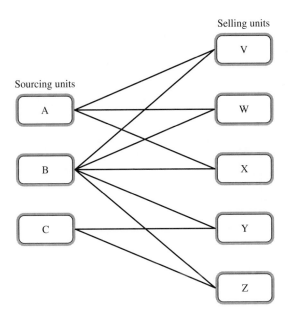

Selling units

Sourcing units

units. In some cases sourcing units manufacture goods that are sold in only a few markets, but in others this is not the case. For Unilever, its Dove soap is made in only one factory, which supplies some 80 selling units around the world. As Unilever sharply reduces the number of its brands (by about 75 percent), the number of selling units supplied by each sourcing unit will also grow.

The key question for MPC design is how are selling units best connected to sourcing units? Figure 17.17 depicts the way the sourcing units at Unilever/Nestlé (the back end) are connected to the selling units (front end). In this simplified case we have three sourcing units (A, B, C) supplying five selling units (V, W, X, Y, Z). Sourcing unit A supplies three selling units, C supplies two, and B supplies all five. The five selling units can be expected to have different ways of approaching their marketplaces and different MPC systems as well. The key here is that selling units V, W, and X can provide their data to sourcing unit A in whatever ways they wish, as long as the resultant data are input into an appropriate e-based B2B system linkage. In essence, each sourcing unit–selling unit connection is a specific dyad, needing to be optimized in its unique way according to how the selling unit operates. For example, perhaps V has an ERP system from which it extracts its requirements. W, on the other hand does its planning with a spreadsheet. Both sets of data can be input into an e-based B2B system linkage to A. The transactions for data transfer and subsequent timings for deliveries depend on the particular dyad. Perhaps A is in France and so is V, whereas W is in Nigeria. The general approach for data sequencing and subsequent shipments would be the same, but the timings would be different. For instance, requirements passed from V to A might be filled in 24 hours, while those from W to A might take two weeks.

To the extent that the sourcing units operate in uphill skier position to the selling units, the sourcing units are free to ship as they please to the selling units, but the inventories at the selling units are managed on a VMI basis (title to the goods does not pass to the selling units until they ship them). This requires that the sourcing units have visibility into the

FIGURE 17.18 **Extending the Dyad Linkages**

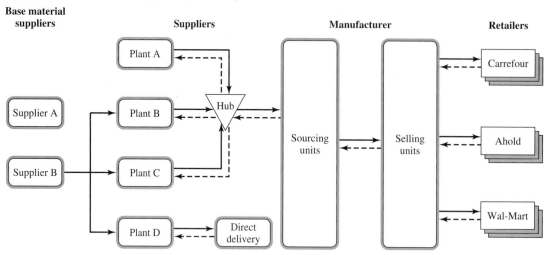

inventory balances at the selling units. The sourcing units need to be able to support data input in two or three different forms (Microsoft, Java, etc.) but this is not overly onerous. The rules for transaction processing between sourcing units and selling units can be established with relative ease. Moreover, once the rules are in place and both parties are used to them, it is relatively easy to switch patterns, as when a sourcing unit is closed. It is also straightforward to change the timings as new distribution methods are implemented, since the general approach for how sourcing units are tied to selling units is transparent.

Figure 17.18 extends the approach used for the sourcing unit–selling unit dyads. Here the individual sourcing unit and selling unit dyads are coordinated as described above. The selling units in turn can be connected to their key customers, such as Carrefour or Wal-Mart with a similar dyad-based approach, to support the ways in which the customers do business. This is primarily a matter of passing demand data back—perhaps starting in the form of orders—but over time moving to the passing of information and uphill-skier-type execution. But it is important to understand that the bundle of goods and services provided to Wal-Mart will be different than that provided to Carrefour; they each see their business differently, with different performance metrics and internal systems. Moreover, at first there are often unnecessary dyad transactions needed to support existing internal systems (e.g., after-the-fact sales orders to create invoices). These might be required to transact the passage of title for the goods in a manufacturing company to its customers. These transactions can be included, but they clearly show the need (and potential value) for intercompany business process reengineering.

The information passing from the major retailers to the manufacturing company in Figure 17.18 does not necessarily imply that the physical flow of goods needs to be the same. The sourcing units can indeed ship directly to the retailers, the retailers can pick up the goods from the sourcing units, or the physical distribution can be arranged by a third party. Also, the information coming from the retailers needs to be visible to the sourcing units. This supports better planning and coordination of manufacturing and physical distribution.

The dyad-by-dyad approach can be extended from the sourcing units back to their suppliers, and even back to the base material suppliers. The basic approach is the same: How do the two parties increase the chain value/cost ratio? How should they do their scheduling, and how can they best be coordinated? Where are there extra inventories, longer lead times than necessary, the possibility to utilize VMI, the potential for joint scheduling, and the opportunities to sharply reduce logistics costs? Figure 17.18 shows the potential use of a hub between some sourcing units and some suppliers, as well as direct delivery from supplier plant D to one or more sourcing units. Any and all of these improvements in dyad performance are possible. The key is to focus improvement efforts on a one-by-one, dyad-by-dyad approach. A final observation here is that the dyad-by-dyad approach needs to be continually improved. One needs to migrate the learning from one dyad to another. Where are there extra transactions that could be eliminated? How can the two firms better share information? Is the VMI working as well as it might? Are there "just in case" inventories that can be eliminated? What are the truly best practices? Are we designing the dyad processes and systems in a modular fashion so that new dyad relationships can be more easily implemented?

Figure 17.19 depicts one way for a dyad to implement vendor-managed inventory, but with the two firms using classical function-based MPC systems. In this case, the customer creates plans in manufacturing, which are passed to a materials planning process, which yields a projected outflow of raw materials. Those supplied by this supplier are passed in the usual e-based B2B dyad to the sales organization at the supplier. This unit proposes a replenishment shipment to the customer that is evaluated and confirmed. Then the supplier sales organization creates a consignment stock order that is picked and shipped to the customer. The supplier plans manufacturing to satisfy the proposed replenishment orders on the basis of the projected finished goods inventory balances. The shipments are received into raw materials inventory at the customer, and thereafter issued to manufacturing as needed. This issue is passed to the purchasing department to create a purchase order to match the quantity issued to manufacturing. This process essentially passes ownership of the goods from the supplier to the customer. On the supplier side, the receipt of the purchase order allows the supplier to create a sales order and update its VMI inventory held by the customer. The sales order in turn passes to the finance function to create an invoice, which is paid by the customer. Also shown in Figure 17.19 is joint inventory reconciliation between the customer and supplier to be sure that the amount actually consumed by the customer matches that issued to manufacturing. Figure 17.19 illustrates how cumbersome the processes often are to implement supply chain management. The problems come from needing to match transactions to existing functional processes (and thinking).

Figure 17.19 includes X marks in many of the activity boxes. These are the transactions that can be eliminated with joint business process reengineering work. The result is that the customer's manufacturing plan passes directly to the supplier's manufacturing planning. The dotted arrow depicts the new linkage to create the VMI stock order. Thereafter the stock is picked and shipped to the supplier, and issued to manufacturing. Completion of manufacturing now is linked with another dotted line to finance to pay the amount for the materials consumed. The differences are great: There no longer are sales orders, purchase orders, or invoices. All of these require human intervention to create them. Similarly, several human intervention processes for shipments are eliminated. The supplier operates in "uphill skier" position.

FIGURE 17.19 Classical Functional Transaction Limitations

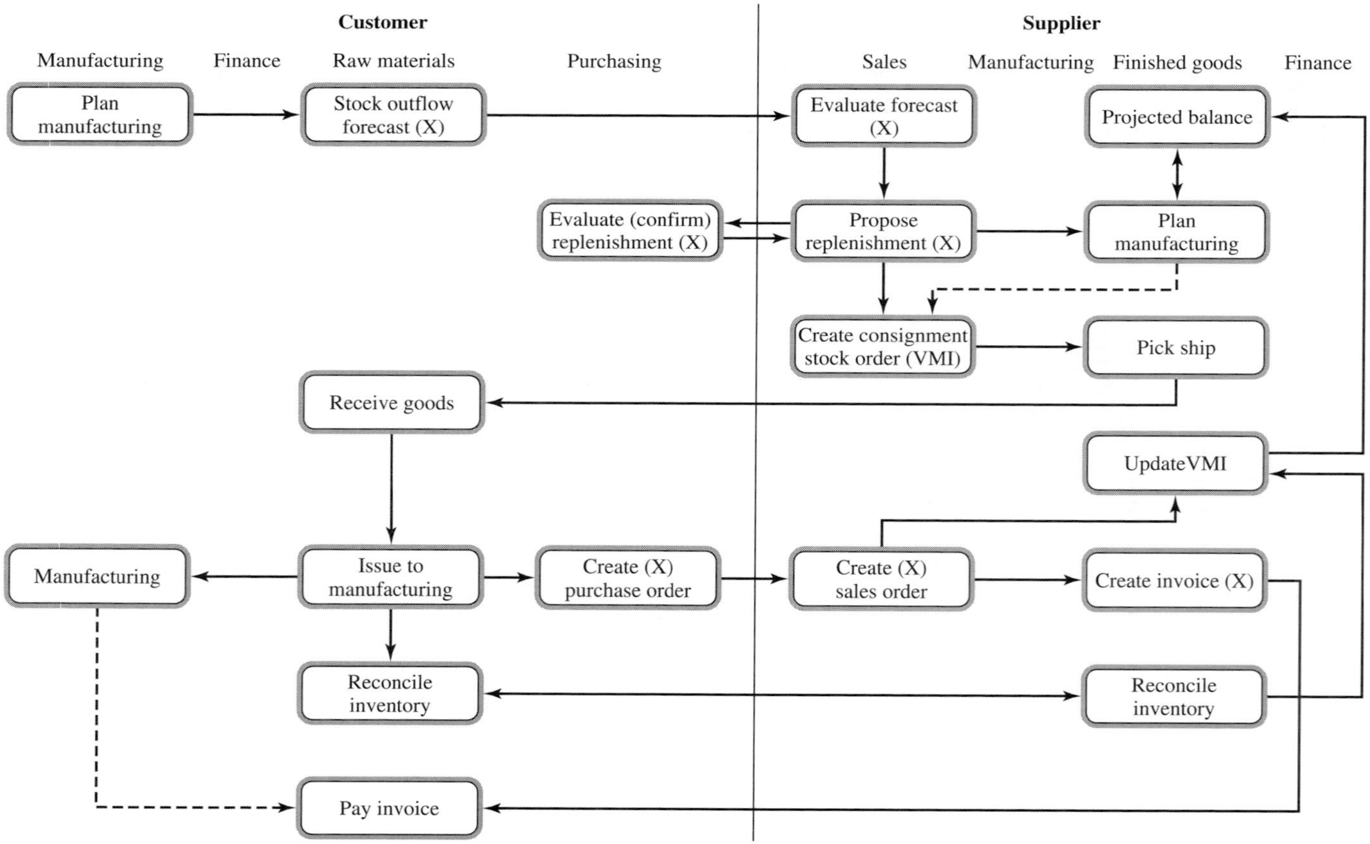

It is obvious that the elimination of excess transactions is very cost-effective. But doing so requires joint business process reengineering actions in the dyad. It is not enough to change only the processes on one side. The dyad will need improvement projects to take out these costs. It may be necessary to closely examine who will need to incur the change costs, and who will be the immediate recipient of the benefits. Perhaps the dyad will need to include the resultant information in subsequent price negotiations.

Mass Customization

Mass customization essentially means providing individualized solutions to fit the exact needs of different customers—but doing so with the benefits of mass production rather than with higher-cost craftlike approaches. Since each customer need is a bit different, how does the firm provide differentiated bundles of both goods and services? The jar of Nescafé on the shelf at one supermarket chain is the same as that at another. But the bundle is different. Each supermarket chain has its own ways of ordering, MPC systems, ways of interacting with suppliers, ways to go to market, and individual measures of performance (e.g., sales per square meter of shelf space, inventory turns, stockouts, or customer service). The smart supplier (Nestlé in this case) helps each of these firms achieve *its* objectives. It needs to design/implement MPC systems that support "mass customization." In fact, firms like Nestlé and Unilever need to implement dyad-based MPC systems that reflect the realities of their relationships with different customers. Moreover, these e-based systems need to evolve over time to keep pace with the ongoing strategic moves of the important customers. Thus, the globalization strategy of Wal-Mart will need to be reflected in the detailed MPC systems that connect it to its major suppliers.

Figure 17.20 comes from work by Andy Boynton and his colleagues (Paul Strebel, ed.). The model depicts products on the *y* axis and processes on the *x* axis. In both cases they are seen as either stable or dynamic. In the top right corner, we find dynamic-dynamic, which is labeled "Invention." In this situation, we find the high-technology start-up firms, such as

FIGURE 17.20
Mass Customization

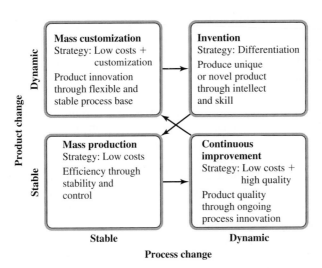

electronics or biotech. They are not quite sure what they will make or how they will do so, but they have a concept that they wish to pursue. This is also called the *craftsmanship stage*. The workplace is a laboratory or craft shop, and the people are discovering what to make and how to make it. The MPC systems that support invention are highly informal, perhaps based on the backs of envelopes or at best on spreadsheets. Product volumes are low and expectations as to deliveries and support of customers are similarly low.

At some point in a successful start-up company, a product idea comes to life. At that point it is imperative to move from the top right of Figure 17.20 to the bottom left. That is, it is necessary to transform this enterprise from a laboratory into a factory. It is necessary to change the way we work from chaotic to stable. The product must be standardized and tightly controlled; the only way to do so is to tightly design and control the processes for making the products. The bottom left is the world of Henry Ford (make them any color as long as it is black). Mass production allows the firm to produce a highly standardized product at low cost and high efficiency. This is the world of statistical process control, ISO 9000, and the classic MRP-based MPC systems. It is fundamentally responsible for the style of life we all enjoy today.

The next transformation is from mass production to continuous improvement. The product stays stable, but the process becomes dynamic. The process now incorporates new levels of quality into the product by continually enhancing the ways in which we work. This is the Toyota transformation. Henry Ford did not want his workers to think. They were paid high wages to do exactly as they were told. At Toyota people are not allowed to park their brains at the door. Everyone is expected to have improvement ideas, to be incorporated in the way the work is done. At Toyota, it is said that there are 3 million improvement suggestions per year. This raises the question of how Toyota handles all these suggestions. The way 3 million suggestions are "handled" is that every employee is a member of a small team, perhaps 5 or 6 people. If one person has an idea, he/she explains it to the others; if they all think it is a good idea—then just do it! The MPC systems and overriding philosophy in continuous improvement are also transformative. Now the tools and approach of TQM and JIT are dominant. Teams of empowered workers, receiving more highly aggregated requirements data from the MPC systems, control manufacturing on the basis of cellular approaches. Instead of centralized MPC planning done at the level of detail of individual operations, it is now only done at the level of planning assemblies. Part and operation planning is performed by the workers. Does this work? Of course—the results can be seen on the roads of the world. The Japanese built better automobiles for many years, and now others are copying the improvement ideas.

The next transformation shown in Figure 17.20 is from continuous improvement to mass customization. Here the empowered workforce can use its competencies to increase the range of products offered—in fact, unique bundles of goods and services. That is, one moves back to a new form of stability, one based on cellular manufacturing with empowered work teams that have the ability to develop dynamic final products as the customers deem necessary. If a customer wishes a variation on some standard product, or some improvement in the dyad-based MPC system, an empowered work team can make it easily, with little need for supervision and at little to no extra cost. So the goal in mass customization is to provide a wider product range, augmented by a wider range of services, that supports the provision of solutions to customer perceived problems. The solutions are tailored to explicit customer needs, while still achieving the benefits of mass production as well as the ongoing improvements inherent in continuous improvement. The unique solutions must be supported by customer driven MPC systems. These will be specific dyad-based systems that are responsive to new customer requirements, and robust enough to support many different kinds of customer requests easily.

One key to successfully achieving mass customization is to design business processes and MPC systems with the same concepts of modularity used in product design. A good example is the Premier pages used by Dell. If an employee of some company such as Ford wished to order a new computer, he/she would connect to the Dell Web page, and then to the special page for Ford. It might have the Ford logo and it would be very user friendly. It would tell the person which computers were compatible with others at Ford, what the options are, which software would come installed on the machine in order to make it work immediately in the Ford environment, and it would be easy to place the order. Moreover, when the computer arrives, one has only to take it out of the box, turn it on, and it works! No need for IT specialists to reach the proper operating level. The MPC systems in this case are highly customized to Ford, but more than 90 percent of the underlying software is the same as that for other clients. Adding a new client is easy for Dell.

Mass customization is better understood by examining some examples. In all of these cases, the fundamental shift is to start with the specific needs of the customer and then design a supply chain (and MPC systems) that can provide them.

> Some years ago a major hotel chain awarded its entire worldwide business to a telecom equipment supplier, requesting common equipment in all hotels. The supplier's immediate response was joy, followed by puzzlement: How was this account to be served? What were the MPC systems needed? The telecom supplier was organized geographically while this required global account management. This was debated for a long time, with the account finally treated as an exception to normal business. This cannot be, since soon some customer like the state of Montana might ask for handsets, long lines, fiber optics, and digital switches—as one contract in their eyes but crossing several supplier business divisions. The firm transformed itself from one organized by function to a process focus, and finally to one organized by customer.

The company needs to sell as the customers wish to buy (making it easy for them). This has to be the driving force. Moreover, the company needs to do so accurately and at low cost (routine things done routinely); in essence, it needs a mass customization approach to running its business. This has to embody an internal coordination led by sales/marketing responding to the customer needs, which in turn must be supported by customer service, order fulfillment and distribution, then manufacturing, and finally procurement. The overall supply chain has to support the particular customer segment. MPC system development starts with sales, focusing on order entry, but soon focuses on connecting customer needs to supplier schedules.

> Another example comes from work with a food additive company. Each business unit was asked what it needed to do to clearly win the customer orders. The first group to respond was one that sold spices. It replied that a new snack food company in its market was expected to dominate the market in a few years and was now looking for supplier partners. This was regarded as a "smart" customer, since it was asking the right questions, such as: Can you do an ABC costing exercise and then tell us your cost drivers? We will try to do business with you to reduce those costs, with us receiving a share of the savings. Can you help us uniformly apply spices to the snacks so that every bite tastes the same and we use the minimum amount

of spices? Can you formulate our spices with no exotic ingredients so we will not receive any unpleasant surprises about cost increases? In essence the customer was quite specific as to its needs and the customized bundle of goods and services it wished to be provided. The customer was asking for much more than spices.

The food ingredients company needed to sell the way the customer wished to buy, and to back that up with consistent processes for sales support, logistics, distribution, manufacturing, and procurement activities. All of this had to be executed with new MPC systems.

> Another example is in a firm selling personal computers. Here the firm wished to sell its personal computers to retailers. It found, however, that its selling modes just did not support this goal effectively. A salesperson called on a retail account, developed a proposal, and thereafter had to have it approved by his/her supervisor. Even then the proposed order next had to pass through manufacturing and distribution to see when it might arrive at the retailer. Finally the salesperson had to reconfirm with the retailer—many ups, overs, and downs. This was clearly not supportable. Sales people had to be empowered, trained, and equipped with laptop computers and modems. They had to be empowered to make deals and close sales. The MPC tools developed allowed them to determine if a proposed sale was inside their range of allowable decisions and by what margin it was inside. The sales agreements in turn needed to connect to the detailed MPC execution systems.

Implementing mass customization raises some fundamental issues for MPC systems design. Figure 17.21 shows the match between MPC systems and the four phases of the product/process cycle mass customization model. In the invention phase, the systems are highly informal, perhaps consisting largely of spreadsheets. This is because the focus of attention is on creativity, based on highly individualized actions. It is not clear exactly what is to be made or the processes by which it will be made. The transformation from invention to mass production requires a major change in MPC systems. In order to achieve stability and the related efficiencies, it is necessary to implement almost draconian controls over the actions of everyone. No action, no matter how worthy, is worth it if it comes at the expense of a mismatch between what the MPC systems see as reality and what exists on the shop floor. The MPC systems that support this matching are master planning, MRP, shop scheduling, etc. Mass production is based on command/control management with functional hierarchies.

The transformation to continuous improvement is equally dramatic. Instead of controlling those "idiots and thieves" who work for us, the premise is that we are dealing with

FIGURE 17.21

Mass Customization and MPC Systems Cycle

Invention	Mass Production	Continuous Improvement	Mass Customization
Informal systems	MRP, MRP II, ISO 9000	JIT, TQM, Practice sharing	Customer driven systems, robust, responsive to new requirements
To support creative, individualized workers	To **control** actions of everyone	To encourage evolution, empowerment, simplicity, and thinking	To support a "portfolio" approach to demand chain linkages

intelligent, well-motivated teams of workers that are empowered and will make many changes. These changes will introduce simplifications—both in processes and in the MPC systems to control those processes. That means that MPC systems here are not static. Many of the MPC systems that support mass production can remain, such as the need for some form of MRP system, but JIT has its own MPC requirements as well. Moreover, worker empowerment implies MPC systems that support wider interpretations of allowable actions. The workers are intelligent enough to act with fewer system constraints. For example, workers work in teams to support multiple operations and even multiple part/assembly steps without the MRP inventory transactions.

The transformation from continuous improvement to mass customization is, however, a major step for MPC systems. The MPC systems must be responsive to new customer requirements, and in fact be proactive—that is, offer new MPC functionality to customers before they ask for it. Now the focus is on a "portfolio" approach to demand chain linkages. Mass customization *is* the way customer segmentation is achieved. Different customers require different MPC systems support. This implies a major increase in projects and the need for MPC systems to support project management excellence. Providing the overall MPC support is a challenge for systems design. The best way to support mass customization in MPC design is to focus on modularity in systems design. In today's world, one needs MPC system solutions that can be assembled with mostly common e-based system elements

The transformations in mass customization are even more interesting when the focus is not on one firm but two linked (a dyad) in a supply chain. Mass customization adds another set of partnership requirements. The two firms need to jointly develop understanding for how the *customers of the customer* firm are to be won and the implications for mass customization features. Which ones of these are to be provided by the customer firm and which by the supplier? Which has abilities to provide mass customization and what joint MPC features will support true mass customization?

The most important lesson here is that genuine supply chain partnerships need to understand the implications of mass customization. If this is where customers are headed (and we see the series of shifts as quite universal), then it is imperative that the customer and its key suppliers develop a joint focus for achieving mass customization. The people who will need to work together are different, the MPC systems designs need to support joint actions, and what was formerly good may now be wrong.

Concluding Principles	Superior supply chains are one of the best ways to compete in today's marketplaces. Achieving a dominant supply chain requires more than lofty ideas and pet terms such as "partnership." In the end, supply chains require the right infrastructure to make them work. Cross-organizational MPC systems must be developed, implemented, continually improved, and then replaced—again and again—by new MPC systems that support the next transformation. We see the following principles as particularly useful:

- Supply chain management is based on a definitive shift from intrafirm optimization to interfirm optimization.
- Supply chain management cannot be a vague concept. In the end, it has to be supported by concrete MPC systems (but new ones).

- Overall supply chain evaluation needs to include the bullwhip effect. Reducing it by decreasing the number of stages in the supply chain can sometimes more than offset what appear to be higher manufacturing costs.

- Orchestration of a supply chain should be driven by the party that is best positioned to make a major improvement in total chain value/cost. New orchestration requires new MPC systems.

- The goals for new supply chain management include more than the standard MPC metrics. In many cases these now include new product development, faster market response, early supplier involvement, and quality management across the chain.

- Good results require new ways of working and new MPC approaches. These are not always possible to achieve.

- Making it easy to do business for your customers is an important objective for supply chain management.

- Interfirm MPC is not a simple extension or connection of intrafirm MPC systems.

- Standardization of working methods, data, and systems is an essential underpinning to multiple-organizational-unit (e.g., regional buying) supply chain management.

- Dyad-based MPC approaches represent an emerging way of thinking in supply chain management.

References

Bovet, David, and Joseph Martha. *Values Nets: Breaking the Supply Chain to Unlock Hidden Profits.* New York: John Wiley & Sons, 2000.

Carr, A. S., and John N. Pearson. "Strategically Managed Buyer–Supplier Relationships and Performance Outcomes," *Journal of Operations Management* 17, no. 5 (August 1999), pp. 497–519.

Crabtree, Ron. "World-Class Procurement and the Small Manufacturer," *APICS—The Performance Advantage,* September 2002.

Gilbert, S. M., and Ronald H. Ballou. "Supply Chain Benefits from Advanced Customer Commitments," *Journal of Operations Management* 18, no. 1 (December 1999), pp. 61–73.

Hill, C. A., and Gary D. Scudder. "The Use of Electronic Data Interchange for Supply Chain Coordination in the Food Industry," *Journal of Operations Management* 20, no. 4 (August 2002), pp. 375–387.

Hoover, W. E., Jr.; E. Eloranta; J. Holmstrom; and K. Huttunen. *Managing the Demand-Supply Chain: Value Innovations for Customer Satisfaction.* New York: John Wiley & Sons, 2001.

Johnson, M. Eric, and David F. Pike (eds.). *Supply Chain Management: Innovations for Education.* Production and Operations Management Society, 2000.

Knolmayer, Gerhard; Peter Mertens; and Alexander Zeier. *Supply Chain Management Based on SAP Systems.* Springer Verlag, 2001.

Lawrence, F. Barry, and Anoop Varma. "Integrated Supply: Supply Chain Management in Materials Management and Procurement," *Production and Inventory Management Journal,* 2nd quarter 1999.

Lambert, Douglas M., and Terrance L. Pohlen. "Supply Chain Metrics," *International Journal of Logistics Management* 12, no. 1 (2001), pp. 1–19.

Mahajan, J.; Sonja Radas; and Asoo J. Vakharia. "Channel Strategies and Stocking Policies in Uncapacitated and Capacitated Supply Chains," *Decision Sciences Journal* 33, no. 2, pp. 191–222.

Monczka, Robert; R. Trent; and R. Handfield. *Purchasing and Supply Chain Management,* 2nd ed., Southwestern, 2002.

Narasimhan, Ram, and Ajay Das. "Manufacturing Agility and Supply Chain Management Practices," *Production and Inventory Management Journal,* 1st quarter 1999.

Narasimhan, R., and Soo Wook Kim. "Effect of Supply Chain Integration on the Relationship between Diversification and Performance: Evidence from Japanese and Korean Firms," *Journal of Operations Management* 20, no. 3 (June 2002), pp. 303–323.

Persson, Fredrik, and Jan Olhager. "Performance Simulation of Supply Chain Designs," *International Journal of Production Economics* 77, no. 3 (June 11, 2002), p. 231.

Pine, B. J.; B. Victor; and A. C. Boynton. "Making Mass Customization Work," *Harvard Business Review,* September–October 1993.

Rudberg, Martin, and Jan Olhager. "Manufacturing Networks and Supply Chains: An Operations Strategy Perspective," *OMEGA* 31, no. 1 (February 2003).

Shapiro, Jeremy F. *Modeling the Supply Chain.* Duxbury Press, 2000.

Simchi-Levi, David; Philip Kaminsky; and Edith Simchi-Levu. *Designing and Managing the Supply Chain,* 2nd ed., New York: McGraw-Hill, 2003.

Singhal, J., and Kalyan Singhal. "Supply Chains and Compatibility among Components in Product Design," *Journal of Operations Management* 20, no. 3 (June 2002), pp. 289–302.

Stock, G. N.; Noel P. Greis; and John D. Kasarda. "Enterprise Logistics and Supply Chain Structure: The Role of Fit," *Journal of Operations Management* 18, no. 5 (August 2000), pp. 531–547.

Strebel, Paul, ed. *Focused Energy: Mastering Bottom-Up Organization.* Chicester, U.K.: John Wiley & Sons Ltd., 2000.

Swaminathan, J. M.; Stephen F. Smith; and Norman M. Sadeh. "Modeling Supply Chain Dynamics: A Multiagent Approach," *Decision Sciences Journal* 29, no. 3 (summer 1998), pp. 607–632.

Zhao, X.; Jinxing Xie; and Jerry C. Wei. "The Impact of Forecast Errors on Early Order Commitment in a Supply Chain," *Decision Sciences Journal* 33, no. 2 (spring 2002), pp. 251–280.

Discussion Questions

1. Suppose Microsoft is launching a new game, the Y Box.
   a. What are the costs/benefits and risks of making it in house?
   b. How do these change if Microsoft has it made by an EMS outsourcing firm such as Flextronics?

2. Assume that Microsoft in Question 1 did outsource the manufacturing of the Y Box to Flextronics.
   a. What are the cost/benefits and risks of also outsourcing the physical distribution of the product?
   b. How do these change if a third-party logistics provider does this work?
   c. If the logistics is outsourced, what information might Microsoft want to know on a timely basis?

3. In what ways does the Nokia supply chain management approach foster cross-functional and cross-organizational communications?

4. In what ways can knowledge of a customer's exact build schedule provide an advantage over forecasting for a supplier to improve its operations?

5. How does a hub allow two firms in a supply chain to work more effectively? What MPC system linkages need to be provided by the hub operator? What else does the hub need to provide to the supplier and customer?

6. What are the reasons for a firm to outsource? As a supplier, what must you do to get your customers to outsource?

7. What does mass customization mean for Dell? What are the bundles of goods and services it is offering and how are they changing? What does all this mean for MPC systems design?

8. Why is quality an important part of MPC design in supply chains? Can you identify a recent quality issue in the press, and does it have supply chain issues?

9. Why do many dyad-based B2B systems have cumbersome transaction processing?

10. Why is "demand chain management" a better goal than "supply chain management?" What is the key distinction?

Problems

1. A factory makes a special sweater that is sold in a retail store at a rate of five units per 5-day week (50 weeks/year). The store is supplied through a field warehouse. Each of these operates an EOQ/ROP system with the following features:

	Factory	**Warehouse**	**Retail**
EOQ	100	50	10
Lead-time	2 weeks	3 weeks	1 week
Safety stock	20	10	2
ROP	30	25	7

a. What is the total inventory in the supply chain, and the inventory turnover ratios for the factory, warehouse, and retail? How long will it take to introduce a new product?

b. The company has just reengineered its factory so it can make-to-order, with a lead-time of one day. Moreover, it has implemented an agreement with a third-party logistics provider to deliver directly to the retailer in two days. What should be the ordering policy at retail? What will be the total inventory in the chain, and how long will it take to introduce a new product?

2. The sweater in problem 17.1 is now made in three additional colors, with weekly sales of 4, 3, and 1 unit each. Assume that the same EOQ/ROP parameters were used for all four sweaters.

a. What is the total inventory in the chain under the original polices of problem 1? What are the inventory turnover ratios?

b. How different is this answer with the reengineered conditions?

3. Assume that for the original conditions in problem 17.1, the orders from retail are sent by mail and fax. Also assume that the replenishment orders from the field warehouse are sent this way.

a. How many orders per year would be sent from retail to the field warehouse?

b. How many orders per year would be sent from the field warehouse to the factory?

c. How many orders per year would be scheduled by an MRP system?

d. How does all this change with the reengineered conditions?

e. What might the result be if sales terminals at retail are connected by an e-based system directly to a factory JIT system?

4. A manufacturing site is supplied from three suppliers, A, B, and C. They ship to the site, using a trucking company that has a depot in the vicinity. The distances between these entities is as follows:

			To		
From	**A**	**B**	**C**	**Depot**	**Site**
A		10	20	5	25
B	10		15	6	20
C	20	15		30	10
Depot	5	6	30		20
Site	25	20	10	20	

a. Assume that when A wishes to ship to the site, a truck comes from the depot, then after loading goes on to the site, and then returns to the depot. The same pattern is repeated for shipments from B and C. What is the total distance traveled to bring lots from all three suppliers to the site?

b. What is the percentage saving in travel time if the truck picks up all lots in one pass, traveling from depot to A, then to B, then to C, then to site, and then back to depot?

c. Suppose the site had four additional suppliers and the average distance between them and the site and depot were equal to the average distances between A, B, and C and the site/depot. Also assume that the average distance of these suppliers from each other and from A, B, and C is the same as the average distance between A, B, and C. What is the total distance traveled to bring lots from all seven suppliers to the site? What is the percentage saving in travel time if the truck picks up from all seven suppliers in one pass?

5. Returning to Figure 17.4, redo the analysis with policies for both the company and its supplier of holding three periods of sales in inventory instead of two. What are the minimum and maximum quantities ordered by the company on its supplier and by the supplier on its part supplier? How do these compare with the results in Figure 17.4?

6. The XYZ beer company sends its sales people to call on major accounts once per week. The salesperson typically takes a buyer out to lunch, at which they discuss how much beer the customer will order for delivery the following week. The salesperson thereafter writes up the order and mails it to the factory, where it is entered into the order entry system (overnight batch) and the next day scheduled for manufacturing, then delivery. Final delivery to the customer warehouse is typically one week after the sales call, but it can vary as much as plus or minus two days from this norm. One major retail account has 10 stores, supplied from a central warehouse on a weekly basis. The stores are open six days per week, with average daily sales per store of 5, 5, 5, 6, 7, 8 cases of beer. Safety stock in each store is set at four cases. The central warehouse orders weekly, and carries a safety stock of two days' supply in order to offset the variability in replenishment timing.

a. What is the average weekly quantity ordered by each store?

b. What is the average weekly quantity ordered by the central warehouse?

c. What is the total average inventory in the system?

7. The customer in problem 17.6 now plans to replenish its stores on a daily basis, cutting the safety stock for each of them in half.

a. What is the average quantity ordered by each store? What is the total average inventory in the total supply chain?

b. Now the customer is asking XYZ to replenish the central warehouse on a daily basis, with a lead time of one day (it too will reduce its safety stock to one day). What is the average order quantity ordered by the central warehouse, and the total inventory in the system?

8. An automotive parts supplier in Detroit is the supplier for an electronics product provided to one of the major automakers. The product is a combination radio, CD player, telephone, and GPS navigation system. The navigation system is the most expensive portion of the product. It incorporates a GPS chip made in Austin, Texas, which is assembled into a module in Bangkok, and thereafter combined with other parts in an EMS firm located in Chula Vista, California. In Detroit, the unit is combined with some other products such as a telephone and CD changer to fit in the trunk. Figure 17.22 shows the four firms, the flow of materials, and the inventories in the system. As indicated the sales are 10,000 units per week.

a. What is the total inventory in the supply chain?

b. What is the total inventory in weeks of sales?

FIGURE 17.22 Flow of Materials (All Quantities in Thousands)

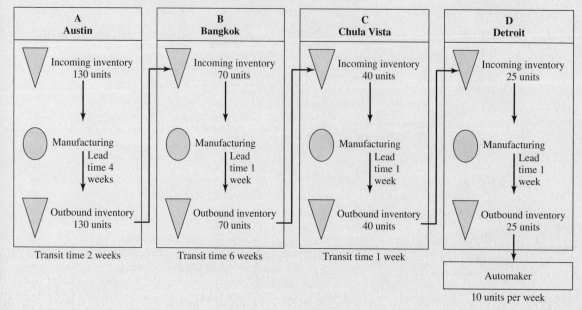

c. What is the total lead time from the start of manufacturing at A until the delivery to the automaker?

9. The EMS company in problem 17.8 has now contracted with a third-party logistics provider that will put in hubs at D, C, and B. All inventories and transactions will be posted in real time to an e-based system that is accessible to all parties in the chain. One major impact is the ability to eliminate all outbound inventories at A, B, and C.

   a. Assuming that no changes are made in inbound inventory levels, what is the change in total chain inventory?

   b. If the use of the hubs is implemented immediately, what is the impact on the orders from D to C? From C to B? From B to A?

10. Continuing with problems 17.8 and 17.9, let us assume that the cost of the chip passed from A to B is $35, and that B buys another $2 of materials and services. When B includes its value added plus profit, it passes the module on to C at a cost of $40. C buys another $5 of materials and services, and then passes the unit on to D at a cost of $50. D buys other fairly standard products and services at a total cost of $40. With its value added and profit added, it passes the package to the automaker at a cost of $100.

   a. The EMS company has studied this cost structure, and now believes that it could take over the module assembly work done in Bangkok (its manufacturing lead time would not be increased). But whereas Bangkok has a value added/profit of $5, this work would need to be priced at $6 if done in Chula Vista. Further analysis, however, finds that there would be an offset in shipping costs of $0.50. How much would the total lead time be reduced if the module were now made at C (assume shipping time from A to C is 1 week)?

   b. What is the change in total chain inventory? Assuming an inventory carrying cost of 10 percent, is this change desirable?

11. The following data are for a portion of the 42 products sold in the Souper Soup example of the chapter:

Product	Forecast (Weekly)	Inventory	Safety Stock
1	100	60	50
2	86	70	45
3	85	20	38
9	20	35	30
10	18	40	30
11	18	25	30
23	6	50	40
24	6	10	40
25	6	5	40

Construct the build schedule to be used at Alpha for these items.

12. Figure 17.6 and the accompanying narrative described a specialty chemicals producer in stage 1, which wished to coordinate fulfillment of customer promises. Let us assume that this company received the following sales orders from a distributor over a 3-week (15-day) period, that shipments were made immediately from stock, and that the sales department issued the following manufacturing orders to replenish their inventory. The firm starts with a beginning inventory of 200, and manufacturing orders are completed in two days (e.g., an order issued on day 1 arrives on day 3, and is available for satisfying sales in day 4).

Day	Sales Order	Manufacturing Order
1	30	100
2	20	
3	10	
4	50	
5	30	100
6	30	
7	25	
8	60	100
9	20	
10	40	
11	30	100
12	10	
13	40	
14	20	
15	30	

a. What are the daily manufacturing deliveries, inventories, and average inventory?

b. Let us now assume that a logistics activity replaces the receipt of sales orders and issuance of manufacturing orders. Now, logistics receives customer orders and makes exactly that quantity in one day (quantities manufactured in day 1 are available for shipping on day 3). Since the largest quantity ordered by the customer is 60, the firm now starts with inventory (a delivery of 35 is scheduled for day 1). What are the day-to-day manufacturing quantities, inventory levels, and average inventory?

c. Let us now assume that the firm can take customer orders, and thereafter manufacture and deliver them in the same day. What are the day-to-day manufacturing quantities, inventory levels, and average inventory in this scenario?

13. Continuing with problem 17.12a (not b and c), let us now assume this specialty chemicals company moves up to stage 2 in Figure 17.6. Its customer (a distributor) also starts with a beginning inventory of 200 units. It has the following set of demand data from its several customers, which it passes to the specialty chemicals company with a delay of three days (customer orders in day 1 are totaled and thereafter placed as an order to the specialty chemicals producer in day 4 and received immediately).

Day	Customer Orders	Replenishment Orders
1	50	30
2	30	20
3	30	10
4	25	
5	60	
6	20	
7	40	
8	30	
9	10	
10	40	
11	20	
12	30	
13	40	
14	20	
15	50	

a. What are the day-to-day replenishment quantities ordered by the distributor (the first three days are provided), the inventory levels, and average inventory?

b. What are the combined inventories of both firms (problem 17.12a)?

14. If we now combine problems 17.12a and 17.13, suppose the two firms eliminated all inventory at the specialty chemicals manufacturer—that is, the customer orders at the distributor as generated in problem 17.13 are directly passed to the specialty chemicals producer and that they are delivered to the customers the following day. What would be the impact on final customer demand? What is the impact on total supply chain inventory?

15. Supposing the specialty chemicals firm now operated under the conditions of problem 17.12c, and the orders from final customers of the distributor are e-based and visible to the specialty chemicals company. They in turn ship directly to the end customers, while the distributor concentrates on sales—holding no inventory. What are the daily total supply chain inventory levels in this case?

Chapter 18

Implementation

This chapter is concerned with implementation issues in MPC systems. At the end of the day new MPC systems change the ways in which people work as well as their understanding of how to serve their customers. There are some key implementation concepts and procedures to learn, and there are existing ideas and procedures that need to be definitively replaced. Implementation of MPC systems is not a one-time event. There is always room for improvement, and the best companies continuously enhance their MPC systems to provide more effective ways to satisfy their customers. Moreover, the enhancements are often somewhat different for different business units in a company. Each business unit tends to define its customer base, segmentation, and bundles of goods/services in unique ways. Finally, there are two fundamental approaches to enhancing MPC systems: One can focus on improving the MPC systems that integrate internal operations; alternatively, one can focus on the MPC systems that integrate between companies—that is, with suppliers/customers. In fact this is not an either/or question. MPC systems improvements can and should take place in both internal and inter-firm systems. These issues are explored in this chapter with the following five key questions:

- *Internal integration:* What are the key implementation issues for enhancing MPC systems within a company?
- *Interfirm integration:* What is the change in approach when the MPC focus is on inter-firm integration?
- *Transformation:* Why does implementation of major MPC improvements need to be seen as "doing better things," not just "doing things better?"
- *Project management:* How does project management play an essential role in the implementation of MPC systems?
- *Benchmarking and auditing:* How should one audit existing MPC systems and benchmark other systems in order to drive continuous improvement?

This chapter has linkages with all the other chapters in that there is an implementation issue in every one. But the key linkages are with Chapter 1, where the scope of MPC is defined, Chapter 4, which concentrates on ERP systems, Chapter 9, where the issue is implementing JIT-based systems, Chapter 17 with its focus on supply chains, and Chapter 19, where we deal with the next frontier of MPC systems.

Internal Integration

Internal integration is concerned with implementing MPC systems that better plan and control the operations within a firm. The driving force for internal integration is largely one of cost reduction, and the implementation journey often now revolves around ERP systems. But the actual implementation of specific MPC systems must reflect the business model of the particular organization (typically focused on a business unit).

From Lean Manufacturing to Lean Organization to Lean Enterprise

Lean manufacturing has as its focus excellence in the factory. Typical improvement objectives are to make significant reductions in inventory levels, throughput times, and responses to customer needs, all with less people and other resources. These objectives are supported by new processes and systems (MPC) and—importantly—by changes in practices to achieve flawless execution.

Flawless execution is an important concept in MPC implementation. This term has the following meaning:

- *Zero defects:* As much as is humanly possible, MPC systems need to operate with few or no mistakes. The best way to ensure this is to design and implement MPC systems in which mistakes are very difficult to make.

- *Routine schedule execution:* One needs to make a schedule and then precisely execute it. To the extent that this is not the case, it is very costly to coordinate other activities with this schedule. There will be broken promises unless large buffer inventories are held.

- *Sufficient planning horizon:* The plans coming from an MPC system need to have a planning horizon long enough for others to readily coordinate their activities with the schedule.

- *No buffers:* Inventories are to be avoided. They tend to take the focus off routine schedule execution and database accuracy. This only hides mistakes and poor practices.

- *Information linkages:* MPC systems have to provide the information to integrate work and decisions in different places and different firms. The data have to be correct, but it is also critical to provide the data. If suppliers are not told of production plans, they need to guess!

- *Recovery mechanisms:* Murphy's law is always in operation (when something can go wrong, it will). There will be defects and schedule misses. The questions are how well is the system able to recover and does this require heroic means?

These flawless execution goals have subordinate goals to support them as well: accuracy in bills of materials, stockroom inventory balances, detailed schedule achievement, and all transaction processing. Additionally, lean manufacturing focuses on quality improvements and additional forms of improving execution in the factory. Basically, the goal is to be able to routinely handle the demands of the marketplace faster, better, and at less cost than the competition.

Lean organization extends this concept by moving beyond pure manufacturing (factory) issues. Now the goal is to achieve excellence in the business unit. Included are better methods for order entry, logistics, after-sales service, and even internal issues such as accounting and human resource management. Additionally, lean organization includes a more comprehensive view of the customers, often including distinct market segmentation, with different approaches and metrics for different customer groups. All of this implies changes in the MPC system to one with a wider focus. In fact, MPC for lean organizations is largely defined by ERP-based systems that focus on the integration of virtually all functional areas of the business unit, supported with an integrated database.

Lean enterprise is one more extension of this thinking, since lean organization usually takes as its focus the entire company. This focus recognizes that there are major improvements to be made from better integration among business units in the same firm. Different business units in the same firm can have common suppliers, customers, and distribution systems. Significant synergies can often be achieved through cross-business unit efforts, but then the MPC systems need to reflect this integration. A key example is seen in recent developments in purchasing. Companies such as Unilever have integrated their procurement activities, at least by region. This started with integration of factory purchasing in the same general business. For example, all major packaging for ice cream products was centralized for Europe.

Thus the MPC system needed to be centralized and requirement information needed to be gathered from multiple locations. A natural follow-on is to integrate the purchasing of major items across all Unilever business units, such as milk powder or packaging in Europe. This again necessitates a broader reach for the MPC systems to determine future requirements. Eventually some of this integration will also become global, and this has happened in some industries and firms. Nokia, for example, does global buying for many of its components. But again, lean enterprise requires MPC systems that support its achievement. For example, if Nokia wishes to buy a particular component globally, it must plan, control, and coordinate—flawlessly—the need/use for this component in all of its business units.

Regional and global linkages are also being driven from the customer side. Supply chain management works both ways, with one's suppliers and one's customers. Thus the customers of Unilever and Nestlé, such as Carrefour and Wal-Mart, now wish to purchase on a regional basis with the expectation that this will move to global purchasing in the not-too-distant future. For Nokia, there is a similar trend toward customer concentration with the big telecom operators such as Vodaphone.

The potential payoffs from consolidated purchasing are large. It is not unusual to see firms reduce the number of SKUs purchased by 75 percent or more as similar (or the same) items are identified and reduced to a common SKU. With this new commonality, the number of suppliers is often reduced by an equal amount. These reductions support great economies of scale as well as potentially closer coordination with fewer suppliers for joint value/cost improvements (such as in new product design). A 75 percent reduction in both items and suppliers implies a 16-fold average increase in volume per supplier! Thus consolidated purchasing means consolidated selling for the suppliers.

Implementation needs to follow a common path or roadmap, whether to achieve lean manufacturing, lean organization, lean enterprise, or lean supply chain. In every case one always needs to address the following set of issues:

- What are the improvement goals? What will this do for the customers?
- What are the resultant MPC systems that will be needed?

- What are the new ways of working? Who will implement the changes?
- What is the business process reengineering required, and who will do it?
- What are the organizational changes required to make this work?
- What are the IT requirements?
- What is the scope of the project to bring this to fruition? Who owns it?
- Are the timings, resource requirements, and scope realistic?

MPC Implementation for Lean Manufacturing

Figure 18.1 depicts the movement from lean manufacturing to lean organization to lean enterprise. The key point here is that implementation depends on what one is implementing and from where one is coming. Implementation of MPC systems to support lean manufacturing (factory excellence) is greatly different from MPC systems for lean organization and even more so from MPC systems for lean enterprise. It is essential to be quite clear as to what are the objectives and by what measures success will be evaluated.

MPC systems for basic manufacturing—in support of lean manufacturing objectives—have their own set of implementation problems and constraints. One extreme is a factory run by informal methods, as is often the case for a new company with a successful new product. The factory has been essentially a laboratory or craft shop, but now it needs to change into one based on manufacturing of higher volumes with tight controls. Here the MPC implementation starts with basic scheduling, supported by bill of materials design and actions to achieve inventory accuracy. Without inventory accuracy, no MPC system can plan effectively. So implementation starts with very basic changes such as limited-access stockrooms and frequent cycle counts. The analog is to a bank: No one in a bank can rummage around in the vault as he/she pleases, taking cash as needed, and the teller's cash is closed out several times per day.

Our implementation "roadmap" needs to reflect the unique aspects of lean manufacturing in finding the answers to the roadmap questions. First of all, if the approach is lean manufacturing, the focus is on the factory, where cost reduction, improved quality, and better delivery performance are the objectives. This implies change in the ways people work and

FIGURE 18.1 From Lean Manufacturing to Lean Enterprise

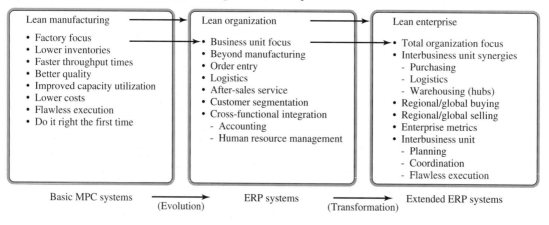

in the systems/processes used to support their work. Implementation of MPC systems goes hand in hand with business process reengineering (BPR). New processes have to be adopted and implemented. Old ways of working need to be unlearned. Thus, implementation is far more inclusive than the adoption of some new information technology (IT). In fact, it is very important that IT be a fast follower but not the driver for MPC decisions/implementation. New work patterns need to be defined and followed precisely. For lean manufacturing, it is usually the work processes to support basic MRP systems that have to be implemented. These determine which components are to be withdrawn from the stock rooms at which times and sent where. These processes and systems must be followed. Any problem solved at the expense of data accuracy—no matter how important—is just not worth it. The organizational changes are largely within the manufacturing function, including shop scheduling, logistics, and links to customer service. A lean manufacturing project needs to be owned by the senior executives in manufacturing who are willing to make whatever changes are necessary to implement the use of new formal systems and processes.

Implementation of MPC processes always implies changes in work methods (i.e., BPR). This is so if the goal is lean manufacturing, lean organization, lean enterprise, or lean supply chain. But the work changes are different, as are the processes and systems. The starting point is the set of objectives for the MPC implementation. Lean manufacturing requires work methods that support flawless execution in the factory following classic MRP-based approaches: A master production schedule, explosion to yield time-phased material and capacity plans, detailed shop scheduling to execute the plans, and purchasing planning/execution to support the detailed shop schedules. Lean manufacturing objectives are followed up by MPC systems to support total quality management and other manufacturing improvement programs.

Implementation of JIT approaches for factory excellence provides another approach to manufacturing processes, which again require the right supporting work methods and MPC systems. JIT does work for some kinds of firms, but the shift to JIT from the traditional informal or even MRP-based manufacturing approaches to JIT mandates major changes in processes, systems, metrics, and flawless execution. Typically the factory needs to be reconfigured into manufacturing cells, amounts and placements of inventory need to be determined, and rules for when to produce—in what quantities—need to be established. The primary point here is that the manufacturing processes and the MPC systems need to support the new ways of manufacturing, which in turn satisfy particular marketplace objectives.

There are many ways to execute the classic MRP-based approaches as well as JIT approaches. The differences reflect the use of different processes and systems to do the job. The choice again needs to depend on what the company wishes to accomplish in the marketplace, identifying those processes that provide unique benefits. But an important principle here is that the choice should not be overly constrained by present processes. Many companies have invested large sums to design systems to support unique processes that add little value over some common or available process/system. There is a good maxim for this: Choose simple systems that are "good enough" to satisfy the customers. Do not develop elaborate MPC systems unless they provide some unique marketplace value! Change an existing complex process to match a common process/system, rather than customize a readily available system to match a complex process. The choice of processes/systems needs to be driven with a strategic perspective. The selection should be by managers.

Information system specialists can help, but in the last analysis those who understand the objectives, as well as the current processes, should make the process design choices.

MPC Implementation for Lean Organization

Implementation of MPC systems for lean organization objectives is very different from that for lean manufacturing. The emphasis is on the overall business unit, so the typical approach follows implementation of ERP-based approaches. This implies a functional approach where ERP is implemented function by function, and the overall ERP system architecture allows the functional systems to be integrated. ERP can start with manufacturing, essentially following the ways of lean manufacturing, or it can start with another function. In some cases today, ERP systems are being implemented in firms that do not even have true manufacturing. Regardless of how started, the ERP structure provides an integrated approach to business unit operations that yields a database and platform for running the business.

For any manufacturing company, MPC systems must be an integral part of the ERP implementation process. ERP and lean organization implies implementing processes and systems to support work practices in marketing/sales, product design/development, after-sales service, distribution/logistics, finance/accounting, and human resource management, in addition to the basic manufacturing processes. The principle relating to constraints of existing systems applies even more here—think simplicity! One needs to determine which functional areas are truly important and whether unique work methods/processes will provide a competitive advantage. Again, this choice should be driven by those who best understand the marketplace, and what needs to be done to achieve some competitive advantage. For example, we once worked with a company implementing ERP in a newly created business unit based on a merger of three former units. At first there was a plan to create a very complex payroll system to satisfy the historically different ways of payment. This investment in complex systems would add nothing to the business unit's competitive advantage. A packaged payroll system was adopted, and everyone was thereafter paid in the same way.

The need for managers to drive process/system choices is even more critical for lean organization. The strategic objectives of the business unit have to be reflected in the choice of which functional areas to implement first, as well as in the particular MPC systems to be implemented. ERP systems should facilitate these objectives, implying that those processes that are unique be carefully chosen. That is, it is strategically important to identify which processes and supporting MPC systems will allow the firm to achieve something unique in the marketplace. Unfortunately, this is far too often not the case. We have seen many ERP implementation projects where at the outset the project defined key business process reengineering to support new ways to provide new bundles of goods and services to the customers, with limited attention given to routine processes that have little competitive impact. But at the end, the relative efforts were reversed. Too many managers insisted that some existing ways of working needed to be retained. The flow of ideas needs to be toward marketplace and customer objectives—these drive work design and processes. These in turn drive system design. And the choices are tempered by always using existing or commonly available processes/systems when they will do the job. One clearly needs to differentiate between "essential," "nice to have," and "good enough."

Again, the implementation roadmap and its set of questions need to be tailored to the key issues associated with lean organization. The clear implication for implementing ERP is that one needs a business unit perspective based on what the business unit sees as its unique customer segments and marketplace opportunities. Thereafter this perspective should allow the implementation team to set priorities: What are the critical customer segments and how do we win the orders in these segments? Which functional areas will yield the best results quickly? Where do we need unique ways of doing business to increase customer loyalty? What do we need to change in terms of the ways we work? What processes and systems best support these ways of working? What are the readily available processes/systems in existing ERP packaged solutions? When are these "good enough"? In lean organization the scope of the implementation project becomes more critical since the project cuts across functional lines. There are many constituencies to serve, and project creep is a real danger.

MPC Implementation for Lean Enterprise

The shift to lean enterprise, as shown in Figure 18.1, is perhaps even more dramatic than that from lean manufacturing to lean organization. Now, the objective is on how to achieve synergies across the entire company, or at least a set of business units. As shown in Figure 18.1, the change is transformative. That is, it is not sufficient to do the same things better. We will see that in order to truly attain lean organization excellence, one again needs new MPC systems and processes, executed flawlessly. Implementing these MPC systems involves a new set of challenges, ones that should not be taken lightly.

Many firms approach lean enterprise—perhaps without calling it so—through a focus on purchasing. Lean enterprise encompasses much more than purchasing, but consolidated purchasing is often seen as a "quick win"; unfortunately, the quick win turns out to be quite a bit more complex than anticipated. A necessary first step is to rationalize the items being purchased. The implications for MPC are huge. If ERP systems have been implemented separately in the business units, there will undoubtedly be different specifications for items purchased, different suppliers, different processes and systems, and different ideas for what is important. These need to be brought into a common framework and a common MPC system.

An example is a firm selling a well-known brand of ice cream bar. To the customers this product was the same all over the world. But in fact, it was packaged in 300 different wrappers. Why? This company was organized geographically (by country), so that Greece could decide that the red color in the wrapper would be better received in its market if it were slightly more orange. Every geographic region manufactured this product as it saw fit. If Italy had Italian packaging equipment that worked well with aluminum foil, then it would develop an aluminum foil wrapper. The English product came with an English language wrapper. Even the ice cream bar itself was a bit different from place to place: some area managers preferred their vanilla ice cream to be more yellow than others, for example.

It is interesting to again see the differences in the way the implementation roadmap play out here. Implementing lean enterprise in this case required massive changes. Manufacture of the particular ice cream bar was concentrated in a few countries—not all. In order to achieve purchasing leverage it was necessary to select one type of wrapper, even if this meant retooling the packaging lines. The wrappers needed to have multilanguage packaging. This went hand in hand with developing a regional orientation to production/distribution (that is, the demands of each country had to be balanced so as to best satisfy selected customer segments as well as to maximize total group financial performance, not that of individual country units). The country form of organization had to give way to a regional form. This in turn affected MPC systems design in that production in any country did not automatically belong to that country, particularly in case of a shortage. The demands from every region needed to be stated correctly, with no padded forecasts, all inventories in the countries had to become visible, and all data elements in country MPC systems needed to be common. Manufacturing at the various factories needed to be coordinated. This required joint capacity planning both in the short term and for the longer term. The transit packaging (for cases of ice cream bars) needed to have multiple bar coding that supported the distribution systems in each country, each of the third-party distribution partners, and the various major customer groups.

In fact, for a long time it was not possible to make the changes necessary to achieve lean enterprise for this company. Everyone knew that the 300 different wrappers were a big problem. But the problem could not be solved by the purchasing organization. Nor could it be solved by interactions among the country organizational units. Too often the response would be "Let's rationalize—you change and do it like I do it!" Finally, a senior manager said "I no longer want to hear why we cannot do this. I only want to hear what each of you is going to do to do it." He also changed the country-based performance system to one based more on regional performance and sanctioned a region-based MPC system to coordinate the lean organization. The payoffs? This firm achieved major savings in purchasing, but there were even more important payoffs: During the first year the regional MPC system was working, the summer was colder than usual in the northern part of Europe and warmer than usual in the southern part. This allowed—for the first time—shipments of excess inventories from north to south, instead of holding those stocks for an entire year while unable to fill demand in the South.

This example is about regional optimization, not global optimization, but it was a major step forward for the company. There may well be other steps that are more global in nature, but food does seem to be a product with more regional characteristics than most other products. The primary point of the example is that lean enterprise does indeed pay off. But implementation requires breaking organizational constraints that focus on business units or geographical areas at the expense of the overall enterprise. The MPC systems to support lean enterprise are integrated to provide coordination across common company boundaries. Manufacturing has to be planned at a central level, and allocations may be necessary: The focus is on overall enterprise optimization, not that of particular organizational units.

Herein lies an interesting dilemma. Should a company centralize in order to achieve the benefits of lean enterprise—or does this negate local optimization, make it more difficult to appeal to specific customer segments, and create a feeling of bureaucracy? One approach to this dilemma has been to try to separate the "back end" (purchasing, manufacturing, distribution) from the "front end" (sales, marketing). The separation potentially allows for economies from lean enterprise while supporting more localized and focused sales/marketing. The overall objective is to preserve the unique nature of the business unit focus while still gaining the benefits of coordinated execution. An example we know well is a large food service firm with many different business units, each appealing to a local client base and market segment. The menus for these units can be quite different, but they all can use the same chicken.

The difficult part of this front end–back end separation is to design the MPC systems to pass the needs of the front end to the back end and thereafter execute all parts flawlessly.

Component and Database Commonality/Rationalization

Implementing MPC systems always involves database cleanup and standardization of components, processes, and bills of material. But achieving lean enterprise requires a new level of cleanup, common definitions, and new dictates for flawless execution. In essence, the enterprise has to have enterprise-wide unambiguous definitions and complete matching between MPC system quantities and actual quantities (including shared forecast accuracy). This requirement is almost universally underestimated in terms of the time and effort required, as well as the necessary organizational commitment and leadership necessary. However, there are large economies to be gained through reducing the number of items in the database.

A major telecom firm has attempted implementation of an enterprise-wide ERP system three times. Now the company's managers think they have "probably" done it right. Implementation in each of the factories was relatively straightforward, achieving lean manufacturing in every case. Putting these ERP systems together by business unit also was reasonably straightforward, and lean organization was thereby achieved. But then it was necessary to integrate regionally with the two major product divisions, and thereafter expand the regional approach to a single global approach. These changes required major modifications in databases as well as MPC standardization efforts. The biggest challenge came when the company wished to jointly plan and control all purchasing, manufacturing, and logistics in all factories, on a global basis, for both business product divisions. A major problem encountered was that one product division operated with accurate forecasts and passed quite exact requirements back to its suppliers, while the other one tended to pass optimistic requirement forecasts to its suppliers (often the *same* suppliers). These suppliers were smart enough to know that the requirements from one part of the company were right while the others were overstated. But now—if these two sets of demands were combined—the suppliers would become confused. It was necessary for the telecom company to eliminate the overoptimistic planning in one division and for the personnel in that division to clearly understand the implications for their MPC systems.

A critical point in rationalizing components and the resultant MPC database is the need to move beyond specifications that come from suppliers. A large food service company found that it bought 16 kinds of frozen peas. In its analysis it found that two or three kinds would be sufficient. But if a particular business unit specified its peas as "Supplier X peas" then it is not possible to rationalize. If instead of the Supplier X specifications, the specifications are exact—but in fact they *are* those of Supplier X, we have the same problem (e.g., peas with 0.056 percent sodium content). Component specifications set by suppliers is a very common phenomenon, and needs to be broken. This implies hard work on the part of the *users* of the components to determine what is the best (and widest) specification. This does not necessarily mean establishing a low-quality specification. In the case of the food service firm, it wished to set the specification for frozen peas so that the purchasing organization could have considerable freedom to buy the best-quality peas for its meal planning.

Achieving the necessary level of component commonality typically requires an interorganizational task force that has the explicit goal of significantly reducing component variety and the size of the supplier base. In the latter case, a good starting point is to prepare a list of all suppliers who provide only one item. The obvious question is "Who can also provide this item?" In the case of the food service firm, its U.S. restaurant unit created

FIGURE 18.2

An Example of Analysis of Purchases

Country/Product Category	Range	Percentage of Spend in Range (e.g., Top 10 Items Represent 17% of Spend)			
		Top 10	Top 25	Top 50	Top 300
U.K. nonproduct	2,371	17	30	42	80
U.K. mechanical	2,014	15	26	37	74
U.K. electronic	3,012	14	25	36	71
U.K. systems	882	19	34	50	94
U.K. packaging	4,345	12	22	32	68
France nonproduct	903	25	41	60	95
France mechanical	602	24	44	74	90
France electronic	1,220	24	45	65	92
France packaging	1,350	20	35	53	80
Spain all products	5,451	11	18	28	63

a "food council" that specifically focused on rationalizing items and suppliers. This group was able to quickly reduce the number of items purchased by one-half and the supplier base by a similar amount. It is now trying to do it again—another 50 percent reduction in both categories. The next moves for this company are to extend the thinking, geographically and across business units. Lean enterprise implies rationalizing the item and supplier base for the whole enterprise. Something like an enterprise food council will be needed, but there surely will be the same sort of organizational barriers, like those encountered by the ice cream manufacturer.

One firm that we know mounted a company-wide effort to rationalize the purchasing activities in Europe. The effort was started independently in each of the geographical divisions. The initial effort was to separate the purchased items into product groupings and collect information on the distribution of purchasing costs. Figure 18.2 shows the results shortly after the project was started. Focusing on the first line in Figure 18.2, one sees that the U.K. business unit purchases 2,371 unique nonproduct items (such as office supplies), but just 13 percent of them (300 SKUs) account for 80 percent of the total purchasing costs for this category. The same pattern can be seen in all three divisions for each of the categories. This is typical of most purchasing profiles, with a small percentage of the items accounting for a large percentage of the costs. The French division purchases substantially fewer items than the U.K., but still has the same purchasing profile, with just a few items accounting for a large percentage of the costs. For example, in the nonproduct category, the French buy only 903 different items, but one-third of them account for 95 percent of the buy. This means that they buy another 603 items to fill out their needs for nonproduct items. Note that Spain has yet to break down the items purchased into categories.

Product rationalization is hard work, but it does offer great potential for being able to concentrate purchasing power and achieve major cost savings. Figure 18.2 focuses on rationalization within a country unit, and there are large potential savings in reducing the

FIGURE 18.3
Number of Divisions Making Copy Paper Purchases from Each Vendor

Vendor

Specifications	1	2	3	4	5	6	7	Specification Totals
80 bright, 20 weight	1		3	1	6			11
82 bright, 20 weight		1						1
84 bright, 20 weight			2	2		3		7
80 bright, 22 weight	12	3	4		4		1	24
80 bright, 22 weight	1							1
82 bright, 22 weight		1						1
Vendor totals	14	5	9	3	10	3	1	45

number of items purchased in each division. But in the spirit of lean enterprise, it is necessary to rationalize *across* the country units. That is, even greater savings are possible if the number of items purchased is reduced in total, with higher volumes for the reduced supplier base. Figure 18.3 shows a method for doing this. For a category and an item type, say nonproduct copy paper, list all vendors and item specifications purchased. These are the rows and columns of Figure 18.3. The entries in each cell are the number of divisions that purchase the item. Promising places to start the rationalization process are with those specifications that have multiple users. Potential vendors are those that have high totals. Going further into the analysis provides information on the products that represent a high portion of the purchase costs. These are candidates for becoming standard items. Thus, Figure 18.3 seems to indicate that three of the six specifications as well as three of the seven vendors are immediate candidates for rationalization, since they appear to account for a small amount of the total purchasing activity. This conclusion, however, would need to be carefully checked. There could be a large volume associated with one vendor or specification—or the particular item might have some unique benefit.

There is one further issue in rationalization that is critical to implementation of MPC systems. In far too many cases we have seen that rationalization has been put off for later efforts, rather than tackled first. This is usually a mistake. By not rationalizing, the problems faced are much more complex and the MPC systems to deal with them are similarly overly complicated and difficult to implement. Several years ago one of us was asked by a food additives company if it should implement a state-of-the-art ERP system that was at that time being implemented in several sister companies. We strongly advised them not to do so, because they had an enormously complex product structure For example, they had 300 "standard" strawberry yogurt flavors plus "special" strawberry yogurt flavors. The bill of materials design and maintenance for their product structure using classic ERP approaches would be a nightmare. Instead they were advised to restructure their product records, using modular building blocks. Unfortunately, they did not get around to doing so, and a few years later decided to implement a state-of-the-art ERP system. The company was essentially unable to run the business and experienced a drop in sales of more than 50 percent.

Interfirm Integration

In some ways, a natural extension of lean enterprise is to move toward a lean supply chain, through working across companies to increase the value/cost ratio. But in fact, whereas the move from lean organization to lean enterprise is transformative, the move on to lean supply chain is probably better seen as revolutionary. This is particularly so for the MPC systems required to support lean supply chains.

A New Paradigm

Lean enterprise is a desirable prerequisite to lean supply chain, since it should incorporate rationalization and thereby increase the potential benefits to the partners in a supply chain relationship. But lean enterprise does not have to precede lean supply chain, and many firms are indeed working on this endeavor. In fact, the good news is that one can achieve benefits from lean supply chain with a modest investment in time, whereas the ERP system implementation for lean enterprise is a long and tedious process.

Implementation of lean enterprise typically focuses on developing ERP-based processes and systems on an overall company basis or on implementing complex middle-ware to connect ERP systems. This usually follows from earlier implementation of ERP systems at the business unit level. Implied are not only MPC systems that can accumulate demands from all enterprise needs. One also needs enterprise based metrics and processes that optimize the total benefits to the organization, not to each organizational unit independently.

Dyad Relationships

The key building block for the new MPC paradigm to support supply chain management is to base the MPC systems on support of joint efforts between two particular supply chain entities. For our purposes, a dyad can be defined as a critical supply chain relationship between two firms that is designed to achieve a significant joint benefit.

The major shift in approach for lean supply chain is that the focus is on MPC systems to support a *specific* dyad in whatever unique ways best support the relationship. The dyad is made up of two business units operating as supplier and customer, and it is not necessary to create a dyadic relationship with *every* supplier or customer. One can choose to work with an important supplier of some particular component, as well as with a customer who is seen as important.

The choice of which suppliers/customers to work with—which dyads to form—is complex. At the end of the day the criteria of lean enterprise still come into play, but now the focus is on value/cost in a specific chain—that is, for the two firms combined. The obvious first choice is to find where costs can be taken out of the chain. This requires careful analysis and understanding of the difference between costs, prices, and margins. Any cost in the chain should be removed if possible, with attendant benefits shared by the dyad partners. If at all possible margins should be preserved or even increased. If your supplier increases its margin by working with you, it will devote more of its energy/brainpower to you to do so.

Conversely, squeezing a supplier's margins makes you a less desirable customer. You should obviously want to increase your own margins and competitive ability, but it makes sense to share the benefits with those who help create them. Moreover, smart suppliers evaluate margins by customer, not only by percentage of sales. This means that by significantly increasing the amount purchased from a supplier, that supplier might indeed accept lower unit margins, while significantly increasing the total margin achieved from this customer.

In many interfirm improvement projects, one needs to invest in one part of the dyad to achieve benefits in the other. This is because most firms have already made the investments where they also achieve the benefits. The interesting potentials are where a supplier does something that makes it much easier for the customer to do business and vice versa. For example, a supplier can provide materials to a customer on a vendor-managed inventory (VMI) basis, so the customer does not need to order, transactions are reduced, and the inventory comes off the customer's books. Similarly, the customer can provide accurate detailed demand data for the supplier's items, allowing the supplier to provide them at their discretion, thereby providing flexibility to factory schedules and logistics.

Dyad-based lean supply chains again imply MPC systems—of a different kind—to support new processes; the processes require business process reengineering (BPR), now in *both* dyad companies. It is critical to understand that the reengineering *must* be in both companies and that different changes in thinking and implementation are required. It will also be necessary to find ways to get around rigidities of some processes that are built into ERP-based MPC systems.

Implementation of dyad-based interfirm integration often requires exchanging key people between the two firms for temporary assignments. Often, someone from one company needs to work inside the dyad partner company for six months or so. The work is on BPR that crosses the dyad: What has to be changed in each company? Where are the benefits and what has to change to achieve them? How do we extract data from existing systems, pass it back and forth, and integrate our MPC systems? People who think they are engaged in supply chain partnering when they only mandate changes from their suppliers are usually mistaken!

MPC systems for interfirm integration are increasingly utilizing the Internet, that is, e-based B2B systems. This allows conditions in each part of the dyad to be visible in essentially real time, and for joint planning to be carefully synchronized (e.g. the next week's demand is always passed on Monday, confirmed on Tuesday, etc.). Taking time delays out of interfirm planning is in itself a source of benefits. This can be particularly important in responding to surprises in end customer demands and in new product introductions. At a more basic level is the ability to eliminate dual transaction processing in the dyad and to reduce the bullwhip effect. Sometimes this requires subversion of existing MPC system processes—for example, changing ERP systems that require orders, invoices, and other transactions to authorize movement of materials from a supplier to a customer, and subsequent payment for those materials. Indeed, most of these transactions require manual intervention; someone has to process them. The problems are compounded when the system does not reflect the reality of the actual process. For example, many times suppliers are promised payment of invoices within 30 days but in fact they are paid later, and with variability in the delay.

Implementation of e-based systems for interfirm integration follows a much different pattern than that of ERP-based systems. Instead of a functional approach, now the focus needs to be around certain key dyad processes, such as demand creation, supply planning, order fulfillment, and project management. Each of these cuts across the functions in both dyad firms. Moreover, developing the interfirm integration—processes and systems—has to be driven by the specific objectives, and must be integrated with other systems in each enterprise.

In practice, implementation of interfirm e-based systems tends to be rather short. There is not an immediate need to create an all-encompassing system. Instead, our experience is that a dyad can establish and implement an e-based system in about six months. This system will then evolve as new forms of cooperative MPC efforts are developed. It will also evolve when new dyad relationships are added. What works well in one dyad, for one set of objectives, may need to be modified in another.

The specific dyad relationship depends on two basic ideas: trust and objectives. Assuming that trust exists, we focus on how the objectives must drive design of the MPC dyad. In any company, the relationships with specific suppliers and customers will be somewhat special. There will be some common problems/issues, but others may be different. It is essential that the dyad partners identify the key objectives for working together, and quickly determine what are the MPC implementation issues in each of the companies. A fairly common example is the identification of separate inventories in both companies (finished goods at the supplier and the same items held as materials by customers). Eliminating at least one inventory can take significant costs out of the chain. It will also increase the speed to respond to new challenges such as product innovation. But eliminating one inventory level requires joint planning, information visibility across the chain, and flawless execution of the chain. The MPC systems for both dyad partners need to be based on accurate and clearly communicated information, and the partners must execute according to agreed-on time schedules.

In one recent case, we worked with an electronic manufacturing services (EMS) company that was building a new consumer electronics product that was expected to have great consumer acceptance. The final design for the product was being established as one part of the interaction between the EMS and the customer. This meant that changes in product configuration needed to be one part of the e-based MPC systems to link the EMS and the customer. Design changes needed communication in essentially real time. A second objective related to the inability to predict consumer acceptance. This drove a key objective for the dyad: great flexibility in ramping up production to whatever levels were necessary. But to avoid the bullwhip effect, it was necessary for the EMS to have visibility of actual consumer sales, since there was a need to build the pipeline inventories, especially since the product launch was to be for the Christmas season.

The e-based linkages with suppliers were also driven by specific objectives. Fast linkages were critical to implementing the changes in product design, and to knowing immediately the extent of obsolescence in components/products (in the total chain) caused by any design change. It was also necessary for the EMS to have enough visibility in its suppliers' factories to know the extent to which production could be ramped up and over what time horizon. The customer also wished to have access to this level of planning detail. A special case came from one major module of the device. It had a high defect rate, which largely resulted from one component of the module. It became necessary to modify the e-based

MPC systems so that all quantities of this module and its components were visible to the EMS and to the customer. Visibility required knowledge of total quantities, quantities rejected, and status of rejected materials in several different firms in the supply chain. All changes in the status of rejected materials needed to be reflected in the MPC systems at all levels of the chain.

On the other hand, the specific e-based planning tools needed by the EMS to interact with the majority of its suppliers were quite similar. It was necessary for the EMS to extract data from its ERP systems (more then one plant), combine these data in ways that were not too dissimilar, and transmit them to the various key suppliers. The relationships with suppliers varied somewhat, with several suppliers using VMI and others working with more conventional systems. In some cases it was necessary to jointly develop unique planning linkages between the EMS and a supplier. This was particularly the case when the supplier used multiple plants; the EMS wished to have visibility into the chain, and the supplier needed to determine how best to partition the demand to its factories.

Partnership/Trust

We started the last section by stating that implementing dyad partnerships must be founded on trust and clear objectives. Let us now turn to the trust issue. The bottom line here is that a dyad relationship that is not based on trust and mutual understanding does not have a good chance of success. If costs are to be incurred by one partner in the dyad and the benefits received by the other, there must be some means to make this attractive to both parties. If one party talks "partnership" but this is only another form of bargaining, again this will not result in taking cost out of the chain. Zero-sum approaches have indeed been widely used to good results, and we should not expect negotiation to become extinct. But in many cases there is much less ability to decrease prices through bargaining than through mutual efforts to design cost out of the chain. Eliminating an entire inventory level in the chain, moving goods from start at the supplier to finish at the customer in one week instead of three, significantly reducing the bullwhip effect on the chain, and slashing distribution costs—all of these can be achieved through combined (dyad) efforts. But they need to be implemented jointly, with new work methods and MPC systems in both companies, and with mutual benefits received.

To many readers, concepts of trust, partnership, shared values and joint efforts are completely naïve and counter to their experience. This is sadly true, but only makes the potential payoffs from cooperative efforts larger and the implementation challenges even greater. We have had many conversations with suppliers to the auto industry. In general, these suppliers have been bruised and beaten by sharp negotiators for years. They now tend to be extremely careful as to the information they are willing to share with their customers. We recently did a study of two manufacturers of rear hatch doors for two different compact cars. The study was based on one metal door (made in this case by the car company) and one made from composite materials (made by a supplier firm). Both firms in the study understand that there are important insights we can give them if they are willing for us to identify in each case the other firm and bring them together to share the details of the study. But each firm (the supplier in particular) is extremely reluctant to share the information, feeling that doing so might put it at some disadvantage in a future contractual negotiation.

Automotive suppliers are equally cagey as to promises from their customers. Volumes often do not materialize, but this can be forgiven if the marketplace so dictates. But sometimes volumes are promised, prices are set accordingly, and thereafter the volumes are given to others. Finally there are the working processes and supporting MPC systems. Far too often suppliers are promised clear and accurate information, limitations to changes, and frozen time horizons that just do not turn out to be the case. Several suppliers have told us that Toyota receives the lowest prices in the industry. But this is not because Toyota bargains harder; Toyota says what it is going to do—and then does what it says. Other well-known automotive customers continually change the timings and amounts of materials demanded from their suppliers, often with very short notice. Toyota gets better prices because it is easy to do business with. In essence this means that interfirm integration with Toyota works; the work processes and MPC systems in the dyad companies execute flawlessly, and costs are removed from the chain, to the benefit of both supplier and customer.

Nokia has a particularly interesting viewpoint on the subject of partnership/trust. It says that *the* single most important criterion in choosing a supply chain partner is "shared values." If it feels this is not the case, there is no point in investing the time and energy to develop a dyadic relationship. Nokia is a very large customer for many of its suppliers, and it also feels that, in general, it is only large suppliers that can be their supplier partners. The supplier partners need to have global operations, Nokia wishes to be a preferred customer, and the dyad needs to have excellent work processes and connected MPC systems. The investment in implementing a well-functioning dyad is seen by Nokia as significant. However, the cost of *not* having a well-functioning dyad is even greater. It is essential that the processes and MPC systems support rapid new product development with minimal obsolescence, that ramp-up can be extremely rapid, and that surprises are few and fixed quickly. None of this is possible without excellent MPC systems, built on a foundation of trust and mutual interest.

Third-Party Logistics Providers

Third parties, particularly logistics companies, often play an important role in implementing supply chain management and interfirm integration. They are responsible for moving the goods between dyad partners, and sometimes for storing the inventories (in **hubs**). Supply chain optimization can be enhanced by use of hubs between the stages in the chain. A hub can be seen as a physical warehouse, or in fact a virtual warehouse where a third-party distribution provider takes possession of the goods but can keep them anywhere—including on trucks! The use of hubs is particularly useful in the case of a finished goods manufacturer such as Hewlett-Packard or an EMS and its immediate suppliers. All inventories are best placed in one place, near the point of use (the finished goods manufacturer or EMS). Having finished goods inventories at the suppliers as well as at the EMS will aggravate the bullwhip effect and impede joint efforts to develop MPC orchestration of joint work.

The logistics activities need to be driven by state-of-the-art work processes and MPC systems. In some cases, it is the logistics partner that in fact orchestrates the chain. Moreover, in some cases it makes a great deal of sense for the logistics provider to play a key role in implementation. To whatever extent a series of product movements and storages (transportation and hubs) can be integrated with an existing set of movements and storages, the incremental costs will tend to be quite modest. If the logistics chain is coordinated well, the total inventories in the chain can be reduced, transportation costs can be cut, and flexibility can be increased for the partners in the dyad(s).

In the nonintegrated approach, a supplier calls a trucking company to take a consignment of goods to a customer, and the truck might travel half empty. In one potential integrated approach, the supplier knows that the truck will pass its factory every Tuesday at 10 A.M. and Thursday at 4 P.M. (arriving at the customer plant 24 hours later). The supplier can put whatever it wishes on the truck, enough to last the customer for a few days or weeks. The materials are held in a hub by the third-party logistics provider, and supplied to the customer on a VMI basis with all inventory values visible to the supplier and the customer. The trucking cost now becomes essentially a fixed cost, irrespective of the quantity hauled, and the truck can pick up additional materials at very little incremental cost. A potential follow-up on the part of the supplier is to eliminate all finished goods inventories for the materials moving through this supply chain. The costs to hold the inventories are paid by the supplier to the third-party logistics provider according to the amounts held. The costs are thus visible and variable; there will be good reason to sharpen the scheduling of manufacturing to reduce them.

The third-party logistics provider should also ideally handle outbound freight from the customer to the customer's customers. That is, after unloading supplier materials at the customer, the truck should be immediately loaded with goods on the way to market. The larger the transportation integration becomes, the greater the savings potential. However, it is important to understand that it is the logistics company that now takes on a key role in designing, implementing, and orchestrating the supply chain.

Transformation

One primary driver in lean manufacturing is continuous improvement, or kaizan. But continuous improvement is based on the idea of essentially doing the same things better. Transformation, on the other hand, recognizes that continuous improvement is necessary but not sufficient. One needs to also do better things: Break the barriers. Change the rules of the game. Make a quantum step. Set the goals in business process reengineering to double some metric, or cut it in half if reduction is the goal.

We live in a world of transformative change, since the only way to outpace competitors is to move beyond mere improvement of current thinking. But implementation of transformative change is different from that where one evolves in a continuous improvement mode. Implementation of transformation typically requires a senior management commitment, a shared consensus as to the expected results and marketplace impact, an understanding as to the impact on those most affected by the transformation, and a well-defined project with detailed plans and objectives.

Figure 18.4 depicts the need for *continuous* transformations and how each of these has to be supported though new ways of working. Transformations in the supply chain need to be seen in a strategic context; they need to support conscious decisions made with respect to preferred customers and market segments. Which customers will we target and how will we win the orders? What are the bundles of goods and services we can offer that will make us immune from competitors? In each transformation, there is a need to work differently—to reengineer key processes—usually interfirm processes. But the bottom line is that in every case new processes must be supported by new MPC systems that are specifically oriented to the new ways of thinking. What is the MPC infrastructure required to deliver this

FIGURE 18.4 **Continuous Transformations Require New Organizational Capabilities and Thinking**

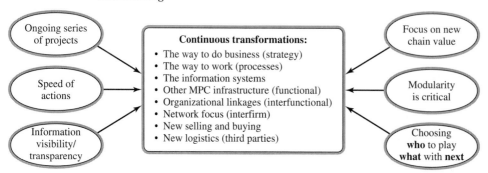

promise? This new MPC infrastructure is the key difference between vague ideas about supply chain management and concrete results! We now examine some of these transformations and MPC changes.

Stair-Step Transformations

Stair-step transformation is a way to emphasize the need for *joint* transformation of a supply chain. It is imperative for any company to understand that to view a supply chain problem as "theirs" instead of "ours"—"they" not "we"—is shortsighted thinking. The big payoffs in value/cost are achieved through joint developments. Figure 18.5 shows the necessary joint efforts in a series of supply chain transformations. Here we have an automotive company working with a major supplier to implement modular assembly. The module is the cockpit module—the firewall of the car with whatever can be attached to it, such as steering wheel, dashboard, brake cylinder, pedals, etc. The first transformation depicted in Figure 18.5 shows the need for the automotive company to outsource this work to the module supplier. Outsourcing is by definition different from subcontracting. In the former, one divests the assets, the people, and the competencies. Outsourcing implies giving up the ability to perform this work. Figure 18.5 shows the supplier as needing to develop the competencies for assembly, with a performance criterion of conformance. That is, the supplier needs to assemble cockpit modules with no defects. Of course, this can only be accomplished with the MPC systems for linking with suppliers, as well as those for organizing internal processes. At the same time, the automotive manufacturer needs to outsource, and it needs to reduce costs by doing so. This again implies changing its ways of working and the MPC infrastructure to support the new ways of working. If it did not truly outsource, then duplicate capacities are held and obsolete MPC processes are maintained, with extra supply chain system costs.

The next transformation shows the supplier needing to gain competencies in logistics. This transformation is shown as a discrete step—a definitive shift up in competencies and achievements from the earlier step. In this case, the firm needs to develop a set of just-in-time suppliers and the MPC systems/infrastructure so that component part inventories are carefully managed. This is, of course, in addition to the competency of assembly and criterion of conformance. Now the additional criterion for evaluation is "assembly schedule support." That is, the supplier must support whatever level of output the automotive manufacturer establishes, including ramp-ups and slowdowns. Moreover, this has to

FIGURE 18.5   **Auto Industry: Stair-Step Partnering**

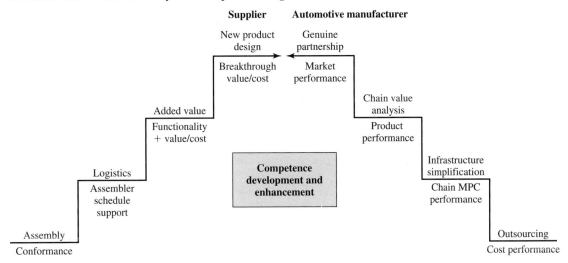

occur with minimal inventories and no stockouts. The automotive manufacturer, in turn, needs to simplify its infrastructure, divesting whatever systems and people were used to coordinate the flow of materials. The MPC linkages between the automotive manufacturer and the supplier will also need to be more closely integrated. The exact build schedule will need to be passed in real time to the supplier, and any product enhancements need to be planned in advance so that they can be jointly implemented. Clearly this work will require combined efforts and new MPC systems jointly developed/implemented by both parties.

One next possible step shown in Figure 18.5 on the supplier side is to provide "added value." Here the idea is that after the supplier has achieved flawless execution of both assembly and logistics, the partners might agree to increase the value added by the supplier in this module—for example, by including additional features to an existing integrated circuit. This might occur by buying a newly available component, or even by the module supplier taking over manufacturing of a component previously purchased. Perhaps in doing so, one stage can be taken out of the supply chain, reducing the total inventory in the chain. The objective is increased value, and the evaluative criteria are functionality and value/cost. The module must be at least as good as before in functionality, and the value/cost ratio should increase. On the customer side, the objective is joint value analysis/reengineering, and the measure of success is product performance. The automobile needs to perform as well at less cost, or better at an acceptable increase. Again, achieving this transformation will require significant changes in MPC infrastructure to support new working relationships.

The final set of possible stair steps depicted in Figure 18.5 focuses on new product design. It is here that breakthrough value/cost benefits can be achieved. The two firms need to work together in ESI for the next model, concentrating on design for manufacture (DFM) issues in both firms, as well as the features that will be of most importance to the marketplace. This final step on the automotive side has a goal of "genuine partnership": The customer needs to find the ways to truly leverage the competencies of its tier one and tier two suppliers. This implies much more than negotiation. At the end of the day, the *real* question is market performance—market share—that determines whether a new model is profitable. Here we see the evolution in supply chain management evaluative criteria. We move way beyond the classical intrafirm MPC metrics.

The stair steps in Figure 18.5 show a *sequence* of transformations. Moreover, the objectives and measures of effectiveness are different in each; the key players in both companies will also need to be matched to the particular transformation. Most important, Figure 18.5 illustrates the need for senior management in both firms to have a shared understanding and to play a key role in driving implementation of each stair step. This understanding must be deeper than some sense of good feelings, mutual working, or shared destiny. There must also be an understanding at the senior management level that the two firms will need to engage in an ongoing series of transformative efforts that will require significant resources. Let us now examine another stair-step example that will illustrate this principle.

Figure 18.6 is based on the kinds of developments taking place in large consumer goods companies today. This example focuses more directly on the kinds of joint efforts required. On the right-hand side of Figure 18.6 is a consumer goods company such as Nestlé or Unilever. At the first step, this firm wishes to concentrate purchasing in order to reduce the prices paid for its components. The left-hand side is depicted as a packaging supplier; let us say one who manufactures cardboard transport packaging. The first step comes from the customer's desire to reduce unit cost, through awarding a single-source contract. From the supplier's point of view this can be desirable if the resultant economies of scale support a volume-based cost reduction. The interaction depicted as necessary to conclude this agreement is the traditional purchasing-sales relationship. That is, this agreement is largely a matter of negotiation. In fact, this view is a bit shortsighted, since it ignores the new MPC systems necessary to support the sole-source relationship. For example, in order to truly achieve economies of scale it will also be necessary for the consumer goods firm to

FIGURE 18.6 **Consumer Goods Stair Steps: Joint Actions**

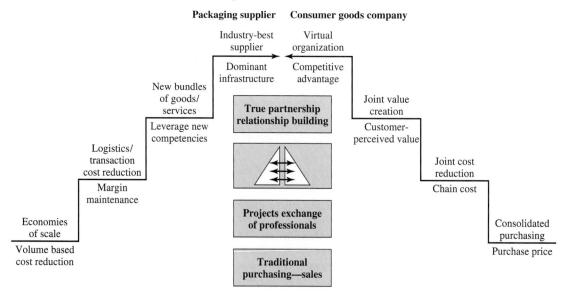

standardize its packaging material, as well as the ways in which requirements are generated at each of the consumer goods factories. In many cases we have seen, the packages vary minutely from customer plant to plant because of slightly different packaging equipment, and they do not incorporate multilingual printing. The combined requirements from the set of customer factories need to be fed to the supplier, which needs to determine which to manufacture in which factory.

The next stair step shown in Figure 18.6 derives from the customer's desire to take cost out of the supply chain (which again will lead to a reduced price). The supplier could be interested in this effort, providing it is not a zero-sum game. That is, the supplier would want to maintain its margins, which could be possible if transaction and logistics costs can be reduced. Perhaps a joint MPC system can eliminate orders, passing requirements from the consumer goods factories directly to the supplier with an e-based system, allowing the packaging supplier more latitude as to when it can manufacture as well as reducing transportation costs. If all of these can be achieved, a true win-win might be possible: Both firms can be better off with higher profits. But achieving this result is not a matter of only negotiations between buyer and seller. Implementation requires significant joint project efforts, which we depict as an "exchange of professionals:" Each firm may need to have one or more employees working full time in the partner firm for a year or more, to in fact design and implement the joint MPC system enhancements. That is, joint cost reduction cannot be achieved by the two firms working independently—and certainly not by only asking the supplier to make improvements. Implementation of this step clearly shows the need for top management consensus and shared vision in both companies. Each firm will have to make transformative changes, find new ways to cooperate, and abandon zero-sum thinking.

In the next stair step in Figure 18.6, the customer now focuses on the numerator of value/cost. This firm wishes to find ways to work more closely with its supplier to create greater value in the chain. The evaluative criterion for this would be customer perceived value, which could be that of the immediate customer of the consumer products firm (supermarkets) or the end customer. In this case it would probably be the former since our example is transport packaging. Perhaps the packaging supplier can develop a new box that is easier to open, has less cardboard to be disposed of, or can be used to display the product in the store. But why would the packaging firm desire to do this? Perhaps the new package is so good the consumer products company is willing to pay more. Perhaps the price is the same but the package has less material. But even more interesting, perhaps the packaging company regards this customer as especially smart, so that working with it will allow the packaging firm to develop new competencies that can be leveraged with other customers. To implement the necessary changes, we once more need to redefine the roles played by the two firms and who will need to be involved. Here we see an evolution in the criteria used to evaluate the supply chain partnership. The change in emphasis is depicted in Figure 18.6 by the two triangles; the implication is that there are interactions across many functions and levels in the two firms (and that new MPC systems support will be needed). The opposite situation is the two triangles with only their points (sales-purchasing) touching (the bow-tie model).

Finally, we speculate a fourth stair step where the customer wishes to achieve virtual integration with this supplier, implying joint package design, early supplier involvement (ESI), linked e-based computer systems, new joint MPC design work, etc. The consumer products company wishes to enter this world because it perceives this supplier to be one of its best-run suppliers (smartest). Whatever it learns here can be leveraged with its other suppliers. The supplier has a similar view: This is one of my smartest customers, so I am willing to devote significant resources to work with this customer. By so doing I will achieve the best (dominant) infrastructure in the industry, and be able to compete success-fully with anyone. Moreover, the MPC systems I develop can perhaps become industry standards. That is, the supplier can go to other customers and tell them that using it as a sole supplier will generate clearly provable benefits—but the new customers will need to change their internal MPC systems in prescribed ways to match those of the supplier. Now the two firms enter new MPC connections and thinking, where the supplier is willing to invest because the resultant MPC systems can be used with other customers. Examples that come to mind are the early efforts of Procter and Gamble working with Wal-Mart to invent cross docking and new ways to work more effectively. Cross docking passes the point of sale (POS) data from Wal-Mart to P&G on a daily basis to execute a form of "today for tomorrow," but with another twist: P&G goods for each store are sent to Wal-Mart ware-houses such that they never go into stock—they just go straight "across the dock" out to the stores.

The two stair-step examples demonstrate the need for transformative thinking, and the extent to which implementation needs to be tailored to the particular goals of each stage. Each step is more then continuing to do what was done before only better. Better things are essential. These can be implemented only through joint efforts. It is the supply chain that must be transformed with new MPC systems. Stair-step transformations require significant work. One should work only with the smartest partners!

Moving up the Value Chain

Another important supply chain transformation is what we call **moving up the value chain.** Increasingly, the winning competitor provides an improved bundle of goods and ser-vices, largely by helping the customer to solve its problems and taking on complexity to make life easy for the customer. This approach also recognizes the changes in customer operating practices as well as new customers with different needs. Making this a reality implies major enhancements to MPC systems.

Nokia has moved up the value chain in its telecom systems business. The traditional customer for telephone switching equipment was a publicly owned telephone/telegraph (PTT) operator. These firms knew the technology, had engineering specialists on their payrolls, and could integrate equipment from different suppliers. Moreover, being established and publicly owned, they had no major financial problems. But now there are new private operators of mobile phone networks, with core competencies in marketing, who know little about the equipment (and do not care to learn), have the need to quickly establish coverage over a wide geographical area, and are very concerned with cash flow. This means that a successful equipment supplier will "move up the value chain," taking over some tasks typically the province of the customer: Included are where to locate base stations, when to upgrade them, what kinds of antennas and microwave radios are needed for particular locations, and even turnkey operations, where entire network planning and installation is done by the supplier. The customer pays only when the system is making revenues! The relationships with the traditional customer were supported by classic MPC systems, where customers placed orders for specific catalog items, which were thereafter shipped and invoiced. The customers could compare suppliers on prices, delivery, after-sales service, and other common measures. For the new customers, MPC systems need to coordinate the delivery, installation, and handover of operating systems comprising multiple items, many of which are not manufactured. In fact, for these customers the MPC systems need to support implementation of the equipment at the customer sites and subsequent revenue generation with that equipment. The bundle also needs to include educating the customer and its personnel in best-practice operations of the system. Customer satisfaction is making money—and no problems! MPC scheduling is much more complex, with a greatly expanded set of processes that are uniquely established for each customer installation. Invoicing is only one aspect of the customer-based MPC systems, but even here new complexities are faced, such as when a deliverable is agreed on as complete. MPC systems now need to include significant emphasis on project management. In essence the new MPC requirements for Nokia are similar to those required by the EMS firms: Nokia is asking its customers to outsource! Moreover, Nokia needs to make it easy for the customers to do business with them. It is Nokia who takes on the complexity!

Moving up the value chain also implies outsourcing for the company moving up. Taking on new activities implies giving up others in order to focus on key competencies needed to win customer orders. For Nokia, providing enhanced bundles of goods and services and working with outsourcing partners has entailed major changes, particularly in MPC systems to support purchasing and joint supply chain developments with suppliers.

Figure 18.7 shows how the entire value chain shifts up as new services are provided to the end users. As indicated, each player in the chain develops new competencies and outsources activities that are better done by its suppliers.

A medical equipment supplier had a similar experience in moving up the value chain. Traditional purchase of an x-ray machine was by a radiologist in a hospital. Now, the hospital business manager makes this decision. He/she wants to know: How much does it cost? What is the payback period? What is the economic life? Will you finance it? How is it to be maintained and at what cost? How does it integrate with existing information systems for patient billing, record keeping, and scheduling? Can we have the outputs in digital form and can you help integrate analysis of the data with others such as blood analysis? Can we obtain a record that will protect us against malpractice suits? All this implies major changes in the way the product is sold, designed, and maintained. It also implies a need for new competence development for the medical equipment supplier, an explicit outsourcing policy, restructuring of work done internally and externally, and major revisions to MPC systems and practices. The MPC systems must support the sales and delivery of a much more complex bundle of goods/services (including user education). The bill of materials (BOM) must be designed accordingly. Each customer will have somewhat unique needs that must be expressed in some extended form of customer order and tailored BOM. The procurement of services as well as goods needs to be reflected in purchasing practices and supporting

FIGURE 18.7   **Moving up the Value Chain in Telecommunications**

| Component manufacturers: Developing increasing functionality in components | Contract manufacturers: Building global presence and taking over increasing share of manufacturing services | Technology suppliers: Moving forward to take over operators' traditional activities | Operators: Strong end-user focus to increase the variety of services | End users: Constantly looking for new services |

FIGURE 18.8   **Moving up the Value Chain in Medical Equipment**

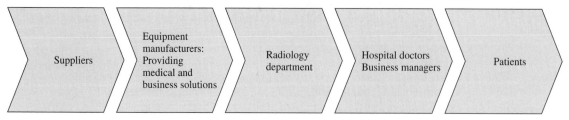

Suppliers

Equipment manufacturers: Providing medical and business solutions

Radiology department

Hospital doctors Business managers

Patients

systems. Customer service and satisfaction must be measured in new ways with inputs from a variety of customer use points. Figure 18.8 shows the similar shift up the value chain for this example.

Project Management

Project management is increasingly becoming a way of life. Management is less and less concerned with routine execution and more concerned with implementing constant change. This can be attained only through better project management. Evolution, transformation, and revolution in MPC systems are prime examples of the need for improved project management. Implementation of new ways of working—supported by new infrastructure—is essential, and the pressure is on to accomplish these changes faster and better. Historically, implementation of MPC systems, such as ERP, has been a long process. Three-year time frames are common, with actual results often stretching out to four or five years. Considering that in many cases there was also a significant time period for MPC system design and approval, the real time can often be six or seven years. This time lag is simply frightening; it could mean that we are implementing a system today that was designed before we knew much at all about the Internet! For intercompany e-based B2B systems, the right implementation time frame needs to be no longer than six months for a dyad. That is, we need to define and execute joint company projects that achieve results quickly. Thereafter, we can improve them, learning from results achieved in other dyads.

Continuous MPC Enhancements

There have always been enhancements to MPC systems, and these usually require projects and teams of people to implement them. Changing the ways in which work is done, the processes that support the new ways of working, and the underlying information systems requires the skills and coordinated efforts of many people in a company. When the projects move from a focus on lean manufacturing to lean organization and then to lean enterprise, the focus for the project team necessarily becomes ever larger. Moreover, with the efforts now on the interfirm dyad approach, the degree of change is even higher. For dyads, it is essential that the partner firms share a common sense of destiny so that joint project work can proceed quickly, with the right commitment of key people—those who can indeed implement the necessary changes in both companies.

A good example was when the Albert Heijn supermarket chain introduced a concept it called "today for tomorrow." The basic idea was that it would tell each of its major suppliers such as Unilever and Heineken exactly what had been shipped from its warehouses to its stores at the end of each day, and the suppliers were to exactly replace those amounts the following day. At first glance, this policy can be seen as simply passing the costs of maintaining inventory from Albert Heijn to its suppliers. But this viewpoint is shortsighted. For the suppliers, this enhancement allowed them to redefine several key business processes and supporting MPC systems. For example, it was no longer necessary to conduct sales in the same way; the new approach has significant potential cost savings. Moreover, it was also possible for the suppliers to manage their distribution and logistics in new ways. But achieving these economies required changes in *both* Albert Heijn and in the supplier companies. Joint company project teams needed to define and implement the new ways of working, new processes, streamlined transactions, and new ways of passing information to coordinate the flows on information and materials between the two companies.

Continuous MPC enhancements through ongoing projects implies an important but often overlooked objective for project management. Projects are typically evaluated in terms of timing, budget, and objectives: Was it on time, on budget, and did it achieve the stated objectives? But another key objective is personal: Did each of the project team members feel that participating in the project was fun, stimulating, personally rewarding, and a useful learning experience. The significance of this personal objective is seen in the light of the ongoing series of projects that will be required to improve MPC systems, as well as the general growth in projects in all companies. If key personnel see projects as exciting and personally rewarding, they will be more inclined to participate in future projects. The opposite is equally true. If at the end of the project one feels that he/she had to respond to unreasonable demands, implement a poorly thought out project, serve under an incompetent project leader, or deal with other unpleasant conditions, that person will be less likely to volunteer for the follow-on project. In the final analysis, the most successful company will be able to take on—and implement—more projects than its competitors. Project success is directly linked to the speed of learning.

MPC Project Justification

A key issue in implementation is to first justify the commitment to the MPC project, with as clear as possible an understanding of the goals. What is the project expected to deliver in benefits, where are those benefits to be realized, and when will they be achieved? Equally important is clear knowledge of the costs, timings, and, most important, the necessary commitments of internal resources to the effort. Who is going to own the project, who will make key choices, and what is the process for both making the choices and reviewing progress?

Justification for internal integration is often based on the need to essentially create a stable, predictable manufacturing environment. This is especially so if the MPC focus is at the beginning—perhaps a basic MRP-based system that focuses on a particular factory with the goal of lean manufacturing. When the intent is to optimize the operations of the business unit, then the project scope typically includes MPC modules that focus on more general management issues such as sales and operations planning systems—to connect the business unit strategy with detailed execution. When the goals include integration with suppliers and/or customers, again the focus is necessarily different in terms of the work to be done, the people who will do it, the expected timings, the desired results, and the personal commitments of those who implement the MPC systems.

Goals for MPC projects almost always include inventory reduction, faster throughput times, better capacity utilization, fewer stockouts, reduced obsolescence costs, and improved customer service. More global MPC objectives include faster new product development, ramp-up, coordination with other enterprise objectives such as human resource planning, and fostering value/cost in supply chains. There are significant differences in how these are formulated, depending on the scope of the project, and one needs to select measurements that match the objectives in the MPC project. Some classic measures include:

- Production schedule performance
- Shipping budget performance
- Labor utilization rates
- Productivity measures
- Obsolete inventory
- Cycle count accuracy
- Overtime hours
- Purchased component costs
- Vendor delivery performance
- Premium shipment costs
- Customer delivery promise performance
- Days of inventory (by category—e.g., raw materials)
- Safety stock levels
- Lead-time reduction

In addition, there are some more general measures that are important—even if they cannot always be made with great precision (it is better to be approximately right than exactly wrong). Many firms implementing MPC systems assess the following issues:

- Customer relations
- Competitive position and market share
- Customer based delivery performance
- Product quality and safety
- Employee morale and esprit de corps
- Learning (and unlearning)

It is critical to not underestimate the scope of an MPC project. This is particularly so with large ERP projects. They often take several years, cost more than $100 million. All too often the costs are more than planned, the actual timings are longer than expected, and the benefits are not quite what was expected. A key driver in all of this is a tendency to underestimate the time requirements for key internal people to plan and execute the MPC project. In many cases we have witnessed MPC projects that have started correctly—driven by key users—but thereafter they have slipped into the hands of consultants and IT people. These individuals can be of enormous help in MPC system implementation, but the direction and key choices need to remain with those senior managers who will live with the results. Costs for MPC projects include the following:

- Training of MPC users, as well as those who will interface with the new MPC systems. It is also essential to provide management education, not only on the use and expectations for the new systems but also for the roles that senior managers need to play. This is particularly important when the scope of the MPC project extends to interfirm integration.

- Database cleanup. There seems to always be an underestimation of the need to clean up databases and substitute formal methods for what was formerly done informally. This is so if the scope of the project is limited to lean manufacturing as much as if it involves interfirm planning/scheduling.

- Rationalizing the product and component base. Especially in lean enterprise, there is a great source of potential savings by reducing the number of items sold, the number of items bought, and the number of vendors from whom we buy. This is very hard work, typically underestimated, but well worth the efforts.

- Personnel expenses. For most MPC projects it is necessary to use the best/brightest people in the organization. Typically these folks are not in need of something to do. Best practice is often to insist that these people hire and train a replacement before joining the MPC project team. This category also can include outside help such as consultants and temporary workers.

- Support for the personnel. In this category we have new information system devices such as computer terminals, bar-code readers, and handheld terminals. It also includes revised pay schemes for those who will do the work and new job definitions. Implementing good MPC systems needs to be seen as hard work but an excellent means for personal advancement.

- Software packages. This includes new computer systems, installation expenses, and whatever is required to ensure that the information technology personnel are not going to be the bottleneck to the MPC project success.

- Hardware. In most large MPC projects one often needs new or expanded computer power. For interfirm MPC one needs the equipment as well as the support for e-based execution systems.

Project Planning and Resource Commitment

Projects in general, and MPC projects specifically, often fail in terms of the classic metrics. They take much longer than the original time estimates, cost significantly more than the budgets, and deliver less than promised. A large part of the explanation for these problems is the underestimation of resource requirements. Too often MPC projects are seen as being largely a matter of information system design, with insufficient attention to work process redesign. Moreover, the resources for information systems design often come from consulting and other outside firms, whereas the resources for changing the ways in which the work is to be done must be largely internal. These resources are usually in short supply, so it is critical to use them wisely. Perhaps more important, it is essential to be realistic as to the match between supply and demand. In far too many firms we find too many projects chasing too few resources.

A closely related issue is the tendency toward "project creep." That is, projects are often not tightly defined as to goals, definitions, and deliverables. It is so easy to not include key features in the initial project specification, then subsequently need to add large amounts of work, resources, and time. These additions frequently are made informally, with the impact seen only later, in the form of missed schedules and overstressed employees. To the extent that the initial project definitions are fuzzy or incomplete, this problem is magnified. One firm we know has been able to make substantial progress against project creep by clearly placing responsibility for project completion on a particular individual. Each project leader in this company knows that the key to success is being extremely tight on the project definition in the first place. The general rule is to not accept responsibility for a project unless the person feels 95 percent sure that he/she knows all the ins and outs of the project, has the project planned for a short time completion (three months), has the necessary resources available, and has a team committed to achieving success. This company strongly believes in separating development projects (that can be specified) from discovery projects (that can not be planned).

These ideas are particularly relevant to MPC projects, especially those for intercompany supply chain management. State-of-the-art practice in these dyad-based projects is a six-month maximum length project. The specific objectives, changes in work practices, new processes, and supporting information systems infrastructure should be very clear before starting. Equally clear should be the commitment of resources by both dyad companies to implementing the specified project. There again will always be a tendency toward project creep, but this can be avoided by putting these desires into subsequent projects. In essence, it is useful to take smaller bite-sized projects, where the resource commitments are clear, and where the outcomes can be evaluated quickly.

Goldratt's Critical Chain Concepts

Eli Goldratt's critical chain concepts expand his earlier bottleneck concepts to project management. A key idea is that one needs to consider not only the critical path, but also the use of resources in the project. This results in the critical chain—the bottleneck of activities augmented by the resources needed to achieve those activities. The concept is directly analogous to advanced planning and scheduling (APS) systems, where the capacity limitations of a machine are taken into account, as well as the lead times, in determining when jobs/products will be completed.

But the critical chain has several other key ideas. Goldratt notes that time estimates for project activities are universally made for worst-case scenarios, so that one should have an excellent chance of achieving the plans. In fact just the opposite occurs because the start dates for subsequent activities will be incorrectly planned. Figure 18.9 illustrates the idea. This example project consists of four activities (t_1, t_2, t_3, t_4), each with an estimated time of 10 days. The standard deviations for these estimates are 2, 3, 4, and 5 days as shown. The sum of the four time estimates is 40 days, and the standard deviation for this estimate is 5.2 days, as indicated. The lower part of Figure 18.9 shows a typical way one might schedule the overall project, in this case first basing each of the activity time estimates as the mean plus slack time—estimated in each case as two standard deviations. The result is an estimated time for the project of 68 days.

Goldratt shows that this very conservative time estimation process usually leads to poor project completion. The best estimate for when activity 1 will be completed is its mean

FIGURE 18.9
Example of Time Estimates for Activities

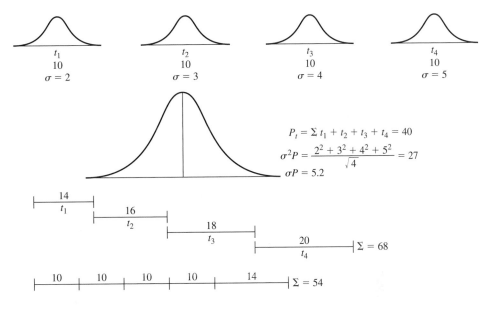

$$P_t = \Sigma\, t_1 + t_2 + t_3 + t_4 = 40$$

$$\sigma^2 P = \frac{2^2 + 3^2 + 4^2 + 5^2}{\sqrt{4}} = 27$$

$$\sigma P = 5.2$$

time, 10 days. This is then, by definition, the best time to schedule the start of activity 2. But the conservative approach assumes that activity 1 will finish at time 14, so this is when the resources for activity 2 are thought needed. This means that if activity 1 finishes at any time earlier than 14, the project will usually wait until time 14 before activity 2 can be started. Another way of looking at the situation is that more than 95 percent of the time, activity 1 will be completed before time 14; the earlier this occurs, the greater the problems this will create in trying to start activity 2 at the completion time of activity 1. Early completion times will be very hard to incorporate in the overall project time.

The last portion of Figure 18.9 depicts the critical chain approach: schedule all activities at their mean times. Take the total slack time from before (68 − 40 = 28 days), divide this in half, and put all of that slack at the end of the project. That is, do not incorporate slack into the individual activities—put it in the overall project. As shown, this results in an estimated completion date of 54 days. More important, since the individual activities are scheduled at their most likely finish dates, it will be much easier to coordinate the start of subsequent activities with the completion of their predecessor activities. This means that the math underlying the calculation of the project standard deviation (5.2 days) is based on reality. Note that the project now has a 97 percent chance of meeting its due date, which is 14 days earlier than the conservative estimate (which will usually not be met).

There are several other insights in the critical chain, including what is called the "student syndrome." This is based on the fact that homework assignments are always done the night before they are due. Extending the due date from one week to two weeks has no impact, since in either case the homework is done the night before it is due. In project management this means that, for example, activity 1 will not be started before the end of time 4, since the person believes he/she can do it in 10 days. In fact, the work might start quite a bit later because the person believes that it can easily be expedited. The result is extra time in the system, more project work than necessary, and increased need to prioritize project work. This is directly analogous to releasing more work in process earlier in the mistaken belief that giving work to the factory early will enable it to finish the work on time.

Benchmarking and Auditing

The final issue we see as critical in MPC system implementation is the need to strive for perfect execution, then to always seek improvement, to never be satisfied with what is, and to continually see MPC systems improvements as key to attaining—and maintaining—customer loyalty. Leading-edge companies continuously examine MPC best practices in other industry and company settings, always looking for those insights that can be internally captured. Benchmarking is a critical activity that needs to be continually sharpened. One can always learn from examining the work of others, both good and poor. Moreover, there is an equal need to audit and examine internal practices. The question is not whether it can be done better, it is how best to do it better (and do better things).

Flawless Execution and Database Integrity

A key issue in benchmarking and auditing concerns the extent to which the company does not make mistakes. As noted above, flawless execution implies minimal defects, hitting the schedule routinely, a sufficient planning horizon to support activities in other organizational entities, minimal buffer inventories, good IT systems, and the means to recover from the inevitable surprise. Database integrity means that the numbers in the computer match those in reality, and the firm says what it does—and does what it says. It is important to compare these qualities on a relative basis with other business units and companies. It is also important to continually measure them, expecting steady progress with no relapses.

Perhaps the first and foremost imperative for MPC systems is that they need to work, and work well. This can occur only when the systems are supported with a high level of database integrity. MPC systems are designed to support specified ways of working: We must work according to the specified ways, and the systems need to provide the correct information to make the right decisions. This implies execution according to the dictates of the MPC systems, dictates that are not overridden by informal planning (such as occurs when end of accounting period financial demands are met by informally expediting products scheduled later by the MPC systems). The need for accuracy also needs to be supported by correctness in all elements in the database. In fact, MPC is often seen as management *by* the database and management *of* the database. If this is not the case the resultant decisions will not be "transparent" to all users. Everyone has to believe that the numbers are right without costly cross-checking and extra control procedures. This dictate is absolute, irrespective of the MPC system being implemented. Whether the data pertain to a single operation in the factory or to the amount of inventory in a customer's warehouse, without data accuracy wrong decisions can result and the "fix" to the problem usually makes the underlying situation worse.

Both benchmarking and auditing should be applied to flawless execution and database integrity. It is critical to know the extent to which the company makes errors and the problems with data accuracy. Having this knowledge implies routine auditing to check the numbers and to make all errors/problems visible. It is only in this way that root causes can be identified and corrective actions initiated. Benchmarking is still another source of information: How does our company compare to others in terms of errors, database accuracy, auditing procedures, and corrective actions?

A strong principle that comes from experience is that any problem solution, no matter how worthy it may seem, that comes at the expense of data integrity must be avoided. Costs of ignoring this principle are high; they include collapse of the system and a return to firefighting as the means to survival. In MPC systems with poor data accuracy, one often finds people who attend to customer needs in spite of the systems, not by using the systems.

Achieving and maintaining database accuracy is aided when the work done by users is supported by the transactions processed by the same users. If data collection is only an added burden to an existing job with no immediate effect if it is wrong, the chances for errors increase dramatically. Obviously, the best form of transaction processing is *no* transactions, or at least automatic transactions passing all information electronically. Paper and pencils are to be avoided! Similarly, with electronic means it is possible to do computerized cross-checking, matching transactions from one place with those with which they should be in agreement (e.g., is this a valid part number, is it part of an open shop order, has it been withdrawn from inventory?).

Evolution and Revolution

This chapter has outlined a series of phases through which MPC systems might pass. There are profound differences between optimizing with a factory focus (lean manufacturing), a business unit focus (lean organization), a company-wide focus (lean enterprise), and a cross-business focus (supply chain management). When one sees implementation of supply chains as dyad based, there is an even more revolutionary change. Instead of larger integration and more complex systems, one chooses specific dyads and focuses only on how to make the interface work flawlessly; the individual firms in the dyads can work in whatever ways they wish. The vastly different changes and resultant implementation routes imply the need to always understand the differences and to be unambiguous as to which route one is taking.

The project team to lead an add-on capability to an existing MPC system does not need to have the same horsepower and approach as one that will fundamentally alter the ways in which the firm works and the ways in which it cooperates with its suppliers and customers. Composition of the project team needs to reflect the MPC process to be implemented. This also implies selecting the right managerial group to oversee the project. Those managers having areas where work will be profoundly different need to be closely involved with the project. This implies more than lip service; if the same manager is to be in charge in a very different way of working, he/she needs to understand the reasons for the change, anticipate the likely reactions of key personnel, and plan the implementation with the project team. Often, especially in MPC projects focusing on interfirm integration, people need to unlearn some inbred ideas: The suppliers and customers are not enemies! It is imperative that interfirm MPC systems not be driven with zero-sum thinking! The benchmarking and auditing activity needs to match the MPC systems being implemented. If one shifts from a lean manufacturing orientation to one of lean manufacturing, lean organization, or lean supply chain, then the auditing must match the execution: What are the critical points, changes in metrics, transactions, database elements, etc.? Are we achieving database accuracy? What are the execution problems (errors)? When we benchmark, do we choose comparable firms? Where is the best practice for the particular MPC systems?

Benchmarking versus Industrial Tourism

In keeping with the ideas of matching MPC project definitions to the desired outcomes and to different implementation agendas, benchmarking activities should be tailored in their approach. Clearly, the primary activities in benchmarking an MPC project are on the techniques, work practices, processes, changes required, information systems, and management of the overall project—all this with an eye to what can be learned and implemented in one's own firm. But in examining implementation of an MPC project, it can be equally valuable to seek out the original project definition and scope and map these to what has followed. How tightly has the company followed its plans? Were the original plans realistic? How might they have been improved? Where did the project team go off its plans, and what would the team members do if they had it to do over again?

True benchmarking requires keeping an open mind as well as working hard to minimize defensive thinking. In far too many cases, supposed benchmarking trips result only in "feel good" exercises where a team returns convinced of its own superiority. This is clearly faulty. One can always learn from almost any benchmarking visit. The trip needs to be set up right in the first place, but the key here is an attitude that is based on the premise that there *is* something to learn and each of us needs to seek it out. If nothing can be found there is something wrong with our efforts.

A few practical ideas for a benchmarking visit are to study the publicly available materials on any company you will visit, ask questions and request materials before making the visit, specify carefully what it is you wish to benchmark with explicit questions, identify who is on your team (with short resumes if possible), divide the efforts so that some people ask questions while others take notes as to answers, immediately meet after the session to share materials and reach conclusions, ask any follow-on or clarification questions very soon after the visit (within a day or two), decide on the actions indicated for your firm, and respond to the company visited, explaining what you have learned.

Another key issue in benchmarking is that one can always learn from *being* benchmarked. Moreover, any visitors to your operations are potential sources of new ideas. A typical visit for any of us to a Japanese factory is followed by a question and answer session where the visitor is asked what he/she saw that could be improved. Attending the session are 10 to 15 people from the company taking notes on our ideas. These are thereafter sifted and examined for whatever can be learned. Any learned person visiting an operation will have some thoughts as to improvements that can be easily gathered by the representatives of the firm visited, if they have the right attitude. But far too often visitors are not asked. One of the authors took a large group of food service executives from a major food manufacturer through the kitchens in one of the world's largest amusement parks. The hosts never asked any of us if we had any improvement ideas, which was a shame since there were many hundreds of years of experience looking at their practices.

Auditing

Auditing is slightly different from benchmarking. Benchmarking can lead to transformation, while routine auditing is primarily oriented to "doing the same things better." Routine measurements of MPC effectiveness [key performance indicators (KPIs)] should form the base for routine auditing. Continual improvements should be expected in those metrics.

Additionally, one always needs to ask if the KPIs are right. What are the key issues facing us as a company and how are they manifested in our measurements? Is it time for a transformation?

A more fundamental form of auditing involves a periodic deep look at the operations (and MPC systems) in each factory or business unit of the company. This is a key practice in many large companies, such as Nestlé, where a team of company experts comes in to examine the operations of the unit, matching them with the current marketplace conditions as well as known best practices. This exercise is good for the business unit examined as well as for the team members who do the examinations. The right spirit is that the audit will not be seen as threatening. On the contrary, the business unit should see this as an opportunity for a talented group of company experts to help it make a quantum leap in operational effectiveness.

A similar exercise can involve outside experts. We have often been asked to perform a thorough audit of MPC practices in an organization. Our approach is first to take whatever time is needed to understand the systems in place, how they are supposed to work, who uses them in what ways, and a more basic question of the extent to which the present approaches are appropriate for the marketplace. What are the main problems facing the firm? What keeps executives awake at night? What are the problems of the key customers and are we helping them solve these problems? These questions are worth pursuing to some depth, since they can lead to identifying a mismatch between the basic MPC systems and the current set of problems facing the business.

Moving on to the existing MPC systems, we want people to explain what are the systems and the work processes they plan/control, and then we want to examine the actual outputs from the MPC systems. We take an initial view of ignorance, since we want the managers (not IT people) to explain what they see as the daily problems/issues, and how they solve them using the MPC systems. Most actual systems tend to be unique in their presentation, but MRP logic is MRP logic, as are other concepts such as available-to-promise logic, advanced planning systems, and vendor-managed inventory (VMI). All of these can be compared to best practices.

After gaining understanding of how the MPC systems are supposed to work, it is critical to see if this is actually the case. We examine several records in a system to see if there are logical inconsistencies such as negative inventory balances (a bit difficult to cycle count), records with all zeros in some field, missing data, seriously past due scheduled receipts, shop orders that are open before the lead time would indicate, VMI records that cannot match with reality, etc. It is also informative to see if data from different functional systems match; for example, do manufacturing, sales, and finance all have the same data for last month's shipments of a particular product? As a side issue, we sometimes find that in-house experts cannot explain how documents are created, what they contain, how they are used, or who will use them.

With a basic understanding of the MPC systems, it is most useful to see if the reality matches the model. If told how a certain shop scheduling system works, it is useful to ask a foreman to show you today's schedule in the system and where the department is at this point in time. This can sometimes lead to blank stares, while at other times one gets exactly the right answer. It is also interesting to see if we can gain entrance to the stockroom without any formal authorization and rummage around in the bins. Could one do this in a bank? No one should be allowed free access and the ability to remove goods without proper transactions being processed. To audit stockroom record accuracy, we often ask for computer records for several parts—records indicating how many are in stock and where they are. Then we want to check the accuracy of the inventory information. The on-hand balance drives all MRP calculations. If it is wrong, virtually all MPC systems are at risk. Other impolite questions to ask include:

- Is there an end-of-the-month shipping bulge? If so does it match the schedule or are high-value jobs from the subsequent month "cherry picked?"
- How often does the assembly department run out of parts? Does it use the official methods to get more?
- How many days is the master production schedule met? Is there an end-of-the-week or -month catch-up period?
- Do many people know how the overall MPC system works in detail, or is it some mystery?
- Are senior managers knowledgeable about MPC systems? Have they been educated in this area or do they only send their subordinates?

In sum, one part of the audit of existing MPC systems starts with the idea of believing nothing unless proved. The objective is to find out what is supposed to be the case and whether actuality matches the system. In the last analysis, an MPC system is effective only when used as it is designed.

Concluding Principles

We see the following principles emerging from this chapter:

- The approach to MPC implementation depends on the particular objectives of the company, which change over time.
- Business process reengineering is always part of MPC implementation; one needs to change work, processes, and the supporting information systems.
- New processes need to be evaluated to see when a process is "good enough."
- Rationalization of the supplier and product base is an important prerequisite for simplified MPC system implementation.
- Implementation of transformative change requires significant top management support, particularly when the MPC systems coordinate interfirm activities.
- Project management plays a key role in MPC implementation. The costs and benefits need to be justified.
- Implementation of interfirm MPC systems is fundamentally different from that for intrafirm implementation.
- Costs often need to be incurred in one part of the dyad, with the benefits received in the other. The savings need to be shared.
- Benchmarking MPC systems can provide breakthrough concepts as well as ideas for improving existing systems.
- Auditing MPC systems needs to be an ongoing process—a key part of continuous improvement.

References

Anderegg, Travis. *ERP: A–Z Implementer's Guide for Success.* Cibres Inc., 2000.

Camp, Robert C. *Business Process Benchmarking.* Milwaukee, WI: American Society for Quality, 1995.

Carroll, Brian J. *Lean Performance ERP Project Management—Implementing the Virtual Supply Chain.* Boca Raton, Fla.: CRC Press, 2002.

Cooper, R. *When Lean Enterprises Collide: Competing through Confrontation.* Cambridge, Mass.: Harvard Business School Press, 1995.

Cordon, C., and T. E. Vollmann. "Building a Smarter Demand Chain," *Financial Times Mastering Information Management,* February 1999.

Galbraith, Jay R., *Designing Organizations,* 2nd ed., San Francisco, Jossey-Bass, 2001.

Goldratt, Eliyahu M. *The Critical Chain.* Great Barrington, Mass.: The North River Press, 1997.

Goodson, R. E. "Read a Plant—Fast." *Harvard Business Review* 80, no. 5 (May 2002), pp. 105–113.

Hensley, R.; Z. J. Irani; and A. Satpatthy. "Better Purchasing for Auto Suppliers," *McKinsey Quarterly,* no. 3 (2003).

Kerzner, H. *Project Management: A Systems Approach to Planning, Scheduling, and Controlling.* 8th ed. New York: Wiley, 2003.

McCormack, R. A. *Lean Machines: Learning from the Leaders of the Next Industrial Revolution.* Publishers & Producers, 2002.

McCutcheon, D., and F. Ian Stuart. "Issues in the Choice of Supplier Alliance Partners," *Journal of Operations Management* 18, no. 3 (April 2000), pp. 279–301.

Shah, R., and Peter T. Ward. "Lean Manufacturing: Context, Practice Bundles, and Performance," *Journal of Operations Management* 21, no. 2 (March 2003), pp. 129–149.

Teed, Nelson J. "Origins and Reality of Lean Manufacturing," *APICS—The Performance Advantage,* January 2001.

Vollmann, Thomas E. "Systems Are Never Good Enough," *Financial Times Mastering Management,* November 20, 1995.

Wallace, Thomas F., and Michael H. Kremzar. *ERP: Making It Happen: The Implementers' Guide to Success with Enterprise Resource Planning,* 3rd ed. New York: John Wiley & Sons, 2001.

Womack, J. P.; Daniel T. Jones; and Daniel Roos. *The Machine That Changed the World: The Story of Lean Production,* HarperCollins, 1991.

Discussion Questions

1. What are the major differences between lean manufacturing, lean organization, and lean enterprise?

2. Why is supply chain management implementation based on dyads?

3. What makes the implementation of transformation different from that of continuous improvement?

4. What is the concept of "shared values" at Nokia and why is it important?

5. Why do stair-step transformations necessarily involve both supplier and customer?

6. What is "moving up the value chain?" Can you name any other examples?

7. Why is database accuracy so critical for MPC systems?

8. How is the implementation of interfirm project management different from that of intrafirm project management?

9. Why does "project creep" occur in MPC systems implementation and how can it be avoided?

10. Why does use of the critical chain concepts increase the probability of project success while cutting the budgeted time for the project?

Problems

1. The set of data in Figure 18.10 is for packaging material, a nonproduction category purchased item for a firm with five divisions in southern Europe. Each of the geographical divisions operates independently, making their own purchasing decisions. Managers of the firm are wondering what the data tell them about the potential for implementing a sourcing rationalization program for the company. As a start, develop the percent of spend information for each of the five divisions, using the top two and top five items for each.

2. Using the data from problem 18.1, determine what percent of the total purchasing spend for packaging material is covered by each the items? What percent of the spend does each vendor have?

3. Using the data from problem 18.1, perform an analysis like that shown in Figure 18.10. How many countries buy a particular item from what vendor?

FIGURE 18.10
Purchasing Records for Packing Material

Number	Location	Item	Vendor	$ Amount
1	Spain	36-5817	Frantoni	21,731.18
2	Spain	36-5817-A	Frantoni	41,429.73
3	Spain	36-3220-B	Melitas	69,450.50
4	Spain	36-4221	Melitas	4,674.14
5	Spain	36-3154	Todas	13,843.76
6	Spain	36-5133	Melitas	5,534.43
7	Spain	36-5444-C	Todas	49,570.98
8	Spain	36-8820	Ajax	35,336.76
9	Spain	36-2481	Melitas	21,891.68
10	Spain	36-2886	Mercur	70,511.92
11	France	36-8840	Frantoni	24,679.80
12	France	36-5417	Mercur	6,446.85
13	France	36-3365	Mercur	22,870.02
14	France	36-3365-A	Frantoni	38,716.64
15	France	36-3220-B	Mercur	55,892.10
16	France	36-4559	Melitas	53,217.97
17	France	36-4827	Frantoni	4,093.87
18	France	36-4835	Melitas	17,683.21
19	Portugal	36-2886	Frantoni	32,456.66
20	Portugal	36-4744	Mercur	56,844.32
21	Portugal	36-3220-B	Todas	21,133.12
22	Portugal	36-5271	Melitas	7,182.92
23	Portugal	36-2553	Todas	4,913.29
24	Portugal	36-8820	Ajax	27,971.85
25	Portugal	36-4644	Todas	19,929.81
26	Greece	36-3220-B	Hellion	10,293.92
27	Greece	36-5444-C	Frantoni	22,967.49
28	Greece	36-2481	Hellion	2,553.57
29	Greece	36-8820	Ajax	19,891.23
30	Greece	36-5817-A	Frantoni	23,109.32
31	Greece	36-8871	Hellion	3,967.85
32	Italy	36-2553	Todas	2,266.03
33	Italy	36-5817-A	Frantoni	10,034.32
34	Italy	36-8840	Frantoni	14,120.67
35	Italy	36-4827	Todas	1,796.10
36	Italy	36-3220-B	Frantoni	4,959.34

4. In Figure 18.3, there are three specifications that are provided from a sole-source vendor. How would the figure change if these specifications were combined with the dominant specification in each weight (20 and 22)? What actions would be required to implement this change?

5. Continuing with problem 4, supposing the three sole-source vendor specifications were in fact the highest-usage items with attractive pricing. How would your answer to problem 4 change?

6. The XYZ company has reduced its supplier base from 2,000 to 850, while at the same time reducing the number of SKUs purchased from 7,500 to 3,000. What is the average increase in the amount bought per supplier?

7. The ABC Food Service Company buys paper products from three local suppliers in one of its countries. The overall annual spend for these supplies is $1.2 million. ABC has 100 restaurants, and each of them orders twice per month, and carries a safety stock of one-half month's use of the products. ABC buys monthly, choosing the supplier that offers the best price, requesting next day delivery into its warehouse. ABC carries a safety stock of one month's supply in its warehouse. If each of the three suppliers carries enough stock to meet an order from XYZ, how much average stock will be held in the overall supply chain?

8. XYZ has decided to make a single-source contract for the paper products, which will thereafter be delivered weekly (four times per month) directly to the restaurants by a third-party logistics provider. Assuming that the restaurants now hold a one-week safety stock, how does this change affect the total chain inventory?

9. Hoover Electric Company is considering implementation of a basic MRP system. The estimated costs for hardware, software, and training are $100,000, and the implementation costs are $50,000 (per year). The system is expected to be completed in one year and save $20,000 per year in operating cost, while increasing the inventory turnover from 2.5 to 4 times per year. The present sales level is $1,000,000. If the cost of carrying inventory is 20 percent, what is the expected payback period for the investment? What is the first-year cash flow?

10. Returning to problem 9, what happens to the analysis if the MRP project takes two years instead of one to implement?

11. The Teltech Company is a medium-size firm in the telecom business (annual sales of $730 million). Its current inventory level is $120 million. An industry rule of thumb is that a reduction of 10 days of inventory will return 1 percent net profit as a percentage of sales. Teltech has identified 10 customers that account for 50 percent of its sales, and now is building dyad-based relationships with these firms, similar to that illustrated in Figure 18.5. Teltech expects that this approach will decrease the inventories it holds to support these customers by 15 days on average. What is the potential increase in profits?

12. Continuing with problem 11, Teltech is now working with one of its main customers, using an e-based B2B system similar to Figure 18.5. The following business process reengineering study has been made for the portion of Figure 18.5 that starts with customer planning manufacture and ends with the customer receiving the goods:

    - Plan manufacturing and determine stock outflow forecast (Monday)
    - Evaluate forecast at supplier and propose replenishment (Tuesday)
    - Evaluate (confirm) replenishment at customer (Wednesday)
    - Plan manufacturing at supplier (Thursday)
    - Create consignment stock order (VMI) (Friday)
    - Pick, ship (Monday of week 2)
    - Receive goods (Tuesday of week 2)

    a. Assuming this customer is typical of the others in Teltech's top-ten list, what would be the payoff from redesigning the process with these customers to eliminate the X's in Figure 18.5?

    b. What if Teltech also operates on the "uphill skier" concept with these customers?

13. In Figure 18.4 Plant A has made the following weekly shipments to the hub, and received the following payments from the sourcing unit for the uses of its item (the agreement between A and the sourcing unit is VMI but immediate payment on use):

Week	Plan A Shipments	Sourcing Unit Payments
1	10	8
2	10	10
3	20	10
4	0	8
5	10	10
6	20	12

Assuming the hub started with an inventory of 10 units, what should be the inventory at the hub at the end of period 6?

14. Jones Manufacturing Company estimates that it costs $6,000 per year in administration costs for each of its 1,000 vendors. Jones now plans to implement a new MPC system that will be directly linked to each supplier.

   a. If Jones has a budget of $1 million for vendor education and training, how much does it need to reduce the number of suppliers to pay for the education and training?

   b. Suppose Jones reduces its supplier base to 300, but continues to spend $1 million per year in developing new ways to work with vendors. How much do these efforts have to return per vendor to break even?

15. Louis Gordon is in charge of implementing a new MPC module. There is considerable grumbling about the new module, and he wonders if this is just the usual adjustment problems or if something is going wrong. After two weeks the call center has received the following log of calls to resolve problems:

Day	Calls	Day	Calls
1	95	6	180
2	125	7	190
3	140	8	180
4	130	9	195
5	140	10	190

Weekly data for four other MPC modules that have been implemented are:

Week	A	B	C	D
1	400	800	25	150
2	300	900	15	95
3	150	400	5	60
4	50	100	0	20
5	5	50	0	10

What should Louis do?

19

MPC: The Next Frontier

In this final chapter, we focus on what we see as the next major area for definitively different MPC developments. An important issue in describing this next frontier is that manufacturing planning and control (MPC) systems *remain* the key focus. Ultimately, all work to coordinate flows of information and materials for manufacturing comes down to detailed MPC processes and the information technology systems that support them. Firms will continue to implement MRP, JIT, and ERP, but these are essentially well known. Moreover, they are not going to provide any significant competitive advantage. Everyone has these capabilities; they are required to remain in business. A sustaining competitive advantage requires MPC systems that cross organizational boundaries, coordinating company units, which traditionally have been independently working with key suppliers/customers. The focus has to be on extending the concepts of supply chain management (i.e., lean supply chain) that are just now coming to fruition. These improvements necessarily will focus on a dyad-by-dyad approach—that is, pairs of organizations.

A dyad-by-dyad approach means that pairs of organizations jointly develop the new processes and MPC systems that allow them to ever more effectively integrate their detailed operations. It is dyad-by-dyad because the joint working and definitions of improvement projects will tend to be unique to the dyad. This said, best practice will be to learn as much as possible from each dyad improvement effort, and then imbed the MPC thinking, processes, and systems into modular approaches to whatever extent possible. That is, one should work hardest with smart partners where new chain benefits are achieved, but then try to leverage the learning in other dyads. In this chapter we develop a framework for thinking about these efforts, as well as the benefits to be achieved, supported by examples of leading edge practices.

This chapter is organized around four topics:

- *A supply chain development framework:* What is a framework for understanding the cross-organizational challenges, the necessary responses, the resulting new ways of working, and the infrastructure to support these ways of working? Moreover, all this needs to be seen as a continuum of changes—one in which we are only today at the beginning.

- *Competitive drivers/challenges:* What are the current challenges and forces for cross-organizational MPC development? What are the objectives for these developments and the transformative changes required?

- *Cross-firm MPC design:* What are the most critical cross-organizational coordination mechanisms that are being implemented, and how are best practices evaluated? What are the cooperative efforts needed by the dyad partners? What are the major barriers to implementation?
- *Examples and techniques:* What are some leading edge examples, and for which application areas are new techniques being developed? What might be the developments in the future?

This chapter has links to several other chapters, most notably Chapters 8, 13, 17, and 18. Chapter 9 also deals with cross-firm coordinated efforts to implement JIT. Chapter 9 also makes an important point in that JIT involves much more than classic MPC tools; one also needs to redesign products, processes, and work methods. We will see similar needs here. Chapter 13 describes some of the key choices in MPC integration including issues for interfirm integration. Chapter 17 presents the basics in supply chain management as well as many best practices. Chapter 17 also examines the detailed processes used in interfirm e-based business-to-business (B2B) systems. We extend those ideas here, where our focus is on the future and frontiers of application. Chapter 18 is devoted to implementation, and one part of that chapter differentiates between implementation of intrafirm MPC systems and interfirm MPC systems (our focus in this chapter).

A Supply Chain Development Framework

Supply chain improvements have been evolutionary, and will continue to be so. The definitive problems, overriding strategic objectives, changes in work practices/processes, and supporting infrastructure are understood only in a primitive form. It is useful to develop a historical perspective on supply chain development so that the frontiers for major improvements can be seen more clearly.

Supply chains are often visualized as linkages between several firms, such as suppliers of the suppliers, suppliers, the firm, its customers, and their customers. The result is a long chain or more often a network of many companies working together to satisfy end-customer needs. Optimizing the entire network is a laudable objective. We see, however, that state-of-the-art improvements in supply chains are achieved by working in dyads—pairs of companies that commit to joint new ways of working, new processes, and new MPC systems. Success in implementing one dyad naturally leads to others and to attempts to capitalize on the learning in one dyad in working with subsequent dyads. But it also necessarily leads to internal transformation of work methods. The first dyad might be an experiment or pilot, where the joint efforts are not considered mainstream for the company; it still operates largely with arm's-length relationships with suppliers and customers. But success in the dyad work will likely at some point force the company to realize that this is the future, not the present, mainstream. The result will be a need for major change—transformation (not just doing the same things better). Let us now develop a framework for the dyad-focused improvement process that shows the necessary interactions between the objectives, the transformative changes required in both organizational units of the dyad, the need for cross-organizational project management, and chain-based measures.

Historical Perspective for MPC Development

It is useful to briefly review the history of classic MPC development, in order to establish the present state of the art in cross-organizational MPC implementation. Figure 19.1

FIGURE 19.1
Historical View of MPC Development

1970s From chaos to order	1980s Systems to support operating processes	1990s Operating processes to support systems

- Implement formal systems
- From paper to computer
- Problem structuring
- Execution accuracy
- Bill of materials processing

- Tailored solutions
- Integrated operations
- New processes/practices
- Match systems to operations
- MRP/MRPII

- Standard solutions
- Company integration
- Implement packages
- Match operations to systems
- ERP

depicts this history in three blocks: the 1970s, 1980s, and 1990s. In the first decade (building from developments in the 1960s), there was a major push to move from informal planning methods for manufacturing to computer-based systems. This activity involved several key changes. The first was to design/implement formal systems. Factory schedules were no longer based on long experience, in highly unstructured ways, using implicit knowledge. Knowledge was made explicit, and informal paper-based systems were replaced with explicit computer-based systems. The major enabler for all this was bill-of-materials (BOM) processing. BOM processing permitted the gross-to-net arithmetic of the first MRP systems, which was possible only with the advent of random-access computing. BOM processing was just not feasible with sequential files for manufacturing firms having more than a few levels in the bill of materials and several thousand active part numbers. BOM processing provided a new structure for scheduling work in a manufacturing company. Problems in almost any manufacturing company could be structured in this way. Executing MRP with BOM processing required a computer, and IBM led the world in selling hardware to implement MRP systems.

Internally, once the hardware and formal planning systems were in place, attention necessarily turned to execution. People had to change the ways in which they worked, and discipline had to be instilled to ensure that the numbers in the computer matched the reality on the factory floor. Joe Orlicky, often cited as the "father of MRP," used to say that data accuracy was not difficult: It was like losing weight—we *know* how to do it, it is just a matter of discipline.

The second decade depicted in Figure 19.1 is that of the 1980s, which we label as "Systems to support operating processes." This was the heyday of firms such as Andersen Consulting that helped companies implement MRP systems and its advanced forms (MRPII). Now the primary emphasis was on solutions that were tailored to match the ways in which a company ran its operations and reached its marketplace. The focus of MRPII was on integrating the various MPC activities. Again this required changes in the ways people worked, supported by uniquely defined processes/practices and underlying IT systems.

Finally, we reach the third decade, where the emphasis shifts from developing systems solutions to developing operating processes that support standardized systems. Now we have firms like SAP selling software packages as "standard" solutions. Tailoring is still required, but best practice here is to use standard packages and solutions as much as possible. That is, instead of allowing unique ways of working to dictate unique processes and tailored supporting systems/infrastructure, now the approach is to utilize packaged solutions whenever possible—as well as "plain vanilla" processes. The packages now embody ERP, with a larger company-wide integration perspective. Work is transformed to support systems, not vice versa.

The new frontier should not be seen as an extension to this approach. There are people today who see supply chain management as an extension to ERP, achieved by connecting ERP systems between companies. This is *not* going to be sufficient. Fundamentally, the evolution depicted in Figure 19.1 is based on integration *within* a firm. The frontier is to integrate *between* firms. This requires new thinking—and new transformations (work, processes, and MPC systems). That is, firms will have different ways of working in dyads, the underlying processes will be different as well, the business process reengineering efforts will be different, and the resultant MPC systems will also be new.

However, we are now entering into what appears to be a similar evolutionary cycle to that depicted in Figure 19.1, one that will probably proceed faster. We find dyad pairings of companies that are starting to make order from chaos in joint working. Suboptimal working such as ordering, extensive transaction processing, duplicate inventories, and multiple quality checks are being eliminated. E-based systems are replacing faxes, telephone calls, paper-based systems, and other informal communication methods.

The second decade of Figure 19.1 is also being entered. New ways of joint working are being implemented. The necessary changes in thinking (not zero-sum) are taking place. In dyads, new processes are being established, and new information systems support these processes. But these changes are akin to those in the 1980s decade of Figure 19.1; there are not yet standard processes and systems available for all to implement. We are still in the early stages, not in the standard software implementation phase.

Interorganizational (Chain) Design

Figure 19.2 provides an overview for supply chain development. The figure is composed of two parts: strategy development and infrastructure development. The left-hand part depicts four necessary strategic activities. The first box, strategic positioning, is concerned with the purpose for the dyad efforts. Essentially, what will this dyad bring to the marketplace; what are the payoffs for successful joint development? The second box, transformation, reflects the need to fully understand, in both dyad firms, the need for transformative change. Success here will not be achieved by simply doing the same things better; both firms need to embrace changes in ways of working, processes, and infrastructure. The third box, project management, focuses on the critical need to not only develop a cross-company project team, but also to ensure that the team works effectively, with minimal parochial constraints. The final box in the left-hand side of Figure 19.2, metrics, focuses on the need to establish clear measures of chain effectiveness. These need to reflect a win-win mentality, where both dyad firms see benefits from the joint work that they can leverage in other dyads.

FIGURE 19.2   **Interorganizational (Chain) Design**

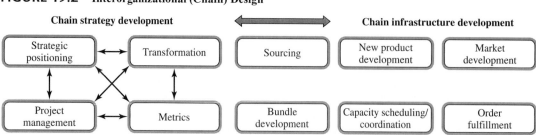

The right-hand side of Figure 19.2 focuses on the particular arenas for developing joint infrastructure. This list should not be seen as definitive; rather, it is the most likely areas where dyad efforts will take place. The first box, sourcing, reflects efforts to optimize working with suppliers in new ways to create breakthrough benefit/cost improvements. The third box, market development, should be seen as the other side of the same coin. In one case the dyad is with a supplier; in the other it is with a customer—but the focus is quite similar. In fact, if it is *not* similar, this usually indicates shortcomings on the strategic side (e.g., win-win mentality). The second box in Figure 19.2, new product development, is clearly an activity where the dyad can produce impressive results. Combining product design competencies with those of suppliers and/or customers is one of the best ways to achieve better designs, to get them to market faster, and to continuously improve them before your competitors do so. Box four, bundle development, implies joint efforts to enhance the bundles of goods and services provided to customers. Efforts here often focus on providing "solutions" in which specific needs of key customers are met in tailored bundles, but creating (and evolving) these bundles using relatively standard (modular) infrastructure. The box titled "Capacity scheduling/coordination" is the most straightforward extension of classic MPC. But here the focus is on joint scheduling and uses of capacities in the dyad to achieve better utilization, increased speed, greater flexibility, improved response to Murphy's law events, and reduced chain inventories. The final box, "Order fulfillment," is similar to the previous box, but now the focus is definitively external and downstream, rather than internal and upstream. Here the intent is for the dyad to focus on the best ways to jointly meet the needs of end customers.

Chain Strategy Development

Figure 19.3 is an expanded view of the left-hand side of Figure 19.2—that is, chain strategy development. Within the "Strategic positioning" box there are several key questions that need to be addressed by the dyad:

- What is the unique value proposition: What might the dyad offer to the marketplace that will provide a definitive competitive advantage, one not easily copied?

FIGURE 19.3
Chain Strategy Development

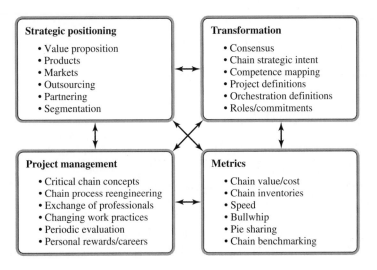

- What are the products to be provided and how will they be evolved over time? More fundamentally, what are the bundles of goods and services?
- What markets is the dyad going to serve? How are those markets changing, and what is required to win the orders?
- What is the strategic positioning on outsourcing? Who can do what—better? Where should each of the dyad firms be headed in competency development to optimize the chain? How do we get our customers to outsource to us?
- What does "partnering" really mean? Are both firms in the dyad serious about this, or are we engaged in some new form of negotiation? Do both firms believe they are working with a smart partner, someone with whom they are learning?
- What specific market segments is the dyad going to serve? What is needed to dominate each segment? How will the segment evolve, and how can *we* drive the evolution?

The "Transformation" box raises a similar set of questions that the dyad needs to address:

- Do *we* have consensus—a shared view—on where we are going, why we are doing it, and what we each will attain by doing so?
- Can we specify an explicit statement of strategic intent for the immediate dyad efforts? This needs to be much more than some vague statement such as "maximizing shareholder value" or "being the preferred supplier."
- What are the explicit competencies that each of the dyad firms needs to develop? More important, what are the joint competencies? Can we map these to see how they fit and whether they are mutually compatible?
- Have we specified explicit projects, both within each dyad company and jointly, that have to be achieved to reach the stated objectives? Do we understand what has to be "unlearned" in each firm?
- Do we jointly understand the concept of "orchestration" of the chain? Is this seen as some kind of power game, or as an issue of which partner can most effectively coordinate certain work in the chain?
- Have we specified the key roles and commitments in the dyad companies? Are there specific individuals charged with making the changes in working, processes, and information systems?

"Project management" also is expanded in its meaning:

- Does project management in the dyad embrace the latest thinking on how to achieve projects in the planned times?
- Is a key part of the project focused on reengineering joint chain processes? Are these efforts seen as requiring transformative changes in *both* firms?
- Are both firms ready and willing to exchange personnel for significant time periods in order to achieve the cross-company business process reengineering? That is, will key people work in the other company for a year or so to implement the necessary changes?
- Are the dyad companies ready to drastically change work practices if necessary? Are they committed to take on the necessary changes in personnel, education, and training?

- Is the project subject to periodic reporting and evaluation? Is this a joint effort by senior managers in both companies? Is there an ongoing commitment to these efforts—or is this a project that is supposed to take place during someone's spare time?
- Do the people who work on this project see it as personally rewarding and exciting? Will they receive appropriate recognition for a job well done? Will there be some sanctions for a job not well done?

Finally, the "Metrics" section has its set of detailed issues that need to be resolved in order to have a well-developed strategic approach to supply chain development:

- Does the set of metrics include some definition of value/cost for the chain? It is important to attempt this definition, recognizing that approximately right is much better than exactly wrong. Efforts must be focused on both the numerator and denominator.
- Are inventories in the total chain measured and continually monitored? Parochialism is to be avoided, and the benefits from chain inventory reduction need to be rewarded to the entity that bears the costs of reducing them.
- How is speed going to be explicitly defined and monitored? Will the measure be time to market? Manufacturing lead times? Delivery times? Response times? Are our goals here as ambitious as they should be? Fifty percent time reduction objectives force transformative changes.
- Is the bullwhip effect clearly understood and seen as an important objective for reduction? Do the dyad companies realize that reducing the bullwhip effect requires more than mere exchange of information?
- Is "pie sharing" seen as less important than "pie growing?" It is important to have all employees in the dyad focus on making the transformative improvements a reality, rather than on haggling over who should receive which specific benefits. Pie sharing should be periodic, at a high level.
- Does the dyad do chain benchmarking and auditing? What are seen as best practices in dyad development, and is this dyad achieving what it should? Are senior managers aggressively asking this question, and who is answering it?

Chain Infrastructure Development: Work

Figure 19.4 is a similar expanded view of Figure 19.2, now focused on the right-hand side—chain infrastructure development. The objective in Figure 19.4 is to provide more depth in the specific activities being undertaken in interorganizational chain design. These fall into two categories: the top three boxes in Figure 19.4 focus on the new work that needs to be done, while the bottom three focus on infrastructure: the processes and systems.

As indicated above, sourcing has to do with joint efforts with a supplier to develop new ways of working, processes, and supporting infrastructure. The following are some key areas for joint work:

- *Prospecting/assessing:* How can the dyad improve its abilities to understand the products, services, and underlying competencies of both existing and potential suppliers? What needs to be done to leverage those competencies with those of the dyad?

FIGURE 19.4 Chain Infrastructure Development

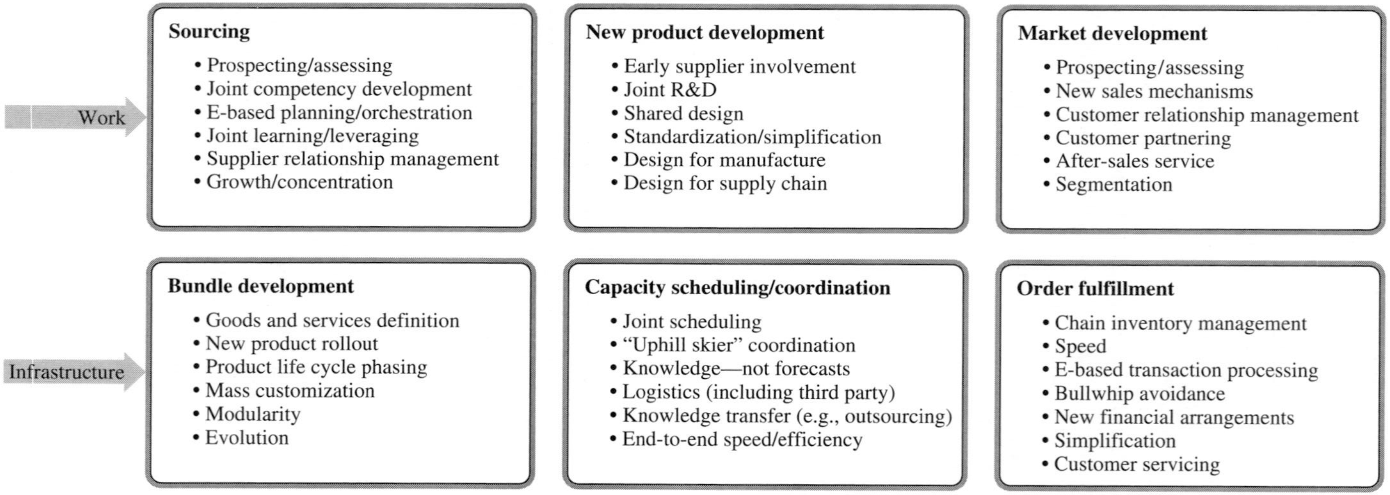

Sourcing
- Prospecting/assessing
- Joint competency development
- E-based planning/orchestration
- Joint learning/leveraging
- Supplier relationship management
- Growth/concentration

New product development
- Early supplier involvement
- Joint R&D
- Shared design
- Standardization/simplification
- Design for manufacture
- Design for supply chain

Market development
- Prospecting/assessing
- New sales mechanisms
- Customer relationship management
- Customer partnering
- After-sales service
- Segmentation

Bundle development
- Goods and services definition
- New product rollout
- Product life cycle phasing
- Mass customization
- Modularity
- Evolution

Capacity scheduling/coordination
- Joint scheduling
- "Uphill skier" coordination
- Knowledge—not forecasts
- Logistics (including third party)
- Knowledge transfer (e.g., outsourcing)
- End-to-end speed/efficiency

Order fulfillment
- Chain inventory management
- Speed
- E-based transaction processing
- Bullwhip avoidance
- New financial arrangements
- Simplification
- Customer servicing

Work

Infrastructure

- *Joint competency development:* What might the dyad do to develop distinctive new joint competencies? What is next? A true partnership always has an aggressive improvement agenda.
- *E-based planning/orchestration:* Where are the transactions and hidden costs in the chain? How do we eliminate them? What is the extent of joint e-based system development? Are our efforts focused on better coordination of the chain, or merely pushing problems from one side to the other? Do the dyad partners agree on this?
- *Joint learning/leveraging:* Do both partners see this relationship as one of the best sources of learning for their company? Is the learning being leveraged with other dyad partners? Are both parties not only aware but also supportive of the other leveraging the learning?
- *Supplier relationship management:* Is this a term with the same amount of meaning and focus as the term *customer relationship management?* Why are there any differences? Is the customer partner's strategy to be the most attractive customer to its supplier partners?
- *Growth/concentration:* Does the customer see supplier reduction as a key objective? Is part of the reward for a supplier partner a major increase in business (perhaps tenfold)?

New product development is a major opportunity in which joint working can yield major improvements. In fact, firms such as the electronic manufacturing services (EMS) companies see new product development support as one of their critical competencies. In many cases, time to market is much more important than long-run product cost improvement. Some key areas where joint work is being done include:

- *Early supplier involvement:* This has been an important source of competitive advantage to many companies. Involving the suppliers early on in product design allows faster times to market, better products, and lower costs, leveraging the competencies of the suppliers.
- *Joint R&D:* There are increasing examples of how suppliers are working with major customers to create the products of the future—better, faster, and more economically.
- *Shared design:* In many products the basic product design itself can be jointly done, with the dyad partners clearly defining which aspects of the design can be done independently and where the teams need to come together for joint design work.
- *Standardization/simplification:* Often we encounter firms with overly complex supply chains, such as 85 percent of suppliers furnishing only one item, a global company that buys almost all of the same items from different suppliers in each market, processes that generate individual purchase orders for items that are almost the same (e.g., capacitors). There are major opportunities here, but they take hard work and unlearning.
- *Design for manufacture:* Clearly suppliers can help in design efforts to make manufacturing better and more efficient. But this also applies to designs that are easier to manufacture in the supplier companies because of their unique processes and equipment.
- *Design for supply chain:* Best practice now realizes that some designs are much better adapted to various packages, means of distribution, and flows of materials between supplier networks.

Market development is the flip side of sourcing. State-of-the-art practices here are truly transformative, essentially changing the ways a firm goes to market and the "working" of sales personnel:

- *Prospecting/assessing:* How can the dyad improve its abilities to learn what products, services, and offering enhancements that current potential customers will buy? What changes will be needed to improve this ability for the dyad?
- *New sales mechanisms:* Dyad developments here often find ways to eliminate ordering, replace forecasting with exact knowledge of customer needs, and coordinate the capacity utilizations in the chain to mutual benefits.
- *Customer relationship management:* Making this widely shared objective into more than a slogan requires solid MPC systems, with jointly designed new processes and new ways of working in the dyad.
- *Customer partnering:* Partnering must actually mean something and not just be some buzzword. Making customer partnering a reality is hard work, backed by solid MPC systems.
- *After-sales service:* Here there are some very interesting recent supply chain developments—often using third-party logistics providers—to pick up, rapidly repair, and return products to their owners. Again the key questions seem to be "Who can do what best?" and "What new competencies need to be developed?"
- *Segmentation:* Here we see the same issue as in strategic positioning, but at more of a microlevel. The issue now is more focused on which specific customers and small segments can be captured through joint coordinated efforts of the dyad.

Chain Infrastructure Development: Infrastructure

We have now examined the top three boxes of Figure 19.4, which are organized in terms of three basic activities, work, or functions in a company: buying, product development, and selling. The bottom three boxes are oriented toward processes. In fact, the two parts of the figure can be thought of as a matrix: activities and processes, where some of the interactions are more important than others (such as interactions between order fulfillment and market development). Let us examine these processes and some of their connections to the top three function boxes.

Starting with bundle development, the dyad processes necessarily focus on important, but not very well structured, development opportunities:

- *Goods and services definition:* Dyad developments in defining the bundle of goods and services need to develop better means (processes) through which dialogue can take place between partners on what will achieve lock-on to specific customer segments and how joint efforts can achieve this lock-on. That is, the focus now is how the dyad can develop explicit processes, and continuously improve them, to support the segmentation aspect of market development.
- *New product rollout:* The focus is again to develop specific processes to support new product rollout, and to explicitly learn/update the processes after each new product rollout experience. These dyad-based processes need to develop explicit steps in new product rollout, focus on what each party needs to do during the step, determine who drives orchestration during the step (and how), and how progress is to be assessed during the rollout. The processes would have a clear intersection with many of the activities listed in the new product development activity/function.

- *Product life cycle phasing:* Best-practice firms manage their product life cycles, obsoleting their own products before the competitors do it. This implies a set of processes to manage the product life cycle, which need to be closely coordinated in the dyad. These would clearly intersect with many activities in the sourcing function.
- *Mass customization:* Mass customization is the supporting mechanism for finer degrees of market segmentation. In order to make mass customization a reality, it is essential for the dyad to establish (and evolve) processes that allow mass customization to take place with maximum efficiency and speed.
- *Modularity:* Modularity in product design is better known than modularity in process design, but both are needed to support mass customization, rapid new product development, new sales mechanisms, and e-based planning/orchestration. Again, these efforts need to be concentrated and codified into processes that become more explicit over time.
- *Evolution:* Rapid evolution in bundle development is a key competitive issue, which supports customer relationship management, new sales mechanisms, and joint learning/leveraging. Codified processes should speed evolution.

Capacity scheduling/coordination must be achieved through processes that are more explicit than those for bundle development. Now the emphasis is on how the dyad partners can move materials through the dyad with minimal dyad inventory, maximum speed, minimal transactions, minimal/automatic coordination, and zero mistakes.

- *Joint scheduling* implies operations in two firms coordinated as if this were one cellular activity.
- *The uphill skier* idea in essence passes the decision on when and what quantities to ship from the customer to the supplier. This allows the supplying firm flexibility as long as the customer firm schedule is not disrupted; it is supported with VMI.
- If the supplier has explicit *knowledge* of what a smart customer will need, the supplier does not need to guess (forecast) nor wait until the customer orders (ordering should be eliminated).
- *Logistics* firms and other third parties can support many innovative dyad processes. The larger the area in which a logistics firm operates, the greater the potential for optimization, but this does not come without smart (predictable) dyad operations.
- Outsourcing needs to be driven by which enterprise can do what better—but in many cases an explicit *transfer of knowledge* is required to support the new processes.
- The overall objectives should be expected to at some point encompass dyad *end-to-end speed* and dyad efficiency as the true metrics for supply chain management.

Order fulfillment focuses on those downstream processes that provide whatever the customers want—and whatever they *might* want—perhaps before they even know they want it! Thus, what we have here is the response to prospecting/assessing in market development: At some point the firm needs to develop and deliver the bundles that deliver what is foreseen. Implementing state-of-the-art processes for order fulfillment requires major changes in the *work* in both selling and buying. Within one firm, transferring a customer need into a satisfactory experience for the customer often involves separate processes for demand forecasting, sales planning, order entry, credit checking, order configuration management, inventory analysis and allocation, picking, shipping, delivery, invoicing, and reordering from the supplier. When examined across a dyad, one sees that a similar process must take place in the supplier firm. The potential for dyad-based process reengineering is high. The time required in the classic functional approach, extra inventories, and poor customer service are great targets of improvement. But as always, the need is for joint new work processes, supported by appropriate infrastructure. Further, the most significant improvements come from not just replicating the former processes. For many dyads this implies creating the mass customization processes that support continual evolution in the bundle of goods and services provided to end customers. There are several key goals for dyad-based order fulfillment processes:

- The focus needs to be on *inventory in the chain,* in this case, the dyad inventory. Making all of the inventories completely visible is a first step.
- Chain inventory reduction is directly related to *speed.* The objective is to satisfy customer wants much more quickly, without large inventories. For Nokia, this was expressed as "plan for capacity, execute to order."
- *E-based transaction processing* is the only way to coordinate joint dyad processing. Moreover, the e-based processes need to be designed with modular structures and transparency, so that other dyad links can be easily added.
- Reducing/eliminating the *bullwhip effect* is also a key objective. This requires much more than information transfer. Since uncoordinated work processes cause bullwhip problems, it follows that new, jointly designed, work processes will be required.
- *New financial arrangements* will be needed to support the dyad-based work. It is quite usual for one party to take on work or inventory expenses that were formerly borne by the other.
- *Simplification* is a major source of added value, but it is never easy. Simplification involves reducing product complexity, but it also is achieved by concentrating the supply base—buying more from fewer suppliers, with dyad-based work processes.
- Finally, *customer care or servicing* has to be one of the most important issues for dyad-based process redesign. At the end of the day, it is not only winning the customer orders, it is also achieving a long-term customer business commitment.

Competitive Drivers/Challenges

Many of the forces driving dyad-based supply chain management are similar to those that were driving earlier MPC improvements, e.g., increased competition, cost reduction, faster response, shorter product life cycles, and greater goods/service bundle variety. Today, these battles just cannot be won with conventional thinking alone. Moreover, there are some additional challenges and improvements that are uniquely associated with cross-firm working.

Outsourcing

Critical thinking about outsourcing is on the agendas of many enlightened companies. There is a real need to decide what activities should be maintained and which should be done by others. Unfortunately, all too often outsourcing starts by eliminating noncritical work, such as by no longer operating the company cafeteria. The more significant forms of outsourcing take place in dyads, where a key question is which partner can do what better? Another common misconception, or starting position, on outsourcing is that one should retain those things that are core while divesting those that are noncore. Unfortunately this can easily become a tautology: If we outsource it, it must be noncore, while if we keep it, it must be core. For example, DuPont de Nemours found itself at one point in an odd position: It had classified plastic compounding as core in Europe and noncore in the United States. In reality, outsourcing of plastic compounding made good sense in the United States and did not in Europe, for the basic reason that there had been different historical developments with suppliers in the two locations.

Outsourcing needs to be seen as a strategic choice. A firm needs to periodically redefine its mission and the resultant set of deliverables (the bundle of goods and services) that it wishes to provide to its customers. What will win the customer loyalty? How do we achieve unbeatable customer loyalty? In many cases this implies a move up the value chain, taking over some activity customarily performed by the customer. In fact, what is implied here is redefining the value proposition so that the customer will outsource to us! Moving up the value chain often results in outsourcing as well. This is a matter of focus as well as one of resources. No company can be expected to be excellent in everything. Choices need to be made and they are influenced by the availability and competencies of key suppliers. Thus, for Hewlett-Packard, the use of electronic manufacturing services (EMS) firms such as Solectron and Flextronics makes a great deal of sense. HP can concentrate on marketing, new design, and enhancing its brand name. For a company growing rapidly, such as Nokia, outsourcing at some point becomes a necessity, unless the company is willing to hire many thousands of new people every year. The bottom line to this is that outsourcing needs to be seen in a strategic context. Where should we be positioned in the value chain? Where can we add unique value and leverage the competencies of others?

Implementing outsourcing requires a strategy, new competencies, new ways of working, new processes, and new supporting infrastructure. This typically begins on a dyad basis. Pilot projects are created to provide specific new bundles to a specific customer and to work with specific suppliers in new ways. When effective, most firms try to leverage the learning gained in one dyad to their other dyads—to roll out the strategy on a dyad-by-dyad basis.

Significant forms of outsourcing require much more than typical purchasing. The dyad usually needs to be adjusted so that customer work becomes supplier work, and the supplier may not have the knowledge to do this. It is often necessary to identify tacit knowledge at the customer and transfer that knowledge to the supplier. The classic purchasing approach focuses on supplier selection: Which supplier can provide this good at the lowest price? But now it is more than a good—it is an evolving bundle of goods and services. The focus thus needs to shift to supplier development and finally to *dyad* development. What is the work to be performed by the dyad? Which partner does what? What are the processes/systems in each company (and the joint processes/systems)? How does all this evolve over time?

Evolution of the dyad relationship raises two interesting strategic issues. First, new joint working, processes, and systems imply transformation and hard work. The payoffs need to be there for both parties. One payoff is more volume through supplier reduction programs; the best suppliers often achieve tenfold increases in volume. This dyad should be much more efficient, thereby delivering better value/cost to the customer. Moreover, the supplier will be smart enough to measure total contribution per customer. Another joint payoff is in learning: This dyad is where both parties work, each with a smart partner, and the learning can be leveraged in other dyads. The second strategic issue is related. The dyad has to be based on trust and a win-win mentality. Nokia expressed this well by specifying the overriding issue in choosing true partnerships as "shared values." Without a fundamental match in thinking between the dyad partners, no outsourcing relationship will survive over the long haul.

Regionalization/Globalization

A different sort of challenge facing many supply chains today is the move toward more regional and in some cases global operations. In Europe, for example, it was traditional for food companies such as Nestlé or Unilever to have factories in virtually every country. The product ingredients were grown and bought in the country, and thereafter manufactured, sold, and consumed there as well. This has all changed, mainly because of the European Economic Union. Now the pasta might be made in Italy, ice cream bars in France, ice cream bricks in Holland, and one brand of chocolate bars in the United Kingdom. All these products are in turn sold throughout Europe—and elsewhere as well.

Regionalization requires many changes in supply chain operations, including new work, processes, and systems. In addition, regionalization demands simplification and standardization. To whatever extent possible, the *same* pasta, ice cream bars, ice cream bricks, and chocolate bars need to be made. Otherwise, the economies of scale will not be achieved. When the same products are made in more than one factory, again the result must be identical, or else the customers will develop a preference for products from a particular factory. Simplification mandates common packaging, standard bar coding, multilingual labeling, and any other practices that allow any product to be sold in any market.

Regionalization/globalization has major implications for MPC systems and the work they support. Regional MPC systems must be developed. Demands from all sources need to be integrated and used for MPC planning systems. Regional logistics systems must be developed. Visibility of all inventories is required. Production and inventories may be reassigned as needed. If, for example, a season is much warmer than expected in northern Europe and colder in southern Europe, then products may need to be reassigned. If more than one manufacturing source is used for a product, one needs to allot the joint requirements to the individual production units. Shortages also need to be assigned: Which customers will not be served?

Regional metrics must be developed. One needs to cure the "country disease," where each country unit optimizes its results, often at the expense of sister operating units. The goal is to maximize the returns for the overall region or globally; measurement systems that impede this overall focus must be changed. Moreover, the culture of the firm needs to undergo a similar metamorphosis. In practice this usually requires cross-boundary assignments, joint projects, and much greater efforts on networking. It is imperative that everyone recognizes the need for standardized regional MPC systems and working methods.

The problems (opportunities?) are magnified when global operations are to be coordinated. In many cases, the supplier choice itself becomes limited—to those suppliers that can indeed support the global operations. They well may need colocated manufacturing units, but they also need codeveloped ways of global working, processes, and information systems.

Customer Concentration

Another competitive challenge facing many supply chains today comes from concentration. This is easily seen in the development of the large retail customers such as Wal-Mart. For its suppliers, Wal-Mart is first regarded as having great bargaining power. But there is more to the story. Wal-Mart increasingly has a global strategy for its marketplace and wishes to work with large selected suppliers to support this strategy. It is in the process of developing sophisticated systems for working with its dyad partners. This mandates integration of these systems internally by the suppliers in order to achieve maximum dyad effectiveness.

Wal-Mart, like any smart customer, has selected several smart suppliers to work with jointly on dyad MPC systems. Procter & Gamble has traditionally been one of the companies with which Wal-Mart has had a strong partnership relation and shared values. But today Wal-Mart works with several other dyad partners in developing new ways of working, processes, and systems.

The opportunities for improved operations by the big retailers are significant. They sell in larger volumes, over greater geographic areas, to more diverse populations. Moreover, they are largely responsible for redefining the bundles of goods and services offered to consumers. Supporting these bundles implies new dyad relationships and ways of working.

Other forms of concentration also imply changes in the ways firms need to support markets. The out-of-home eating market continues to expand. This implies new solutions for this market and the MPC systems to support the solutions. For the big food companies like Unilever and Nestlé, customers such as Disney are becoming ever more important. This requires not only new food products. For example, the packages for these products need to be designed for optimal effectiveness, as does the food preparation itself. For example, a pizza supplied by Nestlé and sold at a Disney park needs to be quickly prepared in facilities that can easily expand to meet maximum demand. Moreover, that pizza must be suitable for easy eating without utensils if necessary. Many people will in fact eat the pizza while walking or standing in line. The product must taste good, but also be adaptable to unorthodox eating practices. Nestlé has designed a unique "solution" for Disney, which implies close working relationships. Moreover, the supply of that product and the MPC systems for working in the dyad are also important. They are always being investigated to find new ways to take costs out of the dyad.

So we see that the Disney/Nestlé dyad needs joint work in product design and continual improvement based on feedback from actual use. What could be done to cook it faster/ better? How could it stay warm longer? What tastes are most liked/not liked? What is being thrown away (the garbage cans are a great source of information)? But there are other linkages as well. How is this product replenished? How is it scheduled in manufacturing at Nestlé? What is the dyad inventory? Where is it located? Should it be held by Nestlé or by Disney? Finally for both firms, what has been learned in this dyad and how can that be leveraged, both for other Nestlé-Disney business and for other dyad relationships?

There are many other forms of concentration, and they seem to be growing. Intel is a powerful chip manufacturer that increasingly influences the way its suppliers must develop their bundles of goods and services. Several automotive companies mandate that their suppliers colocate and also provide worldwide agreements. Wal-Mart and others are pushing for European-wide agreements, regional supply chains, common pricing in euros, common e-based B2B systems, and joint improvement efforts. All of these imply new dyad relationships: work, processes, and systems.

Lock-on

A final current challenge that defines state-of-the-art dyads is what we call "lock-on." Lock-on is the extent to which one has a particularly favorable position with another dyad party. It should not be thought of as "lock-up," where one creates a monopolistic or contractual situation with choice eliminated. Rather, lock-on is achieved by providing a superior bundle of goods and services and continuing to enhance that bundle so that it is very difficult for a competitor to capture this business. Lock-on thus becomes a strategic objective. We say: "If you are in the commodity business—you deserve it!" The way *not* to be in the commodity business is to achieve lock-on by providing much more than a commodity.

Lock-on can be seen as being gained between a consumer products company and its end customers through branding and superior products. It is also being achieved today through websites and other e-based communications. Thus, for example, Club Nokia is a net-based system that provides end mobile phone users with a series of benefits that in the end enhance the brand name of Nokia. That brand image creates a strong pull through demand for Nokia products.

A different form of lock-on is to enlist more direct customers. For Nokia this could be a phone company such as Vodaphone or a retailer such as Wal-Mart. In either case, lock-on is enhanced by providing better performance in terms of customer measures: lowering the customer investment in inventory, increasing customer return per cubic meter of shelf space, reducing end customer stockouts, better supporting customer market initiatives, better coordination of new product introduction and subsequent obsolescence, improving the after-sales support, finding new ways to process warranties, lowering end customer returns, and other forms of "being easy to do business with."

For many companies, lock-on with suppliers may be an even more important source of competitive advantage. Lock-on with suppliers means better deliveries, preferred customer status during periods of shortage, joint design efforts, leveraging of supplier competencies in the customer company, sharing of best practices, and joint improvement efforts. The customer that is considered "most attractive" to its suppliers will be able to focus the supplier's brainpower on finding solutions to *the customer's* problems. Although supplier lock-on can and is in fact achieved through muscle power, the most attractive customer can achieve supplier lock-on more naturally. Whether the supplier will respond better to fear than friendship is a tough question. But we believe attractiveness to indeed be an important source of supplier lock-on.

Lock-on requires more than an attitude or agreement. Once more we come back to MPC systems. Lock-on can be effective only if the dyad partners have the necessary working relationships and supporting MPC systems to make it a reality—that is, to orchestrate the chain. Moreover, lock-on can be maintained only through continuous improvement. Lock-on needs to be seen in a relative sense—the extent to which working with *me* is superior to working with my competitors.

Cross-Firm MPC Design

As noted above, cross-firm MPC design is not a natural extension from ERP, which is functionally organized with a command and control mentality. Cross-firm MPC needs to be organized by process, and often by specific customer. Moreover, best practice has the dyad partners acting in each other's interest, without any explicit rules that dictate actions.

E-Based Systems

The infrastructure to support cross-firm MPC optimization has to be e-based. E-based MPC systems link companies via the Internet, which essentially allows for real-time coordinated planning. There simply is no other intelligent choice. A dyad might start by using e-based software to process transactions, essentially replacing EDI. But soon the dyad needs to communicate about product knowledge, joint planning, product life cycles, chain demands/inventories, and joint improvement projects. Figure 19.5 depicts some key issues in the information flows under e-based MPC.

The first and most basic issue is that the dyad has the goal of processing *all* transactions electronically, with no human intervention. This may never be completely achieved, but having this as a clear goal focuses attention on working practices that do not conform. The rollout of dyad-based, e-based MPC will always lead to the need for transformative change in work practices. E-based processing also commits the dyad to instantaneous linkages. This is important, not only because the exact status for dyad requirements is known but also because, with real-time connectivity, the natural amplification induced by traditional cross-company linkages can be reduced. Moreover, the true implications of problems are known immediately and their solutions follow accordingly. Not all human interventions and decisions can be automated. But there are great possibilities to reduce the degree of human intervention, as well as to make the resultant decision making more straightforward.

E-based MPC can eliminate the need for ordering and forecasting. With exact knowledge of the customer situation, the supplier does not need to forecast (guess) the customer needs, nor does the supplier have to wait for orders in order to know them. The chain is orchestrated in ways that allow the individual parties to work more independently, but with full knowledge of the true needs and the implications of various actions. This implies a

FIGURE 19.5
E-Based MPC: Information Flows

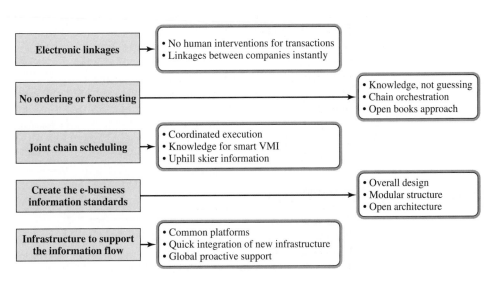

sharing of knowledge, shown in Figure 19.5 as "Open books approach." However, we would warn against the classic demand for open books often made by purchasing organizations. All too often their interest is in knowing the profitability of their business with the supplier in order to bargain harder. Sound advice for a supplier faced with this request is to agree with the philosophy and general sentiment for sharing information, but focus initially on sharing other information—both ways—with the intention to share cost data as well *when* the cooperative efforts advance to this step.

Joint chain scheduling is a key goal of cross-firm MPC design. Coordinated execution will allow the chain to respond to end-customer demands in greatly reduced time frames, with minimal inventory levels. "Smart VMI" (vendor-managed inventory) goes hand in hand with uphill skier information for joint scheduling. Customer knowledge establishes the constraints: what *has* to be available (and when) to support the customer schedule. The uphill skier basis for joint work allows the supplier to send more than the requirements, and as soon as wished, but payments are based on VMI. The result is increased flexibility for the supplier at virtually no extra cost to the customer.

E-business information standards and infrastructure to support the information flow note the need for compatible systems, with the ability to support evolution in dyad relationships. This is achieved in practice through modular designs for processes and systems, open architecture, and common platforms.

Figure 19.6 extends the e-based MPC thinking from the information flows to the physical flows of materials, planned/coordinated by the information flows/systems. Here we see the key objectives, and the innovations that are being implemented. New logistics providers are offering new services—in some cases by combining flows from several suppliers to multiple customers. All of this is taking place in a more global context and amid increased use of outsourcing.

FIGURE 19.6
E-Based MPC:
Physical Flows

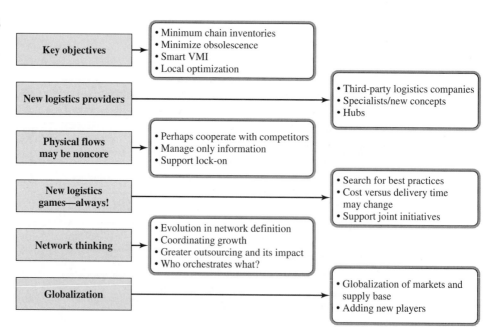

Orchestration

Orchestration is a key issue in supply chain management. The key question is "Which partner will orchestrate?" That is, which dyad partner makes the key decisions? Some firms unfortunately see this as a power game. *We* want ourselves to be the "orchestraters" and the other dyad parties to be the "orchestratees." This is erroneous thinking. It is the dyad that needs to be coordinated through orchestration, but the choice and extent as to *which partner* does the orchestration should be based again on whichever can do a particular task better. Figures 19.7 and 19.8 illustrate the process by which an OEM (original equipment

FIGURE 19.7 **Different Phases of a Product Life Cycle Require Different Coordination Means (Systems/Processes)**

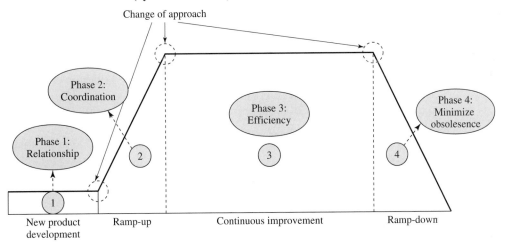

Phases of cooperation with volumes of production

FIGURE 19.8 **OEM and EMS Need to Bring Diverse Capabilities to the Relationship in Different Phases**

Capabilities required for successful management of product life cycle

Company	New product development	Ramp-up	Continuous improvement	Ramp-down
OEM	• Relationship building • Cooperation of different functions • Engineering capabilities • Project management	• Relationships with supplier • Coordination • Flexible organization • Rapid design evolution	• Demand visibility • SC capabilities • Being the premium customer	• Accurate forecasting • Market intelligence • Flexible organization • Relationships between people
EMS	• Engineering capabilities • Quality management	• Project management • Responsive operations • Engineering capabilities • Quality management	• Efficient manufacturing • Flawless execution • IT integration • SC capabilities	• Project management • Flexibility • Managing across the supply chain

Orchestration

manufacturer) works together with an EMS (electronic services manufacturer) supplier through a product life cycle.

Figure 19.7 depicts the product life cycle as broken into four explicit phases. This model would be used by an OEM-EMS dyad to be quite clear as to the particular work at hand. Each phase requires different coordination mechanisms. More important, the model shows three defined changes in the approach and mechanisms to be used. The implication is that at each change point, a transformation occurs in the work to be done and those who will do it. The model allows the dyad to identify the shifts, make them as needed, and identify best practices in each phase.

Figure 19.8 carries the model one step further. Here some key capabilities for the dyad firms are listed—those that are required for successful management of the four phases in the product life cycle. Also shown is a shaded line depicting orchestration. The two firms need to work together (i.e., their MPC systems are closely coordinated), but at some phases one firm or the other will be more suited to take on the coordination/orchestration of the joint efforts. Figure 19.8 shows the OEM as having a greater role in the new product development phase, since it is the partner that has identified the product and its value proposition for the end customers. The orchestration roles are shown as shifting to about 50-50 in the ramp-up; both firms need to work together to rapidly bring the production volumes up to the desired levels. The continuous improvement phase is shown as being more orchestrated by the EMS. It is the one that necessarily is closest to the action for reducing cost and improving the product design. Finally, in ramp-down, the orchestration might shift back to the OEM, which decides when to phase out the product, often by bringing out a replacement product.

> When Figure 19.8 was shown to a senior executive at the EMS company, Solectron, he made an interesting observation: The shaded line in Figure 19.8 needs to be thought of as a series of such lines that are parallel and based on the competency of the OEM. Managing a product life cycle with a highly skilled OEM implies a parallel line higher up; the OEM does more relative orchestration. At the other extreme, a new-venture OEM with little or no manufacturing expertise implies a lower parallel line; it is the EMS that would have the superior ability to orchestrate the dyad. Thus, the orchestration issue is best examined as to what is to be orchestrated (explicit phases) and *which partner* can do *what* better? The bottom line is that MPC systems exist in both dyad firms, and the more they operate as an integrated whole the better the dyad performance. There are natural points where one dyad partner might take a more dominant role. However, this thinking needs to be modified by MPC experience of the dyad partners. The more competent should take on a larger role in orchestration.

Hubs

Hubs are another key innovation in dyad-based relationships. Their use is growing dramatically, with excellent results. A hub is most often manifested as an inventory location, such as a warehouse. But the location is less important than the function. One key is that the hub must be secure, with transparency as to inventory and transactions. Best-practice use of hubs can eliminate one level of inventory in a dyad. Instead of the supplier holding finished goods and the customer the same goods as raw materials, production can go directly to the hub, and from there into subsequent conversion at the customer site. This implies that the hub is physically located close to the customer, which has the ability to retrieve goods from there almost as easily as if the goods were on site at the customer.

In fact, at some point it makes no difference where the hub is located, and it can become "virtual." For a third-party logistics provider the inventory can be almost anywhere—in warehouses or in trucks—as long as it is secure. The third-party logistics provider provides materials as needed, where needed, and when needed. Often the hub is replenished with VMI and the uphill skier concept. The uphill skier idea is that just as it is the job of the uphill skier to look out for those heading downhill, a dyad can be established so that it is the supplier who orchestrates—decides when to ship and in what quantities—not the customer. The customer is invoiced only when the goods are used, and accurate transactions are maintained. The hub often plays a key role in this relationship, providing all the benefits of holding finished goods for the supplier, along with other significant advantages: The inventory offers protection against stockouts where they could occur, physical movement is reduced, total chain inventory can be lowered, and transportation costs might be reduced.

Hubs also allow for consolidated shipments to joint customers. For example, Unilever uses a hub in The Netherlands to receive output from several of its factories. These factories used to separately deliver to large customers such as Albert Heijn, the largest Dutch retailer. Now, deliveries from the hub can combine many Unilever products. Moreover, there is no particular reason why the hub could not also consolidate deliveries of products from other, non-Unilever, companies to the same customers. In the longer term, if the volumes from the hub become high enough, it might be possible to bypass the distribution system for the large customers, delivering directly from the hub to the individual supermarkets.

Another example is seen in the hubs used by EMS firms, such as Flextronics. In its Hungarian location, Flextronics operates within an industrial park, where several subsuppliers are physically located, such as a carton manufacturer, and a sheet metal fabricator. Information can be shared with all these players, and with close proximity all requirements can be met with minimal response times and inventories. The site also has a hub (owned and managed by a part of Flextronics) where all materials can be identified—down to individual serial numbers and bar-code numbers—which in turn can be passed to Flextronics customers so they can know total chain inventories as well as the relative states of completion of those inventories. The hub can be used as part of the overall scheduling process, with authorization to remove materials as a signal to commence production. Ownership of the actual hub inventories can also be managed in various ways. Under some circumstances, it might be the suppliers who own the inventories (VMI). In other cases it might be the customers of Flextronics that have taken ownership of the inventories as part of their contractual arrangements with suppliers and with Flextronics. In any case ownership of exact materials (perhaps with different costs) might pass from either the supplier or the customer to Flextronics and then back to the customer on completion of the products. The hub offers great flexibility in this regard, with tight processes to clearly pass ownership, to create product cost information, and to be able to account for all materials in real time.

In a similar vein, there is a large hub under construction in Beijing that will serve several electronics OEM companies as well as several large suppliers, including an EMS. The basic idea is to have only one inventory, with e-based visibility to all interested parties. With only one warehouse and elimination of multiple safety stocks, the overall efficiency of the system can be quite high. But again, this works only with accurate inventories, excellent information supplied by smart dyad partners, and clear rules for usage.

Examples and Techniques

As noted above, cross-organizational supply chain management is in an early stage. It is not an extension to work based on existing (ERP) systems; by definition, cross-organizational supply chain management is transformational. Let us now examine the ways in which some companies have proceeded in this quest for definitively different MPC systems.

ChemUnity

ChemUnity is an e-based company that in essence helps the work of purchasing transform from informal to formal. ChemUnity, like many early purchasing e-business ventures, started with the idea that firms wanted to adopt auction-based buying. That is, by proposing to buy some goods, various suppliers would bid for their purchase order. In fact, almost all of these schemes are failures, for the obvious reason that they do not support better utilization of interfirm capacity management. On the contrary, auctions increase the uncertainty as to whether one will receive business (demands for capacity), which in the end results in less intensive capacity utilization and higher chain costs.

ChemUnity was originally designed for the purchase of the odd truckload of chemicals. For the buyer, this was a problem, since knowledge of this marketplace would be limited. ChemUnity would allow access to many firms that might be able to satisfy this need. On the other hand, ChemUnity was useful for the supplier who on occasion had some extra chemicals to sell. Note here that ChemUnity did not start out to satisfy purchasing of one's major supplies. These were believed to be already a matter of historical development between the customer and supplier; it would be naïve to think some simple auction would replace this relationship.

Figure 19.9 depicts what ChemUnity now offers to its customers. Instead of an auction, the product has evolved into essentially an "extranet" where the informal purchasing part of MPC—based on telephone calls, papers, and faxes—is now made formal and incorporated with other MPC systems. All purchasing contacts are now in a common system that supports the work of purchasing. ChemUnity has moved from selling an e-based marketplace to selling software that facilitates the matching of buyers and sellers. The system essentially extends the MPC approach based on classical internal systems (ERP) to include those activities before formal purchasing takes place, such as material specification, search for suppliers, request for quotation, and price negotiation. The status of all requirements is known and routinely updated, on a common basis, with an e-based system.

Further enhancements to the ChemUnity software have included what it calls the "sourcing portal," which helps streamline certain work before the purchasing decision is made. In use, the system is much less oriented toward finding the supplier who will offer the lowest price than toward communication and coordination with the suppliers. All information on scheduling, deliveries, and new customer demands are integrated through the normal ERP system. But the results of these transactions need to be communicated to the suppliers, along with planning for subsequent buying decisions. The ChemUnity software provides a convenient means for a purchasing organization to accomplish its traditional work better and faster. Moreover, once in use it supports new efforts to streamline the buying process. Let us now turn to another example, which clearly shows this kind of streamlining.

FIGURE 19.9
ChemUnity:
Formal
Systems

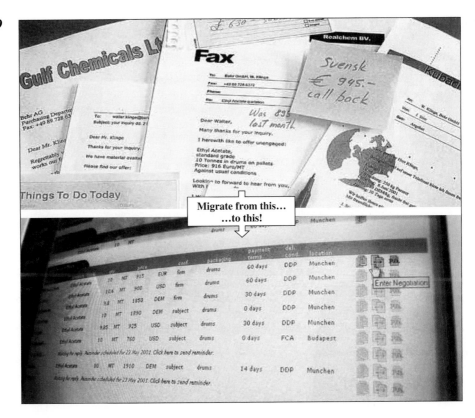

SourcingParts

SourcingParts is another purchasing e-business venture. It too started with the idea that at least one key part of its appeal would be auctions. And again, this has proved to be false. SourcingParts provides a customer-supplier interface for complex build-to-order parts, such as those used in complex machines. The software is organized so that suppliers can specify the capabilities of their particular equipment, such as a four-axis milling machine for parts with maximum size of 1.2 meters. Customers in turn can specify the kinds of equipment needed to fabricate their parts. They can also pass design requirements, part drawings, and computer-aided design/computer-aided manufacturing (CAD/CAM) data over the Internet. One additional part of SourcingParts' offering is a system to convert CAD/CAM data from one software system to another.

SourcingParts supports more complex interfirm interactions than ChemUnity. These include joint design discussions between the firms, purchasing to sales communications, resolution of order administration/fulfillment issues, and status as to payments/deliveries/guarantees, quality/delivery performance, vendor assessments, and references. However, there is a similarity to ChemUnity in that the offering is shifting from an e-based marketplace to more of an Internet-based software package—one that supports communications between various parties in the customer company and that of the supplier. Examples include the ability of a highly specialized supplier to move from guessing/forecasting of a

FIGURE 19.10   **Nextrom Local Purchasing**

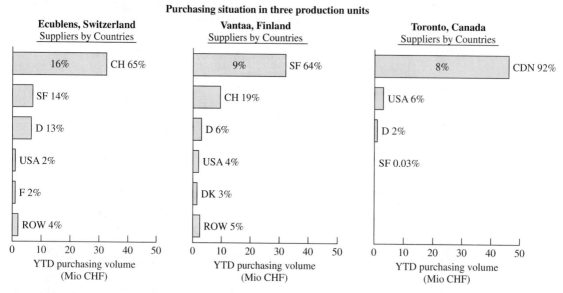

Purchasing situation in three production units

Note: CH = Switzerland, SF = Finland, D = Germany, CDN = Canada, ROW = rest of world. Mio CHF = millions of Swiss francs.

Source: Nextrom/Global Procurement Database.

particular customer's needs to having knowledge of those needs. The two firms converse about the utilization of particular special machine capacity. It is in the interest of both firms to better manage this capacity.

An interesting example of how SourcingParts has helped to streamline buying is well-illustrated by one of its customers, Nextrom, which was in the process of a major transformation of its supply chain. In essence, Nextrom wished to globalize procurement, reduce its complexity, concentrate the supply base, and develop a strategic sourcing process based on outsourcing. Figure 19.10 shows the potential. Manufacturing was based in three countries, each of which had developed its own (highly local) supply base. As can be seen, for example, in Finland, 64 percent of the purchases came from Finnish sources, only 9 percent of which were from international companies having Finnish operations. Nextrom manufactures highly complex machines to fabricate fiber-optic cables. These machines use some very complex manufactured parts. Concentrating procurement of these parts is a good idea, but it first requires common part specifications, unified product design approaches, completely accurate integration of all part requirements, and centralized buying. On the supply side, the key suppliers have very expensive machines that need to be utilized effectively. SourcingParts provides some key infrastructure to support these initiatives.

Dyator

Dyator is a provider of e-based infrastructure to support interorganizational supply chain management. Rather than focus on e-based marketplaces like many other e-business ventures, Dyator focuses on dyad relationships. One of its primary initiatives is called Electronic Key Account Management. The idea is for a firm to begin with a customer dyad (a key account). In one early example, a manufacturer of electronic components was in an allocation situation with a customer key account. This global account had eight receiving factories that were supplied by six factories of the manufacturer (supplier). The need was to obtain full visibility of the customer requirements, the supplier's commitments to those requirements, the current status of all goods in transit, and data on quality/yields. The system developed, iPlan, provides goods-in-transit visibility, global and factory forecast tracking, and workflow management using e-mail and SMS (the short messaging system used in mobile phones) to inform all interested supply chain parties of changes in either the information or physical flows. The system also has security and definitions of who can see what and who can do what, managed by access levels.

The supplier implemented this new way of working and supporting infrastructure in its relation with this one key customer during a time of crisis. After seeing how well this works, the supplier implemented it with other key customers and at the time of this writing this MPC system supports 50 percent of the sales for the electronic components manufacturer. But, it is important to note, making this a reality required *major* changes in the way this firm worked: how it sells; *what* it sells (this bundle is definitely not a commodity), the ways in which orders are tracked, forecasting, and the whole communications approach with the customers.

Dyator has, as one would expect, incorporated further capabilities into its e-based software, essentially focusing on visibility of information and inventories between supply chain dyad parties. By building on the base of goods-in-transit visibility, it could add global and factory forecast tracking, allocation logic, and workflow reporting. Accompanying these features, an important addition has been to include key performance indicators reporting on service levels, stock levels, and forecast accuracy. These can be made at all levels of location and product hierarchy. A second major enhancement has been to create logic for recommended weekly replenishment quantities from suppliers to hubs to best support the detailed downstream factory operations on the basis of latest factory forecasts and inventory positions. These are only recommendations, since the hubs are often replenished with uphill skier and VMI logic. But the recommended replenishment quantities provide a good benchmark for what might provide good downstream support with minimal chain inventories.

Another enhancement has been to connect firms in ways that go beyond the usual concept of supplier commitment. A smart customer wants to *know* that suppliers will honor their commitments. Dyator has developed a collaborative planning system that provides visibility to the customer of the supplier's manufacturing operations and its supply chain. This allows the customer to make more intelligent predictions as to the supplier's ability to meet a major ramp-up in production. It also allows the customer to estimate the impact on the upstream supply chain if volumes are reduced.

The next enhancement developed by Dyator was for a mobile phone company to share new product development plans with several key suppliers, such as a major integrated circuit manufacturer. The MPC system to support this activity is called iProject. This software module, essentially a collaborative project management system, allows the supply chain partners to conduct net-based meetings to foster joint engineering. The iProject module has been extended from some suppliers to their own key suppliers. A key benefit is to provide an integrated "one-face" view of new product development that is necessarily based on interfirm development. This is an absolutely key competitive element in this business.

There are several further enhancements currently under development, and these will continue. After all, we truly are only in the beginning stages of interorganizational supply chain management. The enhancements include jointly developed technology roadmaps, enhanced quality information, new ways to manage hub inventories, shipment mode optimization (fast versus cheap), chain capital optimization (the firm with the lowest cost of capital should finance inventories), and open books options.

Concluding Principles

Superior supply chains are the emerging competitive weapons of the future: the best way to compete today. We are at an early state today, but it is clearly possible to see some emerging trends. The following are some principles we see important to their successful development.

- We are at a beginning state in interfirm MPC development. A large part of the efforts will focus on converting informal approaches into formal systems and joint-firm processes.

- Interfirm optimization is attractive in today's competitive world for delivering effective long-term results.

- An effective starting point in interfirm cooperation is with processes and e-based systems that plan and coordinate interfirm product movements.

- The processes and systems developed in the future will go beyond the classical approaches of MPC that mostly focus on the flows of goods.

- Lock-on with key supply chain partners (customers and suppliers) provides the way to definitively move away from the commodity business.

- The new MPC systems that cross company boundaries need to be driven with a new set of metrics and a set of shared values in each dyad.

- Implementation of interfirm supply chain linkages is not easy. It must be focused on explicit dyads, thereafter finding ways to leverage the learning to other dyads. One should not underestimate the efforts involved in transforming the supply chain. It is essential to link new ways of working to the processes that support this working and to the systems that allow the processes to function.

- E-based systems are being designed and implemented in various dyad relationships. Any firm that wishes to be at the cutting edge should be studying these systems extensively, finding the ways to modify and apply them to their own environment.

- Perhaps the single most important principle in developing the new MPC approaches is to not be limited by parochial thinking. One must always start by asking what breakthrough would truly capture (lock on to) the end customers.

References

Cordon, C., and T. E. Vollmann. "Building a Smarter Demand Chain." *Financial Times Mastering Information Management,* February 1999.

Guide, V. D. R., Jr. "Production Planning and Control for Remanufacturing: Industry Practice and Research Needs," *Journal of Operations Management* 18, no. 4 (June 2000) pp. 467–483.

Hoover, W. E.; E. Eloranta; J. Holmstrom; and K. Huttunen. *Managing the Demand-Supply Chain.* New York: John Wiley & Sons, 2001.

Meyer, M. H., and R. Seiglier. "Product Platforms in Software Development." *Sloan Management Review* (summer 1998), pp. 61–74.

Orlicky, Joseph, and George W. Plossl. *Orlicky's Material Requirements Planning.* New York: Mc-Graw-Hill Trade; 2nd edition, 1994.

Robertson, D., and K. Ulrich. "Planning for Product Platforms." *Sloan Management Review* (summer 1998), pp. 19–31.

Sunday Business (KRTBN), "Wal-Mart Wants All Suppliers to Switch to New Supply Chain Technology." June 15, 2003.

Discussion Questions

1. Why is interorganizational supply chain management much more than the next extension to ERP and related systems?

2. Suppose XYZ Electronics is to provide a new DVD player for an enhanced computer game box to be sold by the ABC Consumer Products Company. In regard to Figure 19.7, how might the dyad best work jointly on new product development? What might be most important? Who should orchestrate?

3. Continuing with Question 2, what are the most important joint efforts and orchestration in the ramp-up phase? How might this change in the third phase, continuous improvement?

4. What are the metrics that might be used to evaluate the dyad during the different phases of Questions 2 and 3?

5. What features of the systems offered by Dyator would be most useful in the dyad of Questions 2, 3, and 4?

6. What makes e-based systems more effective than electronic data interchange (EDI)?

7. How do hubs support better dyad capacity utilization? What processes and information have to be in place?

8. In what ways does the ChemUnity approach support formalization of purchasing?

9. What has to be changed internally at Nextrom (Figure 19.10) to reduce the supplier base?

10. The Dyator iPlanning module provides systemwide visibility of stocks. Why might quality reporting be important here?

Problems

1. ABC makes a product using a component bought from DEF. ABC sells 100 units per week, manufactures the same amount each week, and buys 100 units per week from DEF as well. ABC keeps a one-week inventory of raw materials as well as a one-week inventory of finished goods. DEF follows a similar set of rules, except that it has a two-week lead time for manufacturing plus a one-week time to deliver the goods to ABC. What is the total inventory in the dyad?

2. Continuing with problem 1, what happens if the finished goods held by XYZ are eliminated, with XYZ having visibility of its component inventory held downstream? Of what else would XYZ like to have visibility to operate more effectively?

3. Ajax passes orders to Batesville through the mail and by fax. These are confirmed by Batesville and then entered into internal Batesville information systems. The normal time for this process to occur is two weeks. Now an e-based system linkage is to be established between the two firms, so that this process is achieved—flawlessly—in a matter of minutes. Assuming the inventory turnover in the dyad is 4.0, what would be the possible effect on the inventory turnover from achieving these results?

4. Continuing with problem 3, let us assume that the total inventory held by the Ajax-Batesville dyad is $100,000. If Batesville is a typical supplier, and represents 5 percent of the purchases from Ajax, what is the potential supply chain savings for Ajax and its suppliers from implementing the e-based system with all of them?

5. Figure 19.10 shows Nextrom buying approximately CHF35 Mio (35 million Swiss francs) in Switzerland by its Swiss factory. The similar numbers for Finland are CHF33 Mio, and for

Canada CHF47 Mio. Of these amounts, 16, 9, and 8 percent, respectively, are purchased from international suppliers. Let us assume that through purchasing consolidation these amounts can be doubled and centralized, and that through more effective dyad work the costs to the dyad firms could be reduced by 5 percent. What are the potential savings?

6. End of the Trail (EOT) makes an electronic hiking aid that shows altitude, distance traveled, and directions. The major component for this device is an application-specific integrated circuit (ASIC) made by Chips-R-Us (CRU). EOT sells 1,000 units per month, and orders components from CRU at the beginning of each month for delivery at the beginning of the month after next (two-month lead time). The two-month lead time is made up of two weeks (0.5 months) for shipping from CRU to EOT, and 1.5 months for manufacturing at CRU. EOT keeps one extra month of component stock, as well as one extra month of finished goods inventory. Manufacturing at EOT is based on monthly buckets. That is, lead time is one month. CRU also keeps one month of finished goods inventory of the chips. If both firms follow first-in, first-out processing, how long is it before a new chip manufactured at CRU leaves EOT as a finished device? What is the total inventory of chips held in the dyad? What is the dyad inventory turnover?

7. Continuing with problem 6, assume that a VMI hub exists between CRU and EOT. What is the time from removal of chips from the hub to shipments of completed units? What is the inventory turnover for EOT?

8. Please assume (incorrectly) that the answers to Question 6 are 4 months, 4,000 units, and a turnover of 3. Let us now suppose that EOT's customers hold two months of stock, and a competitive product appears on the market. The response by EOT has to be to reduce the retail price by $50 until a new chip can be designed and implemented (three months). What is the total amount of the price reduction that must be absorbed by EOT, its suppliers, and its customers, before a new model can be introduced?

9. Katch-Em-Quick (KEQ) sells security devices. The company has asked EOT (problem 6) to develop a version of its product that can be hidden in the body of an automobile. If this car is stolen, the device will tell the police exactly where to find the car. Implementing this request requires a small change in the ASIC chip, which CRU will be able to accomplish. Assume that the same processes are used for this product as for the hiking product (but the volume for the KEQ product is 2,000 units per month). What happens to the total dyad inventory between CRU and EOT?

10. Major Motors has the dubious distinction that one of its cars is the most widely stolen model in the United States. The company wishes to install the KEQ chip (problem 9) in all of its cars at the factory. This order would be for 5,000 units per month. What happens to the dyad inventory between CRU and EOT if the same processes are used?

11. Please assume (incorrectly) that with the conditions of problems 6, 9, and 10, the total demand for EOT products is 10,000 units per month, and the total dyad inventory for CRU plus EOT is 50,000 chips (in two varieties). CRU and EOT have decided to change the ways in which they work, and the supporting infrastructure. Now, production at EOT will be in weekly buckets (2,000 per week), with the hiking device made one day and the automotive device made the other four days of the week. CRU will also work in weekly buckets, reducing its time to manufacture to four days and its delivery time to one day. CRU will deliver the weekly quantities of chips needed to EOT one week in advance of production needs. Neither company will hold other chip inventories. EOT will also reduce its finished goods levels to one week of stock. How long is it before a new chip manufactured at CRU leaves EOT as a finished device? What is the total inventory of chips held in the dyad? What is the dyad inventory turnover?

12. Whistle-Your-Missile (WYM) is a defense company specializing in cruise missiles. It now wishes to use several new versions of the EOT (problem 6) guidance system for its missiles. Specifically, WYM has asked EOT to supply 10 new guidance systems, each of which requires a

new ASIC chip. Combined with the hiking and automotive markets, this means EOT will produce 12 chips and 12 end products. The quantities for the missile chips are less than the others, averaging 200 chips per missile (10) per month. But the demand is expected to be highly variable, depending on how many wars are being launched by various WYM country customers. WYM has asked EOT to maintain a safety stock inventory of three months' stock in finished products, as well as another three months' safety stock of chips. Assume that EOT and CRU now implement a joint e-based planning system where EOT produces 12,000 products per month: 2,000 hiking devices, 8,000 automotive, and 2,000 of the 10 missiles. The hiking and automotive devices are produced as indicated in problem 11. What is the total inventory of chips in the dyad? What is the dyad inventory turnover?

13. Continuing with problem 12, EOT and CRU have worked in a new chip design (IC—not ASIC) that has much greater capacity. With this chip, all the end-product varieties can be accommodated with software. On this basis, EOT and its customers have agreed that EOT will carry a one-week supply of each end product (12), plus one week of chips that can be programmed in whatever way is needed. The flow conditions between EOT and CRU are the same as in problem 11. What is the total dyad chip inventory? What is the dyad inventory turnover?

14. Returning to the basic conditions of problem 6, let us now assume that the EOT sales of 1,000 units per month are growing by 100 units per month. Also, assume the dyad firms start with the inventory conditions indicated. What are the orders that must pass from EOT to CRU to retain the conditions as stated (assume that desired inventory values in the next month are based on the most immediate demand usage from the next downstream manufacturing, sales, or inventory stage)? Make any other assumptions you find useful (but state them). Process six months of increasing demands through the chain and explain what happens. Finally, if you have the time you might try this with a spreadsheet and a longer time horizon.

15. Continuing with problem 14, do the exercise again but introduce a forecast error, where you flip a coin to see if the error is +100 units or −100 units. What happens and what does this imply for how CRU and EOT need to interact?

Appendix

Areas of the Standard Normal Distribution

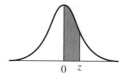

An entry in the table is the proportion under the entire curve that is between $z = 0$ and a positive value of z. Areas for negative values of z are obtained by symmetry. Using Microsoft Excel these probabilities are generated with the equation:

$$.5 - \text{NORMSDIST} (z).$$

z	.00	.01	.02	.03	.04	.05	.06	.07	.08	.09
0.0	.0000	.0040	.0080	.0120	.0160	.0199	.0239	.0279	.0319	.0359
0.1	.0398	.0438	.0478	.0517	.0557	.0596	.0636	.0675	.0714	.0753
0.2	.0793	.0832	.0871	.0910	.0948	.0987	.1026	.1064	.1103	.1141
0.3	.1179	.1217	.1255	.1293	.1331	.1368	.1406	.1443	.1480	.1517
0.4	.1554	.1591	.1628	.1664	.1700	.1736	.1772	.1808	.1844	.1879
0.5	.1915	.1950	.1985	.2019	.2054	.2088	.2123	.2157	.2190	.2224
0.6	.2257	.2291	.2324	.2357	.2389	.2422	.2454	.2486	.2517	.2549
0.7	.2580	.2611	.2642	.2673	.2703	.2734	.2764	.2794	.2823	.2852
0.8	.2881	.2910	.2939	.2967	.2995	.3023	.3051	.3078	.3106	.3133
0.9	.3159	.3186	.3212	.3238	.3264	.3289	.3315	.3340	.3365	.3389
1.0	.3413	.3438	.3461	.3485	.3508	.3531	.3554	.3577	.3599	.3621
1.1	.3643	.3665	.3686	.3708	.3729	.3749	.3770	.3790	.3810	.3830
1.2	.3849	.3869	.3888	.3907	.3925	.3944	.3962	.3980	.3997	.4015
1.3	.4032	.4049	.4066	.4082	.4099	.4115	.4131	.4147	.4162	.4177
1.4	.4192	.4207	.4222	.4236	.4251	.4265	.4279	.4292	.4306	.4319

(Continued)

z	.00	.01	.02	.03	.04	.05	.06	.07	.08	.09
1.5	.4332	.4345	.4357	.4370	.4382	.4394	.4406	.4418	.4429	.4441
1.6	.4452	.4463	.4474	.4484	.4495	.4505	.4515	.4525	.4535	.4545
1.7	.4554	.4564	.4573	.4582	.4591	.4599	.4608	.4616	.4625	.4633
1.8	.4641	.4649	.4656	.4664	.4671	.4678	.4686	.4693	.4699	.4706
1.9	.4713	.4719	.4726	.4732	.4738	.4744	.4750	.4756	.4761	.4767
2.0	.4772	.4778	.4783	.4788	.4793	.4798	.4803	.4808	.4812	.4817
2.1	.4821	.4826	.4830	.4834	.4838	.4842	.4846	.4850	.4854	.4857
2.2	.4861	.4864	.4868	.4871	.4875	.4878	.4881	.4884	.4887	.4890
2.3	.4893	.4896	.4898	.4901	.4904	.4906	.4909	.4911	.4913	.4916
2.4	.4918	.4920	.4922	.4925	.4927	.4929	.4931	.4932	.4934	.4936
2.5	.4938	.4940	.4941	.4943	.4945	.4946	.4948	.4949	.4951	.4952
2.6	.4953	.4955	.4956	.4957	.4959	.4960	.4961	.4962	.4963	.4964
2.7	.4965	.4966	.4967	.4968	.4969	.4970	.4971	.4972	.4973	.4974
2.8	.4974	.4975	.4976	.4977	.4977	.4978	.4979	.4979	.4980	.4981
2.9	.4981	.4982	.4982	.4983	.4984	.4984	.4985	.4985	.4986	.4986
3.0	.4987	.4987	.4987	.4988	.4988	.4989	.4989	.4989	.4990	.4990

Index